ASIAN AMERICAN PLAYWRIGHTS

ASIAN AMERICAN PLAYWRIGHTS

A Bio-Bibliographical Critical Sourcebook

Edited by
Miles Xian Liu

Emmanuel S. Nelson, Advisory Editor

GREENWOOD PRESS
Westport, Connecticut • London

Library of Congress Cataloging-in-Publication Data

Asian American playwrights : a bio-bibliographical critical sourcebook / edited by Miles
Xian Liu.
    p.   cm.
    Includes bibliographical references and index.
    ISBN 0–313–31455–1 (alk. paper)
      1. American drama—Asian American authors—Bio-bibliography—Dictionaries. 2.
Dramatists, American—Biography—Dictionaries. 3. Asian Americans in
literature—Dictionaries. 4. Asian Americans—Biography—Dictionaries. I. Liu, Miles
Xian.
    PS338.A74 A9   2002
    812'.509895'03—dc21
    [B]   2001037680

British Library Cataloguing in Publication Data is available.

Library of Congress Catalog Card Number: 2001037680
ISBN: 0–313–31455–1

First published in 2002

Greenwood Press, 88 Post Road West, Westport, CT 06881
An imprint of Greenwood Publishing Group, Inc.
www.greenwood.com

Printed in the United States of America

The paper used in this book complies with the
Permanent Paper Standard issued by the National
Information Standards Organization (Z39.48–1984).

10 9 8 7 6 5 4 3 2 1

Contents

Preface

During the embryonic stage of Asian American writings in the 1880s, Asian American authors mainly detailed the customs, lifestyles, and traditions of their Asian homeland. In contrast to the early novels and autobiographies, however, Asian American drama made its debut with the spotlight firmly on the lives and struggles of Asians in North America. In what might be considered the earliest Asian American dramatic works in the United States—*Confucius, Buddha*, and *Christ*—which Sadakichi Hartmann wrote between 1889 and 1897, the playwright attempted to transform the American theater of the late Victorian period by employing a fusion of poetry, music, and mystic elements. Ling-ai (Gladys) Li, the first Asian American woman playwright on record, focused on the conflict between two sets of equally compelling values from the cultures of America and China in *The Submission of Rose Moy* (1924). Coincidentally, or perhaps not so coincidentally, their works together started a tradition still evident today in Asian American dramatic literature, namely, challenging the limitations of established theater conventions and directing popular attention to issues and experiences that might otherwise be ignored or marginalized.

But the continental U.S. theater was not ready for Asian American plays when they first appeared. Although Li wrote and reportedly produced her first play without incident in Hawaii, Hartmann's scripts never saw production. Instead, he saw the inside of Charles Street Jail in Boston because his *Christ* was deemed "vicious and salacious according to American ideas," and all its copies were confiscated.[1] He was fined $100 for violating the community's sensibilities. Yet Asian American drama as a literary canon has been composed and produced for domestic consumption. From the commercially successful productions, such as *M. Butterfly* by David Henry Hwang and *Tea* by Velina Hasu Houston, to staged readings of scripts unheard of outside the field, the wide-ranging themes like identity struggles, cultural adjustment, immigration stigma, racism within, and the joys and hardships of diasporan experience as well as the possibilities and limits of multiethnicity continue to be appreciated by the multicultural audience more than by a homogeneous crowd. The diverse voices that Asian American plays present not only have enriched the American stage, but also have delineated the struggles of all Americans in an ever-changing racial landscape.

However, an overview of ethnic drama yields an unfortunate fact. While Asian American literature has come into full efflorescence in the past two and a half decades, Asian American drama has yet to receive the kind of critical attention it warrants. Its production is discussed primarily in the theater reviews of newspapers; its writers are known only to the scholars, producers, and acting professionals of ethnic and academic theaters; and most of its scripts remain unpublished despite the warm reception of their productions. This reference book is intended to serve as a versatile vehicle for exploring the field of Asian American drama from its recorded conception to its present stage.

The selection of playwrights and performance artists for this volume is based on a combination of recommendations from theater scholars, the existing record of publication or production, and a playwright's ethnicity. While the first two criteria are more or less self-evident, the ethnicity test deserves explanation. The intent of this book is to reflect the demographics of the diverse Asian American communities in North America, but in an era when ethnicity is becoming increasingly a matter of personal choice rather than heritage, neither geography nor nationality helps define what constitutes "Asian American." Playwrights of the Pacific islands would be excluded if the term were defined geographically; the latest talents of Asian immigrants would be ignored if the term were delimited by citizenship; and it would go against everything this undertaking stands for if the term were prescribed by a playwright's percentage of "Asian blood." This dilemma exposes the very fallacious nature of defining artists, and humanity, by race. While the best-defined racial labels must be mutually exclusive in theory, they will be the least accurate in reality. Yet an all-inclusive category is not feasible because of space constraints. With the recognition of "Asian American" as a bureaucratic and editorial convenience rather than a precise racial category, this volume has thus included fifty-two established and emerging American playwrights and performing artists of origins from India, Pakistan, Vietnam, the Philippines, Japan, Korea, and China in order to articulate a presence that has been traditionally appropriated for the tourist gaze in the collective mind of North American audiences.

As a reference tool, this book is designed to provide a comprehensive but practical resource to educators and scholars engaged in teaching and researching Asian American drama and to students and theater practitioners interested in reading and producing new plays. The fifty-two entries—one for each playwright—are arranged alphabetically. Each entry consists of four sections: Biography, Major Works and Themes, Critical Reception, and Bibliography. At the end of the book, a general Selected Bibliography compiles, separately, both the primary and secondary sources for further reading.

The Biography within each entry is a succinct narrative that places the accomplishments of a playwright in a cultural context. Major Works and Themes is an interpretive description of plays that highlights recurring themes and plots. Critical Reception is an overview that provides the most up-to-date critical assessment of the playwright under discussion. Bibliography is a compilation that lists both the published and unpublished works of the playwright, their selected production history, and sources of critical studies. Although each entry makes no claims to being definitive, it does strive to be comprehensive enough for advanced scholars and general readers alike in their inquiry into each playwright.

The selected production history of an entry serves a dual purpose. On the one hand, it gives credit to the crucial role of theaters to playwrights like that of publishers to authors; on the other, it documents the vitality and struggles of Asian American plays. The successful development of Asian American drama would not have been possible without the establishment of Asian American theaters across the nation. The East West Players in Los Angeles (1965), the Kumu Kahua Theatre in Hawaii (1971), the Asian American Theater Company in San Francisco (1973), the Northwest Asian American Theatre in Seattle (1976), the Pan Asian Repertory Theatre in New York (1977), the New WORLD Theater in Amherst (1979), and Theater Mu in Minneapolis (1992), to name just a few, have all helped create a permanent space on the American stage for Asian America. Although many of them were founded primarily as alternatives to mainstream-dominated venues for Asian American acting professionals, the circuitous trail they blazed has not only galvanized Asian American playwriting to emerge, but has also provided the continuity of that asserted presence in flesh and blood. The postcolonial gaze of Asians is being transformed into an appreciative eye for their cultures and hopefully an eventual embrace of their humanity. While the selected production history credits and honors these theaters and professionals, it is not meant to be complete or comprehensive, but illustrative of the vivacity of Asian American drama in its efforts to reach a larger audience.

On behalf of all the contributors, I wish to acknowledge the playwrights and performance artists for their patient cooperation. My gratitude also goes to all the contributors. Their dedication to Asian American dramatic literature, commitment to original research, and attention to detail have made this reference volume a reality. Appreciation is due as well to Professor Emmanuel Nelson of the State University of New York at Cortland and Dr. George Butler of Greenwood Press for their trust and support throughout the project. In its completion, I must pay special tribute to Roberta Uno, Josephine Lee, and Jie Tian for their field-tested expertise, professional guidance, and generous assistance.

NOTES

1. Harry Lawton and George Knox, Introduction, *Buddha, Confucius, Christ: Three Prophetic Plays*, by Sadakichi Hartmann, ed. Harry Lawton and George Knox (New York: Herder and Herder, 1971) ix–xliv.

ASIAN AMERICAN PLAYWRIGHTS

Brenda Wong Aoki

(1953–)

Melinda L. de Jesús

BIOGRAPHY

Brenda Wong Aoki was born in Salt Lake City, Utah, on July 29, 1953, and was raised in Los Angeles. She is of Japanese, Chinese, Spanish, and Scots descent. Aoki studied dance and majored in community studies at the University of California at Santa Cruz, graduating with a B.A. (with honors) in 1976. An Asian American actress, singer, and musician, Aoki grew tired of the stereotypical roles available to her; during the 1970s and 1980s, she became a founding member of the Asian American Dance Collective and the Asian American Theater Company. She then studied commedia with the Dell'Arte Players as well as Noh and Kyogen (Japanese classical theater) with Yuriko Doi's Theatre of Yugen and later traveled to Japan to work with Noh master Nomuro Shiro and Kyogen master Nomura Mansaku at Chusonji Temple. Aoki also cofounded SoundSeen, an "extraordinary, if short lived, zen-jazz-performance ensemble" (Hurwitt, "Brenda" 266). Since 1988, Aoki has concentrated primarily on solo performance. She and her partner, composer/musician Mark Izu, are the artistic directors of First Voice, a San Francisco–based nonprofit arts organization dedicated to the "music and stories of people caught between cultures, speaking in their own voice" ("About Us"). Currently, Aoki is a member of the Theater-arts faculty at the University of California at Santa Cruz.

MAJOR WORKS AND THEMES

Eclecticism, individuality, and diversity are the hallmarks of Aoki's work. Her plays are inspired by Japanese folktales and her own autobiography and delve into the themes of secrets, betrayal, danger, passion, love, forgiveness, and family. In regard to theatrical form, Aoki's work "is a distinctive melding of dance, music and theatre from both Western and Japanese dramatic traditions" (Perkins and Uno 14).

Obake! Some Japanese Ghosts (or *Obake! Tales of Spirits Past and Present*) (1988) is a unique synthesis of Asian, Asian American, and autobiographical storytelling. Aoki presents five distinct vignettes here: "Black Hair," the story of what happens when a samurai deserts his devoted wife; "Dancing in California," adapted from Hisaye Yamamoto's short story "Miss Sasagawara," which tells of a Japanese American ballerina's struggle to maintain her sanity while interned during World War II; "Havoc in Heaven," a retelling of the Monkey King's epic battle; "The Bell of Dojoji" (an adaptation of Noh and Kabuki plays), in which a woman's passion transforms her into a snake; and "Grandpa," based on Aoki's recollections of her Chinese immigrant grandfather.

The Queen's Garden (1992) is an autobiographical work that describes Aoki's adolescence on the fringes of Asian and Pacific Islander gang life in Long Beach. It explores her romance with gangster Kali, her inability to escape her past, despite graduating from college and moving north, and her desperate but futile attempts to save Kali from his destiny. Kali's entanglements in drugs and crime foretell a tragic firestorm at the play's end.

Random Acts of Kindness (1992) continues Aoki's autobiographical musings. It is a story of a single woman solo performer, "consumed with worries about aging and her own ethnopolitical relevance . . . beset by Christian fundamentalist protesters who suspect that her Japanese children's songs might be satanic incantations" (Hurwitt, "Brenda" 266).

Mermaid Meat (1997) is a fantastic and sensuous tale of love, betrayal, and forgiveness that melds Aoki's unique brand of storytelling with live symphonic accompaniment. Drawing upon the Japanese folkloric belief that one can gain eternal life by eating mermaid meat, Aoki embellishes the story, creating what she calls "nouveau myth": an old fisherman reels in a mermaid from the sea, and they fall in love (Telephone interview). They live happily together with the fisherman's daughter for many years, until the day the daughter notices herself aging. In a moment of insanity, she cuts a slab of flesh from the back of the mermaid and devours it; meanwhile, a giant turtle comes forth to rescue the wounded mermaid and return her to the sea. The final scene depicts the daughter's great remorse and the mermaid's forgiveness, a powerful vision of transformation and love.

Aoki returns again to autobiography in *Uncle Gunjiro's Girlfriend* (1998). This one-woman show explores Aoki's discovery of and reactions to her family's secret: the 1909 interracial marriage of her granduncle, Gunjiro Aoki, to Gladys Emery, daughter of the archdeacon of San Francisco's Grace Cathedral. Fleeing angry mobs and the anti-miscegenation laws hastily passed to prevent their union, Gunjiro and Gladys settle in Seattle. The piece documents their family's persecution through World War II, when the widowed Gladys and her children hide in the Sierra to avoid internment. Thematically, *Uncle Gunjiro's*

Girlfriend, like much of Aoki's work, explores how family secrets and shame haunt generations of a family, and how the act of uncovering and reclaiming family history offers healing as well as a means to honor and celebrate one's past. Aoki is currently writing a novel based on this play.

CRITICAL RECEPTION

Recently anthologized, Aoki's work has received considerable acclaim. In 1992, *The Queen's Garden* garnered four Dramalogue awards for Best Performance, Best Writing, Best Original Music, and Best Lighting as well as a San Diego Critics Circle Award; likewise, both of Aoki's two spoken-word CDs, *Dreams and Illusions: Tales of the Pacific Rim* (1990) and *The Queen's Garden* (1999), have received the National Association of Independent Record Distributors (NAIRD) Indie Award for "Best Spoken Word Album of the Year." *Mermaid Meat* received an American Society of Composers, Authors, and Publishers (ASCAP) special award in 1998.

Nancy Churnin describes Aoki's storytelling talents in *The Queen's Garden* as "formidable" and "extraordinary" ("Memories" F1), and Cheryl North proclaims *Mermaid Meat* to be "impressive" (1). However, Robert Hurwitt notes that the ambitious scope of *Uncle Gunjiro's Girlfriend* undermines its effectiveness: "Too many characters, too many themes and too many performance styles compete for our attention" ("Tale" D1).

By virtue of her mixed heritage and through the content and the formal aspects of her solo work, Aoki has been heralded as the literal embodiment of multicultural American theater. An iconoclastic, daring American playwright whose work continues to astound, Brenda Wong Aoki consistently redefines the concept of Asian American cultural fusion.

BIBLIOGRAPHY

Works by Brenda Wong Aoki

Drama

The Queen's Garden. Contemporary Plays by Women of Color. Ed. Kathy A. Perkins and Roberta Uno. New York: Routledge, 1996. 14–31.

Mermaid Meat: A Piece for Symphony. Excerpt. *Extreme Exposure: An Anthology of Solo Performance Texts from the Twentieth Century.* Ed. Jo Bonney. New York: Theatre Communications Group, 2000. 271–75.

Random Acts of Kindness. Excerpt. *Extreme Exposure: An Anthology of Solo Performance Texts from the Twentieth Century.* Ed. Jo Bonney. New York: Theatre Communications Group, 2000. 267–70.

Unpublished Manuscripts

Whisperings. 1985.

Obake! Some Japanese Ghosts (or *Obake! Tales of Spirits Past and Present*). 1988.

Tales from the Pacific Rim (*The Phoenix and the Dragon*). 1988.
Random Acts of Kindness. 1992.
Uncle Gunjiro's Girlfriend. 1998.

Selected Production History

Obake! Some Japanese Ghosts (or *Obake! Tales of Spirits Past and Present*)

Solo performances, dir. Jael Weisman. National Storytelling Festival, Jonesborough, TN, 1988.
———. Foot of the Mountain Theatre, Minneapolis, 1988.
———. Kennedy Center, Washington, DC, 1990.
———. Whitney Museum of Art, New York City, 1990.
———. Aaron Davis Hall, New York City, 1991.
———. Solo Mio Festival, Climate Theatre, San Francisco, 1991.
———. East/West Center, Honolulu, 1992.
———. San Diego Repertory Theatre, San Diego, 1992.
———. Smithsonian Institution, Washington, DC, 1992.
———. New Victory Theatre, New York City, 1996.
———. Graz Festival, Graz, Austria, 1999.
———. Sapporo University, Sapporo, Japan, 1999.

The Queen's Garden

Solo performances, dir. Jael Weisman. Solo Mio Festival, Climate Theatre, San Francisco, 1992.
———. East/West Center, Honolulu, 1992.
———. San Diego Repertory Theatre, San Diego, 1992.
———. Smithsonian Institution, Washington, DC, 1992.
———. Highways Performance Space, Santa Monica, CA, 1995.
———. Asia Society, New York City, 1996.

Random Acts of Kindness

Solo performances, dir. Jael Weisman. La Peña, Berkeley, CA, 1992.
———. Dallas Theater Center, Dallas, 1994.
———. National Storytelling Festival, Jonesborough, TN, 1994.
———, dir. Amy Mueller. Field Museum, Chicago, 1998.

Mermaid Meat

Solo performances, dir. Jael Weisman; monodrama with Berkeley Symphony, cond. Kent Nagano, and composer Mark Izu. Zellerbach Hall, Berkeley, CA, 1997.
———, dir. Jael Weisman; monodrama with Torrance Symphony, cond. Frank Fetta, and composer Mark Izu. Armstrong Theater, Torrance, CA, 1997.
———, dir. Patricia Pretzinger; composer Mark Izu. Fringe Club, Hong Kong, 1999.

Uncle Gunjiro's Girlfriend

Solo performances as work in-progress, dir. Paolo Nuñez-Ueno. New American Playwrights Festival, Villa Montalvo, San Jose, CA, 1997.
———, dir. Diane Rodriguez. Bay Area Playwrights Festival, Intersection, San Francisco, 1998.

Solo performaces. Solo Mio Festival, Yerba Buena Center for the Arts, San Francisco, 1998.
————. Japan America Theatre, Los Angeles, 2000.
————. McCallum Theatre, Palm Desert, CA, 2000.

Interviews

Telephone interview. 6 Dec. 2000.
Salovey, Todd. "Interview with Brenda Wong Aoki." *San Diego Repertory Theatre News.* Nov.–Dec. 1992: 1+.

Recordings

Dreams and Illusions: Tales of the Pacific Rim. Perf. Brenda W. Aoki. Rounder Records, 1990.
Black Hair: Some Japanese Ghost Stories. Perf. Brenda W. Aoki. Audiocassette. Pele Records, 1997.
The Queen's Garden. Perf. Brenda W. Aoki. Asian Improv Records, 1999.

Studies of Brenda Wong Aoki

"About Us." Home page. 21 June 2000. First Voice. 5 Jan. 2001 <http://www.firstvoice.org/about_firstvoice.html>.
Cheng, Scarlet. "Speaking of the Unspoken: Brenda Wong Aoki Bases Her *Uncle Gunjiro's Girlfriend* on a Long-held Family Secret." *Los Angeles Times* 30 Apr. 2000, Calendar: 48+.
Churnin, Nancy. "Memories of the Gang Trap." Rev. of *The Queen's Garden. Los Angeles Times* 6 Nov. 1992: F1.
————. "Storyteller Stirs Myth, Memory." Rev. of *Obake! Some Japanese Ghosts. Los Angeles Times* 5 Nov. 1992: F1.
Helig, Jack. Rev. of *Random Acts of Kindness. Reader: Chicago's Free Weekly* 27.2 (17 Apr. 1998): 2.
Hurwitt, Robert. "Brenda Wong Aoki." *Extreme Exposure: An Anthology of Solo Performance Texts from the Twentieth Century.* Ed. Jo Bonney. New York: Theatre Communications Group, 2000. 265–66.
————. "One Woman's Tales Paint a Portrait of a Nation." *San Francisco Chronicle* 23 Aug. 1998: D7.
————. "A Tale of Love and Racism." Rev. of *Uncle Gunjiro's Girlfriend. San Francisco Chronicle* 12 Oct. 1998: D1.
North, Cheryl. "It's a Scream at Berkeley Symphony." Rev. of *Mermaid Meat* with composition by Mark Izu. *Oakland Tribune* 17 May 1997, Cue: 1, 5.
Perkins, Kathy A., and Roberta Uno, eds. *Contemporary Plays by Women of Color.* New York: Routledge, 1996.
Winn, Steven. "Aoki's *Garden* Needs Weeding." Rev. of *The Queen's Garden. San Francisco Chronicle* 10 Oct. 1992: C6.
————. "Aoki Tells Adult Tales with Flair." Rev. of *Obake! Some Japanese Ghosts. San Francisco Chronicle* 14 Sept. 1990: E7.

Jeannie Barroga
(1949–   )

Jie Tian

BIOGRAPHY

Jeannie Barroga was born in Milwaukee in 1949. She graduated with a B.A. in fine arts from the University of Wisconsin at Milwaukee in 1972. After graduation, she moved to northern California and felt a connection with this place that hosts rich and diverse cultures and people from different backgrounds. Since then, the San Francisco Bay Area has been home for Barroga and a prominent stage for her career as a playwright. Barroga started playwriting in 1979 as a personal response to her father's passing. Later she explored her own Filipino heritage and a broad range of cultural, political, racial, and ethnic issues in her plays.

In two decades, she has written more than fifty plays, including five that have been broadcast on cable television. Her work has been published, anthologized, and produced nationwide. Today, Barroga plays an active role in many theater groups in northern California and in the nation: the Dramatists Guild, Theater Bay Area, Marin Theater Lab, Quarry (A.C.T.), New Works Forum (formerly Playwright Forum), TheaterWorks, and Teatro Ng Tanan.

Since the 1990s, Barroga has been teaching playwriting in colleges, universities, and theater groups. She has taught playwriting for California State University at Monterey Bay and Colorado College and for theater groups such as Pintig Group in Chicago, Peninsula Civic Light Opera in San Mateo, Teatro Ng Tanan, and the Asian American Theater Workshop in San Francisco, as well as for numerous Bay Area high schools and universities.

A playwright and teacher, Barroga is also a producer, director, and literary manager. In 1983, Barroga founded the Playwright Forum in Palo Alto, California. She has served as literary manager for the Oakland Ensemble Theater.

Since 1985, she has been the literary manager/spectrum artist of TheaterWorks in Palo Alto. Barroga has directed and produced many plays, including *When Stars Fall* for the Playwright Forum, *Bubblegum Killers* at TheaterWorks and Il Teatro in San Francisco, *Kin* at the Asian American Theater Company in San Francisco, Horner Performance Center in Portland, and El Teatro Campesino in San Juan Baustista, and *Kenny Was A Shortstop* for Brava! Women for the Arts in San Francisco. Assisting Amy Gonzalez, Barroga directed *Voir Dire* by Joe Sutton at TheaterWorks in Palo Alto, as well.

Barroga's accomplishments have placed her on grants panels, won her commissions, and garnered her numerous awards. They include the Maverick Award from the Los Angeles Women's Festival, the Joey Award from TeleTheatre, the Tino Award from TeleTheatre, and Work of Excellence from Cupertino, as well as awards from the Bay Area Playwrights Festival Ten-Minute Play Contest and the Inner City Cultural Center Short Play Competition in Los Angeles.

MAJOR WORKS AND THEMES

Barroga writes with passion, perseverance, and a blend of stylistic innovations. Her plays are an ardent quest into the self, the Filipino American experience, and American national identity. They embrace the personal and the public, individual lives and public history, and spheres personal, cultural, and political.

Intergenerational conflict, the tension between tradition and assimilation, ethnic culture, and mainstream culture are the focus of Barroga's earlier plays. *Eye of the Coconut* (1986) epitomizes the classic conundrum through the stories of a Filipino American family in Milwaukee. Dad, who came from the Philippines as a child to pursue a career as a musician, is confronted with three teenage daughters who have minds and dreams of their own. They prefer to date Caucasian men rather than Filipino men, for example. Their preference inevitably intensifies the struggle of assimilation their parents themselves are encountering. In *Rita's Resources* (1995), Barroga uses highly symbolic devices to capture the reality of the Filipino immigrant family in Milwaukee of the 1970s and the illusion of the pursuit of the American dream. As symbols of the American dream and materialism, the Statue of Liberty, the car, Big Bird, and the spaceman present a contrast to the plight and challenges of Rita, the Filipino American seamstress.

Barroga's plays also move beyond the tale of assimilation to portray immigrant groups' quest for identity, truth, and understanding. Her recurrent use of newspaper reporters as the main characters in her plays is a bold device. Her Asian American female characters are active, inquisitive, conscious, and awake, quite the opposite of Asian females stereotyped as geishas, ornaments, prostitutes, or submissive human beings. They are engaged in a search for meaning of personal, cultural, and historical magnitude, sometimes in angry, confounded, tormented, and emotionally charged states. In *Talk-Story* (1992), Dee, a Filipino

American heroine, is a copy girl striving to be a newspaper columnist in order to uncover new angles and write stories featuring her father and uncle in the Philippines and in California. Cora in *Kenny Was a Shortstop* (1990) is a newspaper reporter who covers the story of a young Filipino killed in a gang accident. In the process, she also uncovers hidden angers and resentments of Kenny's mother as well as her own painful memories.

Barroga's exploration of the complexity of politics, race, and ethnicity in America unfolds more deeply in *Walls* (1989), a play inspired by Jan Scrugg and Joel Swerdlow's book *To Heal a Nation*. Vi, a Chinese American reporter, probes the controversial and entangled issues centered around the Vietnam War Memorial and challenges the war of indifference and prejudice on race and ethnicity. The play reflects multicultural America. Barroga creates in the play racially diverse characters—five Asian Americans, three African Americans, and six Caucasians—in representative roles as patriotic veteran, army nurse, protester, and others who were wounded or victimized. In touching and powerful ways, the play acknowledges the traumatic history of the war, probes divisions arising from it, and examines the power of politics over art, the victimization of white and ethnic Americans, and the building of "walls" of division and separation. Despite her use of walls as a metaphor denoting multiple levels of separation and gap between mainstream Americans and ethnic Americans, Barroga urges the necessity to break down the walls and presents her hope and vision for healing, reconciliation, and understanding.

CRITICAL RECEPTION

Productions of Jeannie Barroga's plays have drawn critical attention from theater reviewers in the mainstream media, ethnic newspapers, and magazines published in English, as well as more serious examination recently from scholars in academic institutions. Theater reviews written for the mainstream media can hardly be counted as rigorous studies of Barroga's plays. The reviewers demonstrate some understanding of the issues and struggles of the characters. However, they seldom achieve an insight, depth, or empathetic understanding that is satisfying. The reviews are impressionistic and episodic, revealing little about the characters, the plays, or the playwright. They can be read as phantasmagoria—mainstream America holding a mirror to ethnic America and startled to discover a foreign and unfamiliar assemblage, very much unlike their own, and not knowing what to make of it except labeling it as wild, comic, and absurd.

Criticism from theater reviewers centers on the plays' structural and character development. In a *Seattle Times* article, Wayne Johnson praises the Northwest Asian American Theatre production of *Eye of the Coconut* as "boisterous" and "spirited" (E9). Laurie Winer of the *Los Angeles Times* writes of the anthologized *Talk-Story* as a "thin work." While Winer acknowledges that Dee, the heroine of the play, has "personality and integrity," she questions the internal logic of the character and her actions and terms one of the most passionate speeches of Dee as "impossible to imagine" (42). In his review for the *San Francisco Chronicle*, Steven Winn comments that characters in *Eye of the Coconut* are "unmotivated" "synthetic emblems" lacking "an authentic human ring" (C7).

Theater critics seem to urge plausible actions and dialogue to achieve unity in artistic creation. In the *San Francisco Examiner*, Robert Hurwitt sees *Eye of the Coconut* as evidence of the harm sitcoms have done to theater. He sees the performance as "generally ringing from underdeveloped to amateurish mugging" (C1). In his review for the *Village Voice*, Luis H. Francia deftly captures the conflicts and central issues of the play *Rita's Resources* as revolving around the racially divided America of the early 1970s and the disappointments in the character's quest for the American dream. Yet he questions the play's artistic creation and views the play as "largely predictable" and the portrayal of the family's world and the larger American society as "sketchy" and "more uttered than shown" (90).

Ethnic newspapers published in English—*A. Magazine, Filipino Reporter,* The *Filipino Express, International Examiner*, the *Asian Reporter, AsianWeek,* and *Filipinas Magazine*—offer another source for the reception of Barroga's plays. Devoid of derogative perceptions like those in the mainstream media, the reviews in ethnic periodicals center on the themes, productions, and casts of the plays. However, they are brief and are more factual than critical or analytical.

In the academic arena, a generation of scholars and writers has become conscious of new ethnic and women's literature. These scholars collect, publish, study, and teach less represented writers as a deliberate effort to expand boundaries and lift new artistic creation out of the shadow of silence, denial, and misunderstanding. Jane T. Peterson and Suzanne Bennett dedicate a bio-bibliographical entry to Jeannie Barroga in *Women Playwrights of Diversity*. Roberta Uno at the University of Massachusetts is outspoken and bold in voicing the sensibilities and experience of Asian American women playwrights. She places Barroga's *Walls* among the best dramatic literature written by Asian American women since the 1970s. In her introduction to *Unbroken Thread: An Anthology of Plays by Asian American Women* (1993), Uno powerfully and convincingly argues for a place for Asian American theater and justifies "the ongoing battle by Asian Americans to interpret their own images in both the popular media and the stage" (3). Uno sees the plays and performances as a thread, "a cultural continuum" and a "continuing sense of cultural connection" that "marks the dynamic response of Asians in America" (8–9).

In 1997, Barroga's *Talk-Story* was anthologized in another important collection, *But Still, Like Air, I'll Rise: New Asian American Plays*, edited by Asian American playwright, activist, and scholar Velina Hasu Houston of the University of Southern California. Though the collection is not an analytical study of Barroga's play, Houston offers rich historical, social, and cultural contexts in which to view new Asian American plays. Her primary goal is to redress a critical history that is written from "the heterosexual, patriarchal, Euro-centric perspective" that "presents itself as unchallengeable, immortal, and righteous" (Houston xv). She claims the playwrights of Asian descent residing in the United States as a liberating force: "They lift stereotypes to the wind, broaden the perspectives of ethnic identities of color, and flood people's understanding, in the hope of greater ethnic tolerance" (Houston xvi).

Josephine Lee, associate professor of English at the University of Minnesota, devotes the first scholarly and critical attention to Barroga's *Walls* in her book *Performing Asian America: Race and Ethnicity on the Contemporary Stage*. Lee discusses the performance of race and ethnicity on the stage, the varying perceptions of Asian American performance, and the value of constructing race and ethnicity in theater and American culture. She speaks of the exploration of "Asian Americanness" as necessary not only in forming a "pan-ethnic identity" but also in the "formation of alliances across racial, gender, and class lines . . . to combat racism, sexism, poverty, and systematic discrimination that hurt society as a whole" (209). While Lee acknowledges the complexity in the portrayal of racial, social, cultural, and personal differences in *Walls*, she sees the value of the play in particular as "helping to define relationships among dominant and minority cultures . . . and envision situations in which some understanding can take place" (210).

BIBLIOGRAPHY

Works by Jeannie Barroga

Drama

Two Plays: Kenny Was a Shortstop and The Revered Miss Newton. San Francisco: Philippines Resource Center, 1993.
Walls. Unbroken Thread: An Anthology of Plays by Asian American Women. Ed. Roberta Uno. Amherst: U of Massachusetts P, 1993. 201–60.
Talk-Story. But Still, Like Air, I'll Rise: New Asian American Plays. Ed. Velina Hasu Houston. Philadelphia: Temple UP, 1997. 1–47. Excerpts.
Monologues for Actors of Color: Men. Ed. Roberta Uno. New York: Routledge, 2000. 137–38.

Unpublished Manuscripts

Gets 'Em Right Here. 1982.
Donato's Wedding. 1983.
The Flower and the Bee. 1983.
Reaching for Stars. 1983
Wau-Bun. 1983.
Bachelorettes. 1984.
The Deli Incident. 1984
Pigeon Man. 1984.
Waiting Room. 1984.
Batching It. 1985.
Lorenzo, Love. 1985.

Night before the Rolling Stones Concert 1981. 1985.
Paranoids. 1985.
When Stars Fall. 1985.
Eye of the Coconut. 1986.
Sistersoul. 1986.
Angel. 1987.
Adobo. 1988.
Family. 1988.
Musing. 1989.
My Friend Morty. 1989.
Kin. 1990.
Letters from Dimitri. 1992.
King of Cowards. 1993.
Shades. 1993.
Sabi-Sabi. 1994.
Remnants. 1995.
Rita's Resources. 1995.
A Good Face. 1996.
Passkey of Hearts. Screenplay. 1996.
The Seed. Screenplay. 1997.
Bubblegum Killers. Musical. 1998.
Gadgets. 2000.
Returns. 2000.
Tracking Kilroy. 2000.

Selected Production History

Eye of the Coconut

Production, dir. Bea Kiyohara. Northwest Asian American Theatre, Seattle, 1986.
————, dir. John Shin. Asian American Theater Company, San Francisco, 1987.
————, dir. Ann Fajilan. Asian American Theater Company, San Francisco, 1991.
————, dir. Cary Haguchi. East West Stage, Berkeley, CA, 1993.
————, dir. Maria Zaragoza. Asian American Repertory Theatre, Modesto, CA, 1995.

Lorenzo, Love

Production, dir. Jeannie Barroga. Foothill College Theatre, Los Altos Hills, CA, 1986.

When Stars Fall

Production, dir. John McDonough. Playwright Forum, San Francisco, 1986.

Sistersoul

Production, dir. Kathleen Woods. Playwrights Center Blue Bear Theatre, San Francisco, 1988.
————, dir. Kathleen Woods. TheatreWorks, Palo Alto, CA, 1988.
————. Crystal Springs Uplands School, Hillsborough, CA, 1988.
————. San Jose State Theatre, San Jose, CA, 1988.
————. Inner City Cultural Center, Los Angeles, 1988.

Family

Production, dir. Gary Martinez. Northside Theatre Company, San Jose, CA, 1989.

My Friend Morty

Production, dir. Jeannie Barroga. Playwrights Center, San Francisco, 1989.

Walls

Production, dir. Marian Li. Asian American Theater Company, San Francisco, 1989.
————, dir. David Kurtz. Stanford Drama Department, Stanford, CA, 1991.
————, dir. Michael Birtwhistle. New WORLD Theater, U of Massachusetts, Amherst, 1991.
————, dir. Ray Newman. Asian American Repertory Theatre, Stockton, CA, 1993.
————. Asian American Repertory Theatre, Modesto, CA, 1994.
————, dir. Roberta Uno. Shipboard Education, International Dateline, 1995.
————, dir. Sharon Bandy. Oakes Acting Troupe, Santa Cruz, CA, 1995.

Kenny Was a Shortstop

Production, dir. Jeannie Barroga. Brava! Women for the Arts, San Francisco, 1990.

Kin

Production, dir. Chris Millado. Teatro Ng Tanan (Cowell Theatre), San Francisco, 1991.
————, dir. Jeannie Barroga. Asian American Theater Company, San Francisco, 1991.
————. Horner Performance Center, Portland, OR, 1991.
————, dir. Ann Fajilan. TheatreWorks, Palo Alto, CA, 1991.
————. El Teatro Campesino, San Juan Bautista, CA, 1991.

The Revered Miss Newton

Production, dir. Alissa Welch. San Francisco State U, San Francisco, 1991.
————, dir. Amanda Egron. San Francisco State U Film Department, San Francisco, 1992.

Talk-Story

Production, dir. Marc Hayashi. TheatreWorks, Palo Alto, CA, 1992.
————, dir. Kati Kuroda. Pan Asian Repertory Theatre, New York City, 1995.
————. Kumu Kuhua Theatre, Honolulu, 1995.
————, dir. B. Sellers-Young. Theatre/Dance Department, U of California, Davis, 1999.

Sabi-Sabi

Production, dir. Edgardo de la Cruz. Pintig Cultural Group, Chicago, 1994.

Rita's Resources

Production, dir. Kati Kuroda. Pan Asian Repertory Theatre, New York City, 1995.

A Good Face

Production, dir. Kathleen Woods. Mark Taper Forum, Los Angeles, 1997.
————, dir. Pam McDaniels. 450 Geary Studio/Theatre of Yugen, San Francisco, 1997.
————, dir. Kathleen Woods. Stanford U, 1998.
————. Quarry (A.C.T./Berkeley Repertory), San Francisco, 1998.
————. Warehouse Repertory Theatre, Fort Bragg, CA, 1998.

Tracking Kilroy

Production, dir. Kelvin Han Yee. ODC Theatre, San Francisco, 2001.

Essays

"One Fil-Am's Experience in American Theatre." *Fil-Am: The Filipino American Experience.* Ed. Alfred A. Yuson. Makati City: Publico, 1999. 158–59.

Television

Reaching for Stars

Production, dir. Judith Abend. Viacom Cable Television, Mountain View, CA. 1983.
——, dir. Bruno Borello. Midcoast Cable Television, Half Moon Bay, CA. 1985.

The Deli Incident

Production, dir. Bruno Borello. United Cablevision, Cupertino, CA. 1984.
——, dir. Bruno Borello. Midcoast Cable Television, Half Moon Bay, CA. 1985.

Pigeon Man

Production, dir. Bruno Borello. United Cablevision, Cupertino, CA. 1984.
——, dir. Bruno Borello. Midcoast Cable Television, Half Moon Bay, CA. 1985.

Sistersoul

Production, dir. Kathleen Woods. Viacom Cable Television, Mountain View, CA. 1989.

Batching It

Production, dir. Jean Slanger. Viacom Cable Television, Mountain View, CA. 1991.

Studies of Jeannie Barroga

Francia, Luis H. "Colored Too." *Village Voice* 40.20 (1995): 90.
Houston, Velina Hasu, ed. *But Still, Like Air, I'll Rise: New Asian American Plays.* Philadelphia: Temple UP, 1997.
Hurwitt, Robert. "Coconut Falls from Sitcom Tree: Asian Theater Play Finds the Laughs Are Hard to Come By." *San Francisco Examiner* 31 Jan. 1991: C1.
Johnson, Wayne. "*Eye of the Coconut* Takes a Warm Look at a Filipino-American Family in Transition." *Seattle Times* 15 Oct. 1987: E9.
King, Jennifer, and Thomas A. Gough, eds. *Reflections of Diversity: A Scenebook for Student Actors.* Davis: U of California, 1997.
Lee, Josephine. "Walls." *Performing Asian America: Race and Ethnicity on the Contemporary Stage.* Philadelphia: Temple UP, 1997. 208–15.
Peterson, Jane T., and Suzanne Bennett, eds. *Women Playwrights of Diversity: A Biobibliographical Sourcebook.* Westport, CT: Greenwood P, 1997.
Uno, Roberta, ed. *Unbroken Thread: An Anthology of Plays by Asian American Women.* Amherst: U of Massachusetts P, 1993.
Weiner, Bernard. "A Dramatic Reflection of the Wall." *San Francisco Chronicle* 28 Apr. 1989: E8.
Winer, Laurie. "A Collection with Much Missing." Rev. of *But Still, Like Air, I'll Rise: New Asian American Plays*, ed. Velina Hasu Houston. *Los Angeles Times* 31 Aug. 1997, Calendar: 42.
Winn, Steven. "An Ethnic Comedy That Loses Its Way." *San Francisco Chronicle* 2 Feb. 1991: C7.

Mei-Mei Berssenbrugge

(1947–   )

Martha J. Cutter

BIOGRAPHY

Mei-Mei Berssenbrugge was born in Beijing, China, on October 5, 1947, to a Chinese mother and a Dutch American father. Berssenbrugge grew up in Massachusetts and received a B.A. from Reed College in 1969 and an M.F.A. from Columbia University in 1973. She has lived and/or worked in New Mexico, Rhode Island, Ohio, Massachusetts, Oregon, New York, and numerous other locations. It is not surprising, then, that one strong theme of her drama is cultural and geographical crossings—from the past to the present, from China to the United States, and from the world of the parents to the world of the children.

Berssenbrugge has authored one play but is known primarily for her poetry and her collaborations with visual artists such as Kiki Smith and Richard Tuttle. She has won numerous awards, including the American Book Award (1980, 1984), National Endowment for the Humanities awards (1976, 1981), the Before Columbus Foundation Book Award (1980), and the Asian American Writers' Workshop Annual Literary Award (1997). Her poetry has been featured in journals such as *East-West Journal, Partisan Review, American Rag*, and *River Styx* and has frequently been anthologized. Her only play, *One, Two Cups*, highlights themes of her work as a whole and articulates dilemmas that are central for many Asian American women writers such as Maxine Hong Kingston.

MAJOR WORKS AND THEMES

Ian Hamilton calls Berssenbrugge "a philosophical poet" who questions "being and language simultaneously" (43). The same can be said of Berssenbrugge's poetry and drama in general. Her poetry blurs the boundaries between visual art and words, between music and language, and between self and other. For example, one of her books, *Mizu*, tells a Japanese folktale about a boy who disappears underwater; the book is structured as an accordion and unfolds to almost fourteen feet so that the poem itself becomes visual art. Berssenbrugge has also collaborated with choreographers and has had her poems set to music, once again undermining boundaries between "different" art forms. A poem such as "Sphericity," written just before and after the birth of Berssenbrugge's daughter Martha, blurs gradations between "self" and "other": "The time of having her becomes an absorptive surface, instead of when the person was alive/ . . . As if a person being was like hearing" (*Sphericity* 26).

Like Berssenbrugge's poetry, *One, Two Cups* (1974) experiments with form and with the blurring of boundaries and borders. This densely lyrical, abstract play questions identity through the merging of the three principal characters, Lily, Lillian, and Leilani, and questions language and storytelling through its musings on this very subject: "They put the stories inside you, wrapped in cloth. But then the threads began to rot away, and the stories and the rags lie jumbled in the bottom of the jar" (68). At times it is difficult to tell who is speaking to whom, or whether the dialogue is actually enunciated to another person. In her "remarks," Berssenbrugge herself says that sometimes the speaker is a voice and not a character; she also comments that perhaps neither mother should speak (51). Furthermore, the characters of the two mothers (Lillian and Emily) are deliberately blurred into the characters of the two daughters (Lily and Leilani). The play also shifts from a contemporary time period in the United States to Beijing in the 1940s and back to what seems to be the United States.

These shifts and blurrings underscore the play's major theme: the confusion of identity between mothers and daughters and the difficulty of hearing the stories of the past that actually construct us in the present. Like Maxine Hong Kingston's mother in *The Woman Warrior*, these mothers are difficult to know, difficult to hear. Yet their voices are crucial since it is precisely the stories of the mothers in the play that create the daughter/author: "What is this but being switched on us as if we were invented by them and without their consulting us?" (*One, Two Cups* 51). We are "invented" or created at least in part by the past—and by the stories of our relatives in the past even when they remain unarticulated. We must therefore struggle to hear these allusive and elusive voices.

CRITICAL RECEPTION

Berssenbrugge's poetry has been reviewed favorably and frequently. For example, Jackson Mac Low states that "calmly and convincingly she leads our attention from confidence of passion or attention itself to ice crystals, gulls, fireworks, or apple trees and to very specific qualities of perception, especially vision . . . in poetry that always speaks equally about 'the world' and 'herself.' " Rosemarie Waldrop calls *Empathy* a "dialogue of an extremely fine-tuned intelligence with the world" and argues that it "is not just a fine book. It is an event. An important event." To date, however, Berssenbrugge's drama has received no critical attention.

BIBLIOGRAPHY

Works by Mei-Mei Berssenbrugge

Drama

One, Two Cups. *Summits Move with the Tide: Poems and a Play.* Greenfield Center, NY: Greenfield Review P, 1974. 51–68.

Selected Production History

One, Two Cups

Production. Basement Workshop, New York City, 1979.
————. Northwest Asian American Theatre, Seattle, 1980.

Poetry

Fish Souls. San Francisco: Greenwood P, 1972.
Summits Move with the Tide. Greenfield Center, NY: Greenfield Review P, 1974.
Chronicle. N.p.: Basement Editions, 1978.
Random Possession. New York: I. Reed Books, 1979.
The Heat Bird. Providence, RI: Burning Deck, 1983.
Pack rat sieve. New York: Cambridge Graphic Arts, 1983.
Hiddenness. Drawings by Richard Tuttle. New York: Library Fellows of Whitney Museum, 1987.
Tan Tien. Tucson: Chax P, 1988.
Empathy. Barrytown, NY: Station Hill P, 1989.
Mizu. Art by Cynthia Miller. Tucson: Chax P, 1990.
Sphericity. Drawings by Richard Tuttle. Berkeley: Kelsey Street. P, 1993.
Endocrinology. Art by Kiki Smith. Berkeley: Kelsey Street P, 1997.
Four-Year-Old Girl. Berkeley: Kelsey Street P, 1998.

Studies of Mei-Mei Berssenbrugge

Bernstein, Charles. Rev. of *Empathy.* 1989. 3 Dec. 2000. <http://www.stationhill.org/Fauthor.html>.
Fisher, Dexter, ed. *The Third Woman: Minority Women Writers of the United States.* Boston: Houghton Mifflin, 1980.
Hamilton, Ian, ed. *The Oxford Companion to Twentieth-Century Poetry in English.* New York: Oxford UP, 1994.
Mac Low, Jackson. Rev. of *Empathy.* 1989. 3 Dec. 2000 <http://www.stationhill.org/Fauthor.html>.
Tabios, Eileen, ed. *Black Lightning: Poetry-in-Progress.* Philadelphia: Temple UP, 1998.

Waldrop, Rosemarie. Rev. of *Empathy*. 1989. 3 Dec. 2000 <http://www.stationhill.org /Fauthor.html>.

Wang, L. Ling-chi, and Henry Yiheng Zhao, eds. *Chinese American Poetry: An Anthology*. Seattle: U of Washington P, 1991.

Eugenie Chan
(1962–   )

Sean Metzger

BIOGRAPHY

A fifth-generation Chinese American, Eugenie Chan grew up in San Mateo, California. Her parents lived and initially met among the congested streets of Chinatown in nearby San Francisco. The local church provided a social connection for them and proved formative, in Chan's estimation, of much of their community's cohesiveness. While her parents came of age in a relatively bilingual environment, she spent her youth in the suburbs speaking English along with a smattering of Cantonese. However, during my interview with her, she discussed at length her family trips to Arizona. If the southwestern landscape looms large in her writings, it may well be her early experiences in that region that contribute to its significance. For Chan, such early travel enhances her knowledge of and insight into the interracial dynamics that help construct Chinese identities in the United States.

Chan studied literature at Yale University and subsequently became a Yale-China teaching fellow, which enabled her to teach English at the Chinese University of Hong Kong in the mid-1980s. Such experience apparently proved valuable, for she currently holds a position at the Marin Academy, where she teaches various courses in English literature and creative writing to high-school students. In the period between these positions, Chan worked as a dramaturge and literary manager at the Magic Theatre in San Francisco (1988–91) and helped with Berkeley Repertory's production of Maxine Hong Kingston's *The Woman Warrior* at the Mark Taper Forum in Los Angeles.

In spite of Chan's involvement with the theater and her composition of choreopoems in college, she did not write her first play until the age of twenty-nine, as part of the prerequisite for entering graduate school. Chan received her

M.F.A. in dramatic writing from New York University in 1993. Her awards include winning the Mixed Blood versus America Playwriting Contest (1994) and a New York University graduate achievement award in screenwriting and playwriting (1993). Her screenplay *Willy Gee!* was a 1997 CineStory Competition finalist as well as a semifinalist for the Nicholl Fellowship.

MAJOR WORKS AND THEMES

Chan's corpus consistently engages the intersecting issues of class, religion, sexuality, gender, and ethnicity. By setting the majority of her dramatic productions in the western or southwestern United States, she exposes the often-contradictory affiliations that help to construct Chinese identities in the "American" landscape. Her works thus deal with the specific material and fantastic relationships among Chinese immigrant, Latino, and native American populations.

Characteristic of Chan's writings, *Novell-Aah!* (1993) examines the position of two Chinese women in a world structured by men, particularly in the realm of male fantasies materialized through popular culture. The women in the play seem capable of nothing more than reproducing the milieu of clichés established by the narrating voice-over of El Locutor as they await the presence of a man to activate their lives. The one-act's conclusion, however, finds the women establishing a relationship with one another; female homoeroticism offers an alternative to the futile and endless wait for a man.

Departures and arrivals, of course, mark the immigrant experience also. Chan most explicitly explores the comings and goings that buttress contemporary concerns such as migrancy, diaspora, and borders in *Emil, a Chinese Play* (1994). Using the device of the mother-daughter dyad along with the absent father and pseudoincestuously driven relative (a cousin, whom the audience may view as an actual member of the protagonist's clan or the son of an "uncle" or "auntie"— paper or otherwise), this drama bears a certain intertextual resemblance to some of Chan's other works, but in this play, the stage suggests movement. The title character, a "foreign" man from "South America," begins his journey in Miami through the South, the Midwest, and Disneyland, eventually arriving in San Francisco's Chinatown. In a cinematic type of construction, the scenes in the first half of the piece crosscut between Emil and a young Chinese woman named Maggie (the daughter of the mother/daughter pair). The three principal characters come together and split apart in the space of Chinatown through the theatrical devices of a comic panorama of the United States in act 1 and a bizarre love triangle in act 2. Mother and Maggie alternate investment in Emil. The love story provides a unique vision of interracial romance. From food to offspring to chopsticks, *Emil, a Chinese Play* interrogates what constitutes the boundaries of "Chinese" and the forces invested in constructing a "Chinese" lineage.

A more rustic landscape sets the stage for *Willy Gee!* (1994), a Depression-era tale of a Chinese family in California. Perhaps the closest piece to a history play, this work interrogates the Chinese mythology of the American West. Lily and Augustine Gee run a brothel, with grandma and their adolescent son Willy on the premises. Exposing the hypocrisy of the white "Anglo" establishment, the screenplay comically shows the entrepreneurial ingenuity of a Chinese family in the midst of racial and religious misunderstanding. At the center of the narrative, Willy comes of age and works toward a better understanding of his peers, his family and their business, and his own sexuality.

Chan's full-length play *Rancho Grande* (1997) opens in "a desert expanse in the American Southwest." Mixing Spanish, English, and Chinese, the protagonist Mamie begins with a narrative variant of the Chinese Mid-Autumn Festival (*zhongqiu jie*). The folktale informs the audience specifically about the role of women and coming of age in the lives of a Chinese family of sojourners, but Chan complicates the very notion of home for this nonnuclear familial unit. In addition to interacting with two deities that seem infused with Chicano and Native American influences as much as Chinese ones, Mamie develops cognizance of her sexuality and its attendant expectations in and through the absence of her father. To confuse this scenario even further, Mamie's brother, Sammy, queerly identifies with his sibling, in whom he displays an incestuous interest, as well as his father, who is mostly absent from home. This tension between and within gender characterizes the bulk of Chan's dramatic storytelling.

Given her proclivity for producing work concerned with generations of gendered Asians, audiences may expect perplexing parental figures and meandering men to recur as figures and themes throughout many of Chan's productions. In the short film *Paradise Plains* (1993), Chan again addresses the topic of incest. This time, the relationship occurs between an uncle and niece. Although Chan does not deal at all with Chinese characters in this film, she said in my interview with her that an Asian American play is anything that falls "within the imagination and experience" of a writer who might identify with such a label. Chan thus expands the boundaries imposed by a theater of cultural nationalism in favor of a more expansive definition of the term "Asian American." In so doing, she helps add a new chapter in Asian American theater history by moving beyond the conventions established in the 1960s and 1970s to a more fluid conception of Asian American identity and concomitant cultural production.

The screenplay *Athena Adrift* (1997) also uses Chinatown as a setting. However, this scenario invokes Chinatown as an ambivalent space. Living with her mother Flora and her brother Nelson, Athena longs to find romance. While she dreams through the literature that she teaches—be it through the words of Sor Juana or a Brontë—her quixotic fantasies eschew a Chinese cultural connection, much to the chagrin of her mother, whose own suitor is a wealthy Chinese entrepreneur. The play explores the dynamics of heterosexual relationships of different generations and across racial lines. Nelson engages in an affair with a South American named Cleopatra, while Athena's dating attempts find her in bed with a Japanese-identified Italian. By the end, Athena must negotiate her own relationship to her Chinese heritage both emotionally and professionally. Her final confrontation with her obnoxious and mysterious admirer takes her through San Francisco into Chinatown's crowds.

The brief piece *Sticks and Stones* (1999) comments on gender and sexual difference in a slightly different way. This work stages the attempts of two characters ("Girl" and "Boy") to communicate with one another. Moving from their verbal misfires, the pair eventually finds some sort of connection through one another's corporeality. A similar theatrical device seems to inform the one-minute drama *Esmerelda* (1997). This pithy monologue presents the physical processes of a woman's waiting for someone who never arrives.

Chan's current project *Snakewoman* (2001) is a taiko percussion piece. The story concerns a half woman, half snake with three breasts and three children (one black, one white and one lemon), whose fathers are gods. This latest work continues Chan's exploration of the diverse myths and fantasies that impinge on any conception of reality.

Central to all of Chan's works, issues of family, gender, and identity continually resurface in a variety of contexts. Family, in particular, is a well-worn trope in Asian American drama. Chan's remarkable ability to affirm and interrogate Chineseness in a multiethnic landscape both enriches and problematizes any attempt to claim cultural membership and thus refigures old familial models of ethnicity. In other words, Chan's writings attest to the complicated material and psychic affiliations that render the term "Asian American" both meaningful and highly contentious.

CRITICAL RECEPTION

Because only two of Eugenie Chan's works have been published, critical literature on her work remains minimal.

BIBLIOGRAPHY

Works by Eugenie Chan

Drama

Novell-aah! Seattle: Rain City Projects, 1993.
Esmerelda. Seattle: Rain City Projects, 1997.

Unpublished Manuscripts

The Fan. Choreopoem. 1984.
Tour Sino: A Short Radio Play. 1992.
Emil, a Chinese Play. Ms. 345. Roberta Uno Asian Women Playwrights Scripts Collection 1924–1992, Special Collections and Archives, W.E.B. Du Bois Library, U of Massachusetts, Amherst, 1994.
Paradise Plains. 1995.
Rancho Grande. Ms. 345. Roberta Uno Asian Women Playwrights Scripts Collection

1924–1992, Special Collections and Archives, W.E.B. Du Bois Library, U of Massachusetts, Amherst, 1997.

Sticks and Stones: A Short Play. 1999.

Snakewoman. 2001.

Selected Production History

The Fan

Production, Yale U, New Haven, 1984.

————. Chinese U of Hong Kong, Hong Kong, 1985.

Emil, a Chinese Play

Workshop, Pan Asian Repertory Theatre, New York City, 1992.

————, dir. Tim Bond. Seattle Group Theatre's Multicultural Playwrights Festival, Seattle, 1992.

————, East West Players, Los Angeles, 1993.

Novell-aah!

Production. Brava! For Women in the Public Theatre, San Francisco, 1993.

————, dir. Rebecca Patterson; perf. Michelle Ching, Pin-Pin Su, and Angela Fitzgerald. Perishable Theatre, Providence, RI, 1996.

Tour Sino

Production (radio), dir. Eugenie Chan. WBAI, New York City. 1993.

Rancho Grande

Workshop, dir. Phyllis S.K. Look; perf. Kerri Higuchi, Dian Kobayashi, Sean San Jose, and John Cho. Bay Area Playwrights Festival, Magic Theatre, San Francisco, 1994.

————, perf. Kerri Higuchi. PlayLabs at the Playwrights Center, Minneapolis, 1995.

————. Asian American Theater Company, San Francisco, 1996.

————, dir. Phyllis S.K. Look; perf. Kerri Higuchi, Dian Kobayashi, Radmar Agana Rao, Tamlyn Tomita, Stan Egi, and Jim Ishida. East West Players, Los Angeles, 1997.

Production, dir. Jane Kaplan; perf. Leilani Wollam, Tony Colinares, Mona Armonio Leach, Vera Wong, Jose Abaoag, and Chris San Nicholas. Northwest Asian American Theatre, Seattle, 1999.

————, dir. Tony Kelley. Thick Description, San Francisco, 2001.

Paradise Plains

vox i Productions, dir. Elizabeth Schub. VHS. 1995.

Production. Bilbao International Film Festival, 1995.

————. Cinequest Film Festival, 1995.

————. Mill Valley Film Festival, 1995.

————. Warner Prize, New York U, New York City, 1995.

Esmerelda

Performance. "Night of 1,000 Playwrights," Rain City Project, Seattle, 1997.

Snakewoman

Workshop. New Music Theatre Project, San Francisco, 1998.

————. Brava! For Women in the Arts, San Francisco, 2000.

Sticks and Stones

Staged reading. Djerassi Foundation, Woodside, CA, 1999.

Interview

Personal interview. 6 May 2000.

Screenplays

Winnie's World. Fifteen-minute short film. 1992.
Paradise Plains. Short film. 1993.
Street X. Series of shorts. 1993.
Willy Gee! Feature film. 1994.
Athena Adrift. Feature film. 1997.

Studies of Eugenie Chan

Peterson, Jane T., and Suzanne Bennett, eds. *Women Playwrights of Diversity.* Westport, CT: Greenwood P, 1997.

Frank Chin

(1940–   )

Guiyou Huang

BIOGRAPHY

Few Asian American writers are as controversial as Frank Chin and yet as influential as he is in his own way on Asian American literary and cultural discourses. Born in Berkeley, California, on February 25, 1940, Chin graduated from the University of California at Berkeley. At an early age, he moved to Oakland to realize "big ideas." He was the first Chinese American brakeman on the Southern Pacific Railroad, an experience that he masterfully sketches in various works of fiction and drama. Chin also takes pride in being the first Asian American playwright to have a play produced at the American Place Theatre in New York in 1972, when Asian American writing as literature had hardly been heard of, not to mention recognized.

Chin became a playwright by chance. In 1970, he went to Maui, Hawaii, where he worked with friends in construction. When the East West Players in Los Angeles held a playwriting contest, Chin, prompted by an urge to get off the island, wrote *The Chickencoop Chinaman* in six weeks, won the $500 contest, and left the island. Then Chin met Randy Kim, a Chinese/Korean American actor who made his writing "fast, fun, and sharp," and with Kim in mind he wrote his second play, *The Year of the Dragon*, which was also staged at the American Place Theatre (Davis 86).

In 1988, Chin published a collection of short stories under the title *The Chinaman Pacific & Frisco R.R. Co.*, which received the American Book Award from the Before Columbus Foundation. In the early 1990s, Chin turned his creative energy to writing novels, publishing *Donald Duk* in 1991 and *Gunga Din Highway* in 1994. Chin's novels were influenced by writers such as the renowned African American novelist Ishmael Reed as well as by classical Chinese writers like Luo Guanzhong and Shi Nai'an, respective authors of *Romance of the Three Kingdoms* and *Water Margin*, and Sun Tzu, whose *Art of War* is a must read for all Chinese military academies and many U.S. military institutions. Indeed, Chin's thinking on social, cultural, intellectual, and racial issues has benefited from these masterpieces. To say that Chin emulates the black revolutionaries of the 1960s is to underestimate the shaping power of Chinese classics.

Chin is a controversial figure in the Asian American literary and cultural communities. Some have recognized him as the "Godfather" of Asian American writing (*The Big Aiiieeeee!* 529); others have called him an acrimonious critic. In any case, Chin has contributed to almost every major literary genre as playwright, novelist, essayist, critic, and editor. He was first editor of the groundbreaking Asian American anthology *Aiiieeeee!*, second editor of *The Big Aiiieeeee!*, and author of such widely cited essays as "This Is Not an Autobiography" and "Come All Ye Asian American Writers of the Real and the Fake," though he is primarily regarded as a playwright and a novelist.

MAJOR PLAYS AND THEMES

The themes that Chin explores in his plays, novels, stories, and essays all concern Asian America, which he handles in such a way that they do not seem to be intended to please any one particular group or another. In his plays, Chin writes about historical, social, and intellectual issues relevant to Chinese and Asian American cultural heritages, expressing concerns over race relations, racial stereotyping, identity, family, history, and Hollywood.

The Chickencoop Chinaman (1971) is noteworthy for being the first play by an Asian American produced at New York's American Place Theatre, where it opened on May 27, 1972, and closed on June 24 "after a limited engagement of 33 performances" (Willis, vol. 28, 129). The play follows one main story line: The search for a father figure starts the play, and the failure to find one concludes it. The dramatic plot involves major U.S. races: Caucasian, Native American, black, Asian, and in-between products of interracial marriages; it explores issues such as assimilation, the social and political predicament of Asians in the United States, their cultural and racial identities, and their struggle to debunk racial stereotypes, especially of Asian men, who are believed to make "lousy fathers." Complicating these issues are the endangered condition of the Asian American family and the persistent presence of racial violence on and prejudice against minority groups and individuals.

In the play, the viewer/reader cannot find a complete, unbroken family that symbolizes unity and happiness. Tam Lum, a writer and filmmaker whose first name is often mocked for its resemblance to Tampax and the Anglo name Tom, flies out of Oakland, California, to Pittsburgh, Pennsylvania, in search of the father of Ovaltine Jack the Dancer, a former lightweight champion, for his documentary film, only to find that Charley Popcorn is not Ovaltine's father but a

former boxer trainer who now runs a porno movie house, and who is a "bigot
. . . nothing but a black racist when it comes to yellow people" (42). Even though
Tam is looking for someone else's father, he misses a real father and is himself
not a good father because he is divorced from his Caucasian wife and his two
children do not miss him. He tells Lee, the Eurasian girl who lives in Kenji's
apartment, "Chinamans do make lousy fathers. I know. I have one" (23); he
even insults Lee with an ethnocentric observation: "I reminded you of your
Chinese husband" (23). Thus the manhood of Chinese American males is drawn
into question.

Kenji, a research dentist and Tam's longtime Japanese American friend, is
not married to Lee but plays the role of a surrogate father to Lee's son Robbie.
Robbie claims that he has several fathers, though he knows not which one is
his biological dad. Tom, Lee's former Chinese husband, wants to be Robbie's
father and remarry Lee, but neither seems genuinely interested in returning to
him. When the curtain finally falls on the audience, one is made to realize that
the search for a father figure results in no hit, thus exposing the lack of manhood
in Asian American males.

Robbie is a male child under twelve, but he talks like a man. He has no
innocence and cooks for all the adults under the roof of Kenji's apartment. Tam,
who went out of his way to Pittsburgh to locate Ovaltine's father, in the end
finds himself cooking in Kenji's kitchen, too, while thinking about the ears his
grandmother had for trains. Asian American men's habitual use of the kitchen
as a terrain of work, Chin seems to imply, results from the mainstream culture's
emasculation of them—thus Chin's satirical portrayal of their loss of manhood.

Another theme closely interwoven with the loss of Asian American manhood
in the play is Chin's concern with American racism and race relations. Representing white American racism is the Lone Ranger, who, with his faithful Indian
companion Tonto, shoots Tam in the hand, calls himself "the law" and Asians
"honorary white," tells them to be "legendary obeyers of the law, legendary
humble, legendary passive," and directs them to go back to Chinatown to pre-
serve their culture (37). The Lone Ranger offers Helen Keller as a compact
model for all minorities (36). Tam sarcastically sums up this racist mentality:
"Helen Keller overcame her handicaps without riot! She overcame her handicaps
without looting! She overcame her handicaps without violence! And you Chinks
and Japs can too" (11). Tam's anger at racist America affects his perceptions
of all races, including people of his own Chinese race such as Tom and the
part-Chinese Lee.

Tom is writing a book called *Soul on Rice* about Chinese American identity.
He insists that he is not prejudiced against Chinese, that he is assimilated and
accepted in white America, and that Lee is non-Chinese. Tom's assimilationist
attitude causes Tam to accusingly call him an "ornamental Oriental": "You
wanted to be 'accepted' by whites so much, you created one to accept you. You
didn't know Lee's got a bucket of Chinese blood in her? At least a bucket? . . .
You wanted a white girl so bad, so bad, you turned her white with your magic

eyes. You got that anti-Chinaman vision" (59–60). On the other hand, Lee appears to be more egalitarian in her views of race relations—she has married Chinese, white, and black; now she is living with a Japanese and claims that she is on her way to Africa. Lee is not as race sensitive as Tam, nor is she as biased as Tom; she does not seem perfectly comfortable with her mixed identity, nor does she know what to do with it; hence the purposelessness of her life and her inability to acquire an identity that fits her.

Also salient in *The Chickencoop Chinaman* is the role that language plays in defining identities. In Tam's dialogue with the Hong Kong Dream Girl during his flight to Pittsburgh, the latter narcissistically believes that she has rid herself of her Hong Kong accent when speaking English, hoping that she sounds and will be considered Americanized. Like Tom, the Hong Kong–born stewardess yearns for assimilation and acceptance, though Tam offers her no such affirmation. On the other end of the linguistic spectrum, however, Tam's and Kenji's ebonic accent due to growing up in Oakland's black ghettos confuses black men like Charley Popcorn. In fact, Tam's black speech offends Popcorn because Popcorn never dreams that a Chinaman like Tam can speak his language, which causes him to mistake him for a black man on the phone, a mistake that is not corrected until the two actually meet in person at Popcorn's porno movie house. It is obvious in Chin's play that language can help both make and break one's cultural identity, and that it bears little on the formation of identities. Tam and Kenji can fluently use different accents to sound like Helen Keller, like blacks or whites, but they are Americans of Asian descent. As Elaine Kim asserts, culture is not passed down through the blood (68).

Chin's second play, *The Year of the Dragon*, was also first produced at the American Place Theatre, where it opened on May 22, 1974, and closed on June 15 after thirty performances (Willis, vol. 30, 98). In January 1975, PBS aired the play as a ninety-minute television drama, with George Takei in the leading role (Kurahashi 73). Like Chin's novel *Donald Duk*, the play unfolds its events on the Chinese New Year of the dragon, and like his first play, this one treats the Chinese American family from inside San Francisco's famous Chinatown, though it looks more gloomily into the disintegration of the family.

The drama revolves around several significant events occurring to the Eng family during the New Year: Pa Wing Eng's imminent death; the arrival of China Mama, Pa's Chinese wife; the return of the daughter Mattie (Sis) with her white husband Ross on a tour promoting her cookbook; the completion of little brother Johnny's probation for possessing a gun; and the central character Fred Eng's last tour of Chinatown. The play ends with Pa's expected death and Fred's continuation as a Chinatown tourist guide.

The play is close to what may be called a modern tragedy, not unlike Arthur Miller's *Death of a Salesman*, which also centers on the family and father/son relationships and features the death of the father. The most tragic dimension of Chin's play is not the expected and even anticipated death of the tyrannical father, but rather the disintegration of the Chinese American family as a result of societal and political circumstances beyond their control. Pa Eng is a bigamist and brings his Chinese wife over for the mere sake of dying Chinese. His American Chinese wife, Hyacinth, has no control over her husband's decisions or her children's (one of them, Fred, is not her biological son), but she seems capable of finding release from her stress by hiding in the bathroom, the only quiet spot in her Chinatown apartment. China Mama, though physically present, remains motionless and speechless for the majority of the duration of the play. Her dramatic name symbolizes the remote, ancient China that the Eng family has left behind and that is now brought back by the tyrannical wish of the dying father.

Mattie, who wanted to be just people and not Chinese and married a white guy to live her philosophy, is assimilated into the mainstream culture in Boston, and now she wants her family to move out, too. Johnny, on the other hand, hates white people and refuses to leave Chinatown because that is where he feels at home. Fred, stuck between these two positions, sacrificed his youth and his dream to become a writer by helping Mattie out of Chinatown; now he wants to do the same for Johnny by trying to prevent him from becoming a tourist guide like himself and urging him to marry a white girl while he is young. But Johnny turns out to be a Chinatown tourist guide despite Fred's opposition. Pa Eng's death wish for Fred to become Chinatown's mayor is shattered; Mattie presumably returns to Boston; Fred and Johnny both work as tourist guides in Chinatown. Fred in the end "appears to be a shrunken Charlie Chan, an image of death" (141). Elaine Kim's reading of Jeffery Paul Chan's "Auntie Tsia Lays Dying" seems pertinent here: "Chinatown is a 'fraud,' a place of death where listless celibacy and sterile incompleteness are thinly veiled by a cheap facade for tourists" (73).

The fact that Fred hates his job and swears so much indicates that he feels confused about his identity: Chinese or American, neither or both? His father wants him to be Chinese and responsible; indeed, Fred has been responsible and even filial, despite Pa's accusation of him otherwise. In contrast, his American Ma seizes opportunities to remind him, "Don't forget you're 'Chinese of American descent' " (92). As a result, Fred has to struggle in this "catch-22" situation—after his father's death he is expected to take care of both his biological China Mama and his American Ma, being forced by familial circumstances to be both Chinese and American. He understands his American mother perfectly, but he cannot even say a word and make sense to his Chinese mother. Out of frustration and anger, Fred tells China Mama: "I'm not Chinese. This ain't China. Your language is foreign and ugly to me, so how come you're my mother?" (115). Through disclaiming China Mama, Fred dissociates himself from China and its culture. But because the woman is his biological mother and now a U.S. citizen, she constitutes a new burden to Fred, so his never-stable identity is made even more insecure by this responsibility.

The problematic identity issues are further dramatized in Mattie's willingness to assimilate through interracial marriage. Mattie left Chinatown not to return until fifteen years later, and now she calls Boston with Ross her home, not Chinatown with her folks in it. Fred enlightens his white brother-in-law about assimilation: "It's the rule not the exception for us to marry out white. Out in Boston, I might even marry me a blonde" (85). This marrying out, to Chin, contributes to the disintegration of the Chinese American family, and ultimately to the extinction of Chinese American culture. It is an end result of assimilation, an issue that Chin drives home in his novel *Gunga Din Highway*, in which he relentlessly attacks Chinese Americans who take the highway of assimilation for white acceptance.

Chinatown, for good or bad, betokens Chinese American culture, and for Fred it is "as real as China," but if he steps out of its customary boundaries, he fears that he will become nobody (116). Chinatown itself is also in the process of disintegrating, however, because the people who inhabit and represent this coop are dying out. Pa Eng, for example, as Chinatown's mayor, is sick and decrepit, losing not just health but also respect and control. When Fred answers no to his recurrent question "You my son yes or no?" Pa hits him and then collapses. Fred not only beats on his dead body but calls him " 'Mayor of Chinatown' Flop" (140). Chinatown therefore is also a flop and should be abandoned, but fear of becoming a nobody outside it propels Fred to pathetically continue his existence as a tour guide in Chinatown for its performance value.

CRITICAL RECEPTION

Critical discourse on Frank Chin's work varies from gender to gender. An investigation of the reception of his plays is inseparable from critics' perceptions of his work in other genres. However, Chin's views on Asian American history and culture and on specific issues such as family, assimilation, and racism were first formed and expressed in his two plays under discussion here.

Reviews of *The Chickencoop Chinaman* are mixed. Jack Kroll views the play as an addition to "the roster of alienation coming out of our theatre and fiction," though he is disappointed about the play's roughness (55). "This first play needs more work—the basic emotional tone of hysteria is too unmodulated, the action is too thin, and awkward structure wrenches the play in and out of fantasy. But there is real vitality, humor and pain on Chin's stage" (55). Responding to Betty Lee Sung's charge reported in Dorothy Ritsuko McDonald's introduction to Chin's plays that the audience did not enjoy the play and kept dwindling, Joseph S.M. Lau writes that the reason for the dwindling was that "no one could possibly finish watching the play without feeling scathed. . . . Language offends as much as the smell of Wing Eng's long turd" (101). Chin is unpopular because, according to Lau, "the work of a writer suffering from self-contempt naturally makes unpleasant reading. . . . In a solitary way, however, Chin has fulfilled the essential moral obligations of a negative serious writer" (104).

David Leiwei Li offers a more sympathetic reading: Chin's play "exemplifies his tenacious drive to combat the discursive modes of domination that encode the object position of the minority. . . . Chin wages war against the hegemonic exercise of power in the form of language" (215). Though Li is critical of Chin's partial blindness to "the multiplicity of contemporary Chinese American reality," he lauds Chin's sense of responsibility as a writer. "There is little question that Chin is everywhere motivated by this sense of moral integrity" (221). Erik Mac-Donald reads *The Chickencoop Chinaman* as Chin's effort to "create a location and a politics of identity amid a world that both shatters his identity and tries to provide instead a ready-made 'Chinese American' character" (142); in the end, "Chin discards the icons offered to the Asian Other, disemboweling the language, and thus apparently places Tam at once both inside and outside his society" (149).

Elaine Kim views Chin's work more critically, as an attempt "to reassert male authority over the cultural domain and over women by subordinating feminism to nationalist concerns," and therefore "Chin's indisputable status as pioneering advocate for Asian American literature and culture is undermined by his insistence on a system of binary oppositions that denies women an autonomous selfhood" (75). King-Kok Cheung agrees and considers Chin's work as an effort to redefine "both literary history and Asian American manhood" (234), though she finds it disturbing that Chin "should lend credence to the conventional association of physical aggression with manly valor" (237).

The Year of the Dragon has garnered similarly mixed receptions. Clive Barnes finds Chin's second play an exploration of identity: how Chinese or how American is the Chinese American? Barnes appreciates Chin's fascination with bicultural and generational issues, "especially if we think of his play in the terms of that American melting pot that never seems to be properly heated and never seems to be properly stirred" (39). Like some reviewers of *The Chickencoop Chinaman*, Barnes finds gaps and a lack of energy in the new play. Jim Moore, though not impressed with the performance of some actors, praises the play's sophisticated presentation of Chinatown life: "It's an angry, biting, funny, despairing play about real, invisible people struggling to escape stereotypes. Chin's version of America's Chinatowns is utterly convincing" (19). Dan Sullivan also faults the play for lacking a beat and being "a bit choked by all the stories Chin wants to tell"; nonetheless, Sullivan finds that Chin's "Chinatown from the inside is much more interesting than it is from the bus" and that the play is "easily the strongest full-length script East/West has done" (17).

Yuko Kurahashi views the play as Chin's attempt to reclaim Chinese American manhood as well as a criticism of the assimilation of Chinese Americans. Chinatown thus is a contested battleground. Chin's view of Chinatown is twofold: "Chin regards Chinatown as the center of Chinese American life, which preserves ancient Chinese culture and traditions. On the other hand, he also views Chinatown as a product of American racism" (73). Therefore, neither leaving Chinatown nor remaining there is a desirable and winning option. As David Leiwei Li points out, Chinatown is treated as "a special hegemonic creation of the Chinese American sociogeographic space," but the drama does not focus on "Chinatown as an exotic setting but on the burden and dilemma it poses as an existential space for the Chinese Americans there" (217).

Even though Li construes Fred's rebellion as "an act of resistance to the authoritarian father figure of the dominant" (218), the rebellion is not productive, for Fred in the end chooses to stay in Chinatown and becomes a Charlie Chan, who constitutes the most favorite target (created out of the white imagination) of Frank Chin's scathing barrages of verbal attacks in almost all of his writings—novels, stories, essays, interviews, and last, but also the most important, his plays.

BIBLIOGRAPHY

Works by Frank Chin

Drama

"Act I of *The Chickencoop Chinaman.*" *Aiiieeeee! An Anthology of Asian-American Writers.* Ed. Frank Chin, Jeffery Paul Chan, Lawson Fusao Inada, and Shawn Hsu Wong. Washington, DC: Howard UP, 1974. 49–74.
The Chickencoop Chinaman and The Year of the Dragon. Seattle: U of Washington P, 1981.

Selected Production History

The Chickencoop Chinaman

Production, dir. Jack Gelber, perf. Randall (Duk) Kim. American Place Theatre, New York City, 1972.

The Year of the Dragon

Production, dir. Russell Treyz; perf. Randall (Duk) Kim. American Place Theatre, New York City, 1974.
———, perf. George Takei. *Television-Drama.* PBS. 1975.

Essays

"This Is Not an Autobiography." *Genre* 18 (Summer 1985): 109–30.
"Come All Ye Asian American Writers of the Real and the Fake." *The Big Aiiieeeee! An Anthology of Chinese American and Japanese American Literature.* Ed. Jeffery Paul Chan, Frank Chin, Lawson Fusao Inada, and Shawn Wong. New York: Meridian, 1991. 1–92.
"Uncle Frank's Fakebook of Fairy Tales for Asian American Moms and Dads." *Amerasia Journal* 18.2 (1992): 69–87.
Bulletproof Buddhists and Other Essays. Honolulu: U of Hawai'i P, 1998.

Interviews

Davis, Robert Murray. "Frank Chin: An Interview with Robert Murray Davis." *Amerasia Journal* 14.2 (1988): 81–95.

———. "West Meets East: A Conversation with Frank Chin." *Amerasia Journal* 24.1 (1998): 87–103.

Novels

Donald Duk. Minneapolis: Coffee House, 1991.
Gunga Din Highway. Minneapolis: Coffee House, 1994.

Short Stories

The Chinaman Pacific & Frisco R.R. Co. Minneapolis: Coffee House, 1988.
"The Only Real Day." *The Big Aiiieeeee! An Anthology of Chinese American and Japanese American Literature*. Ed. Jeffery Paul Chan, Frank Chin, Lawson Fusao Inada, and Shawn Wong. New York: Meridian, 1991. 529–62.

Studies of Frank Chin

Barnes, Clive. "*Year of the Dragon* Is New Frank Chin Play." *New York Times* 3 June 1974: 39.

Cheung, King-Kok. "The Woman Warrior versus the Chinaman Pacific: Must a Chinese American Critic Choose between Feminism and Heroism?" *Conflicts in Feminism*. Ed. Marianne Hirsche and Evelyn Fox Keller. New York: Routledge, 1990. 234–51.

Huang, Guiyou. "Frank Chin." *Asian American Novelists: A Bio-bibliographical Critical Sourcebook*. Ed. Emmanuel Nelson. Westport, CT: Greenwood P, 2000. 48–55.

Kim, Elaine H. " 'Such Opposite Creatures': Men and Women in Asian American Literature." *Michigan Quarterly Review* 29.1 (Winter 1990): 68–93.

Kroll, Jack. Rev. of *The Chickencoop Chinaman*. *Newsweek* 19 June 1972: 55.

Kurahashi, Yuko. "Gender, Cultural Nationalism, and Between Worlds: *The Year of the Dragon* and *The Soul Shall Rise*." *Asian American Culture on Stage: The History of the East West Players*. New York: Garland Publishing, 1999. 69–89.

Lau, Joseph S.M. "The Albatross Exorcised: The Rime of Frank Chin." *Tamkang Review* 12.1 (1981): 93–105.

Li, David Leiwei. "The Formation of Frank Chin and Formations of Chinese American Literature." *Asian Americans: Comparative and Global Perspectives*. Ed. Shirley Hune, Hyung-chan Kim, Stephen S. Fugita, and Amy Ling. Pullman: Washington State UP, 1991. 211–23.

MacDonald, Erik. " 'The Fractured I ≠ the Dissolved Self': Ethnic Identity in Frank Chin and Cherríe Moraga." *Theater at the Margins: Text and the Post-Structured Stage*. Ann Arbor: U of Michigan P, 1993. 137–72.

McDonald, Dorothy Ritsuko. Introduction. *The Chickencoop Chinaman and The Year of the Dragon*. Seattle: U of Washington P, 1981. ix–xxix.

Moore, Jim. "East-West Players' *Year of the Dragon*." *Los Angeles Herald Examiner* 10 October 1974: 19.

Sullivan, Dan. "The Scrutability of Frank Chin." *Los Angeles Times* 4 Oct. 1974: 17.

Willis, John. "Season 1971–1972." *Theatre World* 28 (1972): 129.

———. "Season 1973–74." *Theatre World* 30 (1974): 98.

Ping Chong

(1946–)

Douglas I. Sugano

BIOGRAPHY

Ping Chong was born on October 2, 1946, in Toronto, Canada, but grew up in New York City's Chinatown. After high school, he went on to study filmmaking and graphic design at Pratt Institute's School of Visual Arts. From 1964 to 1966, Chong started his theatrical career with Meredith Monk's House Foundation, where he collaborated with Monk on several major works, including *The Travelogue Series* and *The Games*, for which they shared an Outstanding Achievement in Music Theatre Award in 1986.

Chong's first independent theater work was *Lazarus*, which was produced at the Lee Nagrin Studio in New York City. Since that time, he has created dozens of works for the stage, several of which have won prestigious awards, including *Humboldt's Current*, which won an Obie Award in 1977, *A.M./A.M.—The Articulated Man*, which won a Villager Award in 1982, *Kind Ness*, which won a USA Playwrights' Award in 1988; and *Brightness*, which garnered two 1990 Bessie awards. In 2000, Ping Chong received an Obie Award for Sustained Achievement from the *Village Voice*.

Ping Chong and Company was formerly called the Fiji Theatre Company, which Chong founded in 1975 to explore performances that combine contemporary theater, multicultural issues, movement, and art. It is difficult to categorize Chong's works, as they are all, to some degree, multimedia projects on wide-ranging and eclectic subjects. In 1990, Ping Chong created *Deshima*, the first of a series of performance works that explore East-West relations. In 1992, at New York City's Artists' Space, Chong created *Undesirable Elements*, an ongoing series of performance pieces that explore the effects of culture, history, and ethnicity on the lives of people in different communities. Chong created different versions of the show for Chicago, Cleveland, Minneapolis, Seattle, Rotterdam, and Tokyo. *Deshima* was followed by *Chinoiserie* (1995) and by *After Sorrow* (1997). His two latest shows are *Pojagi*, which is about Korean history, and *Truth and Beauty* (1999). In 1998, Chong further demonstrated his versatility when he collaborated with set designer Mitsuro Ishii and puppet artist Jon Ludwig to create *Kwaidan*, a puppet-theater work based on three Japanese ghost stories by Lafcadio Hearn.

Chong's other multimedia projects include directing television specials— *Paris* with Meredith Monk for KCTV in Minneapolis and *Turtle Dreams* for WGBH in Boston, which won the Grand Prize at the Toronto Video Festival. His other original video works include *I Will Not Be Sad in the World* and *Place Concrete* for both WNET and WGBH. Chong has also created many video installations for museums and galleries: *In the Absence of Memory* (Hartford, Connecticut), *Tempus Fugit* (Marquette University), *A Facility for the Containment and Channeling of Undesirable Elements* (New York City), and *Testimonial* (Venice). Even though he has created dozens of plays, multimedia works, and performance works, Chong's published theatrical works include only *Kind Ness, Snow*, and *Nuit Blanche*.

MAJOR WORKS AND THEMES

As indicated earlier, Ping Chong's dramatic work is difficult to categorize and to describe because it combines performance art, multimedia installations, dance, and conventional theater. His influences, hence, are many, and his works are filled with allusions to history, philosophy, science, religion, and popular culture. It is unfortunate that just three of his dozens of performance works are available in print. Much of the performance's effect may be diminished on the printed page anyway, because of the technical and choreographic nature of his work, but the three printed plays will receive most of the attention in this entry.

Chong's first major dramatic production was *Nuit Blanche: A Select View of Earthlings* (1981), which premiered at New York City's La Mama in 1981. This play, like all of Chong's, takes advantage of various media to give a cosmic view of colonial oppression and imperialism around the world. In *Nuit Blanche*'s eleven scenes, the audience is treated to a dramatic lens that yields a cosmic view of earth and zooms in on specific, yet paradoxically generic, locations: a South American estancia, a prehistoric cave, the Carolinas, and an undesignated third-world location. The audience moves through an ever-accelerating chronology as well. Scenes 1–5 encompass six years in the 1800s; scenes 6–8 take in a few days; the last three scenes take place in a matter of hours. The first scene begins with a fund-raiser who is "handling" the (imaginary and real) audience with flattery and with dire descriptions of the world's extreme needs. Scene 2 presents a slide sequence of earth from space. Scenes 3–5 concern colonialism, classicism, and slavery on an unnamed South American plantation. Scene 6 is a slide sequence of a prehistoric cave with a soundtrack of bat sounds.

Scene 7 leaps into the 1960s in the Carolinas, but the issues (with different characters) still involve the effects of slavery in the South. Scene 8 recalls the slides of earth from scene 2, but the last three scenes take place in a third-world resort in a country on the verge of revolution. As in the previous two locations, these scenes reveal the colonial attitudes of tourists through mundane conversations and interactions. The last scene (11) depicts in dumb show how consumerism and colonialism are destroying indigenous cultures.

Kind Ness (1986) premiered in Boston and New York. Unlike *Nuit Blanche, Kind Ness* takes place in American suburbia of the 1960s and 1970s. Chong parodies American popular culture to reveal the ludicrousness of cultural constructs and the exploitation of intelligent animal life. The striking first scene is a slide show of paired disparate ideas with a humorous narration that contrasts images that are "like and . . . not alike. . . . What is harmonious and what is dissonant" (5). The rest of the play follows the loves and changes in five children and one precocious gorilla, named Buzz, as they grow up together through grade school and high school. Throughout the play, Buzz is taken to be one of the human group of friends, even though he speaks in his own primate language. The scenes take the audience through common school experiences—dances, dating, and learning about ethnic, physical, and class differences. There are two slapstick routines (scenes 4 and 7) that satirize popular American notions about colonialism and the great White Bwana, a scene that alludes to Buzz's jungle roots. The last scene takes place in a zoo where Buzz and Daphne, now married, visit a captive gorilla and make ironic comments about his ungainly size and appearance. The couple wrongly believes that they understand the differences between themselves and the primate in captivity.

Snow (1988) leaps forward and backward in time, beginning and ending in postwar Berlin (1946), but also covering World War I's western front, Meiji Japan, seventeenth-century France, prehistory, nineteenth-century Massachusetts, and suburban Minnesota of the 1980s. If the play can be characterized, it seems to be, much like *Nuit Blanche*, a tone poem or meditation. *Snow* considers how all people of all different cultures and time periods are linked by life's certainties: everyone's struggle for survival interspersed by occasional acts of mercy. As in Chong's other plays, there is a mix of media: projected images of snow and music that link the various scenes. The first scene reveals the grimness of postwar survival and the random oppression of the occupying Russian army. Scene 2 introduces Meiji Japan and the appearance of the Yuki Onna ("Snow Demon") who sucks life out of the living. In most scenes, the falling snow reminds the audience of this common thread that connects all people of all times, all subject to the inclement weather and to death. An exception appears in scene 6 (near the middle of the play, the end of act 1) when seventeenth-century French nuns find and care for an abandoned baby boy, but the other scenes remind us that such grace derives from others' profound suffering.

Scene 7, the beginning of act 2, takes place at Mt. Chocorua in 1992 (four years in the audience's future) and portrays a meeting of census takers. Each member reports, some humorously so, on the number of surviving indigenous peoples, location by location. In the last three scenes (9 through 11), the figure of Death takes the place of the snow and makes timely appearances, showing the mundanity and banality of each situation. The play ends with snow falling, a boy's narration recounting epic events in world history, concertina music, and a parade of people. As in *Nuit Blanche* and *Kind Ness*, Chong problematizes the survival of humanity and endangered species, as well as universal notions of otherness that both describe and perpetuate human suffering.

CRITICAL RECEPTION

Critics have responded to Ping Chong in a variety of ways: first, as a multivalent performance artist/director; second, as an Asian American; and third, as an avant-garde metaphysical playwright. In the first category, audiences have noted his training as a cinematographer, his collaborations with choreographer Meredith Monk, and his penchant for stylized visual-effect performance art rather than "conventional" theater. Noel Carroll observes: "Chong embellishes the themes of loneliness and alienation by utilizing several distinct techniques. . . . Even a normal movement like walking is de-familiarized" with an actor pacing across the stage repetitively, and "[a] familiar pose such as resting an arm on a table is alienated by sustaining it for a very long time" (Carroll, "Earthlings," 74–75).

Several of the numerous interviews with Chong mention his ethnic identity and his development as an artist. Many theater reviews have noted his jolting visual effects and the multicultural themes of his work. It is apparent that his body of work accentuates ideas of "culture and the other" (Chong, "Notes" 63). But Chong is careful to add that his work is not just "ethnic," or Asian American. "I'm addressing an American audience, whoever they might be. . . . The basic issue of how our culture deals with another is primal, basic" (Chong, "Notes" 64–65). That intercultural relationship is another important key to appreciating Chong's work. His plays reveal cultural tensions—a relational push and pull—that exist in all relationships and all cultures. That effect is largely responsible for his being classified as "a postmodern playwright of a dreamlike bricolage" (Moynihan 105). In his plays, characters converse, but do not actually respond to each other: scene changes also indicate radical shifts in perspective and time; rather than being sequential, scenes leap, and the audience is forced to find unity of tone, mood, or ideology. Kent Neely astutely notes, "Obfuscation of logic and reliance on intuition is precisely Chong's intent. . . . [H]uman beings exist in a universe governed by coincidence and randomness or, in Chong's terminology, fate" (Neely, "Ping" 131).

Again, what is most impressive about Ping Chong's work is the ingenuity and variety of media that he uses to convey complex, engaging, and enduring ideas. His sizable contributions to the fields of performance art, art installations, video, and film cannot be realistically separated from his contributions to the theater. All of his contributions can be seen in his dramatic works, but they alone cannot represent the complex corpus of his work.

BIBLIOGRAPHY

Works by Ping Chong

Drama

Kind Ness. Plays in Progress 8.9 (1986): 1–43.
Snow. Plays in Progress 10.9 (1988): 1–62.
Nuit Blanche. Between Worlds: Contemporary Asian-American Plays. Ed. Misha Berson. New York: Theatre Communications Group, 1990. 2–28.

Unpublished Manuscripts

Lazarus. Uncataloged. Ping Chong and Co., 1972.
Humboldt's Current. 1977.
Brightness. Uncataloged. Ping Chong and Co., 1990.
Deshima. Uncataloged. Ping Chong and Co., 1990.
Undesirable Elements/Japan. Uncataloged. Ping Chong and Co., 1992.
Chinoiserie. Uncataloged. Ping Chong and Co., 1995.
After Sorrow. Uncataloged. Ping Chong and Co., 1997.
Kwaidan. Uncataloged. Ping Chong and Co., 1998.
Pojagi. Uncataloged. Ping Chong and Co., 1999.
Truth and Beauty. Uncataloged. Ping Chong and Co., 1999.

Selected Production History

Lazarus

Production, dir. and perf. Ping Chong and Company. Lee Nagrin Studio, New York City, c. 1973.

Kind Ness

Production, dir. and perf. Ping Chong and Company. Northeastern U, Boston, 1986.
———. La MaMa Annex, New York City, 1986.
———. Central Park Summerstage, New York City, 1988.
———. Milwaukee Repertory Theater, Milwaukee, 1988.
———. Lafayette College, Easton, PA, 1989.
———. Syracuse U, Syracuse, NY, 1989.
———. Amherst College, Amherst, MA, 1989.
———. Painted Bride Art Center, Philadelphia, 1990.
———. Trinity College, Hartford, CT, 1990.
———. U of Nebraska, Lincoln, 1991.
———. District Curators, Washington, DC, 1991.
———. Théâtre 95, Cergy-Pontoise, France, 1992.
———. Illusion Theatre, Minneapolis, 1992.
———. Seattle Group Theatre, Seattle, 1993.

Snow

Production, dir. and perf. Ping Chong and Company. Illusion Theatre, Minneapolis, 1988.

Nuit Blanche

Production, dir. and perf. Ping Chong and Company. La MaMa E.T.C., New York City, 1981 and 1985.

Undesirable Elements/New York

Production, dir. and perf. Ping Chong and Company. Artists' Space, New York City, 1992.
————. Rutgers U, New Brunswick, NJ, 1993
————. Henry Street Settlement, New York City, 1993.
————. American Museum of Natural History, New York City, 1994.
————. McCarter Theatre, Princeton, NJ, 1994.
————. Art Awareness, Lexington, NY, 1994.
————. West Kortright Center, East Meredith, NY, 1994.
————. Staller Center, SUNY Stony Brook, 1994.

Undesirable Elements/Cleveland

Production, dir. and perf. Ping Chong and Company. Performance Art Festival, Cleveland, 1993.
————. Kent State U, Kent, OH, 1994.

Undesirable Elements/Twin Cities

Production, dir. and perf. Ping Chong and Company. Illusion Theatre, Minneapolis, 1994 and 1995.

Undesirable Elements/Seattle

Production, dir. and perf. Ping Chong and Company. Group Theatre, Seattle, 1995.

Undesirable Elements/Tokyo

Production, dir. and perf. Ping Chong and Company. Tokyo Metropolitan Art Space, Tokyo, 1995.
SlutForArt. With Muna Tseng. *Tokens? The NYC Asian American Experience on Stage.* Ed. Alvin Eng. New York: Asian American Writers' Workshop, 1999. 377–406.

Interview

"Response." Interview. *Yellow Light: The Flowering of Asian American Arts.* Ed. Amy Ling. Philadelphia: Temple UP, 1999. 204–12.

Screenplays

Tempus Fugit. Dir. and prod. Ping Chong and Company. Videocassette. 1990.
I Will Not Be Sad in the World. Dir. and prod. Ping Chong. Videocassette. 1992.

Television

Paris. Dir. Meredith Monk and Ping Chong. KCTA, Minneapolis. 1982.
Turtle Dreams. Dir. Meredith Monk and Ping Chong. PBS. WGBH, Boston. 1982.
"Plage Concrete." Dir. and prod. Ping Chong. *New Television Series.* PBS. WGBH, Boston. 1989.

"Plage Concrete." Dir. Ping Chong. Prod. Susan Dowling. *New Television Series*. PBS. WNET, New York. 1998.

Studies of Ping Chong

Adcock, Joseph. "Group Theatre's *Kind Ness* Shows Beauty's Many Sides." *Seattle Post-Intelligencer* 22 Apr. 1993, final ed.: C6.

———. "Meditating on Seattle's *Elements*; Ping Chong's Work Is a Contemplative Delight." Rev. of *Undesirable Elements*. *Seattle Post-Intelligencer* 13 Feb. 1995, final ed.: C1+.

———. "Ping Chong Finds Art in a World of Differences." *Seattle Post-Intelligencer* 27 Jan. 1995, final ed.: 15.

———. "Playwrights Take a Quizzical Approach toward American Life." *Seattle Post-Intelligencer* 16 Apr. 1993, final ed.: 7.

Auslander, P. Rev. of *Kwaidan*. *Theatre Journal* 50.4 (1998): 521–523.

Bacalzo, Dan. "SlutForArt." Rev. of *SlutForArt*. Apr. 1999. 26 Jan. 2000 <http://www.leftnet/~gapimny/newsletter/apr99/slutforart.html>.

Berson, Misha. "Collage of Culture—*Undesirable Elements* Explores Seattle Faces." *Seattle Times* 3 Feb. 1995: H26.

———. "*Undesirable Elements*: Crisscrossing of Cultures." Rev. of *Undesirable Elements*. *Seattle Post-Intelligencer* 13 Feb. 1995, final ed.: E1.

Carroll, Noël. *The Philosophy of Horror, or, Paradoxes of the Heart*. New York: Routledge, 1990.

———. "A Select View of Earthlings: Ping Chong." *Drama Review* 27.1 (1983): 72–81.

Chong, Ping. "Notes for 'Mumblings and Digressions: Some Thoughts on Being an Artist, Being an American, Being a Witness. . . . ' " *MELUS* 16.3 (1989–90): 62–67.

Dillon, John. "Three Places in Asia." *American Theatre* 13.3 (1996): 19–22.

Feingold, Michael. "Culture Shakes." *Village Voice* 43.39 (1998): 141.

Francia, Luis H. "Outside Looking In." *Village Voice* 34.44 (1989): 43–44.

Frieze, James. "Channelling Rubble: *Seven Streams of the River Ota* and *After Sorrow*." Rev. of *After Sorrow*. *Theatre Journal* 49.3 (1997): 352–54.

Gussow, Mel. "*Nuit Blanche*." *New York Times* 23 Jan. 1981: C8.

Hardy, C. "Ping Chong and Company, Muna-Tseng Dance Projects." *Dance Magazine* 71.5 (1997): 78.

Hargraves, Kelly. "*Chinoiserie*." Rev. of *Chinoiserie*. 16 Nov. 1995. 26 Jan. 2000 <http://www.danceonline.com/rev/chong.html>.

Hawes, Jennifer B. "Kwaidan: Into an Imaginary Realm." Rev. of *Kwaidan*. 7 June 1999. 26 Jan. 2000 <http://www.charleston.net/pub/spoleto/sponews/kwaidan0607.htm>.

Hering, D. "Ping Chong and Company." *Dance Magazine* 65.2 (1991): 115–16.

Howard, Beth. "Ping Chong: Creating a Visual and Aural Feast." *Theatre Crafts* 24.3 (1990): 27–31, 59–60.

Lee, Josephine. "Between Immigration and Hyphenation: The Problems of Theorizing Asian American Theater." *Journal of Dramatic Theory and Criticism* 13.1 (1998): 45–69.

———. "Performance Review: *Undesirable Elements*—Twin Cities/River of Dreams." *Theatre Journal* 47.3 (1995): 424.

Lee, Thomas. "By Definition, Being an Artist Means Taking Risks." Interview with Ping Chong. *Arts Spectrum* Sept. 1999. Harvard U, Cambridge. 26 Jan. 2000 <http://www.fas.harvard.edu/~ofa/spectrum/sep99/ping.html>.

McLennan, Douglas. "Review: *Undesirable Elements* Offers Personal Stories about Heritages." Rev. of *Undesirable Elements*. *News Tribune* (Tacoma) 11 Feb. 1995: SL16.

Moynihan, D.S. "Ping Chong's *Nuit Blanche*." *Drama Review* 25.1 (1981): 101–5.

Neely, Kent. "Ping Chong's Theatre of Simultaneous Consciousness." *Journal of Dramatic Theory and Criticism* 6.2 (1992): 121–35.

———. "Theatre Review—*Snow*." *Theatre Journal* 41.2 (1989): 234.

Sandla, Robert. "Practical Visionary: Ping Chong." *Theater Week* 2.20 (1989): 26–33.

Wentworth, Anna. "Improvisation on Stage as in Real Life." Rev. of *American Gothic*. 1 Oct. 1999. 26 Jan. 2000 <http://www.roanoke.com/marquee/stage/100199.html>.

Westfall, Suzanne. "Ping Chong's *Terra In/Cognita*: Monsters on Stage." *Reading the Literatures of Asain America*. Ed. Shirley Geok-lin Lim and Amy Ling. Philadelphia: Temple UP, 1992. 359–73.

Govindas Vishnudas Desani

(1909–2000)

Uppinder Mehan

BIOGRAPHY

Govindas Vishnudas Desani was born in Nairobi, Kenya, on July 8, 1909, to a merchant father and mother who had him educated privately. He made his way to the United Kingdom in 1926, where he started a career as a journalist that spanned roughly three decades and took him to India. He became a correspondent of the *Times of India* in 1934 and a broadcaster for the BBC in 1936. In 1948, Desani published his most important work, the novel *All about H. Hatterr*, followed by the play *Hali* two years later. After a year of touring and lecturing in India, Desani spent the years between 1952 and 1966 in various monasteries and retreats studying Buddhist and Hindu culture in India and Burma. Also doing some writing during the last few years of his study, Desani contributed to the *Illustrated Weekly of India* and the *Times of India* group of publications from 1960 to 1968. He taught philosophy from 1969 to his death in 2000 at the University of Texas at Austin, where he was appointed professor emeritus in 1979.

MAJOR WORKS AND THEMES

Although Desani wrote only one novel, only one play, and a handful of short stories, he is assured a prominence matching that of his more prolific contemporaries such as Mulk Raj Anand, R.K. Narayan, and Raja Rao and his most direct heir, Salman Rushdie, in postcolonial Indian writing. Desani's *All about H. Hatterr* has been hailed as a comic masterpiece. The plot is fairly conventional in that it follows the picaresque adventures of a young man in India as he searches for Truth. What is distinctive, and what has earned Desani his high place, is his remaking of the English language. The language is a remarkable hybrid of the various Englishes (most notably the queen's and the babu's) available to Desani and his characters. As Hatterr tries the teaching of one guru after another, one Western scheme after another, and finds them all lacking, one of Desani's major themes emerges: the impossibility of reducing multifarious life to any one master narrative. Ultimately, life is not a riddle to be solved but a process to be lived.

In contrast to the linguistic acrobatics of *All about H. Hatterr*, Desani's play *Hali* (also referred to as a prose-poem) settles on a hieratic language that tells the allegorical story of a man seeking solace after the death of his beloved. The play is structured as a series of monologues delivered by the young man Hali, his biological mother, his adoptive mother, his beloved, and some mythic figures. *Hali* is Desani in full tragic mode. Gone are the comic digressions, the playful languages, and the biting satires on the religious and psychic charlatans. In their place, Desani exhibits an earnestness that comes close to being self-mocking.

The story of *Hali* brings into play all of creation as Desani takes as his starting point the creation of the creator of the cosmos. The cosmology is based on ancient Upanishadic mythology, but the image of the creator as an alienated artist is his own. Shortly after the creation of the world, Hali is created as the perfect being. He lives in a paradisiacal world in the hills with his mother and pet deer until the gods take them both away suddenly. Hali is found by a good woman, Maya, and she raises him as her own. Reaching adulthood, Hali falls in love with the perfect image of a woman, Rooh, but she too is suddenly taken away. One can get a sense of Desani's mythic language and the severity of the tests Hali undergoes in the narration of Hali's meeting with Rooh: "Then he found a beloved being, the most beloved being God ever made. Rooh was her name. And Rooh is dead" (*Hali* 18). The rest of the short play is a series of horrific and terrible images of death and destruction as Hali searches for some sense of meaning behind his loss. The only meaning he can find is that life is best lived in a state of involved detachment from the world, or, as Hali puts it: "I seek no love of the living, I seek no commerce with the dead. But I wish to be nigh, I wish to be nigh, as air, as air bearing love" (*Hali* 52).

Although it is difficult to have the final word on complex artistic work, it is almost impossible in Desani's case because he was always revising. Molly Ramanujan notes that he made some sixteen hundred changes between the first version of his novel and the last (52). The 1950 version of *Hali* and the 1991 version differ in many small ways that ultimately make the language less poetic. The latter version also has a preface by Desani in which he asks the reader to contemplate the wonder of the creative act in the midst of the hellishness of this world. What makes possible creativity and joy is the realization for Desani's characters that reality is not a set of contrary absolutes but a constant oscillation between them.

CRITICAL RECEPTION

Almost all the critical attention Desani receives is directed to his novel *All about H. Hatterr*, but *Hali* has drawn some brief commentary, beginning with T.S. Eliot and E.M. Forster, whose favorable few lines form the foreword of the 1950 edition of the play. Both Eliot and Forster see the play as poetry, and both point to its alienness for Western readers. Most reviewers of the play have followed in a similar vein, even those who had an opportunity to read the 1991 revised version of the play, in which Desani added an explanatory preface and postscript. Desani continually revised his play throughout his life. Sybil Steinberg finds it an ornate, rapturous meditation (134), and Michael Dirda states that it is written in "dithyrambic prose that verges on the incomprehensible and sometimes doesn't stop there" (X5).

However, the most sustained examination has been by Molly Ramanujan. In a volume devoted to all of Desani's fiction, Ramanujan provides a scene-by-scene commentary on *Hali* along with some of Desani's own words about his artistic intentions. Ramanujan finds that the play manages to be both universal and highly personal. Her commentary is particularly aimed at making the play's sense more accessible to readers not versed in either Vedantic metaphysics or Desani's symbolism.

BIBLIOGRAPHY

Works by Govindas Vishnudas Desani

Drama

Hali, a Play. Foreword. T.S. Eliot and E.M. Forster. London: Saturn P, 1950.
Hali and Collected Stories. Kingston, NY: McPherson, 1991.

Selected Production History

Hali

Production. Watergate Theatre, London, 1950.

Fiction

All about Mr. Hatterr. London: F. Aldor, 1948. Published as *All about H. Hatterr, a Gesture*, New York: Farrar, Straus, 1951. Published as *All about H. Hatterr: A Novel*. Introd. Anthony Burgess. New Paltz, NY: McPherson, 1986.
Mainly Concerning Kama and Her Immortal Lord. New Delhi: Indian Council on Cultural Relations, 1973.

Studies of Govindas Vishnudas Desani

Aravamudan, Srinivas. "Postcolonial Affiliations: *Ulysses* and *All about H. Hatterr*." *Transcultural Joyce*. Ed. and introd. Karen R. Lawrence. Cambridge: Cambridge UP, 1998. 97–128.

Bardolph, Jacqueline. "Language and Madness in G.V. Desani's *All about H. Hatterr.*" *Commonwealth Essays and Studies* 8.1 (1985): 1–13.

Dirda, Michael. "All about G.V. Desani." *Washington Post* 9 Feb. 1992: X5.

Goers, Peter. "King's English: Whole Language and G.V. Desani's *All about H. Hatterr.*" *New Literature Review* 4 (1978): 30–40.

Harrex, S.C. "The Novel as Gesture." *Awakened Conscience: Studies in Commonwealth Literature.* Ed. C.D. Narasimhaiah. New Delhi: Sterling, 1978. 73–85.

————. "Shakespeare: 'Almost an Indian of My India.' " *Literary Criterion* 29.4 (1994): 1–14.

Jussawalla, Feroza. "Beyond Indianness: The Stylistic Concerns of Midnight's Children." *Journal of Indian Writing in English* 12.2 (1984): 26–47.

Naik, M.K. "Colonial Experience in *All about H. Hatterr.*" *Commonwealth Novel in English* 1.1 (1982): 37–49.

Naikar, Basavaraj S. "*All about H. Hatterr*: A Philosophical Comedy." *Studies in Indian Fiction in English.* Ed. G.S. Balarama Gupta. Gulbarga, India: JIWE Publications, 1987. 25–35.

Ramanujan, Molly. *G.V. Desani: Writer and Worldview.* New Delhi: Arnold-Heinemann, 1984.

Riemenschneider, Dieter. "G.V. Desani's *All about H. Hatterr* and the Problem of Cultural Alienation." *The Literary Criterion* 20.2 (1985): 23–35.

Sharrad, Paul. "Musings on the Hats of the Hatterr." *ACLALS Bulletin* 7.4 (1986): 79–85.

Srinath, C.N. "G.V. Desani: *All about H. Hatterr.*" *Literary Criterion* 9.3 (1970): 40–56.

Steinberg, Sybil. "*Hali and Collected Stories.*" Rev. of *Hali and Collected Stories. Publishers Weekly* 238.16 (5 Apr. 1991): 134.

Stilz, Gerhard. " 'Truth? Hell, You Will Get Contrast, and No Mistake!': Sanitizing the Intercultural Polylemma in G.V. Desani's *All about H. Hatterr* (1948/72)." *Hybridity and Postcolonialism: Twentieth-Century Indian Literature.* Ed. and introd. Monika Fludernik. Tübingen, Germany: Stauffenburg, 1998. 79–101.

Williams, Haydn. "Hatterr and Bazza: Post-colonial Picaros." *Commonwealth Review* 2.1–2 (1990–91): 204–11.

Louella Dizon

(1966–   )

Lucy Mae San Pablo Burns

BIOGRAPHY

Louella Dizon was born in 1966 in Cebu City, the Philippines. In 1968, her family immigrated to the United States and settled in Detroit, Michigan. Dizon's parents came from humble families in the rural areas of the Philippines. They came to the United States as young doctors, believing that living in the United States would create better opportunities for them and their children. The Dizon family arrived at a time when immigration by overseas professionals was welcomed and sought in order to fulfill the demands of labor in the United States. Thousands of Filipinos came at that time, marking the "third wave" immigration of Filipinos to the United States. (The "first wave" is noted at the turn of the century, and the "second wave" in the early 1930s.)

Dizon's artistic interest began at a young age. She directed her first production and wrote her first book when she was in elementary school (Perkins and Uno 127). These years were followed by continued participation in the multidisciplinary arts—writing plays, composing music, and performing. In 1989, Dizon graduated from Princeton University with a B.A. in English, magna cum laude. Soon after, she moved to New York City.

After a long hiatus from writing so that she might finish an advanced degree in computer science, Dizon recently returned to the task and is in the midst of writing a novel (Burns interview). She speaks of writing with longing, even when she is writing. In an interview with Roberta Uno and Lucy Mae San Pablo Burns, she defined a writing writer as "someone who writes everyday. I'm constantly searching to put myself in an environment where I am inspired, and forced, to write."

MAJOR WORKS AND THEMES

Dizon wrote, directed, and produced her first full-length play, *The Color Yellow: Memoirs of an Asian American* (1989), at Princeton University as her thesis project. In this first play, Dizon was searching for a distinct voice but also taking the world of the stage to create a world meant for her. Thematically, she drew from autobiographical experiences with themes such as coming into oneself as an artist of color and as an adult, changing relationship with family. Artistically, Dizon looked to explore the economy of language, influenced by Samuel Beckett, presenting continuous time and concurrent motions. The impetus for this piece was David Henry Hwang's *Sound of a Voice*, in which Dizon was a part of the Yale Drama Department production in 1987. In the interview with Uno and Burns, Dizon shared her experience upon reading for Hwang's *Sound of a Voice*: "It was like a revelation. When I read the script, it was words I knew how to say. . . . It was as though I had walked into a world that was meant for me." That sense of connection with reality has kept Dizon from leaving playwriting.

The creative vein that was opened in *The Color Yellow* pumps greater energy into the works that follow. *Till Voices Wake Us* (1992), published in *Contemporary Plays by Women of Color*, premiered in New York City on September 22, 1994. It was produced by the Ma-Yi Theatre Ensemble at the Soho Repertory Theater. The play is set in Brooklyn, New York, and Cebu City, the Philippines. It looks at the life of the Macadaeg family, a Filipino American family, slightly yet forever altered after a visit by Granma Rosamunda Vilamin. The play shows an ancestral bond connecting a long line of strong women further back than Granma Rosa to young Rosie through clairvoyance. This bond reveals the unanswered in the history of this family.

In *Till Voices Wake Us*, one can see the continuation of what Dizon began in *The Color Yellow*, particularly her interest in collapsing present, past, and future into present realities that are happening at the same time. *Till Voices Wake Us* strongly portrays the power of spirituality, crossing time, borders, and spaces. Dizon negotiates the experience of fragmentation from the dislocation of this Filipino American family with the continuity of bloodlines through ancestral time. In her personal statement published in *Contemporary Plays by Women of Color*, Dizon writes that writing *Till Voices Wake Us* allowed a reconnection with distant familial and cultural ties: "It's odd, and a little tragic, that I never really wanted to know my grandparents until I had to start writing about a particular one. . . . So I wrote—in penance, in tribute, in search of something better than real life" (128).

The two unfinished plays after *Till Voices Wake Us*, *The Sweet Sound of Inner Light* and *Practical Heart*, push further Dizon's interest in the past, in memory, and in simultaneous reality. Although she has not written music for her plays after *The Color Yellow*, Dizon draws from her musical training to experiment with language. Her attention to the rhythms and tonality of languages—Cebuano accent on English, American English on French—reveal her training as a musician. Overlapping and simultaneous dialogue, short and abrupt exchanges between the characters, and lyrical prose are some of the ways in which the music in Dizon's plays is often presented.

CRITICAL RECEPTION

In the early to mid-1990s, Dizon's plays were read and produced. *Till Voices Wake Us* is anthologized in the collection *Contemporary Plays by Women of Color*, edited by Kathy A. Perkins and Roberta Uno. Excerpts from this play are also reprinted in Marsh Cassady's *Great Scenes from Minority Playwrights: Seventy-four Scenes of Cultural Diversity*. The manuscripts of Dizon's plays are archived in the Uno Collection of Plays by Asian American Women in the W.E.B. Du Bois Library, University of Massachusetts at Amherst. Playbills and correspondence are included in this archive.

Dizon's works remain largely unreviewed, but critical works on performance and cultural works in Asian American studies such as Josephine Lee's *Performing Asian America* and Lisa Lowe's *Immigrant Acts* are useful in contextualizing her works for a deeper understanding of the issues that her plays explore. Works on the Filipino diaspora, such as Epifanio San Juan's *Hegemony and Strategies of Transgression* and *After Postcolonialism: Remapping Philippines–United States Confrontations*, are also helpful readings. Recent scholarship in Filipino American studies, including *Amerasia Journal*'s two special issues *Essays into American Empire in the Philippines*, edited by Enrique de la Cruz, also provides insights into Dizon's works.

BIBLIOGRAPHY

Works by Louella Dizon

Drama

Till Voices Wake Us. Contemporary Plays by Women of Color: An Anthology. Ed. Kathy A. Perkins and Roberta Uno. New York: Routledge, 1996. 127–56. Rpt. in *Great Scenes from Minority Playwrights: Seventy-four Scenes of Cultural Diversity*. Ed. Marsh Cassady. Colorado Springs: Meriwether, 1997. 297–338.

Unpublished Manuscripts

The Color Yellow: Memoirs of an Asian American. Ms. 345. Roberta Uno Asian Women Playwrights Scripts Collection 1924–1992, Special Collections and Archives, W.E.B. Du Bois Library, U of Massachusetts at Amherst, 1989.
The Sweet Sound of Inner Light. Ms. 345. Roberta Uno Asian Women Playwrights Scripts Collection 1924–1992, Special Collections and Archives, W.E.B. Du Bois Library, U of Massachusetts at Amherst, 1994.
Practical Heart. Ms. 345. Roberta Uno Asian Women Playwrights Scripts Collection

1924–1992, Special Collections and Archives, W.E.B. Du Bois Library, U of Massachusetts at Amherst, 1995.

Selected Production History

Till Voices Wake Us

Staged reading, dir. Kay Gayner; prod. Ma-Yi Theatre Ensemble. Soho Repertory Theater, New York City, 1992.

Production, dir. Kay Gayner, perf. Lou Ann Lucas, Ralph Peña, John Pfeiffer, Jose San Juan, Lerrick Santos, and Geralyn Yabut, prod. Ma-Yi Theatre Ensemble. Soho Repertory Theater, New York City, 1994.

The Color Yellow: Memoirs of an Asian American

Production, dir. Louella Dizon. Princeton Drama Department, Princeton, NJ, 1989.

————. La Mama E.T.C., New York City, 1990.

————, prod. Lahi Philippine Performing Company. Philippine Consulate, New York City, 1990.

The Sweet Sound of Inner Light

Staged Reading. New Works Festival at the Public Theater, New York City, 1994.

————. Monday Night Reading Series, Ma-Yi Theatre Ensemble, New York City, 1994.

Interview

Interview with Roberta Uno and Lucy Mae San Pablo Burns. New York City. June 1995. Videocassette. Ms. 345. Roberta Uno Asian Women Playwrights Scripts Collection 1924–1992, Special Collections and Archives, W.E.B. Du Bois Library, U of Massachusetts at Amherst, 1995.

Studies of Louella Dizon

De la Cruz, Enrique, ed. *Essays into American Empire in the Philippines*. Spec. issues of *Amerasia Journal* 24.2 and 24.3 (Summer and Winter 1998).

Dizon, Louella. E-mail to the author. Feb. 2001.

Gonzalez, N.V.M., and Oscar V. Campomanes. "Filipino American Literature." *An Interethnic Companion to Asian American Literature*. Ed. King-Kok Cheung. Cambridge: Cambridge UP, 1997. 62–124.

Lee, Josephine. *Performing Asian America: Race and Ethnicity on the Contemporary Stage*. Philadelphia: Temple UP, 1997.

Lowe, Lisa. *Immigrant Acts: On Asian American Cultural Politics*. Durham, NC: Duke UP, 1996.

Perkins, Kathy A., and Roberta Uno, eds. *Contemporary Plays by Women of Color*. New York: Routledge, 1996.

Root, Maria P. *Filipino Americans: Transformation and Identity*. Thousand Oaks, CA: Sage, 1997.

San Juan, Epifanio. *After Postcolonialism: Remapping Philippines–United States Confrontations*. Lanham, MD: Rowman & Littlefield, 2000.

————. *Hegemony and Strategies of Transgression: Essays in Cultural Studies and Comparative Literature*. Albany: State U of New York P, 1995.

Maura Nguyen Donohue
(1970–   )

SanSan Kwan

BIOGRAPHY

Maura Nguyen Donohue is a dancer and choreographer. She was born on July 19, 1970, amid the turmoil of war in Saigon, Vietnam, to a Vietnamese mother and an Irish American father. When she was only a few months old, she was brought by her parents to Barrington, Rhode Island, where she was raised the oldest of six children. Donohue's early movement training was rich and diverse. As a girl, she enrolled in the customary children's dance classes, where she was introduced to creative movement: tap, jazz, modern, and ballet. Later, as an adolescent, she took stage combat lessons with her brother and competed with the gymnastics team at her high school. Donohue continued her ballet training into her teenage years, spending two summers at the intensive Boston Ballet Summer Program. When she reached Smith College, she began her choreographic career in earnest. While she was studying for degrees in anthropology and dance, she directed the student dance troupe, Celebrations, for which she acted as director and choreographer for three years. Her work at Smith was informed by a growing feminism and, in particular, an allegiance to the cause of women of color.

After graduating cum laude from Smith in 1992, Donohue moved to Seattle, Washington, pursuing life as a dancer/choreographer. She spent two years there choreographing several pieces for such local presenters as OntheBoards, Dance Centre/Seattle, Dance on Capitol Hill, and the Bumbershoot Arts Festival. At this time, Donohue's work and life experienced a considerable shift and began to take on a new set of driving concerns. While she was in Seattle, her mother called one day and disclosed a family secret: Mrs. Donohue, while still young back in Vietnam, had been married off to another man, and they had had a child. Later, that marriage had disintegrated, and she had been forced to escape. The older boy who Maura Donohue had always thought was a distant cousin was actually her Vietnamese half brother.

These revelations became a milestone in Donohue's artistic development. They inspired Donohue to take a deeper interest in her Vietnamese heritage and the full story of her family in Vietnam. As a way to better understand her own personal history as well as her place in the American racial landscape, she involved herself with various Asian American artists and art organizations and began to develop work that spoke to her mixed-race identity and to issues of Asian Americanness. She helped to establish the organization Fertile Ground, an Asian American artists' alliance in Seattle. Toward the end of her stay on the West Coast, Donohue joined the cast and eventually re-created movement for the Berkeley Repertory Theatre's touring production of Laurence Yep's *Dragonwings*, a play depicting the lives of Chinese Americans in California in the early twentieth century.

In 1994, Donohue left Seattle for New York City. She first landed work dancing for Chen and Dancers. After two years of touring with this Asian American dance company, however, she ended her contract in order to devote her energies to creating and performing her own work. She established a dance company, Maura Nguyen Donohue/In Mixed Company, and began to choreograph and present intensively. Because of her training in Beijing opera, experimental theater, contact improvisation, and karate (a brown belt soon to receive her first-degree black-belt ranking), Donohue's work began to take mature shape under the influence of these varied movement forms. Maura Nguyen Donohue/In Mixed Company, now five years in existence, currently presents at least one new work per season and continues an active touring season. It is safe to say that Donohue, as a relatively new artist, will continue to produce and to develop her craft for some time to come.

MAJOR WORKS AND THEMES

As a dancer/choreographer, Donohue is a newcomer, but as a cultural interpreter, she has begun distinguishing herself on the stage of racial and gender exploration through her unique artistry. Her major works might all be seen as shifting, evolving answers to the same large question: What does it mean to be a *hapa*—a biracial Asian American woman—in a society inclined toward oversimplified categorizations of color, sexuality, and gender? At its most basic level, the evolution of Donohue's work has been an expression of the development of her own sense of identity as a half-Vietnamese, half–Irish American woman living in America. Of course, as her work has matured, it has come not only to tell the story of her own journey, but to represent a larger exploration of the unremittingly complex personal, social, and political facets of race and gender as they play out in the contemporary United States.

In one of her earliest pieces, *When You're Old Enough* (1992), Donohue lays bare the painful, personal story of her search for a sense of being. In this full-hour, one-woman piece, she spins the tale of how her once comfortably white-aligned identity becomes forever shaken by the revelation of a family secret. The secret involves her mother's previous marriage to a Vietnamese man and the news that Donohue has a Vietnamese half brother. This discovery awakens in Donohue a consciousness of her Asian heritage. She is forced to examine her childhood experiences with race and racial prejudice and to seek answers to her early choices of assimilation and denial. It is by coming to understand the story of her mother that Donohue is able to move from a place of shame for her yellow skin to a place of growing pride. In telling the story of this revelatory moment, Donohue explores the conflicts of belonging and difference, pride and denial, that define the experience of biraciality in America. In its form, *When You're Old Enough* marks the beginning of Donohue's work with mixed-media performance. Aside from vigorous, athletic choreography, the piece relies on performed text, dramatic story, and slides.

Donohue takes up her concern with biraciality again three years later in a group piece called *Islands: a hapa wet dream* (1995). *Islands* moves beyond the autobiographical, narrative angle of *When You're Old Enough* and explores the *hapa* experience at a broader and more abstract level. The piece unfolds as a kind of dreamlike journey from a watery, womblike beginning into an explosion of light, sound, and furious movement. The dancers start in blue-hued semidarkness, each standing apart while attempting to break out of embryonic skins. They struggle with themselves and each other. Carried onstage, they begin to dance blankly like shop mannequins vogueing behind Plexiglas. Along the journey, the choreography is accompanied by imagistic poetry recalling the Vietnam War and childhood memories of xenophobic prejudices and, later, by the driving sound of live Japanese taiko drumming. At the sound of the drumming, the dancers swirl and race across the stage in waves, lured by the intensity of the beat. The piece ends with a ritualistic arrival at acceptance and belonging. The dancers approach bowls of clear water and are mesmerized by their own reflection in them; they baptize each other with the droplets. Water as both isolator and redeemer serves finally as a recurring trope.

For *Lotus Blossom Itch* (1997), Donohue begins to move away from specifically *hapa* concerns to the wider arena of Asian American women and the issue of their sexual exploitation. With this piece, Donohue indulges in the appeal of pop music and rock 'n' roll and engages in the slippery but potent area of theatrical parody. Taking as its cue and victim American popular culture's images of the exotic, erotic Oriental whore, Donohue pummels the audience with over-the-top choreographic imitations of hula girls, Madame Butterflies, Bangkok boys, belly dancers, lotus-blossom babes, Miss Saigons, and jungle kittens. The piece is built on the pretense of an amusement-park tour of the Orient led by three wisecracking, Hawaiian-shirt-wearing tour guides, who are, incidentally, members of the Asian American male performance troupe Slant. Throughout the so-called tour, the performers sustain a raucous, hyperbolic attitude of grinning and showboating. At the culmination of the work, however, the dancers and actors break down, revealing the destitution and emptiness of their masked, prostituted personas. The piece ends on a somber note and delivers a lesson to any who might suffer from "lotus blossom itch."

SKINning the surFACE (1998) takes as its centerpiece the plight of the *bui doi*—the 30,000 half-American children fathered by GIs during the Vietnam War and then abandoned after the United States pulled out in 1975. In 1987, the Amerasian Homecoming Act allowed these children entry to the United States, often based solely on the passport of their physically "American" traits, that is, their brown hair, bigger noses, or lighter skin. *SKINning the surFACE* continues Donohue's inquiry into the *hapa* experience; she uses this historical episode as a springboard into a heated exploration of the biracial body—its personal and political significance and reverberations. The piece tells the difficult story of the three main players in the *bui doi* phenomenon: father, mother, and child. Through simple, poignant movement, the dancers represent the pain of separation and loss—a hand once held in another and suddenly empty, a look to a spot once occupied and now abandoned. The choreography also powerfully expresses the confusion of biracial identity—furious spinning, swirling, and slashing like a battle in one's own veins; the peeling of skin; and, most beautifully, desperate, risky, and ultimately fragile partnering. *SKINning* continues the collaborative process that Donohue established in *Islands* and *Lotus Blossom Itch*: it incorporates live music, text, bold visual designs, and an athletic combination of traditional Asian and contemporary movement forms.

Donohue's latest work, *Righteous Babes* (2000), is a provocative exploration of gender roles and issues set to songs by punk folk maverick Ani DiFranco. In a series of duets, solos, and group works, *Righteous Babes* uses DiFranco's music and spoken-word pieces such as *Not a Pretty Girl, Tiptoe, In or Out, I'm No Heroine, 'Tis of Thee, Hello Birmingham,* and *My IQ* as accompaniment to an exhaustive physical interrogation of the heated terrain of antichoice violence, domestic abuse, race relations, sexual alliances, traditional gender roles, and cross dressing. As such, it furthers her examination of the state of race and gender relations in America. In fact, Donohue's artistry, from her earliest to her latest works, consistently takes a bold, provocative stance toward racial and sexual injustice and intermixes that political stance with a sensitive, nuanced examination of personal identity.

CRITICAL RECEPTION

Because Donohue has only been working professionally for six or seven years, she has not yet received a great deal of published critical attention. All of the written work on her artistry has come in the form of reviews or short profiles. The reviews, however, have been generally consistent.

Choreographically, Donohue's work has been praised for its blend of power and sensuality. Marilyn Abalos characterizes *Islands* as "overflow[ing] with movement both striking in its athleticism and alluring in its aggressive sensuality" (9). Speaking of a solo by Donohue, Tobi Tobias calls her work "enormously powerful, alternately voluptuous and frenetic" (45). Gia Kourlas writes, "Donohue's style is a blend of the erotic and violent" (25). At the very worst, some critics have accused Donohue's choreography of being repetitive.

Critics have agreed that the central concerns in Donohue's work are both gripping in their intensely personal nature and moving in their passionately political message. "Donohue's dances deliver a sociopolitical wallop," writes Chris Dohse (143). Reviewers often cite the power of the compelling narratives and heart-rending stories that Donohue tells through her choreography and applaud her ability to speak the political through the personal. Jack Anderson states of *SKINning*, "Her work's emotional intensity captured one's attention and conveyed a real sense of political and emotional turmoil" (E7). If reviewers criticize, it is to say that a particular work may have been overly ambitious or overly stated. Lisa Jo Sagolla, writing about *SKINning*, is particularly harsh: "The heavy-handed text is preachy and unconvincingly delivered, while the flowing, repetitious movement phrases, constantly interrupted by handstands, prove tiresome" (31).

Susanna Sloat, however, provides a more balanced viewpoint: "*Islands: a hapa wet dream* seems to try to encapsulate a huge swathe of Maura Nguyen Donohue's experience in one dance. The details of *Islands* can be hard to remember . . . almost too many props, too many changes, almost too many performers in several media (dance, poetry, music). Yet as it unrolls, *Islands* has beauty and meaning and the piece seems complete and resolved" (36). Sloat's reading, in fact, might summarize the bulk of critical work on Donohue. Most find her artistry, if sometimes overeager to deliver a message, mostly intensely effective—a skillful, intelligent blend of both "beauty and meaning."

BIBLIOGRAPHY

Works by Maura Nguyen Donohue

Unpublished Manuscripts

When You're Old Enough. 1992.
Trap. 1993.
Islands: a hapa wet dream. 1995.
Exchanges. 1996.
Exotic Dancers. 1996.
Quilt of Johatsu. 1996.
21 Year Spill. 1996.
Aperitifs at Exotica Lounge. 1997.
Lotus Blossom Itch. 1997.
Repossession. 1997.
SKINning the surFACE. 1998.

a dime for 2 nipples. 1999.
Grin 'n Bare It. 1999.
Righteous Babes. 2000.

Selected Production History

When You're Old Enough

Solo performances, perf. Maura Nguyen Donohue. Dance Centre/Seattle, Seattle, 1992.
————. Room 608, Seattle, 1993.
————. Association for Asian Studies, National Conference, Oakland, CA, 1995.
————. Montgomery Theater, San Jose, CA, 1995.
————. Scott Studio Theater, Smith College, Northampton, MA, 1997.
————. Cornell U, Ithaca, NY, 1998.
————. Lawrence U, Appleton, WI, 1998.
————. Brown U, Providence, RI, 1998.
————. Wesleyan U, Middletown, CT, 1999.
————. U of Missouri, Columbia, 1999.
————. American Museum of Natural History, New York City, 1999.

Islands: a hapa wet dream

Production, perf. Maura Nguyen Donohue/In Mixed Company. Dance Theater Workshop,
New York City, 1995.
————. Schaeffer Theater, Bates College, Lewiston, ME, 1996.
————. Scott Studio Theater, Smith College, Northampton, MA, 1996.
————. Mulberry Street Theater, New York City, 1996.
————. Hampden Theater, U of Massachusetts, Amherst, 1996.
————. Lyte Auditorium, Millersville U, Millersville, PA, 1996.

Exotic Dancers

Production, perf. Maura Nguyen Donohue and Marc Morozumi. Schaeffer Theater, Bates
College, Lewiston, ME, 1996.
————. Cunningham Studio, New York City, 1996.
————. Mulberry Street Theater, New York City, 1996.
————. La Mama E.T.C., New York City, 1999.

Quilt of Johatsu

Production, chor. Marc Morozumi; perf. Maura Nguyen Donohue and Marc Morozumi.
Cunningham Studio, New York City, 1996.

21 Year Spill

Production, chor. Marc Morozumi; perf. Maura Nguyen Donohue and Marc Morozumi.
Bates Dance Festival, Bates College, Lewiston, ME, 1996.

Aperitifs at Exotica Lounge

Production. Theater 14 and Scott Studio Theater, Smith College, Northampton, MA,
1997.

Lotus Blossom Itch

Production, perf. Maura Nguyen Donohue/In Mixed Company. Dance Theater Workshop,
New York City, 1997.

SKINning the surFACE

Production, perf. Maura Nguyen Donohue/In Mixed Company. New York City, 1998.
————. New WORLD Theater, U of Massachusetts, Amherst, 1998.
————. Dance Theater Workshop, New York City, 1999.
————. Vassar College Studio Theater, Poughkeepsie, NY, 1999.
————. Madison Civic Center, U of Wisconsin, Madison, 1999.

a dime for 2 nipples

Production, perf. Maura Nguyen Donohue/In Mixed Company. Danspace Project, St. Mark's Church, New York City, 1999.

Righteous Babes

Production, perf. Maura Nguyen Donohue/In Mixed Company. P.S. 122, New York City, 2000.

Studies of Maura Nguyen Donohue

Abalos, Marilyn. "*Islands: a hapa wet dream* Opens at DTW." *Asian/New Yorker* Nov. 1995: 9.
Abbott, Susan. "Skins More Than the Surface." Rev. of *SKINning the surFACE. Massachusetts Daily Collegian* 17 Nov. 1998: 6.
Anderson, Jack. "Children with Lives Predetermined by War." Rev. of *SKINning the surFACE. New York Times* 18 Mar. 1999: E7.
Asaf, Dawn. "Fertile Ground: Redefining Asian American Art." *Northwest Asian Weekly* 16 Oct. 1993: 4.
Ben-Itzak, Paul. "Boy in Babeland: Donohue's Righteous Dance." Rev. of *Righteous Babes. Dance Insider* 12 May 2000. 22 December 2000. <http://www.danceinsider.com/f512.html>.
"Dance Troupe Focuses on Cross-over Culture." Prev. of *Islands. Daily Hampshire Gazette* 12 Nov. 1996: 24.
Dohse, Chris. "Bare Fictions." Rev. of *Exotic Dancers* and *Grin 'n Bare It. Village Voice* 44.2 (1999): 143.
Gangatirkar, Seema. "Hampden Theater to Host Dance Troupe." Prev. of *Islands. Massachusetts Daily Collegian* 14 Nov. 1996: 6.
Hargraves, Kelly. "Choreo-history: Mixed Results from In Mixed Company." Rev. of *SKINning the SurFACE. Dance Insider* 5 Sept. 2000. 22 December 2000 <http://www.danceinsider.com/f95_2.html>.
Hong, Binh Ha. "Maura Nguyen Donohue." Profile. *Vietnow Magazine* Sept./Oct. 1995: 48.
Jung, Jean. "Maura Nguyen Donohue Explores Her Vietnamese/American Family History." Rev. of *When You're Old Enough. Northwest Asian Weekly*, 12 June 1993: 11.
Kourlas, Gia. "Night and Day." Prev. of *Lotus Blossom Itch. TimeOut/New York* 13–20 Mar. 1997: 25.
Sagolla, Lisa Jo. "Maura Nguyen Donohue: *SKINning the surFACE.*" *Back Stage* 2–8 Apr. 1999: 31.
Sloat, Susanna. "Split Stream: Aleta Hayes/Patricia Davila/Maura Nguyen Donohue." Rev. of *Islands. Attitude* 11.1 (1996): 36–37.

"Things to Say In Mixed Company." *Asian American Arts Alliance Newsletter* Nov./
  Dec. 1996: N. pag.
Tobias, Tobi. "Track Work." Rev. of *Hai. Village Voice* 40.19 (1995): 45.
Wolf, Sara. "Mermaids, a Madman, and the Open Road." *LA Weekly* 6 Oct. 2000. 22
  December 2000 <http://www.laweekly.com/ink/00/46/dance-wolf.shtml>.

Linda Faigao-Hall
(1948–   )

Gary Storhoff

BIOGRAPHY

Born on July 3, 1948, in the Philippines, Linda Faigao-Hall immigrated to America in 1973. She received a B.A. in English at Silliman University, the Philippines, and an M.A. in English at New York University, where she is currently a Ph.D. candidate in educational theater. Faigao-Hall has been employed as a language-arts instructor at the College of New Rochelle, La Guardia Community College, and other community colleges in New York. She has been a full-time computer-systems analyst since 1983. She married Terrence Hall in 1984, and they have one son, Justin.

Faigao-Hall's plans for the future include expanding her playwriting concerns beyond ethnic issues. "I see myself writing more plays about people other than Asian-Americans," she explains, "and all of them dealing with personal issues in relationships but placing these conflicts against a larger cultural context" (E-mail). She also hopes to have her plays rewritten as screenplays for film.

MAJOR WORKS AND THEMES

Attracted to "the educational aspect of theatre," Linda Faigao-Hall introduces Filipino mythologies and folklore into Asian American theater while commenting on contemporary issues: America's relations with third-world poverty, neocolonialism, homophobia, hate crimes, religious alienation, sexism, domestic abuse, and the difficulties faced by Filipino immigrants in the United States (E-mail). Faigao-Hall also dramatizes other more mundane troubles—dating problems, finding reliable baby-sitters, and surviving at jobs that barely pay the minimum wage. Her audience is most impressed by the audacious sweep of the topics covered in her plays, especially in *Woman from the Other Side of the World* (1997), *God, Sex, and Blue Water* (1998), *The 7th of October* (1999), and *Pusong Babae (Heart of a Woman)* (2000). Not surprisingly, she considers herself most influenced by Anton Chekhov in his "ostensibly conversational and sometimes banal" dramatic action "where the subtext is always about something devastating" (E-mail).

This ambitious range is matched by her innovative, postmodernist dramatic technique. Her dramaturgy might well be described as "magic realism"—a mode of writing that is often associated with marginalized writers. As the oxymoron "magic realism" implies, fantasy and magic coexist in the text with their antithesis, realism; yet magical elements are not textually subordinate to a realistic scene but are organically connected to the whole work, neither more nor less privileged than the play's realistic components. The boundaries between the fantasy world and the real world in Faigao-Hall's plays are gradually erased, eliding the audience's presumption that a commonsense, rationalist interpretation of events can easily be discovered. The realist narrative is disrupted by the interception of magic and the supernatural. Thus the audience is challenged to revise a traditional, Western distinction between a Cartesian epistemology of a rationally knowable world governed by natural law and a supernatural vision of a world controlled by fantasy, dream, and myth.

Her plays, then, are radically structured to explore metaphysical questions. The very title of her play *Woman from the Other Side of the World* expresses Faigao-Hall's extreme vision of a world spiritually infused. Other versions of experience than the rationalist, commonsense view compete for the viewer's attention. The play concerns the ordinary life of Emilya, a Filipino mestiza who, as a "stressed out working mother," has to contend with the problems of "a string of babysitters and a confusing love life" (8). With her son Jason, Emilya seems eager to adopt the American culture as her own, saying, "I love this country more than I ever loved [the Philippines]" (16). Her ambivalence toward her ancestral heritage is rendered problematic, however, by her choice of a boyfriend, George, who is also of Filipino descent.

On the surface, this seems unpromising dramatic material: a woman who disavows her past, embracing instead a familiar life of crass materialism and ordinary reality: "This is America," Emilya says, "there's no magic here" (16). But the eponymous character Ines brings magic with her, transforming Emilya's life by recalling her troubled past. Although Ines's ostensible purpose is to be Jason's baby-sitter (his *yaya*), Ines's magic brings Emilya's buried life to the surface. Emilya, coerced in the Philippines to marry the sugar magnate Don Leon, suffered from emotional and physical abuse and eventually murdered her husband. Her guilt over this undetected crime has blighted her life in America. Ines employs a *duwende*, "a magical gnome," to assist her in confronting the extremity of her situation and releasing her from her guilt. The *duwende* actually performs an exorcism to rescue Emilya and Jason from their shared misery.

The play's magic thus provides the narrative's thematic meaning of transcendence. Faigao-Hall implies with Ines that "there is so much to wonder about. Life is extraordinary" (64). A person from the Philippines, Faigao-Hall suggests, should appreciate life's spiritual dimension that may be inaccessible to many Americans because of their cultural commitment to pragmatic experience. Faigao-Hall's play promotes a different way of responding to the world, one based on the acceptance of dreams, myth, and the occult. This thematic emphasis is dramatized by George, an electrical engineer. He discloses the limitations of a strictly rational, scientific approach to life, since even he is persuaded to believe in Ines's ability to defy natural law. The play's conclusion unites George and Emilya in a shared reverence for the transcendent values the play celebrates.

God, Sex, and Blue Water explicitly stresses Faigao-Hall's commitment to a mystic, spiritual level of existence. The play's narrative center is the *payson*, the passion play that originated in the sixteenth century and is still performed in the Philippines during Easter. During *payson*, volunteers are nailed to the cross. Laling and Clarita (mother and daughter) wish to enact the *payson* in Manhattan, to the consternation of the Catholic church. The plot is complicated by Clarita's stigmata and her mysterious healing powers, which provoke a mother-daughter rivalry over their relative holiness. Yet both mother and daughter agree upon the sterility of contemporary American life; as they say, "The secret of happy living in America is to avoid extreme behavior" (*God*).

Ironically, the play's most compelling character, Brian, embodies the American materialist spirit along with the sense of his own vacuousness: "I have a life but when I strip it down there's really nothing there" (*God*). Brian is a marine insurance broker whose staid business life is disrupted when he falls in love with Clarita. Inspired by her, he begins to question his own moral values. Although the cultural divide between Clarita and Brian is never overcome, Brian rescues his own integrity by making a moral business decision, with the guidance of Clarita.

This predominance of the spiritual is expressed again in *Pusong Babae (Heart of a Woman)*. The seriousness of the spiritual dimension of life is in this play argued by its absence, since the preeminence of the spiritual is enacted not through character but through staging. Faigao-Hall's stage is divided between real, narrative time and Adelfa's memory of her life three years earlier, when she emigrated from the Philippines. Her "real time" is unrelieved misery, while her "memory time" reveals her dreams and hopes in the Philippines. The time shifting exposes the multiplicity of experiential meanings available to people comfortable with their nonrational, intuitive, and mystic capacities. Adelfa is such a character. Having left the Philippines, where she and her symbolically named brother Anghel formerly resided in a vast garbage heap, Adelfa has become a mail-order bride in order to emigrate. She has married Roger, a real-estate magnate, and experiences horrific sexual and physical abuse (onstage) even as she attempts to work out her family's salvation through her sacrifice.

Though she constantly suffers for her family, Adelfa struggles to heed Anghel's message: "To stop dreaming is to die" (*Pusong*). Ironically, however,

Anghel has forgotten his own advice. Instead of persisting in his dream to succeed as a dancing teacher, he has prostituted himself just as his sister has done. He has become a male "macho dancer" and is now dying of AIDS-related tuberculosis. Both Adelfa and Anghel are eager to sacrifice themselves for their family, yet their sacrifice brings a meager "reality" into their lives—a television, VCRs, and Sealy Posturepedic beds. Confronted with this empty consumerism, Adelfa becomes a "lost soul" and expresses Faigao-Hall's judgment on consumerist America: "There's something to be said for poverty" (*Pusong*).

Roger Gold, whose name signifies his love of money, is Faigao-Hall's representative of a patriarchal, consumerist America. Roger is the husband from hell. He is an alcoholic, beating and raping his wife whenever he drinks too much. As a mail-order bride, Adelfa has little choice but to submit to his excesses, even when he requires that she cry out, "Save me, white man!" during sexual intercourse (*Pusong*). Yet her commitment to a world of diversity ultimately saves her, for she finally leaves Roger to survive in America without material comforts, perhaps, but with dreams and memories of devoted family love.

The 7th of October seems a departure for Faigao-Hall, since the play adheres to realistic conventions. Nevertheless, Faigao-Hall injects a strong sense of spirituality with her symbolically named character Angel. The play is organized around Angel's homosexual love for Michael, whose name implies that he too is an angel, the divine messenger who brings a message of acceptance and love to straight America. Michael's message coheres to the date of October 7, when Matthew Shepard was killed in Wyoming. Angel and Michael, prompted by this hate crime, are led to reevaluate their lives in the closet, and when Michael "outs," he provokes a homosexual panic among his Manhattan construction workers. Urged to conceal his homosexuality, Michael refuses for patently political reasons: "Every gay man is a revolutionary" (*7th*). The tragic ending of the play—when Angel sacrifices his life for Michael—seems to bring home Faigao-Hall's political purpose: the need for federal hate-crimes legislation.

The 7th of October, then, marks an artistic transition for Faigao-Hall. No longer centering her work on ethnicity, she challenges her adoptive nation to confront social injustice. Nevertheless, she does not abandon her commitment to a transcendent set of values. "I think of my playwriting," she reflects, "as some kind of ministry" (E-mail).

CRITICAL RECEPTION

Faigao-Hall's theatrical works have achieved measured success according to the influential reviewers on both coasts. Mel Gussow of the *New York Times*, for example, wrote that "both the play [*State without Grace*] and the playwright are marked by their potential" (C21). The Los Angeles critic Philip Brandes found *Woman from the Other Side* extraordinarily "compelling" (20). But most of her plays, though widely produced at various theaters in New York City, have received unfortunately little attention from theater critics and scholars. Critical studies of her works will not only benefit ethnic curricula on college campuses, but also add yet another perspective to the national debates on cultural issues, values, immigration, and social justice.

BIBLIOGRAPHY

Works by Linda Faigao-Hall

Drama

Woman from the Other Side of the World: A Full-Length Play. Woodstock, IL: Dramatic Publishing Co., 1996.

Unpublished Manuscripts

State without Grace. Ms. 345. Roberta Uno Asian Women Playwrights Scripts Collection 1924–1992, Special Collections and Archives, W.E.B. Du Bois Library, U of Massachusetts, Amherst, 1984.

Requiem. Ms. 345. Roberta Uno Asian Women Playwrights Scripts Collection 1924–1992, Special Collections and Archives, W.E.B. Du Bois Library, U of Massachusetts, Amherst, 1986.

Americans. Ms. 345. Roberta Uno Asian Women Playwrights Scripts Collection 1924–1992, Special Collections and Archives, W.E.B. Du Bois Library, U of Massachusetts, Amherst, 1987.

Men Come and Go. Ms. 345. Roberta Uno Asian Women Playwrights Scripts Collection 1924–1992, Special Collections and Archives, W.E.B. Du Bois Library, U of Massachusetts, Amherst, 1987.

Sparrow. 1990.

And the Pursuit of Happiness. 1991.

Burning Out. 1991.

Manilla Drive. 1992.

Pidgin' Hole. 1996.

The Interview. 1997.

Duet. 1998.

God, Sex, and Blue Water. 1998.

He & She. 1998.

The 7th of October. 1999.

Pusong Babae (Heart of a Woman). 2000.

Selected Production History

State without Grace

Production, dir. Aida Limjoco. Pan Asian Repertory Theatre, New York City, 1984.

————, dir. James Chew. Asian American Theater Company, San Francisco, 1985.

Requiem

Production, dir. Aida Limjoco. Henry Street Theater Arts Center, New York City, 1986.

Staged reading. Pan Asian Repertory Theatre, New York City, 1989.

————. East West Players, Los Angeles, 1990.

Americans

Production. Chelsea Theater Arts Center, New York City, 1987.
————. Catskills Reading Society, Ellenville, NY, 1991.

Men Come and Go

Production. Actors' Institute, New York City, 1987.

Sparrow

Staged reading as work in-progress. Dramatists Guild, New York City, 1987.
————. Henry St. Settlement House, New York City, 1988.
Staged reading. Catskills Reading Society, Ellenville, NY, 1991.

Manilla Drive

Staged reading. Working Theatre, New York City, 1993.

Pidgin' Hole

Production. Women's Project and Productions, New York City, 1996.

The Interview

Production, dir. Gail Noppe-Brandon. Clark Studio Theatre, New York City, 1997.

Woman from the Other Side of the World

Production, dir. Alberto Isaac. East West Players, Los Angeles, 1997.
————, dir. Jorge Ledesma. Ma-Yi Theatre Ensemble, New York City, 1994.

Duet

Production, dir. Gail Noppe-Brandon. Clark Studio Theater, New York City, 1998.

God, Sex, and Blue Water

Production, dir. Suzanne Bennett. Lark Theater Company, New York City, 1998.

He & She

Production, dir. Elaine Smith. Expanded Arts, New York City, 1998.

The 7th of October

Staged reading, dir. Mark Plesent. American Place Theatre, New York City, 1999.
Production, dir. Gail Noppe-Brandon. Working Theatre, New York City, 2000.

Pusong Babae (Heart of a Woman)

Production, dir. Gail Noppe-Brandon. Clark Studio Theater, New York City, 2000.

Letter

E-mail to the author. 27 Nov. 2000.

Studies of Linda Faigao-Hall

Brandes, Philip. "Cultures Clash in Haunting *Woman from the Other Side.*" *Los Angeles Times* 13 June 1997: F20.
Gussow, Mel. "Pan Asian's *State without Grace.*" *New York Times* 28 Nov. 1984: C21.
Uno, Roberta. Appendix. *Unbroken Thread: An Anthology of Plays by Asian American Women.* Amherst: U of Massachusetts P, 1993. 309–28.

Alberto S. Florentino
(1931–   )

Andrew L. Smith

BIOGRAPHY

Alberto "Bert" S. Florentino was born on July 28, 1931, in a "barrio" or cluster of nipa huts in the Philippines. Soon after, the family moved to a satellite city, Cabanatuan, some kilometers away. His father, a teacher, had an extracurricular interest in play directing and organizing school choir groups. He enlisted the younger Florentino as his typist, turning out multiple copies of plays using a lightweight portable typewriter. "I read those plays as I typed them and probably learned playwriting dialogue in that manner" (Personal interview). Some years later, the Florentinos moved again, to Manila, where he would live for the next forty years. Florentino graduated from Torres High School in Manila. Prior to college (1948), Florentino's main interest was science. Using "war surplus" optical lenses then available, he made his own microscopes and telescopes, viewing tiny paramecia and amoebas, as well as the grand planet of Jupiter, with its dancing moons. By chance, he saw his name in print in a Manila paper when a letter he had written to the editor was published. Encouraged, he submitted a political parody of Robert Browning's "Pippa Passes," which also was printed. Soon after, he won fifteen pesos in a short-short-story contest in the *Daily Mirror*, a weekly newspaper.

Florentino pursued his modest education at the U.S. Information Service Escolta, Manila's first university without walls, and then at the University of the East at twenty-three. He was a conscientious student, as his mother was paying for his tuition out of her grocery money. He continued at the University of the Philippines and Far Eastern University. But it was at the University of the East that his interest in playwriting began to develop. He saw plays written by elder playwrights Nick Joaquin, Wilfrido Guerrero, and Severino Montano, who were the powerhouses of Philippine drama in the 1950s and 1960s.

At the University of the East, Florentino wrote *The World Is an Apple* and submitted it for the first annual postwar Carlos Palanca Memorial Awards for Literature (Drama in English). Although he was hoping for the third prize of three hundred pesos, enough to buy a portable typewriter, the play won first prize. *Cadaver*, the other play he submitted, was also vying for first prize in the same contest. Florentino says, "That started it all." In 1954, his first serious attempt at playwriting caused him to abandon his schooling. Eventually, he went on to write more than fifty plays for the stage and more than one hundred for television, first in English, then in Tagalog (Filipino).

Following the Palanca Award in 1954, *The World Is an Apple* was published in the *Sunday Times Magazine* that same year. It was premiered at the Civic Theatre in Manila early the following year. Four years later, the play was adapted for television and published as the title play in Florentino's own collection, *"The World Is an Apple" and Other Prize Plays* (1959).

While Florentino continued to pen award-winning plays and television scripts, he went into book publishing in 1962, eventually turning out the Peso Book series by numerous prewar/postwar authors led by seven national artists in literature, the most notable of whom was José García Villa, in 1973. His writing career also includes serving as editor of numerous literary magazines such as *Short Story International*, and as a visiting writer and professor at various universities in the Philippines and the United States throughout the 1970s. He and his family immigrated to the United States in 1983. He now lives in New York City and continues to publish small-run chapbooks by Philippine, Philippine American, Asian American, and mainstream writers. He also serves as editor of *Illustrado*, a weekly online literary magazine that may be accessed through the *Manila Post*.

MAJOR WORKS AND THEMES

At the age of seventeen, Florentino started reading the fiction and plays of American writers of the 1930s. Among his favorites were Theodore Dreiser, Erskine Caldwell, Eugene O'Neill, John Steinbeck, William Saroyan, and Clifford Odets. They were the culturally piqued writers, playwrights, and essayists who fomented ideas in Florentino. "They were all writing my sentiments; I'm a socially conscious writer because I read those authors" (Personal interview), and that awareness presents itself in Florentino's work in the sense that his plays are all realist problem pieces involving social issues. He catalogs the common side of the city just as Steinbeck did in *The Pearl, Cannery Row*, and *The Grapes of Wrath*, for instance. Later, he was to meet Arthur Miller and John Updike and, later still, correspond with Norman Mailer.

Resilience seems to have the thematic claim in his early plays. After all, it is a national character that has long been associated with the Filipino people. *The*

World Is an Apple (1954), by general consensus the most produced play written by a Filipino playwright, portrays resilience in the especially ugly world of the Manila slums. Gloria, Mario's wife, tries to prevent him from resuming the criminal activities of his single days. Gloria would rather die of starvation than live off of dirty money. The play is one of contrasts; amid the graft and vice of their impoverished world, there are men, women, and children whose feelings and thoughts are beautiful.

Oli Imapan (c. 1959), which means "holy infant," is based upon the eviction by the mayor of Manila of the squatters in the slums of Interamuros and Binondo five days before Christmas 1958. Resilience in this play is illustrated through the dialogue of two children, a girl and a boy, who do not understand why their shantytown is being destroyed by the government contractor. Those who try to prevent the government from ejecting the occupants are summarily arrested. The children, not being able to understand any of the reasons why the government is bulldozing their community, begin to sing "Silent night, holy night! All is calm, all is bright."

The composition and production of Florentino's first political play, *Memento Mori* (1971), can themselves be deemed examples of resilience. The play was not only written during the social upheaval of the early 1970s, but was also produced on *Balintataw* (a weekly television drama, based upon Filipino literary writings) almost on the eve of the declaration of martial law. To get past the government censors, the director, Lupita Kashiwahara, set the play in a mythical Latin American country. Between 1972 and 1984, Florentino wrote *The Death and Martyrdom of José Abad Santos, Mariang Makiling*, and *Doña Teodora Alonzo*, also during the martial-law years, when the Philippine government was discouraging public readings and performances of his earlier plays.

However, the themes spanning Florentino's entire oeuvre can be distilled to the playwright's "reaction to the world I never made" (Personal interview). Authoritarianism, rebellion against poverty, unequal distribution of wealth, and exploitation of the masses are among the recurring subjects in his work. The Philippines is a land of paradoxes in his eyes. A few blocks from places similar to Manhattan, Florentino reflected during my interview, "one can quickly be transported to the third, if not the fourth world, with its open sewers, disease, malnutrition. It's a world I never made" (Personal interview). Thus his dolorous characters particularly speak to the disparities: the wife in *Cadaver* (1953), the younger sister in *Cavort with Angels* (1958), the mother in *Lunsod* (1968), and the son in *Katapat ng Langit* (1973), or "kingdom on earth," loosely translated.

CRITICAL RECEPTION

In the Philippines, Florentino is considered a cultural icon; his works have been read and performed widely. In fact, his name always appears at the top of the list of the most celebrated contemporary Filipino playwrights. However, as an Asian American, living and working in the United States, he is marginalized.

In part, his relative anonymity in American culture can be attributed to limited publishing and distribution of his work by Philippines publishers. Like the works of many talented writers, his plays have appeared mainly through academe— De La Salle University Press, which has virtually no budget for marketing and distribution.

Among his works, *The World Is an Apple* has garnered the most significant following. Severino Montano described Florentino as having "a poetic vision of social protest" (i), while others have suggested that the playwright is a poet of Manila's slums. A member of the Society of Jesuits once wrote that reading one single play by Florentino is a good primer for society's ills (Florentino, Home page). After all, Florentino chooses to write about the dispossessed, the poor, and the disadvantaged. But then the essayist suggested that he might not recommend a dosage of more than any one Florentino play to young people for fear of inordinately depressing them. In the essayist's view, all five plays in *"The World Is an Apple" and Other Prize Plays* most certainly reflect reality— the human condition, pained, challenged, humored—yet, at the finale, Florentino's characters offer audiences studies in resilience, hope, and eventually, victory (Florentino, Home page).

Although Florentino has been credited with departing from the mainstream plays that traditionally offered Filipino audiences romantic story lines, his work has generated little critical interest in the United States so far. The public's limited access to his plays may partially be to blame, but the complacency on the part of U.S. audiences about subjects and themes that do not seem immediately related to their lives may be the real reason for the lack of interest in his work. Ironically, though his works are set in Filipino society, they are about Good battling Evil, where Good is often crippled by a deteriorating environment. Like the medieval morality play *Everyman*, Florentino's plays offer audiences studies in fellowship and good deeds. In the final analysis, his plays are always as timely as newspaper headlines, because his characters are squatters and this world is someone else's apple.

BIBLIOGRAPHY

Works by Alberto S. Florentino

Drama

And Now Comes the Night. Philippine Review 2.10–11 (1953): 23–56.
"The World Is an Apple" and Other Prize Plays. Manila: Philippine Cultural Publishers, 1959.
The World Is an Apple. Philippine Contemporary Literature. 2nd ed. Ed. Acuncion David-Maramba. Intro. Teodoro Evangelista. Manila: Bookmark, 1965. 134–45.
Balintataw *Teleplay Series.* Manila: Bookmark, 1968.
Oli impan. 3 Filipino Playwrights: Alberto S. Florentino, Wilfrido D. Nolledo [and]

Jesus T. Peralta. By Alberto S. Florentino, Wilfrido D. Nolledo, and Jesus T. Peralta. Manila: Philippine Educational Theater Association, 1968. 7–13.

Wedding dance. 3 Filipino Playwrights: Alberto S. Florentino, Wilfrido D. Nolledo [and] Jesus T. Peralta. By Alberto S. Florentino, Wilfrido D. Nolledo, and Jesus T. Peralta. Manila: Philippine Educational Theater Association, 1968. 15–21.

Sangyugto. Manila: Philippine Educational Theater Association, 1970.

Memento Mori: More Short Plays. Manila: MCS Enterprises, 1971.

Panahon ng Digma. Mandaluyong: Cacho Hermanos, 1973.

Huling Habilin. Ed. Alejandrino Hufana. *Multicultural Creative Writing Journal*. Spec. issue of *Likhaan* 1 (Dec. 1979): 11–34.

The Portable Florentino: Seven Representative Plays. Manila: De La Salle UP, 1998.

Unpublished Manuscripts

Information unavailable

Selected Production History

Information on stage productions unavailable.

Interview

Personal interview. 12 May 2000.

Television

The World Is an Apple

Production, dir. Lupita Concio. *Balintataw* television drama. Manila. 1968.

Bannatiran

Production (stage adaptation of Amador T. Daguio's "The Woman Who Looked out the Window"), dir. Lupita Concio. *Balintataw* television drama. Manila. 1968.

Cañao

Production (stage adaptation of Amador T. Daguio's "Wedding Dance"). *Balintataw* teleplay series. Manila. 1968.

Laarni

Production (stage adaptation of Loreto Paras Sulit's "A Dream"). *Balintataw* teleplay series. Manila. 1968.

May Day Eve

Production (stage adaptation of Nick Joaquin's "May Day Eve"). *Balintataw* teleplay series. Manila. 1968.

Mir-i-nisa

Production (stage adaptation of José García Villa's "Mir-i-nisa"). *Balintataw* teleplay series. Manila. 1968.

Studies of Alberto S. Florentino

Alegre, Edilberto N., and Doreen G. Fernandez. *Writers and Their Milieu*. Manila: De La Salle UP, 1987.

Bernad, Miguel. "The World of the Slums." *Philippine Studies* 8.3 (1960): 56–64.

Bernardo, Gabriel. *A Critical and Annotated Bibliography of Philippine, Indonesian, and Other Malaysian Folk-lore*. Ed. Francisco Demetrio Y. Radaza. Cagayan de Oro City, Philippines: Xavier U, 1972.

Casper, Leonard. "Alberto S. Florentino." *New Writing from the Philippines: A Critique and Anthology*. Syracuse, N.Y: Syracuse UP, 1966.

Chung, Yu. "An Evaluation Analysis of Eight Plays of Alberto Florentino." M.A. thesis. U of San Carlos, 1973.

Cruz, Isagani. *Beyond Futility: The Filipino as Critic*. Quezon City: New Day, 1984.

Cultural Center of the Philippines. *Philippine Theater*. Vol. VII of *Encyclopedia of Philippine Art*. Manila: CCP Special Publications Office, 1994.

De La Torre, Visitacion, ed. *A Survey of Contemporary Philippine Literature in English*. Manila: National Bookstore, 1978.

Demetillo, Ricaredo. *Major and Minor Keys*. Quezon City: New Day, 1987.

Dizon, Fe S. *Seventy Years of Philippine Theater: An Annotated Bibliography of Critical Works, 1900–1970*. Manila: U of the Philippines, 1972.

Egipto, Filour. "A Comparative Study of the Characterization and Theme of Alberto Florentino's *The World Is An Apple* and Hendric Ibsen's *A Doll's House*." M.A. thesis. Isabela State U, 1984.

Florentino, Alberto S. Home page. 2 October 2000. 13 December 2000 <http://hometown.aol.com/bertflorentino/myhomepage/index.html>.

Gonda, Catalina. "The Naturalistic Aspect of Six Selected Plays: Their Social Impact." M.A. thesis. Golden Gate Colleges, 1989.

Gruenberg, Estrellita B. "The Perceived Canon of Philippine Literature." *DLSU Graduate Journal* 13.1 (1988): 1–24.

Lachica, Lourdes. "An Analytical and Evaluation Study of (15) Selected Plays of Alberto Florentino, Wilfrido Nolledo, and Jesus Peralta." M.A. thesis. U of Santo Tomas, Philippines, 1981.

Lao, Armando, and Fanny García. *Pitong Teleplay*. Manila: Anvil, 1995.

Lumbera, Bienvenido, and Cynthia N. Lumera, eds. *Philippine Literature: A History and Anthology*. Manila: National Book Store, 1982.

Manguerra Brainard, Cecilia, ed. *Fiction by Filipinos in America*. Quezon City: New Day, 1993.

Medina, B.S., Jr. *Confrontations: Past and Present in Philippine Literature*. Manila: National Book Store, 1974.

Mejorada, Ma. Flor. "*The World Is An Apple* and Other Prize Plays: A Study of the Conflict of Human Values." M.A. thesis. St. Louis University, Philippines, 1972.

Mella, Cesar T., Jr. *Directory of Filipino Writers: Past and Present*. Manila: CTM Enterprises, 1974.

Montano, Severino. Introduction. *The World Is an Apple and Other Prize Plays*. Manila: Filipiniana Publishers, 1959. i–iv.

Polotan, Kerima, ed. *An Anthology of Carlos Palanca Memorial Awards Winners, English Division*. 4 vols. Manila: Bustamante P, 1976.

Tiongson, Nicanor. *Dulaan: An Essay on Philippine Theater*. Manila: Sentrong Pangkultura ng Pilipinas, 1989.

Philip Kan Gotanda

(1951–   )

Randy Barbara Kaplan

BIOGRAPHY

Since the 1970s, Philip Kan Gotanda has been at the center of the Asian American theater movement, creating a body of theatrical work that speaks in the many voices of Japanese America and encompasses a broad spectrum of dramatic styles. Along with David Henry Hwang, Momoko Iko, and Wakako Yamauchi, Gotanda was one of a core of "second-wave" dramatists to follow in the footsteps of pioneer Frank Chin to develop a viable Asian American theater. Since his initial theatrical effort, a musical entitled *The Avocado Kid, or Zen and the Art of Guacamole* (1979), debuted at Los Angeles's East West Players, Gotanda's works have been successfully produced at both Asian American and culturally nonspecific theaters across the United States.

Born and raised in Hawaii, Gotanda's father, Wilfred Itsuta Gotanda, came to the U.S. mainland to study medicine at the University of Arkansas. After embarking upon a successful medical career serving the large Japanese American community of Stockton, California, the elder Gotanda ironically found himself forced to return to Arkansas when, during World War II, he was interned at Rohwer Camp. After the war, he resumed his life in Stockton, marrying schoolteacher Catherine Matsumoto and starting a family. Philip Kan Gotanda was born the youngest of three sons to his nisei parents on December 17, 1951, in Stockton, California.

Gotanda's formative years were characterized by an ongoing tug-of-war between two opposing drives: a "creative, artistic" side that battled with a "serious, professional" counterimpulse (Omi xii). Throughout his adolescence, Gotanda, like many baby boomers who came of age during the turbulent 1960s, was drawn to rock music, writing his own songs and performing with local bands.

After high school, however, academia beckoned. With an eye toward becoming a psychiatrist, Gotanda enrolled at the University of California at Santa Cruz (1969), although he continued to write lyrics and perform music. After a year of university studies, Gotanda's creative side gained the upper hand. He left the United States for Japan, where he spent a year studying ceramic techniques with artist Hiroshi Seto. Gotanda's knowledge of the pottery-making process would inform his work years later in *Ballad of Yachiyo* (1996), a play inspired by the true-life story of his paternal aunt's suicide, and *Yohen* (1997), a drama of domestic conflict between a nisei woman and her African American husband of thirty-seven years. But more than simply providing materials for dramatic plots, Gotanda's Japan experience gave him the opportunity to experience for the first time "a sense of racial anonymity": immersing himself in a culture in which he was not defined as "Other." Gotanda realized then and there the effort required of Americans of Asian descent to maneuver themselves psychologically in order to deflect the impact of racism. Simultaneously, he came to appreciate the extent of his "Americanness," a cultural positioning that would never permit him to assume an entirely Japanese identity, thereby forcing him to forge his own (Omi xiii).

Upon returning from Japan, Gotanda completed his undergraduate studies at the University of California at Santa Barbara (1973), this time majoring in Japanese arts. The next two years were a heady time for the Asian American arts community on the West Coast. The Asian American theater scene in Los Angeles had been established with Mako's East West Players (1965), and Frank Chin was launching San Francisco's Asian American Theater Company (1973). Asian American musicians, artists, and writers declared themselves actively committed to creating and promoting a uniquely Asian American aesthetic rather than reproducing traditional Asian art forms. Gotanda took his first steps toward playwriting through his music, penning the lyrics to songs he entitled "Ballad of the Issei" and "All-American Asian Punk" (Omi xiv) and continuing to perform. When his conflicting urges surfaced once more, Gotanda enrolled in Hastings School of Law, where he completed a law degree (1978). Nevertheless, he continued to create music, penning and performing original material informed by the Asian American experience. For a brief time Gotanda played guitar in Bamboo, a rock band that also featured fellow playwrights David Henry Hwang and R.A. Shiomi.

Gotanda's first theatrical piece was a musical inspired by the well-known Japanese folktale "Momotaro the Peach Boy." *The Avocado Kid, or Zen and the Art of Guacamole* caught the eye of veteran actor Mako, then serving as artistic director of East West Players, who invited Gotanda to come to Los Angeles and develop the piece for the company. As Omi describes the play, it manifests Gotanda's growing awareness of the value of drawing upon Asian root cultural traditions without slavishly reproducing them in order to generate an Asian American performance aesthetic: it is "a distinctively Asian American play—tak[ing] familiar elements drawn from Asian and Asian American culture and subvert[ing] them. Its 'hip' dialogue and style, combined with aggressive music and dance, celebrate the spirit that playfully captures the ongoing Asian American engagement with popular culture" (Omi xv). Though the production did not elicit enthusiastic responses from several reviewers, presumably because of its frank treatment of sexuality, that did not stop the piece from finding favor with audiences at both East West Players (1979) and Asian American Theater Company (1981; revival, 1988) (Kurahashi, "*Avocado*" 116). His experience with *The Avocado Kid* convinced Gotanda to close the door on his legal career forever.

Gotanda's next play was written in loving tribute to his father. *A Song for a Nisei Fisherman* (1980) traces the life of Itsuta "Ichan" Matsumoto from an impoverished Hawaiian childhood through his World War II internment to maturity and old age as husband and father. The poignant drama, which demonstrated the skill and sensitivity with which Gotanda was able to articulate the nisei experience, was produced at four professional Asian American theater companies: Asian American Theater Company, where David Henry Hwang directed its world premiere (1980), Pan Asian Repertory Theatre (1983), East West Players (1984), and Northwest Asian American Theatre (1991).

With *Dream of Kitamura* (1982), Gotanda experimented with surrealism, a style to which he would return in a later work about the midlife crisis of a sansei law professor, *Day Standing on Its Head* (1994). While *Kitamura* played on the West Coast, New York's Pan Asian Repertory Theatre produced another surrealistic Gotanda work about a sansei rock musician, *Bullet Headed Birds* (1981). While these early works spelled the beginning of success for Gotanda, it was his bittersweet drama about the dissolution of a nisei marriage, *The Wash* (1985), that placed him firmly in the public's eye as a playwright of standing.

Originally, *The Wash* was workshopped at the Mark Taper Forum's New Theatre for Now Festival (1985). Two years later, the play had its world premiere at San Francisco's Eureka Theatre. It was filmed for American Playhouse (1990), with a powerful cast that included Mako as Nobu Matsumoto, a nisei husband consumed with anger and self-loathing; Nobu McCarthy as Masi, Nobu's wife who leaves him to seek a meaningful and independent life for herself; and Sab Shimono as Masi's lover Sadao. With its frank but tender and thoughtful treatment of the death of a marriage, Gotanda carved out a dramaturgical place for himself as the creator of distinctly nonstereotypical, realistic characterizations of Japanese Americans and their lives.

With his next play, a bitingly ironic examination of the impact of racism on the lives of two Asian American actors, *Yankee Dawg You Die* (1986), Gotanda tackled casting discrimination in the entertainment industry. (The piece coincidentally foreshadowed issues that would surround the "*Miss Saigon* controversy" in 1990, resulting from British theatrical producer Cameron Mackintosh's decision to cast Jonathan Pryce, a Caucasian actor, as a Eurasian pimp in a musical retelling of *Madame Butterfly* set during the Vietnam War.) To call attention to the extent of both historical and contemporaneous inequities faced by Asian

American actors, Gotanda created an intergenerational conflict between the older Vincent Chang, an actor who had made a career of playing "Oriental" stereotypes, and the self-consciously militant young Bradley Yamashita. The play traces a year in their occasionally amicable but often-acrimonious relationship during which time the two men clash, grow, learn, and ultimately reverse philosophical and professional positions.

By the early 1990s, it had been some time since Gotanda had performed with a band, but he had never lost his love for music, and all of his dramas utilize musical performance or sound effects as an integral element of dramatic action. With *in the dominion of night* (1993), a "spoken word play with music," Gotanda returned to musically driven performance art. The piece features Gotanda himself as retro-hip poet joe ozu with his backup band, the new orientals, comprised of Dan Kuramoto, of the sansei jazz fusion band Hiroshima and with whom Gotanda had maintained an artistic relationship since his student days, Danny Yamamoto, and Taiji Miyagawa. The new orientals "are very 50's bohemian with a 90's sense. A kind of neo romantic post yellow meditation" (*in the dominion of night* 4). Against a jazz background that recalls 1950s coffeehouse bravado punctuated with sansei chic, Gotanda performs a lengthy poem that is by turns tongue-in-cheek, wildly erotic, self-deprecating, and deeply reverent toward life and love.

Gotanda is equally at home writing for the stage or the camera. Weary of Hollywood producers expressing lukewarm enthusiasm for his ideas, Gotanda overcame the obstacle by creating his own production companies. He wrote, produced, directed, and starred in his first short film, *The Kiss* (1992), as an office "nebbish" whose heroic moment transcends boundaries that define people as Others (it is worth noting that Gotanda is a delightful actor who takes a role in all of his films). *The Kiss* was shown at a number of film festivals, including the Sundance Film Festival and the Berlin and Edinburgh film festivals. Gotanda also wrote, directed, and produced *Drinking Tea* (1996), a thirty-minute film about the dying process and its effects on an elderly nisei couple. His most recent film, *Life Tastes Good* (1999), is by turns amusing and painful; the action revolves around a retired nisei mobster and his last attempt before suicide to reconcile with his estranged children, a cokehead dentist daughter and her brother, an incompetent but gentle guitar player. The film has been shown at Sundance, along with film festivals in San Francisco, Hawaii, Fort Lauderdale, Los Angeles, and Toronto.

Gotanda's plays demonstrate his ability to write in a wide range of styles. In the surreal *Day Standing on Its Head* (1994), the audience journeys into the mind of Harry Kitamura, a man struggling to find his way through a labyrinth of mid-life regrets and lost dreams. *Fish Head Soup* (1995) is a dark examination of a Japanese American family's deeply rooted dysfunctional behaviors. *Ballad of Yachiyo* (1996), an impressionistic memory play set in Hawaii, tells the story of a love triangle gone disastrously wrong. *Sisters Matsumoto* (1997), a Chekhovian-style realistic drama, portrays the psychological scars suffered by a nisei family in the aftermath of their incarceration in World War II as they return to their childhood home to rebuild their lives. *Yohen* (1997) depicts another marriage in crisis, this time between a nisei woman and her African American husband.

The Wash and *Yankee Dawg You Die* signaled a significant shift in Gotanda's popularity (Omi xvi). His work continued to be produced by Asian American theater companies, and Gotanda has always acknowledged his indebtedness to them, often describing his relationship with the Asian American Theater Company, for example, as a connection to his "life's blood." However, since the early 1990s, Gotanda's plays have also been developed and produced by culturally nonspecific theaters. *Fish Head Soup* premiered at Berkeley Repertory Theatre under the direction of Oskar Eustis (1991); Eustis also directed the East West Players' production (1993) and Gotanda's next play, *Day Standing on Its Head*, at the Manhattan Theatre Club (1994). *Ballad of Yachiyo* (1996) was cocommissioned by Costa Mesa's South Coast Repertory and Berkeley Repertory Theatre, where it received its world premiere (1995), subsequently traveling to South Coast Repertory in Costa Mesa (1996). *Sisters Matsumoto* was codeveloped by the Asian American Theater Company with San Jose Repertory Theatre and Seattle Repertory Theatre, which later coproduced Boston's Huntington Theatre Company production (2000).

Gotanda's work has been recognized with numerous awards, honors, fellowships, commissions, and grants. He is the recipient of Guggenheim, McKnight, National Endowment for the Arts, and a number of Rockefeller fellowships, in addition to the National Artist Award from the PEW Charitable Trust and Theatre Communications group. He has also received a Gerbode Foundation Grant and a Lila Wallace-Reader's Digest Writer's Award. Gotanda serves as an associate artist at the Seattle Repertory Theatre and Mark Taper Forum.

It is to Gotanda's credit that he remains uncompromisingly committed to creating a uniquely and specifically Asian American vision instead of seeking to ensure commercial success outside the Asian American theater world by diluting his writing to accommodate the sensibilities of non–Asian American audiences. Michael Omi astutely assesses Gotanda's work when he describes the playwright's "cultural specificity . . . [as] strategically utiliz[ing] . . . a way of affording his audience a more expansive look at who and what America really is" (xvii).

MAJOR WORKS AND THEMES

Philip Kan Gotanda is the creator of influential Asian American dramas that reflect the state of contemporary Asian American theater and, indeed, often influence the course of its development. As such, considered as a body of work, Gotanda's plays can be said to address a broad spectrum of Asian American, and specifically Japanese American, experiences, encompassing a variety of theatrical styles, including realism, surrealism, and the eclectic style of the American stage musical. Considered separately, each of Gotanda's works makes a distinct claim for the diversity of Japanese America.

Gotanda's major works are thematically driven by his excavation and public naming of the deeply rooted effects of racism on Japanese Americans so as to move toward a state of healing. To this end, the internment camps figure prominently in his plays, although Gotanda, born after World War II, was not himself an internee. Nevertheless, the internment's impact on his writing and life is palpable; as he has said, "Whether you speak about the Camps or don't speak about them, the experience is passed on generationally. . . . It's a psychic scar" (Berson, "Philip Kan Gotanda" 30).

While playwrights such as Wakako Yamauchi (*12–1-A*) and Lane Nishikawa (*Gila River*) have written camp dramas that depict life in the camps, Gotanda's work focuses on the long-term effects of the camp experience on the Japanese American psyche in the aftermath of the war. Gotanda's treatment of the camp experience ranges from the overt and immediate, as in *Sisters Matsumoto*, to the implicit and far reaching, as in his earlier plays *A Song for a Nisei Fisherman, The Wash*, and *Fish Head Soup*.

In *Sisters Matsumoto*, Gotanda positions the camp experience as the central force behind the dramatic action. "Acutely aware of how this theme had been brought to the public's attention in popular film and novel form, I had taken great pains to insure that the telling was not only as impactful and dramatic as the story inherently demanded, but that it be told through forms of behavior and communication that I knew to be authentic, i.e., 'as it was lived', which I felt were ignored in those popularized forms" (Gotanda, Letter). The play takes place in Stockton in 1945 as the Matsumoto sisters and their husbands return from Rohwer to find their once-proud family homestead crumbling into a shameful eyesore; the words "Japs Go Home" have been scrawled across one wall. As the action unfolds, and the characters must make decisions about how to resurrect their lives, they slowly come to realize that internment has become part and parcel of their very selves; closing the emotional door on their victimization will never be an option. The camps are demonstrated to be omnipresent even in the play's finely drawn moments: when Henry, the proverbial "boy next door," and Rose, the youngest Matsumoto sister, meet for the first time in many years, they refer to Poston and Rohwer camps as where they live, not where they were involuntarily held.

The psychological internalization of the camp experience—an effect Gotanda has described as similar to that of abused child syndrome (Berson, *Between Worlds* 30)—runs through Gotanda's earlier plays. In this group of works, the dramatic action transpires years after World War II but clearly references internment as a watershed for Japanese Americans. Omi notes Gotanda's progressive depiction of racism through his "family dramas," *A Song for a Nisei Fisherman, The Wash*, and *Fish Head Soup*. Moving through this series of plays, Gotanda portrays the psychological effects of racism as cutting deeper and deeper into the Japanese American community, beginning with forces outside individuals that act upon them and moving to individuals who internalize racism to the point of participating in their own victimization (Omi xxi).

The life of Itsuta "Ichan" Matsumoto, the protagonist of *A Song for a Nisei Fisherman*, parallels that of Gotanda's own father, Wilfred Gotanda. Indeed, Itsuta comments on the irony of having pursued medical studies at the University of Arkansas and then being forcibly returned to the same state for incarceration (*Song* 240). As Itsuta describes Rohwer, Gotanda notes in a stage direction that his monologue "gradually builds up in intensity of feeling, passion, and anger, but it is always controlled" (241). That operative phrase, "always controlled," is Itsuta's means of keeping his justifiable rage in check and confining it to a subterranean place in his emotional life. As a result, its toxins undoubtedly leak into the psyche of the individual, the family, and the Japanese American community at large. However, Gotanda is concerned that that operating sentiment of the play, and of the Japanese American culture, is widely misunderstood: "The Japanese American world is formulated in a tradition that can easily be perceived as flat and lacking in strong dramatic action when compared to works of the more overt and direct tradition, and as a consequence, easy to dismiss" (Letter).

In *The Wash*, which traces Masi Matsumoto's liberating journey from emotionally neglected wife to independent woman, the camps loom large in the nisei characters' psychology. Here the dramatic action occurs some forty years after World War II. The characters do not openly refer to the physical, emotional, and financial deprivations of the experience, referring instead to camp sock hops and old friends. Nevertheless, the experience has had a profound impact on the characters' behaviors. For Nobu, Masi's emotionally withholding husband, it has been one of the defining elements of his manhood. He is incapable of scaling the internment's psychological walls, and his accompanying emotions of guilt and inadequacy cause him to act out his feelings on Masi. She is ultimately left to choose between allowing Nobu to abuse her or salvaging what is left of her life. Unlike many nisei women who sacrificed themselves in the name of husband and family, Masi chooses to save herself.

"Victim mentality" (Lee, "*Fish Head Soup*" 181) figures prominently in *Fish Head Soup* (1991). *Nisei Fisherman* embraces its characters in all their triumphs and shortcomings, and the tone of *The Wash* is bittersweet without being bitter. *Fish Head Soup*, however, holds the audience's feet to the fire; it is not, as Gotanda has said, a "self-congratulatory" family play. Instead, this drama lays bare "the manner in which racism is internalized and manifested in our familial relationships, the generational effect of this legacy, and the ugly reality of anti-Asian sentiments and violence" (Omi xxii).

Mat Iwasaki, the younger son, returns to his San Joaquin Valley home some years after faking his own suicide to find his father mentally and physically incapacitated and his mother seeking solace in an affair with a Caucasian. His older brother Victor is a Vietnam veteran who desperately attempts to maintain a semblance of normalcy, feverishly rushing to repair the family's ever-disintegrating home. In order to heal itself and be reborn, the family must undergo a powerful and transformative naming and exorcism of the effects of racism that have infected them from the inside out like a putrid, unhealed wound. In the final moments of the play, the walls of the decaying house are "blown away by the fury of the wails," and a clean infrastructure of glowing pipes and wires is revealed within. The last image the audience sees is the Iwasaki family, having shed its destructive past, exposed to the full moon, a window to their future (*Fish Head Soup* 66–67).

Another characteristic of Gotanda's dramatic treatment of racism fearlessly goes to the heart of the Japanese American community itself. While the camp experience demonstrates the victimization of Japanese Americans by forces outside the community, Gotanda also turns the magnifying glass on racism within the community. In *Nisei Fisherman*, Itsuta suffers the prejudice of whites, having been taunted by classmates in medical school, robbed by white taxi dancers, and incarcerated in Rohwer, yet he brings ethnic bias to bear on his own family. Learning that his eldest son is living with a Chinese American woman, he is outraged: "A Chinese? My son's going around with a damn Shin-san! Jesus Christ, Robert, you know better than that! . . . Michiko, I don't want any damned Shin-san in this house!" (*Song* 246–48).

Similarly, in *The Wash*, Nobu's refusal to tolerate racial difference goes beyond his mere muttering about *kurochan* ("blacks") and Mexicans moving into his neighborhood. His younger daughter Judy is married to an African American and is the mother of a baby boy. Nobu refuses to recognize the marriage or see Timothy, who is his only grandchild: "Japanese marry other Japanese, their kids are *Yonsei* [fourth generation Japanese American]—not these damned *ainoko* [biracial people]" (*The Wash*, in *Fish Head Soup and Other Plays* 182). Only Timothy, the personification of the future, has the power to crack Nobu's isolation. In a powerful moment of transracial, transgenerational love and acceptance, Judy offers Timothy to Nobu to hold in his arms for the first time. As Nobu holds the infant to his chest, he softly sings a lullaby to this new face, so familiar and yet so strange to him.

In his popular take on casting discrimination in the entertainment industry, Gotanda presents Japanese Americans who struggle with identity issues and self loathing. *Yankee Dawg You Die* revolves around Bradley Yamashita, a brash young Asian American actor whom Gotanda contrasts with the older and more refined Vincent Chang. Against a background of Hollywood-generated racist images of Asians, Bradley and Vincent wrestle with the Asian American actor's ethos and media representation. Bradley, who all along has considered Vincent to be a sellout to whites, a "Chinese Steppin' Fetchit," eventually undergoes cosmetic surgery and accepts a movie role as a monster who is "half Chinese, half rock." Vincent, on the other hand, finds self-validation in the world of nonprofit Asian American theater, playing a role for no pay about a character not unlike his own father.

Gotanda is unusual for his redefinition of Japanese American gender issues in a culture that does not allow Asian American people to define these in meaningful, dignified ways. In *Yankee Dawg You Die*, Gotanda extends his examination of gender concerns to issues of sexual preference, becoming one of the first Asian American playwrights to create a dignified gay Asian American male in the character of Vincent Chang and contrasting him favorably with his heterosexual antagonist.

Gotanda's honest and dignified treatment of Asian American sexuality, in fact, runs throughout his work and is especially remarkable in his plays that focus on nisei characters: *The Wash, Yohen*, and *Fish Head Soup*. The depiction of sexual behavior in older characters that is not lampooned as ugly at worst or inappropriate at best is rare indeed in American popular culture, which typically reserves portrayals of erotic desire for the young and physically beautiful. Gotanda's sensitivity toward this aspect of nisei life is all the more remarkable because of his own age; at the time of writing *The Wash*, for example, he had not yet turned forty.

Though the stage version of *The Wash* does not feature the lovemaking scene between Masi and Nobu, as does Michael Uno's film adapation, erotic desire between characters is clear without being explicit. The scene where Masi massages Nobu's back demonstrates a true, albeit unspoken, intimacy between a man and a woman who have shared their lives:

NOBU: Just breakfast. Then in the morning when we get up you can go back to your place. (Masi stops, realizing he is asking her to spend the night. Masi does not move. Nobu stares ahead. More silence. Then, tentatively, she moves her hands forward and begins to massage him. A faint smile appears on Nobu's face. Dim to darkness.) (*The Wash*, in *Fish Head Soup and Other Plays* 180–81)

From the action of the play it is clear that Masi also has a sexual relationship with Sadao Nakasato. Though her elder daughter Marsha's inadvertent "morning after" intrusion on Masi and Sadao arouses predictable laughter, the amusement derives from Gotanda's turning the tables generationally, not from demeaning older characters engaged in inappropriate behavior.

Besides Masi, sexuality extends to other nisei women in the play. Nobu's female companion Kiyoko talks to her friend Chiyo openly about the loss of her husband and its impact on her life:

It's not easy for me, Chiyo. (Silence.) When Harry died . . . I started taking the bus to work. I had a car. I could drive. It was easier to drive. I took the bus. For twenty-five years you go to sleep with him, wake up next to him, he shaves while you shower, comes in from the yard all sweaty. Then he's gone. No more Harry in bed. No more smell of aftershave on the towel you're drying off with. No more sweaty Harry coming up and hugging me. . . . I missed the smell of men. Every morning I would get up and walk to the corner to take the bus. It would be full of all these men going to work. And it would be full of all these men coming home from work. I would sit there pretending to read my magazine . . . (Inhales. Discovering the different smells.) Soap . . . just washed skin . . . aftershave lotion . . . sweat. (*The Wash*, in *Fish Head Soup and Other Plays* 189–90)

Gotanda's writing demonstrates his remarkable understanding of nisei women acculturated to render their own needs invisible before those of their children and husbands. It is also worth noting that Gotanda's depiction of nisei men as objects of feminine desire has otherwise been unheard of in American culture, which relegates sexual depictions of Asian American men of any age to sexually neutered eunuchs or hyperhormonal predators.

CRITICAL RECEPTION

In her review of Gotanda's *Fish Head Soup and Other Plays*, which appeared in *Amerasia Journal* (1997), Josephine Lee briefly examines *The Wash, A Song for a Nisei Fisherman, Yankee Dawg You Die*, and *Fish Head Soup*. However, most of Gotanda's works have received scant scholarly attention. Though his works are certainly worthy of such consideration, the majority of critical response to his plays must be sought in newspaper reviews written in response to specific productions rather than to the literary value of his dramaturgy. These are numerous indeed, and, given the subjective nature of such writing, range from positive to lukewarm to—rarely—outrightly negative. Even when reviewers find fault with the length of a performance, they tend to appreciate the risks Gotanda takes in his writing, the level of sophistication his political thinking exhibits, and the number of subjects he tackles within a single script. His artistic collaborations with directors Sharon Ott (*Ballad of Yachiyo, Yankee Dawg You Die, Sisters Matsumoto*) and Oskar Eustis (*Day Standing on Its Head*) have been especially successful.

Of Gotanda's films and theatrical works, none seems to have aroused more scholarly critical interest than *Yankee Dawg You Die*. Presaging as it did the acrimonious "*Miss Saigon* controversy," the play, in its exposing of institutionalized racism in the American entertainment industry, has inspired a broad range of critical response from negative to appreciative.

James Moy's article, "David Henry Hwang's *M. Butterfly* and Philip Kan Gotanda's *Yankee Dawg You Die*: Repositioning Chinese American Marginality on the American Stage" (1990) evolved into the chapter entitled "Flawed Self-Representations: Authenticating Chinese American Marginality" in Moy's full-length study *Marginal Sights: Staging the Chinese in America* (1993). Moy pairs Gotanda's work with David Henry Hwang's *M. Butterfly* (1988), which also seeks to displace Asian stereotypes by, in Hwang's words, "deconstructing" them. Nevertheless, Moy considers debunking stereotypes by appropriating them to be extremely dangerous. He asserts that such a dramaturgical strategy validates rather than defuses the power of the stereotype for Euro-American audiences when the stereotypes are "authenticated by Asian American authorship" ("Flawed" 126). Gotanda's play is acknowledged to be sensitive in addressing the extent to which Asian Americans are forced to go to seek viable role models: in one scene, for example, Bradley describes his adolescent yearning for a role model to be such that he assumes Jewish pop singer Neil Sedaka to be Japanese American. However, Moy objects to the conclusion of the play, in which the two actors "trade places," which Moy interprets as simply reinforcing the marginalization of the Asian American actor as a "given" of the acting business. He considers Vincent Chang to be a "disfigured" actor and objects to Vincent's prophecy that Bradley will become "just like 'Chinese' actor Vincent Chang" ("*Flawed*" 124). According to Moy, *Yankee Dawg You Die*, as well as *M. Butterfly*, represents the "genesis of a new representational strategy, one in which the words offer a clear indictment of the cultural hegemony of the West, while the characters empowered to represent and speak on behalf of the Chinese or Asianness are laughable and grossly disfigured" (125). As such, they are merely "old wine in new bottles"—recycled stereotypes—since they constitute no threat to the Euro-Americans watching the show.

Josephine Lee considers the co-opting of negative stereotypes in order to neutralize their power in *Yankee Dawg You Die* to be more productive. In "The Seduction of the Stereotype," chapter 4 of her study *Performing Asian America* (1997), Lee concedes that it is nearly impossible to rupture entirely the connections between any stereotype and the ugly historical facts of the racism that engendered them. However, she parts ways with Moy's assertion that Gotanda's "self-subverting Asian American tendency" (Moy, "Flawed" 128) has simply resulted in a new stereotype easily digested by whites. Lee does not consider Asian performance stereotypes to be "playful or neutral" (*Performing* 98), but rather argues that Gotanda's approach has neutralized their racist implications by shining the light on the facts of their sociohistorical emergence. Thus, while the audience sees Vincent Chang portray the bowing and scraping Asian male character, Gotanda is able to delineate the reasons for its historical existence in the context of the play. According to Lee, Gotanda also plays off the "stereotype's inability to account fully for the body of the Other" by writing this role specifically for an Asian American actor (30). Finally, Gotanda seeks to enlighten spectators to share their ethnicity with his characters by relying upon the self-conscious acknowledgment that Asian Americans in the audience position themselves in different ways relative to the stereotype (98).

Lee identifies Gotanda's use of stereotypes as unique in their construction for theatrical roles, which actors Vincent and Bradley must play as necessitated by the racism of the industry, rather than as actual persons. Gotanda succeeds because he "insist[s] that the actor has a coherent self distinct from the stereotype he plays," constantly evoking the mask that is taken on and off (103). The fallacies that the actors within the play expose make use of the stereotypes a reasonable dramaturgical technique. In other words, Gotanda successfully "parod[ies] the stereotype in order to reveal a true, authentic self," showing the "Asian body as something that can be seen through the stereotype as real" (119–20).

Robert Vorlicky contributes the most positive, and a distinctly ethnically non-specific, scholarly response to *Yankee Dawg You Die* in his study of all-male-cast plays, *Act Like a Man: Challenging Masculinities in American Drama* (1995). Instead of focusing on Asian American concerns, Vorlicky instead considers Gotanda's representation of male-gendered objectivity and subjectivity, analyzing the gendered and sexual anxieties depicted in the play. This is an area no other critic has considered; given that Gotanda has made a point of creating Vincent as a gay character, it is a worthy analysis and fills in a much-overlooked blank. Vorlicky sees the play's central issue as the "impact of racial and gender codings upon the development of the self-identified, marginalized American character" (195).

Vorlicky applauds Gotanda's portrayals on a number of levels. Rather than seeing the reversal that occurs at the end of the play as a sellout to Euro-American sensibilities, Vorlicky interprets it as enabling the men to comfort each other after grappling "publicly with the ethical issues involved in accepting roles that are racist portrayals of Asian Americans" (193). Noting that male-to-male confrontation in other American plays derives predominantly from alcohol abuse and violence, Vorlicky applauds Gotanda's sensitive handling of the same-sex relationship, which enables both characters to move to the center of their own histories.

For Vorlicky, the play proceeds from a point of racial and ethnic concern to a consideration of "gender codings" among men of color (196). Unlike Moy, who considers Vincent to be "disfigured," Vorlicky sees Vincent as empowered by his ability to embrace his sexuality and thereby redefine himself. The role reversal of Vincent becoming empowered and Bradley becoming artistically and politically compromised is necessary in order to define and highlight the sexual conflict. Vorlicky applauds the depiction of a homosexual and heterosexual male in which the gay man serves as the "elder role model" who is capable of "deeply mov[ing]" Bradley through Bradley's recognition of Vincent's power (198).

The debate surrounding *Yankee Dawg You Die* provides varying fascinating perspectives, to be sure, but the general lack of scholarly attention to Gotanda's body of theatrical work can prove frustrating indeed for the student of his dramaturgy. Quite possibly the notoriety of the *"Miss Saigon* controversy," which publicized the issues Gotanda had previously addressed in *Yankee Dawg*, has led critics to consider the work to be his most popularly accessible. Nevertheless, with thirteen plays and five films produced over twenty years' time, Gotanda is a prolific playwright of artistic stature. Gotanda has his own take on the critical consideration of *Yankee Dawg* to the exclusion of all his other works:

I think the incentive for critics unaware of the Japanese American experience to understand the nature of unspoken, non-verbal, restrained, indirect, repressed, internalized racist psychological and behavioral dynamic—is not there. "Why leave my house, when what I see is what is there and what I don't see, is not there." . . .

Perhaps . . . academicians are to some degree also guilty of a similar bias. That is, looking to the plays that are the easiest to access, like a *Yankee Dawg*, because it requires on the surface no need of shifting of psychological and cultural reference point, due to its mainstream references, and provides a story telling that is more direct and immediate, instead of looking at a piece like *The Wash* or *Sisters Matsumoto*, which demand a stepping out of worlds known and stepping into worlds of the other, worlds where communication is perhaps done in a different modality—through indirection and unspoken argument, in forms of seemingly unaffected delivery, inappropriate restraint with sudden explosions of intensity. A language of behavior which, though not as readily apparent to the unschooled eye, is not any less humanly expressive in depth, pain and complexity. (Letter)

Gotanda's treatments of the nisei generation, Asian American sexuality and gender-related concerns, the positioning of the internment and post–World War II racism in relation to the Japanese American community, and the dynamics that configure Japanese American families all provide worthy opportunities for future critical analyses. Further studies examining Philip Kan Gotanda's plays are warranted indeed and would shed much-needed light on both Gotanda's interpretations of the Asian American experience and his practice of theater.

BIBLIOGRAPHY

Works by Philip Kan Gotanda

Drama

The Dream of Kitamura. West Coast Plays 15/16. Ed. Robert Hurwitt. Los Angeles: California Theatre Council, 1983. 191–223.

The Wash. West Coast Plays 21/22. Ed. Robert Hurwitt. Los Angeles: California Theatre Council, 1987. 119–65. Rpt. in *Between Worlds: Contemporary Asian-American Plays*. Ed. Misha Berson. New York: Theatre Communications Group, 1990. 27–43; *Fish Head Soup and Other Plays*. New York: Dramatists Play Service, 1991; Portsmouth, NH: Heinemann, 1992; Intro Michael Omi. Seattle: U of Washington P, 1995. 131–98.

Fish Head Soup. Fish Head Soup and Other Plays. Intro. Michael Omi. Seattle: U of Washington P, 1995. 1–67. Excerpts. *Monologues for Actors of Color: Men*. Ed. Roberta Uno. New York: Routledge, 2000. 67–68.

A Song for a Nisei Fisherman. Fish Head Soup and Other Plays. Intro. Michael Omi. Seattle: U of Washington P, 1995. 199–258.

Yankee Dawg You Die. New York: Dramatists Play Service, 1991. Rpt. in *New American Plays*. Introd. Peter Filichia. Portsmouth, NH: Heinemann, 1992. 77–124; *Fish Head Soup and Other Plays*. Intro. Michael Omi. Seattle: U of Washington P, 1995. 69–130; *Playwrights of Color*. By Meg Swanson and Robin Murray. Yarmouth, ME: Intercultural P, 1999. 129–57; Excerpts. *Monologues for Actors of Color: Men*. Ed. Roberta Uno. New York: Routledge, 2000. 151–52.

Day Standing on Its Head. New York: Dramatists Play Service, 1994. Rpt. in *Asian American Drama: 9 Plays from the Multiethnic Landscape*. Ed. Brian Nelson.

New York: Applause, 1997. 1–42; *But Still, Like Air, I'll Rise*. Ed. Velina Hasu Houston. Philadelphia: Temple UP, 1997. 49–87.

Ballad of Yachiyo. *American Theatre Magazine* Feb. 1996: 27–42. Rpt. New York: Dramatists Play Service, 1997; Rpt. New York: Theatre Communications Group, 1997. Audiocassette. Los Angeles: LA Theatre Works, 1996.

in the dominion of night. Coauthors: Dan Kuramoto, Danny Yamamoto, and Taiji Miyagawa. Published privately by the author, 1996.

Unpublished Manuscripts

The Avocado Kid, or Zen and the Art of Guacamole. 1979.
Bullet Headed Birds. 1981.
Sisters Matsumoto. 1997.
Yohen. 1997.
Floating Weeds. 2000.

Selected Production History

The Avocado Kid, or Zen and the Art of Guacamole

Production, dir. Mako; chor. Shizuko Hoshi; perf. Keone Young, Clyde Kustasu, Sab Shimono, Julie Inouye, Dom Magwili, and Emily Kuroda; band, Glen Chin (also music dir.), Alan Furutani, Philip Kan Gotanda, Scott Nagatani, and Bob Stover. East West Players, Los Angeles, 1979.

———, dir. Dee K. Carmack; prod. Eric Hayashi; perf. Ken Narasaki, Mitzi Abe, Jay Chee, Brenda Wong Aoki, Art M. Lai, Amy Hill, Dennis Dun, Bernadette Cha, Bill Hammond, Marc Hayashi, Lane Nishikawa, Emilya Cachapero, Randall Akira Nakano, and Kent Hori. Asian American Theater Company, San Francisco, 1981.

A Song for a Nisei Fisherman

Workshop, dir. David Henry Hwang; prod. Asian American Theatre Project; perf. David Pating. Stanford U, Palo Alto, CA, 1980.

Production, dir. David Henry Hwang; prod. Wilbur Obata; perf. Marc Hayashi, James Hirabayashi, Suzie Okazaki, Judith Nihei, Lane Nishikawa, Mitzie Abe, Kent Hori, Ken Narasaki, William Ellis Hammond, Taylor Gilbert, Peggy Ford, and John Nishio. Asian American Theater Company, San Francisco, 1980.

———, dir. Mako and Shizuko Hoshi; perf. Mako, Diane Kobayashi, Ernest Harada, Josie Pepito, Keone Young, Leigh Kim, Nelson Mashita, and Jim Ishida. New Theatre for Now Festival, Mark Taper Forum, Los Angeles, 1982.

———, dir. Raul Aranas; perf. Ron Nakahara, Tom Maatsusaka, Wai Ching Ho, Stan Egi, Mariye Inouye, Alvin Lum, and Ronald Yamamoto. Pan Asian Repertory Theatre, New York, 1983.

———, dir. Shizuko Hoshi and Mako; perf. Ernest Harada, Diane Kobayashi, Jim Ishida, Leigh Kim, Keone Young, and Josie Pepito. East West Players, Los Angeles, 1984.

———, dir. Philip Kan Gotanda; perf. Marc Hayashi, Richard Haratani, James Hirabayashi, Sharon Iwai, Francis Jue, Ron Muriera, Lane Nishikawa, Colette Ogle, Betty Porter, and Diane Emiko Takei. Asian American Theater Company, San Francisco, 1988.

————, dir. Marc Hayashi; perf. Ken Mochizuki, Robert Lee, Masaye Okano Nakagawa, Michael H. Su, David Kobayashi, and Michael A. McClure. Northwest Asian American Theatre, Seattle, 1991.

Bullet Headed Birds

Production, dir. Judith Nihei; prod. Wilbur Obata; perf. Marc Hayashi, Kent Hori, Bernadette Cha, Dennis Dun, June Mesina, Ken Narasaki, and Ron Muriera. Asian American Theater Company, San Francisco, 1981.

————, dir. Tisa Chang; perf. Christopher Odo, Gedde Watanabe, Raul Aranas, Lynette Chun, Jessica Hagedorn, Ching Valdes, Geoff Lee, Susumu Akiyama, Chi On, Tsuyoshi Tampo, and William Ogilvie. Pan Asian Repertory Theatre, New York City, 1981.

The Dream of Kitamura

Production, dir. David Henry Hwang; prod. Pamela A. Wu and Wilbur Obata; perf. Marc Hayashi, Amy Hill, William Ellis Hammond, Diana Tanaka, Victor Wong, Emilya Cachapero, and June Mesina. Asian American Theater Company, San Francisco, 1982.

————, dir. Mako. East West Players, Los Angeles, 1982.

————, dir. Jean Erdman and Philip Kan Gotanda; prod. Open Eye Productions; perf. Chris Odo, Maureen Flemmings, Stanford Egi, Glenn Kubota, Jodi Long, William Akamine Ha'o, and June Angela. Asian American Theater Company, San Francisco, 1987.

————, dir. Jean Erdman and Philip Kan Gotanda; perf. Chris Odo, Maureen Flemmings, Stanford Egi, Glenn Kubota, Jodi Long, William Akamine Ha'o, and June Angela. Japan America Theatre, Los Angeles, 1987.

————, dir. Shelley Souza; perf. Sonya Sweeney, Trent Bright, Buck Stevens, Mikael Salazar, Jane Spigarelli, Kira Spreng, and Andrew Wesson. U of California, Irvine, 1991.

Workshop, perf. Taka Aizawa, Rose A. David, Victor Koga, Michael Lee, Simon Lee, Todd Nakagawa, Naomi Noda, Susie Takeda, Nancy Wong, Peter Wong, and Shan Shan Wu. Asian American Theater Company, San Francisco, 1992.

————, dir. Lane Nishikawa; perf. Victor Koga, Michael Lee, Simon Lee, Susie Takeda, Nancy Wong, and Peter Wong. Asian American Theater Company, San Francisco, 1993.

————. Seattle Repertory Theatre, Seattle, 1996.

The Wash

Workshop as work in-progress. New Theatre for Now Festival, Mark Taper Forum, Los Angeles, 1985.

Production, dir. Richard Seyd; perf. Nobu McCarthy, Woody Moy, Hiroshi Kashiwagi, Judy Momii Hoy, Sharon Omi, Diane Emiko Takei, Amy Hill, and Art Lai. Eureka Theatre, San Francisco, 1987.

————, dir. Sharon Ott; coprod. Mark Taper Forum; perf. Sab Shimono, Nobu McCarthy, George Takei, Shizuko Hoshi, Diane Emiko Takei, Jodi Long, and Carol A. Honda. Manhattan Theatre Club, New York City, 1990.

————. Northwest Asian American Theatre, Seattle, 1990.

————, dir. Sharon Ott; perf. Sab Shimono, George Takei, Nobu McCarthy, Jodi Long,

Diane Takei, Shizuko Hoshi, Carol A. Honda, and James Saito. Mark Taper Forum, Los Angeles, 1991.
————. Studio Theatre, Washington, DC, 1994.
————. Teoriza Company Theatre, Tokyo, 1999.

Yankee Dawg You Die

Workshop. East West Players, Los Angeles, 1986.
————. Bay Area Playwrights Festival, San Francisco, 1987.
Production, dir. Sharon Ott; perf. Kelvin Han Yee and Sab Shimono. Berkeley Repertory Theatre, San Francisco, 1988.
————, perf. Sab Shimono and Stan Egi. Playwrights Horizons, New York City, 1989.
————, dir. Lane Nishikawa; prod. Eric Hayashi; perf. Ken Narasaki and Kelvin Han Yee. Asian American Theater Company, San Francisco, 1990.
————, dir. Eric Hayashi; perf. Lane Nishikawa and David Kim. State U of New York, Geneseo, 1990.
————, prod. Eric Hayashi; perf. Lane Nishikwa and David Kim. New WORLD Theater, U of Massachusetts, Amherst, 1990.
————, perf. Ken Narasaki and David Kim. El Teatro Campesino, San Juan Bautista, CA, 1990.
————, dir. Lane Nishikawa; prod. Eric Hayashi; perf. Ken Narasaki and David Kim. Julia Morgan Theatre, Berkeley, CA, 1991.
————. InterAct Theatre Company, Philadelphia, 1995.

Ballad of Yachiyo

Workshop. South Coast Repertory Theatre, Costa Mesa, CA, 1989.
————. Berkeley Repertory Theatre, San Francisco, 1994.
————. South Coast Repertory Theatre, Costa Mesa, CA, 1995.
————. Berkeley Repertory Theatre, 1995.
Production, dir. Sharon Ott; perf. Lane Nishikawa, Sala Iwamatsu, Greg Watanabe, Sab Shimono, Diane Kobayashi, Emily Kuroda, and Annie Yee. Berkeley Repertory Theatre, San Francisco, 1995.
————. South Coast Repertory Theatre, Costa Mesa, CA, 1996.
————. New York Shakespeare Festival, Public Theater, New York City, 1997.
————. Seattle Repertory Theatre, Seattle, 1997.
————. Gate Theatre, London, 2000.
Staged reading, dir. Randy Barbara Kaplan. GENseng, State U of New York, Geneseo, 2001.

Fish Head Soup

Production, dir. Oskar Eustis; perf. Alberto Isaac, Diane Kobayashi, Stan Egi, and Kelvin Han Yee. Berkeley Repertory Theatre, San Francisco, 1991.
————, prod. Nelson Handle; perf. Sab Shimono, Stan Egi, Nelson Mashita, and Diane Kobayashi. East West Players, Los Angeles, 1993.
————, dir. Philip Kan Gotanda; prod. Eric Hayashi and Pamela A. Wu; perf. Randall Nakano, Diane Emiko Takei, Greg Watanabe, and Kelvin Han Yee. Asian American Theater Company, San Francisco, 1993.
————. Contemporary Theatre, Seattle, 1994.

in the dominion of night

Production. East West Players, Los Angeles, 1993.

————, dir. Diane Emiko Takei; prod. Pamela A. Wu. Asian American Theater Company, San Francisco, 1994.

Day Standing on Its Head

Production, dir. Philip Kan Gotanda and Marya Mazor; presented by Berkeley Repertory Theatre; perf. Bonnie Akimoto, Juliette Chen, David Furumoto, William Ellis Hammond, Michael Chih Ming Hornbuckle, Michael Edo Keane, Ken Narasaki, Diana C. Weng, and Jennie S. Yee. Asian American Theater Company, San Francisco, 1994.

————, dir. Oskar Eustis; perf. Tamlyn Tomita, Stan Egi, Keone Young, Kiya Ann Joyce, Liana Pai, Kati Kuroda, Glenn Kubota, and Zar Acayan. Manhattan Theatre Club, New York City, 1994.

Yohen

Production, dir. Timothy Douglas. Berkeley Repertory Theatre, San Francisco, 1997.

————, dir. Ann Bowen; prod. East West Players and Robey Theatre; perf. Nobu McCarthy and Danny Glover. David Henry Hwang Theatre, Los Angeles, 1999.

Sisters Matsumoto

Staged reading. Yerba Buena Center for the Arts, San Francisco, 1998.

Workshop, dir. Judith Nihei. Asian American Theater Company, San Francisco, 1998.

Production, dir. Sharon Ott; perf. Lisa Li, Stan Egi, Kim Miyori, Nelson Mashita, Sala Iwatmatsu, Ryun Yu, and Will Marchetti. Seattle Repertory Theatre, Seattle, 1999.

————. San Jose Repertory Theatre, San Jose, CA, 1999.

————, perf. Stan Egi, Sala Iwamatsu, Christine T. Johnson, Will Marchetti, Nelson Mashita, Kim Miyori, and Ryun Yu. Huntington Theatre Company, Boston, 2000.

————, dir. Edu. Bernadino; perf. Ruth Yamamoto, Marissa Quintos, and Judy Chen. Asian Stories in America (ASIA) Theatre, Washington, DC, 2000.

Screenplays

The Wash. Dir. Michael Toshiyuki Uno. Perf. Mako, Sab Shimono, and Nobu McCarthy. American Playhouse and Lumiere Productions, 1988.

The Kiss. Dir. Philip Kan Gotanda. Perf. Philip Kan Gotanda and Marc Hayashi. Joe Ozu Films, 1992.

Drinking Tea. Dir. Philip Kan Gotanda. Perf. Nobu McCarthy and Sab Shimono. Joe Ozu Films, 1996.

Life Tastes Good. Dir. Philip Kan Gotanda. Perf. Sab Shimono, Tamlyn Tomita, Greg Watanabe, and Philip Kan Gotanda. Life Tastes Good Productions, 1999.

in the dominion of night. Dir. Philip Kan Gotanda. Perf. Philip Kan Gotanda, Dan Kuramoto, Danny Yamamoto, and Taiji Miyagawa. Joe Ozu Films, unreleased.

Studies of Philip Kan Gotanda

Ahlgren, Calvin. "Autobiographical Drama: Gotanda Explodes out of Writer's Block; Playwright Restirs *Soup*, Others." *San Francisco Chronicle* 7 March 1993: 36.

Berson, Misha. "Coming Home: New Play Explores Life for Japanese Americans after Internment." *Seattle Times* 7 Jan. 1999: E1.

————. "Fighting the Religion of the Present: Western Motifs in the First Wave of Asian American Plays." *Reading the West: New Essays on the Literature of the Amerian West.* Ed. Michael Kowalewski. New York: Cambridge UP, 1996. 251–72.

————. "Gotanda's Plays Explore Lives of Asian-Americans." *American Theatre* Sept. 1988: 54–55.

————. "Role Model on a Role: Philip Kan Gotanda's Work Grabs Mainstream Attention and Inspires Younger Artists." *Seattle Times* 10 Oct. 1996: D1.

————. "*Sisters* Recounts Sad Time in U.S. History." Rev. of *Sisters Matsumoto. Seattle Times* 12 Jan. 1999: E1.

Brantley, Ben. "A Midlife Crisis as a Hallucinogenic Mystery Story." Rev. of *Day Standing on Its Head. New York Times* 26 Jan. 1994: C13.

Carroll, Jerry. "Family Secret Revealed on Stage." Rev. of *Ballad of Yachiyo. San Francisco Chronicle* 5 Nov. 1995: 26.

Drake, Sylvie. "*Fish Head* Flounders in Excess." Rev. of *Fish Head Soup. Los Angeles Times* 16 Jan. 1993: F1.

Ellis, Kirk. "*Fisherman* Anchors at East/West." Rev. of *A Song for a Nisei Fisherman. Los Angeles Times* 2 Nov. 1984, sec. 4: 7.

Eustis, Oskar. "Writing for a New America." *American Theatre* Oct. 1994: 30–31, 111–12.

Feingold, Michael. "Rife in the Theater." Rev. of *Yankee Dawg You Die. Village Voice* 34.21 (1989): 98.

Foley, F. Kathleen. "An Earthen Vessel Cracks under Fire." Rev. of *Yohen. Los Angeles Times* 15 Jan. 1999: F1.

————. "A Non-Linear Night Fuses Poetry, Jazz." Rev. of *in the dominion of night. Los Angeles Times* 26 Jan. 1995: F6.

Gotanda, Philip Kan. Letter to the author. 6 Aug. 2000.

Gussow, Mel. "Theatre: *Fisherman*." Rev. of *A Song for a Nisei Fisherman. New York Times* 11 Dec. 1983, sec. 1: 109.

————. "Wife Is Dutiful Though Separated." Rev. of *The Wash. New York Times* 8 Nov. 1990: C28.

Harth, Erica. "Literature of Shame: Recent Fiction and Drama on the Japanese American Internment." *Brandeis Review* 20.4 (2000): 28–31.

Hartigan, Patti. "Digging Out the Secrets." Rev. of *Sisters Matsumoto. Boston Globe* 2 Jan. 2000: L1.

Harvey, Dennis. "*Life Tastes Good*." Rev. of *Life Tastes Good. Variety* 8–14 Mar. 1999: 62.

Hurwitt, Robert. "Song of a Sansei Playwright: An Interview with Philip Kan Gotanda and Richard Seyd." *West Coast Plays 21/22.* Ed. Robert Hurwitt. Los Angeles: California Theatre Council, 1987. 166–74.

Hwang, David Henry. "Philip Kan Gotanda." *Bomb* Winter 1998: 20–26.

Kirkpatrick, Melanie. "Theatre: Asians in America." Rev. of *The Wash. Wall Street Journal* 9 Nov. 1990: 8.

Koehler, Robert. "*Dream of Kitamura*—An Eye for the Visual." Rev. of *Dream of Kitamura. Los Angeles Times* 8 June 1987, sec. 6: 7.

Kurahashi, Yuko. "*The Avocado Kid.*" *Asian American Culture on stage: The History of the East West Players.* By Yuko Kurahashi. New York: Garland, 1999. 114–17.

———. "Philip Kan Gotanda's Personal Saga, *A Song for a Nisei Fisherman.*" *Asian American Culture on stage: The History of the East West Players.* By Yuko Kurahashi. New York: Garland, 1999. 162–66.

Lee, Josephine. "*Fish Head Soup and Other Plays.*" Rev. of *Fish Head Soup and Other Plays.* Intro. Michael Omi. *Amerasia Journal* 23.1 (1997): 181–83.

———. *Performing Asian America: Race and Ethnicity on the Contemporary Stage.* Philadelphia: Temple UP, 1997.

Mahoney, John C. "*Avocado Kid* at East/West." Rev. of *The Avocado Kid. Los Angeles Times* 2 Feb. 1979: V14.

Metzger, Sean. "*Yohen.*" Rev. of *Yohen. Theatre Journal* 51.4 (Dec. 1999): 468–70.

Moy, James. "Asian American Visibility: Touring Fierce Racial Geographies." *Staging Difference: Cultural Pluralism in American Theatre and Drama.* Ed. Marc Maufort. New York: Peter Lang, 1995. 191–200.

———. "David Henry Hwang's *M. Butterfly* and Philip Kan Gotanda's *Yankee Dawg You Die*: Repositioning Chinese American Marginality on the American Stage." *Theatre Journal* 42 (March 1990): 48–56.

———. "Flawed Self-Representations: Authenticating Chinese American Marginality." *Marginal Sights: Staging the Chinese in America.* Iowa City: U of Iowa P, 1993. 115–29.

Omi, Michael. "Introduction." *Fish Head Soup and Other Plays.* By Philip Kan Gotanda. Seattle: U of Washington P, 1995. xi–xxvi.

Rich, Frank. "Two Asians and Hollywood's Bias." Rev. of *Yankee Dawg You Die. New York Times* 15 May 1989: C13.

Robinson, Marc. "Rights and Passage." *American Theatre* Sept. 1992: 18.

Rothstein, Mervyn. "A Playwright's Path to His Play." *New York Times* 7 June 1989: C17.

Schiffman, Jean. "Three's Company." Development of *Sisters Matsumoto. American Theatre* Feb. 1999: 65–67.

Shirley, Don. "The Life Cycles of Gotanda's *Wash.*" Rev. of *The Wash. Los Angeles Times* 19 Jan. 1991: F1.

Siegel, Ed. "Exiled (in)side America: *Sisters Matsumoto* Explores a Family Wounded by Internment in World War II for Japanese Ethnicity." Rev. of *Sisters Matsumoto. Boston Globe* 7 Jan. 2000: C1.

Siegel, Nina. "*Ballad of Yachiyo.*" Interview with Philip Kan, Gotanda. *American Theatre* Feb. 1996: 25–26.

Stanley, John. "Gotanda Ladles Out Another Family Drama." Rev. of *Fish Head Soup. San Francisco Chronicle* 3 Mar. 1991: DAT38.

Sullivan, Dan. "*Nisei Fisherman* by New Theatre for Now." *Los Angeles Times* 16 Apr. 1982, sec. 4: 1.

———. "Stereotypes Skewered in *Yankee Dawg.*" Rev. of *Yankee Dawg You Die. Los Angeles Times* 6 June 1988, sec. 6: 1.

———. "*Wash* and *Legends*: A Box Score of Contrasts." Rev. of *The Wash. Los Angeles Times* 27 Nov. 1985, sec. 6: 1.

Swanson, Meg, and Robin Murray. "Yankee Dawg You Die." *Playwrights of Color.* By Meg Swanson and Robin Murray. Yarmouth, ME: Intercultural P, 1999. 107–28.

Tajima, Renee. "Postmarital Sex." Rev. of *The Wash. Village Voice* 33.34 (1988): 61.

Vorlicky, Robert. "Realizing Freedom: Risk, Responsibility, and Individualization." *Act like a Man: Challenging Masculinities in American Drama.* By Robert Vorlicky. Ann Arbor: U of Michigan P, 1995. 190–200.

Weinraub, Judith. "Philip Kan Gotanda: His Japanese American Spin on *The Wash.*" Rev. of *The Wash. Washington Post* 3 Apr. 1994: G2.

Winn, Steven. "Gotanda Composes a *Ballad* on Sexual Awakening." Rev. of *Ballad of Yachiyo. San Francisco Chronicle* 10 Nov. 1995: C5.

———. "Gotanda's *Day* in Midlife: Surreal Confessions at the Asian American Theatre." Rev. of *Day Standing on Its Head. San Francisco Chronicle* 31 Mar. 1994: F1.

———. "*Sisters* Shows Toll of Internment." Rev. of *Sisters Matsumoto. San Francisco Chronicle* 3 May 1999: D1.

———. "*Yankee Dawg* Still Has Bite: A Timely Revival of Play on Stereotyping Asian Americans." Rev. of *Yankee Dawg You Die. San Francisco Chronicle* 12 Sept. 1990: E2.

Jessica Tarahata Hagedorn

(1949–)

Victor Bascara and Miles Xian Liu

BIOGRAPHY

Jessica Tarahata Hagedorn was born on May 22, 1949, in Manila, the Philippines, which she left with her mother and brothers in 1963. The family emigrated to San Diego and soon moved to San Francisco. Not only did she spend her teenage years and early adulthood there, she also received her education in theater arts at the American Conservatory Theater. She moved to New York in 1979. Hagedorn has been a significant voice in the world of Asian American literature for more than a quarter of a century. Her work ranges from poetry, film, and music to novels, essays, and drama. Since the late 1980s, she has emerged as one of the main faces of Asian American literature through such work as her 1990 National Book Award–nominated novel *Dogeaters* (1990) and her edited anthology *Charlie Chan Is Dead: An Anthology of Contemporary Asian American Fiction* (1993).

As the popularity and critical acclaim of her novel *Dogeaters* inaugurated her rise in national and international literary prominence, her career can be broken up into two parts: pre-*Dogeaters* and post-*Dogeaters*. Prior to *Dogeaters*, she was primarily known for her poetry and her plays, particularly their eclecticism. Her poems were championed by Kenneth Rexroth in his anthology *Four Young Women* (1973). Among those produced works are *Where the Mississippi Meets the Amazon* (with Thulani Davis and Ntozake Shange, 1977) and *Mango Tango* (1978). Her performance pieces incorporated the pleasures of melodrama into the lucidity of performance, as exemplified in *Chiquita Banana* (1972), *Tenement Lover* (1981), and *The Art of War/Nine Situations* (1984). Her work with the Gangster Choir, an on-again, off-again performance group of which she is a founding member, did not go unnoticed, either. Yet as a playwright, she remained less well known throughout this pre-*Dogeaters* period.

A by-product of her *Dogeaters* success was her editorship of the first-ever collection of Asian American fiction, *Charlie Chan Is Dead: An Anthology of Contemporary Asian American Fiction*. From the 1970s through the 1990s, in what may come to be seen as a golden age of ethnic American literature anthologies, Hagedorn herself fast became a staple of the Asian American canon through such poems as "The Song of Bullets" and "Motown/Smokey Robinson." The collection of her early poems, *Danger and Beauty* (1993), displays both a facility with modernist poetry's technique and a deep appreciation for mass- and popular-culture forms. Her prose nonfiction articulates a deep respect for the tradition of writers of which she is a part as well as a wariness of the pitfalls of being flavor of the month at a time of multiculturalism.

Hagedorn's relocation to New York City and her subsequent association with New York's Public Theater allowed her to continue to develop and display her dramatic talents. The two major post-*Dogeaters* theatrical pieces were *Airport Music* and the stage-adapted *Dogeaters*. Produced in 1993, *Airport Music* was a collaborative two-person performance piece with fellow Filipino-American playwright Han Ong. The piece premiered at the New York Shakespeare Festival and was also staged at the Berkeley Repertory Theater that same year. While these pieces helped cement her status as a figure in New York's experimental theater world, Hagedorn has long been a committed and tireless voice of the emergence of Asian American literature.

MAJOR WORKS AND THEMES

Throughout the mainstream success with her novel, Hagedorn has continued to explore the formal and topical horizons of Asian America onstage. "Despite the protean quality of her achievement, a spirit of ethnic consciousness and an undercurrent of social protest serve to unite much of her work," as George Uba has observed (373). Among the themes she frequently explores are "colonialism, violence, and psychological debilitation" (Uba 373). If Hagedorn's earlier theater pieces come across as playful flashes of brilliance, delightful pastiches irreverently refracting contexts and references, her more recent theatrical work successfully adapts novelistic elements such as the broad canvas and narrative arch to the appeal of immediacy onstage.

In *Airport Music*, Hagedorn used the liminal space of an airport terminal to ironically capture the simultaneity of the rootless for subjects in the new global village. On a spare stage with a row of chairs to intimate the dull monotony and uniformity of a terminal waiting area, Ong and Hagedorn strode about taking turns delivering acerbic monologues about always seeming to be in between locations and never quite situated. In this piece, as in much of her earlier work, Hagedorn manages to deploy the trappings of postmodernism, particularly the aesthetics of playful referentiality, narrative fragmentation, and epistemological instability, without being pretentious and opaque. The formal inventiveness is always in the service of making visible the unique condition of postcolonialism and neocolonialism. The well-received "word concert" effectively uses slides, scrims, and sound effects to convey the rootlessness felt by the new migrants of globalization who no longer fit the model of the old immigrants.

While *Airport Music* was a spare word concert, *Dogeaters* (1998) is an epic involving many and multiple virtuosic performances and palimpsests of dramatic action. This dramatic adaptation of her novel *Dogeaters* is in fact her most brilliant theater work to date. While her novel had made ingenious use of the-atrical elements, the play managed to transform the epic sweep made possible by the novel form into a succession of dioramas that render the historical layers of colonialism, imperialism, postcolonialism, and neocolonialism. The stage al-lows for the spatial layering, and hence the characters' development, that the novel could only render by jump-cutting.

For example, Rio Gonzaga (the quasi-autobiographical writer figure) would be in the foreground in the 1950s standing on her bed reciting an 1899 speech by William McKinley while sex workers in the 1980s would be putting on a show in the rear portion of the stage as other characters in an intermediate position sat watching the sex show. The play holds such an assemblage together by having the sex performers alter their coital positions in sychronization with the "four options" for the Philippines that Rio reads. The missionary intentions of the past are aligned with the missionary and other positions that have man-ifested themselves in the present. Further still, as Rio (played by Sandra Oh) reads the speech, she begins to weep uncontrollably until she can no longer continue. Such dramatic palimpsests as this pervade the play from its opening with miscellaneous voices on catwalks speaking humorous observations about the colonization of the Philippines to the final reassemblage.

Like *Airport Music, Dogeaters* could be called a word concert, but *Airport Music* is a duet in recital, and *Dogeaters* is grand opera. Every part of the stage is used in the latter, from the catwalks and scaffolds to center stage, frequently simultaneously. The result is not a confusing mess, at least no more confusing and messy than life in Manila. These two works are indicative of Hagedorn's style of inventive staging and hip, popular-culture referentiality. It is through this kind of simultaneity of the multiple stages that Hagedorn makes evident the fragmentary consciousness of neocolonialism in the United States and the Phil-ippines.

CRITICAL RECEPTION

Provocative in theme and staging, Hagedorn's work in general, and her theater pieces in particular, defy simple categorization of genre and style. They are often "marked by leaps across artistic genres by collage-like effects, and by other maneuvers that run the risk of confusing or alienating her audiences" (Uba 374). Not surprisingly, they tend to receive mixed reviews.

Chiquita Banana (1972), a one-act television play, approached the exploitation of women of color by featuring takeoffs on many Hollywood figures. "The work effectively evokes anger and militance, while experimenting with fragments of song, poetry, and dance" (Uba 374).

The Art of War/Nine Situations (1984) reminded Jennifer Dunning of the *New York Times* of the metaphor of warfare in everyday work and life when she saw the performance. Though the subject is Sun Tzu's treatment of proper strategies for war games in the third century B.C., the piece has "brief moments of recognizably heedless humanity" through soldiers, spies, business men, women, and children who "move through the nine scenes with equally chill efficiency" (C20). The relevancy of Sun Tzu's winning strategies to the life of modern America is "hard to look away from" yet "almost impossible to watch" (C20). But *Airport Music* was too much for the *Nation*'s critic Hal Gelb. Reviewing the Berkeley Repertory production, Gelb maintained that the piece's perspective is "more than critical, it's sour. And whiny" (325).

Critics generally lauded *Dogeaters* for its brilliant fusion of an impressive array of discourses to render and revisit colonial and postcolonial Manila. Compared to much of the increasingly formulaic treatments of multiculturalism in the United States, *Dogeaters* onstage was a revelation. It was "a bridge to the Philippines," as Jan Breslauer saw it, because it helped take Americans out of their perception of that country as "an indistinct collection of tropical islands: exotic, agricultural and beset with frequent political upheaval" (79).

By playfully engaging with the theatricality of everyday life, Hagedorn's work has shown the capabilities that Asian American cultural production makes possible. Rather than exhibiting Asian Americans as simply another flavor of the month in American literature, she uses the sensibilities emerging from the historical and cultural conditions that created "Asian Americans" to enlighten through entertainment and entertain through enlightenment.

BIBLIOGRAPHY

Works by Jessica Tarahata Hagedorn

Drama

Chiquita Banana. Teleplay. *Third World Women*. Ed. Toni Cade Bambara. San Francisco: Third World Communications, 1972.

Mango Tango. *Y'Bird Magazine* 1.1 (1977): 58–74.

Teenytown. *Out from Under: Texts by Women Performance Artists*. Ed. Lenora Champagne. New York: Theatre Communications Group, 1990. 89–117.

Tenement Lover: no palm trees/in new york city. Television play. *Between Worlds: Contemporary Asian American Plays*. Ed. Misha Berson. New York: Theatre Communications Group, 1990. 75–90.

Unpublished Manuscripts

Where the Mississippi Meets the Amazon. With Thulani Davis and Ntozake Shange. 1977.
Petfood. 1981.
Tenement Lover: no palm trees/in new york city. 1981.
Crayon Bondage. 1982
Peachfish. 1983.
The Art of War/Nine Situations. With Blondell Cummings. 1984.
Ruined: A Beach Opera. 1985.
Holy Food. Radio play. 1988.
A Nun's Story. Teleplay, with Blondell Cummings. 1988.
Airport Music. With Han Ong. 1993.
Dogeaters (adapted for the stage from the novel). 1998.

Selected Production History

Where the Mississippi Meets the Amazon

Production. Public Theater/New York Shakespeare Festival, New York City, 1977.

Mango Tango

Production. Public Theater/New York Shakespeare Festival, New York City, 1978.

Tenement Lover: no trees/in new york city

Production. The Kitchen, New York City, 1981.

Crayon Bondage

Performance. Real Art Ways, Hartford, CT, 1982.

Peachfish

Production. Basement Workshop, New York City, 1983.

The Art of War/Nine Situations

Production, perf. Blondell Cummings, Laurie Carlos, Jessica Hagedorn, Evangeline Johns, Mindy Levine, Trinket Monsod, John Rusk, and Leslie Yancey. Dance Theater Workshop, New York City, 1984.

Ruined: A Beach Opera

Production. Art on the Beach, New York City, 1985.

Holy Food

Production. *Radio Stage* series. WNYC-FM. Aired nationally, 1988.
———. Cornell U, Center for the Performing Arts, Ithaca, NY, 1989.

A Nun's Story

Performance. "Alive from Off Center." PBS-Thirteen/WNET. New York City, 1988.

Teenytown

Production. Franklin Furnace, New York City, 1988.
———. Danspace Project, New York City, 1988.
———. L.A.C.E., Los Angeles, 1990.
———. Intersection, San Francisco, 1990.

Airport Music

Production, perf. Jessica Tarahata Hagedorn and Han Ong. Los Angeles Festival, Los
    Angeles, 1983.
————, dir. Sharon Ott; perf. Jessica Tarahata Hagedorn and Han Ong. Joseph Papp
    Public Theater, New York City, 1994.
————, perf. Jessica Tarahata Hagedorn and Han Ong. Berkeley Repertory Theatre,
    Berkeley, CA, 1994.

Dogeaters

Production, dir. Michael Greif; perf. Sandra Oh, Alec Mapa, Tess Lina, and Seth Gilliam.
    La Jolla Playhouse, U of California, San Diego, 1998.
————. Public Theater/New York Shakespeare Festival, New York City, 2001.

Anthology

Charlie Chan Is Dead: An Anthology of Contemporary Asian American Fiction. Ed.
    Jessica Hagedorn and pref. Elaine Kim. New York: Penguin, 1993.

Essays

"On Theater and Performance." *MELUS* 16.3 (Fall 1989): 13–15.
"Jessica Hagedorn." *Between Worlds: Contemporary Asian-American Plays.* Ed. Misha
    Berson. New York: Theatre Communications Group, 1990. 76–79.
"Imelda Sings Again." Editorial. *New York Times* 13 Jan. 1992, late ed.: A15.
"Charlie Chan Is Dead." Letter. *New York Times* 23 Jan. 1994, late ed., sec. 7: 27.

Interview

"Fuel." Interview. *The NuyorAsian Anthology: Asian American Writings about New York
    City.* Ed. Bino A. Realuyo and Rahna R. Rizzuto. New York: Asian American
    Writers Workshop, 1999. 350–58.

Novels

Dogeaters. New York: Pantheon, 1990.
Two Stories. Minneapolis: Coffee House P, 1992.
The Gangster of Love. Boston: Houghton Mifflin, 1996.

Poetry

"Jessica Tarahata Hagedorn." *Four Young Women: Poems by Jessica Tarhata Hagedorn,
    Alice Karle, Barbara Szerlip, and Carol Tinker.* Ed. and intro. Kenneth Rexroth.
    New York: McGraw-Hill, 1973. 1–43.
Dangerous Music. Collection of poems and fiction. San Francisco: Momo's P, 1975.
"Natural Death," "Poem for the Art Ensemble of Chicago," and "Solea." *Time to Greez!
    Incantations from the Third World.* Ed. Janice Mirikitani, Luis Syquia, Jr., Buriel
    Clay II, Janet C. Hale, Alejandro Murguia, and Roberto Vargas. San Francisco:
    Glide, 1975. 28–32.
The Woman Who Thought She Was More Than a Samba. San Francisco: Momo's P,
    1978. Rpt. in *Breaking Silence, an Anthology of Contemporary Asian American
    Poets.* Ed. Joseph Bruchac. New York: Greenfield Review P, 1983. 46–48.
"Canto de Nada." *American Born and Foreign: An Anthology of Asian American Poetry.*

Ed. Fay Chiang, Helen W. Huie, Jason Hwang, Richard Oyama, and Susan L. Yung. New York: Sunbury Press Books, 1979. 105–107. Rpt. in *Stealing the Language: The Emergence of Women's Poetry in America.* By Alicia Suskin Ostriker. Boston: Beacon P, 1986. 203–204.

Pet Food and Tropical Apparitions. Collection of poem and fiction. San Francisco: Momo's P, 1981.

"Ming the Merciless." *Breaking Silence, an Anthology of Contemporary Asian American Poets.* Ed. Joseph Bruchac. New York: Greenfield Review P, 1983. 49.

"Motown/Smokey Robinson." *Breaking Silence, an Anthology of Contemporary Asian American Poets.* Ed. Joseph Bruchac. New York: Greenfield Review P, 1983. 45. Rpt. in *The Woman I Am: The Literature and Culture of Contemporary Women of Color.* Ed. D. Soyini Madison. New York: St. Martin's P, 1994. 74–75.

"Song for My Father." *Breaking Silence, an Anthology of Contemporary Asian American Poets.* Ed. Joseph Bruchac. New York: Greenfield Review P, 1983. 50–52. Rpt. in *Early Ripening: American Women's Poetry Now.* Ed. and intro. Marge Piercy. London: Pandora P, 1987. 91–93.

"Loft Living." *Portable Lower East Side* 4.1 (1987): 3–4.

"The Song of Bullets." *Early Ripening: American Women's Poetry Now.* Ed. and intro. Marge Piercy. London: Pandora P, 1987. 94–95.

Danger and Beauty. New York: Penguin, 1993.

"Smokey's Getting Old" and "Yolanda Meets the Wild Boys." *The Open Boat: Poems from Asian America.* Ed. Garrett Hongo. New York: Anchor Books, 1993. 104–10.

Visions of a Daughter, Foretold: Four Poems (1980–1993). With Paloma Hagedorn Woo. Milwaukee: Woodland Pattern Book Center, 1994.

Screenplays

Fresh Kill. Dir. and prod. Shu Lea Cheang. Independent Television Service, 1994.

Short Stories

"Film Noir." *Charlie Chan Is Dead: An Anthology of Contemporary Asian American Fiction.* Ed. Jessica Hagedorn and pref. Elaine Kim. New York: Penguin, 1993. 122–31.

Nonfiction

Burning Heart: A Portrait of the Philippines. Photography by Marissa Roth. New York: Rizzoli International, 1999.

Studies of Jessica Tarahata Hagedorn

Birkerts, Sven. "In Our House There Were No Chinese Things." Rev. of *Charlie Chan Is Dead: An Anthology of Contemporary Asian American Fiction. New York Times Book Review* 19 Dec. 1993: 17.

Breslauer, Jan. "A Bridge to the Philippines." Rev. of *Dogeaters* (play). *Los Angeles Times* 13 Sept. 1998, Calendar: 79.

Bush, Catherine. "A Culture Caught at Breakpoint." *Globe and Mail* (Toronto) 21 July 1990: C15.

Champagne, Lenora. "Laurie Carlos, Jessica Hagedorn, Robbie McCauley." *Out from Under: Texts by Women Performance Artists*. Ed. Lenora Champagne. New York: Theatre Communications Group, 1990. 91–94.

Coates, Joseph. "Manila: The Price of Imperialism." Rev. of *Dogeaters*. *Chicago Tribune* 13 Apr. 1990, sec. 5: 3.

Corrigan, Maureen. "Yo-Yo in a Rock Band." Rev. of *The Gangster of Love*. *Nation* 263.13 (28 Oct. 1996): 64–66.

D'Alpuget, Blanche. "Philippine Dream Feast." Rev. of *Dogeaters*. *New York Times* 25 Mar. 1990, late ed., sec. 7: 1.

De Manuel, T.L. "Jessica Hagedorn." *Encyclopedia of Post-colonial Literatures in English*. Ed. Eugene Benson and L.W. Conolly. London: Routledge, 1994. 620.

Duncan, Erika. "Jessica Hagedorn: Creating a Powerful Collage." *Ms. Magazine* 7.2 (Sept.–Oct. 1996): 81.

Dunning, Jennifer. "Dance: *The Art of War* by Cummings and Hagedorn." Rev. of *The Art of War*. *New York Times* 15 Nov. 1984, final ed.: C20.

Eder, Richard. Rev. of *Mango Tango*. *New York Times* 30 May 1978, sec. 3: 6.

Farley, Christopher John. "Have Guitar, Will Travel—An Immigrant's Tale with a Rock and Role Twist." Rev. of *The Gangster of Love*. *Time* 148.13 (16 Sept. 1996): 80–81.

Gelb, Hal. Rev. of *Airport Music*. *Nation* 259.9 (26 Sept. 1994): 321–25.

Gussow, Mel. "3 'Satin Sisters' Spin a Poetry of Nostalgia at Stage Cabaret." Rev. of *Where the Mississippi Meets the Amazon*. *New York Times* 20 Dec. 1977: 44.

Hughes, Kathryn. "Sweet-Sour." Rev. of *Dogeaters* by J. Hagedorn and *The Kitchen God's Wife* by A. Tan. *New Statesman and Society* 12 July 1991: 37–38.

"Interview with Jessica Hagedorn." *Dispatch* 6.1 (Fall 1987): 14–16.

James, Caryn. "Manila Pop." *New York Times Book Review* 14 Mar. 1993: 12.

Lehmann-Haupt, Christopher. "Life (and It's Cheap) in a Colonized Culture." Rev. of *Dogeaters*. *New York Times* 22 Mar. 1990, late ed.: C21.

Loo, Jeffrey. "Navigating Dynamics of Filipino and American Culture." Rev. of *The Gangster of Love*. *Philadelphia Inquirer* 13 Oct. 1996: Q5.

Mackey, Mary. "The Restless Heart of a Poet." Rev. of *Danger and Beauty*. *San Francisco Chronicle* 28 Feb. 1993, Sunday ed.: 3.

Partnow, Elaine T., and Lesley Anne Hyatt. *The Female Dramatist: Profiles of Women Playwrights from the Middle Ages to the Contemporary Times*. New York: Facts on File, 1998. 97–98.

Pearlman, Mickey, ed. "Jessica Hagedorn." *Listen to Their Voices: Twenty Interviews with Women Who Write*. New York: Norton, 1993. 134–42.

Prose, Francine. "Foxy Ladies." Rev. of *The Gangster of Love*. *New York Times* 15 Sept. 1996, late ed., sec. 7: 14.

Radner, Rebecca. "Dark, Gossipy Novel about the Marcos Era." Rev. of *Dogeaters*. *San Francisco Chronicle* 29 Apr. 1990, Sunday ed.: 3.

San Juan, E., Jr. "Mapping the Boundaries: The Filipino Writer in the U.S.A." *Journal of Ethnic Studies* 19.1 (Spring 1991): 117–32.

Sengupta, Somini. "At Lunch with Jessica Hagedorn—Cultivating the Art of the Melange." *New York Times* 4 Dec. 1996, late ed.: C1.

Shih, David. Rev. of *Charlie Chan Is Dead*. *Amerasia Journal* 21.3 (Winter 1995): 210–13.

Steinberg, Sybil S. Rev. of *The Gangster of Love*. *Publishers Weekly* 10 June 1996: 86.

Tobias, Tobi. Rev. of *The Art of War*. *New York* 17 (19 Nov. 1984): 76.

Uba, George. "Jessica Tarahata Hagedorn." *Reference Guide to American Literature*. 3rd ed. Ed. Jim Kamp and introd. Warren French, Lewis Leary, Amy Ling, Marco Portales, and A. LaVonne Brown Ruoff. Detroit: St. James P, 1994. 373–75.

Amy Hill
(1953—   )

Yuko Kurahashi

BIOGRAPHY

Amy Hill was born on May 9, 1953, in Deadwood, South Dakota, to a Japanese mother and a Finnish American father. From her early childhood, Hill loved acting and occasionally performed as all of the characters she encountered on television before the audience of her family and neighbors. From infancy, she was fascinated by her own ability to change voices, speech patterns, and mannerisms. In 1959, the family moved to Seattle, where she continued to pursue her "acting and dancing career" on her family's front porch. In 1971, she went to Japan to find the other "half" of her ethnic roots. There she became a bohemian. Her experiences as an international student at Sophia University and later as an entertainment reporter and television actor in Tokyo formed the basis of her first solo performance piece, *Tokyo Bound*.

Upon returning to Seattle in 1975, Hill received her B.A. in Japanese and art (fine art) at the University of Washington. In her Japanese-language class at the University of Washington, she met Garrett Kaoru Hongo, one of the founders of the Asian Exclusion Act, now known as the Northwest Asian American Theatre. This led her to accept her first stage-managing job for Frank Chin's *Year of the Dragon*. She also performed in Wakako Yamauchi's *And the Soul Shall Dance* and Momoko Iko's *Gold Watch*. In 1976, Hill again visited Japan, where she married and worked as a private English tutor and a reporter of weather and entertainment for a Japanese cable television station.

During her second stay in Japan, Hill had an opportunity to travel alone throughout Asia, the Middle East, and Europe. Once again she incorporated her world-tour experiences into a solo performance piece, called *Deadwood to Hollywood*. Some of these experiences, for instance, receiving "second-degree burns" from eating with her fingers in Sri Lanka, honestly examine her naïveté and shock in encountering various cultures (*Deadwood*).

Upon returning to the United States in 1978, Hill took professional theater training at the American Conservatory Theatre in San Francisco. She also started acting at the Asian American Theater Company. In 1987, Hill moved to Los Angeles to broaden the horizons of her acting career. In San Francisco and Los Angeles, Hill played a variety of roles in such plays as *Dream of a Common Language* by Heather McDonald at Berkeley Repertory Theater, *Tea* by Velina Hasa Houston at the Asian American Theater Company, *Lettice & Lovage* by Peter Shaffer, *Hiro* by Denise Uyehara, and *Golden Child* by David Henry Hwang at the East West Players, and *Twelfth Night* by William Shakespeare at Lincoln Center. She also appeared in a number of films and television programs, including *Dim Sum, Singles, Rising Sun, Seinfeld, All American Girl* (regular), *Maybe This Time*, and *The Naked Truth*. Hill was a staff writer for *The Puzzle Place* on PBS and was nominated for a regional Emmy as writer/host of *Get Real*, a half-hour talk show that was geared toward Pacific Islander American teenagers.

MAJOR WORKS AND THEMES

Tokyo Bound (1991), Hill's critically acclaimed solo piece, premiered at the East West Players under the direction of Anne Etue in 1991. This play depicts Hill's six-year life experience in Tokyo from the age of eighteen through twenty-three. It examines her faux pas at encountering cultural differences, her desperate effort to become a "genuine" Japanese, the prejudice she faced, and her evolving friendship with her Japanese fiancé's mother, who is biracial Japanese/Indian. Hill presents these serious issues with her unique sense of humor and fast-paced rhythmical language through fifteen different characters, generating a vivid picture of a young American girl struggling to adjust to Japanese cultural mores.

Beside Myself (1992) is Hill's provocative assessment of what it means to grow up as a mixed-race child in the United States. It was first staged at the Mark Taper Forum in Los Angeles. In this piece, Hill eloquently narrates her journey in search of her identity. Beginning with her innocent, happy girlhood in a small town in South Dakota, Hill parallels her physical relocation to Seattle with her quest of "herself." Hill imagines that she is like her mother—a petite, beautiful Japanese woman. At the same time, she also wishes to be just like a "normal" American girl. With the "encouragement" of her family and friends, she desperately tries to become "someone" who is not herself. The piece is particularly powerful because she relentlessly questions hypocrisy, vanity, the mainstream notions about beauty in the United States, and her struggle to claim and affirm her unique identity in a humorous and energized narrative.

In *Reunion* (1995), which premiered at the Actors Theatre of Louisville in 1995, Hill depicts her mother, Ayako Yoneoka Hill, who grew up in pre–World War II Japan as a motherless child and later crossed the ocean as a "war bride."

Hill wraps her mother's memories around gentle and sometimes-outrageous yet profound and insightful jokes that reveal her mother's struggles and ability to survive by seeing circumstances with hope and humor. This piece exposes the unexamined cultural clashes she, like many other multicultural people, has in her own family and American society. In *Out of the Light/Into the Fire* (1997), which premiered at Highways in Santa Monica, California, in 1997, Hill satirically depicts various forms and values of rituals in the traditions of her Japanese/Finnish cultural life.

Most recently, Hill completed a solo performance piece, *Deadwood to Hollywood* (1999). It premiered at the West Coast Ensemble in Los Angeles in 1999. The piece is a compilation of issues she considered in *Beside Myself*: her life in Deadwood, South Dakota, on the West Coast, and during her long visit to Japan, and her struggle as an Asian American actor in theater, film, and television. Through familiar anecdotes, Hill draws not only a picture of the life journey of herself, but also of those who surround her, including her parents and friends. Compared with *Beside Myself, Deadwood* focuses more on the personal growth that she garnered from her life journeys. She presents her childhood as an "evil" but also creative circumstance that pushed her to seek answers, to hone her ability to think critically, and to express herself loudly but clearly and without fear.

For instance, she looks candidly at the constant remarks about her not looking Asian enough. Hill illustrates the point with an anecdote about being asked to play a Nicaraguan nun on the soap opera *Santa Barbara*. She goes on to comment, with wit, sarcasm, humor, and warmth, on the absence of Asians in common television shows such as *Suddenly Susan*, which takes place in San Francisco, a city "that is 30 percent Asian" (*Deadwood*). She continues, "There are more cartoon characters, aliens, even dogs on television than Asian Americans" (*Deadwood*). She also recounts her constantly being mistaken for an extra at film locations. Hill concludes the piece by discussing her role as Maria in *Twelfth Night* at Lincoln Center, where she became the "first AA" (*Deadwood*). These anecdotes serve as Hill's critical observation of current show business as well as her determination to maintain her artistic visions and identity as a solo performer.

CRITICAL RECEPTION

All of Hill's solo pieces have been well received by both critics and audiences. The critics have particularly appreciated Hill's ability to use her life journey to examine the confusion, disappointment, and eventual acceptance of her cultural heritage. About *Tokyo Bound*, Sylvie Drake of the *Los Angeles Times* observes that as the play unfolds, "it broadens and blossoms, ultimately becoming an affecting journey into love and marriage in Japan that leads to an acceptance and appreciation of the richness and complexity of her uncommon heritage" (F1). Steven Winn of the *San Francisco Chronicle* states that the details of

Hill's life in *Tokyo Bound* provide a "natural touch" that "proves more artful and resonant, in the end, than you anticipate" (E2). In fact, it played to sellout houses in various cities across the country and was chosen as a critic's choice in Seattle, San Francisco, and Los Angeles. It was later included in the Festival of New Voices at the Public Theater in New York and was nominated for a 1995 Cable Ace Award.

Reunion was also positively reviewed by major newspapers. Scott Collins of the *Los Angeles Times* stated, "diverting as the material sometimes is—especially in Hill's affectionate, impeccably timed performance—in the end it's as illuminating as a visit to grandmother's house" (F26). About *Beside Myself*, Jan Breslauer of the *Los Angeles Times* commented on Hill's strength in identifying with characters who are "beside herself," although she pointed out her weakness in portraying herself: As her Japanese mother, she is "brilliant and hilarious. But Amy as Amy actually reveals less about the cultural displacement that is Hill's topic" (F18). Breslauer's comment exemplifies Hill's excellent artistry in "becoming" others while revealing Hill's constant negotiation and struggle with her multiple identities and positions as a biracial artist in the United States.

BIBLIOGRAPHY

Works by Amy Hill

Drama

Tokyo Bound. Asian American Drama: 9 Plays from the Multiethnic Landscape. Ed. Brian Nelson. New York: Applause, 1997. 43–70.

Unpublished Manuscripts

Beside Myself. 1992.
Reunion. 1995.
Out of the Light/Into the Fire. 1997.
Deadwood to Hollywood. 1999.

Selected Production History

Tokyo Bound

Solo performances, dir. Anne Etue. East West Players, Los Angeles, 1991.
———, dir. Anne Etue. Asian American Theater Company, San Francisco, 1991.
———, dir. Anne Etue. Public Theater, New York City, 1991.

Beside Myself

Solo performances. Mark Taper Forum, Los Angeles, 1992.

Reunion

Solo performances. Actors Theatre of Louisville, Louisville, KY, 1995.

Out of the Light/Into the Fire

Solo performances. Highways Performance Space, Santa Monica, CA, 1997.

Deadwood to Hollywood

Solo performances. West Coast Ensemble, Los Angeles, 1999.

Studies of Amy Hill

Breslauer, Jan. "*Beside Myself:* Formulaic Look at One's Identity." *Los Angeles Times* 23 July 1993: F18.

Collins, Scott. "Amy Hill Portrays Mother in *Reunion.*" *Los Angeles Times* 28 Apr. 1995: F26.

Drake, Sylvie. "*Tokyo Bound* Soars toward Comical Cultural Collisions." *Los Angeles Times* 15 Aug. 1991: F1.

Fong-Torres, Ben. "Bound and Determined Portrait of Japanese Actress Aims Past Stereotypes in *Tokyo Bound.*" *San Francisco Chronicle* 21 Apr. 1991, Sunday Datebook: 22.

Suravech, Glenn. "Teens Reluctant to 'Get Real' on New Talk Show." *Rafu Shimpo* 1 Apr. 1993: 1.

Winn, Steven. "A Japanese Transplant's Story: Amy Hill's Comic *Tokyo Bound* at Asian American Theater." *San Francisco Chronicle* 10 Apr. 1991: E2.

Velina Hasu Houston

(1957–)

Masami Usui and Miles Xian Liu

BIOGRAPHY

Velina Avisa Hasu Houston was born on May 5, 1957, in Tokyo, Japan, as the second child of an African Native American (Blackfoot) father, Lemo Houston, from Linden, Alabama, and a Japanese mother, Setsuko Takechi, from Matsu-yama, Ehime, a provincial town in Shikoku Island. Identifying herself as "an Amerasian," Houston is one of the children born of the many interracial couples during the U.S. occupation of Japan after World War II. Setsuko first met Lemo in 1946 in Kobe, whose international port played an important role for the U.S. occupation. Lemo returned to the United States in 1949 and then served in the Korean War in 1951. Setsuko and Lemo married after nine years of courtship, but Satsuko's father committed suicide partially because of her relationship with Lemo. In 1959, Houston moved to the United States with her parents, elder sister Hilda Rika Hatsuyo, and adoptive elder brother Joji Kawada.

After a temporary stay with Lemo's family in New York, the Houstons settled in Junction City, Kansas, as Lemo was transferred to nearby Fort Riley. He died in 1969 of combat-related stress and alcoholism. Houston stayed there with her mother and sister until her mother remarried. Because both Setsuko and Lemo cut their family ties when they married, Houston was brought up primarily within a sphere of her immigrant mother's lifestyle, with little influence of American culture from any extended family. Her brother Joji disappeared in 1984 and lost contact with Houston until 1999. Houston's childhood and ado-lescence experiences were shaped by her family's destiny—being entirely re-jected and harshly discriminated against by the Japanese and Americans both inside and outside her extended families. She experienced firsthand the racial prejudices of whites, blacks, and Asians. Her Amerasian heritage in predominantly white middle-class towns of the Midwest was an object of constant gaze and suspicion. In fact, when she scored well on grade-school IQ tests, according to *People Weekly*, "her teachers thought she had cheated and insisted that she take them over" ("Playwright" 168). Ironically, it was childhood experiences such as these that enabled her works to speak to all Americans.

Houston went to Kansas State University, where she was an honors student and graduated in 1979 with a B.A. in journalism, mass communications, and theater and a minor in philosophy. She moved to Los Angeles and earned her M.F.A. in theater arts with a minor in screenwriting in 1981 from the University of California School of Theater, Film, and Television in Los Angeles. Her M.F.A. thesis, "Asa Ga Kimashita (Morning Has Broken)," became a workshop production at Studio Theater of UCLA in the same year. Since then, Houston has shared her America in person with audiences at schools and universities across the country. Included on the list of campuses where she has worked are the Junction City Senior High School as visiting artist in 1989; UCLA as guest lecturer in 1993 and 1998; the University of Hawaii, Manoa, as guest mentor in 1994–95; the Padua Hills Playwrights' Festival as master class mentor in 1995; and the University of California at San Diego as guest lecturer in 1997. Since 1990, Houston has been teaching at the University of Southern California. She is currently associate professor, resident playwright, and director of the Playwriting Program at the USC School of Theatre and is working on her doctoral dissertation, entitled "All Mixed Up with Nowhere to Go: Cinema, Popular Culture, and the Mythology of Multiracial Identity" at the USC School of Cinema-Television. Houston is now a mother of two children.

Houston's dramatic works caught the attention of the mainstream theater with the successful production of *Tea* by Manhattan Theatre Club in 1987. Ever since, her plays have been staged across the country and around the world. In her prolific career, eight of her plays have been commissioned by such well-known projects and foundations as the Mark Taper Forum, the Manhattan Theatre Club, the Asia Society, the Honolulu Theatre for Youth, the Lila Wallace–Reader's Digest Foundation New Generations Play Project, the Kennedy Theatre, the Hawaii State Foundation on Culture and the Arts, the Jewish Women's Theatre Project, and the Cornerstone Theatre Company.

In addition to playwriting, Houston has edited the journals *Multiracial Asian Times* and *Amerasia Journal*, has compiled literary anthologies, and has written for film and television. The most noted volumes and scripts include *The Politics of Life* and *But Still, Like Air, I'll Rise, Hishoku* for Alternate Current International, and *Kalito* for the American Film Institute, as well as "Golden Opportunity," "Leon for President," "Pretty Perfect," and "The Rest Test" for the PBS series called *The Puzzle Factory* in 1993.

Houston's works also gained critical attention internationally, especially in Japan. She was put under the spotlight of the media during her short visit in 1995. Invited as a lecturer by Akira Wakabayashi, a representative of the Kokusai Seinen Engeki Center, which produced *Tea* at Theatre X in Tokyo, Houston had the opportunity to collaborate with Japanese theater artists and share with the Japanese audience her American experience as a person of Japanese descent. During the production of *Tea*, she delivered her widely publicized lecture entitled "A Daughter of Imperialism: Notes of Identity as an Amerasian" at the Japan Foundation and the Tokyo Metropolitan Culture Foundation for the fiftieth-anniversary year. In May 1995, Nippon Hoso Kyokai (NHK) or Japan Broadcasting Corporation produced a two-night documentary entitled "Setsuko to Velina—Amerika ni lkita Sensou Hanayome" [Setsuko and Velina—A War Bride Who Has Been Living in America]. Both Mainichi Broadcasting Company and TV Tokyo produced television documentaries of Houston's works and family.

As one of America's prominent contemporary playwrights, Houston has served as a Rockefeller Foundation playwriting fellow twice, a California Arts Council fellow, a Los Angeles Endowment for the Arts fellow, a James Zumberge fellow twice, and a Japan Foundation fellow. She also served as a national judge for the 20th Century Playwrights' Festival in New York in 1994, the PBS Keepin' It Real Youth Script-writing Competition in 1998, and the Contemporary Theatre's National Women's Playwriting Award in 1998. She is now a member of Phi Beta Kappa, an artistic associate of the Sacramento Theatre Company, and a member of the Women's Project and Productions, the Dramatists Guild, and the Writers Guild of America, West.

The long list of the most noted national and international awards she has garnered includes the first prize for the Lorraine Hansberry Playwriting Award (1982), the first prize for the David Library Playwriting Award (1982), *LA Weekly* Drama Critics Award for *Asa Ga Kimashita* (1984), Who's Who in American Women (1985), best ten plays written by women worldwide for *Tea* by the Susan Smith Blackburn Prize of London (1986), *DramaLogue* Outstanding Achievement in Theatre Award for the Old Globe production of *Tea* (1988), the McKnight Foundation fellow (1989), the Japanese American Women of Merit 1890–1990, the Critics Choice Awards from both the *Los Angeles Times* and *DramaLogue* (1991), the inaugural recipient of the Remy Martin New Vision Award (1992), and the Po'okela Award (1996).

MAJOR WORKS AND THEMES

Thematically, Houston's plays focus on interracial and multicultural conflicts as exhibited in life from daily incidents to struggles with identity. Cross-cultural politics are an integral part of her work. However, the allegiance her plays pledge is to humanity, not any geopolitical entity. Houston's forte is often the depiction of a domestic space where women's struggle is often buried and ignored. The library of her theatrical works may be categorized into two mutually inclusive groups: those that examine stories inspired by her family, and those that explore race, gender, class, and culture issues beyond the confines of family, generations, and national borders.

The representatives of the first group are mostly her earlier biographical plays, often referred to as the trilogy: *Asa Ga Kimashita* (1980), *American Dreams* (1983), and *Tea* (1983). The trilogy restages the path through which "war brides" have proceeded and depicts the life that Houston, as a daughter of a Japanese "war bride," has lived in "the home of the brave and justice for all." *Asa Ga Kimashita* is a grandfather's story in Japan, *American Dreams* a father's story in America, and *Tea* a story of mothers in silence.

Framed within Japan's forced democratization after the long nightmares of the war, *Asa Ga Kimashita* is plotted around the painful changes that the Shimada family has to endure from the prewar patriarchal household, which suppressed both class and gender conflicts, to the postwar collapsed yet liberated sphere, which enabled the powerless—women, maids, and peasants—to break free from tradition. The play begins with two grunting male figures, Kiheida Shimada, the patriarch of the Shimada estate, and his tenant peasant, Hajime Takemoto, but ends with two insightful and perceptive female characters, Fusae, Kiheida's wife, and their independent-minded daughter, Setsuko. The other characters—Haruko, Setsuko's narrow-minded elder sister; Fumiko, Kiheida's bilingual Americanized niece; and Creed Banks, an African American soldier, Setsuko's forbidden love—are all symbolic voices of the era. Like the changing times they must adapt to for survival, the play spares no one in its ironic twists and reversals.

As a stark defender of the Japanese civilization, Kiheida resents the occupation government's policies restricting lumber sales, refuses to acknowledge the pending land reform, does not believe that his tenant peasants might know what to do with the land they would get, and cannot fathom his youngest daughter's affection for "a Yankee soldier" (*Asa* 270). To him, the old ways are best; the Japanese way is the right way; and what has been "managed to perfection . . . from father to son for millennia" should be left alone (228). In his defiance of the forced social changes, he finds a political ally and a possible son-in-law in an otherwise unlikely person, Hajime Takemoto, his tenant for years.

The Takemotos have toiled at the Shimada estate for generations. Although Hajime is an obvious beneficiary of "MacArthur's land resettlement," he cannot talk about the Americans without calling them "pigs" (224). To him, they are corrupting Japanese women, culture, and tradition. As patriotic as Kiheida, Hajime cannot stand Fumiko because "she does not work for the Empire" (244). It turns out that Hajime cannot stand Kiheida's oldest daughter, Haruko, either, though she has been promised to be his bride. Hajime goes after Setsuko as soon as he gets the two tracts of Kiheida's land through the government decree. His argument is that Setsuko might marry out if she is not spoken for now, while Haruko will always marry a Japanese. Setsuko is then promised to him despite her vehement protests, because marrying one's own kind honors a way of living that Kiheida believes is worth the sacrifice of his daughter's happiness.

Dying with a chest tumor, Fusae Shimada, Kiheida's wife, is a charismatic figure who understands the importance of change and appreciates the value of dreams. Though she chose "a reliable mule" over "a wild horse" in her life, the last wish she makes to her self-righteous husband is "the freedom of my youngest child" (266). She encourages Setsuko not only to have dreams but also to "hold on to them" because "the present moment, the one we can grasp in our fists and feel," is what matters in life (272–74). The play ends with Setsuko by Fusae's side contemplating her life in America.

Although Houston calls *Asa Ga Kimashita* a "peculiarly Japanese play," it encompasses a wide range of themes such as class, gender, race, and, most profoundly, the humanistic approach to love and life beyond national borders (210). In fact, the play calls into question the allegiance that the patriarch and the patriot pledge to their fine civilization and proud empire through their own actions. Kiheida, in defense of his "civilized" lifestyle, is more than willing to disown his youngest daughter (248), while Hajime, the self-made protector of Japanese women, is more than ready to dismiss the relationship between Setsuko and Creed, but to get his hands on Setsuko, all in the name of his love for Nippon. In contrast, neither Fusae nor Setsuko proclaims loyalty to a tradition or country, yet both are strong in character and reflective in action, exemplary human beings of any culture. Even Fumiko, frivolous as she may seem from time to time, offers a thoughtful analysis of Japan's downfall in the heated exchange with Kiheida: "This provincial closed-mindedness and arrogance is what brought our country to its knees" (248). Thus *Asa Ga Kimashita* is also a play with its sympathies firmly rooted in humanity rather than nationality.

In *American Dreams*, nationalism, racism, class conflict, sexism, and interracial oppression are all put on display again as Setsuko undergoes anguish and humiliation in contesting the racial and sexual inequality in the new world. Little did Setsuko know at the end of *Asa Ga Kimashita* that her dream of a life with her African Native American husband would lead to her experience of imprisonment and homelessness during the four-night stay with her in-laws in a New York apartment. *American Dreams* details Setsuko and Creed's struggle with racial hostility and cultural intolerance while the couple tries to make its home in America. Like *Asa Ga Kimashita*, where the culturally oppressed in postwar Japan resorted to nationalism and racism to exert their self-worth, *American Dreams* shows the couple least tolerated by the casualties of racial inequality, namely, Creed's relatives. But, unlike *Asa Ga Kimashita*, this play offers a thread of hope beyond Setsuko's personal future, because some of Creed's relatives begin to realize by the end of the play that they themselves are both the victims and the products of a racist society. Racism and cultural supremacy exist not only in white America but also in the heart of racial victims like themselves.

Tea becomes Houston's signature play as it transcends her mother's biographical stories to examine the silenced lives of five Japanese "war brides" who have made their homes in a small midwestern town near a military base. In the name of honoring Himiko Hamilton, who shot herself recently after killing her abusive husband several years earlier, four Japanese women—Setsuko Banks, Chizuy Juarez, Eruko MacKenzie, and Atsuko Yamamoto—get together reluctantly to have tea in the home of the deceased. "We're here today," as Chizuy puts it, "because we're scared" (172). Himiko's violent suicide does not make the occasion any easier. Nevertheless, her death serves unexpectedly as a catalyst for the living to reflect on their own husbands, children, and lives as foreigners in America.

Though the four women are all Japanese, they would have nothing in common if they were in Japan because of their widely different social and cultural backgrounds. In this military town of Kansas, however, they come to share a life between the two worlds—"a casualty the Japanese do not care to count" and "[e]xcess baggage Amerika does not want to carry" (181). Love and separation, excitement and frustration, hope and despair, happiness and loneliness are the buried lives they have lived since their arrival in the new world. But their respective excuses have kept them apart until Himiko's death. The tea ceremony is thus transformed in the play from a uniquely Japanese ritual of improving eyesight into a metaphor of women's spirits enhancing insight. *Tea* therefore gives voice to the silenced stories of these women in both English and Japanese.

Waiting for Tadashi (1999), a play completed during Houston's Kyoto stay in 1999, may be considered as an addition to the trilogy. It reconstructs a story not too different from that of Houston's brother, Joji. An Amerasian orphan by the name of Tadashi Lane is abandoned by his single mother, sent to an ill-operated orphanage in Tokyo, adopted by an African American GI who marries a Japanese woman, and taken to the United States with his new family. After years of his disappearance as a form of revolt against his adoptive mother, Tadashi decides to find her in search of his roots. During his efforts to locate his stepmother, he journeys back into the tragic past. Tadashi realizes that his odyssey is a quest to find himself. Like *Tea, Waiting for Tadashi* is created in a carefully manipulated domestic space. The tragic past—personal and collective—is discovered and articulated with the shared fate of political homelessness and psychological imprisonment. Its characters from Setsuko to Tadashi are all engaged in a desperate search for a place they can feel and call home.

The typical plays of the second group include *The Matsuyama Mirror* (1979), *Kokoro* (1989), *Christmas Cake* (1990), *Cultivated Lives* (1994), *Hula Heart* (1994), and *Ikebana* (1999). Characters in these plays are more emblematic than biographical in their approach to conflicts of identity, gender, class, and race.

Set in the Edo feudal period of Japan, *The Matsuyama Mirror* portrays a twelve-year-old girl, Aiko, who wants so much to remain a child with her dolls that she refuses to become a woman. She lets go of her mirror and dolls only after her mother's sudden death, her father's remarriage to her aunt, and her first menstrual cycle. Symbolically, the vicissitudes have transformed Aiko from a child obsessed with toys to a woman passionate for life.

Kokoro (True Heart) engages in the exploration of cultural conflicts in contemporary America. *Kokoro* examines the Japanese traditional practice of *oyako-shinju* (parent-child suicide) in a transnational context. Based on an *oyako-shinju* incident in which the Japanese mother survived and her child drowned in Santa

Monica, California, in 1985, the play depicts the agonizing struggle within the Yamashitas' house to keep their marriage and make some sense of their life in the United States. The internal conflict between Yasako (wife) and Hiro (husband) is finally brought out in the open six years after they left Japan. As a couple, they no longer trust each other because of Hiro's three-year-long affair with another woman; and as parents, they differ in their opinions about their daughter's education and home training. In desperation, Yasako resorts to *oyako-shinju* by jumping into the sea with her daughter.

Written with carefully researched materials, the play not only articulates a tragic consequence of Japanese female immigrants transplanted to America, but also studies the pitfalls of using one country's legal assumptions to judge another nation's behavior, as in the case of *oyako-shinju*. The disparity between Yasako's motive and Angela Rossetti's (Yasako's attorney) legal reasoning forms the play's subplot of law and culture. With the public's gradual recognition of *oyako-shinju* as an accepted Japanese cultural practice, the play ends with the court handing down a lighter sentence in order to give Yasako a chance to regain her will to live.

A similar fact-based approach is used in *Christmas Cake* to explore a Japanese invention, "bachelor schools." Though the play is a satire on ethnic correctness, it presents a California version of a serious Japanese problem: Bachelors are experiencing enormous difficulties finding women who would play the role of wives as defined by tradition. As women become more professionally oriented in their life decisions, a bachelor in his forties, coerced by his concerned parents, decides to go to a bachelor school to brush up on his dating skills in order to find a suitable bride. In the end, it is neither the curriculum of the bachelor school nor his parents' plans, but love itself that wins out for those ready for a committed relationship.

Cultivated Lives is another picture of postwar Japan at the crossroads, where opposing values clash between generations and genders. Misao Itamura, a young woman from a well-to-do family, and her Eurasian maid, Sadako Kitabayashi, attempt to run away from Misao's father and two bachelor medical residents in his hospital. While the Itamuras' mansion may be a symbol for the cultivated lives of carp and flowers, beneath its elegant facade are the patriarchal values that once held Misao's late mother hostage, are making Misao's aunt a housemaid for the family, and will imprison Misao when she comes of age. Misao's escape from her own father thus becomes an ultimate expression of rebellion against the tyranny of the old tradition and yearning for change.

Ikebana (Living Flowers), a sister version of *Cultivated Lives*, employs the sophisticated metaphor of ikebana—Japanese traditional flower arrangement— to explore the paths of two young women in a quest for a room of their own in Tokyo. Ayame Itamura and her Amerasian maid Hanako are confronted with the male-dominant views of women: Ayame, as a daughter of a wealthy doctor, is being coerced to get married to one of her father's young colleagues, while Hanako, as an exotic beauty, suffers the constant harassment of three men. In a status-conscious society like Japan, Ayame and Hanako are not likely to share a room under normal circumstances, but their shared experience as women unites them to pursue a room of shared living space together.

In both groups, Houston clearly challenges the social biases on race, gender, class, and culture as human conditions. They exist in the different times, generations, and societies on both sides of the Pacific. While the male-dominated Japanese culture lends itself well to Houston's themes of gender disparity, racially mixed America becomes an ideal stage for Houston's theatrical portrayal of the limits and possibilities of ethnic labeling. A culture, along with its myths and prejudices, defines as well as confines the individual and community—a reoccurring theme that Houston invokes throughout her works on behalf of humanity.

CRITICAL RECEPTION

Although Houston's works are among the most widely produced Asian American plays in the United States, they have yet to receive systematic critical examinations. Among the few scholars who have studied her are Roberta Uno, Juli Thompson Burk, and Josephine Lee. Uno not only has always supported Houston professionally, but also introduced her into the American classrooms of theater through *Unbroken Thread*, one of the first anthologies devoted to Asian American women playwrights. Burk has been instrumental in production assistance and has spoken highly of Houston in her various conference presentations. Josephine Lee uses *Tea* to discuss the potential and limitations of racial, sexual, and generational "passing" both on the stage and in reality. While *Tea* celebrates the interracial marriages of its characters, none comes about without high human cost. Lee believes that the play "holds up racial difference as an impassable boundary" in these relationships (200). The departure of these war brides from Japan is "linked, literally and symbolically, to death," and their arrival is marked by the endless sacrifice they must make for their relationships while they feel "suspended between two worlds" (201). The best two marriages—Chizuy's and Setsuko's—tragically result in the premature death of their respective husbands, suggesting the inevitable "loss of personal satisfaction" for interracial coupling in the play (201). It is thus on a mournful note that *Tea* "investigates the tragic dimension of passing" both as an ideal and as a social practice (204).

The theater reviews in all major U.S. newspapers have been mostly favorable. Edith Oliver of the *New Yorker* calls Houston a "talented dramatist" (104), and *People Weekly* calls her work "literally, dramatic proof of American hybrid vigor" ("Playwright" 168). Like her other plays, *Tea*, for example, strikes a note with American audiences, at least partially because this is a country of immigrants. The blind faith and the devastating loneliness it captures are not exclusive to the lives of the international war brides in Kansas, where "[t]hey were no longer Japanese and not allowed to feel American" (Siegel D1). Like these women, most of the immigrants come as if, in Houston's words, "walking into a black hole and holding tightly onto someone's hand" (Churnin, "Play" 1), but despite the circumstances, they all take that chance in America. Therefore, her works, though largely rooted in Japanese American cultural tradition, speak to multiracial America with special effectiveness.

In Japan, Houston has also received critical attention. Unlike Houston's critics and reviewers in the United States, Japanese scholars bring their insight of Japanese tradition and culture into their Houston studies. Yuriko Murakami, a Japanese free-lance writer and specialist in Asian American theater, points out Houston's overwhelming aesthetic inclination to Japan expressed in her works (1997). Yasuko Kawarasaki, the first scholar in Japan to write an academic article on Houston, evaluates her inclination to the war-bride issue in her thorough discussion of *Tea*. Based on research into the lives of Japanese "war brides," she sees the play as a revelation of a silenced yet gradually recognized history. Masami Usui focuses on the aftermath of World War II as reflected in *Asa Ga Kimashita, American Dreams, Tea*, and *Kokoro*. Her interpretations are often constructed from a feminist transnational perspective. In *Kokoro*, for example, Yasako (mother) resorts to *oyako-shinju* (parent-child suicide) when her marriage is falling apart in America. To a Japanese, her decision, tragic as it is, can be considered normal, because options are culturally more limited for a woman to dissolve a marriage in Japan, and parent-child suicide is an accepted practice in Japanese traditional culture. However, when Yasako transplants her Japanese solution to her American problem in a land where suicide itself is not even entertained as part of any conflict resolution, her action becomes not only immoral and unacceptable but also subject to criminal prosecution. The play focuses precisely on the disparity between the outcry of the American public over the incident and Yasako's Japanese reasoning for her decision in order to demonstrate the importance of cross-cultural communication. Therefore, *Kokoro* is best read as a transnational feminist drama. In this global and transnational era, it is clear that Houston will gain more critical appreciation among the theater audience and in academia on both sides of the Pacific Ocean as her work continues to provoke new perspectives on perennial issues such as race, gender, class, and identity.

BIBLIOGRAPHY

Works by Velina Hasu Houston

Drama

Asa Ga Kimashita (Morning Has Broken). *The Politics of Life: Four Plays by Asian American Women*. Ed. Velina Hasu Houston. Philadelphia: Temple UP, 1993. 205–74.

Tea. Unbroken Thread: An Anthology of Plays by Asian American Women. Ed. Roberta Uno. Amherst: U of Massachusetts P, 1993. 155–200.

The Matsuyama Mirror. Short Plays for Young Actors. Ed. Craig Slaight and Jack Sharrar. North Stratford, NH: Smith and Kraus, 1996. 77–106.

As Sometimes in a Dead Man's Face. Asian American Drama: 9 Plays from the Multiethnic Landscape. Ed. Brian Nelson. New York: Applause, 1997. 71–125.

Kokoro (True Heart). *But Still, Like Air, I'll Rise: New Asian American Plays.* Ed. Velina Hasu Houston. Philadelphia: Temple UP, 1997. 89–129.

Hula Heart. Eight Plays for Children: The New Generation Project. Ed. Coleman A. Jennings. Austin: U of Texas P, 1999. 77–104.

Unpublished Manuscripts

Switchboard. 1976

Nobody like Us. 1979.

Zyanya. 1979.

Thirst. Ms. 345. Roberta Uno Asian Women Playwrights Scripts Collection 1924–1992, Special Collections and Archives, W.E.B. Du Bois Library, U of Massachusetts, Amherst; also at the Joyce Ketay Agency, New York City, 1981.

Amerasian Girls. 1983.

American Dreams. Ms. 345. Roberta Uno Asian Women Playwrights Scripts Collection 1924–1992, Special Collections and Archives, W.E.B. Du Bois Library, U of Massachusetts, Amherst; also at the Joyce Ketay Agency, New York City, 1983.

Child of the Seasons. 1984.

Shinseku. 1984.

The Legend of Bobbi Chicago. Musical. 1985.

Albatross. Ms. 345. Roberta Uno Asian Women Playwrights Scripts Collection 1924–1992, Special Collections and Archives, W.E.B. Du Bois Library, U of Massachusetts, Amherst; also at the Joyce Ketay Agency, New York City, 1988.

My Life Is a Loaded Gun. 1988.

O-Manju. 1989.

A Place for Kalamatea. 1989.

Cactus Bloom. 1990.

The Canaanite Woman. 1990.

Christmas Cake. 1990.

The Confusion of Tongues. 1990.

Kapi'olani's Faith. 1990.

The Melting Pot. 1990.

Necessities. 1990.

Princess Kaiulani. 1990.

Broken English. 1991.

Plantation. 1991.

Tokyo Valentine. Ms. 345. Roberta Uno Asian Women Playwrights Scripts Collection 1924–1992, Special Collections and Archives, W.E.B. Du Bois Library, U of Massachusetts, Amherst; also at the Joyce Ketay Agency, New York City, 1991.

Alabama Rain. Ms. 345. Roberta Uno Asian Women Playwrights Scripts Collection 1924–1992, Special Collections and Archives, W.E.B. Du Bois Library, U of Massachusetts, Amherst; also at the Joyce Ketay Agency, New York City, 1992.

Kumo Kumo. 1992.

Once Every Christmas. 1992.

The Sky Is Falling. 1992.

Word for Word. 1992.
Snowing Fire. 1993.
Cultivated Lives. 1994.
Sentimental Education. 1997.
Lotus of the Sublime Pond. 1998.
Ikebana. 1999.
Shedding the Tiger. 1999.
Waiting for Tadashi. 1999.

Selected Production History

Nobody like Us

Production. Ebony Theatre Company, Manhattan, KS, 1979.

Switchboard

Production. Purple Masque Theatre, Manhattan, KS, 1979.

Asa Ga Kimashita

Production. Studio Theater, UCLA, Los Angeles, 1981.
————, prod. Keone Young. East West Players, Los Angeles, 1984.
————. Pacific Rim Productions at Nova Theater, San Francisco, 1985.
————, dir. Gene Shofner. Kumu Kahua Theatre, Honolulu, 1991.
————. Massman Theatre, U of Southern California, Los Angeles, 1991.

American Dreams

Production, dir. Samuel P. Barton; perf. Nancy Hamada, Reuben Green, Sandra Reaves-Phillips, Count Stovall, Kim Yancey, Ching Valdes, Walter Allen Bennett, Jr., and Ron Auguste. Negro Ensemble Company, New York City, 1984.
———— (radio). LA Theatre Works and National Public Radio–KCRW, Los Angeles, 1991.

Thirst

Staged reading. Lee Strasberg Creative Center, Hollywood, CA, 1984.
Production, dir. Mitzie Abe. Asian American Theater Company, San Francisco, 1986.

Tea

Staged reading. East West Players, Los Angeles, 1985.
Workshop, dir. Judith Nihei. Asian American Theater Company, San Francisco, 1985.
Staged reading. Seattle Group Theatre, Seattle, 1986.
————. Manhattan Theatre Club, New York City, 1987.
Production, dir. Julianne Boyd; perf. Takayo Fischer, Lily Mariye, Jeanne Mori, Natsuko Ohama, and Patti Yasutake. Manhattan Theatre Club, New York City, 1987.
————, dir. Julianne Boyd; perf. Gerrielani Miyazaki, Lily Mariye, Shuko Akune, and Diana Tanaka. Old Globe Theatre, San Diego, CA, 1988.
————, dir. Julie Akers. Interstate Firehouse Cultural Center, Portland, OR, 1988.
————, dir. Olympia Dukakis. Whole Theater, Montclair, NJ, 1989.
————, dir. Julianne Boyd. Philadelphia Theatre Company, Philadelphia, 1989.
————, dir. Yuriko Doi. TheatreWorks, Palo Alto, CA, 1990.
————, dir. Yuriko Doi. Menlo Park's Burgess Theatre, San Francisco, 1990.
————, dir. Ellen Polyphronopoulou. Kumu Kahua Theatre, Honolulu, 1990.

————, dir. Julianne Boyd. Odyssey Theatre Ensemble, Los Angeles, 1991.

————. Apple Island Theatre, Madison, WI, 1991.

————. Mount Holyoke College, South Hadley, MA, 1991.

————. Syracuse Stage, Syracuse, NY, 1991.

————, dir. Yuriko Doi. Theatre of Yugen, San Francisco, 1992.

————, dir. Leslie B. Jacobson. Horizons Theatre, Washington, DC, 1993.

———— (radio). LA Theatre Works and National Public Radio–KCRW, Los Angeles.
     1993.

————, dir. Sakiko Taoka. Amagasaki Piccolo Theatre, Hyogo, Japan, 1993.

————, dir. William Wilday. Morgan-Wixon Theatre, Santa Monica, CA, 1995.

————, dir. Peggy Shannon. A Contemporary Theatre, Seattle, 1995.

————, dir. Akira Wakabayashi. Theatre X, Tokyo, Japan, 1995.

————, dir. Stuart E.W. Smith. Nevada Theatre, Nevada City, CA, 1996.

————, dir. Chil Kong. San Diego Asian American Repertory Theatre, 1997.

————. Asian Theatre Network, Stanford U, Stanford, CA, 1998.

————, dir. Julianne Boyd. Barrington Stage Company, Sheffield, MA, 1999.

————, dir. Pamela Berlin. Pittsburgh Public Theater, Pittsburgh, 2001.

Amerasian Girls

Production. Ensemble Studio Theatre, Los Angeles, 1987.

The Legend of Bobbi Chicago

Staged reading. Mark Taper Forum, Los Angeles, 1987.

Albatross

Staged reading, dir. Velina Hasu Houston. Playwrights' Theatre, Los Angeles, 1988.

————. Manhattan Theatre Club, New York City, 1989.

————. Arizona Theater Company, Tucson, 1991.

————. Theatre/Theatre, Los Angeles, 1992.

My Life Is a Loaded Gun

Staged reading. Old Globe Theatre, San Diego, 1988.

Necessities

Staged reading. Old Globe Theatre, San Diego, 1990.

Production, dir. Julianne Boyd. Old Globe Theatre, San Diego, 1991.

————. Purple Rose Theatre, Chelsea, MI, 1993.

Broken English

Staged reading. Odyssey Theatre Ensemble, Los Angeles, 1991.

Christmas Cake

Staged reading. East West Players, Los Angeles, 1991.

Workshop. Kumu Kahua Theatre, Honolulu, 1992.

The Confusion of Tongues

Production, dir. Susan Mott. St. Augustine's by-the-Sea Episcopal Parish, Santa Monica,
     CA, 1991.

Kapi'olani's Faith

Staged reading. Kumu Kahua Theatre, Honolulu, 1991.

Production. Kumu Kahua Theatre, Honolulu, 1994.

Tokyo Valentine

Staged reading. East West Players, Los Angeles, 1992.

Kumo Kumo

Staged reading. East West Players, Los Angeles, 1993.

The Matsuyama Mirror

Staged reading, dir. Brian Nelson. East West Players, Los Angeles, 1993.
————. Lincoln Center Institute, New York City, 1993.
Production. John F. Kennedy Center for the Performing Arts, Washington, DC, 1993.
————, dir. Pamela Sterling. Honolulu Theatre for Youth, Honolulu, 1995.

Rain

Staged reading, dir. Tina Chen. Women's Project & Productions, New York City, 1993.

As Sometimes in a Dead Man's Face

Staged reading. East West Players, Los Angeles, 1994.

Japanese and Multicultural at the Turn-of-the-Century

Production (radio). Asia Society–National Public Radio, 1994.

Kokoro

Production, dir. Yuriko Doi. Lila Wallace Theatre, New York City, 1994.
————, dir. Yuriko Doi. Theatre of Yugen, San Francisco, 1994.
————, dir. Tina Chen. 28th Street Theatre, New York City, 1995.
————, dir. Jan Lewis. Odyssey Theatre Ensemble, Los Angeles, 1996.
————, dir. Peggy Shannon. Sacramento Theatre Company, 2000.
————, dir. Noelle Ho. Asian Theater Project of Williams College, Williamstown, MA, 2000.

Snowing Fire

Staged reading. Cornerstone Theatre Company, Los Angeles, 1994.
————. Massman Theatre, U of Southern California, Los Angeles, 1994.

Hula Heart

Staged reading, dir. Peter C. Brosius. Honolulu Theatre for Youth, Honolulu, 1994 and 1995.
Production, dir. Peter C. Brosius. Honolulu Theatre for Youth, Honolulu, 1996.

Cultivated Lives

Production, dir. Juli Thompson Burk. Kennedy Lab Theatre, U of Hawai'i, Manoa, 1996.
————, dir. Karin Williams. Asian American Repertory Theatre, San Diego, 1999.

Sentimental Education

Staged reading. 24th Street Theatre, Los Angeles, 1997.

Lotus of the Sublime Pond

Staged reading. 24th Street Theatre, Los Angeles, 1998.

Ikebana

Production, dir. Shirley Jo Finney. Pasadena Playhouse, Pasadena, CA, 2000.
————, dir. Pamela Berlin. Pittsburgh Public Theater, Pittsburgh, 2000.
————, Santa Monica College Concert Hall, Santa Monica, CA, 2000.

Shedding the Tiger

Production, dir. Peggy Shannon. Sacramento Theatre Company, Sacramento, CA, 2000.

Waiting for Tadashi

Production, dir. Peggy Shannon. Wyatt Pavilion Theater, U of California, Davis, 2000.
————, dir. Hannah Fujiki DeVorkin. George Street Playhouse, New Brunswick, NJ, 2000.

Anthologies

The Politics of Life: Four Plays by Asian American Women. Philadelphia: Temple UP, 1993.
But Still, Like Air, I'll Rise: New Asian American Plays. Philadelphia: Temple UP, 1997.

Essays

"On Being Mixed Japanese in Modern Times." *Pacific Citizen* 20–27 Dec. 1985: B1–B3.
"The Japanese Women of Kansas." Program Notes of *Tea.* Old Globe Theatre production, San Diego, 1988. OG2–OG6.
"Counterpunch: The Fallout over *Miss Saigon*; It's Time to Overcome the Legacy of Racism in Theater." *Los Angeles Times* 13 Aug. 1990, Calendar: F3.
"The Past Meets the Future: A Cultural Essay." *Amerasia Journal* 17.1 (1991): 53–56.
"The Challenge of Diversity for African Americans and Asian Americans." *Multiracial Asian Times* 16 Nov. 1991: 1–2.
Introduction. *The Politics of Life: Four Plays by Asian American Women.* Ed. Velina Hasu Houston. Philadelphia: Temple UP, 1993. 1–31.
"Home." *Homemaking: Women Writers and the Politics and Poetics of Home.* Ed. Catherine Wiley and Fiona R. Barnes. New York: Garland, 1996. 277–81.
Introduction. *But Still, Like Air, I'll Rise: New Asian American Plays.* Ed. Velina Hasu Houston. Philadelphia: Temple UP, 1997. xv–xxii.
"No Passing Zone: The Artistic and Discursive Voices of Asian-Descent Multiracials." With Teresa Kay Williams. *Amerasia Journal* 23.1 (1997): vii–xii.
"To the Colonizer Goes the Spoils: American Progeny in Vietnam War Films and Owning Up to the Gaze." *Amerasia Journal* 23.1 (1997): 69–84.
"Uphill Fight for Asian American Plays." *Los Angeles Times* 15 Sept. 1997: F3.
"Kyakuin Kyoju/Kyakuin Kenkyuin no Peiji" [About visiting professor and visiting scholar]. *Doshisha University International Center News Letter* 1 (Dec. 1999): 5.

Interview

"Response." Interview. *Yellow Light: The Flowering of Asian American Arts.* Ed. Amy Ling. Philadelphia: Temple UP, 1999. 236–40.

Poetry

"Amerasian Girl." *Echoes IV* (1984): 25. Rpt. in *Pacific Citizen* (20–27 Dec. 1985): B2; *GIDRA* 1990: 111.
"Song of an Ainoko Granddaughter." *Echoes IV* (1984): 25. Rpt. in *Pacific Citizen* 20–27 Dec. 1985: B1.
"Half-Japanese." *Pacific Citizen* 20–27 Dec. 1985: B11.

"I Was Japanese Before It Was Cool." *Pacific Citizen* 20–27 Dec. 1985: B10.

"To My Japanese Grandfather on Seeing His Reflection in My Eyes." *Pacific Citizen* 20–27 Dec. 1985: B1.

"a taste of Honey." *Pacific Citizen* 19–26 Dec. 1986: B14.

"Blood." *dlSorient* 5 (1997): 69.

"Green Tea Girl in Orange Pekoe Country." *Amerasia Journal* 23.1 (1997): 161–62.

"Rearview." *Touchstone* Winter-Spring 1997: 35.

"The Soprano's Father: A Letter." *Intersecting Circles: The Voices of Hapa Women in Poetry and Prose*. Ed. Marie Hara and Nora Okja Keller. Honolulu: Bamboo Ridge P, 1999. 317–18.

Screenplays

"Journey Home." Wonder Works. PBS. KCET, Los Angeles. 1984.

War Brides. Taft Entertainment, 1984.

Kalito. American Film Institute, 1991.

Hishoku (Not Color). Adaptation from *Hishoku* by Sawako Ariyoshi. Prod. Margaret Smilow. Alternate Current International, 1992.

"Golden Opportunity." *The Puzzle Factory*. PBS. 1993.

"Leon for President." *The Puzzle Factory*. PBS. 1993.

"Pretty Perfect." *The Puzzle Factory*. PBS. 1993.

"The Rest Test." *The Puzzle Factory*. PBS. 1993.

Hothouse Flowers. Blue Turtle Films, 1994.

Studies of Velina Hasu Houston

Arkatov, Janice. "Playwright Draws on Experience of Growing Up in an Interracial Household." *Los Angeles Times* 27 Jan. 1991, Calendar: 94.

Arnold, Stephanie. "Dissolving the Half-Shadows: Japanese American Playwrights." *Making a Spectacle: Feminist Essays on Contemporary Women's Theatre*. Ed. Lynda Hart. Ann Arbor: U of Michigan P, 1989. 181–94.

"Beihei ni totsuida anna tachi no Jinsei" [The lives of women who married American GIs]. Review of *Tea*. *Asahi Shimbun* [Evening] 21 Feb. 1995: 12. Original in Japanese.

Berger, John. "*Mirror* Reflects on Maturation." Rev. of *The Matsuyarma Mirror*. *Honolulu Star-Bulletin* 4 March 1995: B2.

Berson, Misha. "*Tea*: Symbolism beyond the Beverage." Rev. of *Tea*. *Seattle Times* 15 Sept. 1995: G1–G2.

Birchall, Paul. "*Kokoro* (True Heart) at the Odyssey Theatre." *BackstageWest* 25 Apr. 1996: N. pag.

Breslauer, Jan. "Hues and Cries." Rev. of *Necessities*. *Los Angeles Times* 7 July 1991, Calendar: 3+.

Campbell, Bob. "Steeped in Tradition." Rev. of *Tea*. *Star-Ledger* [Newark] 27 Oct. 1989: 47+.

"Cha no Joen" [Production of *Tea*]. Rev. of *Tea*. *Hokubei Hochi* 6 Sept. 1995: 1. Original in Japanese.

Chinen, Karleen. "*Asa Ga Kimashita* (Morning Has Broken): A Moving New Production by Kumu Kahua." Review. *Hawaii Herald* 1 Feb. 1991: A13.

Churnin, Nancy. "Author's Heavy Hand Puts Bit of a Damper on *Tea*." Rev. of *Tea*. *Los Angeles Times* 28 Mar. 1988, sec. 6: 1.

————. "Play Steeped in Memories of a War Bride's Daughter." Interview with Velina Hasu Houston. *Los Angeles Times* 25 Mar. 1985, sec. 6: 1.

Colicchio, V.C. "*Asa Ga Kimashita/Tea*: Shattering an Honorable Triad." Rev. of *Asa Ga Kimashita* and *Tea*. *Daily Californian* 3 Apr. 1985: 13–14.

Drake, Sylvie. "Two Blistering Commentaries on Brutalization." Rev. of *Coming into Passion/Song for a Sansei* by Jude Narita and *Tea* by Velina Hasu Houston. *Los Angeles Times* 24 Apr. 1988, Calendar: 47.

D'Souza, Karen. "Cultures Clash: Sacramento Theatre Company Presents *Kokoro*—The Tragic Story of a Japanese Immigrant in America." Rev. of *Kokoro*. *Sacramento Bee* 9 Jan. 2000: EN18.

Foley, F. Kathleen. "*Kokoro* Goes to Heart of Mother's Woes." Rev. of *Kokoro*. *Los Angeles Times* 18 Apr. 1996: F10.

Green, Juliet. "*Tea* Steeped in Cultural Struggle." Rev. of *Tea*. *San Jose Mercury News* 9 Jan. 1990: 3D.

Gussow, Mel. "Stage: Negro Ensemble." *New York Times* 2 Feb. 1984: C17.

Harada, Wayne. "Casting About in the Sea of Humanity." Rev. of *Cultivated Lives* and *Hula Heart*. *Honolulu Advertiser* 10 Apr. 1996: D1+.

Hoang, Hahn. "Amazing Grace: Valina Hasu Houston Draws Strength and Inspiration from the Hard Adventure of Growing Up Black and Japanese." *Transpacific* July/ Aug. 1991: 37–45.

Holdcroft, Leslie. "*Curtain Call*." Rev. of *Tea*. *Alaska Airlines Magazine* Nov. 1995: 39–43, 67.

Hongo, Florence M. "Velina Hasu Houston: Truly Japanese and American." *Strength and Diversity: Japanese American Women, 1885 to 1990*. San Francisco: National Japanese American Historical Society, 1990. 29–30.

Hunt, Phil. "Firehouse Troupe Serves Stimulating Round of *Tea*." Rev. of *Tea*. *Oregonian* 25 Apr. 1988: C6.

Johnston, George. "Houston's *Tea* Proves a Strong, Strange Brew." Rev. of *Tea*. *Pacific Citizen* 12 May 1989: 3.

Kawarasaki, Yasuko. "Tatakau Onnatachi: Velina Hasu Houston no *Tea* ga Egaku Sensou Hanayome no Kisseki" [Women's struggles in Velina H. Houston's *Tea*]. *AALA Journal* 2 (1995): 47–55. Original in Japanese.

"Kokoro." Rev. of *Kokoro*. *New Yorker* 33 Apr. 1995: 16.

Kreisworth, Sandra. "Amerasian Playwright Steeps Work in Own Life's Experiences." *Santa Monica Outlook* 25 Jan. 1991: D3.

————. "Japanese War Brides Serve Up a Satisfying *Tea* at Odyssey." Rev. of *Tea*. *Santa Monica Outlook* 1 Feb. 1991: D16+.

Lee, Josephine. *Performing Asian America: Race and Ethnicity on the Contemporary Stage*. Philadelphia: Temple UP, 1997.

Ling, Amy. "Velina Hasu Houston, Playwright and Poet." *Yellow Light: The Flowering of Asian American Arts*. Ed. Amy Ling. Philadelphia: Temple UP, 1999. 236–40.

Matsumoto, Jon. "Surviving Junction City." *Rafu Shimpo* 13 Mar. 1991: 1+.

Matsuoka, Alan. "*Morning* Breaks on Kumu Stage." Rev. of *Asa Ga Kimashita*. *Honolulu Star-Bulletin* 23 Jan. 1991: B1+.

Miller, Matt. "Amerasian Lit Finally Is Finding Its Voice." *San Diego Union-Tribune* 25 Sept. 1995: D1+.

Murakami, Yuriko. *Ajiakei Amerikajin* [Asian Americans]. Tokyo: Chuo Koronsha, 1997. Original in Japanese.

Njeri, Itabari. *The Last Plantation—Color, Conflict, and Identity: Reflections of a New World Black*. Boston: Houghton Mifflin, 1997.

Ogawa, Ruby. Rev. of *The Politics of Life: Four Plays by Asian American Women*, ed. by Velina Hasu Houston. *Amerasia Journal* 19.3 (1993): 163–67.

Oliver, Edith. "The Theatre: Off Broadway, Explosive Mixture." Rev. of *American Dreams*. *New Yorker* 20 Feb. 1984: 104, 106.

Park, Menlo. "*Tea* Successfully Depicts the Life of Japanese 'War Brides.' " Rev. of *Tea*. *Peninsula Times Tribune* 11 Jan. 1990: 7.

Phillips, Michael. "*Tea* a Fragrant Blend of Comedy, Drama." Rev. of *Tea*. *San Diego Union-Tribune* 24 May 1997: E6.

"Playwright Velina Houston Reaps Sweet Dramatic Fruit from a Complicated Family Tree." *People Weekly* 23 (10 June 1985): 168.

Ramirez, Tino. "Cultural Mix Is Writer's Cup of Tea." *Honolulu Star-Bulletin* 30 May 1991: B1+.

Sawamura, Wataru. "Hito: Berina Hasu Hyusuton" [Profile: Velina Hasu Houston]. *Asahi Shimbun* 5 June 1994: 3. Original in Japanese.

Schneider, Anita. "Tempest Steams in TheatreWorks' *Tea*." Rev. of *Tea*. *Stanford Daily* 11 Jan. 1990: 4.

———. "TheatreWorks' *Tea* Explores Women Trapped between Cultures." Rev. of *Tea*. *Country Almanac* 10 Jan. 1990: 19.

Shimakawa, Karen. "Swallowing the Tempest: Asian American Women on Stage." *Theatre Journal* 47.3 (Oct. 1995): 367–81.

Shirley, Don. "*Tea* and Empathy: Velina Hasu Houston's Heartfelt Stories of Japanese War Brides." Rev. of *Tea*. *Los Angeles Times* 29 Jan. 1991: F1+.

Siegel, Ed. "Souls Struggle in Limbo in the Berkshires." *Boston Globe* 18 Aug. 1999: D1.

Tayler, Robert. "Ethnic Theatre Ensembles Produce a Hit and a Miss." Rev. of *Dreyfus in Rehearsal* by Jean-Claude Grumberg and *Thirst* by Velina Hasu Houston. *Oakland Tribune* 20 Jan. 1986: C1+.

"*Tii* Asukara Tokyo Koen: Senso Hanayome no Yorokobi to Kanashimi EgakJu" [*Tea* will be produced in Tokyo tomorrow: Joy and sorrow of war brides]. *Mainichi Shimbun* [Evening] 20 Feb. 1995: 9. Original in Japanese.

Uno, Roberta. Introduction. *Unbroken Thread: An Anthology of Plays by Asian American Women*. Amherst: U of Massachusetts P, 1993. 1–15.

Usui, Masami. "Creating a Feminist Transnational Drama: *Oyako Shinju* (Parent-Child Suicide) in Velina Hasu Houston's *Kokoro* (True Heart)." *Japanese Journal of American Studies* 11 (2000): 173–98.

———. "Dreams and Nightmares, Nightmares and Dreams in Velina Hasu Houston's *American Dreams*." *Kansai American Journal* 35 (1998): 32–53.

———. "Japan's Post-war Democratization—Agrarian Reform and Women's Liberation in Velina Hasu Houston's *Asa Ga Kimashita* (Morning Has Broken)." *AALA Journal* 5 (1998): 11–25.

———. "Voices from the 'Netherworld': Japanese International Brides in Velina Hasu Houston's *Tea*." *Chu-Shikoku Studies in American Literature* 34 (June 1998): 45–64.

"Velina Hasu Houston." *Women Playwrights of Diversity*. Ed. Jane T. Peterson and Suzanne Bennett. Westport, CT: Greenwood P, 1997. 166–70.

Viotti, Vicki. "Velina Hasu Houston: *Cake* Mix of Drama, Comedy." Rev. of *Christmas Cake*. *Honolulu Star-Bulletin* 8 Jan. 1992: D1+.

Weiner, Bernard. "Japanese War Brides Reflect during *Tea*." Rev. of *Tea*. *San Francisco Chronicle* 10 Jan. 1990: E4.

White, John W. "Good *Morning* Awakens Emotions." Rev. of *Asa Ga Kimashita*. *Honolulu Star-Bulletin* 25 Jan. 1991: B7.

Winer, Laurie. "A Collection with Much Missing." Rev. of *But Still, Like Air, I'll Rise*, ed. Velina Hasu Houston. *Los Angeles Times* 31 Aug. 1997, Calendar: 42.

Shih-I Hsiung
(1902–1991)

Yupei Zhou

BIOGRAPHY

Shih-I Hsiung was born on October 14, 1902, in Nanchang, China. He was educated at Peiping University (now Beijing University). After graduation, he began to be involved actively in theater managing, directing, teaching, and writing in mainland China, Hong Kong, and London. He assumed teaching jobs, each for a period of a year or two, at the Agricultural College and Chung Shan University in Nanchang and at Min Kuo University in Beijing. He started his major writing career after he began to live, on and off, in London, in the 1930s, where he became a lecturer at Cambridge University from 1950 to 1953. His major contributions to education also included his founding and acting as the first president of Tsing Hua College in Hong Kong in 1963, where he spent most of the rest of his life. Besides being an editor for a short period for the Commercial Press in Shanghai early in his life and chairing and serving on the board of directors of Standard Publishers Ltd. in Hong Kong in the 1950s, Hsiung was active mainly as a theater director and manager. Starting as an associate manager of Chen Kwang Theatre in Beijing in 1922, he later became the managing director of Pantheon Theatres Ltd. in Shanghai in 1929 and the managing director of Pacific Films Corporation Ltd. and the director of Konin Corporation Ltd., both in Hong Kong, in the 1950s.

Hsiung wrote in both English and Chinese. Before his first successful major publication, *Lady Precious Stream*, he tried his hand at playwriting by translating into Chinese some of Sir James Barrie's, Bernard Shaw's, and Shakespeare's plays. *Lady Precious Stream*, a play adapted from a classic Chinese tale in English, appeared in London in 1934. The following year, he published his second major play in English, *The Romance of the Western Chamber*, adapted from a classic Chinese play with the same name. He wrote his third major English play with Chinese subject matter, *The Professor from Peking*, in 1939. Besides plays, he also wrote two novels: *The Bride of Heaven* and *The Story of Lady Precious Stream*. His biography in English, *The Life of Chiang Kai-Shek*, was published in 1948.

MAJOR WORKS AND THEMES

Though Hsiung stated that his first play was mainly aimed at commercial success (Afterthought 177), his most important motive for writing plays in English was to introduce classical Chinese drama and authentic Chinese ways of life to the West. As Hsiung discovered, the average European perceived the Chinese as "a sinister monster" (Afterthought 185) and an opium addict (Afterthought 186), capable of black magic and concealing emotions under the mask of his perpetually expressionless face. Hsiung's plays were intended to correct these stereotyping and often-falsifying representations of the Chinese theater and of Chinese culture through staging in typical Chinese dramatic manner and costumes and through truthfully portraying Chinese characters as being capable of living a life of ideals, love, faith, courage, and justice.

While it is hard to say whether such an effect was achieved or not, it is at least true that Hsiung's first play made a quick hit in Europe and America. First staged after many barriers at the Little Theatre in London on November 28, 1934, *Lady Precious Stream*, within a short period of two or three years, was performed more than eight hundred times and was translated into four languages and on tour or in repertory in seven countries ("*Lady Precious Stream*"). Its popularity stemmed partially from Hsiung's talent with language and partially from its authentic Chinese staging, costumes, and subject matter. Hsiung's writing of this play was based upon memory rather than upon a written version of the tale and hence was easily adapted to the verse pattern of Western drama (Afterthought 179). The story concerns a prime minister's daughter, Precious Stream, who chose Hsieh Ping-kuei, her father's gardener, as her husband. Disinherited by her father, she went to live with Hsieh in a cave. Though Hsieh went to fight in a war and was thought to be dead, Precious Stream remained faithful to him. After eighteen years of separation from him, she reunited with Hsieh, who had become the king of the Western Regions. Love and faith won a sweeping victory over villainy and class snobbishness.

Compared to *Lady Precious Stream*, *The Romance of the Western Chamber* (1935) is more of a Chinese drama in that it was translated and adapted from a classical Chinese play with the same name. Whereas "*Lady Precious Stream* is a commonplace melodrama," in the playwright's own words, *The Romance of the Western Chamber* attempted to represent the achievement of classical Chinese drama from the very beginning as well as the ideal side of Chinese life (Afterthought 177). As a translation based on seventeen versions of the Chinese play, *The Romance* is more refined in language than *Lady*. Hsiung retained both the lyric pattern and the dramatic effect typical of classical Chinese drama, achieving both dramatic unity and poetic beauty. This story also tells about the daughter of a prime minister, Ts'ui Ying-ying, and her lover, Chang Chun-jui, who was from a humble family. But this time, the hero was not a warrior but an intellectual, and the reunification between the lovers was successfully carried out with the help of Ying-ying's maid, Hung Niang, who is symbolic of goodness, courage, talent, and justice.

Unlike Hsiung's first two plays, *The Professor from Peking* focuses on the present, but like the first two plays, *The Professor* is also aimed at depicting authentic modern Chinese life, this time through the life story of one man, the professor. The professor is a character of contradiction, both a villain and a hero, representing human nature true to people of all ethnic backgrounds. He pursues political power unscrupulously and lacks moral integrity regarding marriage and sexuality, but he shows love for his country, his children, and especially justice, for which he seems to be willing to sacrifice his son. Hsiung successfully depicted the conflict and disparity between appearance and essence and between the desire for power and the necessity for selflessness in life, private and public. The three-act spatial structure parallels the three important historical stages in China at the beginning of the twentieth century: Yuan Shih-Kai's claiming himself as the emperor of China, Kuo-Min-Tang's gaining power and popularity and cooperating with the Communist party, and Kuo-Min-Tang's massacre of Communist party members. At each stage, the crucial choice the professor faces is whose side to take in politics so that the interest of the country can be served while his own desire for power is also satisfied. The audience is led to believe that the professor is always good at working out a compromise between such selfish desire and the necessity to serve the nation until the last minute, when he expresses willingness to save the country at the sacrifice of his life. Hsiung ingeniously incorporated his hope for China's future into this ending of the play and satirized Europeans for their mistaking the partial for the whole, and the appearance for the essence, in their perception of the Chinese character.

CRITICAL RECEPTION

Current criticism of Shih-I Hsiung is almost a blank. In 1976, James Harbeck did a comparative study of *Lady Precious Stream* and *The Yellow Jacket* by George Hazelton and Harry Benrimo. His article focuses on their differences in regard to their authenticity and faithfulness to the characters of Chinese drama and ethnicity. Harbeck's conclusion is that *Lady Precious Stream* is a much more authentic representation of the Chinese and Chinese drama, though such authenticity was not appreciated at the time. His study is also a review of the reception of the production of the two plays when they were first staged.

Hsiung's plays received some immediate reviews, which were not unanimous in their opinions. Positive reviews, both on the literary merits and on the dramatic effect of the plays, all emphasized the novelty brought about by the Chinese background of the author and of the plays themselves. Just as one critic was deeply impressed by Hsiung's "charming, exotic, different, novel, captivating and refreshing" *Lady* (*Lady*, Advertisement), so was Gordon Bottomley by "the picturesque side of Chinese life" and "domestic scenes" presented by *The Romance* (x). Whereas some critics like Brooks Atkinson noted and gave credit to Hsiung's effort to introduce authentic Chinese drama to the Western world, others did not believe that Hsiung's plays were authentic Chinese because of their literary and artistic merits. When *Lady Precious Stream* came out, some concluded that the author either had an English collaborator or was not Chinese himself. Some negative comments, however, targeted the literary and dramatic weaknesses of the plays. Percy Hammond, for example, defined *Lady Precious Stream* as "a rich and colourful freak, abounding in all the shy innocence and dignity that is said to characterize the mysterious people from which it springs" (12). He stated that from the play "one learns [. . .] that the stage in China is more of a kindergarten than a sophisticated art" and that one could only watch the play "with the mentality of a child" (12). Another critic also commented that the play was a "venture [. . .] wrapped in the silken splendors of an Oriental prank" (*Lady*, Advertisement).

On the one hand, the sentimental ideals in the play do justify to a certain extent these reviewers' negative comments. On the other, their generalized attack was apparently unduly made on the ground that they equated ancient Chinese drama with modern China and that their views of the play were the extension of their stereotypic conception of the Chinese. In fact, the same can be said about most of the contemporary theater reviews of Hsiung's plays. As a result, the reviews may be appropriately used as valuable companion texts to the studies of Hsiung's plays.

BIBLIOGRAPHY

Works by Shih-I Hsiung

Drama

Lady Precious Stream; an Old Chinese Play Done into English according to its Traditional Style. Preface. Lascelles Abercrombie. London: Methuen, 1934.
Mencius Was a Bad Boy. London: Lovat Dickson and Thompson, 1934.
The Romance of the Western Chamber. London: Methuen, 1935.
The Professor from Peking. London: Methuen, 1939.

Selected Production History

Lady Precious Stream

Production. Little Theatre, London, 1934.
————, prod. Ken Spinks. Settlement Players, Letchworth Garden City, UK, 1937.

The Professor from Peking

Production. Highbury Players, Highbury Little Theatre, Sutton Coldfield, UK, 1942.

Biography

Life of Chiang Kai-Shek. London: Peter Davies, 1948.

Essay

"Occidental Fantasy." *New York Times* 9 Feb. 1936, sec. 10: 1+.

Novels

The Bridge of Heaven. New York: Putnam's Sons, 1943.
The Story of Lady Precious Stream. London: Hutchinson, 1950.

Translations

The Autobiography of Benjamin Franklin. Chinese. Shanghai, China: Commercial Press, 1932.

Studies of Shih-I Hsiung

Atkinson, Brooks. "Bards from Cathay." *New York Times* 23 Feb. 1936, sec. 10: 1.
Bottomley, Gordon. "Preface to *The Romance of the Western Chamber*." London: Methuen, 1935. ix–xii.
Hammond, Percy. Rev. of *Lady Precious Stream*. *New York Herald Tribune* 28 Jan. 1936: 12.
Harbeck, James. "The Quaintness—and Usefulness—of the Old Chinese Traditions: *The Yellow Jacket* and *Lady Precious Stream*." *Asian Theatre Journal* 13 (1996): 238–47.
Hsiung, Shih-I. Afterthought. *The Professor from Peking*. London: Methuen, 1939. 163–98.
"Imagination Plays an Important Part in *Lady Precious Stream*." *Boston Herald* 29 Nov. 1936: B5.
"*Lady Precious Stream*." *Booth Theatre Program* 27 Jan. 1936. N. pag.
Lady Precious Stream. Advertisement. *New York Herald Tribune* 29 Jan. 1936: 41.

David Henry Hwang

(1957–   )

Esther S. Kim

BIOGRAPHY

David Henry Hwang was born on August 11, 1957, in Los Angeles, California, and grew up speaking English at home in San Gabriel, a middle-class enclave south of Pasadena. Hwang is the son of a Shanghai-born father and a Chinese mother who was raised in the Philippines. In 1948, Hwang's father as a young man emigrated from Shanghai via Taiwan to California and received a business degree at the University of Southern California. His mother was sent in 1952 by her parents to the University of Southern California to complete her training as a classical pianist. Hwang's parents met at a foreign students' dance on campus and soon decided to get married. His mother's family was, however, devoted Protestant fundamentalist, and the two could not get married until his father converted to Christianity. Hwang and his two sisters were brought up with the fundamentalist teachings. His father became a successful businessman and a founder and owner of a bank. A professional pianist, his mother introduced Hwang to music early in life. He began to play the violin at the age of seven. His earliest experiences in theater were, in fact, playing the violin in pit orchestras for musicals in high school, although he never participated as an actor in the productions. He does remember, however, that he "liked to stay after rehearsal and listen to the director give notes" (Savran 119). The first nonmusical theater production Hwang saw was Arthur Kopit's *Indians* (1969) during his senior year of high school.

In college, he was expected to follow in his father's footsteps and major in business, but he attended Stanford University because it did not offer a business degree (Savran 117). He majored in English and in his sophomore year decided that "playwriting was something [he] could do" (Savran 119). In the same year,

Hwang renounced Christian fundamentalism, which would become a focal point of his plays such as *Family Devotions, Rich Relations*, and *Golden Child*. He had seen some shows at the American Conservatory Theatre and Magic Theater (both in San Francisco) during his freshman year and found the "idea of creating a world and then seeing it come to life" very appealing (Savran 119), so Hwang began to write plays without any formal training in playwriting.

Stanford University did not have a playwriting program at the time, but he found help from the novelist and English professor John L'Heureux, who told Hwang that he was writing "lousy plays because [he] was working in a vacuum" (Savran 119). Hwang took L'Heureux's advice and read as many plays as possible, and in the summer of 1978, before his senior year, he attended the first Padua Hills Playwrights' Festival, where he learned playwriting from Sam Shepard and Maria Irene Fornes, both of whom would continue to have a major influence on him. He learned to "access [his] subconscious" while "reading and seeing a lot of plays" (Savran 119–20). The conception of *FOB* began that summer.

The following spring, Hwang directed *FOB* in his dorm at Stanford and presented the production in front of friends and family. Before seeing the production, his parents had decided that they would approve of his writing career only if the play was good. By the end of the play, Hwang's father was brought to tears, and his parents have supported him ever since. Hwang submitted *FOB* to the 1979 Playwrights Conference of the O'Neill Theater Center, and it was accepted for a staged reading. The artistic director of the program, Robert Alan Ackerman, sent the play to Joseph Papp, who, upon reading and seeing the play, decided to include the play as part of the first Asian American theater showcase at the Public Theater in New York City. The play premiered at the Public Theater in June 1980 and was well received by critics and audiences. *FOB* won an Obie Award in 1980. Also in 1980, Hwang worked briefly at the Asian American Theater Company in San Francisco as a director, beginning a working relationship with other Asian American theater artists. There he directed Philip Kan Gotanda's *Song for a Nisei Fisherman*.

After receiving positive reviews of *FOB*, Hwang was encouraged by Papp to write more plays for the Public Theater. Hwang attended the Yale University School of Drama from the fall of 1980 to the spring of 1981. According to Hwang, he went to Yale for two reasons: "to buy time and to get a firmer grasp of theatre history" (Savran 120). By the end of his first year at Yale, Hwang moved to New York City because *The Dance and the Railroad* had opened off-off Broadway, and *Family Devotions* was scheduled to premiere at the Public Theater. In 1982, *FOB* premiered in Singapore. In 1983, Hwang wrote two "Japanese plays," *The House of Sleeping Beauties* and *The Sound of a Voice*, which premiered together at the Public Theater as "Sound and Beauty."

Around this time, Hwang stopped writing, mainly because of his discomfort with contradictory responses to his plays. At the age of twenty-four, he was not prepared to deal with early success and the emphasis on his ethnic background.

Hwang was inadvertently made a spokesman for Asian America. This, he admits, was inevitable, but he did not like the role. He found the critics and audiences too focused on his Asian heritage, and it caused a "very conflicted emotion" in him (Savran 123). He felt misunderstood as a writer and stayed away from writing for the following two years. He broke out of this period by writing *Rich Relations*, an autobiographical play that did not deal with ethnic issues. When the production was not received well, Hwang had to deal with failure not only as a writer coming out of a period of inactivity, but also doing so with his first non-Asian play.

Despite the negative reception of *Rich Relations*, which he calls "the first really big flop," Hwang was more certain than ever that he wanted to be a writer for the rest of his life (Frockt 131). The failure was actually liberating for Hwang; it gave him "tremendous freedom to say, 'I can do whatever I want'" (Frockt 131). With a renewed commitment to playwriting and sense of freedom, he began to write *M. Butterfly* in 1986. The idea of the play came to Hwang when he read an article in the *New York Times* about a former French diplomat and his Chinese lover of twenty years. The two were sentenced by a French court for spying for China, and during the court trials, the Chinese lover, who was a star of the Beijing Opera, was revealed to be a man. The diplomat testified that this news was shocking to him. Hwang immediately saw a potential play in the story but "purposely refrained from further research for [he] was not interested in writing docudrama" (Hwang, "Afterword" 95).

Using the article as a basic story line, Hwang filled in the details of the play with his imagination. "The story enabled me to pull together various concerns that I have about racism, sexism and imperialism. [It] was like a perfect little jar that could hold all these different subjects" (Gerard 45). With the encouragement of Stuart Ostrow, an independent producer, Hwang wrote the play and sent it to John Dexter, a distinguished theater director famous for his production of Peter Shaffer's *Equus* (1973). Dexter's response was immediate and positive. Dexter and Hwang met in December 1986 and began to work on the production together. *M. Butterfly* premiered at the National Theatre in Washington, D.C., on February 10, 1988. Although the play did not get a positive review in the *Washington Post*, it gained popularity and opened on Broadway on March 20, 1988. After that, the play "found a life of its own" ("Afterword" 97) and became the longest-running nonmusical play on Broadway since the production of Peter Shaffer's *Amadeus* (1980). It grossed over $35 million in box office in the United States and several million dollars more internationally and won the Outer Critics Circle Award and the Tony Award for best play of 1988.

With the immense success of *M. Butterfly*, Hwang found himself back in the same uncomfortable position as before: a spokesman for Asian America. The role was much more demanding than before, but this time around, Hwang was ready and willing to express his views as an Asian American playwright. He began to articulate his "evolution" as a playwright in America and his preoccupation with identity by describing different phases in his life: assimilationist, isolationist-nationalist, and multiculturalist. He argued, "America must not re-strict its 'ethnic' writers to 'ethnic' material, while assuming that white males can master any topic they so desire" ("Introduction," *FOB and Other Plays* xiii). While *M. Butterfly* was still playing on Broadway in 1989, he found himself increasingly interested in a "multiculturalism model" that was "more represen-tative of what this country is becoming" (Hwang, "Evolving" 19). He resisted the "literary segregation" and "cultural limitation" that came with the label "Asian American playwright." However, before Hwang could enjoy the artistic freedom that came with the success of *M. Butterfly* and become a "multicultural" playwright, he had to once again play the role of an Asian American spokesman when the *Miss Saigon* controversy broke out in the summer of 1990.

With other Asian American theater artists such as Tisa Chang and B.D. Wong, Hwang was one of the first to publicly protest against the "yellow-face" imper-sonation in the Broadway version of *Miss Saigon*. To Hwang, the controversy encompassed several complicated issues at both the personal and professional levels. First, living with *M. Butterfly*'s success proved more challenging than his marriage could handle. Hwang divorced his Chinese Canadian wife, Ophelia Chong, whom he had married in late 1985. He acknowledged that the divorce was tied to the success of *M. Butterfly*: "It bugs me that I fall into the cliché about having had some success and your marriage falls apart. But I do, so that's that" (Kelly B92). Second, the story of *Miss Saigon* seemed to overshadow his deconstruction of the opera, *M. Butterfly*, which had closed on Broadway only a few months before the controversy. In response to the pressure of producing a new play that could do better on Broadway, Hwang wrote *Face Value*, a play inspired by the *Miss Saigon* controversy.

Face Value was Hwang's first attempt at writing a farce, and he "made it more difficult for himself by forcing it to say something about political cor-rectness" (Kelly 25). He understood and supported both sides of the controversy: artistic freedom of the producers and discrimination against minority actors, but *Face Value* poked fun at a serious theme—the sociopolitical construction of racial identities in America—by putting Asian characters in whiteface as an impetus for the comic plot. Hwang worked on the first draft for six months and continued to revise it during the tryout process. Despite Hwang's optimism and political urgency, the play closed after eight previews at the Cort Theater on Broadway.

Between 1992 and 1997, Hwang lived a bicoastal life, writing screenplays in Los Angeles and working in theater in New York City. He wrote the film adaptation of *M. Butterfly*, although the final version of the film (starring Jeremy Irons and John Lone) was "more naturalistic" and less metaphoric than he had intended. For Hwang, the director David Cronenberg made artistic choices that differed from Hwang's: "I can't really accept the film as my own child" (Kondo, "Interview" 216). Hwang also wrote other screenplays, including *Golden Gate* (starring Matt Dillon). In theater, Hwang wrote two one-act plays, *Bondage* and *Trying to Find Chinatown*, which challenge the concepts of racial identity. *Bond-*

age premiered at the Humana Festival of New American Plays at Actors Theatre of Louisville in 1992 and starred Kathryn Layng, who graduated with a B.F.A. in acting from the University of Illinois at Urbana-Champaign. Hwang later married Layng, and their first child, Noah, was born in March 1996.

The birth of Noah influenced Hwang to write his most personal play, *Golden Child*. In 1996, Hwang was commissioned by South Coast Repertory of Costa Mesa, California, to write the play and received a Kennedy Center Fund for New American Plays production grant to produce it. *Golden Child* was based on a "novel" Hwang wrote at the age of eleven when he chronicled his family's history told by his Chinese-born maternal grandmother about her father. The story became the main source material for *Golden Child*. In November 1996, the play premiered at the Public Theater in New York City and went on Broadway in 1998. Around this time, Hwang decided to live in New York City permanently. "I feel like I don't have the moral fiber to live in L.A." (Raymond 2). The decision was also based on changes in his personal life, mainly his wish to settle down with his wife and their son.

Hwang's return to New York City was accompanied by favorable reception of *Golden Child*, including the Tony Award nomination for best play in 1998. Also in 1998, Hwang wrote an adaptation of Henrik Ibsen's 1867 dramatic poem *Peer Gynt* as the artist-in-residence at the Trinity Repertory Company. In 1999 and 2000, Hwang turned his attention to music dramas and musicals, writing three librettos for three different artists. He worked with music composer Bright Sheng and choreographer Muna Tseng to create *The Silver River*, a music drama based on a Chinese folk myth. The piece has been described as "fusion opera" and, like Hwang's plays, a mix of Eastern and Western influences. Commissioned by five organizations, including the Kennedy Center for the Performing Arts, *The Silver River* premiered at the Spoleto Festival in Charleston, South Carolina, in the summer of 2000. On Broadway, Hwang worked with Robert Falls and Linda Woolverton to write the book for *Aida*, the third Disney musical with music by Elton John and lyrics by Tim Rice. Hwang also wrote an adaptation of *Flower Drum Song*, keeping the Rodgers and Hammerstein score of 1958 but providing a new story line. The musical premiered October 2, 2001 at the Mark Taper Forum in Los Angeles. Currently, Hwang is working on a new play about the life of Paul Gauguin.

MAJOR WORKS AND THEMES

Since his first play, *FOB* (1979), Hwang has been concerned with such themes as ethnicity, identity politics, cultural diversity, Asian American issues, and East/West relations. Early in his career, he stated, "By confronting our ethnicity, we are simply confronting the roots of our humanity" (Savran 118). Indeed, Hwang has confronted the concept of ethnicity and has attempted to transcend sociopolitical limitations by transforming ethnic-specific issues into those of humanity.

FOB explores the cultural differences and tensions between Steve, a recent immigrant or "FOB" (fresh off the boat), and Dale, an assimilated Chinese American or "ABC" (American born Chinese). Caught in between is Grace, Dale's cousin, who is a journalism student at the University of California at Los Angeles. Set in the back room of a Chinese restaurant, the play begins with the meeting of Steve and Grace, who disagree on almost everything, especially their understanding of the Chinese mythic figures Gwan Gung and Fa Mu Lan. They decide to go out together with Dale, who drives a sports car and tries not to be "a Chinese, a yellow, a slant, a gook," but "just a human being, like everyone else" (Hwang, *Trying* 33). Steve plays to Dale's presumptions of "fob" by speaking only in broken English and grinning idiotically. But away from Dale, Steve is an eloquent, confident man who regards himself as the exiled Gwan Gung, god of "warriors, writers, and prostitutes." He echoes the voices of "yellow ghosts" (Chinese immigrants) who felt deceived by "white ghosts" along with their materialistic promises of America. Steve would rather enact his "fobbishness" in a community full of ABCs than show his true identity.

The juxtaposition of reality and myth becomes a major theme in *FOB* and Hwang's subsequent plays. Hwang credits Sam Shepard for influencing him: Shepard is "very conscious that . . . we, as a country, have a collective history" (Savran 120). Hwang traces the collective history of Chinese Americans, the "yellow ghosts" of both reality and myth and of both China and America. *FOB* is quintessentially American precisely because of its dramatization of immigration and assimilation.

Rooted in American theater, Hwang's dramaturgical style combines realism and symbolism but adds elements from Chinese theater. This use of both Western and Eastern theatrical elements has become Hwang's signature style, but Hwang's style was still at its experimental stage in *FOB*. In fact, the Chinese operatic style was not even in the play initially. When Joseph Papp of the Public Theater chose Mako of the East West Players as the director for the New York premiere, they decided to cast John Lone, who has a background in Chinese opera. Hwang worked with Mako and Lone to incorporate the Chinese operatic style into the revised version of the play. But, as Frank Rich of the *New York Times* notes, "If West and East don't precisely meet in *FOB*, they certainly fight each other to a fascinating standoff" ("Theater: *FOB*" C6). The two theatrical styles clash rather than reach a harmonious fusion, as they do in his later plays.

For his next play, Hwang "consciously set out to write a play that would combine Western and Asian theatre forms" (Savran 121). The result was *The Dance and the Railroad* (1981), which was developed with Tzi Ma and John Lone, who choreographed and directed the New York production. Like *FOB*, the play takes place in California, but a century earlier, in 1867, at a transcontinental railroad construction site. Its plot also juxtaposes two characters ("Lone" and "Ma") to explore the Chinese Americans' immigrant experiences of assimilation and exclusion. Lone is the more worldly, cynical, and proud character who has been in America for two years, while Ma is the naïve dreamer who has been in the country for only four weeks. Ma still believes that American mountains are made of gold and that by the time he goes back to China, he will "ride in gold sedan chairs with twenty wives fanning [him] all around" (Hwang, *Trying* 61). Lone, on the other hand, was trained as a child to be a Chinese opera actor, but his career was cut short when his impoverished parents sold him into servitude. After spending ten hours in railroad construction each day, he goes to a vacant mountaintop at night to practice his theatrical techniques so he won't feel like other Chinamen who are "dead" because "their muscles work only because the white man forces them" (*Trying* 66). Lone's practice not only introduces the Chinese operatic elements into the play, but also reinforces the theme that Lone works his muscles for self-betterment and thus to "live" as a human being, not as another coolie slave.

During the series of meetings between the two men on the mountain while they wait out a strike, Ma asks Lone to teach him acrobatic techniques, but Lone does not take Ma seriously. The characters' encounters and exchanges create humorous moments, especially when Ma ineptly tries to imitate Lone's striking movements. In the final section of the play, Ma and Lone improvise their own Chinese opera about "their harrowing sea journey to America and their subsequent adventures in the ostensible promised land" (Rich, "Stage" C5). By the end of this often-funny sequence, the power relation of the characters changes: Ma finds his inner strength and learns to "look at men with opaque eyes," and Lone finds himself dancing "for no reason at all," as if he had lost the illusions of both America and China.

For Hwang, the blending of Western theater and Chinese opera styles makes a political statement (Savran 121). This idea of using theatrical forms to make political statements began with *FOB* and *The Dance and the Railroad* and culminated in *M. Butterfly* (1988) as a powerful dramaturgical tool with an unforgettable theme. Using the form of theater (both Western and Chinese) and the mode of metatheatrical performance, Hwang explores in *M. Butterfly* the discrepancies of gender, sexuality, and Orientalism as they show on the surface as opposed to their truthfulness. This dynamic interplay of perception and deception makes *M. Butterfly* one of the most important American dramas in the twentieth century.

Hwang began writing *M. Butterfly* with the presumption that the French diplomat fell in love not with an actual person but with a fantasy stereotype of the Orient, the Madame Butterfly. *M. Butterfly* is set a few years earlier than the actual espionage story. In the play, the French diplomat (renamed Gallimard) sees the Peking opera star (renamed Song) for the first time at an embassy function where the singer performs the death scene from Puccini's *Madama Butterfly*. Gallimard compliments Song for portraying the "utterly convincing" Butterfly, but Song scoffs at him: "It's one of your favorite fantasies, isn't it?

The submissive Oriental woman and the cruel white man" (17). Song invites him to see "some real theatre," Peking opera, and so begins a relationship that lasts twenty years. In act 3, when the French judge asks Song how he fooled Gallimard, he answers: "One, because when he finally met his fantasy woman, he wanted more than anything to believe that she was, in fact, a woman. And second, I am an Oriental. And being an Oriental, I could never be completely a man" (83). These two points about the characters' relationship metaphorically represent the play's main themes. The first is the West's misunderstanding of the East as exotic, submissive, mystical, delicate, poor, and feminine. Conversely, the West thinks of itself as "masculine—big guns, big industry, big money" (83). Although Hwang had not read Edward Said's *Orientalism* before writing the play, the two texts complement each other as if the play is a dramatic example of Said's critical argument.

Song's second point addresses the West's underestimation of the East. Hwang uses the story line to make a specific commentary on World War II and the Vietnam War: "We didn't figure after the Second War that they'd come back and beat us at our own game. That sort of miscalculation also led us to believe that if we bombed Vietnam enough, they would all give in" (Gerard 44). Indeed, the power relationship between Gallimard and Song resembles a war in which only one winner comes out at the end. At the end of the play, Gallimard admits that he is a "man who loved a woman created by a man" but fails to give up his fantasy. Instead, he becomes the Butterfly and kills himself by acting out the death scene from *Madama Butterfly*. The last image the audience sees onstage is Song, standing as a man and smoking a cigarette and staring at the dead Gallimard. While the play is a deconstruction of *Madama Butterfly*, it is not, according to Hwang, an "anti-America" or anti-West play. "Quite to the contrary, I consider it a plea to all sides to cut through our respective layers of cultural and sexual misperception, to deal with one another truthfully for our mutual good, from the common and equal ground we share as human beings" (Hwang, "Afterword" 100).

In *M. Butterfly*, misperceptions of culture and sexuality are explored with multiple layers of theatrical metaphors, such as Song, who is a Peking opera performer, "performing" a gender and racial stereotype, and Gallimard telling his story in his prison cell and finally dying to the music of Puccini's opera. Hwang's subsequent plays also address the deceptive and performative nature of racial and sexual identities, but instead of using theater as a general metaphor, he uses the image of the mask to represent the powerful dynamic of identity construction and perception. *Bondage* (1992) is about Terri (a dominatrix) and Mark, who play out their fantasies at an S & M parlor "on the outskirts of Los Angeles." Both wear full masks, hoods, and full-body leather outfits "to disguise their identities," and together, they humiliate each other with racial stereotypes. One moment, Terri tells Mark that she is a black woman and he is a white man, and the next moment, Mark labels himself Asian and Terri white, which are their true racial identities. In each combination of role playing, a different set of power relations is formed, and one character humiliates the other for his or her pleasure.

As a result, racial identity becomes a matter of choice, not the color of the skin, and the idea of race becomes blurred to the point of complete confusion. In fact, Mark tells Terri: "I worry when I think about the coming millennium. Because it feels like all labels have to be rewritten, all assumptions re-examined, all associations redefined" (Hwang, *Trying* 277). At the end of the play, Terri and Mark remove their costumes and acknowledge their attraction to each other "beyond the world of fantasy." As Hwang has noted, the play is a romance of the two characters who overcome their fears of racial identity and cultural differences and discover each other's "human essence" (Frockt 145).

Hwang again redefines racial labels in *Trying to Find Chinatown* (1996) by moving even further away from the essentialist notions of race. In the play, Benjamin is a Caucasian male who was adopted and raised by Chinese American parents, and Ronnie is an Asian American male who plays "Hendrix-like virtuoso rock 'n' roll riffs" with his jazz violin on New York streets. Benjamin knows about Chinese American history and Chinese mythology and calls the Chinese American community "home," while Ronnie criticizes him as one of the "ethnic fundamentalists, always settling for easy answers" (Hwang, "Trying" 291). The characters' biological racial identities as "Asian" or "Caucasian" are only incidental, and their cultural identities are up for grabs. For Hwang, the play was "born out of [his] growing conviction that in the not-too-distant future, cultural identity will be a matter of personal choice" (qtd. in Wu).

Hwang chooses to define all of his work as "Asian American" because he defines himself as such, but he also recognizes the complexity the term carries (Hwang, "Response" 224). He deals with these and other personal identity issues in three autobiographical family plays: *Family Devotions* (1981), *Rich Relations* (1986), and *Golden Child* (1996). Hwang has admitted that the first two family plays "represent an attempt to deal with a lot of psychological issues from my past which may or may not be interesting to the general public" (Cooperman, "Across" 368). In *Family Devotions*, Hwang uses the ambiguity of the title to focus on the destructive influence of Christian fundamentalism on Asian culture and tradition. Echoing Sam Shepard's family plays, *Family Devotions* is a comically absurd play about a dysfunctional Chinese American Christian family that obsessively quarrels over who owns more material possessions. Hwang parodies the foundation of his family's faith and creates a "spiritual farce" that is "funny in the first act then turns dark and gets ritualistic in the second act" (369).

Rich Relations is similar to *Family Devotions* in many ways, including the characters who are consumed by vacuous Christian fundamentalism and accumulation of wealth and possessions. Although the ethnicity of the characters is not specified, the play dramatizes the absurdities Hwang observed in his own family. The main character, Hinson, is similar to Robert in *Family Devotions*, both of whom are modeled after Hwang's father, but in *Rich Relations*, "Hinson happens to be white" (369). Hinson and other members of the dysfunctional family play out their surreal tragicomedy in loud and chaotic ways and end up "resurrecting" to a hellish existence.

Hwang's third family play, *Golden Child*, provides a positive and realistic look at the influence of Christianity on his family. Written ten years after *Rich Relations* and after the success of *M. Butterfly*, *Golden Child* uses the style of Chekhovian naturalism to examine how his great-grandfather converted to Christianity. The play begins with the main character, Andre Kwang, being visited by his grandmother, Eng Ahn (the title character). Unfolding is a story about Eng Tieng-Bin, Eng Ahn's father and a wealthy Chinese merchant in Southeast China, who decides to convert to Christianity and adhere to Western ideas about love and individuality in the premodern China of 1918. Eng has three wives who show their subservience to him but often clash with one another behind his back. The first wife is traditional and addicted to opium; the second is crafty and strategizing to westernize; and the third is lovable and naïve. The clash worsens when Tieng-Bin unbinds Ahn's feet and adopts Christianity. His conversion requires that he have only one wife, leading to the wives' fierce and fatal power struggle. Tieng-Bin is advised by Reverend Baines, a Welsh missionary who does his best to introduce Western ideas to the family.

According to Hwang, the central issue in the play is "change as both a negative and positive force" (Berson, "Raising" M1). Indeed, the play is about one family's complex reaction to modernization and predicts China's fate in the following decades. Hwang has compared *Golden Child* to Anton Chekhov's *Three Sisters* for its ensemble cast and to Tennessee Williams's *Glass Menagerie* as a memory play. The play is also Hwang's most conventional play in terms of its dramatic structure and character development. Whereas his earlier plays deal with two characters in dialectic confrontation over identity and culture, with the weaker one often winning at the end, *Golden Child* is "more three-dimensional and emotional, and . . . more about people rather than ideas" (Raymond 3).

CRITICAL RECEPTION

From the beginning of his career, Hwang was recognized for asking questions about the Chinese American identity and combining Western theater conventions with those of the East. For theater reviewer Frank Rich, *FOB* was the "first show that [had] ever attempted to marry the conventional well-made play to Oriental theater and to mix the sensibilities of Maxine Hong Kingston and Norman Lear" ("Theater: *FOB*" C6). Maxine Hong Kingston, who saw the Public Theater production of *FOB*, understood what he was trying to do but also knew that he could do better: "The main question he asks [in *FOB*] is, What is Chinese-American? Is there a separate identity? In *FOB* there's a bit of borrowing from Chinese theater, but it's not Chinese theater. He's searching, and he hasn't found it yet" (Gerard 88). Other Asian American critics were not as encouraging. An Asian American newspaper review criticized Hwang and *FOB* for setting "Asian America back ten years" (Frockt 133). The majority of such criticism focused on Hwang's use of Asian stereotypes and his alleged failure to portray positive images of Asian Americans. While non-Asian critics often praised Hwang for his literary and dramaturgical styles and his ability to address political topics nondidactically, the Asian American community was understandably focused on what Hwang presented and represented. This crevice in critical reception widened as Hwang's commercial success increased.

M. Butterfly is by far Hwang's most successful and most discussed play. Although Hwang never compromised by making the play "more Broadway," some critics—mostly heterosexual Asian American men—questioned its intended audience and the use of the "effeminate" stereotype of the Asian man. Theater historian James Moy has criticized Hwang for perpetuating, rather than subverting, Asian stereotypes. Moy understands that Hwang's intention is to "offer a truer view of what it means to be Asian in the space created by the tension between the audience's stereotypical perception and his 'slangy and jarring' contemporary reality" (54). However, Moy points out that the character of Comrade Chan is "perhaps even more stereotypical and cartoonish than the worst of the nineteenth-century stereotypes," and Song Liling is "at best another disfigured stereotype": "s/he finally comes across as little more than a disfigured transvestite version of the infamous Chinese 'dragon lady' prostitute stereotype" (54). Therefore, Moy concludes that the play "affirms a nefarious complicity with Anglo-American desire in its representation of otherness, both sexual and racial" (54).

Equally critical is Frank Chin, who has maintained that Chinese American writers like Maxine Hong Kingston, Amy Tan, and David Henry Hwang "so boldly fake . . . Asian literature and lore in history" and cater to the whites by writing stereotypical "Chinese fairy tales" (Chin 2–3). Other Asian American critics have put forward similar arguments in more considerate terms. Josephine Lee in her chapter "The Seduction of the Stereotype" examines *M. Butterfly* using Homi Bhabha's concepts of mimicry and colonization. She concludes that "in [Hwang's] reappropriation of these myths [of cultural difference], no true version of the story emerges to correct the stereotype" (Lee 119–20).

However, for other Asian American theater artists, *M. Butterfly*'s tremendous success, including a Tony Award for best play, affirmed a sense of accomplishment for Asian American theater in general. In mainstream American theater, Hwang is recognized as one of the most important playwrights and, for some, as important as Arthur Miller, Tennessee Williams, and other major figures in American drama. While many critics have described *M. Butterfly* as an angry play in which Hwang condemns Western oppression of the East, an argument Douglas Kerr supports in his article "David Henry Hwang and the Revenge of Madame Butterfly," others agree that Hwang understands both cultures and provides a balanced assessment. Robert Cooperman states that "it is possible to see the emergence of a different, less commercial, and more culturally optimistic

David Hwang" if one focuses on Hwang's work before *M. Butterfly*, "suggesting how the theater can bring cultures together" ("New" 202).

In academia, *M. Butterfly* attracted and encouraged discussions of gender, sexuality, race, and imperialism. Robert Skloot, in "Breaking the Butterfly: The Politics of David Henry Hwang," outlines the play's three political topics: cultural politics, gender politics, and theatrical politics. Hwang "forces the audience of his play into complicity with the discovery, dismantling, and re-establishment of theatrical illusion, while at the same time confronting them with challenges to traditional cultural and gender assumptions" (59). Dorinne Kondo, an anthropologist, uses the play to discuss conventions of essentialist identity: "*M. Butterfly* reconstitutes selves in the plural as shifting positions in moving, discursive fields, played out on levels of so-called individual identities, in love relationships, in academic and theatrical narratives, and on the stage of global power relations" ("*M. Butterfly*" 27). Karen Shimakawa and others have also focused on the unstable nature of gender and ethnicity in *M. Butterfly* in their studies. Shimakawa uses several theoretical frameworks, including Judith Butler's concept of the "performativity of gender" and Jean Baudrillard's postmodern notions of time, space, bodies, and pleasures (349).

No other play by Hwang has matched the amount of critical discourse that *M. Butterfly* has prompted. His latest full-length play, *Golden Child*, received mixed reviews from theater critics, and a conversation in academia is yet to emerge. Fintan O'Toole of the *Daily News* comments that *Golden Child* comes short of being a "powerful evocation of the dilemmas of China's attempts to modernize itself" (59). Many critics agree that *Golden Child* is no match for *M. Butterfly*'s theatricality and success. For instance, Peter Marks of the *New York Times* describes it as "literary" and "novel-like" (E1). However, there are others who see improvement in *Golden Child*. Jerry Patch of South Coast Repertory states that with the play, Hwang may be "coming into a period of maturity where his work may take another quantum leap" (Raymond 1).

While responses to particular plays may vary, the overall positive reception of Hwang's work has not changed. As the only Asian American playwright with a Broadway record, Hwang has been put in an awkward, unsolicited position as a spokesman for Asian America, and this has consistently affected the reception of his plays in both mainstream and Asian American communities. The dynamic grew more complicated as Hwang's success and fame increased. Hwang himself has admitted that he has become a "Broadway playwright" and that having a Broadway play both made him and ruined him. "From the experience of having survived a commercial hit, I was infected, perhaps permanently, with a Broadway virus" ("Worlds Apart" 53). Incidentally, or perhaps not so incidentally, all of Hwang's successful plays feature Asian characters and/or theatrical conventions, while his failures, such as *Rich Relations* and *Face Value*, do not. This pattern seems to indicate an intricate relationship between commercial success and the entertaining values of "Asianness" on American stages. However, all criticisms aside, Hwang has certainly struck the perfect balance as a successful yet political Asian American playwright and has become a spokesman not only for Asian America but also for mainstream American theater.

BIBLIOGRAPHY

Works by David Henry Hwang

Drama

FOB. New York: Theatre Communications Group, 1979. Rpt. in *FOB; and, The House of Sleeping Beauties: Two Plays*. New York: Dramatists Play Service, 1983. 9–51; *Broken Promises: Four Plays*. New York: Avon, 1983. 1–57; *FOB and Other Plays*. Foreword. Maxine Hong Kingston. New York: New American Library, 1990. 2–49; *Trying to Find Chinatown: The Selected Plays*. New York: Theatre Communications Group, 2000. 1–51.

The Dance and the Railroad. The Dance and the Railroad; and, Family Devotions: Two Plays. New York: Dramatists Play Service, 1983. 9–43. Rpt. in *Broken Promises: Four Plays*. New York: Avon, 1983. 59–99; *FOB and Other Plays*. Foreword. Maxine Hong Kingston. New York: New American Library, 1990. 50–86; *Trying to Find Chinatown: The Selected Plays*. New York: Theatre Communications Group, 2000. 53–88.

Family Devotions. The Dance and the Railroad; and, Family Devotions: Two Plays. New York: Dramatists Play Service, 1983. 45–98. Rpt. in *Broken Promises: Four Plays*. New York: Avon, 1983. 101–68; *FOB and Other Plays*. Foreword. Maxine Hong Kingston. New York: New American Library, 1990. 87–146; *Trying to Find Chinatown: The Selected Plays*. New York: Theatre Communications Group, 2000. 89–150.

The House of Sleeping Beauties. FOB; and, The House of Sleeping Beauties: Two Plays. New York: Dramatists Play Service, 1983. 53–84. Rpt. in *Broken Promises: Four Plays*. New York: Avon, 1983. 169–208; *FOB and Other Plays*. Foreword. Maxine Hong Kingston. New York: New American Library, 1990. 147–82; *Trying to Find Chinatown: The Selected Plays*. New York: Theatre Communications Group, 2000. 177–213.

The Sound of a Voice. New York: Dramatists Play Service, 1984. *FOB and Other Plays*. Foreword. Maxine Hong Kingston. New York: New American Library, 1990. 183–209. *Trying to Find Chinatown: The Selected Plays*. New York: Theatre Communications Group, 2000. 151–75.

M. Butterfly. New York: Dramatists Play Service, 1988; Afterword by the Playwright. New York: Penguin, 1989.

As the Crow Flies. Between Worlds: Contemporary Asian–American Plays. Ed. Misha Berson. New York: Theatre Communications Group, 1990. 91–108.

Rich Relations. FOB and Other Plays. Foreword. Maxine Hong Kingston. New York: New American Library, 1990. 211–73.

Bondage. Trying to Find Chinatown; and Bondage. New York: Dramatists Play Service, 1996. 17–46. Rpt. in *Asian American Drama: 9 Plays from the Multiethnic Landscape*. Ed. Brian Nelson. New York: Applause, 1997. 127–55; *But Still, Like Air,*

I'll Rise. Ed. Velina Hasu Houston. Philadelphia: Temple UP, 1997. 157–78; *Trying to Find Chinatown: The Selected Plays*. New York: Theatre Communications Group, 2000. 249–79.

Trying to Find Chinatown. *Trying to Find Chinatown; and Bondage*. New York: Dramatists Play Service, 1996. 5–16. Rpt. in *Tokens? The NYC Asian American Experience on Stage*. Ed. Alvin Eng. New York: Asian American Writers' Workshop, 1999. 3–14; *Trying to Find Chinatown: The Selected Plays*. New York: Theatre Communications Group, 2000. 281–94.

Golden Child. New York: Theatre Communications Group, 1998; New York: Dramatists Play Service, 1999.

Unpublished Manuscripts

Aida. With Robert Falls and Linda Woolverton. Adaptation of *Aida* by Giuseppe Verdi, music by Elton John, lyrics by Tim Rice. 2000.

The Silver River. Libretto. Music by Bright Sheng. 2000.

Flower Drum Song. Musical. Adaptation of *Flower Drum Song* by Richard Rodgers and Oscar Hammerstein. 2001.

Selected Production History

FOB

Production, dir. David Henry Hwang; perf. Loren Fong, Hope Nakamura, and David Pating. Okada House Dormitory, Stanford, 1978.

Stage Reading, dir. Robert Alan Ackerman; perf. Ernest Abuba, Calvin Jung, and Ginny Yang. Playwrights Conference of the O'Neill Theater Center, Waterford, CT, 1979.

Production, dir. Mako; perf. Calvin Jung, Ginny Yang, and John Lone. Joseph Papp Public Theater, New York City, 1980.

———, perf. John Lone, Keone Young, and Kim Yumiko. East West Players, Los Angeles, 1980.

———, dir. David Henry Hwang; perf. Dennis Dun, Stan Egi, and Ann M. Tsuji. Pan Asian Repertory Theatre, New York City, 1990.

———, dir. Tzi Ma. East West Players, Los Angeles, 1997.

The Dance and the Railroad

Production, dir. John Lone; perf. John Lone and Tzi Ma. Henry Street Settlement's New Federal Theater, New York City, 1981.

———. Joseph Papp Public Theater, New York City, 1981.

———, dir. Alan Lyddiard; perf. Tom Yang and Unku. TAG Theatre (in collaboration with Singapore's Leling Beijing Opera Troupe), Glasgow, Scotland, 1992.

———, dir. Tzi Ma and Philip Kan Gotanda. East West Players, Los Angeles, 1993.

Family Devotions

Production, dir. Robert Alan Ackerman; perf. Jodi Long, Jim Ishida, Lauren Tom, Tina Chen, June Kim, Helen Funai, Michael Paul Chan, Victor Wong, and Marc Hayashi. Joseph Papp Public Theater, New York City, 1981.

The Sound of a Voice and *The House of Sleeping Beauties*
(produced as "Sound and Beauty")

Production, dir. John Lone and Lenore Kletter; perf. Ching Valdes, Victor Wong, Natsuko Ohama, John Lone, and Elizabeth Fong Sung. Joseph Papp Public Theater, New York City, 1983.

As the Crow Flies

Production, dir. Reza Abdoh. Los Angeles Theatre Center, Los Angeles, 1986.

Rich Relations

Production, dir. Harry Kondoleon; perf. Joe Silver, Keith Szarabajka, Phoebe Cates, Susan Kellermann, and Johann Carlo. Second Stage, New York City, 1986.

————, dir. Simon Fill; perf. Lane Nishikawa, Ken Narasaki, Andrea Stevens, Sharon Iwai, Janis Chow, Lisa Larice, and David Kim. Asian American Theater Company, San Francisco, 1991.

M. Butterfly

Production, dir. John Dexter; perf. John Lithgow, B.D. Wong, John Getz, Lindsay Frost, Lori Tan Chinn, Rose Gregorio, George N. Martin, Alec Mapa, Chris Odo, and Jamie H.J. Guan. National Theatre, Washington, DC, 1988.

————. Eugene O'Neill Theatre (Broadway), New York City, 1988–90.

————, perf. Anthony Hopkins, G.G. Goei, Lynn Farleigh, Tsai Chin, and Don Fellows. Shaftesbury Theatre, London, 1989.

Production (national tour), dir. Stuart Ostrow; perf. Philip Anglim, Alec Mapa, Alma Cuero, Brian Reddy, Rachel Jones, and Jennifer Lam. Colonial Theater, Boston, 1990.

————. Wilshire Theatre, Los Angeles, 1991.

————. Curran Theatre, San Francisco, 1991.

————. Civic Theatre, San Diego, 1992.

Bondage

Production, dir. Oskar Eustis; perf. B.D. Wong and Kathryn Layng. Actors Theatre of Louisville at the 16th annual Humana Festival of New American Plays, Louisville, KY, 1992.

————, dir. Cyndie Mastel. Theatre Off Jackson, Seattle, 1993.

————, perf. Beth Bayless and Robert Dahey. Asian American Repertory Theatre, San José, CA, 2001.

Face Value

Production, dir. Jerry Zaks; perf. Mark Linn Baker, Jane Krakowski, Mia Korf, and Dennis Dun. Colonial Theater, Boston, 1992.

———— (preview); perf. Mark Linn Baker, Jane Krakowski, Mia Korf, and B.D. Wong. Cort Theater, New York City, 1993.

Golden Child

Workshop. Trinity Repertory Company, Providence, RI, 1996.

Production, dir. James Lapine; perf. Tsai Chin, Stan Egi, John Christopher Jones, Jodi Long, Liana Pai, and Julyana Soelistyo. Joseph Papp Public Theater, New York City, 1996.

————. South Coast Repertory, Costa Mesa, CA, 1997.

————. Kennedy Center for the Performing Arts, Washington, DC, 1997.

————, perf. Tsai Chin, Randall Duk Kim, John Horton, Kim Miyori, Ming-Na Wen, and Julyana Soelistyo. Singapore Repertory Theatre, Singapore, 1997.

————. American Conservatory Theatre, San Francisco, 1998.

————. Longacre Theatre (Broadway), New York City, 1998.

————, dir. Sharon Ott; perf. Julienne Hanzelka Kim, James Saito, James Clay, Kim Miyori, Karen Tsen Lee, and Grace Hsu. Seattle Repertory Theatre, Seattle, WA, 1999.

————, dir. Chay Yew; perf. Melody Butiu, Robert Glaudini, Kerri Higuchi, Amy Hill, Daniel Dae Kim, and Emily Kuroda. East West Players, Los Angeles, 2000.

Trying to Find Chinatown

Production, dir. Paul McCrane; perf. Richard Thompson and Zar Acayan. Actors Theatre of Louisville at the 20th annual Humana Festival of New American Plays, Louisville, KY, 1996.

Anthologies

Broken Promises: Four Plays. New York: Avon Books, 1983.

FOB; and, The House of Sleeping Beauties: Two Plays. New York: Dramatists Play Service, 1983.

FOB and Other Plays. Foreword. Maxine Hong Kingston. New York: New American Library, 1990.

Trying to Find Chinatown; and Bondage. New York: Dramatists Play Service, 1996.

Trying to Find Chinatown; The Selected Plays. New York: Theatre Communications Group, 2000.

Essays

"Are Movies Ready for Real Orientals?" *New York Times* August 11, 1985, late city final ed., sec. 2: 1.

"Afterword." *M. Butterfly: With an Afterword by the Playwright*. New York: Penguin, 1988. 94–100.

"Evolving a Multicultural Tradition." *MELUS* 16.3 (Fall 1989–90): 16–19.

"Introduction." *FOB and Other Plays: With a Foreword by Maxine Hong Kingston*. New York: Plume, 1990. x–xv.

"Response." *Yellow Light: The Flowering of Asian American Arts*. Ed. Amy Ling. Philadelphia: Temple UP, 1999. 222–27.

"Worlds Apart." *American Theatre* 17.1 (Jan. 2000): 50–56.

Librettos

1000 Airplanes on the Roof: A Science Fiction Music-Drama. Music by Philip Glass. Beverly Hills, CA: Virgin Records, 1989. Rpt. in *FOB and Other Plays*. Foreword. Maxine Hong Kingston. New York: New American Library, 1990. 275–302.

The Voyage. Music by Philip Glass. *Trying to Find Chinatown: The Selected Plays*. New York: Theatre Communications Group, 2000. 215–48.

Monologue

"From Come." Written for Prince. *On a Bed of Rice: An Asian American Erotic Feast.*
   Ed. Geraldine Kudaka. Foreword. Russell Leong. New York: Anchor, 1995. 456–
   61.

Screenplays

Korea: Homes Apart. Motion picture. Third World Newsreel, 1991.
M. Butterfly. Motion picture. Geffen Pictures, 1993.
Golden Gate. Motion picture. Samuel Goldwyn Pictures, 1994.
Seven Years in Tibet. Motion picture. Tristar Pictures, 1997.

Television

"The Dance and the Railroad." Arts Cable Network. ABC. 1982.
"My American Son." HBO Network. 1987.
"The Monkey King." NBC. 2000.

Studies of David Henry Hwang

Berson, Misha. "The Demon in David Henry Hwang." *American Theatre* 15.4 (1998):
   14–18, 50–52.
———. "Raising the Golden Child." *Seattle Times* 26 Sept. 1999: M1+.
Chang, Williamson B.C. "*M. Butterfly*: Passivity, Deviousness, and the Invisibility of the
   Asian-American Male." *Bearing Dreams, Shaping Visions: Asian Pacific Amer-
   ican Perspectives.* Ed. Linda A. Revilla, Gail M. Nomura, Shawn Wong, and
   Shirley Hune. Pullman: Washington State UP, 1993. 181–84.
Chin, Frank. "Come All Ye Asian American Writers of the Real and the Fake." *The Big
   Aiiieeeee! An Anthology of Chinese American and Japanese American Literature.*
   Ed. Jeffery Paul Chan, Frank Chin, Lawson Fusao Inada, and Shawn Wong. New
   York: Meridian, 1991. 1–92.
Cooperman, Robert. "Across the Boundaries of Cultural Identity: An Interview with
   David Henry Hwang." *Staging Difference: Cultural Pluralism in American The-
   atre and Drama.* Ed. Marc Maufort. New York: Peter Lang, 1995. 365–73.
———. "New Theatrical Statements: Asian Western Mergers in the Plays of David
   Henry Hwang." *Staging Difference: Cultural Pluralism in American Theatre and
   Drama.* Ed. Marc Maufort. New York: Peter Lang, 1995. 201–13.
Deeney, John J. "Of Monkeys and Butterflies: Transformations in M.H. Kingston's *Trip-
   master Monkey* and D.H. Hwang's *M. Butterfly*." *MELUS* 18.4 (Winter 1993–94):
   21–39.
DiGaetani, John L. "An Interview with David Henry Hwang." *A Search for a Postmodern
   Theater: Interviews with Contemporary Playwrights.* New York: Greenwood P,
   1991. 161–74.
Eng, David L. "In the Shadows of a Diva: Committing Homosexuality in David Henry
   Hwang's *M. Butterfly*." *Amerasia Journal* 20.1 (1994): 93–116.
Frockt, Deborah. "David Henry Hwang." *The Playwright's Art: Conversations with Con-
   temporary American Dramatists.* Ed. Jackson R. Bryer. New Brunswick, NJ: Rut-
   gers UP, 1995. 123–146.

Gerard, Jeremy. "David Hwang: Riding on the Hyphen." *New York Times Magazine* 13 Mar. 1988, sec. 6: 44+.

Herman, Jan. "M. As in Metamorphosis." *Los Angeles Times* 3 Nov. 1996, Calendar: 6.

Kelly, Kevin. "Hwang Looks beyond *Face Value*." *Boston Globe* 17 Feb. 1993, Living: 25+.

———. "M. Butterfly, Miss Saigon and Mr. Hwang." *Boston Globe* 9 Sept. 1990: B89+.

Kerr, Douglas. "David Henry Hwang and the Revenge of Madame Butterfly." *Asian Voices in English*. Ed. Mimi Chan and Roy Harris. Hong Kong: Hong Kong UP, 1991. 119–130.

Kingston, Maxine Hong. Foreword. *FOB and Other Plays*. By David Henry Hwang. New York: New American Library, 1990. vii–ix.

Kondo, Dorinne. "Interview with David Henry Hwang." *About Face: Performing Race in Fashion and Theater*. New York: Routledge, 1997. 211–25.

———. "*M. Butterfly*: Orientalism, Gender, and a Critique of Essentialist Identity." *Cultural Critique* 16 (Fall 1990): 5–29.

Lee, Josephine. "The Seduction of the Stereotype." *Performing Asian America: Race and Ethnicity on the Contemporary Stage*. Philadelphia: Temple UP, 1997. 89–135.

Loo, Chalsa. "*M. Butterfly*: A Feminist Perspective." *Bearing Dreams, Shaping Visions: Asian Pacific American Perspectives*. Ed. Linda A. Revilla, Gail M. Nomura, Shawn Wong, and Shirley Hune. Pullman: Washington State UP, 1993. 177–80.

Lye, Colleen. "*M. Butterfly* and the Rhetoric of Antiessentialism: Minority Discourse in an International Frame." *The Ethnic Canon: Histories, Institutions, and Interventions*. Ed. David Palumbo-Lin. Minneapolis: U of Minneapolis P, 1995. 260–89.

Lyons, Bonnie. " 'Making His Muscles Work for Himself': An Interview with David Henry Hwang." *Literary Review* 42.2 (Winter 1999): 230–44.

Marks, Peter. "The Unbinding of Traditions." *New York Times* 3 Apr. 1998: E1.

Marx, Robert. "Hwang's World." *Opera News* 57.4 (October 1992): 14–17.

Moss-Coane, Marty, and John Timpane. "David Henry Hwang." *Speaking on Stage: Interviews with Contemporary American Playwrights*. Ed. Philip C. Kolin and Colby H. Kullman. Tuscaloosa: U of Alabama P, 1996. 277–90.

Moy, James S. "David Henry Hwang's *M. Butterfly* and Philip Kan Gotanda's *Yankee Dawg You Die*: Repositioning Chinese American Marginality on the American Stage." *Theatre Journal* 42.1 (1990): 48–56.

O'Toole, Fintan. "*Golden* Opportunity Lost." *Daily News* (New York) 3 Apr. 1998: 59.

Pace, Eric. " 'I Write Plays to Claim a Place for Asian-Americans.' " *New York Times* 12 July 1981: D4.

Pao, Angela. "The Critic and the Butterfly: Sociocultural Contexts and the Reception of David Henry Hwang's *M. Butterfly*." *Amerasia Journal* 18.3 (1992): 1–16.

Raymond, Gerard. "Good as Gold." *Stagebill* March 1998: 1–3.

Remen, Kathryn. "The Theatre of Punishment: David Henry Hwang's *M. Butterfly* and Michel Foucault's *Discipline and Punish*." *Modern Drama* 37.3 (Fall 1994): 391–400.

Rich, Frank. " 'M. Butterfly,' a Story of a Strange Love, Conflict, and Betrayal." *New York Times* 21 Mar. 1988: C13.

———. "Stage: 'Dance, Railroad,' by David Henry Hwang." *New York Times* 31 Mar. 1981: C5.

———. "Theater: *FOB*, Rites of Immigrant Passage." *New York Times* 10 June 1980: C6.

————. "Theater: Hwang's *Family Devotions*." *New York Times* 19 Oct. 1981: C17.

Savran, David. "David Hwang." *In Their Own Words: Contemporary American Playwrights*. New York: Theatre Communications Group, 1988. 117–31.

Shimakawa, Karen. " 'Who's to Say?' or, Making Space for Gender and Ethnicity in *M. Butterfly*." *Theatre Journal* 45.3 (1993): 349–61.

Skloot, Robert. "Breaking the Butterfly: The Politics of David Henry Hwang." *Modern Drama* 33.1 (March 1990): 59–66.

Street, Douglas. *David Henry Hwang*. Boise: Boise State U, 1989.

Trudeau, Lawrence J., ed. "David Henry Hwang." *Asian American Literature: Reviews and Criticism of Works by American Writers of Asian Descent*. Detroit: Gale Research, 1999. 151–68.

Winer, Laurie. "Tracing a Family's Past, Future through Eyes of *Golden Child*." *Los Angeles Times* 20 Nov. 1996: F1.

Wu, Decker. "Trying to Find Chinatown." *Ten Minute Plays*. 16 Sept. 2001 <http://www.happening.com.sg/performance/features/1996/may/ten-minute-plays/tryingtofindchinatown.html>.

Momoko Iko

(1940–   )

Louis J. Parascandola

BIOGRAPHY

Momoko Iko was born in Wapato, Washington, on March 30, 1940, the daughter of Kyokuo and Natsuko (Kagawa) Iko. In 1942, she and her family of eight were forced to move to the Heart Mountain Concentration Camp in Wyoming for reasons of "military necessity." After being released from the camp in 1945, the family worked as migrant farm workers in New Jersey before arriving in Chicago, where Iko's father took a job as a laborer and her mother did piecework sewing. Iko notes in her prose-poem "And There Are Stories, There Are Stories" that despite having to endure racial taunts as well as "my confusing pain and the stumbling drunken pain of my father," there was comfort and support, particularly from her mother. The family home became a center for other Japanese to gather, and young Momoko absorbed the stories she heard, which would eventually turn into the grist for her writing.

Iko's writing career began while she was at Northern Illinois University and continued at the University of Illinois at Urbana-Champaign, where she received her B.A. in English (with honors) in 1961. She also studied at the Instituto Allende in Mexico and began her M.F.A. at the University of Iowa, where she met author Nelson Algren, whose impact on her is recounted in her essay "A Memorial Service Is Not a Story."

Iko's work originally took the form of poetry, essays, and fiction, but after seeing Lorraine Hansberry's *A Raisin in the Sun*, she realized the political capabilities of drama. Her first play, *Gold Watch*, took shape from an unpublished novel. The play remains her best known work, having had several productions and having been shown on television by PBS in 1975. Iko, however, has written a number of other plays, including *Flowers and Household Gods, Hollywood Mirrors,* and *Boutique Living and Disposable Icons.*

Winner of awards from the East West Players, the Rockefeller Foundation, the National Endowment for the Arts, and the Zellerbach Foundation, she has held a number of positions as an administrator, teacher, and visiting artist in Chicago and Los Angeles, where she moved in the late 1970s and continues to live. She has also written and produced films for the Japanese American Service Committee.

MAJOR WORKS AND THEMES

Although Iko was only a child when she was interned, the experience, kindled by the stories of her parents and others, is the major theme in her work. She explains in an interview with Roberta Uno, "I know I absorbed a lot of the camps. . . . [I]t comes out in dreams, in a sensibility, in senses. . . . when I write that's when it comes out" (106). The incidents leading up to this forced relocation and the valiant resistance to it are vividly rendered in her play *Gold Watch* (1970), loosely based on her parents' struggles. The play, set in 1941–42, deals with a Japanese American farm family and community made to leave their homes shortly after the commencement of World War II. The play, "[p]redating the redress and reparation movement. . . . is an early call to break the silence and end the shame surrounding incarceration" (Uno 109). The central figure, Masu Murakami, is a complex character who proudly refuses to accept charity even as his family struggles. He desperately wants the respect of his son, who wants to return to Japan. When the community is told to move, Masu becomes the leading force of resistance. Eventually, he is killed while fighting nightriders, and the son is left holding his father's broken body and clutching the gold watch given to him by his father, a bitter legacy of Masu's failed dreams of America. Ironically, it is the tragedy of this lost dream, initiated by racism, that finally links the two men (Lee 143–48).

Reviewer Luis H. Francia notes that *Flowers and Household Gods* (1975) has several themes, including "the disintegration of family structure; cultural sterility caused by assimilation; the gap between those born here and those not; identity crises brought about by conflicting cultures" (88). Set in Chicago in 1968, the play focuses on three generations of a Japanese American family, the Kagawas. The play opens with the funeral of the family matriarch, and at its core is an intergenerational and intercultural struggle. The family patriarch has never recovered from his humiliating internment, sinking into alcoholism. His nisei (second-generation) children, Mas, Junko, and Mazie, are trapped between American and Japanese cultures. Camp life had caused a distortion of traditional Japanese values and the family hierarchy (Arnold 187–88).

Whereas the center of *Flowers and Household Gods* is a family gathering at a funeral, the focal point for the sequel, *Boutique Living and Disposable Icons* (1987), is the impending wedding of Mazie's niece, who is to marry a nisei,

Glenn, who desperately wants to be considered an American. The play scrutinizes the often-painful and confusing process of assimilation, particularly in the sharp exchanges between Mazie, an ex-hippie still in search of her identity, and Glenn's father, who clings to his Japanese heritage.

Although Iko's works are generally serious and realistic, there is often a humorous touch to them. The arrogant groom-to-be and his pretentious mother, for example, are poked fun at in *Boutique Living and Disposable Icons*. This biting humor is most evident in *Hollywood Mirrors* (1978), a play written and directed by Iko. Utilizing music and dance, the work satirizes the "stereotypes of Asians from films, TV and comic books" and finally reveals "the real person and real human relations and emotions behind those masks" (Weiner 47). Whether Iko chooses to write in a realistic or a comic style, her major focus is still the same: to demonstrate the need for peoples of different ages, genders, races, and ethnic backgrounds to attempt a better understanding of one another.

CRITICAL RECEPTION

There has been little critical response to Iko's work. Stephanie Arnold, though generally giving a favorable account of *Flowers and Household Gods*, regrets that she is unable to write more about Iko because "only limited access to her work was available" (193). Accessibility remains a problem for Iko's work since only *Gold Watch* is in print and several other typescripts are available in scattered archives. In addition, aside from *Gold Watch*, her plays have seldom been revived.

As a result, critical evaluation of Iko has essentially been confined to reviews of her television and theater productions. John J. O'Connor writes of the television broadcast of *Gold Watch* that the play "is both moving and powerful," even if "[k]ey incidents too frequently take place off stage" (81). Daniel Henninger feels that the play "is a flat-out success, as fine a play as anyone interested in new American playwrights could hope for" (22). Lee Margulies calls it "a powerful and moving statement about the struggle for human dignity" (28).

There have been few reviews of Iko's other theatrical works. Luis H. Francia writes that "[t]hough flawed, [*Flowers and Household Gods*] is genuinely moving. When it focuses on the youngest daughter, an aspiring artist, it becomes resolute, inscribing the circle of wholeness" (88). Mel Gussow of the *New York Times* feels that in the same play "[t]he playwright has given her characters a bedrock of specificity," and he calls it "one of the Pan Asian Theater's most praiseworthy ventures" ("Stage" C7). Gussow is less favorable toward *Boutique Living and Disposable Icons*, saying that it "is neither as moving nor as well written as the original play, and several scenes and characters are conceived with too broad a hand," although he praises Iko's satirical touch in the play ("Ethnic" C20). In contrast, Richard Hornby and Irene Backalenick praise *Boutique Living*. Hornby calls it "a low-key yet insightful and engaging play" (4), and Backalenick observes that despite some confusing moments, "this play is well worth seeing, all the same, for its insights into one particular segment of the American population" (45).

Momoko Iko is the first Asian American woman to have had a play produced in the continental United States. Her work has been produced at several major theaters. She was included in the groundbreaking collection of Asian American literature *Aiiieeeee!* in 1974. It is hoped that the growing interest in Asian American literature in recent years will result in the availability of more of Iko's work and increasing critical examination of this important but undervalued writer.

BIBLIOGRAPHY

Works by Momoko Iko

Drama

Gold Watch. Act 1. *Aiiieeeee!: An Anthology of Asian-American Writers*. Ed. Frank Chin, Jeffery Paul Chan, Lawson Fusao Inada, and Shawn Hsu Wong. Washington, DC: Howard UP, 1974. 88–114.

Gold Watch. *Unbroken Thread: An Anthology of Plays by Asian American Women*. Ed. Roberta Uno. Amherst: U of Massachusetts P, 1993. 111–53.

Unpublished Manuscripts

When We Were Young. East West Players Archives, U of California, Los Angeles, 1973.

Flowers and Household Gods. Ms. 345. Roberta Uno, Asian American Playwrights Scripts Collection 1924–1992, Special Collections and Archives, W.E.B. Du Bois Library, U of Massachusetts, Amherst, 1975.

Second City Flat. Ms. 345. Roberta Uno, Asian American Playwrights Scripts Collection, 1924–1992, Special Collections and Archives, W.E.B. Du Bois Library, U of Massachusetts, Amherst, 1976.

Hollywood Mirrors. Asian American Theater Company Archives, U of California, Santa Barbara, 1978.

Boutique Living and Disposable Icons. NCOF+ 95–9620. Library for the Performing Arts, New York Public Library, 1987.

Selected Production History

Gold Watch

Production, dir. C. Bernard Jackson. Inner City Cultural Center, Los Angeles, 1972.

———. Visions Series. PBS. KCET, Los Angeles. 11 Nov. 1976.

———. U of Washington, Seattle, 1976.

———. Stanford U, Stanford, CA, 1977, 1982, 1987, and 1988.

———. Northwest Asian American Theatre, Seattle, 1998.

When We Were Young

Production. East West Players, Los Angeles, 1974.

———. Asian American Theater Company, San Francisco, 1976.

Second City Flat

Production. Inner City Cultural Center, Los Angeles, 1978.

Hollywood Mirrors

Production. Asian American Theater Company, San Francisco, 1978.

Flowers and Household Gods

Staged reading. Smith College, Northampton, MA, 1979.
Production, dir. Tisa Chang. Pan Asian Repertory Theatre in association with La Mama
E.T.C., New York City, 1981.
————. Pan Asian Repertory Theatre. Videocassette. NCOV 157. Theatre in Film and
Tape Archive, Library for the Performing Arts, New York Public Library, New
York City, 1981.
————. Northwest Asian American Theatre, Seattle, 1984.

Boutique Living and Disposable Icons

Production, Pan Asian Repertory Theatre, New York City, 1988.

Essays

"A Memorial Service Is Not a Story." *Pacific Citizen* 19–26 Dec. 1986: B6+.
"Redress: Act of Atonement So They Can Face Their Gods." *Los Angeles Times* 11 Aug.
1988, sec. 2: 7.

Poetry

"And There Are Stories, There Are Stories." *Greenfield Review* 6.1–2 (1977): 39–46.
Rpt. in *Rafu Shimpo* 20 Dec. 1980: 20–21.

Studies of Momoko Iko

Arnold, Stephanie. "Dissolving the Half Shadows: Japanese American Women Play-
wrights." *Making a Spectacle: Feminist Essays on Contemporary Women's The-
atre*. Ed. Lynda Hart. Ann Arbor: U of Michigan P, 1989. 181–94.
Backalenick, Irene. "Not without Flaws, but Well Worth Seeing." Rev. of *Boutique Liv-
ing and Disposable Icons*. *Westport* (CT) *News* 1 July 1988: 45.
Contemporary Authors: A Bio-Bibliographical Guide. Vol. 14. New Revision Series. Ed.
Linda Metzger. Detroit: Gale Research, 1985. 243.
Francia, Luis H. Rev. of *Flowers and Household Gods*. *Village Voice* 26.18 (1981): 88.
Gussow, Mel. "Ethnic Identity Confusion for Japanese-Americans." Rev. of *Boutique
Living and Disposable Icons*. *New York Times* 30 June 1988: C20.
————. "Stage: Nisei Internment." Rev. of *Flowers and Household Gods*. *New York
Times* 21 Apr. 1981: C7.
Henninger, Daniel. "Visions: Public TV Takes a Chance." Rev. of *Gold Watch*. *National
Observer* 13 Nov. 1976: 22.
Hornby, Richard. "Rich Pacifics." Rev. of *Boutique Living and Disposable Icons*. *New
York Press* 1 July 1988: 3–4.
Lee, Josephine. *Performing Asian America: Race and Ethnicity on the Contemporary
Stage*. Philadelphia: Temple UP, 1997.

Margulies, Lee. "Fight for Dignity in *Gold Watch*." *Los Angeles Times* 11 Nov. 1976, sec. 4: 28.

O'Connor, John J. Rev. of *Gold Watch*. *New York Times* 11 Nov. 1976: 81.

Uno, Roberta. "Momoko Iko." *Unbroken Thread: An Anthology of Plays by Asian American Women*. Ed. Roberta Uno. Amherst: U of Massachusetts P, 1993. 103–9.

Weiner, Bernard. "Taking a Flight from Soul-Pounding." *San Francisco Chronicle* 13 Nov. 1978: 47.

Susan Kim

(1958–   )

Andrew L. Smith

BIOGRAPHY

Susan Kim was born on December 10, 1958, in New York City to well-educated Korean parents who moved to America in the 1950s shortly after the Korean War in order for Kim's father to complete residencies and internships stateside. Kim's mother, from the southern city of Pusan, was the daughter of Kim Marl Bong, a well-known female writer from the earlier part of the twentieth century who had written the popular novel *Gilly Flower* as well as the lyrics to the song "The Swing." Thus writing was in the bloodlines, which may explain, in part, Kim's sense that she could not imagine a profession other than writing.

Kim's father, the third generation of doctors in his family, had previously escaped from the North. The family lived in New York City for two years before moving for the father's next medical assignment in Brookline, Massachusetts, then to Brighton, then to New Hampshire for a summer, and then to Concord. All the while, Kim's parents intended to return to Korea, but as the family grew to five and the children began speaking English at home, Kim's parents surmised that their children should remain in America, the country of their birth.

The family's transience was not easy for the children, who were always "the new kids on the block." Coupled with the rough culture of 1960s and New York City working-class neighborhoods, the constant moves created a family of shy, bookish children. "[R]eading was tremendously important," Kim reflected during my interview, as if that were her refuge. "I read a lot when I was a kid. [My friends and I] did a lot of pretending, and making up stories, and putting on shows. . . . I do the same things now. I read. I make up stories" (Personal interview).

Kim's parents encouraged all her siblings to read and write. As a child of about three or four, Kim folded over a piece of paper, scribbled on all sides, and announced that she had written a book. In junior high school, she discovered Tennessee Williams's *The Glass Menagerie* and *A Streetcar Named Desire* and soon became transfixed on theater. Although she acted in high school and later founded a college improvisation group called Spontaneous Combustion, she found that acting, for her, was "fundamentally interpretive, as opposed to creative" (Personal interview). Writing, not acting, was also a career that her parents supported after she expressed disinterest in pursuing a medical degree. Writing is an honorable profession in their eyes, as Kim explained, and "respecting your parents—even in their wishes for your career—is a very big thing" in Korean culture (Personal interview).

Like some other young and aspiring writers and artists, Kim went through a period of a reaction against her initial proclivity. For several years after she graduated with a B.A. from Wesleyan University in Middletown, Connecticut, she did not write or attend theater performances, but worked as a television producer for Public Television in New York. Although she was already co-producing an eight-part series for PBS within a few years of service, she found the work unfulfilling. She began to take playwriting classes in her spare time. Writing appealed to her again thanks to the challenges of composing dialogue: "the balance between what's said and what's not said, and the dynamics of communication" (Personal interview). A year later, Kim won a Drama League Award for *Open Spaces* (1988), her first full-length play. A year after that, she quit television production. Kim has been working full-time writing commissioned plays and scripts for children's television ever since.

MAJOR WORKS AND THEMES

The ideas of openness and communication pervade Kim's work on the stage and on the screen. Kim's characters are often housed in darker comedies, and her themes center on the psychological rather than the social or political. Kim has always been drawn to characters who find themselves somewhat disconnected within—people who have tried to create a certain world for themselves, or an image of self, that is ultimately at odds with who they really are.

Stuck in a "middle-class hell," Lorraine in *Rapid Eye Movement* (1991) is seized by a nameless terror that manifests itself as a roaming pack of wild dogs just outside her door. Gabby in *Seventh Word, Four Syllables* (1993) flees a husband who tries to carve her into the kind of spouse he believes he must have. Jing-Mei Woo of *The Joy Luck Club* (1993) has to make a journey to China— symbolic of "a voyage toward understanding and accepting the very heritage that makes her a Chinese American," as Kim notes in the program for the North American debut of *The Joy Luck Club* at Long Wharf Theater. In *Where It Came From* (2000), Sara hearkens back to a forgotten childhood to begin to find the source of her aberrant behavior as a grownup. However, Kim's women characters generally share that "strength to suffer silently" and the desire to "question things they always assumed were basic truths" (Personal interview).

But writing as an Asian American does not mean that all of Kim's plays or themes are about Asians or Asian Americans. The tendency in theater as elsewhere to categorize a writer's themes by his or her ethnicity is rather limiting to her. She considers writing, like any other creative pursuit, to be ultimately about self-expression—the self lies underneath class, race, and nationality. Her stage play of *The Joy Luck Club*, commissioned by its author Amy Tan, first and foremost tells human stories, while issues like gender and race, though present, are peripheral to the central story line.

Her work in children's television—the means by which she supports her other writing endeavors—involves finding the juxtaposed place where her young characters of today can speak themselves through the amplifier of her own experiences as a child. It seems to insist on the possibility for growth and acceptance in any age group. Like An-Mei from *The Joy Luck Club*, Kim's young protagonists are often on the path to "learning how to shout" but have not quite arrived (Personal interview). That zone of in-between, cognitive and cultural, is exactly where her theatrical works unfold.

CRITICAL RECEPTION

Although Kim continues to be extraordinarily prolific as a young playwright, critical scholarship on her works has been limited exclusively to mixed theater reviews. Some reviewers complain that her plays are "sprawling, even unwieldy," and difficult "to fully grasp" with "overlong monologue," while in the same breath, they hail her staged works as illuminating that "frustrating sense of things coming apart" (Bruckner B3; Marks B1). Other critics are more positive in affirming her theatrical achievements. Spears regards Kim's stage adaptation of *The Joy Luck Club* as so "reverent, faithful" that it offers theatergoers "an excellent example of why good books deserve a life on the stage" (11–12). Brandi, in his review of *Dreamtime for Alice*, describes the play as "often funny, sometimes hysterical, . . . taking the Off-Broadway circuit by storm" (11). Even Bruckner admits that Kim's stage play of Tan's novel achieves her "stated aims very well: . . . revealing a great range of . . . differences among Chinese Americans that other Americans often do not perceive" (B3). Yet overall, Kim's works have not yet generated substantial criticism in print despite their success on the stage. However, that may be likely to change as she continues to make a name for herself in the literary and theatrical corridors of New York City and beyond. If the degree to which theaters and studios seek her out for special stage projects and television pilots is any indicator, academia will not be long in making its contribution to the study of this imaginative and dynamic playwright.

BIBLIOGRAPHY

Works by Susan Kim

Drama

Scientist Meets Fish. Childsplay: A Collection of Scenes and Monologues for Children.
Ed. Kerry Muir. New York: Proscenium Publishers, 1995. 161–68.
To Bee or Not to Bee. Childsplay: A Collection of Scenes and Monologues for Children.
Ed. Kerry Muir. New York: Proscenium Publishers, 1995. 195–200.
Dreamtime for Alice. Ensemble Studio Theatre Marathon '99: The One-Act Plays. Ed.
Curt Dempster. New York: Faber and Faber, 2000. 99–118.

Unpublished Manuscripts

Open Spaces. 1988.
Death and the Maiden. One-act. 1990.
Rapid Eye Movement. One-act. 1991.
Swimming Out to Sea. One-act. 1992.
The Arrangement. 1993.
The Joy Luck Club. 1993.
Seventh Word, Four Syllables. One-act. 1993.
The Door. One-act. 1999.
Where It Came From. 2000.

Selected Production History

Death and the Maiden

Production, dir. Lisa Peterson. Ensemble Studio Theatre, New York City, 1990.

Rapid Eye Movement

Production, dir. Maggie Mancinelli. Ensemble Studio Theatre, New York City, 1991.
———, dir. Jamie Richards. Samuel Beckett Theater, New York City, 1992.

Swimming Out to Sea

Production, dir. Bill Shebar. Home for Contemporary Arts, New York City, 1992.

The Arrangement

Production, dir. Nela Wagman. Ohio Theatre, New York City, 1993.

The Joy Luck Club

Production, dir. Arvin Brown. Shanghai People's Art Theater, Shanghai, China, 1993.
———, dir. Seret Scott. Long Wharf Theater, New Haven, CT, 1997.
———, dir. Tisa Chang. Pan Asian Repertory Theatre, New York City, 1999.
———, dir. Margaret Booker. TheatreWorks, Palo Alto, CA, 1999.

Seventh Word, Four Syllables

Production, dir. Melia Bensussen. Ensemble Studio Theatre, New York City, 1993.

The Door

Production, dir. Gail Noppe Brandon. Blue Heron Theatre, New York City, 1999.

Dreamtime for Alice

Production, dir. Rich Lichte. Ensemble Studio Theatre, New York City, 1999.

Interview

Personal interview. 12 May 2000.

Studies of Susan Kim

Balingit, JoAnn. Rev. of *Are You Afraid of the Dark?* By Susan Kim. *School Library Journal* 41.2 (1995): 62–63.

Brandi, Nick. "Keeping up the Pace." Rev. of *Dreamtime for Alice. Show Business* 2–8 June 1999: 11–12.

Bruckner, D.J.R. "For These Bonded Souls, Some Luck But Little Joy." Rev. of *The Joy Luck Club. New York Times* 27 Apr. 1999: B3.

Ewald, Laura A. Rev. of *Ensemble Studio Theatre Marathon '99: The One-Act Plays. Library Journal* 125 (2000): 93.

Gussow, Mel. "A First Lady's Fantasy of Travel Back in Time." Rev. of *Seventh Word, Four Syllables. New York Times* 10 June 1993: C18.

———. "Psychological Warfare Claims Two." Rev. of *The Arrangement. New York Times* 22 Mar. 1993: C14.

———. "Several Slices of Life in Festival of One-Acts." *New York Times* 9 June 1991: sec. 1: 60.

———. "Women Taking Their Places, Rightful or Not." Rev. of *Rapid Eye Movement. New York Times* 25 Sept. 1992: C2.

Hartigan, Patti. "A Workmanlike 'Joy' Fails to Captivate." Rev. of *The Joy Luck Club. Boston Globe* 10 May 1997: C6.

Klein, Alvin. "Mothers, Daughters, China, and America." Rev. of *The Joy Luck Club. New York Times* 18 May 1997, late ed.: 13CN.

MacMinn, Aleene. "Tracing the History of 'Television'; 8-Part PBS Series Looks at Development of the Medium in the U.S." Rev. of *Television*, dir. Susan Kim. *Los Angeles Times* 23 Jan. 1988, Calendar: 1.

Marks, Peter. "In 4 One-Acts, The Soul Is Crushed at Every Age." Rev. of *Dreamtime for Alice. New York Times* 25 May 1999: B1.

McGinnis, John. Rev. of *The Joy Luck Club. Wall Street Journal* 19 Aug. 1993: A8.

Ruta, Suzanne. "The Jab of the One-Act." Rev. of *Death and the Maiden. New York Times* 20 May 1990, sec. 2: 12.

Spears, Ricky. Rev. of *The Joy Luck Club. InTheater* 10 May 1999: 11.

Taylor, Markland. Rev. of *The Joy Luck Club. Variety* 367.8 (1997): 104.

Tyler, Patrick E. "Joint Production Takes *The Joy Luck Club* to China's Stages." Rev. of *The Joy Luck Club. New York Times* 27 Nov. 1993, late ed., sec. 1: 11.

Unger, Arthur. "Whizzing through TV's First 40 Years." Rev. of *Television*, dir. Susan Kim. *Christian Science Monitor* 21 Jan. 1988: 21.

Winn, Steven. "Joy Luck' Loses in the Translation." Rev. of *The Joy Luck Club. San Francisco Chronicle* 19 Apr. 1999: C1.

Victoria Nalani Kneubuhl

(1949–   )

Elizabeth Byrne Fitzpatrick

BIOGRAPHY

Victoria Nalani Kneubuhl is a playwright of Hawaiian, Samoan, and Caucasian descent who was born in Honolulu in 1949. As a very young woman, she lived in American Samoa, where she was married, had two children, and taught high school. She returned to Honolulu a few years later and worked as a preschool teacher and then as a coordinator for a wilderness school. In her early thirties, she came to the continental United States to attend Antioch College. She graduated in 1982 with a bachelor's degree in liberal studies, specializing in Hawaiian studies, art, and psychology. For the next several years, she worked as an educator and creator of living history programs at two historical museums in Honolulu.

In the mid-1980s, she went back to school. Planning to pursue a master's degree in psychology at the University of Hawai'i, she happened to take a playwriting class and found her calling. She switched to the theater-arts program, earned a master's degree in 1987, and has been a playwright ever since. Many of Kneubuhl's plays have been produced by Kumu Kahua Theatre Company in Honolulu. She has also written plays for the Honolulu Theatre for Youth and the Hawaii Theatre as well as writing scripts for various historical reenactments, videos, and multimedia events. She writes, teaches, and lectures about theater, often in affiliation with the Women's Studies Department of the University of Hawai'i.

Kneubuhl's activist role in the Hawaiian creative community also includes serving as a longtime board member of Kumu Kahua and lecturing about her role as a Hawaiian woman playwright. She is part of a chain of teachers and students. Two particular mentors were Dennis Carroll, her playwriting teacher at the University of Hawai'i and at the time the artistic director of Kumu Kahua, with whom she collaborated on an early work, and her uncle John Kneubuhl, a well-known Samoan playwright and Hollywood screenwriter who was one of the first Samoans to attend Yale University. John directed her first full-length play. Her own work as a teacher of playwriting is praised by students who comment on her supportiveness. In her efforts to pass the craft of playwriting from generation to generation and her many collaborative projects, Kneubuhl appears to operate within a nonwesternized model of art and the artist. For her, art seems to be an everyday, if powerful, means of cultural expression, not the rarefied practice of individuals working in isolation. She received the Hawaii Award for Literature in 1995.

MAJOR WORKS AND THEMES

Kneubuhl believes in the transformational power of the theater. Drama about social and political issues is an especially potent form of art, as she has written, because the communal experience of a performance, with all its contradictory qualities—riskiness, fragility, forcefulness—compels members of the audience to reexamine what they believe. Most of Kneubuhl's plays, exhibits, and films involve consideration of issues of Hawaiian and Samoan cultural identity. Thematically, her works explore the possibility of growth through the contrast between native Hawaiian culture and white America represented by European Americans.

Her white characters range from the sexually repressed nineteenth-century missionary and the ethnographer who uses pseudoscholarship to justify racist attitudes to the twentieth-century tourist who yearns for an "authentic" return to a Polynesian paradise. The Hawaiians they encounter are not a homogeneous group, either. They represent various points on the spectrum of cultural identification from the purely Hawaiian to the completely Americanized. Mixed descent is often significant: *hapa haole* characters in her plays, as the half white is called in the Hawaiian phrase, tend to be assimilated into white culture to a higher degree. When Hawaiian and white characters meet, they always experience culture clash, but these clashes are not always negative. Often characters find in each other's culture a remedy for deficiencies in their own.

Ola Na Iwi [The Bones Live] (1994), which has been produced but not published, is a lively, comic drama about smuggling an ancient skeleton out of a German museum and back to Hawaii for proper burial. Among other things, it comments pointedly on Western preconceptions of Hawaii as paradise and illustrates ways in which Hawaiians sometimes play into a fictionalized cultural identity as preconceived by outsiders.

The Conversion of Ka'ahumanu (1988), set in nineteenth-century Hawaii, reviews some of the disastrous consequences of contact with the whites. The lucrative sandalwood trade meant that local agricultural practices were neglected, while the first appearance of venereal disease took a huge toll. The all-female cast finds some cultural common ground about gender issues, though, and actually learns to appreciate and adopt some of the traits of the other cultures. Hawaiian Queen Ka'ahumanu likes the American idea that women can have civil rights. Conversely, one of the missionary women learns to appreciate Hawaiian sensuality.

In some sense, Kneubuhl's work is always about acculturation by contrast. One of her best-known plays applies the same dynamic to the formation of a woman's identity. *The Story of Susanna* (1996) is framed by a retelling of the biblical story of a woman falsely accused of adultery by two men whose advances she rejects. The play investigates the cultural shaping of femininity as masculinity's "other." As a girl, Susanna learns femininity by learning to apply makeup and to flirt with men. This knowledge is a source of power and, paradoxically, of vulnerability, as the adult Susanna evokes both worship and abuse by men on account of her femininity.

Kneubuhl's strategy of juxtaposition and contrast allows her characters both to experience a heightened sense of their own identities and to consider—and sometimes adopt—new cultural values. As a result, audiences' own preexisting notions about static sexual, racial, or cultural identities are challenged. Both entertaining and didactic, her work provides rich literary texts for ethnic studies.

CRITICAL RECEPTION

Published commentary on Kneubuhl's work consists mostly of reviews of her plays. In a review of *Ka'ahumanu* when it was produced in Los Angeles, Ray Loynd praises her evenhanded presentation of complex material. She avoids black and white in her depiction of the culture clash of Hawaii in the nineteenth century (Loynd F4). But in his reviews, John Berger criticizes *Ka Wai Ola* (*The Living Water*) (1998) for one-sidedness and *The Story of Susanna* for what he describes as its overly feminist stance. Conversely, a profile and interview in the *Honolulu Star Bulletin* of October 29, 1998, details Kneubuhl's emotional struggle with *Susanna*—the most personal of her plays—and praises its exploration of domestic violence (Ensor). In the profile, Kneubuhl talks about overcoming her early fearfulness as a woman and as a writer, her love for the Hawaiian people and land, and her pride in writing strong roles for women. In an article by Burl Burlingame about Kneubuhl's playwriting class, a reporter by the name of Lee Cataluna describes her as a warm, supportive teacher who is much honored by the creative community in Honolulu.

Recognized as an ethnic and regional playwright, Kneubuhl is more discussed locally than on the national scene. Her work has been included in anthologies of Asian American, Native American, and Hawaiian plays, but news-media stories have tended to focus on aspects of the productions and the playwright's personality instead of providing a serious analysis of her work.

BIBLIOGRAPHY

Works by Victoria Nalani Kneubuhl

Drama

The Conversion of Ka'ahumanu. But Still, Like Air, I'll Rise: New Asian American Plays. Ed. Velina Hasu Houston. Philadelphia: Temple UP, 1997. 179–225.

The Conversion of Ka'ahumanu. Excerpts. *A Hawai'i Anthology: A Collection of Works by Recipients of the Hawai'i Award for Literature, 1974–1996.* Ed. Joseph Stanton. Honolulu: State Foundation on Culture and the Arts, 1997. 150–62.

The Story of Susanna. Seventh Generation: An Anthology of Native American Plays. Ed. Mimi Gisolfi D'Aponte. New York: Theatre Communications Group, 1999. 291–370.

Unpublished Manuscripts

Emmalehua. 1985.

Veranda Dance. 1985.

Ka'iulani. With Dennis Carroll, Robert Nelson, and Ryan Page. 1987.

Tofa Samoa. 1991.

January 1893. 1992.

Just So Stories. Adaptations from Kipling. 1992.

Ola Na Iwi [The Bones Live]. 1994.

Pianolo Spurs. 1994.

Hawai'ian Myths and Legends. 1997.

Annexation Debate. 1998.

Fanny and Belle. 1998.

Ka Wai Ola (The Living Water). 1998.

Selected Production History

Emmalehua

Stage reading. American Samoa Arts Fiafia, American Samoa, 1985.

Production, dir. John Kneubuhl. Kumu Kahua Theatre Company, Honolulu, 1986.

———. Kumu Kahua Theatre Company, Honolulu, 1996.

Veranda Dance

Production. Kennedy Lab Theatre, Honolulu, 1986.

Ka'iulani

Production. Kumu Kahua Theatre Company, Honolulu, 1987.

———. Kumu Kahua Theatre Company, Honolulu, 1988.

———. Kumu Kahua Theatre Company, Honolulu, 1990.

———. Touring Edinburgh, Scotland; Washington, DC; and Los Angeles, 1990.

The Conversion of Ka'ahumanu

Production. Tour of American Samoa, 1988 and 1990.

———. Tour of Edinburgh, Scotland; Washington, DC; and Los Angeles, 1990.

Tofa Samoa

Production. Honolulu Theatre for Youth, Honolulu, 1991.
————. Okinawa International Children's Theatre Festival, Okinawa, 1994.

January 1893

Production. Hawaii Centenary Celebration Street Pageant, Honolulu, 1993.
————. Hui Na'auao, Honolulu, 1993.

Just So Stories

Production. Honolulu Theatre for Youth, Honolulu, 1993.
————. Tour of the Hawaiian Islands, 1993.

Ola Na Iwi [The Bones Live]

Production. Kumu Kahua Theatre Company, Honolulu, 1994.

Hawai'ian Myths and Legends

Production, dir. Cheryl Flaharty. Iona Pear Dance Theatre, Hawaii Theatre, Honolulu, 1997 and 1998.

Ka Wai Ola (The Living Water)

Production. Honolulu Theatre for Youth, Leeward Community College Theater, Honolulu, 1998.

The Story of Susanna

Production, dir. Juli Burk. Kennedy Theatre, U of Hawai'i, Manoa, 1998.

Studies of Victoria Nalani Kneubuhl

Berger, John. "HTY Introduces Water and Land Issues to Youngsters." *Honolulu Star-Bulletin Online* 30 Jan. 1998. 15 May 2000 <http://www.starbulletin.com/98/01/30/features/story2.html>.
————. "Subplots Sap 'Susanna's' Strength." *Honolulu Star-Bulletin Online* 2 Nov. 1998. 15 May 2000 <http://www.starbulletin.com/98/11/02/features/story3.html>.
Burlingame, Burl. "Politics Makes for Good Theater, and Turns a News Anchor into a Playwright." *Honolulu Star-Bulletin Online* 1 Sept. 1998. 15 May 2000 <http://www.starbulletin.com/98/09/01/features/story1.html>.
Cho, Gregory. "*Performing Asian America: Race and Ethnicity on the Contemporary Stage* and *But Still, Like Air, I'll Rise.*" *Journal of Asian American Studies* 1 (1998): 303–8.
Enomoto, Catherine Kekoa. "Modern Myth: Hawaiian Legends Wax Eclectic." *Honolulu Star-Bulletin Online* 27 May 1997. 15 May 2000 <http://www.starbulletin.com/97/05/27/features/story1.html>.
Ensor, Deborah. "Fighting the Fear." *Honolulu Star-Bulletin Online* 29 Oct. 1998. 15 May 2000 <http://www.starbulletin.com/98/10/29/features/story1.html>.
Flanagan, Kathleen. "A Hawai'i Anthology." *World Literature Today* 72 (1998): 456.
Kam, Nadine. "Legendary Effort: Iona Pear Dance Theatre Restages 'Hawaiian Myths and Legends.' " *Honolulu Star-Bulletin Online* 28 May 1998. 15 May 2000 <http://www.starbulletin.com/98/05/28/features/story4.html>.

Loynd, Ray. "Festival '90; Stage Reviews Open Festival; *Ka'ahumanu* Details Mission-
    ary Strife." *Los Angeles Times* 6 Sept. 1990: F4.
Stanlake, Christy. "Book Review: *Seventh Generation: An Anthology of Native American
    Plays*." *Theatre Journal* 52 (2000): 144–45.

Dan Kwong
(1954–)

SanSan Kwan

BIOGRAPHY

Dan Kwong is a veteran performance artist, writer, teacher, and visual artist who has been presenting his solo multimedia performances since 1989. Born in Los Angeles on November 26, 1954, to a Japanese American mother and a Chinese American father, Kwong grew up in a diverse household of sometimes-competing cultures. The legacy of his two families' immigrant histories and encounters with racial prejudice, as well as his own experience as a Chinese Japanese American, has served as the driving force behind his work.

Kwong's training as a solo performance artist derives from numerous sources. As a dancer, he probably first honed his movement skills on the baseball field and in the martial-arts studio. Kwong claims that his ability with set design can be attributed in part to his working-class background: "In my family . . . if you wanted something (a toy, a piece of equipment) and it cost too much (which was just about always the case) you had to try and invent your own version of it from scratch. So I learned how to invent things" ("Questions"). After graduating from high school in Los Angeles, Kwong spent a couple of years at the University of Southern California, then transferred to the School of the Art Institute of Chicago, where he picked up technical training in the visual arts, learned audio and video production skills, and worked as a recording engineer.

Kwong's debut as a performer dates to 1989 when he premiered *Secrets of the Samurai Centerfielder* in Santa Monica. The success of this first solo work launched his career of performing, writing, and teaching. Since *Secrets*, Kwong has presented five major performances, toured extensively across the United States and in London and Mexico City, written pieces for various publications, and taught several popular workshops that have spawned performing groups in

Los Angeles, New York, and Philadelphia. Among them in New York City is Peeling the Banana, dedicated to continuing Kwong's style of autobiographical/ sociopolitical performance. In 1994, he started a performance group called Everything You Ever Wanted to Know about Asian Men in Los Angeles. Kwong is also the founder and curator of Treasure in the House, Los Angeles's first Asian Pacific American performance and visual-arts series. Kwong lives and works in Los Angeles.

MAJOR WORKS AND THEMES

One might say that the major theme of Kwong's work as a solo performance artist is himself. Of course, Kwong's ultimate purpose is not to wallow in solipsism, but to use his personal experience as a way to bring larger social issues to the fore. As a Chinese Japanese American male, Kwong is primarily interested in exploring issues of Asian American identity, particularly through subjects such as the model-minority myth, cultural confusion and discovery in a mixed-heritage family, dysfunctionality in the Asian American family, Asian male identity, Japanese American internment, and the impact of HIV/AIDS on the Asian American population. In terms of form, his work combines storytelling, poetry, martial arts, athletics, dance, slide projection, video, sculptural installation, and music. Kwong is the virtuoso auteur; in addition to writing, directing, and performing all of his material, he also designs the props, costumes, sets, and audiovisual effects.

In *Secrets of the Samurai Centerfielder* (1989), Kwong uses playing center field in baseball as a metaphor for his life as a child of Chinese and Japanese parents. Standing on an Astroturf baseball diamond, he tells the story, through slides and narration, of his Japanese family's immigration to the United States, the life his parents settled into as produce sellers in Los Angeles, his grandfather's title as a judo champ, and the night that FBI agents took his grandparents away to a concentration camp. Kwong depicts the racism that both sides of his family encountered and then goes on to describe the mutual feelings of ethnic supremacism that each side expressed toward the other. Situated in the middle of this antagonistic family dynamic while also a victim of racism by the population at large, Kwong talks confessionally about his ability to deny pain and the consequences of internalized oppression. Center field becomes the place that Kwong yearns for: centered yet far from home, and isolated but broad in perspective of the field.

Secrets was followed by *Tales from the Fractured Tao with Master Nice Guy* (1991). Like *Secrets, Tales* is a multimedia work employing slides, audio montage, martial arts/dance, and narrative. The two principal characters in the piece, both played by Kwong, are his boyhood self in baseball cap and jeans and Master Nice Guy, a sort of Asian guru/New Age shrink. Through gentle humor, Kwong depicts his childhood anguish over his parents' divorce and the pain of separation he felt at the absence of his father. As the stories unfold, Master Nice

Guy uses his Mongolian Mental Fax machine (actually just a simple kitchen colander) to help Kwong sort through his feelings. Along the way, Kwong manages to refract his personal experience into a larger discussion of the pathologies of the American family, as well as society's pressures and expectations for the overachieving Asian American. *Tales* becomes a humorous but pointed social commentary enacted through personal disclosure.

Ranging more widely in content than the previous pieces, *Monkhood in Three Easy Lessons* (1993) continues to develop and expand Kwong's multimedia skills. The piece opens with a hilarious sketch involving Kwong dressed in an ingenious soft-cloth baby's body with movable arms and legs; he responds to questions about playing the game of life as if he were an athlete in a pregame interview. The center of the work involves two monologues about his Chinese and Japanese grandfathers. Again, autobiography is employed in the service of sociopolitical aims. Kwong delves into the lives of his male ancestry in order to explore issues of Asian American manhood. In one poignant moment, he reveals the way that he and his sisters used to make a laughingstock of their unsuspecting, doddering Chinese grandfather. Kwong is torn between anger at having such a weak male family figure and regret for the way he misunderstood his grandfather as a child. In another sequence where he runs ever faster on a quickening treadmill, Kwong depicts the struggle Asian American men face in order to prove their masculinity in a society that finds it easy to emasculate them.

The Dodo Vaccine (1994) presents a moving and stylistically clever piece about HIV/AIDS in the Asian Pacific Islander community. The piece begins with Kwong flailing in darkness at clear balloons that hold inside them fluorescent table-tennis balls—an illustration of the relentless reduplication of HIV-infected T cells. Through a story about his own AIDS test—the excruciating wait for the results, the humiliating personal review of his sexual indiscretions—Kwong examines the state of HIV/AIDS in the Asian Pacific Islander community. He cites horrifying statistic upon horrifying statistic attesting to the fact that AIDS should be a major concern in this community, yet the force of the model-minority myth allows these statistics to be ignored by both the larger population and by Asian Americans themselves. To concede that AIDS is an Asian problem would be to undermine the convenience of the myth. True to his earlier, self-scrutinizing pieces, Kwong does not shy away from interrogating his own homophobia and disavowal. The prominent idea throughout this piece is that, sadly, for whatever self-serving reasons, people are often unable to act on what they know to be true.

A significant departure from his earlier works, *The Night the Moon Landed on 39th Street* (1999) explores the broader questions of human existence itself rather than focusing on issues of race, culture, or gender. The show opens with a childhood recollection of once seeing the moon rise so huge that it looked like it had just landed down the street. Kwong and his older sister ran wildly to catch it. This childlike spirit of hope, belief, and creative imagination pervades the entire piece. Using deliberately low-tech props and sets to hilarious effect, Kwong reveals his lifelong desire to "be the first performance artist in space." A particularly effective sequence shows Kwong on video training to be an astronaut: a merry-go-round prepares him for the extreme G force he will have to withstand in space. Later, as the first interstellar performance artist, he does a song-and-dance number while aerosol spray cans serve as rocket boosters. Throughout, Kwong provides the audience with all sorts of space-buff anecdotes and tidbits; he reminisces about the first moon walk on television; and, finally, he ruminates with a sentimental optimism on questions of ontology.

Beginning with *Secrets of the Samurai Centerfielder*, Kwong's artistry has continued to evolve and mature. Always with a belief in the power of the personal to reflect the political and the political to envelop the personal, Kwong addresses the concerns of his time and place: race, gender, culture, family, human existence. Along the way, he generously offers humor, aesthetic ingenuity, and a disarmingly honest piece of himself.

CRITICAL RECEPTION

Reviewers have all agreed that the key to Kwong's work is his skillful blend of wry comedy, honest self-scrutiny, clever artistry, and potent social commentary. About *Monkhood in Three Easy Lessons*, Steven Leigh Morris writes, "Kwong pulls threads of his existence and weaves metaphors that resonate socially and metaphysically" (99). Of *The Dodo Vaccine*, Philip Brandes notes, "Kwong deploys his multimedia arsenal with startling success, using sound, visual composition, and lighting to drive his point home with more force than unaccompanied narrative could achieve" (F4). Critics have suggested that it is Kwong's personal stories that balance out his political critique and, similarly, his gentle humor that balances out his navel gazing. "Whatever he does, Kwong has fun, and his sunny disposition and relaxed, low-key humor make him a joy to watch" (Weaver 95).

By way of criticism, some have felt that Kwong's work tends to overdo it in one area or another. Some have appreciated his politics, but felt that he was sometimes overly self-absorbed: Artists often rely on their life experiences for materials, "but it's as if Kwong forgot to excise the overly personal bits in the process of creating a more sophisticated work" (Breslauer, Rev. of *Monkhood* F8). Others have enjoyed his stories but have grown weary of his sermons, while still others have felt his message but been distracted by some of his less successful stagings. All of this, of course, can be explained by the whims and varying tastes of reviewers, as well as the risks Kwong takes in juggling so many talents and aims in his work.

BIBLIOGRAPHY

Works by Dan Kwong

Drama

The Dodo Vaccine. Excerpts. *On a Bed of Rice: An Asian American Erotic Feast*. Ed. Geraldine Kudaka. Foreword. Russell Leong. New York: Anchor, 1995. 431–37.

Monkhood in Three Easy Lessons. Excerpts. *Getting Your Solo Act Together*. Ed. Michael Kearns. Portsmouth, NH: Heinemann Books, 1997. 82–88. Rpt. in *Yellow Light: The Flowering of Asian American Arts*. Ed. Amy Ling. Philadelphia: Temple UP, 1999. 266–69.

Unpublished Manuscripts

Secrets of the Samurai Centerfielder. 1989.
Boy Story. 1990.
Instruments of Decision. 1990.
Tales from the Fractured Tao with Master Nice Guy. 1991.
The Warriors' Council. 1992.
Monkhood in Three Easy Lessons. 1993.
The Dodo Vaccine. 1994.
Correspondence of a Dangerous Enemy Alien. 1995.
All for One, One for All. 1997.
Samurai Centerfielder Meets the Mad Kabuki Woman. 1997.
The Night the Moon Landed on 39th Street. 1999.
"Questions and Answers." Essay. n. d.

Selected Production History

Secrets of the Samurai Centerfielder

Solo performances, perf. Dan Kwong; Highways Performing Space, Santa Monica, CA, 1989.
———. Ohio State U, Columbus, 1990.
———. Jan Popper Theater, UCLA, 1990.
———. Sushi Performance Space, San Diego, 1990.
———. Dance Theater Workshop, New York City, 1990.
———. East West Players Theater, Los Angeles, 1990.
———. Diverseworks, Houston, 1991.
———. Seven Stages Theater, Atlanta, 1991.
———. Contemporary Arts Center, New Orleans, 1991.
———. Climate Theatre, San Francisco, 1991.
———. Northwest Asian American Theatre, Seattle, 1992.
———. Dance Place Theater, Washington, DC, 1992.

Boy Story

Solo performances, perf. Dan Kwong. Highways Performance Space, Santa Monica, CA, 1990.
———. Japanese American Cultural and Community Center, Los Angeles, 1990.

Instruments of Decision

Production, perf. Dan Kwong and William Roper. John Anson Ford Theater, Los Angeles, 1990.

Tales from the Fractured Tao with Master Nice Guy

Solo performances, perf. Dan Kwong. Highways Performance Space, Santa Monica, CA,
1991.
————. Theater/Theater, Hollywood, 1991.
————. LA Contemporary Exhibitions, Los Angeles, 1991.
————. Cleveland Public Theater, Cleveland, 1992.
————. Columbia U, New York City, 1992.

The Warriors' Council

Production, perf. Dan Kwong, Linda Frye Burnham, Francisco Letelier, Michelle T.
Clinton, Keith Antar Mason, and G. Collette Jackson. Highways Performance
Space, Santa Monica, CA, 1992.

Monkhood in Three Easy Lessons

Solo performances, perf. Dan Kwong. Japan America Theatre, Los Angeles, 1993.
————. N.A.M.E. Gallery, Chicago, 1993.
————. School of the Art Institute of Chicago, Chicago, 1993.
————. U of Wisconsin, Madison, 1993.
————. Pennsylvania State U, State College, 1993.
————. Highways Performance Space, Santa Monica, CA, 1994.
————. Franklin Furnace, New York City, 1994.
————. Multicultural Center Theater, U of California, Santa Barbara, 1994.
————. New WORLD Theater, U of Massachusetts, Amherst, 1995.
————. Olivet College, Olivet, MI, 1996.
————. The Stage, San Jose, 1996.
————. Kansas State U, Manhattan, 1998.
————. Vassar College, Poughkeepsie, NY, 1998.
————. Painted Bride Art Center, Philadelphia, 1998.
————. U of Illinois, Urbana-Champaign, 1999.
————. Tulsa Center for the Performing Arts, Tulsa, 1999.
————. Multicultural Center Theater, U of California, Santa Barbara, 2000.

The Dodo Vaccine

Solo performances, perf. Dan Kwong. Spitalfields Market Art Project, London, UK, 1994.
————. Luna Park Cabaret, West Hollywood, CA, 1994.
————. San Juan Capistrano Arts Center, CA, 1994.
————. Wellesley College, Wellesley, MA, 1995.
————. Reed College, Portland, OR, 1995.
————. Walker's Point Center for the Arts, Milwaukee, 1995.
————. New School for Social Research, New York City, 1995.
————. Hope College, Holland, MI, 1995.
————. Chicago Cultural Center, Chicago, 1995.
————. Whitman College, Walla Walla, WA, 1995.
————. Eastern New Mexico College, Portales, 1995.
————. Ex-Teresa Arte Alternativo, Mexico City, 1995.

————. Seattle U, Seattle, 1996.
————. Northwest Asian American Theatre, Seattle, 1996.
————. Actors Theatre of Louisville, Louisville, KY, 1996.
————. Duke Institute of the Arts, Durham, NC, 1997.

Correspondence of a Dangerous Enemy Alien

Solo performances, perf. Dan Kwong. Japan America Theatre, Los Angeles, 1995.

Samurai Centerfielder Meets the Mad Kabuki Woman

Production, perf. Dan Kwong and Denise Uyehara. New Langton Arts, San Francisco, 1997.
————. Highways Performance Space, Santa Monica, CA, 1997.

The Night the Moon Landed on 39th Street

Solo performances, perf. Dan Kwong. Highways Performance Space, Santa Monica, CA, 1999.
————. Mark Taper Auditorium, Los Angeles, 2000.
————. Tulsa Center for the Performing Arts, Tulsa, OK, 2000.
————. Japan America Theatre, Los Angeles, 2000.
————. Bangkok Playhouse Theatre, Thailand, 2001.

Essays

"New Season." *High Performance* 15. Special issue (Summer 1992): 20.
"Beyond Victimization." *High Performance* 19.3 (Summer 1996): 28.
Author's note. *Getting Your Solo Act Together.* Ed. Michael Kearns. Portsmouth, NH: Heinemann Books, 1997. 82–83.

Interviews

"Daniel Kit Kwong: Multimedia Artist Exposing Oppression." Interview. *GIDRA Twentieth Anniversary Edition* 1990: 109.
"Destroying the Myth of the 'Model Minority.' " Interview. *Asian Times* 17 May 1994: 17.
"Response." Interview. *Yellow Light: The Flowering of Asian American Arts.* Ed. Amy Ling. Philadelphia: Temple UP, 1999. 261–66.

Studies of Dan Kwong

Adcock, Joe. "Cultural Oppression Strikes Out in Samurai Centerfielder." Rev. of *Secrets of the Samurai Centerfielder. Seattle Post-Intelligencer* 24 Jan. 1992: 10.
Berson, Misha. "*Centerfield* Has Its Hits and Misses." *Seattle Times* 24 Jan. 1992, final ed.: 10.
Brandes, Philip. Rev. of *The Dodo Vaccine. Los Angeles Times* 28 Feb. 1996: F4.
————. Rev. of *Samurai Centerfielder Meets the Mad Kabuki Woman. Los Angeles Times* 27 June 1997: F22.
Breslauer, Jan. "Mixed-Media, Mixed-Heritage: *Samurai Centerfielder.*" *Los Angeles Times* 28 Sept. 1989, sec. 6: 5.
————. Rev. of *Monkhood in Three Easy Lessons. Los Angeles Times* 7 June 1993: F8.

———. Rev. of *Tales from the Fractured Tao with Master Nice Guy*. *LA Weekly* 25 Jan. 1991: 51.

Carbonneau, Suzanne. "Dan Kwong." *Washington Post* 12 Mar. 1992: B4.

Carlson, Lance. Rev. of *Secrets of the Samurai Centerfielder*. *High Performance* 13.1 (Spring 1990): 54.

Curtis, Cathy. Rev. of *Instruments of Decision*. *Los Angeles Times* 30 June 1990: F14.

Dirzhud-Rashid, Rajkhet. Rev. of *The Dodo Vaccine*. *Seattle Gay News* 5 Apr. 1996: 18.

Drake, Sylvie. Rev. of *The Warriors' Council*. *Los Angeles Times* 26 Nov. 1992: F1.

Foley, F. Kathleen. Rev. of *The Night the Moon Landed on 39th Street*. *Los Angeles Times* 24 June 1999: F26.

Greenstein, M.A. Rev. of *Tales from the Fractured Tao with Master Nice Guy*. *Artweek* 7 Feb. 1991: 16–17.

Komai, Chris. Rev. of *Instruments of Decision*. *Rafu Shimpo* 2 July 1990: 3.

———. Rev. of *Monkhood in 3 Easy Lessons*. *Rafu Shimpo* 12 June 1993: 2.

Levy, Joel. Rev. of *Tales from the Fractured Tao with Master Nice Guy*. *LA Reader* 18 Jan. 1991: 52.

Moffet, Penelope. "Going to Bat for an Asian-Pacific Performance Fest." *Los Angeles Times* 14 Aug. 1991: F10.

Morris, Steven Leigh. Rev. of *Monkhood in Three Easy Lessons*. *LA Weekly* 19 Mar. 1993: 99.

Orr, Tom. Rev. of *The Dodo Vaccine*. *Seattle Times* 1 Apr. 1996: E3.

Pasles, Chris. "Kwong Explores Centerfield." Rev. of *Secrets of the Samurai Centerfielder*. *Los Angeles Times* 30 Sept. 1989: F3.

Penn, Roberta. "*Dodo Vaccine* Offers No Immunity from Homophobia." Rev. of *The Dodo Vaccine*. *Seattle Post-Intelligencer* 29 Mar. 1996: 20.

Provenzano, Tom. Rev. of *The Dodo Vaccine*. *LA Weekly* 1 Mar. 1996: 102.

Rago, Carmela. Rev. of *Monkhood in Three Easy Lessons*. *Chicago Tribune* 7 Oct. 1993: 20.

Rauzi, Bobin. "Eclectic, Uneven Look at Asian Identity." *Los Angeles Times* 1 Nov. 1997: F4.

Spiegel, Judith. "Confronting Racism." Rev. of *Secrets of the Samurai Centerfielder*. *Artweek* 9 Nov. 1989: 28.

———. "Patriarchy Forsaken." Rev. of *Boy Story*. *Artweek* 30 May 1990: 1+.

Suravech, Glenn. Rev. of *Tales from the Fractured Tao with Master Nice Guy*. *Rafu Shimpo* 24 Jan. 1991: 3.

Thompson, Mariko. Rev. of *The Night the Moon Landed on 39th Street*. *AsianWeek* 24 June 1999: 24.

Weaver, Neal. Rev. of *The Night the Moon Landed on 39th Street*. *LA Weekly* 25 June 1999: 95.

Welsh, Anne Marie. "Kwong Eloquently Goes Deep, Deep in the Centerfield." Rev. of *Secrets of the Samurai Centerfielder*. *San Diego Union-Tribune* 18 May 1990: D3.

———. "Kwong's *Centerfielder* Catches Plight of the Oppressed Asians." *San Diego Union-Tribune* 19 May 1990: D4.

Winn, Steven. Rev. of *Secrets of the Samurai Centerfielder*. *San Francisco Chronicle* 28 Sept. 1991, final ed.: C5.

lê thi diem thúy

(1972–   )

Roberta Uno

BIOGRAPHY

lê thi diem thúy or thúy lê was born on January 12, 1972, in Phan Thiet, Vietnam, a large fishing community located northeast of Ho Chi Minh City (Saigon). In her play *Mua He Do Lua/Red Fiery Summer*, lê explains that she was given that name because of the fires that scorched the South Vietnamese countryside the year she was born. By 1972, the Vietnam War was supposedly winding down, but for the Vietnamese it was the year when carpet bombing by the Americans provoked retaliatory attacks from the North that turned the lush countryside into "red fiery summer." lê was born two months before that saturation bombing campaign began.

lê and her father left Vietnam in 1979; her mother and two sisters left two years later. Refugees from the war, they landed, via a refugee camp in Singapore, in "the country of California, the province of San Diego, the village of Linda Vista." The lê family lived in a "yellow ghetto" in decaying 1940s–1950s Navy housing, home to several resettled Vietnamese, Cambodians, and Laotians. The compound was eventually demolished for condominium development, and the family once again was dislocated. Her parents struggled adjusting to their loss, separation, and relocation. lê sought refuge in Vietnamese punk music and recalls that as a teenager, she climbed out of the window of her parents' home to start a new life. Speaking with fellow Vietnamese American writer Quang Bao, she stated, "I left in order to write" (Bao 1).

In 1993, while lê was a student at Hampshire College, she spent a spring semester doing a field study on French colonial postcards of Indochina in Paris, France. Her studies at Hampshire focused on postcolonial literature, and her Division III (senior) thesis was the writing of the play *Mua He Do Lua/Red Fiery Summer*, conceived as a solo performance. After receiving her B.A. in cultural studies from Hampshire College, she performed the play *Red Fiery Summer* between 1995 and 1997 at a variety of community spaces and formal theaters across the country from the Third New Immigrants' Play Festival at the Vineyard Theatre in New York and New WORLD Theater at the University of Massachusetts, Amherst, to the Railyard Performance Center in Santa Fe, New Mexico, and the Association for Viet Arts in San Jose, California. She was invited to perform internationally as well at the Asian Heritage Festival, Montreal, Canada, and the International Women Playwrights' Conference in Galway, Ireland.

In 1996, she was commissioned by the New WORLD Theater and the New England Foundation for the Arts to write her second full-length work for theater, a solo performance work entitled *the bodies between us*. The play was developed in 1996 in the New Works for a New World play-development laboratory in Amherst, Massachusetts, and was subsequently produced by New WORLD Theater at its national and international play festival and conference, "New Works for a New World: An Intersection of Performance, Practice, and Ideas." During this same time period, she participated in a number of readings of her poetry and fiction at colleges and arts centers, including the Asian American Writers' Workshop at Cornelia Street Café in New York City; Poets' House, New York City; the Asia Society, New York City; the Brooklyn Museum of Art; the Ellipse Arts Center at Arlington, Virginia; the Geraldine R. Dodge Poetry Festival, Waterloo Village, New Jersey; and Yale University, Smith College, Cooper Union, and the University of California at Berkeley.

In 1998, she was featured in the *Village Voice* in an article titled "Writers on the Verge" by Hugh Garvey. Her poetry, fiction, and theater pieces have appeared in a number of poetry and prose collections, particularly those focused on women's, lesbian, and Asian American writing. The publication of "The Gangster We Are All Looking For" in *Harper's Magazine* in April 1996 (the essay originally appeared in the *Massachusetts Review*) brought her work to a nationwide audience; the piece was subsequently published in *The Best American Essays of 1997*. lê's forthcoming publications include a full-length work inspired by and bearing the same name as "The Gangster We Are All Looking For"; the performance text of *the bodies between us*, to appear in *The Color of Theater: A Critical Sourcebook on Race and Performance*; and excerpts from the play *Mua He Do Lua/Red Fiery Summer* in *Bold Worlds: A Century of Asian American Writing*. lê has been awarded writing residencies at the Headlands Center for the Arts, Sausalito, California; Hedgebrook, Langley, Washington; Hampshire College at Amherst, Massachusetts; and St. Mary's College at St. Mary's City, Maryland.

MAJOR WORKS AND THEMES

The themes of dislocation, fragmentation, memory, identity, and the meaning of language are present in both of lê's works for theater, *Mua He Do Lua/Red Fiery Summer* (1995) and *the bodies between us* (1996). *Red Fiery Summer* is constructed in two contrasting halves—the first in Vietnam and the second in the United States. Unlike other immigrant narratives on the Vietnam War, hers is not the expected story of triumph over adversity, where resolution is equated with arrival in America. Rather, she probes a complex and unresolved conversation between fragmented geographies. Using slides of French colonial postcards and photographs of her parents as the backdrop, lê contrasts her family's life in Vietnam during the war with their life in southern California after the war through dramatic monologue, music, movement, and songs. The decision to use French colonial postcards places the Vietnam War within a larger frame of colonialism and a longer history of political violence. Her approach also raises, from an unexpected angle, the contemporary media issue of how images of Vietnamese bodies have been represented, categorized, and transmitted.

Enacting characters ranging from her young, adolescent, and contemporary selves to her parents in their youth and middle age, lê embodies various people without losing herself. Through this acting device, she beckons her audience to see the narrative through her perspective, through her lens. "I am interested in places within places, people within people" (Bao 2). Her depiction of Vietnam avoids the nostalgic while juxtaposing the destruction of war with the sweetness of ordinary life. It is her parents' love story, the story of a South Vietnamese soldier who would desert his post to be with the woman he adored, that creates frightening dissonance when the same couple careens toward madness and alcoholism in the United States. Observes lê, "For me, Vietnam was always a distant 'there,' a suspended other world, a shifting perception. A lot of it came through the confrontation between learning through school history and movies, which was very spectacular, and that spectacle contrasted with my parents' silence" (Garvey 78).

the bodies between us further interrogates these issues as it holds a magnifying glass to the relationship between lê and her father. lê chose to construct this solo performance piece with both visual and audio materials; the scenic element is comprised of three enormous lengths of white gauze suspended from a hoop. These three lengths of fabric are transformed from waves on the shore to the prow of a boat, a hammock in a refugee camp, a swaddled infant, and so on. Two audiotapes serve as secondary and contrapuntal narratives. The first is a National Public Radio interview of a scientist discussing the mysterious return of indigenous Mekong Delta sarus cranes after the war, and another tape is an English-as-a-second-language English interview with a young Vietnamese girl. Organized in four sections, "orange," "earth," "water," and "sky," the play's narrative speaks achingly of the departure from Vietnam, of the endless hallucinatory state of floating on the ocean, of the waking nightmare of the refugee camp, and of efforts to remember and resurrect images of a lost mother.

As in *Red Fiery Summer*, photographs (in this case unseen but referred to) are critical reference points. The narrator's father shows her a photograph to remind her of her mother's face while they are adrift at sea. Later, in California, they try to take a photo of themselves in front of a car to send to her mother. The narrator states, "I don't argue with my father but there's something in how I hold my shoulders for this picture which is meant as a signal to my mother. So that looking at this picture, she would begin to suspect something was not right. I hold my shoulders, as if to say, I am pinned to this picture. This setting. Don't look for me here in front of this shiny car, this big house. Something is wrong. Look at my bones." Similarly, lê urges her audience to look beyond the surface of pictures and read what is askew.

CRITICAL RECEPTION

As a writer under thirty who has produced a collection of fiction, poetry, two plays, and a forthcoming book, lê is just beginning to receive the critical attention she undoubtedly deserves. Chris Rohmann in his review called *Red Fiery Summer* "a brief jewel of a piece, born of an imaginative intelligence and brought to life by an entrancing stage presence. This episodic memoir is told in sparkling prose-poetry" (29). Quang Bao, a Vietnamese American writer himself, observed, "*Red* challenges the mainstream representation of Vietnamese people as one indistinct lot defined by a single episode in recent history. The idea of Vietnam as war instead of as country has restricted America's ability to fully understand Vietnamese people, which makes *Red* more powerful for its meditation on identity and loss" (1). In a review of performances at the Fourth International Women Playwrights' Conference in Galway, Ireland, Mary Trotter rated the play as the most challenging work presented. "lê performed the piece at a slow, dream-like pace, her voice and movements graceful, rolling, unforced. But this same gentleness, when matched with the horrific violence underlying the story, created in performance the taut energy of a tightly drawn bow" (Trotter 523). *The Color of Theater: A Critical Source Book in Race and Performance* provides *the bodies between us* with extended critical commentary on the text and performance.

BIBLIOGRAPHY

Works by lê thi diem thúy

Drama

Mua He Do Lua/Red Fiery Summer. *Bold Worlds: A Century of Asian American Writing*. Ed. Rajini Srikanth and Esther Yae Iwanaga. New Brunswick, NJ: Rutgers UP, 2001. 387–97.

the bodies between us. *The Color of Theatre: A Critical Source Book in Race and Performance*. Ed. Roberta Uno and Lucy Mae San Pablo Burns. UK: Athlone, forthcoming.

Selected Production History

Mua He Do Lua/Red Fiery Summer

Solo performances. Third New Immigrants' Play Festival, Vineyard Theatre, New York, 1995.

————. Northampton Lesbian Festival, Northampton, MA, 1995.

————. "Off-Center Stage: A Festival of Multicultural Theatre," Bard College, Annandale-on-Hudson, NY, 1996.

————. New WORLD Theater, U of Massachusetts, Amherst, 1996.

————. Railyard Performance Center, Santa Fe, NM, 1996.

————. "Second Sight: East/West/East," Whitney Museum, New York City, 1996.

————. Asian Heritage Festival, Montreal, Canada, 1996.

————. Association for Viet Arts, San Jose, CA, 1997.

————. Fourth International Women Playwrights' Conference, Galway, Ireland, 1997.

the bodies between us

Production. New WORLD Theater, U of Massachusetts, Amherst, 1996 and 1998.

Essays

"Shrapnel Shards on Blue Water." *The Very Inside: An Anthology of Writings by Asian and Pacific Islander Lesbian and Bisexual Women.* Ed. Sharon Lim-Hing. Toronto, Canada: Sister Vision Press, 1994. 2–4.

"The Gangster We Are All Looking For." *Massachusetts Review* 36.4 (1995): 511–23. Rpt. in *Harper's Magazine* Apr. 1996: 15–19; *The Best American Essays of 1997.* Boston: Houghton Mifflin, 1997. 190–202.

"California Palms." *Half and Half: Writers on Growing Up Biracial and Bicultural.* Ed. Claudine Chiawei O'Hearn. New York: Pantheon, 1998. 38–48.

"Shelling Shrimp." *Identity Lessons: Contemporary Writing about Learning to Be American.* New York: Penguin, 1999. 78.

Poetry

From Both Sides Now: The Poetry of the Vietnam War and Its Aftermath. Ed. Phillip Mahoney. New York: Scribner, 1998.

Watermark: Vietnamese American Poetry and Prose. Ed. Barbara Tran, Monique T.D. Truong, and Luu Truong Khoi. New York: Asian American Writers' Workshop, 1998.

Studies of lê thi diem thúy

Bao, Quang. "lê thi diem thúy: A Life of Her Own." *VietMagnet.* Mar. 1997: 1–2.

Garvey, Hugh. "Writers on the Verge: lê thi diem thúy." *Voice Literary Supplement* 43.22 (1998): 78.

Rohmann, Chris. "Reborn in the U.S.A." *Valley Advocate* 19 Dec. 1996: 29.

Trotter, Mary. "The Fourth International Women Playwrights' Conference." *Theatre Journal* Dec. 1997: 523.

Cherylene Lee

(1953–   )

Randy Barbara Kaplan

BIOGRAPHY

For Cherylene Lee, a fourth-generation Chinese American, a childhood career in acting opened the door to playwriting. Born in Los Angeles to a dentist father and a mother who worked as a Hollywood extra, Lee made her acting debut in 1956 at the age of three on the *CBS Playhouse 90* production of "The Family Nobody Wanted." Growing up, she was among the first Asian American actors to appear in popular television situation comedies, including *Bachelor Father*, *Dennis the Menace*, and *My Three Sons*. By age twelve, she had danced along-side Nancy Kwan in the film version of the Rodgers and Hammerstein musical *Flower Drum Song* (1961) and performed with John Wayne in *Donovan's Reef* (1963). As a young woman, Lee added to her résumé the voices for several characters in the short-lived Hanna-Barbera animated cartoon series about Detective Charlie Chan, *The Amazing Chan and the Chan Clan* (1972–74) and appearances on television's popular *M*A*S*H* (1975).

During her teenage years, Lee's volunteer work at the La Brea Tar Pits sparked a keen interest in scientific research. Her experiences there inspired her to pursue successfully a bachelor's degree in paleontology at the University of California at Berkeley (1974). Returning to performing before going on to complete her master's degree in geology from the University of California at Los Angeles (1978), she spent a year with the international touring company of the popular musical *A Chorus Line*, as well as tours of *The King and I* and *Flower Drum Song*.

In the early 1980s, Lee discovered playwriting as a means of connecting the analytic skills she had learned as a scientist with her creative impulses as a performer. Her earliest efforts received numerous readings and workshop presentations, and by the 1990s she emerged as a recognized playwright with productions of *Arthur and Leila* (1992) and *Carry the Tiger to the Mountain* (1998) at both Asian American and culturally nonspecific theater companies across the United States.

MAJOR WORKS AND THEMES

In *Wong Bow Rides Again* (1985), Lee introduced patriarch Wong Bow, using a family gambling junket to connect him to three generations of his Chinese American descendants. As the group hurtles through the night toward Las Vegas on a chartered bus, family secrets and marital anxieties are revealed, intergenerational conflicts are fought, and reconciliations are sought. When the play begins, Wong Bow, among the first Chinese immigrants to arrive in America, the "Gold Mountain," is in his eighties and deceased; he has thus never actually met most of his progeny. Throughout the play, time moves fluidly from the present to the nineteenth century and back as Wong Bow enacts episodes from his life that presage, shape, and bear fruit in the thoughts and actions of his children, grandchildren, and great-grandchildren. By casting Wong Bow in the role of a bus driver who gradually transforms into the historical Wong Bow, Lee creates a theatrical referent for the interconnectedness of generations and the legacy of first-generation Chinese Americans' fearless embracing of adventure and the unknown.

When the play was initially produced by Los Angeles's East West Players in 1987, reviewers were quick to point out *Wong Bow*'s structural shortcomings. The play is nevertheless unique for its depictions of Wong Bow's life with the Yurok Indians, marking it among the first Asian American scripts to portray early Chinese American history and to examine the ramifications of relationships between Chinese immigrants and other American peoples of color.

New York City's Pan Asian Repertory Theatre and Basement Workshop provided Lee with the opportunity to develop her next effort, *Yin Chin Bow* (1986), which toured New York City libraries six years later as part of the Playwright Preview Productions' "Urban Stages" series. In this "prequel" to *Wong Bow Rides Again*, Lee concentrates solely on Wong Bow's life, examining both the lures and dangers of cultural assimilation and the tolls these take upon the individual, a theme to which she would return in her later work.

When the action begins, a twelve-year-old Yin Chin Bow (a Chinese bastardization of the American slang "Injun") has arrived in California. Having braved the treacherous journey across the Pacific Ocean to seek his fortune, Yin Chin Bow finds himself surrounded by more than one alien culture, few fellow Chinese, and even fewer Chinese women. Though he leaves his mining camp to live among the Native American Yurok tribe, marrying a Yurok woman and producing two biracial sons, Yin Chin Bow is unable to overcome his feeling of disconnectedness from Yurok culture. He deserts his Yurok family, marries a Chinese woman, and fathers a daughter by her, but his sense of cultural fragmentation continues to dog him. Acknowledging that his life's experiences have imprinted him with both Caucasian and Yurok values, values he even consciously sought to inculcate in himself, Yin Chin Bow makes another discovery: even by seeking to avow his ethnic identity, he cannot ever be Chinese enough for his Chinese family. Ultimately he is forced to hunt down and bring to justice a Yurok youth accused of killing a white man. Unbeknownst to Yin Chin Bow, it is his own eldest son whom he agrees to capture and betray. At the play's conclusion, Yin Chin Bow has turned to alcohol as the only antidote for the pain of his realization that the price of his cultural ambivalence has been his own destruction.

With *Arthur and Leila* (1992), which Lee developed under the aegis of the Mark Taper Forum's Mentor Playwrights Program in Los Angeles, her playwriting skills became more finely tuned, and she hit her stride as a successfully produced and recognized playwright. In 1992 alone, the play was selected for the O'Neill National Playwrights Conference, was cowinner of Mixed Blood Theatre's Playwriting Contest in Minneapolis, and received an honorable mention in South Coast Repertory's California Playwrights Competition. In recognition of the work, Lee received a substantial Fund for New American Plays Grant from the John F. Kennedy Center for the Performing Arts. The play also garnered a Rockefeller MAP Grant for its 1993 world premiere at San Francisco's Brava! For Women and the Arts and a 1994 Fund for New American Plays Award.

Arthur and Leila revolves around the uneasy relationship between Arthur Chin, a dissipated though not unkind alcoholic gambler approaching old age, and his younger sister Leila Chin-Abernathy, a paragon of Chinese American achievement and assimilation. Rather than simply supporting her destitute elder brother by giving him money, something she can well afford to do, Leila allows Arthur to save face by "purchasing" from him detritus from their family's past: a crust of desiccated food wedged in their deceased mother's toothbrush, a mateless chopstick, a can of peaches. Leila exchanges outrageous sums of money for the junk, believing all the while that Arthur is safeguarding valuable objets d'art that he will eventually sell to her. It is not so much the Chinese antiques she is seeking, however, but rather the legitimization of her selfness that they represent to her, a legitimization she believes has been culturally denied to her by virtue of her status as the younger female child. But buying one's selfness, Arthur points out, is merely an illusion: "A story for your prestige. To give you something to be proud of—a 'rich' family heritage. Wasn't that what you wanted to impress your high-class *Lofon* [foreign] friends?" (29).

Lee is at her best constructing roles within roles, reversals within reversals, and circles within circles, a technique she returns to on a larger scale in *Knock Off Balance* (2000). In act 2, scene 3, of *Arthur and Leila*, the two characters engage in a brilliantly written tour de force of role play that exemplifies this approach. Having met her brother in a public park, Leila hopes to convince Arthur to seek professional help for his drinking and gambling addictions. Arthur, who is, however, far more clever than he seems, easily persuades her that he first requires direction in the appropriate manner of participating in psychotherapy. To that end, he suggests a role-playing game to prepare him for a talk-therapy session. As Arthur enacts and speaks in the voice of the therapist, Leila similarly assumes her brother's persona. The ensuing game puts them on an emotional collision course with secrets about familial and cultural losses of identity and issues of shame, guilt, and denial. Ultimately Arthur as therapist forces "himself" to face the destructive truths of his failures as a son and condemns "himself" to die an unthinkable death alone, unloved, exiled from loved ones and community. Leila, on the other hand, moves beyond her anger to an understanding and acceptance of her brother and herself. In the end, the role reversal empowers both characters to awaken to the possibilities of healing their psychic wounds.

Lee successfully entered the arena of political theater with *Carry the Tiger to the Mountain* (1998), becoming the first playwright to receive a commission from West Virginia's Contemporary American Theater Festival (CATF). The case of Vincent Chin's 1982 brutal beating death in Detroit at the hands of Caucasian autoworkers who mistook him for Japanese politically galvanized the Asian American community and resulted in the first non–African American victim in U.S. history filing a federal civil rights lawsuit. Although filmmakers Christine Choy and Renee Tajima had previously documented the historical facts of the case in their 1988 Oscar-nominated *Who Killed Vincent Chin?*, Lee had seen a still-unexplored angle to the story, that of Chin's mother, Lily. At the encouragement of veteran actress Beulah Quo, Lee wrote her own screenplay entitled *And Justice for All*, but the script was unfortunately never filmed. In 1997, responding to President Bill Clinton's nationwide initiative on race relations, "One America in the 21st Century," and Governor Cecil H. Underwood's statewide "One West Virginia in the 21st Century," CATF Artistic Director Ed Herendeen invited Lee to turn her screenplay into a theatrical piece.

In its fluid use of time and cinematic approach to space, *Carry the Tiger* manifests structural similarities to the earlier *Wong Bow Rides Again* and *Yin Chin Bow*, which also depict dramatic time and space as freely shifting between past and present. With *Carry the Tiger*, however, Lee significantly strengthened visual and aural aspects of her playwriting technique that are missing from the previous works wherein the emotional impact of dramatic action is carried solely by spoken discourse. Throughout this play, Lee requires tai chi chuan (the Chinese martial-arts form from which the title of the play is taken) to be performed by Lily Chin and later, in Lily's imagination, by the deceased Vincent. The slow and continuous movements serve as choreographic metaphors for Lily Chin's connection to her cultural heritage and internal struggles as she metamorphoses from a Chinese picture bride to the Asian American political activist who returns to her homeland after the miscarriage of justice in her son's murder case.

Lee additionally calls for projected slides of vehicles along with narration by a character she designates as the "Car Salesman" to reflect the history of America's—and even Vincent's—love affair with the automobile. She further combines Asian music with popular Motown tunes and contemporary disco rhythms to reinforce the theatrical image of competition between Detroit's depressed automotive industry and lower-priced, fuel-efficient Japanese cars, an economic tug-of-war that resulted in the racist and lethal explosion that took an innocent man's life.

Though the continuous intertwining of Chinese and American, dialogue and action, and sound and spectacle is evident throughout *Carry the Tiger*, Lee shows herself to be especially adept at the technique at the conclusions of both acts, in which plot is unfolded through aural and visual metaphors. At the end of act 1, when accused killers Stetz and Evans enact Vincent's murder in stylized tai chi chuan style, Lee calls for a "driving beat of Chinese wood blocks" that transforms into a Motown hit song as the two men repeatedly swing a baseball bat at Vincent's head. As the wood-block sound accelerates, "red silk ribbons representing blood are thrown around Vincent's head as though spurting blood" until Vincent lies still, and the stage is engulfed in a sea of red. The final scene in act 2 reiterates and expands these effects even further, combining the historical Chinese heroine Fa Mu Lan and tai chi chuan swordplay with that most American of pastimes, baseball:

Sound of Chinese woodblock [. . .] Lily picks up a wooden sword to do Tai Chi swordplay. . . . Vincent Chin enters. . . . leading Stetz and Evans with their hands tied behind their backs and placards around their necks, in the way Chinese criminals in the 1940s were paraded publicly before their execution. . . . Lily stares at the two killers, sword in hand. A Chinese woman warrior enters. . . . She is the legendary Fa Mu Lan who takes revenge on the killing of family. Fa Mu Lan takes the wooden sword from Lily. After circling the two men and demonstrating her prowess with the wooden sword using many of Lily's sword moves, she takes batting practice, . . . then Fa Mu Lan steps up to home plate and with one slow motion swing, beheads Evans and Stetz. The wood block sound stops. The lights flood red, then a rousing chorus of "Take me out to the ball game" . . . as Fa Mu Lan raises her sword in triumph.

The violence and fury of the scene serve as an emotional catalyst for Lily, allowing her to release her anger and begin the healing process, a journey that ultimately returns her to her home village in China, where she establishes a tai chi chuan school named for Vincent.

Following the success of *Carry the Tiger to the Mountain*, which went on to be performed at Pan Asian Repertory Theatre and East West Players, Lee served as the Rella Lossy Playwright in Residence at San Francisco State University, overseeing the first fully staged production of *Knock Off Balance*. The play had previously been workshopped at a number of venues, including the Sundance Playwrights Laboratory (1995), and had received staged readings at New York's Culture Project (1996), Los Angeles's Audrey Skirball-Kenis Theater (1996), and San Francisco's 450 Geary Theater (1997). With *Knock off Balance*, Lee returned to the "role-reversal" technique of *Arthur and Leila*. The play takes place in Los Angeles and Hong Kong in 1997 as Great Britain prepares to hand over Hong Kong to the People's Republic of China. Doris Eng, who runs a third-rate Hollywood-celebrity-lookalike agency, unexpectedly meets Dorris Ango, her younger long-lost cousin from Hong Kong, who claims to be seeking actors for a film about arranged marriages.

Doris and Dorris are related by more than blood, race, and their similar names. Both women struggle with issues of self-identity and failed duty to family. As Doris fumes to her cousin: "I was born and raised in this country. I've worked hard, tried hard, and it bugs the hell out of me, that for all the sweat of three generations, . . . I still end up wearing the imitation knock off Chanel suit, while my Chinese cousin . . . not only wears an original, but lo and behold, she is the original, the real Chinese. I am only a hyphenated American. A clown." As the "real thing," Dorris, on the other hand, is less concerned with her ethnic identity than she is with the grip of her past when, during the Cultural Revolution, she betrayed her own mother. Living in the United States has brought her to her own crucial realization: "You vent and re-in-vent. . . . That's how Americans eliminate shame. Make overs, re-inventions, escape from all bonds with the past. To exist without any guilt—that's the American Dream."

In order for each to create the self she desires, Dorris suggests that the two cousins enter into a pact to become each other, trading names, clothes, and occupations, even relocating—Doris to Hong Kong, Dorris to Los Angeles. The ensuing cultural comedy of errors, with each character confronting recalcitrant actors and ominous government officials from the IRS and the Chinese Communist Party, eventually forces both women to face and make peace with their pasts. Though Doris once deserted her family to marry an African American man, her own "Cultural Revolution," as she calls it, she offers Dorris the new identity she really seeks by enabling her to reconcile with the peasant mother she once publicly reviled. As in *Arthur and Leila*, reversal of identities ultimately effects the rebirth of the self.

CRITICAL RECEPTION

The work of Asian American playwrights historically has been met with resounding silence by scholars and critics, and Cherylene Lee's body of work has been no exception. Such published critical assessment of Lee's drama as exists, therefore, is to be predominantly found in the necessarily attenuated responses to productions of her plays by newspaper reviewers and arts editors. In 1987, Sylvie Drake of the *Los Angeles Times*, for example, dismissed *Wong Bow Rides Again* as a "bumpy ride" for its clumsy intertwining of Wong Bow's stories with those of his descendants (1).

Arthur and Leila and *Carry the Tiger to the Mountain* are Lee's most oft-produced works to date and thus have garnered more, albeit mixed, response than many of her earlier dramas. Steven Winn, writing for the *San Francisco*

Chronicle in 1993, described *Arthur and Leila* as "neither absorbing nor plausible" and not much improved by Nancy Kwan's and Dana Lee's performances,
which he found "stiffly acted" (Winn E1). Two months later, however, *Daily
Variety*'s Julio Martinez reviewed East West Players' production with the same
cast. Though he chided director Karen Maruyama for "unimaginative and static"
blocking, he nevertheless applauded both Lee's and Kwan's performances, adding that the "wonderfully balanced sweep of the play" itself compensated for
the production's shortcomings (Review Section). The following year, *Arthur and
Leila* was produced by New York's Pan Asian Repertory Theatre with veteran
Ron Nakahara directing Tina Chen and Jon Lee in the title roles. D.J.R. Bruckner's *New York Times* review commended Cherylene Lee for her "witty dialogue
. . . [in which] every word is a prism" and noted her skillful handling of the
"emotionally taut contest of wills in which protagonist and antagonist are constantly changing roles" (C16).

   Carry the Tiger to the Mountain has also received mixed reviews. Writing
for the *Washington Post* in response to the Contemporary American Theater's
premiere of the play in 1998, Lloyd Rose described *Carry the Tiger* as a hack-
neyed rehashing of racial conflict (C01). The *New York Times*, on the other
hand, approved of Pan Asian Repertory's 1998 production. Wilborn Hampton's
review suggested that the true Vincent Chin story might not be in and of itself
sufficient to "sustain [the action of] a full-length play," but that Lee had capably
fashioned the devastating incident "to build a taut and sometimes humorous
docudrama" that was remarkable for the scope of issues it addressed and the
deftness of the theatrical techniques it employed (E4). Luis H. Francia, himself
a produced Asian American playwright, concurred in his *Village Voice* review
of the same production, noting that Lee had wisely refrained from dwelling on
the inherent pathos of Chin's murder and had opted instead to craft "a solid
human drama focusing on the deep bond between mother and son and on the
terrible agony she endures upon his death" (139). In 1999, when Los Angeles's
East West Players produced *Carry the Tiger*, Michael Phillips noted that artistic
director Tim Dang's able direction, along with Peter Kwong's graceful tai chi
choreography and Beulah Quo's powerful portrayal of Lily Chin, compensated
for the plot's predictability (2).

   Though traditionally overlooked by the American academy, Lee's work has
been recognized with numerous honors, including a San Francisco Arts Council
Individual Commission and grants from the Ucross Foundation, Djerassi Foundation, and Centrum for the Arts. She has also focused efforts toward reaching
young audiences, serving as a guest speaker for Houghton Mifflin/McDougal
Littell's Literature Center, Learning on Line. She also received a commission
from Los Angeles's TreePeople to develop a children's work about the environment, *Six Drops* (1995). The musical based upon her own life experiences
as a child performer entitled *Lost Vegas Acts* (1997) was workshopped at Z
Space in San Francisco. She has been awarded a Gerbode Foundation Grant
with San Francisco's Magic Theatre for the development of her latest work

Legacy Codes, a play that addresses the issue of Chinese American scientists accused of spying for foreign governments. A member of New Dramatists, the Dramatists Guild, Z Space Studio, and ThroughLine, the San Francisco Bay Area playwrights' group, Cherylene Lee continues to produce new Asian American works that address both historical and contemporary issues of identity and reconciliation.

BIBLIOGRAPHY

Works by Cherylene Lee

Drama

Pyros. Videocassette. Seattle: American Folk Theatre, 1983.
Arthur and Leila. Women Playwrights: The Best Women's Plays of 1993. Ed. Marisa Smith. Newbury, VT: Smith and Kraus, 1994. 4–37.

Unpublished Manuscripts

Aesop's Fantastic Fables. 1984.
Overtones. 1984.
Wong Bow Rides Again. 1985.
Yin Chin Bow. 1986.
The Ballad of Doc Hay. 1987.
Memory Square. Cynthia Leung, coauthor. 1988.
Bitter Melon. Act 3. Jeff Gillenkirk, coauthor. 1989.
Delta Pearl, Acts 1 and 2 of *Bitter Melon*. Jeff Gillenkirk, coauthor. 1989.
In the Spirit. 1993.
City Quest a.k.a Six Drops. 1995.
Knock Off Balance. 1995.
Lost Vegas Acts. 1997
Carry the Tiger to the Mountain. 1998.
Legacy Codes. 2000.

Selected Production History

Overtones

Staged reading. Bay Area Playwrights' Festival VII, San Francisco, 1984.
Production. Kumu Kahua Theatre, Honolulu, 1988.

Yin Chin Bow

Staged reading. Pan Asian Repertory Theatre and Basement Workshop, New York City, 1986.
Workshop, dir. Claire Nomura. Asian American Theater Company, San Francisco, 1987.
Staged reading. Third Step Theatre, New York City, 1990.

The Ballad of Doc Hay

Production. Chinese Cultural Center, San Francisco, 1987.
———. Marin Playhouse Theatre, San Francisco, 1987.

Wong Bow Rides Again

Production, dir. Josie Pepito Kim and Leigh C. Kim. East West Players, Los Angeles, 1987.

Arthur and Leila

Staged reading. Mark Taper Forum, Los Angeles, 1991.

Production, dir. Amy Mueller; perf. Nancy Kwan and Dana Lee. Asian American Theater Company, San Francisco, 1993.

———, dir. Karen Maruyama; perf. Nancy Kwan and Dana Lee. East West Players, Los Angeles, 1993.

———, dir. Ron Nakahara. Pan Asian Repertory Theatre, New York City, 1994.

———, dir. Amy Mueller; perf. Nancy Kwan, Dana Lee, Susan Chen, and Qi-Chou Liu. Theatre Artaud, San Francisco, 1994.

Bitter Melon, Act 3

Staged reading. New Traditions Theatre Company, San Francisco, 1991.

Memory Square

Staged reading. P.F. Flyer Productions, San Francisco, 1991.

———. Asian American Theater Company, San Francisco, 1991.

In the Spirit (With the San Jose Taiko Drummers and Abhinaya Dance Theatre)

Production. Louis B. Mayer Theatre, San Jose, CA, 1993.

Knock Off Balance

Staged reading. Audrey Skirball-Kenis Theater, Los Angeles, 1996.

———. 450 Geary Theater, San Francisco, 1997.

Production, dir. Karen Amano. San Francisco State U, San Francisco, 2000.

Carry the Tiger to the Mountain

Production, dir. Ed Herendeen; perf. Beulah Quo, Marcu Ho, Bonnie Akimoto, Mia Tagano, J.P. Linton, Michael Goodwin, Rudolph Willrich, Paul Sparks, and Jim Ishida. Contemporary American Theater Festival, Shepherdstown, WV, 1998.

———, dir. Ron Nakahara; perf. Wai Ching Ho, Andrew Pang, and Peter Von Berg. Pan Asian Repertory Theatre, New York City, 1998.

———, dir. Tim Dang; chor. Peter Kwong; perf. Kandace Cline, Richard Gallegos, Robert Greenberg, Steve Humphreys, Reggie Lee, Cindy Lu, Benjamin Lum, Matt K. Miller, Kim Montelibano, Beulah Quo, and Barry Sigismondi. East West Players, Los Angeles, 1999.

Lost Vegas Acts

Staged reading, dir. Tisa Chang; prod. Pan Asian Repertory Theatre. Musical Theatre Works, New York City, 1999.

Workshop, dir. Karen Amano; perf. Kimiko Gelman, Linda Shiao-ling Chuan, Mitzie G. Abe, Hollis Audrey Wear, Sophie Tamiko Oda, Kaila O'Neill, Michael Ching, Teli Cardaci, David E. Kazanjian, Bonnie Akimoto, and Sheila O'Neill Ellis. Z Space Studio, San Francisco, 2000.

———, prod. San Jose Repertory Theatre New America Playwright Festival. Villa Montalvo, Saratoga, CA, 2000.

The Legacy Codes

Staged reading. New Dramatists, New York City, 2000.
Production, dir. Ron Nakahara. New Play Festival, Hangar Theatre, Ithaca, NY, 2001.

Short Stories

"Hollywood and the Pits." *American Dragons.* Ed. Laurence Yep. New York: HarperCollins, 1993. 34–47.
"Safe." *Charlie Chan Is Dead: An Anthology of Contemporary Asian American Fiction.* Ed. Jessica Hagedorn. New York: Penguin, 1993. 204–14.

Studies of Cherylene Lee

Adolphson, Sue. "Cultural Clash: Chinese American Brother, Sister Square Off in Award Winning Play." Rev. of *Arthur and Leila. San Francisco Chronicle* 24 Oct. 1993: 37.
Bruckner, D.J.R. "Tell Precious Secrets Just As Children Do." Rev. of *Arthur and Leila. New York Times* 18 Oct. 1994: C16.
Drake, Sylvie. "*Wong Bow* Bumpy Ride to Vegas." Rev. of *Wong Bow Rides Again. Los Angeles Times* 9 Feb. 1987, sec. 6: 1.
Francia, Luis H. "A Death in the Family." Rev. of *Carry the Tiger to the Mountain. Village Voice* 43.48 (1998): 139.
Hampton, Wilborn. "When Cultures Clash, the Results Are Fatal." Rev. of *Carry the Tiger to the Mountain. New York Times* 23 Nov. 1998: E4.
Hong, Terry. "Intertwining Tales." *A. Magazine: Inside Asian America* June/July 1998: 78–79.
Lee, Joann Faung Jean. "Cherylene Lee." *Asian American Actors: Oral Histories from Stage, Screen, and Television.* Jefferson, NC: McFarland, 2000. 194–200.
Martinez, Julio. "*Arthur and Leila.*" Review. *Daily Variety* 5 Jan. 1994: Review section. N. pag.
Phillips, Michael. "*Carry the Tiger* Tells of Chinese Immigrant Family's Tragedy." Rev. of *Carry the Tiger to the Mountain. Los Angeles Times* 27 Feb. 1999, home ed., F2.
Rose, Lloyd. " 'Tiger': Stage Left; Shepherdstown's Star Attraction Fizzles" *Washington Post* 16 July 1998: C01.
Uno, Roberta. "Appendix: Plays by Asian American Women." Ed. Roberta Uno. *Unbroken Thread: An Anthology of Plays by Asian American Women.* Amherst: U of Massachusetts P, 1993. 309–28.
Winn, Steven. "Brother, Sister Spar over Chinese Heritage." Rev. of *Arthur and Leila. San Francisco Chronicle* 6 Nov. 1993: E1.
Zia, Helen. "Detroit Blues: Because of You Motherfuckers." *Asian American Dreams: The Emergence of an American People.* By Helen Zia. New York: Farrar, Straus, and Giroux, 2000. 55–81.

Ling-ai (Gladys) Li
(ca. 1910–   )

Shuchen S. Huang

BIOGRAPHY

Ling-ai (Gladys) Li was born in Honolulu, Hawaii, around 1910. Her parents, Tai-Heong Kong and Khai-Fai Li, known as the first Chinese doctors in Hawaii, immigrated from China to Hawaii in 1896. Ling-ai Li had eight brothers and sisters and was the sixth child of the family. Because of her parents' medical practice, she came into contact with people of different races, classes, and vocations in her early childhood.

Ling-ai Li attended the University of Hawai'i and obtained a bachelor's degree in 1930. When she was a college student at the University of Hawai'i, she already showed her artistic talents. She had some poems and plays published in the school journals, particularly the *Hawaii Quill Magazine* and *Troubador*. After graduating from college, she was busily engaged in various cultural productions. From 1932 to 1936, she studied music and Chinese theatre in China. From 1933 to 1936, she also worked as a director of theater in the Beijing Institute of Fine Arts, Beijing, China.

After the Japanese launched the full-scale invasion of China in 1937, Li's artistic career took on a more patriotic tone. Between 1938 and 1940, she was producing a documentary entitled *Kukan*, which recorded how China stood under Japanese military siege during World War II. The film won her both the professional recognition of an Academy Award and the national honor of meeting personally with President and Mrs. Franklin D. Roosevelt in the White House in 1941. From 1940 to 1946, she undertook the responsibility of creating the theater programs for the American Bureau of Medical Aid to China Fund Raising Program. At the same time, she was also a board member of a Chinese newspaper called *Sun Chung Kwock Bo* (New China News). From 1940 to 1953, she directed some plays for the Far Eastern research division of Ripley, Believe It or Not, Inc., in New York City. From 1958 to 1962, she worked as a consultant to the National Nationalities Program of the National Federation of Republican Women. In 1975, Ling-ai Li was named Bicentennial Woman of the Year by the National Association of Women Artists of America.

MAJOR WORKS AND THEMES

Ling-ai Li started writing plays when she was still a college student at the University of Hawai'i. She published three short plays in the school journal called the *Hawaii Quill Magazine*. The first one, entitled *The Submission of Rose Moy*, was written in 1924, printed in the *Hawaii Quill Magazine* in 1928, and later anthologized by Eric Chock and Darrell H.Y. Lum in *Paké: Writings by Chinese in Hawaii* (1989). *The Submission of Rose Moy* recounts a story about generational and cultural conflicts between Rose Moy and her Chinese immigrant father in Hawaii in the early twentieth century. Rose Moy is a Hawaiian-born college girl with "Western ideas and ideals." She has a dream of becoming a female leader in China advocating women's suffrage. However, her father, Wing Moy, with his traditional and patriarchal values in mind, has another plan for his daughter. He insists on marrying her to a wealthy Chinese merchant, Kwang Wei, in Honolulu, who already possesses three concubines in China and seeks a replacement for his recently deceased first wife. Upon learning of Kwang Wei's marriage proposal and her father's arrangement, Rose Moy debates between complying with her father's decision and defying it by leaving home. Her friend, Mr. Donald, for whom she poses for a Chinese painting, offers to help her pursue her goals of postgraduate studies and a career by sending her to live with his sister in Berkeley, California. The play ends with Rose Moy reading her mother's letter, which desires her to follow the traditional paths for women.

The second play, *The Law of Wu Wei*, published in 1929, also focuses on the theme of cultural conflicts. The author tells a story of an unfulfilled love affair between a Chinese student, Chen Wei, and a Hawaiian-born Chinese girl, Rosie Moy. Chen Wei broke his engagement with Rosie Moy in order to carry out his family's marriage arrangement for him in China. The third play is *The White Serpent* (1932), whose idea derives from a Chinese mythological tale, "Madame White Snake."

In addition to the dramatic work, Ling-ai Li also published several poems, a novel, and an autobiography. Her poems include "My Dowry" (1928), "A Prayer" (1929), "My Kimono Sleeves" (1931), and "No-nau-nau" (1931), all of which were published in the *Hawaii Quill Magazine* and *Troubador*. She wrote a novel for young readers entitled *Children of the Sun in Hawaii* (1944). In this book, she narrates a story about a native Hawaiian boy named Kimo and his friendships with friends of different ethnic backgrounds. In 1972, Ling-ai Li published her autobiography, *Life Is for a Long Time: A Chinese Hawaiian*

Memoir. The book chronicles her Chinese parents' immigration to and settlement in Hawaii in the late nineteenth and early twentieth centuries.

CRITICAL RECEPTION

Ling-ai Li was a versatile artist. She wrote poems, plays, and novels and directed theatrical plays and films. However, her writings have received very little critical attention. Generally speaking, her name is most often associated with her autobiography, *Life Is for a Long Time*. *Publishers Weekly* has a short book review of the autobiography, but provides no more than a summary of the book. In *And the View from the Shore: Literary Traditions of Hawai'i*, Stephen H. Sumida asserts that Ling-ai Li is one of the talented writers in earlier Hawaiian literary history, and her autobiography portrays an atypical Chinese immigrant family story in Hawaii at the turn of the century (203). In their annotated bibliography *Asian American Literature of Hawaii*, Arnold T. Hiura and Stephen H. Sumida include seven publication entries by Ling-ai Li, of which three are the plays (*The Submission of Rose Moy, The Law of Wu Wei*, and *The White Serpent*) composed during her college years and published in the *Hawaii Quill Magazine*. In *An Interethnic Companion to Asian American Literature*, Sau-ling Cynthia Wong's chapter has a very brief comment on Ling-ai Li. Wong states that Li is one of those Chinese Hawaiian student writers who wrote "stories, poems and plays about plantation life, generational conflicts, and other 'local' subjects; some experimented with the use of pidgin" (46). But, all in all, her works have fallen into oblivion, as have many other contributions Asian Americans made in the history of the United States.

BIBLIOGRAPHY

Works by Ling-ai Li

Drama

The Submission of Rose Moy. Hawaii Quill Magazine 1 (June 1928): 7–19. Rpt. in *Paké: Writings by Chinese in Hawaii*. Ed. Eric Chock and Darrell H.Y. Lum. Honolulu: Bamboo Ridge P, 1989. 50–64.
The Law of Wu Wei. Hawaii Quill Magazine 2 (Jan. 1929): 20–26.
The White Serpent. Hawaii Quill Magazine 5 (May 1932): 24–31.

Selected Production History

The Submission of Rose Moy

Production. Arthur Andrews Theatre, U of Hawai'i, Manoa, 1925.

The White Serpent

Production. Arthur Andrews Theatre, U of Hawai'i, Manoa, 1927.
———. McKinley High Auditorium, Honolulu, HI, 1928.

The Law of Wu Wei

Production. Arthur Andrews Theatre, U of Hawai'i, Manoa, 1928.

Autobiography

Life Is for a Long Time: A Chinese Hawaiian Memoir. New York: Hastings House, 1972.

Novel

Children of the Sun in Hawaii. Boston: D.C. Heath, 1944.

Poetry

"My Dowry." *Hawaii Quill Magazine* 1 (Jan. 1928): 19.
"A Prayer." *Hawaii Quill Magazine* 2 (Jan. 1929): 6–7.
"My Kimono Sleeves." *Troubador* 3 (May 1931): 20.
"No-nau-nau." *Troubador* 3 (May 1931): 20.

Studies of Ling-ai Li

Hiura, Arnold T., and Stephen H. Sumida. *Asian American Literature of Hawaii: An Annotated Bibliography.* Aiea, HI: Hawaii Ethnic Resources Center, 1979. 36–37, 168.

Rev. of *Life Is for a Long Time: A Chinese Hawaiian Memoir. Publishers Weekly* 4 Sept. 1972: 44.

Sumida, Stephen H. *And the View from the Shore: Literary Traditions of Hawai'i.* Seattle: U of Washington P, 1991.

Wong, Sau-ling Cynthia. "Chinese American Literature." *An Interethnic Companion to Asian American Literature.* Ed. King-Kok Cheung. New York: Cambridge UP, 1997. 39–61.

Genny Lim
(1946–   )

Miles Xian Liu

BIOGRAPHY

Genny Lim was born on December 15, 1946, in San Francisco, California. Her father, Edward Lim, emigrated with his father to the United States as a young boy and went back to China to marry, as his father had done. Lim's mother, Lin Sun, was also from Guangzhou (Canton), China. Both Edward and Lin were processed at the Angel Island immigration detention center when they came in, as their parents before them had been. Like many of the first-generation immigrants, Edward and Lin struggled together to make ends meet. Working as a janitor at the Fairmont Hotel, Edward one day brought home "little pastries and carpet scraps from the main lobby, thick black pile with magenta *fleur de lys*," as Lim recalls in an online interview with Jaime Wright. Her mother worked as a piecework seamstress and often "sewed into the wee hours of the morning" while raising a family of seven children (Wright). Lim grew up in the Chinese tradition that demands both filial obedience and personal perseverance. Her choice of career and the focus of her works reflect this influence from her life in a first-generation Chinese immigrant family.

Indeed, Lim decided against the conventional women's careers that her parents had intended for her in order to become a poet, performance artist, playwright, and educator. She worked as a musician during the 1960s. After graduation with a certificate in broadcast journalism from Columbia University in 1973, she worked in Chicago, Atlanta, and New York as a free-lance writer, television producer, and media commentator. However, her desire to combine her artistic impulses with her journalistic interest in Asian America took her back to San Francisco. She studied theater arts at San Francisco State University (SFSU) and earned a B.A. (1978) and M.A. (1988) in English with creative-writing emphasis. Despite her parents' attempts to steer their children into jobs with greater economic security, Lim embarked on a career path that was anything but financially stable.

While she was studying creative writing at SFSU, an oral-history project led her to hundreds of poems etched on the walls of the immigration detention center on Angel Island. Her signature play *Paper Angels* (1978) is the result of the project, as is the book she coedited, *Island: Poetry and History of Chinese Immigrants on Angel Island, 1910–1940* (1980). Since then, she has written a dozen plays and performance pieces, edited *The Chinese American Experience: Papers from the Second National Conference on Chinese American Studies (1980)* (1984), and published a bilingual children's book, *Wings for Lai-Ho* (1982), and a collection of poetry, *Winter Place: Poems* (1989). In 1989, she joined the faculty of New College of California and started teaching at Naropa Institute in Oakland.

As a prominent poet, performance artist, playwright, and educator of Chinese American descent, Lim is quick to denounce the practice of relying on a person's ethnic label for a niche in a profession. "Labeling is a preoccupation of mass media, marketers, and politicians" in their efforts to package their products and politics for consumers and constituents (Wright). Although she does not write to fit in, she has garnered numerous awards for her work both on and off the page. In 1980, "Nostalgia" received the Robert Frost Award for Poetry at the San Mateo County Fair. In 1982, *Island: Poetry and History of Chinese Immigrants on Angel Island, 1910–1940* was the winner of the American Book Award, and *Paper Angels* the winner of the Downtown Village Award. She received the Certificate of Honor in Appreciative Recognition of Distinction and Merit from the mayor of San Francisco and the Asian Community Mental Health Services Award, both in 1986. In 1987, the Department of Creative Writing at SFSU presented her the Lee and Lawrence First Prize Playwrighting Award for *XX*. In 1991, the *San Francisco Bay Guardian* recognized her with its Goldie Award for outstanding performance, and in 1996, she received the Distinguished Award for Culture from the San Francisco Chinese Culture Center Foundation for her years of contribution to the Chinese American community. In 1997, *Songlines: The Spiritual Tributary of Paul Robeson and Mei Lanfang*, a cantata on which she collaborated with composers Jon Jang and James Newton, won her the John D. Rockefeller Foundation Award. In 2000, the Zellerbach Playhouse production of *Paper Angels* at the University of California at Berkeley won the James Wong Howe Award.

MAJOR WORKS AND THEMES

Lim is as versatile as a performance artist as she is prolific as a cross-genre writer. Her award-winning book *Island* reminds the nation of its shameful anti-Asian immigration policies in the past. Her anthology *The Chinese American Experience: Papers from the Second National Conference on Chinese American*

Studies (1980) provided the discipline of Asian studies with updated research materials. Among her fourteen theatrical works are two of her best-known plays, *Paper Angels* (1978) and *Bitter Cane* (1989). Most representative thematically, these two plays are noted for their insightful examination of race, gender, and generational relations in general and their bittersweet portrayal of the Chinese immigrant experience in particular.

Paper Angels, which grew from her book project *Island*, chronicles the heart-wrenching plight of seven Chinese immigrants—four men and three women—as they wait and hope to be admitted to the United States. Because the Exclusion Act of 1882 refuses the entry of Chinese laborers, every Chinese that comes to shore must be detained while federal authorities investigate his or her right to enter. The arbitrary process, which relies heavily on the stories of witnesses and immigrants, consequently denies the entry of returning citizens from time to time while creating loopholes for newcomers to lie their way into the United States. Although the play is fact based, as Lim told Christine Koyama, a free-lance writer for the *New York Times*, its setting, plot, and characters are more emblematic of the agonizing nature of the whole Chinese immigrant experience in the United States than truthful to any given incident.

The play is set on Angel Island in 1905, when the Chinese Exclusion Act of 1882 was in full force. As Leland Stanford and the U.S. economy no longer needed the builders of the Great Wall to build the dreams of a transcontinental railroad and a settled West, America was doing its best to keep out cheap Asian labor, even though the number of Chinese immigrants was only 0.02 percent of the country's population. Angel Island, similar in its function to Ellis Island as an immigration processing center, did not welcome the Chinese immigrants with the beacon of liberty or freedom, but instead with weeks, months, or even years of detention. Therefore, unlike Ellis Island as the proud symbol of opportunities for European immigrants, Angel Island stands for a sad chapter of U.S. history in the minds of Asian immigrants.

The seven characters in the play come from all walks of life, but arrive with the single purpose of seeking what they hope will be a better life. They constitute, symbolically, a typical slice of Asian immigrants to the United States. A veteran detainee, Fong, who can "always make the best of a bad situation," is cynical about any versions of American dreams (Uno ed. 29); an idealistic poet, Lee wants to learn English because "I want to become an American" (24); Lum, a hot-tempered, irrational young man, believes that he can defeat the system with violence and dreams of the day when "even the white folks call him 'Mis-tah Lum!' " (24). Chin Gung, a returning citizen, is also among the detained. After forty years of working on the transcontinental railroad, he went back to China, reunited with his wife, and brought her over this time for a better life in America. He has no illusions about the Gold Mountain: "America is just a faraway place in the mind" (25). Every immigrant creates his or her own version of America in order to hang on to his or her dreams.

Among the women detainees, Chin Moo, Chin Gung's wife, cannot stop won-

dering whether someone like herself, content with raising two pigs in the back-
yard, could be happy in America; Mei Lai, with a baby on the way, is full of
hope, not unlike her poetic husband, Lee; Ku Ling, a sentimental young girl,
has not only wide mood swings but also high hopes, though she has no idea
what to expect. The address she has in her pocket promises her a life in a brothel
according to Miss Gregory, a Methodist missionary who is bent on baptizing
everyone admitted into the United States.

Together these characters come, as many before them and many more will
after them, to pursue their own version of the American dream in defiance of
America's discriminatory immigration laws. The only difference between them
and European immigrants is that they happen to be Chinese. Accidental as their
ethnicity may be, it automatically makes them subjects of interrogation in the
detention center of Angel Island rather than men of "unalienable rights" on the
streets of America.

In *Bitter Cane*, the contracted Chinese laborers are lured by a monthly wage
of four dollars to Hawaiian plantations to cut sugarcane. Against the backdrop
of the 1882 Chinese Exclusion Act, Hawaii is as close to the Gold Mountain as
most of these Chinese laborers will ever get, but unlike the immigrant characters
in *Paper Angels*, many of the laborers do not intend to stay once their contract
is up. They are temporary sojourners and, as such, expect to work and live with
a normal social life. However, for many of them on "a land of bitter cane" in
the 1880s, work is their life, gambling their entertainment, opium their relaxa-
tion, and an hour with a prostitute their social life (Houston ed. 170). It is against
the background of such cultural dislocation that the play's main characters—
Wing Chun Kuo, Li Tai, and Kam—grapple with the issues of honor, love, and
identity.

Wing, sixteen years old, sets off for Hawaii to rectify what he and his dying
mother thought was the dishonor of his late father, Lau Hing Juo. Lau's body
was never found. "You must remember, my only son," the play begins with the
dying words of Wing's mother, "never to dishonor yourself. . . . Do not kill me
with shame as did your father" (165). With the family mission to "break the
cycle of pain," Wing arrives at the same sugarcane plantation where Lau used
to work (165). He soon discovers, however, that Lau never intended to return
because he had been cheated out of his share of the land by his own family, all
because Lau's mother was a Polynesian. Lau resorted to opium out of spite for
his arranged marriage and his love for Li Tai, a widow forced into prostitution
by a Chinese foreman. But Li reveals Lau's secrets only after Wing falls in love
with her.

As much as Wing is glad that his father did not abandon him and his mother
dishonorably, he is at a loss about his incestuous love for his father's former
lover. Wing asks Li, as would any man in love, to escape with him to Honolulu
for a better life. Li once turned down the same invitation from Wing's father
because "the idea of freedom was as frightening as death" at that point (198).
Now, lonely days of waiting for men have convinced her that life is about "going

after what you want, no matter what," an outlook that may be native to Americans but foreign to the Chinese (198). However, the ending of the play is far from Hollywood's usual happily-ever-after.

If love is complicated in a land where neither tradition nor law seems to matter, the identity of these Chinese cane cutters is even more unsettling. Kam, Lau's former colleague and Wing's roommate, cannot understand why his virility and savings are not enough for him to start a family in America; Fook, a Chinese foreman, cannot see beyond money and power as the sole purpose in life on a plantation; while Wing knows that he does not want to live as a cane cutter for long and that he, as a "Sandlewood Boy," will not fare any better than his father did back in China, still he has no idea how to begin his journey to a normal family life in America (Houston ed. 193). The play thus brings into focus the struggles that all immigrants have experienced in reestablishing themselves in a new culture where their upbringing seems no longer relevant.

The centerpiece of the screenplay *The Only Language She Knows* (1984) was published under the separate title *The Only Language* in 1986. It captures a heated exchange between Mother and Daughter about what Daughter should be doing at the age of thirty. Writing plays, reading books, being single, and "[l]ighting in da loom all day. And still no makee one peeny" are not exactly in Mother's plan for her talented daughter (34). But the independent-minded Daughter cannot help but laugh when Mother tries to entice her with all her jewelry into marrying a good Chinese boy. The exchange is rendered even more vivid when Mother's impeccable Cantonese English forms a lively contrast with Daughter's idiomatic American English. Contrary to popular expectation, their linguistic and cultural differences only accentuate the harmony of their communication. The play then celebrates the closeness of Mother and Daughter despite all their disagreement in opinion.

Pigeons (1980) is a play about making connections: with nature, one's inner self, and each other. Two nameless characters again—Old Woman and Young Woman—happen to meet on a bench in a park with pigeons congregating all around them. Old Woman is delighted and Young Woman disgusted. The former takes out crumbs, ready to feed her cheerful friends, while the latter gets together her things, ready to leave the noisy pests. But when Old Woman begins calling the pigeons by the names she has given them, Young Woman becomes curious about the relationship between Old Woman and the wild pigeons. Their conversation takes off from there. Young Woman reveals that she prefers living alone without a care in the world—no husband, no children, no pets, and nobody but herself. Old Woman used to live like that when she was young, but now cannot help wondering out loud, "When you ol' like me an haf nobodee den it too late" (65). Old Woman's experience puts Young Woman's life choices in perspective.

Old Woman then pleads with Young Woman to take care of Lo Mo, a pigeon who looks "velly velly tiah" (67). Young Woman bolts at the suggestion at first, but agrees to give it a try for a few days. Her experiment, which begins with

caring for Lo Mo, rewards her with a better understanding of the older generation she used to dismiss, the community she was insensitive to, and her own
life that she thought of as being happy-go-lucky. By the end of the play, the de
facto title characters—the pigeons—become not only the symbol for the invisible and marginalized, but also the medium through whom the old and the
young, the rich and the poor, the past and the present, the individual and the
community get connected and try to communicate. Indeed, not all the attempts
are successful, but the pigeons help get the process under way.

Although Lim does not set out to write history dramas per se, the past experience of Chinese immigrants contextualizes all her major plays. The recurring
themes of race, gender, class, self, and identity are all affected by the specific
history of Asian America. Perhaps what Lim shared with Velina Hasu Houston
in an interview best explains why history is often employed in her plays: "[I]f
we examine history closely, we can learn from our mistakes. . . . Otherwise, like
the cat chasing its own tail, we'll be doomed to doing the same" (qtd. in *Politics*
159).

CRITICAL RECEPTION

The theater reviews of Lim's plays, *Paper Angels* and *Bitter Cane* in particular, have been overwhelmingly positive while full critical examinations from
academia have been sparse, as is the case for most Asian American plays, regardless of the audience response. *Paper Angels* often received favorable reviews along with *Island: Poetry and History of Chinese Immigrants on Angel
Island, 1910–1940*. After all, it is the material for the book that provided the
play with stories and contexts. Fred Ferretti of the *New York Times* called *Island*
"a small, sad and touching book . . . yet oddly exhilarating" (C24). Similarly,
Mel Gussow, reviewing the New Federal Theater's production, saw in the play
"the aspirations and the helplessness of people who want to improve their lives
at the peril of risking everything" (C3). Peter Vaughan of the *Star Tribune*
(Minneapolis) wrote that "this sad chapter of American history . . . deserves a
wide viewing" after Theater Mu produced the play (4E). When KCET of Los
Angeles taped the play for the PBS *American Playhouse* series, Christine Koyama for the *New York Times* could hardly contain her enthusiasm and lauded
the opportunity for the nation to finally hear this untold, but unforgotten, story
of the Chinese immigrants trapped "in this agonizing limbo" of Angel Island
(29). "[T]heir anger and frustration, their loneliness, confusion and fading
hopes" spotlight the tragic truth of the American dream that those unwelcome
immigrants once believed in (29). "I came on a ship full of dreams," as one of
the characters summarizes it, "and landed in a cage full of lies" (Uno ed. 45).

Lim's other theatrical pieces have not been as widely produced, but when
they have been produced, they have received generally favorable reviews. *Bitter
Cane* was hailed as a play, Terry Maloney of *Back Stage* writes, that "consider[s]
fundamental human rights through a personal historic window many of us are

afraid to open" (4W). Lim's latest collaboration with composers Jon Jang and James Newton on *Songlines: The Spiritual Tributary of Paul Robeson and Mei Lanfang* (2000) won high praises for its music, lyrics, singing, and costumes, though "the anticipated story line never got off the ground" (Elwood C7).

Major anthologies and studies of Asian American plays, though few in number, have given Lim's works their due consideration. Roberta Uno places *Paper Angels* as the first play in *Unbroken Thread* (1993) in order to represent in her anthology "a chronology of Asian American experience reflected through Asian American women's eyes" (3). The hope and despair the play depicts articulate, if not inaugurate, a unique experience of Asian immigrants in America, which in many ways defines their feelings about this country. Including *Bitter Cane* in her anthology *The Politics of Life: Four Plays by Asian American Women* (1993), Velina Hasu Houston sees it as a work with multiple themes: "the history of oppression of Chinese laborers," "the history of racism against persons of mixed race in China," "the truth of gender exploitation," and "the burdens of men living apart from their wives and children or unable to begin a family in the first place" (158–59). In other words, the play is about the bittersweet human experience.

In her book *Performing Asian America*, Josephine Lee examines both of Lim's plays in the same way that historian Ron Takaki uses personal diaries, letters, and stories to verify the truth of history. The dehumanizing exploitation of Chinese laborers in *Bitter Cane* is evident not just from the twelve-hour shifts, but more significantly, from the "gambling, opium, and women" that the plantation helped furnish for a price (*Bitter Cane* 171). It would have been best for the plantation if each of the laborers could just move "[l]ike a dumb plow ox" (171). In *Paper Angels*, each character voices a perspective emblematic of a specific viewpoint on race, immigration, and life in America. Consequently, "the choral effects" of these plays "prompt an identification with an individual felt experience as well as with a collective experience" (Lee 150). Lim's best works resonate with the audience precisely because they appeal to the common American experience through distinctly Asian voices.

BIBLIOGRAPHY

Works by Genny Lim

Drama

The Only Language. Excerpt from the screenplay *The Only Language She Knows*. Bamboo Ridge 30 (1986): 34–41.
Pigeons. Bamboo Ridge 30 (1986): 57–79.
Paper Angels and Bitter Cane: Two Plays. Honolulu: Kalamaku P, 1991.
Bitter Cane. The Politics of Life: Four Plays by Asian American Women. Ed. Velina Hasu Houston. Philadelphia: Temple UP, 1993. 163–204. Rpt. in *The Oxford*

Book of Women's Writing in the United States. Ed. Linda Wagner-Martin and Cathy N. Davidson. New York: Oxford UP, 1995. 407–40.

Paper Angels. Unbroken Thread: An Anthology of Plays by Asian American Women. Ed. Roberta Uno. Amherst: U of Massachusetts P, 1993. 11–152. Excerpts. *Monologues for Actors of Color: Men.* Ed. Roberta Uno. New York: Routledge, 2000. 95–96. Excerpts. *Monologues for Actors of Color: Women.* Ed. Roberta Uno. New York: Routledge, 2000. 127–28.

La China Poblana. Excerpts. *Yellow Light: The Flowering of Asian American Arts.* Ed. Amy Ling. Philadelphia: Temple UP, 1999. 216–21.

Unpublished Manuscripts

Daughter of Han. 1983.

I Remember Clifford. 1983.

The Pumpkin Girl. 1987.

XX. 1987.

Faceless. Multimedia, text by Genny Lim. 1989.

Winter Place. 1989.

The Magic Brush. 1990.

SenseUs: The Rainbow Anthems. Poetry and music collaboration with Max Roach, Sonia Sanchez, Jon Jang, Jon Santos, and Victory Hernandez Cruz. 1990.

Pins and Noodles. 1992.

Songlines: The Spiritual Tributary of Paul Robeson and Mei Lanfang. Libretto by Genny Lim and music by Jon Jang and James Newton. 2000.

Selected Production History

Paper Angels

Production, dir. Amy Hill; perf. Wood Moy, Dennis Dun, Art Lai, Kelvin Han Yee, Lynette Chun, Karen Huie, Bernadette Cha, and Kitty Tsui. Asian American Theater Company, San Francisco, 1980.

———, dir. John Lone; perf. Victor Wong, Kitty Chen, William Hao, Mia Katigbak, Matthew Grana, Steve Monroe, Jean Kay Sifford, Toshi Toda, Lilah Kan, Henry Yuk, and Ching Valdez. New Federal Theater, New York City, 1982.

———, dir. Mako; perf. Dana Lee, Ping Wu, Chris Huie, A.M. Lai, Dewi Yee, Jo Yang, Jean Lee Wong, Ron Hardesty, Karen Chew, Harry Rosenbluth, Terry Chow, Katherine Monahan, Sue Lim Yee, Leon Sun, and Harry Wong. Chinese Culture Center, San Francisco, 1982.

———, dir. John Lone; comp. Lucia Hwong; perf. James Hong, Joan Chen, Victor Wong, Beulah Quo, Ping Wu, David Huang, and Rosalind Chao. PBS series *American Playhouse.* KCET production. 1985.

———. Asian Theater Group, Seattle, 1995.

———. Ethnic Cultural Center, Seattle, 1995.

———, dir. Kim Hines; perf. Ying Zhang, Sophronia Liu, Daniel Sach Le, Luu Pham, Paul Lohn, Nelson Williams, Jack Malberg, Paul Juhn, Gretchen Douma, and Graydon Kouri. Theater Mu, Minneapolis, 1995.

———, dir. Tony Mark; perf. Art Lai, Robert Fong, Beau Yep, Rina Dion, Jacie Tsong Vang, Lau Gwok Leung, Dung Tien Nguyen, Bree Becker, Michael S. Gething, and Mac Van Dugan. Asian Pacific Theatre Company, Sacramento, 1996.

———, dir. Valeri Braun; perf. Ming Lo, Gary Murakami, Al Barlaan, Anthony Cuesta, Kelly Miyashiro, Nancy Long, Darren O'Hanvey, Dennis Desling, and Larry Gesling. Morgan-Wixon Theatre Company, Santa Monica, CA, 1997.

———. Zellerbach Playhouse, U of California, Berkeley, 2000.

Daughter of Han

Production, dir. Robert Woodruff. Bay Area Playwrights Festival, 1983.

I Remember Clifford

Production, dir. Robert Woodruff. Bay Area Playwrights Festival, 1983.

Pigeons

Production. Chinese Culture Center, San Francisco, 1985.

———. Hampden Theater, U of Massachusetts, Amherst, 1985.

The Only Language She Knows

Production, adapted for film, prod. Steven Okazaki and Amy Hill; perf. Genny Lim. 1987.

———, adapted for film, perf. Genny Lim, Al Young, and M.J. Lee; comp. Francis Wong. Ishmael Reed Productions, 1992.

XX

Production, dir. Genny Lim; comp. Fred Ho; perf. Brenda Wong Aoki, Don Hart, Koichi Tamano, and Genny Lim. The Lab, San Francisco, 1987.

Winter Place

Solo performance, dir. and perf. Genny Lim; comp. Jon Jang and Francis Wong. Hatley-Martin Gallery, San Francisco, 1988.

Bitter Cane

Production, dir. Gwen Victor; perf. Hiroshi Kashiwagi, William Hammond, Sharon Omi, Willard Chin, and Alex Lee. Bay Area Playwrights Festival, Fort Mason, San Francisco, 1989.

———, dir. Jackie Johnson Debus; perf. Eva Lee, Dante Carpenter, Jr., Gordon Hasegawa, Christian Stephen Wong, and Todd Okuma. Hilo Theater, U of Hawai'i, Manoa, 1991.

———, dir. Steven Avalos; perf. Jo Yang, Kei Hayashi, and Charles Chun. West Coast Ensemble, Hollywood, 1993.

———, dir. William Wilday; perf. Charline Su, Ke'o Woolford, David Chan, James Wong, and William Cockerel. Morgan-Wixon Theatre, Santa Monica, CA, 1997.

Faceless

Performance (multimedia), dir. Arnold Iger and Paul Kwan. Magic Theatre, San Francisco, 1989.

The Pumpkin Girl

Production, dir. Murray Mednick. Bay Area Playwrights Festival, San Rafael, CA, 1989.

The Magic Brush

Production as the "World of Tales," comp. Francis Wong. Children's Touring Company, Marin County, CA, 1990.

SenseUs: The Rainbow Anthems

Performance. Festival 2000, Louise M. Davies Symphony Hall, San Francisco, 1990.

La China Poblana

Performance, dir. Mark Knego; comp. Herbie Lewis, Francis Wong, Clifford Woods, and Victor Mario Zaballa; perf. Genny Lim and Guadalupe Garcia. Intersection for the Arts, San Francisco, 1991.

Pins and Noodles

Performance (multimedia), dir. Arnold Iger and Paul Kwan; narr. Genny Lim. Yerba Buena Center for the Arts, 1993.

Songlines: The Spiritual Tributary of Paul Robeson and Mei Lanfang

Performance, dir. Ellen Chang. Zellerbach Playhouse, U of California, Berkeley, 2000.

Anthologies

The Chinese American Experience: Papers from the Second National Conference on Chinese American Studies (1980). San Francisco: Chinese Historical Society of America, 1984.

Island: Poetry and History of Chinese Immigrants on Angel Island, 1910–1940. Trans. Him Mark Lai and Judy Yung. San Francisco: San Francisco Study Center, 1980. Rpt. Seattle: U of Washington P, 1991.

Unsilenced Voices: An Anthology of Poems. San Francisco: Fine Arts Museums of San Francisco, 1991.

Children's Books

Wings for Lai-Ho. San Francisco: East/West, 1982.

Essays

"A Juk-Sing Opera." *California Childhood: Recollections and Stories of the Golden State*. Ed. Gary Soto. Berkeley, CA: Creative Arts Books, 1988. 32–38.

"Word Up." *Yellow Light: The Flowering of Asian American Arts*. Ed. Amy Ling. Philadelphia: Temple UP, 1999. 213–16.

Poetry

"The Only Language She Knows." *American Born and Foreign: An Anthology of Asian American Poetry*. Ed. Fay Chiang, Helen W. Huie, Jason Hwang, Richard Oyama, and Susan L. Yung. New York: Sunbury Press Books, 1979. 16.

"Wonder Woman." *This Bridge Called My Back: Writings by Radical Women of Color*. Ed. Cherríe Moraga and Gloria Anzaldúa. New York: Kitchen Table/Women of Color P, 1983. 25–26. Rpt. in *Breaking Silence: An Anthology of Contemporary Asian American Poets*. Ed. Joseph Bruchac. New York: Greenfield Review P, 1983. 163–64.

"Visiting Father," "Departure," and "Sweet 'n Sour." *Breaking Silence, an Anthology of Contemporary Asian American Poets*. Ed. Joseph Bruchac. New York: Greenfield Review P, 1983. 159–62.

Winter Place: Poems. San Francisco: Kearny Street Workshop, 1989.

Recordings

"A People's Prayer." *Who Sane, Who Sane.* Live recording at New College of California in protest of Gulf War. Audiocassette. Onda Cultural, 1992.

"The Sea That Carried Me" and "Winter Place." *America Fears the Drum: Rebel Poets II.* Prod. Don Paul. Audiocassette. 1992.

Devotee. Perf. Genny Lim, Francis Wong, Elliot Humberto Kavee, and Glenn Horiuchi. Asian Improv Records, 1997.

Island: The Immigrant Suite No. 1. Comp. Jon Jang. Perf. Genny Lim. Soul Note, 1997.

Studies of Genny Lim

Barlow, Jeffrey G. Rev. of *Island: Poetry and History of Chinese Immigrants on Angel Island, 1910–1940. Journal of the West* 32.4 (Oct. 1993): 103–05.

Dong, Lorraine. Rev. of *Island: Poetry and History of Chinese Immigrants on Angel Island, 1910–1940. Journal of American Ethnic History* 14.4 (Summer 1995): 80–82.

Elwood, Philip. "Tribute to a Pair of Rebels." Rev. of *Songlines: The Spiritual Tributary of Paul Robeson and Mei Lanfang. San Francisco Examiner* 2 June 2000: C7.

Ferretti, Fred. "Calligraphic Cries." Rev. of *Island: Poetry and History of Chinese Immigrants on Angel Island, 1910–1940. New York Times* 20 Feb. 1981: C24.

Froyd, Susan. "Thrills for the Week." *Denver Westword* 5 June 1997: N. pag.

Funabiki, Jon. "Poetic *Paper Angels* Depicts Painful Past." Rev. of *Paper Angels. San Diego Union-Tribune* 12 Aug. 1985, Lifestyle: C1.

Gussow, Mel. "Stage: *Paper Angels*, about West Coast's Ellis Island." Rev. of *Paper Angels. New York Times* 26 Mar. 1982: C3.

Holston, Noel. "Coming to America." Rev. of *Paper Angels. Star Tribune* (Minneapolis) 24 Mar. 1995, metro ed.: 1E.

Houston, Velina Hasu. "Genny Lim." *The Politics of Life: Four Plays by Asian American Women.* Ed. Velina Hasu Houston. Philadelphia: Temple UP, 1993. 151–62.

Koyama, Christine. "A Novice Playwright Finds Inspiration in Her Heritage." Rev. of *Paper Angels* on PBS *American Playhouse. New York Times* 16 June 1985, sec. 2: 29.

Lai, David Chuenyan. Rev. of *Island: Poetry and History of Chinese Immigrants on Angel Island, 1910–1940. Pacific Affairs* 65.3 (Fall 1992): 448–49.

Lee, Josephine. *Performing Asian America: Race and Ethnicity on the Contemporary Stage.* Philadelphia: Temple UP, 1997.

Louv, Richard. "Of Poems Carved in Walls, and Angel Island's Ghost." Rev. of *Island. San Diego Union-Tribune* 6 July 1986, news ed.: A3.

Maloney, Terry. "*Bitter Cane.*" Rev. of *Bitter Cane. Back Stage* 34.43 (Oct. 1993): 4W.

O'Connor, John J. "WNET Drama Looks at Angel Island." Rev. of *Paper Angels* on PBS *American Playhouse. New York Times* 17 June 1985, final ed.: C18.

Rosenberg, Howard. "The Chinese Experience Is Illuminated on KCET." Rev. of *Paper Angels* on PBS *American Playhouse. Los Angeles Times* 17 June 1985, Calendar: 1.

Shirley, Don. "Plays about More Than Doomed Love." Rev. of *Bitter Cane. Los Angeles Times* 1 Nov. 1993, Calendar: F9.

"Trapped in Time." Rev. of *Paper Angels* on PBS *American Playhouse. Arkansas Democrat-Gazette* 17 June 1985: 9.

Vaughan, Peter. "*Paper Angels* Is a Stirring Immigrants Story." Rev. of *Paper Angels. Star Tribune* (Minneapolis) 29 Mar. 1995, metro ed.: 4E.

Winn, Steven. "First Look at Theater Pieces at Yerba." *San Francisco Chronicle* 13 Nov. 1993, final ed.: E1.

Wright, Jaime. "Genny Lim, Poet and Beyond." Interview. Oct. 2000. 14 February 2001 <http://www.comfusionreview.com/intergenny.html>.

Paul Stephen Lim
(1944–   )

Miles Xian Liu

BIOGRAPHY

Paul Stephen Lim was born on January 5, 1944, in Manila, the Philippines. Wanting "the best" for him, his Chinese parents sent him to English-language institutions: an elementary school run by American Jesuits, a high school run by Irish Christian Brothers, and two years of college run by the Jesuits again, until he dropped out of school altogether (Lim, "Paul Stephen Lim" 42–43). But Lim's dream of life as a writer in the English language did not die when he quit school in the Philippines. On the contrary, he emigrated to the United States at the age of twenty-four in order to "go to the source of the language I wrote and dreamed in" (44).

Lim earned both his B.A. (1970) and M.A. (1974) in English from the University of Kansas (KU). He abandoned his work toward a Ph.D. and devoted himself fully to playwriting in 1976 when his first play, *Conpersonas*, won the best original script award from the American College Theatre Festival's eighth annual competition. Since then, eight of his eleven plays have been published and all of them produced. He has also published a collection of short stories, four poems, and several essays. But the crown of his professional accomplishment was the founding of the English Alternative Theatre (EAT) in 1989 on the KU campus. Twelve years later, under his tenure of artistic directorship, not only has EAT fulfilled its promise as an invaluable teaching tool for playwriting students to explore their works on stage, it has also become an inseparable part of campus life by producing seventy-six staged readings and thirty-three full productions by student and professional playwrights alike (Elliott 3). The three jewels in his crown came in three consecutive years: first in 1999 when Lim's handpicked EAT representative—an English graduate student—became the

Women's National Acting Champion and the recipient of the Irene Ryan Acting Scholarship during the Kennedy Center/American College Theatre Festival (KC/ACTF) in Washington, D.C.; then in 2000 and again in 2001, when a ten-minute play and a one-act comedy written by two of his students were performed at consecutive nationals of the KC/ACTF.

Anonymous as Lim may seem outside the plains states, his writing has garnered numerous regional and national awards. They include a second prize in the short-story division of the KU literary competition for "The Third and Final Dream of Samuel Toepffer" in 1974; the Palanca Memorial Award for Literature—the most prestigious literary award in the Philippines—for his play *Password* (second prize) in 1975, "Taking Flight" (a short story, first prize) in 1976, the play *Points of Departure* (second prize) in 1977, "Victor and Other Issues" (a short story, third prize) in 1977, and the play *Hatchet Club* (honorable mention) in 1978; the Shubert Playwriting Fellowship and best original script award from the ACTF for *Conpersonas*, both in 1976; the Midwest Playwrights Laboratory Fellowship in 1979; a Kansas Arts Commission Fellowship in Playwriting in 1989; the Kennedy Center gold medallion for contribution to theater in Region V of the ACTF in 1996; and the top prize for *Report to the River* in the playwriting competition at the Edward Albee Theatre Conference in Valdez, Alaska, and the Phoenix Award in the category of performing arts from the Lawrence Arts Commission, both in 1999.

MAJOR WORKS AND THEMES

Lim's plays are noted for their complex allusions, verbal sparring, puns, palaver, biblical terminology, cinematic history, and music knowledge. Thematically, however, they tend to be autobiographical in connotation, but not ethnic specific in reference. As a gay, Chinese Filipino American playwright and English professor in Kansas, Lim wrestles with issues of gender identity, racial stereotyping, professional marginalization, and cultural provincialism in his works more often than with Asian American themes such as anti-Asian immigration policies, internment-camp experiences, the model minority, or racism within the community.

Written in 1974 and first produced in 1975, *Conpersonas* was performed in the Eisenhower Theater at the John F. Kennedy Center for the Performing Arts in 1976. "Against the masks," in a literal translation of the title, *Conpersonas* is an identity play or, more precisely, a dramatic search for identity.

Set in Upper East Side New York, the play begins with Miles Zeigler's suicide in the bathroom after he puts the last touches on the Thanksgiving dinner and spic-and-span cleans his elegant apartment a few minutes before the arrival of his three guests. They are Jesse Jugenheimer, a successful older businessman and a multilingual world traveler; Shelagh Abrams, the deceased's bride-to-be in December; and her feisty sixteen-year-old daughter, Rhoda. Mark Zeigler, the last guest to come in, was not invited to this gathering, although he is Miles's twin brother and a priest also living in the city. He shows up rather unexpect-edly, goes straight to the bathroom, and finds Mark's body there. Trying to establish the probable cause of his brother's suicide, Mark spends the first part of the night with Jesse, Miles's gay lover, and the second part with Shelagh, Miles's fiancée. As it turns out, Mark barely knows Miles despite their shared genetics as twin brothers. Both Jesse and Shelagh know Miles a lot better. In the end, the search that Mark embarks on for the real person behind Miles's assumed masks concludes with the discovery of the person behind his own priest uniform. The true identity of a person, the play seems to suggest, exists only in his or her relationship with others.

Homerica (1977) deals with the cultural aftermath of sexual liberation in America. Through the love affairs of characters with sexual orientations of all kinds, the play exhibits the gradual disintegration of many social institutions such as traditional ways of life, family, marriage, the Catholic church, and par-enthood. *Points of Departure* (1977) focuses on the social decay of the Philip-pines as a result of the colonial penetration by American culture. To the Filipinos, the American style of living is enticing and devastating at the same time. *Woeman* (1978) is the correct thematic spelling for the protagonist Char-lie's five women: his mother, ex-wife, older mistress, younger girlfriend, and daughter. He is supposed to feel closest to them, but they all want to have a relationship with him that he cannot provide. Yet he would not have a life onstage without their memories. *Flesh, Flash, and Frank Harris* (1980) is a biographical drama of "a self-made rake who seems to have spent his life stand-ing knee-deep in the mucky mire of intellectual and social stews" (Bretz 10). The focal thrust, not unlike that of Lim's other plays, seems to steer the audience to a better understanding of its subject—Frank Harris in this case—whether or not they share his preoccupations and values.

Figures in Clay (1992) depicts the hopes and fears of a love triangle among three gay men, Clark Copeland, Eric Swanson, and David Lee. Set in a psy-chiatrist's office in Lawrence, Kansas, the play is structured around the trio's sessions with the invisible psychiatrist, who never appears on the stage but always sits in the audience. Consequently, the audience becomes their psychi-atrist as it listens to their respective takes on the joys and pains of the triangle relationship.

Well established financially as a travel agent, Clark has over fifty offices around the world. At the age of sixty-four, he is confident and controlling as the provider in his relationship with other men. Twenty-four years old, Eric has been an undergraduate at KU for a few years now. He becomes the recipient of both the Marshall and Mellon scholarships on the eve of his graduation. Since he can accept only one, he must decide between the United States and the United Kingdom to further his education. Going to England would mean the end of his involvement with David. Clark and Eric are both enamored of David's "won-derful sense of the absurd" (41).

David Lee is a Chinese Filipino, twenty years younger than Clark and twenty years older than Eric. He came to Lawrence on account of his relationship with Clark, who not only sponsored his trip and helped to have his tourist visa changed to a student visa, but also provided him with accommodation, books, and entertainment. Completely dependent on Clark, David felt like a helpless child. He took the first opportunity he got to start a new relationship with Eric, in which he regained somewhat his sense of independence by showing the ropes to his young partner.

In the end, the love triangle per se seems less important than the level of maturity that all of them have obtained through the relationship. Clark, who began with David in Manila, realizes that a relationship can last only when it has room for the other to grow. Eric, who agreed to the threesome arrangement, now leaves for England with the conviction that love triangles do not work. David, the center of this experiment, has learned to accept himself as a gay Chinese Filipino American who no longer feels the need to impress others by showing off his knowledge of Western literature, philosophy, music, or Eastern zodiac. The play offers nothing new about love triangles, homosexual or heterosexual, with the exception that audiences are not often put in a psychiatrist's seat to listen to three gay men reflecting on their relationship. What does come as a bit of a surprise, maybe pleasant to some and unpleasant to others, is that a midwestern town like Lawrence comes across as a community fairly tolerant of the characters' lifestyle.

Mother Tongue (1992), though published in the same year as *Figures in Clay*, was written around 1988. The fictional timeline places *Mother Tongue* in the conception stage of *Figures in Clay*. Read side by side, the two plays are stylistically interwoven in a Faulknerian fashion—one of the playwright's acknowledged sources of influence—where the setting, protagonist, and characters of importance are mostly the same. Although none is outrageously named like Flem Snopes or Yoknapatawpha County, David Lee, Clark Copeland, and Eric Swanson appear in both plays with stories from different periods of their lives. Thematically, both plays delve into the contemporary issues of sexuality and gender as well as ethnicity and culture rather than the approaches to racial equality, social justice, or a rock-bottom price that the saga of Yoknapatawpha County presents.

In *Mother Tongue*, David Lee is taking a break from his fourteen-year relationship with Clark, but has not started with Eric. He has just met Eric in his office after the 11:00 A.M. section of English 102 he is teaching. At the backdrop of the love triangle depicted in *Figures in Clay, Mother Tongue* zeros in mainly on David's reflection on his identity in terms of ethnicity and culture, a subject that has apparently been on his mind for some time.

Born ethnic Chinese in the Philippines, David was not eligible for citizenship. In order to travel, he applied for and obtained a Taiwanese passport, which country he had neither been to nor cared to visit. All his training—academic, professional, and social—was in English. He was educated in English from grade school through the first two years of college by American Jesuits and Irish

Christian Brothers in the Philippines. He worked with English-speaking clients for an advertising company and hung out with American soldiers on leave from their duties in Vietnam. Now teaching English in mid-America, he is offended by incorrect usage of English by native speakers and has "no tolerance for students who think they know her [English] when they cannot even tell which end of her they're screwing" (63). Yet despite his impeccable English skills, he has to ask his students the first day of class to spare him the line of thinking, "What's a chink doing, teaching English in Kansas?" just in case they might try to convince themselves that he did not belong in front of the classroom (12).

His feelings of homelessness are further exasperated by his mother's constant reminders against three basic facts of his life that constitute the sum total of who he is. First, David is gay, but his mother, Lilian, makes certain that her son gets the message that he should not let his father die again with him by his refusal to get married, have children, and pass on the family name; second, David is having the time of his life with the English language and American culture in Kansas, while Lilian tells her life story time and again, that "she learned new languages, . . . embraced a new religion" without abandoning her faith in the old ways (82); and third, David has become a naturalized U.S. citizen and pledged to defend the country whose drunken soldiers killed his elder brother with a hand grenade at the end of World War II. Lilian screams at him, "And you dare to ask me to be happy for you" (87) becoming an American? David Lee onstage, perhaps like Lim in life, "never really feels 'at home' anywhere" (Lim, "Paul Stephen Lim" 44). But it is also true that his acceptance of religious, linguistic, and cultural hybridity in himself and others has given him an outlook unique to global sojourners, and his living with contradictions and between cultures has rewarded him with a humanistic identity.

Report to the River (1997) is a social commentary about America's "insatiable obsession with crime and violence" (Lim, "Paul Stephen Lim" 52). The play brings out the saddest ironies in America's approach to law and order. Set on the bank of the Kaw, one of the two rivers that flow through Lawrence, the play, though reflecting on America's sickening appetite for the media's sensational coverage of crime and violence, is ironically a murder mystery based on the court transcripts of an actual case and a sixteen-hour interview with the convicted killer, Jake.

Jake is a homeless man with a tent underneath a highway overpass by the side of the Kaw. Born in Texas, he hit the road as soon as he was eighteen. He has drifted to Kansas through Arkansas, Oklahoma, and Missouri. A man with a turbulent childhood, he was, of course, mistreated by his mother and put through a nonchalant system of social services. He has an IQ of 76 and believes that the Bible is the "only book worth reading." Nick, the other character, is from a financially well-to-do family, but is close to neither of his divorced and remarried parents.

The play's focal character, Mikey, ironically does not have a voice of his own. His life and death are in the unreliable memories of two people: his second-grade nameless teacher (Nick's mother), who had only superficial contacts with him, and his convicted killer, who is making up four stories about Mikey's death. As a victim, Mikey is again at the mercy of others even after death. Mikey first came to his teacher's attention at Grant Elementary when he showed up in class one day "without a coat or jacket" in the middle of January (20). On the show-and-tell bulletin board, Mikey posted his pictures from home: "All those people in the kitchen with cigarettes and beer cans in their hands. Garbage all over the place. Children [his younger brothers] asleep on the floor" (20). But his inadequate living conditions were hardly anybody's business.

The play, almost a parody of the media coverage of the tragedy, proceeds not with the stories about how Mikey lived but how he died. The attention is fixed on the perpetrator, not the victim. The public's energy and resources, as a result, are devoted to the analyses of the killer's motive and behavior, not the victim's needs that had led to their tragic association in the first place. As a "mirror" the playwright is holding up to America, *Report to the River* dispenses one irony after another (Lim, "Paul Stephen Lim" 51). The Bible-waving and God-fearing Jake is ultimately convicted of performing the satanic killing; and the neighbor-loving community on the better-off side of the Kaw could not care less about Jake's mental status, nor does it show any collective interest in the deplorable living conditions of children like Mikey when they are alive. Symbolically, the river in modern America is not a nurturing source of life or cradle of civilization, but the unbridgeable divide between the haves and the have-nots, the evidence of industrial wastes, the scene of horrid crime, and worse, the grave of yet another neglected nine-year-old. When the "package" is found, all officers "report to the river" and the case is solved. Or is it? Like Lim's other works, this play again offers the audience more questions than answers.

CRITICAL RECEPTION

Although eight of his eleven plays have been published, Lim's theatrical works are not widely circulated. Critical examination of his plays is unfortunately confined to theater reviews in newspapers and journals, mostly from the Midwest. Academia has yet to give his plays their due consideration.

His award-winning *Conpersonas*, not surprisingly, received quite a bit of publicity in the Midlands. Lim was a graduate student at KU when *Conpersonas* launched his playwriting career. John Bush Jones, Lim's future colleague at KU, believed that "no play more richly deserves this distinction" ("Theater" N. pag.). Jed Davis, director of the University Theatre, was quoted in the *Lawrence Daily Journal-World* as saying that Lim's success might help "break down the 'vast wasteland' syndrome that people from both coasts tend to have about the Midwest" ("Play" 1). Jones described it as "tough" and "brutal" sometimes, but "always frank"—a good example of "Lim's verbal wizardry and an electrifying theatricality" ("Playwright's" 12).

Points of Departure was Lim's first play produced on the West Coast. Michael

Auerbach, reviewing the East West Players production, noted the play's "weaker" structure (compared with *Bunnyhop* by Jeffery Paul Chan, also in production at the time) but stated that it provided a "brilliant condemnation of the American influence in the Philippines without ever becoming blatantly anti-American" (13). However, Jim Moore of the *Los Angeles Herald Examiner* gave it an all-positive review, saying, "Full of good talk and clearly defined but underplayed symbols, Lim's play is engrossing throughout" (B3). *Woeman*, "rich in resonances, allusions, and symbols," shows the playwright's "literary intelligence," according to Glenn Loney of *After Dark* (Rev. of *Woeman* 96). But Joanne Pottlitzer of *New York, New York* had mixed feelings about the literary gymnastics of the play. While Lim "successfully weaves the informative flashbacks of Charlie's life into the present by simple lighting technique," the stories of his past are "much too long and literary" (N. pag.).

Lim's next play, *Flesh, Flash, and Frank Harris*, received two thumbs up from the *Kansas City Star, Lawrence Daily Journal-World*, and *After Dark*, but a mixed review from the *N.Y. Theater Voice*. Michael McGrath called it a "daring provocative play" from "the most noteworthy of our regional playwrights" (3B); and Lynn Bretz felt "like witnessing historical figures come to life in a wax museum" and suggested, "If ever a local theater production deserves the not-to-be-missed tag, it's the one" (10). Glenda Frank, on the other hand, detected the discrepancy in the play's gender depiction. "Though the male characters are all delineated and completely played, the women tend to disappear into each other without much personality . . . , a weakness in the play" (12). However, Loney applauded Lim's unwavering focus on the story of Harris and his ability to skillfully tell it "with humor, pathos, and dramatic force" by "invoking the spirits of Young, Middle, and Old Frank often simultaneously" (Rev. of *Flesh* 58).

Mother Tongue, another East West Players production, received mostly favorable reviews. Ray Loynd of the *Los Angeles Times* observes that the play "catches the new melting pot, where some immigrants are even stranger to countries they left behind" (4). Chris Komai for the *RAFU* called the play "clever," as the protagonist's life and lingo double up as a pun, while pointing out "the flatness of the ending" (1–2). Similarly, Lim's latest theatrical endeavor, *Report to the River*, is "excruciating to watch at times, but [. . .] also mighty fine theater" in the opinion of Jan Biles of the *Lawrence Daily Journal-World* (76).

It may be an understatement when King-Kok Cheung laments that Lim's "talent has been insufficiently recognized in Asian American cultural circles" (Lim, "Paul Stephen Lim" 41). Partially to blame may be his Lawrence residency, non–Asian American themes, or verbal overkill. All the same, his prolific career contributes significantly to the totality of Asian American dramatic literature, which deserves greater critical consideration.

BIBLIOGRAPHY

Works by Paul Stephen Lim

Drama

Conpersonas: A Recreation in Two Acts. New York: Samuel French, 1977.
Points of Departure: A Play in One Act. Excerpts. *Bridge: An Asian American Perspective* 5.2 (1977): 27–29.
Flesh, Flash and Frank Harris: A Recreation in Two Acts. Louisville, KY: Aran P, 1985.
Hatchet Club. Plays 1.1 (1985): 17–62.
Homerica: A Triology on Sexual Liberation. Louisville, KY: Aran P, 1985.
Woeman: A New Play. Louisville, KY: Aran P, 1985.
Figures in Clay: A Threnody in Six Scenes and a Coda. Louisville, KY: Aran P, 1992.
Mother Tongue: A Play. Louisville, KY: Aran P, 1992.

Unpublished Manuscripts

Chambers: A Recreation in Four Parts. 1977.
Zooks. With Steve Rice. 1980.
Lee and the Boys in the Backroom: A Play in Two Acts. Adapted from the novel *Queer* by William S. Burroughs. 1987.
Report to the River. 1997.

Selected Production History

Conpersonas: A Recreation in Two Acts

Production, dir. David Cook; perf. Paul Hough, Peter Miner, Nancy Flagg, Sheri Schlozman, and Victoria Stevens. William Inge Memorial Theater, U of Kansas, Lawrence, 1975 and 1976.
———. Emporia State U, Emporia, KS, 1976.
———. John F. Kennedy Center for the Performing Arts, Washington, DC, 1976.

Homerica: A Triology on Sexual Liberation

Production, dir. Paul Hough; perf. Maureen Hawley, Steven Silver, Charley Oldfather, Mauny Mesecher, Jim Korinke, Jeff Tamblyn, Cathy Corum, Mindy McCrary, Jim Ivey, Duane LaDage, Gary Bruce Sayles, Sandra Collins, Beth Leonard, Elizabeth Andrisevic, Bob Kahle, and Dan Nichols. Kansas Union Ballroom, U of Kansas, Lawrence, 1977.
———, dir. Paul Stephen Lim. University Theater, Leicester U, Leicester, UK, 1983.

Points of Departure: A Play in One Act

Production, dir. Mako; perf. Alberto Isaac, Gene Bryson, and Sumi Haru. East West Players, Los Angeles, 1977.
Staged reading, dir. Ronnie Alejandro. Philippine Cultural Center, New York City, 1978.
Production, dir. Rodney Kageyama. Asian American Theater Company, San Francisco, 1979.

Woeman: A New Play

Production, dir. Jack B. Wright; perf. Rusty Laushman, Joan Oberndorf, Deborah Moke, Heather Laird, Kathleen Warfel, and Diana Sinclair. William Inge Memorial Theater, U of Kansas, Lawrence, 1978.

———, dir. Judith Joseph; perf. Judith Joseph, Kevin Madden, Mary Charalambakis, Sandra Soehngen, Christy Brotherton, and Anthony Di Novo. Marquee Theater, New York City, 1982.

Chambers: A Recreation in Four Parts

Staged reading, dir. Dale Wasserman. Midwest Playwrights Laboratory, Madison, WI, 1979.

Production, dir. Paul Stephen Lim; perf. Ken Smith, Josh Waters, Arnold Weiss, Scott Crouse, Darcy Schild, Gordon Wright, Mark Knapp, Curt Flowers, and Jeffrey Drake. Lawrence Community Theatre, Lawrence, KS, 1985.

Flesh, Flash, and Frank Harris: A Recreation in Two Acts

Production, dir. Mary Doveton; perf. Ambrose Saricks, Craig Swanson, Charley Oldfather, Gerhard Zuther, Patricia J. Abts, Richard Delaware, Bart Ewing, William Keeler, Steve Mokofsky, Barton Lynn Rolsky, Darcy Schild, Charles Whitman, Susan Kelso Zuther, Pat Schmidt, and Jean Averill. Lawrence Community Theatre, Lawrence, KS, 1980.

———, dir. Judith Joseph; perf. David Kerman, Ray Iannicelli, John David Barone, June White, Richard Boddy, Martin Thompson, Keely Eastley, Rita McCaffrey, and Norma Jean Giffin. Entermedia's Second Story Theatre, New York City, 1984.

Hatchet Club: A Play in One Act

Production, dir. Paul Stephen Lim; perf. Kate Taylor, Stacey Warner, Ambrose Saricks, John Alexander, Mark Kramer, and Dan Dannenberg. Lawrence Community Theatre, Lawrence, KS, 1983.

Lee and the Boys in the Backroom: A Play in Two Acts

Production, dir. Paul Stephen Lim; perf. Charles Whitman, Jay Karnes, Paul Jackson, Rich Crank, Karl Ramberg, Diego Taborda, Joe McCauley, Rudy Burlin, Mark Knapp, and Barb Downing. Lawrence Community Theatre, Lawrence, KS, 1987.

Mother Tongue: A Play

Production, dir. Paul Hough; perf. Alberto Isaac, Estelle Bennett, Kathryn Lee, Gene R. Touchet, Jane Ellen, Diane Dorsey, and Gavin Gannon. East West Players, Los Angeles, 1988.

Staged reading, dir. Paul Hough; perf. Alberto Isaac, Emily Kuroda, Rani Cunningham, Joe McCauley, Charles Whitman, Darcy Schild, and Sally McNall. Theater Conference, U of Kansas, Lawrence, 1988.

Figures in Clay

Staged reading, dir. Paul Hough; perf. Alberto Isaac, Peter Matthey, and Joe McCauley. MLA Convention, Chicago, 1990.

———, dir. Paul Hough; perf. William Kuhlke, Jim Korinke, and Joe McCauley. Asian American Festival, U of Kansas, Lawrence, 1991.

Report to the River

Production, dir. Paul Hough; perf. Michael Senften and Phillip Schroeder. Lawrence Arts Center, Lawrence, KS, 1997.

————. Regional Festival of the Kennedy Center/American College Theatre Festival, Johnson County Community College, Overland Park, KS, 1998.

Staged reading, dir. Paul Stephen Lim; perf. Michael Senften and Phillip Schroeder. Edward Albee Theatre Conference, Valdez, AK, 1999.

Essays

The Complete Poetry and Prose of Chairil Anwar, by Chairil Anwar. Ed. and trans. Burton Raffel. Book review. *Books Abroad* 44.4 (1970): 711–12.

Japanese Poetry Now. Trans. Thomas Fitzsimmons. Book review. *Books Abroad* 46.4 (1972): 727–28.

The Waiting Years, by Fumiko Enchi. Trans. John Bester. Book review. *Books Abroad* 46.4 (1972): 727.

"A Portrait of the Filipino Male as Impotent." *Philippine Panorama* (Manila) 4 (17 Aug. 1975): 8–9.

"Firstborn." *Kansas Alumni* 82 (Jan. 1984): 36–40.

"He Takes with Him Memories of Ourselves." *Dreamtime: Remembering Ed Ruhe, 1923–1989*. Ed. Robert Day and Fred Whitehead. Chestertown, MD: Literary House P, 1993. 5–6.

"EAT in Nebraska." *CLASnotes* Spring 1995: 6–7.

Interview

"Paul Stephen Lim." Interview. *Words Matter: Conversations with Asian American Writers*. Ed. King-Kok Cheung. Honolulu: U of Hawai'i P, 2000. 40–57.

Poetry

"Pulchritude." *Solidarity* (Manila) 8.9 (1974): 80.

"Relationships in the Making." *Solidarity* (Manila) 8.8 (1974): 2. Rpt. in *Bridge: An Asian American Perspective* 3.4 (1975): 39.

"Ode to Discipline." *Irish Times* (Dublin) 21 April 1975: 8.

"Alternatives." *Philippine Panorama* (Manila) 4 (13 July 1975): 30.

Short Stories

"Taking Flight." *Solidarity* (Manila) 9.6 (July–Aug. 1975): 82–97.

Some Arrivals, But Mostly Departures. Intro. F. Sionil Jose. Quezon City, Philippines: New Day, 1982.

"Flight." *Iba: The Filipino American Story*. Ed. N.V.M. Gonzalez. Seattle: U of Washington P, forthcoming.

Studies of Paul Stephen Lim

Auerbach, Michael. "Two Superb and Devastating One-Acts." Rev. of *Points of Departure. UCLA Bruin* 31 Oct. 1977: 13.

Biles, Jan. "Original Scripts Stun Audience." Rev. of *Report to the River*. *Lawrence Daily Journal-World* 10 Oct. 1997: 76.

Bretz, Lynn. "Lim's Frank Harris Play off to 'Flashy' Beginning." Rev. of *Flesh, Flash, and Frank Harris*. *Lawrence Daily Journal-World* 24 Apr. 1980: 10.

Elliott, Robert F. "Considering the Alternative." *Update* (Department of English, U of Kansas) 34 (1999): 1–3.

Frank, Glenda. Rev. of *Flesh, Flash, and Frank Harris*. *N.Y. Theater Voice* Mar. 1984: 12.

Jones, John Bush. "Playwright's Progress: Journey to *Homerica*." *Kansas City Star Magazine* 27 Feb. 1977: 6–12.

———. "Theater in Mid-America." Rev. of *Conpersonas*. *Kansas City Times* 30 Oct. 1975: N. pag.

———. "Winning Playwright Keeps His Modesty." *Kansas City Star* 21 Mar. 1976: 2E.

Komai, Chris. "Lim's *Mother Tongue* in Many Voices." *RAFU* 2 Mar. 1988: 1–2.

Loney, Glenn. Rev. of *Flesh, Flash, and Frank Harris*. *After Dark* July 1980: 58.

———. Rev. of *Woeman*. *After Dark* Dec. 1978: 96–98.

Loynd, Ray. "An Ellipsis of the Son in *Mother Tongue*." *Los Angeles Times* 24 Feb. 1988, Calendar: 1+

McGrath, Michael. "Life's Collage: A Daring Flashy Work." Rev. of *Flesh, Flash, and Frank Harris*. *Kansas City Star* 25 Apr. 1980: 3B.

Moore, Jim. "*Points* Is Sharp." Rev. of *Points of Departure*. *Los Angeles Herald Examiner* 3 Nov. 1977: B3.

O'Neal, Shellie. "The Anxious Double: Twins in Plays of the 1970s, 1980s, and 1990s." Diss. Louisiana State U, 2001.

"Play Written at KU Gets No. 1 Rating." *Lawrence Daily Journal-World* 1 Mar. 1976: 1–2.

Pottlitzer, Joanne. "Breakdown." Rev. of *Woeman*. *New York, New York* 4.14 (Mar.–Apr. 1983): N. pag.

Sandra Tsing Loh
(1962–   )

Lynn M. Itagaki

BIOGRAPHY

Sandra Tsing Loh was born on February 11, 1962, in Los Angeles, California. A multifaceted artist, she expresses her offbeat sense of the region and its absurdities. Exploring the changing nature of race in America, Loh additionally examines her own biracial heritage and multicultural upbringing as fundamental themes of her work. Both of Loh's parents immigrated to the United States: her mother from Germany and her father from China. The youngest of three children, Loh was pushed by her father to finish her degree in engineering, and she eventually majored in both physics and literature at the California Institute of Technology, briefly pursuing a graduate degree in physics. She later pursued graduate studies in English at the University of Southern California, studying under novelist T. Coraghessian Boyle and receiving her M.A. in 1983. She left graduate work in 1990 to lead a varied career: performing, teaching, and writing plays and short stories.

Loh's initial performance pieces showcased her training in classical piano. She first achieved national fame in 1987 with a piano concert above a major freeway in downtown Los Angeles that brought media attention in such diverse venues as the *Wall Street Journal, The Tonight Show, National Enquirer*, and *People*. She recorded her compositions on *Pianovision* (1991) and has composed various short pieces for National Public Radio and the music for two feature-length documentaries. An immensely versatile writer, Loh has received acclaim for her work in other genres, including her short story "My Father's Chinese Wives," which won the Pushcart Prize for Literature in 1995, and her novel *If You Lived Here, You'd Be Home by Now*, which was voted one of the "Best Books of 1997" by the *Los Angeles Times*. In writing articles for top fashion magazines and newspapers, Loh continued to sharpen her trademark witticisms and gift for extracting humor from the ordinary as the writer for "The Valley" column for *Buzz Magazine* in the mid-1990s. Loh's first collection of essays, *Depth Takes a Holiday: Essays from Lesser Los Angeles* (1996), chronicles the oddities inherent to living in Los Angeles.

In the spring of 2000, National Public Radio featured Loh's irreverent humor in a weekly radio spot, *The Loh Life in Los Angeles*, in which she performed a five-minute confessional monologue, a role that has garnered her praise as the "funniest woman in America in under five minutes flat" (Glionna 16). Loh also has television credits as the voice of a character in the Disney animated series *Weekenders*, the writer for one of the original episodes for the series *Clueless*, and the guest columnist for the *New York Times* commenting on the 1999 fall television lineup. Loh's numerous interests and talents in multiple genres and fields have her spanning such diverse settings as the "lowbrow cheese-ball middle class" suburbia that she calls "home" (Lacher E1), the basement of the college radio station where her five-minute spots are taped, hosting the *Later* show on NBC for a week in 1999, and judging at the Sundance Film Festival. In a cover article in the *Los Angeles Times Magazine*, Loh was dubbed the "Queen of Anti-Cool" (Glionna 14).

MAJOR WORKS AND THEMES

Whether as a musician, performance artist, playwright, screenwriter, novelist, essayist, radio commentator, actor, or humorist, Loh mines her past eclectic experiences in her various jobs and careers, on the singles scene in New York City and Los Angeles, and, most poignantly, in her often-difficult childhood with eccentric parents continually at odds with one another. Her works in the different genres document life in southern California through the absurd, odd, and unexpectedly funny. The region serves as fodder for her wide-ranging critiques of contemporary lifestyles crossing such disparate locales as the resort town of Palm Springs and the suburbs of the San Fernando Valley, and Loh spears the culture of materialism and superficiality that thrives on silicone implants and plastic surgery stereotypically endemic to Hollywood. In mainstream media, Loh is most celebrated for chronicling her life experiences as representative of those twenty- and thirty-somethings who are the "disappointed generation"—"the dumpies," as she terms them—the "young, highly trained, downwardly mobile professionals" on the fringes of traditional and stable careers, most likely on the semiglamorous edge of the Hollywood scene (*Depth* 7).

Loh's work is further defined by her love-hate relationship with her miserly, unpredictable, and volatile father. In her first monologue, *Aliens in America* (1995), Loh balances her acerbic wit with bittersweet anecdotes of her family: her father's mail-order brides from China after her mother's death, the ill-fated family vacation in Ethiopia, and her attempt to break away from her family as a college freshman. In her succeeding monologues, *Depth Becomes Her* (1997) and *Bad Sex with Bud Kemp* (1998), Loh details the dating world in New York City, revisiting the ideas of her earlier prose works on stage. Through recounting dates with such memorable men as "Cappuccino Man" and "Tony the Pony" in *Bad Sex with Bud Kemp*, Loh's performance briefly, but importantly, dwells on the struggles with her multicultural identity and biracial heritage: "ME: a vaguely Hispanic-looking girl given a Chinese middle name and sent off to kindergarten in Heidi of the Alps type dirndl and clogs." Indeed, all of Loh's published works discuss interracial relationships; Loh is quoted as seeing herself as the human product of a "Sino-German experiment" (Talvi 24).

Loh struggles with and is frustrated by recent attempts to exoticize her ancestry. She satirizes those performers and writers who attempt to find their roots by "discovering" their "Asian grandmothers" in order to capitalize on the demand for multicultural heritages and the politics of identity (Smith C9). In her essays, Loh has especially criticized the grant-giving world of the arts that funds artists based on their racial labels. Loh argues that she does not fit neatly into categories of race while she endeavors to redefine and explode these limiting and restrictive categories of identity. For example, she sensationally and memorably posits Americans as "mongrels" like herself and is quoted in various interviews defining herself as "radically indeterminate" (Goodale 18; Haithman 46).

With a sometimes-painful, almost ruthless honesty, Loh targets and elicits the offbeat oddities of ordinary people and situations, finding poignant humor in the humdrum. Loh defines the source of her humor as "interior monologue," which she defines as the "craziness of what people really think about during the day" (Talvi 24). However, even in her critique of contemporary life and culture, Loh identifies with the disaffected, those pushed to the margins: "There's the sense of being an outsider, the sense that everyone in L.A. is at some fabulous party, and the parade is passing by and you're left behind. Those are my people" (qtd. in Lacher E1).

CRITICAL RECEPTION

In the late 1990s, Loh began to receive significant mainstream critical attention and academic consideration as a writer, performer, and media personality with the success and critical acclaim of her monologues *Aliens in America, Depth Becomes Her,* and *Bad Sex with Bud Kemp.* Critics and audiences respond enthusiastically to her intelligent performances, noting her engaging, personable style and her friendly and compassionate tone in discussing subjects as distressing as her parents' disastrous marriage or her own dating disasters. One theater critic notes the "NPR-ish quality" and compares Loh to a "young Mary Tyler Moore" (Wasman 66). Although reviewers are generally positive about her performances, they point out that her witty and sophisticated literary prose at times does not adapt well to the spoken rhythms of the stage. In a review of *Depth*

Becomes Her, Charles Isherwood argues that "the material seems to have limped lackadaisically from the page to the stage. . . . The rhythms are still literary, lacking the ease of natural speech" (71). In a *New York Times* review of *Aliens in America*, Ben Brantley critiques Loh's occasional overstatement that unbalances her characteristically dry, deadpan humor: "Each story brims with nicely observed details. . . . It's a shame that Ms. Loh isn't confident enough to let those details speak for themselves. She leans toward Big Statement conclusions that either belabor the obvious or force metaphors" (11).

However, what is most striking and exceptional about Loh's writings and performances is her ability to mark poignant moments in her monologues that show compassion for her subjects such as her father. She intrinsically identifies with them and attempts to understand their troubles. David Schweizer, the director of *Bad Sex with Bud Kemp*, connects Loh's interest in the ordinary and the outsider to her fundamental compassion: she is able to generate "this enormous degree of empathy" because "[s]he's so in touch with the culture of the ordinary"—that feeling lingering within everyone that he or she somehow does not belong (Goodale 18). Ultimately, Loh envisions her work as being "inclusive," reaching out to all members of her audiences in an attempt to forge a community among those who are marginalized. Critics recognize that in this way, Loh is venturing onto uncharted territory in terms of issues of multiracial identity and her empathy for the outsiders in America, whether it is focused on "the dumpies," her family, or others like herself.

BIBLIOGRAPHY

Works by Sandra Tsing Loh

Drama

Aliens in America. New York: Riverhead Books, 1997.

Unpublished Manuscripts

Spontaneous Demographics. 1987.
Too Full for Love. 1987.
Self Promotion. 1988.
Night of the Grunion. 1989.
Music at the Bonus Carwash. 1990.
ShiPOOpeE! The American Musical De-Con-Structed. 1990.
A Freeway Home Companion. 1992.
Depth Becomes Her. 1997.
Bad Sex with Bud Kemp. 1998.

Selected Production History

Spontaneous Demographics

Solo performance. Public places of Los Angeles, 1987.

Too Full for Love

Production. Zephyr Theater, Los Angeles, 1987.

Self Promotion

Solo performance. Public places of Los Angeles, 1988.

Night of the Grunion

Solo performance. Public places of Malibu, CA, 1989.

Music at the Bonus Carwash

Solo performance. Public places of Santa Monica, CA, 1990.

ShiPOOpeE! The American Musical De-Con-Structed

Solo performance. "Two Funny," Backstage Theatre, Irvine, CA, 1990.

A Freeway Home Companion

Solo performance, with Mel Green. Theater/Theater, Hollywood, 1992.
———. U.S. Comedy Arts Festival, Aspen, CO, 1996.

Aliens in America

Solo performance. SOLO/LA, CBS Studio Center, Studio City, CA, 1995.
Production, dir. Steve Kaplan. Second Stage Theatre, New York City, 1996.
———. Tiffany Theater, West Hollywood, CA, 1999.
———. Seattle Repertory Theatre, Seattle, 1999–2000.
———, dir. David Schweizer. San José Repertory Theatre, CA, 2001.

Depth Becomes Her

Solo performance, "Mark Taper Forum Asian Theatre Workshop," dir. Chay Yew. Mark
   Taper, Too, Los Angeles, 1997.

Bad Sex with Bud Kemp

Solo performance, dir. David Schweizer. Tiffany Theater, West Hollywood, CA, 1998.
———. Second Stage Theatre, New York City, 1998.

Essays

Depth Takes a Holiday: Essays from Lesser Los Angeles. New York: Riverhead, 1996.
A Year in Van Nuys. Collection. New York: Crown, 2001.

Novels

If You Lived Here, You'd Be Home by Now. New York: Riverhead, 1997.

Recordings

Pianovision. K2B2 Records, 1991.
Breathing Lessons: The Life and Work of Mark O'Brien. Composer. Dir. Jessica Yu.
   VHS. An Inscrutable Films Production in Conjunction with Pacific News Service.
   Boston: Fanlight Productions, 1996.
The Living Museum. Composer. Dir. Jessica Yu. VHS. La Canada, CA: Living Film-
   works, 1998.

Short Stories

"Modern Caucasian Wedding Dances." *Southern California Anthology* 5 (1987): 121–
    31.
"Mundo Del Box." *Buzz Magazine* (Dec. 1993–Jan. 1994): 90+.
"My Father's Chinese Wives." *Pushcart Prize, XX, 1996: Best of the Small Presses*. Ed.
    Bill Henderson with the Pushcart Prize editors. New York: Pushcart P, 1995.
    131–143. Rpt. in *Norton Anthology of Short Fiction*. 6th ed. Ed. R.V. Cassill and
    Richard Bausch. New York: Norton, 2000. 1034–43.
"Raiding the Larder." *Absolute Disaster: Fiction from Los Angeles*. Ed. Lee Montgomery.
    Los Angeles: Dove Books, 1996. 3–15.
"My Ethiopian Vacation." *Mother Jones* Sept.–Oct. 1997: 64+.

Television

A Freeway Home Companion. HBO New Writers Project. HBO Network. 1995.
"Fixing Up Daddy." *Clueless*. Paramount TV. 1996.
Dates from Hell. Dreamworks. FOX Network. 1998.
Life Is Elsewhere. HBO Independent Productions. HBO Network. 1998.
Viva La Rock. Commentator/Interviewer. VH1. 1998.

Studies of Sandra Tsing Loh

Akst, Daniel. "If You Are Really Unlucky, You Might Hear Her Entire Repertoire." *Wall
    Street Journal* 26 Aug. 1987: 23.
Brantley, Ben. "Ever Wincing at Her Roots yet Unwilling to Let Go." Rev. of *Aliens in
    America. New York Times* 20 July 1996, sec. 1: 11.
Daniels, Robert L. Rev. of *Bad Sex with Bud Kemp. Variety* 11–17 May 1998: 179.
Gates, Anita. Rev. of *Bad Sex with Bud Kemp. New York Times* 6 May 1998: E7.
Glionna, John M. "The Multi-cult Semi-celeb." *Los Angeles Times Magazine* 9 Apr.
    2000: 14+.
Goodale, Gloria. "Ethnic Humor for Everyone." *Christian Science Monitor* 26 Nov.
    1999: 18. Rpt. as "Sandra Tsing Loh" in *Migration World Magazine* 28.4 (May
    2000): 40.
Indiana, Gary. "Moonwalk." Rev. of *If You Lived Here, You'd Be Home by Now. Los
    Angeles Times* 19 Dec. 1997, Book review: 12.
Isherwood, Charles. Rev. of *Depth Becomes Her. Variety* 21 Apr. 1997: 71+.
Lacher, Irene. "In Search of the Real Valley." *Los Angeles Times* 23 May 1996: E1.
Smith, Dinitia. "A Family 'Disaster' as One-Woman Theater." Rev. of *Aliens in America.
    New York Times* 24 July 1996: C9.
Sterngold, James. "Anxious Singles." *New York Times* 12 June 1998: E10.
Talvi, Silja J.A. "Sandra Tsing Loh: Our Kind of Alien." Personal interview. *Fabula* 4.1
    (March 2000): 24–25.
Wasman, Howard. Rev. of *Aliens in America. Variety* 29 July 1996: 66.

Darrell H.Y. Lum

(1950–   )

Masami Usui

BIOGRAPHY

Darrell H.Y. Lum was born of Chinese ancestry on April 2, 1950, in the Alewa Heights area of Honolulu, Hawaii, and has been living on the islands ever since. His grandmother on his mother's side moved to Hawaii when she was an infant and married a Chinese rice-mill manager. Lum's mother was the youngest of seven children from Waikane Valley, Oahu. Lum's father was born in Canton (now Guangzhou), China, and came to Hawaii at age five or six. Lum's grandfather on his father's side was a provincial government official in China, but was invited to be a Chinese-language schoolteacher in Kaimuki, Honolulu. Although his grandfather later became a butcher because he could not support his family as a schoolteacher, he kept writing poetry all his life.

Lum went to Maemae Elementary School and Kawananakoa Intermediate School, and graduated from McKinley High School in 1968. In the same year, he left Hawaii to study engineering at Case Institute of Technology in Cleveland. After his freshman year, he transferred to the University of Hawai'i (UH) at Manoa and started taking creative-writing classes. In May 1972, he received his B.A. in liberal studies, creative writing, and graphic design. In December 1976, he received his master's degree in educational communications and technology from the UH at Manoa (UHM). From 1972 to 1974, Lum was assistant director of Hawaii Upward Bound Program of the UH at Manoa. From 1974 to the present, Lum has served as an academic adviser at the UH Student Support Services. In 1997, Lum received his doctorate in educational foundations from the UH. His dissertation was entitled "What School You Went? Stories from a Pidgin Culture." Lum is married to a Japanese sansei, and they have two children.

In 1978, Lum cofounded Bamboo Ridge Press with Eric Chock, his friend since the first grade. As a nonprofit, tax-exempt literary small press and organization, Bamboo Ridge represents many of Hawaii's pioneering local voices and constitutes a local literature movement. Bamboo Ridge publishes a journal, *Bamboo Ridge: A Hawaii Writers Journal* (later *Bamboo Ridge: Journal of Hawai'i Literature and Arts*), as well as books that present Hawaii's local voices. Since 1978, Lum has served as one of the editors of *Bamboo Ridge* and has played a leading part with Chock in introducing, establishing, examining, and reexamining Hawaii's local literature. With Chock, Lum coedited such anthologies as *The Best of Bamboo Ridge* (1986), *Paké: Writings by Chinese in Hawaii* (1989), *Growing Up Local: An Anthology of Poetry and Prose from Hawai'i* (1998), and *The Best of Honolulu Fiction* (1999). After difficult years to keep Bamboo Ridge alive, the press celebrated its twentieth anniversary in 1998.

As a fiction writer and playwright, Lum has published two collections of his works at Bamboo Ridge: *Sun, Short Stories and Drama* (1980) and *Pass On, No Pass Back* (1990). Lum's first play, *Oranges Are Lucky*, was produced by Kumu Kahua Theatre both in 1976 and in 1981. The script is included in *Talk Story, Sun*, and *Kumu Kahua Plays*. The other theatrical productions include *Magic Mango* at Honolulu Theatre for Youth in June 1980, *My Home Is down the Street* at Kumu Kahua in November 1986, and *A Little Bit like You* at Kumu Kahua in November 1991 and in June 1993. *A Little Bit like You* was commissioned by Honolulu Theatre for Youth through a Rockefeller Foundation grant. *Fighting Fire* was commissioned by Kumu Kahua in 1995. *Oranges Are Lucky* and *Fighting Fire* were both produced at Kumu Kahua in February 1996.

In addition to his fiction and drama, Lum has published stories, essays, and children's books. In his children's books, *The Golden Slipper: A Vietnamese Legend, Hot-Pepper-Kid and Iron-Mouth-Chicken Capture Fire and Wind*, and *A Rice Mystery*, he intends to present a respectful understanding of the Asian heritage. Lum's critical writings "Local Literature and Lunch" and "Local Genealogy: What School You Went?" embody his insistently held view of Hawaii's local literature. His works are included in such anthologies as *The Best of Bamboo Ridge* (1986), *Charlie Chan Is Dead: An Anthology of Contemporary Asian American Fiction* (1993), *Into the Fire: Asian American Prose* (1995), *Growing Up Local* (1998), and *The Best of Honolulu Fiction* and *Yellow Light: The Flowering of Asian American Arts* (1999). Lum also received the Elliot Cades Award for Literature in 1991. For *Pass On, No Pass Back*, Lum was awarded the 1992 Outstanding Book Award in Fiction from the Asian American Studies Association. Both Lum and Chock were awarded the 1996 Hawaii Award for Literature for their work on Bamboo Ridge.

MAJOR WORKS AND THEMES

The themes of Lum's major theatrical works center on the conflicts and resolutions of the first-generation Chinese immigrants and their offspring in Hawaii.

One segment of Lum's works is a trilogy of one-act plays that portrays three generations of Chinese families living within the Chinese community in Hawaii: *Oranges Are Lucky* is the grandmother's story, *Fighting Fire* is the father's story, and the third play, on which he is currently working, is the children's story. The other segment consists of two full-length plays with extended themes of conflicts within the changing scheme of family and community in Hawaii. *My Home Is down the Street* depicts the long-unresolved conflict between the aging Chinese father in a Chinese nursing home in Hawaii and his well-established son who has settled in Boston and works as a doctor there. *A Little Bit like You* explores a secret of an interracial family of Chinese and Japanese locals of four generations. All of Lum's works dwell on the fact that immigrants to Hawaii and their offspring have nourished and affirmed their identity in Hawaii as a home of their own.

Oranges Are Lucky (1976) is set at Ah Po's eighty-first birthday party at a Chinese restaurant in the mid-1970s where her family gathers to celebrate. The play consists of two spaces: one is a stilty conversation between Ah Po in pidgin English and the younger people in Hawaii Creole English, and the other is Ah Po's eloquent internal monologue, presumably in Chinese. The contrast depicts all the tensions within an extended family of three generations, including Ah Po's granddaughter's Japanese boyfriend. Ah Po's monologue reveals all the hardships of her own life as an uneducated young woman with bound feet, her marriage to a scholar, her half-forced immigration with him to Hawaii, and her struggle for identity in a new land.

Ah Po's dominant position as the family's matriarch is reversed when she recalls her past as a submissive and weak vessel of Chinese patriarchy. This play is thus an elegy to the Chinese grandmothers whom Lum as a young local boy refused to understand, embrace, and respect because they could neither speak nor read English and maintained the Chinese traditional manners and customs. Lum first regards his two Chinese grandmothers as "the personification of all things Chinese," but later understands that these women founded the ground of local identity because they "created the practices of being 'Chinese' against the backdrop of a dominant white, Western culture and a native Hawaiian host culture" ("Local Girls" 365–66).

"Oranges are lucky" was what Lum's grandmother used to tell him when she urged him to eat oranges. His boyhood refusal to eat the grandmother's "lucky" oranges is turned into his redemption by presenting her long-inarticulate story. Lum concludes the play with Ah Po's birthday wish, which "is not a concession to assimilation but her coming to an understanding of her role as matriarch of her family in Hawai'i and America" ("Inventory List").

My Home Is down the Street (1986) and *Fighting Fire* (1995) are about the father-son conflict and resolution within Chinese families. In both plays, the flashback to the past is suggested with Chinese firecrackers, symbol of fights between father and son, between generations, and between men. In a series of scenes from a hospital room, the father's old home, to Kaimuki Home, a nursing home for elderly Chinese, the lifelong conflict in *My Home Is down the Street* is gradually resolved between Kwan Choy Lee, now in his late seventies, and his son, Bernard, in his mid-fifties. Bernard's hostility and rejection of his dominant father, who worked hard and used to "catch the bus" instead of buying a car, made Bernard escape from him, Chinatown, pidgin English, and everything involving Chinese heritage in Hawaii. Bernard's success as a doctor in Boston ironically does not help his own father, who needs special care and his own son. In flashbacks to the past in which pidgin English is used, Bernard traces the roots of his conflict with his father. The worse Kwan Choy's condition and memory become, the stronger his wish to live with Bernard during the rest of his life. With his cousin Douglas's help, Bernard's decision to return to his father's house is suggested by two symbolic "boo-look," Chinese grapefruits, which Bernard picks up from his father's neglected garden as a sign of a resolved relationship between father and son.

Set in a basement warehouse of a store in Chinatown, *Fighting Fire* is told by two elderly lifelong yet incompatible friends, "Gunner" Loo and "Cowboy" Lee, who once belonged to the same basketball team while young but who now prepare their coffins for their funerals. Gunner is a successful man with an import-export business and store specializing in the fireworks trade, while Cowboy is a retired salesman and a business failure. Cowboy's failure results from his unresolved relationship with his father, Ah Ba, who appears as a spirit. The play ends with the double resolution—Gunner and Cowboy as friends face the end of their lives, and Cowboy and his father embrace each other with understanding and respect.

Presented in three different English languages (Hawaii Creole, pidgin, and standard), the conflicting relationships of the four generations of a Japanese Chinese family are the subject of *A Little Bit like You* (1991). This play thus deals with the theme of *hapa*, mixed blood, through history but in a contemporary setting. Though Ah Po in *Oranges Are Lucky* and Kwan Choy in *My Home Is down the Street* lament that their granddaughters have Japanese boyfriends, *A Little Bit like You* explores racial bias within a Japanese family. Keiko "Kay" Chang, a teenager born of a Japanese mother and a Chinese father, faces an identity crisis, partially brought on by her grandmother, Kiyoko. Kiyoko often uses the insulting term "pa-ke" for the Chinese and is still opposed to her daughter's marriage to a Chinese. But when Keiko discovers the family secret that her grandmother is half Chinese herself, Kiyoko has to confront her own racist attitude toward Chinese, and ultimately toward herself. The play ends with Kiyoko's efforts to accept herself as a Japanese Chinese, which her granddaughter, Keiko, is ready to pass on as an identity of her own.

The play reveals how strongly Japanese discriminated against Chinese, especially among the first and second generations. When Japanese began immigrating to Hawaii, Japan had invaded China and colonized Manchuria, so that the majority of Japanese felt superior to Chinese. Yet the Japanese immigrants learned the fact that the immigrants from China had settled in Hawaii earlier than the Japanese. Like its title *A Little Bit like You*, the reconciliation at the end of the play gives all the generations a new sense of identity as people with mixed racial, cultural, and social heritage, despite the strong sense of the monoracial tradition among both the Chinese and the Japanese.

Lum's plays examine a multilayered identity search of the people across generations who have made Hawaii their home. Unlike short stories and novels, Lum observes that plays "turn out different every time," and the "whole is a mixture of many elements" (Kam D-1). But, not unlike his characters on stage, Lum has embarked in life on a significant voyage of his own identity search through the playwriting process, which has contributed to the new identity formation in Hawaii.

CRITICAL RECEPTION

In spite of his enormous contribution to establishing Hawaii's local literature, Lum is not as noted for his fiction and drama as he has been for his editorship. Frank Stewart, a writer and faculty member of the UH, praises both Chock and Lum for their effort as editors of Bamboo Ridge (viii). Gayle Fujita Sato and Stephen Sumida, both from Hawaii, evaluate Lum as a local writer at the early stage of his activities for Bamboo Ridge. Sumida remarks that Lum is "a master of local symbols, especially his use of pidgin and creole vernaculars," and also "a master of the Hawai'i childhood idyll" in his work like *Oranges Are Lucky* (98). Sylvia Watanabe, a fiction writer originally from Hawaii, considers Lum to be one of the writers "who have a strong sense of identity with and long-term commitment to a particular locale" (Watanabe and Bruchac ii).

However, Josephine Lee has conducted a more serious study of *Oranges Are Lucky* in her book *Performing Asian America*. Lee focuses on one of Lum's plays and interprets *Oranges Are Lucky* as "resolving years of hardship and racism with a modicum of success" (161). Through the disjointed history and unconnected present, the play stages the tragic impact of the U.S. exclusionary acts on the Chinese immigrant community, hence suggesting "a necessary countering of more idealized visions of an Asian American past" (162).

In Hawaii, Lum's plays have received favorable reviews, especially the 1996 double production of two one-act plays, *Oranges Are Lucky* and *Fighting Fire*. Nadine Kam believes that both plays are "identity problematic at any age" (D-1). But, regretfully, the mainland theaters have not paid much attention to his plays. Lum's plays should be evaluated outside Hawaii because they embody the local/ethnic conflicts that can be shared and apprehended by a wide range of audiences. As Dennis Carroll, a professor of theater at the UHM, has noted, the theme of his works is often "cultural accommodation" (63), and Hawaii happens to be the setting.

BIBLIOGRAPHY

Works by Darrell H.Y. Lum

Drama

Oranges Are Lucky. Talk Story: An Anthology of Hawaii's Local Writers. Ed. Eric E. Chock, Dave Robb, Frank Stewart, Gail Miyasaki, Kathy Uchida, and Darrell H.Y. Lum. Honolulu: Petronium and Talk Story, 1978. 139–56. Rpt. in *Sun, Short Stories and Drama.* By Darrell H.Y. Lum. Honolulu: Bamboo Ridge P, 1980. 44–61; *Kumu Kahua Plays.* Ed. Dennis Carroll. Honolulu: U of Hawai'i P, 1983. 64–82.

Magic Mango. Bamboo Shoots. Ed. Dennis Kawaharada. Honolulu: Bamboo Ridge P, 1982. 4–13.

Unpublished Manuscripts

My Home Is down the Street. 1986.
A Little Bit like You. 1991.
Fighting Fire. 1995.
"Inventory List." Essay. n.d.

Selected Production History

Oranges Are Lucky

Production. Kumu Kahua Theatre, Honolulu, 1976 and 1981.
———, dir. John H.Y. Wat. Kumu Kahua Theatre, Honolulu, 1996.

Magic Mango

Production, dir. Phyllis Look. Honolulu Theatre for Youth, Honolulu, 1980.

A Little Bit like You

Production. Kumu Kahua Theatre, Honolulu, 1991.
———, dir. Keith Kashiwada. Tenney Theatre, Honolulu, 1993.
———. Aloha Performing Arts Center, Kona, Hawaii, 1993.
———. Lihue Parish Hall, Lihue, Kauai, 1993.
———. U of Hawai'i at Hilo Theatre, Hilo, Hawaii, 1993.
———. Windward Community College Little Theatre, Kaneohe, Oahu, 1993.

Fighting Fire

Production, dir. John H.Y. Wat; Kumu Kahua Theatre, Honolulu, 1996.

Anthologies

Talk Story: An Anthology of Hawaii's Local Writers. With Eric E. Chock, Dave Robb, Frank Stewart, Gail Miyasaki, and Kathy Uchida. Honolulu: Petronium and Talk Story, 1978.

The Best of Bamboo Ridge: The Hawaii Writers' Quarterly. With Eric E. Chock. Honolulu: Bamboo Ridge P, 1986.

Paké: Writings by Chinese in Hawaii. With Eric Chock. Honolulu: Bamboo Ridge P, 1989.

Growing Up Local: An Anthology of Poetry and Prose from Hawai'i. With Eric E. Chock, James R. Harstad, and Bill Teter. Honolulu: Bamboo Ridge P, 1998.

The Best of Honolulu Fiction: Stories from the Honolulu Magazine Fiction Contest. With Eric E. Chock. Honolulu: Bamboo Ridge P, 1999.

Quietest Singing. With Joseph Stanton and Estelle Enoki. Honolulu: State Foundation on Culture and the Arts, 2000.

Children's Books

The Golden Slipper: A Vietnamese Legend. Mahwah, NJ: Troll Associates, 1994.

Hot-Pepper-Kid and Iron-Mouth-Chicken Capture Fire and Wind. New York: McGraw-Hill, 1997.

A Rice Mystery. New York: McGraw-Hill, 1999.

Essays

"Local Literature and Lunch." *The Best of Bamboo Ridge: The Hawaii Writers' Quarterly.* Ed. Eric E. Chock and Darrell H.Y. Lum. Honolulu: Bamboo Ridge P, 1986. 3–5.

"On Pidgin and Children in Literature." *Infant Tongues: The Voices of the Child in Literature.* Ed. Elizabeth Goodenough, Mark A. Heberle, and Naomi B. Sokoloff. Detroit: Wayne State UP, 1994. 298–301.

"Local Genealogy: What School You Went?" *Growing Up Local: An Anthology of Poetry and Prose from Hawai'i.* Ed. Eric E. Chock, James R. Harstad, Bill Teter, and Darrell H.Y. Lum. Honolulu: Bamboo Ridge P, 1998. 11–15.

"Local Girls." *Growing Up Local: An Anthology of Poetry and Prose from Hawai'i.* Ed. Eric E. Chock, James R. Harstad, Bill Teter, and Darrell H.Y. Lum. Honolulu: Bamboo Ridge P, 1998. 365–66.

Interview

"Response." Interview. *Yellow Light: The Flowering of Asian American Arts.* Ed. Amy Ling. Philadelphia: Temple UP, 1999. 93–98.

Short Stories

Sun, Short Stories and Drama. Collection of Lum's short stories and plays. Honolulu: Bamboo Ridge P, 1980.

Pass On, No Pass Back. Collection. Honolulu: Bamboo Ridge P, 1990.

"Fourscore and Seven Years Ago." *Charlie Chan Is Dead: An Anthology of Contemporary Asian American Fiction.* Ed. Jessica Hagedorn. New York: Penguin, 1993. 287–95.

"Giving Thanks." *Infant Tongues: The Voices of the Child in Literature.* Ed. Elizabeth Goodenough, Mark A. Heberle, and Naomi B. Sokoloff. Detroit: Wayne State UP, 1994. 294–97. Rpt. in *Into the Fire: Asian American Prose.* Ed. Sylvia Watanabe and Carol Bruchac. Greenfield Center, NY: Greenfield Review P, 1996. 113–17.

"Orphan Annie: Coloring in the Eyes." *Growing Up Local: An Anthology of Poetry and Prose from Hawaii.* Ed. Eric E. Chock, James R. Harstad, Bill Teter, and Darrell H.Y. Lum. Honolulu: Bamboo Ridge P, 1998: 222–31.

"Paint." *Yellow Light: The Flowering of Asian American Arts.* Ed. Amy Ling. Philadelphia: Temple UP, 1999. 98–102.

"What School You Went?" *The Best of Honolulu Fiction: Stories from the Honolulu Magazine Fiction Contest.* Ed. Eric E. Chock and Darrell H.Y. Lum. Honolulu: Bamboo Ridge P, 1999. 169–76.

Studies of Darrell H.Y. Lum

Berger, John. "TV Anchor Lends a Hand as Playwright." *Honolulu Star-Bulletin* 11 Dec. 1997. 10 Dec. 2000 <thttp://starbulletin.com/97/12/11/features/index.html>.

Burlingame, Burl. "Bamboo Thriving—*Bamboo Ridge* Editors Win a State Award." *Honolulu Star-Bulletin* 23 June 1997: B1+.

Carroll, Dennis. "*Oranges Are Lucky*: Editor's Note." *Kumu Kahua Plays.* Ed. Dennis Carroll. Honolulu: U of Hawai'i P, 1983. 63.

"Darrell Lum Double Bill at Kumu Kahua Theatre." *Hawaii Pacific Press* 1 Jan. 1996: 87.

Harada, Wayne. "Past Becomes Present for Her 'Orange' Role." Rev. of *Oranges Are Lucky* and *Fighting Fire. Honolulu Advertiser* 11 Jan. 1996: B5.

Kam, Nadine. "Finding Fodder in Family and Friends." Rev. of *Oranges Are Lucky* and *Fighting Fire. Honolulu Star-Bulletin* 9 Jan. 1996: D1+.

Kua, Crystal. "UH Group: Respect Pidgin in Schools." *Honolulu Star-Bulletin* 20 Nov. 1999: A3.

Lee, Josephine. *Performing Asian America: Race and Ethnicity on the Contemporary Stage.* Philadelphia: Temple UP, 1997.

Ling, Amy. "Darrell Lum, Fiction Writer and Playwright." *Yellow Light: The Flowering of Asian American Arts.* Ed. Amy Ling. Philadelphia: Temple UP, 1999. 92.

Oi, Cynthia. "Bamboo Ridge Celebrates 20." *Honolulu Star-Bulletin* 20 Nov. 1998: D1+.

———. "Bodda you? 'Hybolics' Takes a Big Step in Promoting Pidgin as Legitimate Language." *Honolulu Star-Bulletin* 11 Oct. 1999: D1+.

Okawa, Gail Y. "Resistance and Reclamation: Hawaii 'Pidgin English' and Autoethnography in the Short Stories of Darrell H.Y. Lum." *Ethnicity and the American Short Story.* Ed. Julie Brown. New York: Garland, 1997. 177–96.

Rozmiarek, Joseph T. "Lum Plays Become Character Poems." Rev. of *Oranges Are Lucky* and *Fighting Fire. Honolulu Advertiser* 12 Jan. 1996: C9.

Sato, Gayle K. Fujita. "The Island Influence on Chinese American Writers: Wing Tek Lum, Darrell H.Y. Lum, and Eric Chock." *Amerasia Journal* 16.2 (1990): 17–33.

Stewart, Frank. Preface. *Passages to the Dream Shore: Short Stories of Contemporary Hawaii.* Ed. Frank Stewart. Honolulu: U of Hawai'i P, 1987. vii–viii.

Sumida, Stephen H. *And the View from the Shore: Literary Traditions of Hawai'i.* Seattle: U of Washington P, 1991.

Watanabe, Sylvia. "A Conversation with Darrell Lum and Eric Chock." *Into the Fire: Asian American Prose.* Ed. Sylvia Watanabe and Carol Bruchac. Greenfield Center, NY: Greenfield Review P, 1996. 85–98.

Watanabe, Sylvia, and Carol Bruchac. "Out of the Frying Pan." Introduction. *Into the Fire: Asian American Prose.* Ed. Sylvia Watanabe and Carol Bruchac. Greenfield Center, NY: Greenfield Review P, 1996. i–iii.

Marlane Meyer
(1951–   )

Shuchen S. Huang

BIOGRAPHY

Born on January 23, 1951, in San Francisco and raised in San Pedro, California, Marlane Gomard Meyer comes from a mixed ethnic background. Her Hawaiian father, Robert Punobu Gomard, is of Polynesian and Native American (Cherokee) descent, and her mother, Corinne Gomard, of German and Swedish. Meyer describes her father as "a merchant seaman, union official, 'roughneck, gambler, and know-it-all' " and her mother as "a painter, designer, writer, astrologer, gambler," among many other things (*Partnow and Hyott* 150). As a "fringe family," they "collected off-beat characters in many different ways," from whom the colorful characters in her plays usually derive (Loud 24).

Meyer received a bachelor's degree in theater from California State University at Long Beach, where she studied with Murray Mednick, one of the founders of the renowned Padua Hills Festival. Meyer started engaging herself in playwriting at twenty-three. Before her professional debut with *Etta Jenks*, she had already composed about a dozen plays, which were performed "at the Found Theatre, in the utility room of the Uprising Bookstore at Cal State Long Beach, and in various workshops in Los Angeles" (Herman V8). In 1988, *Etta Jenks* received its world premiere, a coproduction of the Women's Project and the Los Angeles Theatre Center. Since then, her works have been presented not only in Los Angeles, New York City, and Chicago, but also in England.

After her mother's death and a divorce, Meyer moved from Los Angeles to New York in 1989, where she divided her time between writing plays for theater and for television. Her television plays include "Sirens" for ABC, "Better Off Dead" for Lifetime, "Life Stories" for NBC, and "Out of the Sixties" for HBO.

In addition to writing, Meyer has taught playwriting at the Yale School of Drama.

Although Meyer is not yet acknowledged as an important contemporary American or Asian American playwright, her works have been awarded many prizes. *Etta Jenks* won the Kesselring Award and the Dramalogue Award in 1987; *Kingfish* won the Dramalogue Award in 1988 and the PEN Center West Award in 1989; *The Geography of Luck* won the Dramalogue Award in 1989; and *Moe's Lucky Seven* won the Susan Smith Blackburn Prize in 1993. Meyer also received the Brody Foundation Grant for Literature in 1987, the Creative Artists Public Service Grant in 1989, and a National Endowment for the Arts Playwriting Fellowship in 1990. Moreover, Meyer, a former playwright-in-residence of the Padua Hills Playwrights' Workshop, belongs to various literary coteries, such as the Dramatists Guild, the Writers' Guild of America East, PEN Center West, the New York Playwrights' Lab, the Women's Project, and the Polynesian Society.

MAJOR WORKS AND THEMES

A prolific writer, Meyer has only three plays published so far: *Etta Jenks* (1988), *The Geography of Luck* (1989), and *Moe's Lucky Seven* (1993). Her works, generally speaking, deal with gritty reality and lives and relationships between socially outcast characters.

Etta Jenks chronicles a girl's "stardom" journey. With nineteen brief scenes and no standard exposition, this play opens with Etta, a girl from somewhere in the middle of the country, coming to Los Angeles by train to become a movie star. Discouraged by lack of opportunity and money, Etta is coerced by a slimy porno king named Ben into becoming a porno actress. Then she works as an agent who scouts "talented" girls for porno movies. Succeeding in the porno business, Etta avenges her innocence and the "disappearance" of her friend Sheri on Ben. The play ends with a powerful Etta, a porno-film producer, interviewing a young woman interested in working for her.

The Geography of Luck also elides an exposition but consists of eighteen episodic scenes. Centering around an ex–rock star, Dixie, who has just been released from prison, the play delineates the protagonist's relationships with his father, mother, women, and friends in his life. As Meyer notes, "[Dixie's] relationships in the play are the landmarks that guide him, teach him, and move him through the terrain—hopefully toward something like the promised land, to home . . . to yourself" ("Mapping the American Heart"). The primary background of *The Geography of Luck* is Las Vegas; however, some of the scenes, as the dramatist notes, are set in dreams.

Moe's Lucky Seven begins with a prologue in which two narrators, Tiny and Knuckles, at a bar called "Moe's Lucky Seven," tell a modern Adam-Eve-Snake story. The on-again, off-again relationship between Patsy/Eve and Drew/Adam is tautened when Patsy becomes pregnant. The son of the bar proprietor and also a local union organizer, Drew is finally convinced to settle down and proposes to Patsy. On the wedding day, however, thanks to Drake/Snake's seduction, Patsy realizes that she does not really want a normal mortal life with Drew and disappears.

Indeed, Meyer's plays are populated with "fringe" characters, such as prostitutes, pimps, gamblers, alcoholics, bartenders, homosexuals, and ex-cons, to list just a few. This is also true in *Why Things Burn* (1994) and *The Chemistry of Change* (1999). The world of *Why Things Burn* is inhabited by an arsonist (Lon), his bickering parents, a group of white supremacists including an unsavory ex-con, a troubled drifter, and a beautiful but lost girl. *The Chemistry of Change*, set in California in the 1950s, tells a story about a problematic family—a mother who has married nine times for money, a daughter who performs illegal abortions for a living, and a son who is alcoholic and in love with his mother.

Although Meyer has a predilection for the "fringe" characters, her plays are not meant to be realistic or naturalistic. As the playwright asserts, what she writes is "extended realism" (Arkatov V18). This "extended realism" can be seen, for instance, in a porno actress (Sheri) in *Etta Jenks*, who learns to transform her human corporeality into smell of gardenia. In *Kingfish* (1986), another play also not published but staged widely, the "extended realism" is spelled out in the character of "Kingfish." "Kingfish" is lonely old Wylie's dog, which appears on stage as a wooden box with four pegs, but at the end of the play actually attacks Hal, who betrays the old man and threatens to kill his "dog." It is Meyer's dramatic devices such as the mythical transformation of the porno actress (*Etta Jenks*) and the ambiguity of "Kingfish's" identity (*Kingfish*) that transcend simplistic realism and add another dimension to her dramatic world.

CRITICAL RECEPTION

Meyer's plays have received quite mixed theater reviews. These reviews show a spectrum of opinions of her works. John Simon remarks that *Kingfish* is "a work of . . . egregious worthlessness" (Rev. of *Kingfish* 73), and *Moe's Lucky Seven* tells a "story, which does not make much sense" (Rev. of *Moe's* 68). In contrast, Mel Gussow argues that Meyer's "talent for gritty realism" is well demonstrated in *Etta Jenks* but not in *Kingfish* ("Kingfish" C5). While *Etta Jenks* has "the hard-edged intensity of a Martin Scorsese film" (Gussow, "Hollywood" C26), *Kingfish* is regarded as "an exercise in absurdism" because Gussow seems unable to decide whether "Kingfish" is a dog, a black box, or a fish ("Kingfish" C5).

Meyer's other plays have encountered a similarly diverse reception. Jeremy Gerard notes that *Moe's Lucky Seven* recalls William Saroyan's *Time of Your Life* "with another waterfront dive featuring a grungy gaggle of off-the-cuff philosophizers, rough-hewn romantics and walking wounded" (47). Dennis Harvey thinks that *Why Things Burn* has brought up "provocative questions" but failed "to decide where to point the motivational blame" (61). Heather Mackey praises Meyer's *Why Things Burn* for its "fabulist images, intense emotions and the austere beauty of her language" (8). Reviewing *The Chemistry of Change*, Charles McNulty comments that the audience, though entertained by the story, might be confused "about whether [the play] wants to be a fiendish feminist romp or an ultratraditional romantic comedy" (91).

In contrast to the number of theater reviews, scholarship on Meyer's works is scarce. In "Gender, Sexuality and 'My Life' in the (University) Theater," Jill Dolan points out that "Meyer's [*Etta Jenks*] positions itself within the feminist antipornography critique in several ways" (187). For instance, through Etta's career trajectory, the dramatist problematizes gender stereotypes such as women-as-exploited-and-objectified-sex and men-as-dominant-and-subject-sex. Discussing the production of *Etta Jenks* and the students' responses to the play at the University of Wisconsin at Madison in 1992, Stacy Wolf theorizes that her students' "unskilled readings" reflect their positionality and agency and "illuminate assumptions of both theatre and pedagogy" (33). While the reviewers generally find *Kingfish* perplexing in one way or another, Lynne Conner illuminates many aspects of the play in her postmodern reading. She interprets that Meyer, "with her sharp postmodern sensibility" (28), has overturned "the assumption of man's dominance and superiority over animals" and redefined what constitutes a family (25). The black box called "Kingfish" "is Meyer's tool for moving in and out of the realistic tradition" (Conner 30).

In summary, the various opinions of the theater reviews indicate an increased popular interest in Meyer's plays. However, most of them either only scratch the surface of the subjects or have not even given a just opinion. For the richness and complexities of the characters, themes, and plays as a whole, Meyer's works certainly deserve more critical attention and in-depth literary appraisals.

BIBLIOGRAPHY

Works by Marlane Meyer

Drama

Etta Jenks. Plays in Process 9.7. New York: Theatre Communications Group, 1988. Rpt. in *WomensWork: Five New Plays from the Women's Project*. Ed. Julia Miles. New York: Applause, 1989. 115–74.

The Geography of Luck. Plays in Process 11.9. New York: Theatre Communications Group, 1991.

Moe's Lucky Seven. Women Playwrights: The Best Plays of 1994. Ed. Marisa Smith. Lyme, NH: Smith and Kraus, 1995. 117–66.

Unpublished Manuscripts

Kingfish. 1986.
Starfish and Strays. 1986.
Relativity. One-act play. 1991.

Why Things Burn. 1994.
The Chemistry of Change. 1999.

Selected Production History

Kingfish

Workshop. Padua Hills Festival, Claremont, CA, 1986.
Production, dir. David Schweizer. Los Angeles Theatre Center, Los Angeles, 1988.
————. Public Theater, New York City, 1989.
————. Magic Theatre, San Francisco, 1995.

Starfish and Strays

Production. Uprising Theatre, Long Beach, CA, 1986.

Etta Jenks

Production, dir. Roberta Levitow. Los Angeles Theatre Center, Los Angeles, 1988.
————. dir. Roberta Levitow. Women's Project, New York City, 1988.

The Geography of Luck

Production, dir. David Schweizer. Los Angeles Theatre Center, Los Angeles, 1989.
————. South Coast Repertory, Costa Mesa, CA, 1989.
————. Steppenwolf, Chicago, 1990.
————. Gilgamesh Theatre, New York City, 1995.

Relativity (one-act play)

Production. Women's Project at the Judith Anderson Theatre, New York City, 1991.

Lon Shaw (later Why Things Burn)

Staged reading, Public Theater, New York City, 1992.

Moe's Lucky Seven

Staged reading. New Works Festival, Mark Taper Forum, Los Angeles, 1993.
Production, dir. Roberta Levitow. Playwrights Horizons, New York City, 1994.

Why Things Burn

Production, dir. Roberta Levitow. Magic Theatre, San Francisco, 1994.

The Chemistry of Change

Production, dir. Lisa Peterson. Women's Project and Playwrights Horizons, New York
City, 1999.

Interview

"Mapping the American Heart." Interview with Stephen Weeks. *Plays in Process* 11.9.
New York: Theatre Communications Group, 1988. N. pag.

Studies of Marlane Meyer

Arkatov, Janice. "A Think Piece on the Pornography Industry." Rev. of *Etta Jenks. Los
Angeles Times* 15 Jan. 1988. Calendar: 8.

Conner, Lynne. "The Comedy of Perception: Marlane Meyer's *Kingfish.*" *Theatre Studies* 39 (1994): 19–31.

DeRose, David J. Rev. of *Kingfish. Theatre Journal* Dec. 1995: 548.

Dolan, Jill. "Gender, Sexuality and 'My Life' in the (University) Theater." *Kenyon Review* 15 (Spring 1993): 185–200.

Gerard, Jeremy. Rev. of *Moe's Lucky Seven. Variety* 16 May 1994: 47.

Gussow, Mel. "Hollywood Ambitions, Cold Realities." Rev. of *Etta Jenks. New York Times* 14 Apr. 1988: C26.

———. "Kingfish, an Exercise in Absurdism." Rev. of *Kingfish. New York Times* 22 Dec. 1989: C5.

Harvey, Dennis. Rev. of *Why Things Burn. Variety* 7 Feb. 1994: 60.

Henry, William A. "Once Outposts, Now Landmarks." Rev. of *The Geography of Luck. Time* 12 June 1989: 72.

Herman, Jan. "The Tough, Tender World of Playwright Meyer." *Los Angeles Times* 26 Aug. 1989, home ed.: V1+.

Hunt, Mame. "Tension in the Kitchen." Rev. of *The Chemistry of Change. American Theatre* Sept. 1998: 36.

Loud, Lance. Interview with Marlane Meyer. *Bomb* 30 (Winter 1990): 24–25.

Mackey, Heather. "Get to Know Your Demons." Rev. of *Why Things Burn. American Theatre* Feb. 1994: 8.

McNulty, Charles. Rev. of *The Chemistry of Change. Variety* 1 Mar. 1999: 91.

Partnow, Elaine T., and Leslie Anne Hyott. *The Female Dramatist: Profiles of Women Playwrights from the Middle Ages to Contemporary Times.* New York: Facts on File, 1998. 150–51.

Peterson, June T., and Suzanne Bennett, eds. *Women Playwrights of Diversity: A Bio-bibliographical Sourcebook.* Westport, CT: Greenwood P, 1997. 238–41.

Simon, John. Rev. of *Kingfish. New York* 15 Jan. 1990: 73.

———. Rev. of *Moe's Lucky Seven. New York* 30 May 1994: 68.

Wolf, Stacy. "Talking about Pornography, Talking about Theatre: Ethnography, Critical Pedagogy, and the Production of 'Educated' Audiences of *Etta Jenks* in Madison." *Theatre Research International* 19.1 (Spring 1994): 29–36.

Nobuko Miyamoto

(1939–   )

Roberta Uno

BIOGRAPHY

Nobuko Miyamoto is a major Asian American cultural figure and activist whose iconoclastic career has eluded categorization, ironically, often at the expense of her inclusion in discussions of Asian American theater. A dancer, singer, choreographer, actor, playwright, arts producer, and organizer, she has performed on stages and college campuses throughout the United States and has had a career spanning five decades from the Broadway stage to Hollywood and involving activism on both the West and East coasts.

Born in Los Angeles, California, Miyamoto was a year and a half old when she and her parents were evacuated to Santa Anita Assembly Center at the start of World War II. They were then forcefully relocated to a farm in Montana and later to Ogden, Utah. Her father had a trucking company that hauled produce for Japanese farmers in the Imperial Valley before the war; after the war, he was a gardener in Los Angeles. He inculcated in her a great love of music. Her mother, a seamstress and homemaker, also encouraged her passion for the arts, directing her toward dance, Miyamoto's first artistic discipline. Of them she says, "My father, in his real desires, would have loved to be a musician and my mother would have loved to be a visual artist. I think, in their frustration, or their love of this, they wanted to expose me, at first. When I got interested and got serious about it, they really supported me" (Burns).

Miyamoto, along with June Watanabe, was one of the first Asian American dancers to break through professionally in the highly competitive world of dance. Her talent brought her to the attention of some of the most respected American choreographers, including Jerome Robbins and Jack Cole. At the age of fifteen, she debuted professionally in the film version of the musical *The King and I*, starring Yul Brynner. She was a principal dancer in this and other Broadway and film classics, including *Flower Drum Song* and *Kismet*. While she was mentored and inspired by the choreographers she worked with, she found the roles limiting in terms of their exotic portrayals of "Orientals." She also found it impossible to work outside of narrowly defined racial categories. Although her grandmother was Caucasian, she was denied roles because she would "stick out" (Burns). She broke the bounds of racial casting when Jerome Robbins cast her as one of the principal dancers in the movie *West Side Story*.

Her *West Side Story* role featured her as a dancer and singer. She subsequently began to explore her voice as a performer, developing a night-club routine in Seattle, Washington. This was in the late 1960s, a time of social turmoil in the United States, and she began questioning her isolation from the world. Her first introduction to politics was as a volunteer for the Eugene McCarthy presidential campaign in 1960s. In Los Angeles, she met Antonello Branca, an Italian filmmaker who was making a documentary about the Black Panther party, entitled *Sieze the Time*. Working as his assistant, she found herself thrown into the heart of revolutionary politics through her contact with the Black Panthers and then the Young Lords, a parallel Puerto Rican revolutionary organization based in New York City. In Harlem, she met the legendary Japanese American activist Yuri Kochiyama, who introduced her to a group called Asian Americans for Action. Through them, she met Chris Iijima and later Charlie Chin. Together they began to write and perform music that embodied and catalyzed the burgeoning Asian American movement. Performing throughout America from 1970 to 1993, they helped galvanize a national Asian American community through their moving interpretations of cultural identity and social action. Their milestone album *A Grain of Sand: Music for the Struggle of Asian Americans* has been included in the Smithsonian music collection.

In 1978, Miyamoto founded Great Leap Inc. in Los Angeles; it is one of the oldest Asian American arts organizations. Great Leap orchestrates original theater and music productions and tours and organizes residencies in universities, communities, and schools. It was the recipient of the 1998 President's Award for Promising Practices. In the mid-1970s to the early 1980s, she continued to develop as a singer and songwriter, performing with pianist/composer Benny Yee and a group called Warriors of the Rainbow. With Yee she cowrote and produced the musical *Chop Suey* in 1980–81, which toured eight Los Angeles county parks and the Pacific Northwest. Significant among her theater work is her solo performance *A Grain of Sand* (1994), for which she wrote the music and book. She was the codirector and creator of *Laughter from the Children of War* (1996), which launched Club o'Noodles, the first Vietnamese American theater company. She has developed a unique pedagogy stemming from song, movement, and storytelling to engage diverse communities in the creation of theater pieces through her *To All Relations* project.

In addition to her own performance work, Miyamoto serves as the artistic director of Great Leap. She has supported the work of culturally diverse artists like Dan Kwong, Paulina Sahagun, Shishir Kurup, Amy Hill, Chic Street Man, Calvin Jung, Louise Mita, and Arlene Malinowski through her program "A Slice of Rice, Frijoles, and Greens," a multicultural festival of performance and public school residencies. Although she has collaborated with and been a guest artist at several institutions, including the University of California at Los Angeles, the Japan America Theatre, the Senshin Buddhist Temple, and the East West Players, she remains an independent producer through Great Leap and her own record label, Bindu Records.

MAJOR WORKS AND THEMES

The major themes of Miyamoto's theater work include the reclaiming of Asian American communal history, the exploration of personal identity, and the commonalities and conflicts between Asian Americans and other groups of color. Her work exists at a unique intersection that both challenges its audience to activism and beckons it to spirituality. These themes are evident in her earliest artistic work. In the seminal recording *A Grain of Sand*, history is mined through songs like "We Are the Children," whose lyrics—"We are the children of the migrant worker, we are the children of the concentration camps"—made immigrant and oppressed roots a point of pride. Another song, "Nosotros Somos Asiaticos (We Are Asians)," sung in Spanish, articulated a cultural identity to another oppressed minority, evoking a sense of third-world unity.

Miyamoto's scripted multicharacter plays and solo performances are written as plays with music. This is the primary reason anthologists have neglected to include her in the growing number of Asian American drama collections. Her multicharacter plays primarily probe the themes of Asian American history and identity. *Chop Suey*, a musical composed with Benny Yee, is an archetypal Asian American story about a young girl who grows up in Chinatown and yearns to know the world beyond. *Talk Story I and II* (musicals) were a series of stories that reflected various aspects of Asian American life. Characters included a Korean storekeeper, two nisei women reuniting after internment camp, an elderly Filipino migrant worker who reminisces about his dance-hall days, and a Korean immigrant woman who cannot speak English.

Miyamoto's solo performance work moves beyond the genre tendency toward narcissism and self-indulgence in the exploration of personal identity and experience. Whereas most successful solo performance achieves the universal through insight into the specific, Miyamoto's solo performance is meaningful because the canvas of her personal experience is so large. *Joanne Is My Middle Name* (1990) juxtaposed the evolution of her career and name changes with upheavals in the American social landscape. Dancing in musicals with the anglicized and abbreviated moniker Joanne Miya, she sought to obscure her ethnicity, as have many performers from Bob Dylan (Robert Zimmerman) to Madonna (Louise Ciccone).

A Grain of Sand further probes the relationship between self and society; its historical bookends are the Japanese American internment during World War II and the 1992 Los Angeles riots. In this work, she uses her remarkable life to chronicle a hitherto-invisible history—that of Asian American movement activism—and she reveals an Asian American presence in struggles that are previously familiar only in black and white. Unlike some of her earlier theater work, which at times slips into a simplistic depiction of hardship and triumph, *A Grain of Sand* moves toward a troubling, complex, and ambiguous final statement, much like the Los Angeles riots themselves. As she races through the burning streets of Los Angeles, "I stop at a light. A young black man looks at me—fire in his eyes. He sees in me the enemy. No time to say, 'Hey, I loved Malcolm.' Or, 'You could be my son.' " Miyamoto frames the piece ritualistically; her presence, at once powerful and vulnerable, suggests a deep spiritual well from which true artists and long-term activists must drink.

It is this sense of an enduring legacy that reappears in her most recent projects. *Laughter from the Children of War* (1996), cocreated with Hung Nguyen, founding artistic director of the Los Angeles–based Club o'Noodles, was a conscious attempt to mentor younger artists from more recent Asian American communities and to pass on her theater-making techniques. This moving work bears her signature in its use of song, story, and movement to make visible the lives of young Vietnamese Americans. In 1998, she adapted this process to a new project, *To All Relations*, which she designed to bring diverse constituencies together through theatrical exploration. In 1999, she carried out the project at Arizona State University with former Japanese American camp internees, the Chamber of Commerce, and members of the Arizona state police department. These newer projects, derived from the methods she has honed over several decades, have moved her early sung call for third-world unity to a more complex performed reality.

CRITICAL RECEPTION

As mentioned previously, Miyamoto's theater work exists primarily in the musical theater genre; consequently, it has been overlooked by Asian American theater publishing projects and excluded from literary discussions. Although Miyamoto can boast one of the longest careers of any Asian American artist and certainly has achieved visibility in the mainstream through her performance work on Broadway and in Hollywood, her work as a theater artist has largely gone unreviewed because of where she has chosen to locate it. Her conscious decision to create theater for Asian American and other communities of color places her outside the limited radar of mainstream theaters. Thus, despite the fact that she has made theater for two decades in Los Angeles, a major metropolitan city with a daily and several weekly newspapers, her work is rarely reviewed. This neglect by both Asian American studies academics and the press challenges how artistic work is documented and what work enters the official record and the canon. For example, her musical *Chop Suey* (1980) was performed at Los Angeles colleges and eight Los Angeles county parks and toured the Pacific Northwest. Arguably, it had one of the largest Asian American audiences of any work of theater written by an Asian American, yet it (and by extension Miyamoto) has been omitted from Asian American theater histories because it was not produced in either an Asian American or mainstream theater.

Her veritable invisibility within the canon and the critical press may also be observed through a lens of feminism, as she has followed an early Asian American movement precept, "self-determination," through the cofounding of an independent record label and production company. As an independent woman who has created strategies to support activist artistic projects, she may have been doubly marginalized by theater critics and scholars. Finally, her political decision to align herself with other artists of color may also have caused her to be placed outside of more narrowly defined Asian American ethnic theater projects. These are some of the possible reasons why publishing about Miyamoto has been largely limited to human-interest and arts promotional stories and accounts of Asian American movement activism.

BIBLIOGRAPHY

Works by Nobuko Miyamoto

Unpublished Manuscripts

Chop Suey. Musical. Comp. Benny Yee. 1980.
Talk Story I and II. Musicals. Great Leap Archives, 1987.
Joanne Is My Middle Name. Great Leap Archives, 1990.
A Grain of Sand. Great Leap Archives, 1994.
Laughter from the Children of War. With Hung Nguyen. Great Leap Archives, 1996.
To All Relations. A series of unpublished community-created plays, Great Leap Archives, 1998–present.

Selected Production History

Chop Suey

Performances. East West Players, Los Angeles, 1980–81.
———. Pacific Northwest tour, 1980–81.
———. Eight Los Angeles County parks tour, 1980–81.

Talk Story I and II

Production. Japan America Theatre, Los Angeles, 1987–89.
———. Hawaiian Islands tour, 1987–89.
———. Theatre Artaud, San Francisco, 1987–89.
———. Los Angeles Theatre Center, Los Angeles, 1987–89.
———. prod. Maricel Pagulayan. Special satellite program, KPFK, Los Angeles, c. 1990.

Joanne Is My Middle Name

Solo performances. Japan America Theatre, Los Angeles, 1990.
Performances. "Slice of Rice" National College Tour, 1990.

A Grain of Sand

Performances. New WORLD Theater, U of Massachusetts, Amherst, 1994, and a national tour, 1994–present.

Laughter from the Children of War

Production, dir. Hung Nguyen. Club o'Noodles, Los Angeles, 1996, and a national tour, 1996–98.

Recordings

A Grain of Sand. With Chris Iijima and Charlie Chin. Paredon Records, 1973; Bindu Records, 1998.
Best of Both Worlds. Singer and songwriter. LP. Los Angeles: Great Leap, 1983.
To All Relations. Singer and songwriter. Los Angeles: Bindu Records, 1997.

Screenplays

The King and I. Dancer. Dir. Walter Lang. 20th Century Fox, 1956.
Les Girls. Dancer. Dir. George Cukor. MGM, 1957.
West Side Story. Dancer, actress, and singer. Dir. Jerome Robbins and Robert Wise. MGM, 1961.
Gaman. Composer. *Silk Screen* series. Dir. Bob Miyamoto. PBS, 1984.
Gathering of Joy. Composer. Dir. James Seligman. Great Leap, 1986.
Karate Kid II. Composer and choreographer for final scene. Dir. John G. Avildsen. Columbia Pictures, 1986.

Study of Nobuko Miyamoto

Burns, Lucy San Pablo. "Something Larger than Ourselves: Interview with Nobuko Miyamoto." *The Color of Theatre: A Critical Source Book in Race and Performance.* Ed. Roberta Uno. London: Athlone P, forthcoming.

Milton Atsushi Murayama

(1923–   )

Nikolas Huot

BIOGRAPHY

Milton Atsushi Murayama was born of Japanese immigrants in Lahaina, Maui, on April 10, 1923. He grew up in Lahaina and in Puukoli, a sugarcane-plantation camp home to more than six hundred Japanese immigrants. After graduating from Lahainaluna High School in 1941, Murayama attended the University of Hawaii. The bombing of Pearl Harbor and the involvement of the United States in World War II abruptly, but temporarily, halted his education. As a volunteer in the army, Murayama trained at the Military Intelligence Language School in Minnesota and served as an interpreter in India, China, and Taiwan during the latter part of World War II.

After his completion of a B.A. in English from the University of Hawaii and an M.A. in Chinese and Japanese from Columbia University, Murayama worked for the Armed Forces Medical Library in Washington, D.C., the San Francisco Public Library, and the U.S. Customs Office, also in San Francisco. While he was living in New York, Murayama started to write, and by 1959 he had published his first short story, "I'll Crack Your Head Kotsun," in the *Arizona Quarterly*. In 1975, along with his wife, he formed Supa Press, in great part to publish his own novel, *All I Asking For Is My Body*. Among the honors he has received, Milton Murayama was awarded the American Book Award of the Before Columbus Foundation in 1980 and the Hawaii Award for Literature in 1991 by the Hawaii State Foundation on Culture and the Arts.

MAJOR WORKS AND THEMES

Mostly known for his three novels about the Oyama family, *All I Asking For Is My Body* (1975), *Five Years on a Rock* (1994), and *Plantation Boy* (1998),

Milton Murayama is also the author of three plays: *Yoshitsune* (1977), *Althea* (1982), and *All I Asking For Is My Body* (1989). Much like his novels, Murayama's plays deal with the struggles of Japanese in Hawaii and/or with individual dilemmas between loyalty to tradition and loyalty to self. *Yoshitsune* is mostly concerned with the drive for power and the question of who or what deserves one's loyalty. *Althea* deals with the inherent racism toward Asians in Hawaii. *All I Asking For Is My Body*, which stands on its own separate from the novel, considers the problems faced by a debt-ridden Japanese family whose sons desperately try to escape the Hawaiian plantation they live and work on. Although *Yoshitsune* has been produced on stage and *Althea* has had a reading, only *All I Asking For Is My Body* is in the process of being published.

Murayama's first play, *Yoshitsune*, is set in Japan in 1185–89. The play deals with the struggle for power between two brothers, Yoshitsune, who is a military genius "torn between militarism and human compassion," and Yorimoto, the older brother who relies on a "warrior system based on unquestioning obedience" to rule Japan (Rozmiarek B4). Despite winning many important battles for his older brother and helping him conquer most of Japan, Yoshitsune is suspected of being disloyal and a threat to Yorimoto and is forced to flee to a remote domain in order to save his life. In this isolated domain, the only one still unconquered by his brother, Yoshitsune debates whether he should retaliate against his brother, whom he used to regard as a father, or continue to "run away and keep hoping [his brother] will relent" in his pursuit (*Yoshitsune* scene 13, 44). To attack his brother would not only undermine his karma but would also disrespect the memory of his benefactor, as Yoshitsune would need to murder his benefactor's heir and usurp his domain in order to raise an army. On the other hand, in the eyes of his allies, to remain passive and worry about karma would show "a faintness of purpose" and a fear of "power and all the filth which comes with power" (*Yoshitsune* scene 13, 43). If this inner struggle drives the play and shows Yoshitsune as a more humane and honorable character than his brother, it is also ultimately responsible for his defeat at the hands of the unhesitating and purpose-driven Yorimoto.

Quite different from Murayama's first play, *Althea* considers racism in Hawaii and is based on the infamous Massie case of 1931 in Honolulu. In September 1931, two Hawaiians, two Japanese, and one Hawaiian Chinese were arrested and charged with the rape of the young wife of a navy lieutenant and daughter of a prominent Washington family. After three weeks of conflicting testimony and four days of deliberation, the jury was unable to reach a verdict, and a mistrial was declared. A month later, Thalia Massie's husband, her mother, and two navy enlisted men kidnapped, shot, and killed one of the defendants in the rape case. The four were convicted of manslaughter and were sentenced to serve ten years of imprisonment; however, under tremendous pressure from the navy and the threat by Congress to make Hawaii a military outpost, the governor of Hawaii commuted the sentence to one hour in custody. Taking this historical case as a base for his second play, Murayama deals in *Althea* with deep-seated racism against Asians and with a judicial system based along color lines.

Murayama's most recent play, *All I Asking For Is My Body*, deals with the same predominant issues raised in his novels and still uses Hawaiian Creole English to convey realism and "to get as close as possible to the experience" (Murayama, "Problems" 7). Unlike his novels, however, the play does not digress and show the Filipino struggle for equal rights, the story behind the $6,000 debt, or the difficulties facing picture brides arriving in Hawaii. Instead, his play centers mostly on the cultural and generational conflicts that arise between the Japanese parents and the Hawaiian-born sons in the 1930s and 1940s. It presents the story of two Japanese Hawaiian men in their early twenties. The feisty Toshio and the more genial Kiyoshi work as plantation hands on Maui and live with their Japanese parents. Burdened with a $6,000 debt, the parents expect the sons, as part of their filial duty, to repay the debt incurred by the lavish spending of the grandfather and the failed attempt at fishing by the father. An easier way of repaying this immense debt than to work on a sugarcane plantation is for the sons to become professional boxers. Toshio and Kiyoshi train devotedly during their spare hours and dream of making it big (and of leaving behind the oppressive life on the plantation).

However, the early 1940s are difficult times for Japanese, and, as the sons soon find out, not every contender makes it. The sense of cultural and geographical confinement is pervasive for Toshio and Kiyoshi, and the conflicts that arise between the young Hawaiian-born sons and the traditional Japanese parents, especially concerning the responsibility to repay the debt, only add to the desire of the sons to leave the island. Luckily, both brothers manage to escape the plantation and the island. Toshio marries, settles on another Hawaiian island, and starts a family of his own. Kiyoshi enlists in the army and, on his way to the mainland, wins enough money playing cards to repay the entire family debt. The outcome of the play is far from being assured or auspicious of better things to come, however; Toshio's future on the new island is uncertain because he may perpetuate the cycle of poverty he craves so much to escape, and Kiyoshi's safe return is far from being guaranteed because Japanese American units were purposely put in extremely dangerous situations in order to prove their loyalty to their adopted country.

The first version of the play (produced in 1989) was mostly told from Kiyoshi's point of view. The younger son of the Oyama family was actively observing the repressive and confining living conditions on the sugarcane plantation, all the while trying to understand his parents and his brother as they were clashing about filial obligations and the family's duty to repay the debt. Despite glowing reviews of the first production of *All I Asking For Is My Body*, Murayama revised the play and incorporated material from his other books, *Five Years on a Rock* (1994) and *Plantation Boy* (1998). The revised version of the play now integrates more of the father and mother's perspectives and results in a more complex picture of the conflicts between different generations and different cultures. The reader/spectator relies less on Kiyoshi's sole viewpoint to understand the clashes and gets a fuller understanding of both sides. In both versions of the play, however, the question of loyalty to oneself, loyalty to one's family, and loyalty to one's country is repeatedly discussed and debated.

CRITICAL RECEPTION

Murayama's first play, *Yoshitsune*, had a rather unsuccessful student production in Honolulu in 1982. In this single production of Murayama's historical drama set in feudal Japan, the stage was practically bare, the props were kept to a minimum, and the cast performed in jeans and T-shirts. The play received scathing reviews from the two major newspapers in Honolulu. Joseph Rozmiarek, of the *Honolulu Star-Bulletin*, thought that Murayama's script contained little "by way of character development or clearly stated philosophy" (B4), and Pierre Bowman, of the *Honolulu Advertiser*, felt that the play did not "work particularly well as either history or drama" (B12). Also, both reviewers deplored the play's "nontraditional aspects" and its lack of clarity "in stating its historical information" (Bowman B12). After this unsuccessful production, Murayama rewrote the play, had a reading in San Francisco, and rewrote it a second time. After the second rewrite, however, Murayama decided to give up the idea of producing his first play: "The character Yoshitsune is too passive to work on stage. So I'd rather forget the whole thing as a learning experience" (Letter).

Seven years after the production of his first play, the Asian American Theater Company produced *All I Asking For Is My Body* in San Francisco. This time, the reception was much more favorable. Instead of criticizing the lack of character development and longing for more traditional approaches, reviewers praised the "multilayered interactions between [well-defined] characters" and applauded the author's fresh new take on "old forms and concepts" (Hurwitt C14). Although critics felt that the first act needed some work, the use of "peppery slang," the "unromanticized sense of rural Hawaii," and the "leaner, sharper" dialogue of the second act won the critics over (Berson 33).

In 1999, ten years after the first production of *All I Asking For Is My Body*, a revised version of the play was staged in Honolulu. Critics praised the second production of the play even more than the first one. John Berger, of the *Honolulu Star-Bulletin*, writes that of all the different chronicles of the Japanese experiences in Hawaii, "none have addressed the subject more effectively than Milton Murayama has" in this play. Berger continues his review by praising Murayama's complex and skillful depiction of the cultural and generational clash between members of the Oyama family. Other than the somewhat incomplete story behind the family debt, Berger finds no fault with the play and raves about the realistic portrayal of nisei and issei alike. Overall, the play receives the mention of "memorable." It should come as no surprise that the play was included in its entirety in *Writing Project*, a collection of pieces by winners of the Hawaii Literary Arts Council Awards.

BIBLIOGRAPHY

Works by Milton Atsushi Murayama

Drama

Yoshitsune. Scene 11. *Hawaii Review* 10 (1980): 59–73.
————. Scene 13 *Hapa* 1 (1981): 39–48.
All I Asking For Is My Body. Writing Project (title still undecided). Honolulu: State
    Foundation on Culture and the Arts, forthcoming.

Unpublished Manuscripts

Yoshitsune. 1977.
Althea. 1982.

Selected Production History

Althea

Staged reading. Julian Theater, San Francisco, 1982.

Yoshitsune

Production, dir. Sidney Milburn and David Anderson, Hawaii Performing Arts Company,
    Honolulu, 1982.

All I Asking For Is My Body

Production, dir. Phyllis Look. Asian American Theater Company, San Francisco, 1989.
————, dir. Harry Wong. U of Hawai'i, Honolulu, 1999.

Essays

"Author Discusses How to Write Pidgin." *Honolulu Star-Bulletin* 25 Nov. 1976: L24.
"Problems of Writing in Dialect and Mixed Languages." *MELUS* 4.1 (Spring 1977): 7–9.
"A Christmas Memory." *Honolulu Star-Bulletin* 21 Dec. 1980: C1.
"Remarks by Milton Murayama." *Writers of Hawaii: A Focus on Our Literary Heritage.*
    Proceedings from the Writers of Hawaii Conference, October 1980. Ed. Eric
    Chock and Jody Manabe. Honolulu: Bamboo Ridge P, 1981. 59–61.

Letter

Letter to the author. 19 Mar. 2000.

Novels

All I Asking For Is My Body. San Francisco: Supa P, 1975. Honolulu: U of Hawai'i P,
    1988.
Five Years on a Rock. Honolulu: U of Hawai'i P, 1994.
Plantation Boy. Honolulu: U of Hawai'i P, 1998.

Short Stories

"I'll Crack Your Head Kotsun." *Arizona Quarterly* 15.2 (1959): 137–49. Rpt. in *The
    Spell of Hawaii.* Ed. A. Grove Day and Carl Stroven. New York: Meredith, 1968.
    323–35.

"The Substitute." *A Hawai'i Anthology: A Collection of Works by Recipients of the Hawai'i Award for Literature, 1974–1996*. Ed. Joseph Stanton. Honolulu: State Foundation on Culture and the Arts, 1997. 18–30.

Studies of Milton Atsushi Murayama

Berger, John. "Compelling Body of Work." Rev. of *All I Asking For Is My Body. Honolulu Star-Bulletin* 3 May 1999. 17 Nov. 2000 <http://starbulletin.com/1999/05/03/features/index.html>.

Berson, Misha. "A Rocky Start: A Standard Boxing Story Could Develop into a Real Contender." Rev. of *All I Asking For Is My Body. San Francisco Bay Guardian* 11 Oct. 1989: 33.

Bowman, Pierre. "An Unclear *Yoshitsune." Honolulu Advertiser* 12 May 1982: B12.

Burlingame, Burl. "Body and Soul: Kumu Kahua Brings Milton Murayama's Classic Novel to the Local Stage." *Honolulu Star-Bulletin* 29 Apr. 1999. 17 Nov. 2000 <http://starbulletin.com/1999/04/29/features/index.html>.

"An Evening with Author Milton Murayama." *San Francisco Center for Japanese-American Studies Newsletter* Jan. 1976. N. pag.

Hershinow, Sheldon, Arnold Hiura, and Rob Wilson. "Question and Answers." *Writers of Hawaii: A Focus on Our Literary Heritage*. Proceedings from the Writers of Hawaii Conference, October 1980. Ed. Eric Chock and Jody Manabe. Honolulu: Bamboo Ridge P, 1981. 67–69.

Hiura, Arnold. "Comments on Milton Murayama." *Writers of Hawaii: A Focus on Our Literary Heritage*. Proceedings from the Writers of Hawaii Conference, October 1980. Ed. Eric Chock and Jody Manabe. Honolulu: Bamboo Ridge P, 1981. 65–67.

Hurwitt, Robert. "Generations on the Ropes in a Play about Boxing." Rev. of *All I Asking For Is My Body. San Francisco Examiner* 22 Sept. 1989: C14.

Luangphinith, Seri. "Milton Murayama." *Asian American Novelists: A Bio-bibliographical Critical Sourcebook*. Ed. Emmanuel S. Nelson. Westport, CT: Greenwood P, 2000. 251–56.

Odo, Franklin S. "The Hawaii Nisei: Tough Talk and Sweet Sugar." Afterword. *All I Asking For Is My Body*. By Milton Murayama. Honolulu: U of Hawaii P, 1988. 105–10.

Palomino, Harue. "Japanese Americans in Books or in Reality? Three Writers for Young Adults Who Tell a Different Story." *How Much Truth Do We Tell the Children? The Politics of Children's Literature*. Ed. Betty Bacon. Minneapolis: Marxist Educational P, 1988. 125–134.

Romaine, Suzanne. "Hau fo rait pijin: Writing in Hawai'i Creole English." *English Today* 10.2 (1994): 20–24.

Rozmiarek, Joseph T. "*Yoshitsune* Needs Classical Trappings." *Honolulu Star-Bulletin* 11 May 1982: B4.

Wilson, Rob. "The Languages of Confinement and Liberation in Milton Murayama's *All I Asking For Is My Body." Writers of Hawaii: A Focus on Our Literary Heritage*. Proceedings from the Writers of Hawaii Conference, October 1980. Ed. Eric Chock and Jody Manabe. Honolulu: Bamboo Ridge P, 1981. 62–65.

Jude Narita

(195?–   )

Melinda L. de Jesús

BIOGRAPHY

Jude Narita was born in Long Beach, California. She studied acting with Stella Adler in New York and Lee Strasberg in Los Angeles. In the mid-1980s, frustrated with the dearth of quality, nonstereotypical roles available to her as an Asian American actress, Narita turned to solo performance (writing and performing her own work). A writer, performer, producer, and activist, Narita is also an educator: she has been a guest artist at California State University's Summer Arts Program, has taught in the Asian American Studies Program at the University of California at Santa Barbara, and has led writing/acting workshops for many groups, including at-risk youth.

MAJOR WORKS AND THEMES

Narita's one-woman plays explore, through the varied and unique voices of Asian and Asian American women, the joys and sorrows of attempting to carve an Asian, female space in a white male world. With both tenderness and ferocity, they underscore the commonalities of struggle, faith, and perseverance that permeate women's daily lives. Narita's portraits make for exquisitely detailed, respectful, and evocative storytelling: they explode stereotypes and reclaim the lives and voices of Asian and Asian American women as survivors and heroes, not passive, silent victims. Her work manifests a distinct Asian American feminist and third-world feminist consciousness.

Narita is best known as the writer, performer, and producer of *Coming into Passion/Song for a Sansei* (1985), which ran for two years in Los Angeles in the late 1980s. This one-woman show features interlinked vignettes, slices of lives of a diverse group of Asian and Asian American women. The narrator of *Coming into Passion* is an assimilated Japanese American newscaster who cannot recognize any commonalities with other Asian women around her; she disavows her "Asianness" and wants to be seen as wholly "American." The play follows her discovering, through her dreams, just how much she does indeed share with the struggles of the Filipino mail-order bride, the Vietnamese bar girl, the nisei woman interned as a child, the Cambodian refugee, the troubled sansei teenager, and the storyteller who weaves the tale of a little girl caught in the bombing of Hiroshima. Each woman, like herself, must negotiate the colliding cultures of Asia and America in order to become whole.

Narita's *Stories Waiting to Be Told/The Wilderness Within* (1992–93) resembles *Coming into Passion* through its depiction of the lives of ten very different Asian American women characters. This one-woman play, originally conceived as two separate pieces that were then combined into one, explores the theme of mother-daughter conflict across cultures and generations, and the struggle toward achieving the American dream. Narita tackles taboo community topics like drug addiction, lesbianism, and domestic violence here and introduces characters like Korean-born Miyhan, who struggles to fit in at her new American high school and is befriended by an African American girl named Bernice; the Cambodian refugee who marvels at American luxuries like wall-to-wall carpet even as the violence of her past haunts her dreams; the young assimilated Chinese American girl who finds herself connecting to the history of Chinese in America; and the young Japanese American woman who finally learns of the pain her mother suffered in the internment camps and recognizes how this experience has given both of them great strength.

The autobiographical mode of *Celebrate Me Home* (1996) echoes *Coming into Passion* and *Stories*. This one-woman play explores the pervasive and insidious nature of stereotyping of and racism against Asians in American society today. The characters here range from a white British actress who blithely "prepares" to play a Cambodian woman on her television show by watching old movies of whites playing Asians and from a white woman at a cocktail party disparaging Asian American women for "trying to be so hip—and they don't even have accents!" to Asian women struggling to define themselves after spending lifetimes being defined by others—particularly men with an "Asian fetish" (Narita, Press packet). In the end, Narita presents portraits of Asian and Asian American women who have completed a long journey. They have learned to treasure their family histories and to discard what is painful and demeaning in their cultures. They have arrived "home" to their families, communities, and themselves.

Narita traveled to Asia as a member of the 1992 Women's Delegation to Vietnam and Cambodia, sponsored by the Women's Union of Vietnam and the Asia Resource Center in the United States. Her interviews with women there inspired her next solo work, *Walk the Mountain* (1997). This play explores the continuing effects of the Vietnam War on the people of Vietnam and Cambodia, and the legacy of ignorance surrounding this war in the United States today. Narita's creations include a jungle-hospital doctor, a freedom fighter imprisoned in a tiger cage, a mourning mother whose sons died somewhere unknown during the war, and an immigrant who dreams of skulls. The play "powerfully affirms the dignity, humanity, and spirit of the Vietnamese and Cambodian people, showing that despite different cultures, languages, or even being on different sides of a war, we are all involved in the common struggle to make life better for ourselves and the ones we love" (Narita, Press packet).

Recently, Narita developed a new piece entitled *Safe Passage toward This Fertile Ground* (2000). This work is "about the Japanese Latin Americans kidnapped in South America by the United States who were used in a hostage trade with Japan for white Americans, at the beginning of World War II" (Narita, Press packet). At the end of 2000, Narita also began performing her newest work, *With Darkness behind Us, Daylight Has Come* (2000), a "multi-media one-woman play about the effects of the internment camps on three different generations of Japanese American women: Issei, Nisei and Sansei" (Narita, "Performances").

CRITICAL RECEPTION

Narita's works have yet to be published or anthologized, nor has she been made the focus of a scholarly study; nevertheless, it would be remiss to assume that her plays have gone unnoticed. She has established herself as a strong writer and a fine actress with a particular facility in vocal accents. Overall, her work has been received very favorably. *Coming into Passion* garnered Dramalogue awards for creation and performance, the Los Angeles Drama Critics Circle Award, a James Wong Howe "Jimmie" from the Association of Asian Pacific American Artists, and a Vesta Award from the Women's Building of Los Angeles, was featured in the PBS/Smithsonian episode "Gender," and was chosen to represent American theater in the Mark Taper/U.S. Information Agency (USIA) tour of Poland. Of this play, Robert Koehler writes, "Narita has found an equilibrium between race and humor, while burning cultural stereotypes on a celebratory pyre" ("*Passion*" 6). In contrast, Juli Thompson Burk contends that *Passion*'s "ideological naivete" might explain its popularity: "[It] promises an examination of the racism and sexism encountered by Asian women and delivers instead a celebration without critique and difference without dissent" (114–15).

In 1990, Narita taught a free acting/writing workshop in Los Angeles to encourage other Asian American actresses to write and perform their own original material. From this she produced the women's ensemble piece entitled *The Tiger on the Right/The Dragon on the Left* (1991), which includes her work entitled "Strong Heart." This show garnered Narita and the other actresses—Lauren Tom, Patty Toy, Szu Wang, and Michelle Emoto (aka Darling Narita)—the 1991

Dramalogue Award for Performance. Narita also received a Dramalogue Award as producer for the ensemble.

While Steven Winn finds Narita's *Coming into Passion: Song for a Sansei* to be "heavy handed" and "simplistic" (D5), Scott Collins admires the stories exactly for their "plain-spoken simplicity and emotional sophistication that will touch nearly everyone" (F31). Similarly, Sylvie Drake calls them "American stories, intimate stories of cultural adoption. . . . Narita's work is always fresh, always precise and . . . larded with just enough philosophical reflection to make us sit up and take notice" (F7). Clearly, Jude Narita is an innovative and gifted American playwright and solo performer whose detailed, compassionate renderings of the lives of the contemporary Asian and Asian American "Everywoman" continue to inspire.

BIBLIOGRAPHY

Works by Jude Narita

Unpublished Manuscripts

Coming Into Passion/Song for a Sansei. Ms. 345. Roberta Uno Asian Women Playwrights Scripts Collection 1924–1992, W.E.B. Du Bois Library, U of Massachusetts, Amherst, 1985.
Stories Waiting to Be Told. 1992.
Stories Waiting to Be Told/The Wilderness Within. 1993.
The Wilderness Within. 1993.
Celebrate Me Home. 1996.
Walk the Mountain. 1997.
Safe Passage toward This Fertile Ground. 2000.
With Darkness behind Us, Daylight Has Come. 2000.

Selected Production History

Coming into Passion/Song for a Sansei

Solo performances, dir. Peter Flood. Powerhouse Theater, Santa Monica, CA, 1987.
———. Fountain Theatre, Los Angeles, 1988.
———. Theatre 6111, Los Angeles, 1989.
———. People's House, New York City, 1989.
———. Whitefire Theater, Sherman Oaks, CA, 1990.
———. Vancouver East Cultural Center, Vancouver, BC, 1990.
———. Tenny Theatre, Honolulu, 1990.
———. East West Players Theatre, Los Angeles, 1990.
———. Storefront Theater, Portland, OR, 1991.
———. Anderson Theater, New York City, 1991.
———. Japan America Theatre, Los Angeles, 1991.
———. Mamiya Theater, Honolulu, 1992.
———. New WORLD Theater, U of Massachusetts, Amherst, 1992.
———. Harold Washington Theatre, Chicago, 1992.

————. Substation Theatre, Singapore Repertory Theatre, Singapore, 1993.
————. Gene Autry Museum, Los Angeles, 1994.
————. Washington Center for the Performing Arts, Olympia WA, 1994.
————. Singapore Repertory Theatre, Singapore, 1995.
————. 24th Street Theater, Los Angeles, 1999.
————. Flushing Town Hall, Flushing, NY, 2000.

The Tiger on the Right/The Dragon on the Left

Production, prod. Jude Narita; perf. Lauren Tom, Patty Toy, Szu Wang, Michelle Emoto
    (aka Darling Narita), and Jude Narita. Fountain Theatre, Los Angeles, 1991.

Stories Waiting to Be Told

Solo performances, dir. Jude Narita. Stages Theatre, Los Angeles, 1992.
————. Los Angeles Theatre Center, 1993.
————. Highways, Santa Monica, CA, 1993
————. Smithsonian Institution, Washington, DC, 1993.

Stories Waiting to Be Told/The Wilderness Within

Solo performances, dir. Jude Narita. Los Angeles Theatre Center, Los Angeles, 1993.
————. Los Angeles Theatre Center, 1995.
————. California Plaza Presents, Los Angeles, 1997.
————. Madison Civic Center, Madison, WI, 2000.

The Wilderness Within

Solo performances, dir. Jude Narita. Japanese American Museum, Los Angeles, 1993.
————. Los Angeles Theatre Center, 1993.

Celebrate Me Home

Solo performances, dir. Charlie Stratton and Darling Narita. McCadden Place Theatre,
    Los Angeles, 1996.
————. Dept. of the Interior, Washington, DC, 1998.

Walk the Mountain

Solo performances, dir. Charlie Stratton. Stella Adler Theater, Hollywood, 1997.
————. "Treasure in the House" Festival, Highways, Santa Monica, CA, 1997.

Safe Passage toward This Fertile Ground

Staged reading, dir. Jude Narita. National Civil Liberties Conference, Sacramento, CA,
    1998.
————. dir. Jude Narita. Legacy Center, Japanese American Historical Building, Los
    Angeles, 2000.

With Darkness behind Us, Daylight Has Come

Solo performances, dir. Darling Narita. Highways, Santa Monica, CA, 2000–2001.

Studies of Jude Narita

Arkatov, Janice. "Narita's *Song* Looks at Roles of Asian Women." Rev. of *Coming into Passion/Song of a Sansei. Los Angeles Times* 28 Aug 1987, sec. 6: 3.

Burk, Juli Thompson. Rev. of *Coming into Passion/Song for a Sansei. Theatre Journal* 43.1 (1991): 114–115.

Collins, Scott. "*Stories*: A Moving One-Woman Show." Rev. of *Stories Waiting to Be Told. Los Angeles Times* 14 Apr. 1995: F31.

Drake, Sylvie. "Intimate, Profound Telling of *Stories*." Rev. of *Stories Waiting to be Told. Los Angeles Times* 4 Dec. 1993: F7.

Foley, F. Kathleen. "Wry Monologues Help *Celebrate*." Rev. of *Celebrate Me Home. Los Angeles Times* 4 Oct. 1996: F29.

Koehler, Robert. "Narita's *Tiger* Is Released from the Lab Too Soon." Rev. of *The Tiger on the Right/The Dragon on the Left. Los Angeles Times* 28 June 1991: F18.

———. "*Passion* for Plights of Asian Women." Rev. of *Coming into Passion/Song for a Sansei. Los Angeles Times* 5 June 1987, sec. 6: 6.

Loynd, Ray. Rev. of *Stories Waiting to Be Told. Daily Variety* 26 July 1995: Review section, n.p.

Morris, Rebecca. "Jude Narita: No Exotic Flower." Rev. of *Coming into Passion/Song for a Sansei. American Theatre* 10.4 (Apr. 1993): 28.

Narita, Jude. "Jude Narita's Performances." Online posting. 2 Jan. 2001. AAAS Community List. 4 Jan. 2001 <http://www.egroups.com/group/aaascommunity/>.

———. Press packet/memo to the author. 1 July 2000.

Shirley, Don. "*Coming into Passion* at Theatre 6111." Rev. of *Coming into Passion/ Song for a Sansei. Los Angeles Times* 4 July 1989, sec. 6: 4.

Winn, Steven. "Narita's Women: From Vietnam to Valley Girl." Rev. of *Stories Waiting to Be Told. San Francisco Chronicle* 14 Oct. 1993: D5.

Lane Nishikawa

(1956–   )

Randy Barbara Kaplan

BIOGRAPHY

Playwright, producer, director, actor, and theater educator Lane Nishikawa is a consummate man of the theater who has won accolades for his trilogy of one-man shows exposing stereotypes of Asian American men: *Life in the Fast Lane* (1980), *I'm on a Mission From Buddha* (1989), and *Mifune and Me* (1994). Born in Wahiawa, Hawaii, he relocated with his family to San Diego when he was a child. Every summer, however, Nishikawa returned to Hawaii for an extended visit with his grandparents, who would inspire much of his writing as an adult. Coming of age in Hawaii, where the predominance of Asian American culture was a commonly accepted fact of life, and simultaneously on the mainland, where the marginalization of Asian Americans was equally pervasive, Nishikawa grew up understanding both the joys and difficulties of what it meant to be sansei, a third-generation Japanese American.

Nishikawa began his college education at San Francisco State University but in the early 1970s fell in with a rough crowd. He credits the fortuitous intervention of a conscientious counselor at the university, Sue Hayashi, with guiding him toward a more positive outlet for his energies—the theater. By this time, Nishikawa had had some experience with San Francisco's Kearny Street Workshop and at the Japantown Art and Media Workshop and was confident in his writing abilities. Seeking to inspire him to expand his potential as a theater artist, Sue Hayashi introduced Nishikawa to her two sons, who were active in San Francisco's then-budding Asian American theater movement. Their meeting led to a lifelong friendship that provided fertile ground for numerous successful artistic collaborations. Marc Hayashi, an actor-director, would eventually direct and act with Nishikawa in numerous productions at Asian American Theater

Company and later coauthor with Nishikawa and R. A. Shiomi a play entitled *Once Is Never Enough* (1984). Marc's older brother Eric, a lighting designer, would direct Nishikawa's second one-man show, *I'm on a Mission From Buddha*, eventually becoming a prominent producer, director, and mentor of numerous Asian American theater artists.

In the early 1970s, Marc and Eric Hayashi were working with the newly founded Asian American Theater Workshop established by the intrepid Chinese American playwright Frank Chin. The group's mission was to provide training for Asian American performers, who had historically not been made to feel welcome in traditional acting programs, while developing a repertory of dignified roles for them to play. In 1973, the workshop evolved into the Asian American Theater Company (AATC), the third professional Asian American performance company, following in the footsteps of Los Angeles's East West Players (founded in 1965) and Honolulu's Kumu Kahua Theatre (1971). Sue Hayashi's guidance proved to be both invaluable and prophetic: AATC became Nishikawa's artistic home for over twenty years.

Nishikawa's first acting role of note was in Amy Sanbo's and Lonny Kaneko's *Lady Is Dying* (1977), in which he was directed by Frank Chin. By 1979, he was performing in virtually every AATC mainstage production as well as learning to direct for the stage himself. Though he was acclaimed and accomplished as a performer, Nishikawa soon came face-to-face with the pandemic casting discrimination that infected the American entertainment industry: casting directors and agents insisted upon relegating him to the Asian stereotypes—houseboy, cook, gook, nerd.

With a host of opportunities that were neither acceptable nor meaningful, Nishikawa needed to call his own shots by creating his own characters to perform. His fledgling playwriting attempt, a pastiche of nine monologues about the Asian American experience, scored a major hit. *Life in the Fast Lane*, the one-man show that Nishikawa not only wrote but directed and performed, made its world premiere in March 1981 as part of AATC's New Playwrights Series. The show was revived for the company's subsequent mainstage season and toured to Seattle's Northwest Asian American Theatre in 1982. Eric Hayashi took over as the show's producer and through his independent company, Sansei Productions, booked the show in countless theaters and universities. Nishikawa performed the play to sellout crowds and uniformly enthusiastic reviews on a national and international tour of the United States, Canada, and Europe that lasted four years, recording his experiences in 1982–83 in a series of essays for the San Francisco–based Japanese American newspaper *Hokubei Mainichi*.

Throughout the 1980s and 1990s, Nishikawa was actively working at the heart of San Francisco's emerging and vital Asian American theater scene with such influential Asian American theater artists as Frank Chin, Momoko Iko, David Henry Hwang, Philip Kan Gotanda, Edward Sakamoto, R. A. Shiomi, Warren Kubota, and Melvyn Escueta. In 1986, Nishikawa assumed artistic directorship of the Asian American Theater Company. He spent the next eight years directing some of the most important Asian American plays of that period: R. A. Shiomi's *Yellow Fever* (world premiere, 1982; revived, 1983), *Rosie's Café* (1989), and *Uncle Tadao* (1992); David Henry Hwang's *Family Devotions* (West Coast premiere, 1987); Laurence Yep's *Pay the Chinaman* (world premiere, 1987); and Philip Kan Gotanda's *Yankee Dawg You Die* (1990) and *The Dream of Kitamura* (1993). Throughout his tenure at AATC, Nishikawa continued to act, direct, and produce, creating production venues for the next wave of Asian American writers that included Cherylene Lee, Jeannie Barroga, Han Ong, Canyon Sam, and Charlie Chin.

Nishikawa had created his second one-man show, a sequel to *Life in the Fast Lane* entitled *I'm on a Mission From Buddha*, in 1989. *Buddha* develops in greater detail the themes introduced in *Fast Lane*, examining more deeply the ironies of being an Asian American actor and attacking Asian stereotypes. Eric Hayashi directed the stage version, again overseeing a standing-room-only national tour. The play's success was such that the Public Broadcasting System's San Francisco affiliate KQED produced it for television; it continued to be aired across the United States through 1994.

While Nishikawa was playing a small supporting role in American Conservatory Theatre's 1993 production of *The Duchess of Malfi*, he made the acquaintance of fellow actor Victor Talmadge. With plenty of backstage time on their hands between appearances in the lengthy production, the two men found themselves sharing stories about their lives. Nishikawa had begun developing a theater piece about the all-nisei 442nd Regiment in World War II, a subject in which he had been interested all of his life and that he had previously addressed in both solo shows. Casual conversation evolved into artistic collaboration; Nishikawa and Talmadge hit upon an idea wherein they could combine their talents, drawing upon their personal interests and experiences. The result, *The Gate of Heaven* (1994), which depicted the half-century-long relationship between a nisei soldier and the Jewish prisoner he liberates from the Dachau concentration camp, starred the two playwrights and was given its first public performance at the Osher Jewish Community Center in Marin, California. But with David Henry Hwang as dramaturge, the play received its professional debut at the Old Globe Theatre in San Diego in 1996 before embarking on a successful national tour.

Two years later, Nishikawa undertook an extensive artistic project inspired by his *Gate of Heaven* experience when he began work on a film trilogy about the role played by nisei soldiers in World War II entitled *When We Were Warriors*. *When We Were Warriors, Part I* retells the Sam and Leon story and was completed in 1999. The second two parts of the trilogy are in progress as of this writing: part 2 is devoted to nisei soldiers of the 100th Battalion and 442nd Regiment; part 3, to nisei soldiers in the Military Intelligence Service (MIS) who served in the Pacific theater of World War II.

The La Peña Cultural Center and Cal Performances of the University of California at Berkeley commissioned Nishikawa's third solo show, *Mifune and Me* (1994). By this time, Nishikawa was not altogether unsuccessful in the film industry, having acted in Steve Okazaki's *Living on Tokyo Time* (1987) and Wayne Wang's *Eat a Bowl of Tea* (1989); eventually Okazaki would cast him in *American Sons* (1998). *Mifune and Me* wrestles with a cruel and inequitable fact of theatrical life for Asian American actors: roles for Asian American men were, on the whole, not much better than they had been fifteen years earlier when Nishikawa wrote *Life in the Fast Lane*. As before, Nishikawa traveled throughout the United States with a successful *Mifune and Me* tour (1997–99).

Nishikawa's commitment to honoring the historical contributions made by Japanese Americans continues to be reflected in his current works. *When We Were One*, which has been underwritten by a National Endowment for the Arts Millennium Grant and a Mid-Atlantic Arts Foundation Artists and Communities Grant, will become the basis of a trilogy about the history of immigrant communities in Hawaii and will tell the story of Nishikawa's issei grandparents. *Gila River*, which was commissioned by the Scottsdale Center for the Arts, depicts the impact of World War II on two nisei brothers: Takeo Wakabayashi is the elder, a kibei son sent to Japan before the war to complete his education; his younger brother Masao is a self-made baseball star interned at Gila River Camp in Arizona. *Lone Wolves* brings together the ghosts of Medal of Honor winner Sadao Munemori and Ira Hayes, a marine memorialized in the famous image of the soldiers who raised the American flag on Iwo Jima; few Americans, however, are aware that Hayes was of Native American descent. With these works, Nishikawa continues the work he began in *The Gate of Heaven* by educating audiences and honoring the memory of those nisei soldiers who fought for the United States in the Pacific theater of World War II.

MAJOR WORKS AND THEMES

Although Nishikawa has recently turned his dramatic eye to writing traditionally structured playscripts in which action unfolds through conflicts among multiple characters, the creative core of his body of work is best represented by his trilogy of solo shows: *Life in the Fast Lane* (1980), *I'm on a Mission From Buddha* (1989), and *Mifune and Me* (1994). The marginalization of the Asian American actor is the structural and thematic motif unifying the plots of all three plays, with Nishikawa hitting head-on issues of race and discrimination in fearless, poetic language. Another distinguishing feature of Nishikawa's writing is his celebration of and overwhelming love for Asian America. Whether he is honoring his Japanese American heritage or smiling at its ironies, Nishikawa acknowledges and values his heritage as fundamentally his own, the very essence of himself.

To that end, all production elements in these three plays are streamlined to focus on the actor himself rather than presenting elaborate scenic, costume, or lighting effects. A single ordinary chair is placed at stage center next to a small table with a pitcher of water and a glass. Nishikawa enters the stage space as himself, clothed entirely in black. Costume changes, when they are called for at all, are simple and performed in full view of the audience, using one or two pieces that can be easily added or removed: an army hat, a suit jacket. Throughout each performance, Nishikawa transforms himself into eight to ten characters as he performs poetic monologues interspersed with direct audience address.

Life in the Fast Lane takes place at an audition-interview. Nishikawa introduces himself to the audience, which fulfills the dramatic function of an imaginary casting director who can neither pronounce nor spell Nishikawa's Japanese surname. Each succeeding attempt to make the "casting director" understand why he feels compelled to write for the theater to share his voice—a voice that is quintessentially Asian American—leads Nishikawa to perform a monologue that enables him to speak more vibrantly and convincingly than any prosaic conversation. Thus, after responding to imaginary questions about his background, Nishikawa performs a loving tribute to his Oba-chang, the issei grandmother who nurtured both his spirit and his stomach as a boy. The succeeding monologue grows out of Nishikawa's delineation of Asian media stereotypes as enemies to be killed or houseboys to be dominated: he portrays a Texas redneck whose children are driving him to racial distraction with their romantic entanglements with Asian Americans. As a sly twist, at the end of the monologue, Nishikawa turns the tables on the audience, transforming himself into a Japanese father who is outraged to learn that his son is marrying a *hakujin* (Caucasian), demonstrating that the door of prejudice swings both ways.

The solo shows also allow Nishikawa to set historical records straight while rendering historical events of enormous scope as uniquely and individualistically human. Chapters of Japanese American history that had long been, and continue to be, entirely neglected or deliberately downplayed in American history texts become the focus of intensely emotional monologues about the psychological scars of shame visited upon Japanese Americans incarcerated in internment camps during World War II. The monologue "They Was Close, Those Brothers" introduces Nishikawa's beloved Uncle Blackie, who fought with the all-nisei 442nd Regiment, the most decorated unit in American military history. Uncle Blackie and his comrades in arms reappear in more than one of Nishikawa's later dramas and screenplays. *Life in the Fast Lane* ends with "I Was Born," the style of which became a prototype for the concluding monologues of Nishikawa's subsequent solo shows: "Born Again Buddhaheads" in *I'm on a Mission From Buddha* and "Home of the Brave" in *Mifune and Me*. In these theatrical "summaries," Nishikawa assesses the impact of major events in Asian American history on the current state of Asian America.

I'm on a Mission From Buddha, *Fast Lane*'s sequel, continues to develop these themes. For this script, Nishikawa abandoned the technique of casting the audience in an imaginary role in favor of acknowledging the audience qua audience, an approach that allows him to engage the spectators personally. Nishikawa opens by cataloging the heroes of the movie industry—Bogart, Gable, Brando, De Niro—Caucasians all. Though he is equally capable of playing any of their roles, it is his face, not his talent, that bars him from success, restricting him to "Jap . . . Chink . . . gook . . . Viet . . . ass-kissin', kung-fu fighting, chop-chop-'til-ya-drop, why can't they just say, 'male'?" (*Buddha*). The neon lights and the silver screen hold so few dignified possibilities for Nishikawa that he seeks refuge in the world of nonprofit theater, where he feels embraced and nurtured rather than excluded—and always poor. Only there, however, can he breathe life into meaningful characters from which the film industry excludes him.

In *Buddha*, Nishikawa returns to several of the characters he created in *Fast Lane*, including Uncle Blackie, whom Nishikawa portrays. In Blackie's heartfelt address to his dead comrades in Hawaii's Punch Bowl Cemetery, where many nisei heroes are interred, Nishikawa goes beyond merely teaching a history lesson to validate the heroism of the forgotten fighters of the 442nd. Together with "They Was Close, Those Brothers," "Uncle Blackie" forms the basis for the character of Sam in *The Gate of Heaven*.

A new theme Nishikawa explores in *Buddha* is his connection to his Japanese roots. Spending a goodly part of his young life in Hawaii surrounded by a dominant Asian American culture, Nishikawa was enabled to view his Asian heritage as empowering rather than embarrassing. Thus, when he confronts his Japanese roots, he appreciates their cultural ironies, admires Japanese economic finesse and achievements, and takes pride in owning his ethnicity: "I'm not just sansei, I'm Buddhahead to the bone" (*Buddha*). Indeed, in "Born Again Buddhaheads," *Buddha*'s concluding monologue, Nishikawa gently chides Asian Americans who live in the suburbs, "assimilating faster than the sound of a 300ZX," as they cheerfully consume "Cajun Korean . . . French Japonais . . . Viet Tex-Mex" (*Buddha*). Acknowledging artistic debts owed to pioneers Mako, Yuki Shimoda, Nobu McCarthy, John Okada, and Bruce Lee and applauding accomplishments of recent successes Connie Chung, James Hong, David Henry Hwang, Wayne Wang, and Steve Okazaki, Nishikawa urges his baby-boomer peers to celebrate, not assimilate, Asian America.

Of Nishikawa's three one-man shows, *Mifune and Me* is technologically and dramaturgically the most complex. Nishikawa repeats his call for simple scenic requirements—the ever-present chair, table, and pitcher of water—but in this play he interweaves his performance with video clips from films starring Toshiro Mifune, Bruce Lee, and Chow Yun Fat, along with Mickey Rooney's repulsive Japanese landlord from *Breakfast at Tiffany's*. Here the videotapes provoke, respond to, and contrast with the actor's words, maintaining an ongoing emotional and political dialogue with them. Using the structure of Miyamoto Musashi's well-known work on samurai ethics, *The Book of the Five Rings*, as a means of organizing the plot of the play, Nishikawa has created a work in which he successfully marries form to content.

Mifune and Me was inspired by Nishikawa's lifelong admiration for Toshiro Mifune, the acclaimed Japanese actor of samurai warrior roles who died in 1997, three years after Nishikawa's first draft of the play. For Nishikawa, both as child and adult, Mifune represents a power to be reckoned with, a man to be emulated as a person and as an actor: "A little violent, you say? Sure. But you have to understand, he was one of the only strong role models I had growing up. He fought for justice, the underdog. He was defiant and witty. He had guts. He had compassion. And he got women. And we had the same color hair. The same color eyes" (*Mifune*). Compared to the simpering images promoted in the popular media—*McHale's Navy*'s Fuji, *Bonanza*'s Hop Sing, a man married to his wok when "even fat ass Hoss had a woman" (*Mifune*), and the nameless Asian on *The Courtship of Eddie's Father*—Mifune inspired with sinew and guts, muscle and nerve. As the personification of the ultimate samurai warrior advocated by Musashi in *Five Rings*, he led the way for Bruce Lee, another Asian American hero to whom Nishikawa pays loving tribute in the play's monologue entitled "I Remember Bruce" (14–18).

Mifune's drive to perform inspires Nishikawa to examine and contrast it with his own theatrical obsessions, lampooning nearly every aspect of an actor's life in the theater business: ending up on the cutting-room floor, jockeying with recalcitrant fellow actors for laughs, getting sent up by his agent for stereotyped roles, and directing incompetent actors in the nonprofit theater. In a series of hilariously enacted auditions, Nishikawa demonstrates the professional dilemmas unique to Asian American actors as he is variously penalized by racist casting directors for not speaking with a Chinese accent, not having a high-enough voice, and not being short enough to play Oriental.

As the samurai circle is completed, Nishikawa closes the production with "Home of the Brave," celebrating the breadth and diversity of Asian American experience. Compared to those Asian American achievements chronicled in Nishikawa's previous works, the list of highly visible and influential Asian Americans has grown exponentially. Yet, for all the tenacity and glory, ugly truths about persistent discrimination force Nishikawa to leave the audience with an unanswered question: "Back when I light incense for my ancestors / cause they'll be there at my grave / when I'm finally free on this land / cause it's the home of the brave. America, will you love me too?" (39).

It is a long way from the hip and sometimes-sardonic humor of his solo shows to the tender drama of *The Gate of Heaven*, which Nishikawa coauthored with Victor Talmadge. *The Gate* traces a half-century-long relationship between Kiyoshi "Sam" Yamamoto, a nisei soldier, and Leon Ehrlich, a Jew Sam has liberated from Dachau. Beyond shedding light on yet another forgotten corner of American history, *The Gate* is remarkable for the sweetness with which it portrays its two male protagonists, a relationship that is unique in that its protagonists are neither sexually involved nor engaged in aggressive competition. Instead, the play portrays two men of disparate backgrounds who discover the power of mutual love and respect to complete themselves as human beings. It need hardly be said that a similar relationship between two heterosexual males is rarely depicted on the American stage or screen, regardless of the ethnicity of the characters. The opening scene is a visual and visceral metaphor for the characters' interdependence. As the lights come up, Sam cradles Leon in his arms. When his attempts to feed Leon fail, Sam chews up a piece of chocolate for the emaciated man, spits it into his own hand, and spoon-feeds Leon.

The action proceeds from a point ten years later when Leon, now a psychiatrist and American citizen, tracks Sam down, until Leon's death in 1996. A series of twelve scenes serves as freeze frames in the lives of the two men, who manage to disagree deeply on issues ranging from the innocuous to the unanswerable yet somehow find within themselves an ability and need to love each other profoundly. Though gentle laughter aroused by cultural misunderstanding cannot help but be part of this cross-cultural relationship, as when Sam and Leon stage a Japanese bar mitzvah for Sam's son, the authors are unafraid to examine issues that evoke interracial discomfort. It is more than a mere irony that for Sam, Leon's white skin entitles him to be treated as though he were born in America, whereas Sam's Asian features mark him forever as an outsider; it is a source of never-to-be-resolved rage. In the end, Leon dies in Sam's arms as Sam recites the Kaddish, the Jewish prayer for the dead. The human and cultural commonalities of Sam's life experience as a Japanese American soldier and Leon's as a Jewish Holocaust survivor prove more powerful than any cultural misunderstanding or ethnic mistrust.

CRITICAL RECEPTION

Lane Nishikawa's works, like those of many Asian American playwrights, have not been the subject of academic inquiry. Instead, the student of Nishikawa's dramaturgy must look to newspaper theater reviews; these, on the other hand, are numerous. Because newspaper reviewing serves to advise the theatergoing public as to whether a production is worth its entertainment dollar rather than to carry out scholarly analysis, critical reception of Nishikawa's productions exists primarily in the form of responses to performances rather than consideration of their literary merits. Reviewers judging Nishikawa's solo performances are uniformly enthusiastic, lauding his vibrant poetic imagery, razor-sharp humor, explosive energy, and consummate ability to transform himself into numerous characters. Although Nishikawa was not the first Asian American to create solo works, it must be said that his incredible success and tenacity have been instrumental in paving the way for another generation of Asian American solo performers, including Byron Yee and Margaret Cho.

Nishikawa's work has been recognized with numerous awards and honors. He is the recipient of a Solo Performance Fellowship from the National Endowment for the Arts, as well as a National Japanese American Citizens League (JACL) Ruby Yoshino Schaar Playwright Award and a Profiles of Excellence Award from ABC-TV in San Francisco (1995). In addition, he has received the JACL Henry and Chiyo Kuwahara Award and a Japanese American Community Cultural Center Humanitarian Award. Nishikawa has also taught at San Francisco State University, the University of California at Santa Barbara, California State University at Monterey Bay, Stanford University, and the Asian American Theater Company.

BIBLIOGRAPHY

Works by Lane Nishikawa

Drama

The Gate of Heaven. With Victor Talmadge. *Asian American Drama: 9 Plays from the Multiethnic Landscape.* Ed. Brian Nelson. New York: Applause, 1997. 161–208. Excerpts. *Monologues for Actors of Color: Men.* Ed. Roberta Uno. New York: Routledge, 2000. 77–79.

Unpublished Manuscripts

Life in the Fast Lane. 1980.
Once Is Never Enough. With R. A. Shiomi and Marc Hayashi. 1984.
I'm on a Mission From Buddha. 1989.
Mifune and Me. 1994.
The Heartbeat of America. 1996.
Gila River. 1999.
Lone Wolves. 2000.
When We Were One. 2001.

Selected Production History

Life in the Fast Lane

Production, dir. and perf. Lane Nishikawa; prod. David Young. Asian American Theater Company, San Francisco, 1981.
————. New WORLD Theatre, U of Massachusetts, Amherst, MA. 1982.
————. Odyssey Theatre, Los Angeles, 1982.
————. dir. Marc Hayashi; perf. Lane Nishikawa; prod. Eric Hayashi. Zephyr Theatre for Asian American Theater Company, San Francisco, 1988.
————. dir. Wilbur Obata; perf. Greg Watanabe; Asian American Theater Company, San Francisco, 1993.

Once Is Never Enough

Production, dir. Marc Hayashi; perf. Lane Nishikawa and Sharon Omi. Asian American Theater Company, San Francisco, 1984.
————. dir. Raul Aranas; perf. Henry Yuk, Carol A. Honda, Alkis Papuchis, Glenn Kubota, Natsuko Ohama, Richard Voigts, Ron Nakahara, and Sam Howell. Pan Asian Repertory Theatre, New York City, 1985.

I'm on a Mission From Buddha

Production, dir. Eric Hayashi; perf. Lane Nishikawa. Asian American Theater Company, San Francisco, 1990.
————. In association with El Teatro Campesino, San Juan Bautista, CA, 1990.

————. New World Festival, Berkeley, CA, 1990.

————. New WORLD Theatre, U of Massachusetts, Amherst, MA, 1990.

————. (videotaped), dir. Deborah Gee; perf. Lane Nishikawa. KQED-TV, San Francisco, 1990.

————, dir. Eric Hayashi; perf. Lane Nishikawa. State U of New York, Geneseo, 1991.

————. Los Angeles Theatre Company, Los Angeles, 1991.

————. Caminito Theatre and Julia Morgan Theatre, Berkeley, CA, 1991.

————, dir. Eric Hayashi; perf. Lane Nishikawa. Julia Morgan Theatre, Berkeley, CA, 1992.

————. U of California, Santa Cruz, 1993.

————. Cowell Theatre, Fort Mason Center, San Francisco, 1993.

————, dir. Wilbur Obata; perf. Lane Nishikawa. Asian American Theater Company, San Francisco, 1993.

The Gate of Heaven

Production, perf. Lane Nishikawa and Victor Talmadge. Osher Jewish Community Center, Marin, CA, 1994.

————. U.S. Holocaust Museum, Washington, DC, 1995.

————, dir. Jack O'Brien; perf. Lane Nishikawa and Victor Talmadge. Old Globe Theatre, San Diego, 1996.

————. Japanese American Cultural and Community Center, Los Angeles, 1997.

The Heartbeat of America

Workshop, dir. Lane Nishikawa. New WORLD Theatre, U of Massachusetts, Amherst, MA, 1996.

Gila River

Staged reading. Scottsdale Center for the Arts, Scottsdale, AZ, 1998.

Workshop, dir. Lane Nishikawa. California State U, Monterey Bay, 1999.

————. Gila River Indian Reservation Arts and Crafts Center, Gila River, AZ, 2000.

Mifune and Me

Production, dir. Lane Nishikawa. Julia Morgan Theatre, Berkeley, CA, 1999.

————. Stanford U, Stanford, CA, 1999.

————. Scottsdale Center for the Arts, Scottsdale, AZ, 2000.

Lone Wolves

Staged reading, dir. Lane Nishikawa. Kerr Center, Scottsdale, AZ, 2000.

When We Were One

Staged reading, dir. Lane Nishikawa. Maui Cultural Center, Honolulu, 2000.

Essays

" 'Life in the Fast Lane' " Cruises the U.S." *Hokubei Mainichi* 5 Nov. 1982: 1.

————. *Hokubei Mainichi* 10 Nov. 1982: 1.

————. *Hokubei Mainichi* 30 Nov. 1982: 1.

————. *Hokubei Mainichi* 4 Dec. 1982: 1.

————. *Hokubei Mainichi* 29 Jan. 1983: 1.

————. *Hokubei Mainichi* 1 Feb. 1983: 1.

Poetry

"Fluid Movement." *Time to Greez!: Incantations from the Third World.* Ed. Janice Mirikitani. San Francisco: Glide, 1975. 54.
"Deneguan." *Ayumi: A Japanese American Anthology.* Ed. Janice Mirikitani. San Francisco: Japanese American Anthology Committee, 1980. 223–24.
"Oba-chan." *Ayumi: A Japanese American Anthology.* Ed. Janice Mirikitani. San Francisco: Japanese American Anthology Committee, 1980. 225–29.
"They Was Close, Those Brothers." Excerpts. *American Dragons.* Ed. Laurence Yep. New York: HarperCollins, 1993. 132–41.

Screenplays

When We Were Warriors, Part I. With Lane Nishikawa and Victor Talmadge. Dir. Lane Nishikawa. Mission from Buddha Productions, 1999.
When We Were Warriors, Part II: "Forgotten Valor." Dir. Lane Nishikawa. Work in progress. 2001.
When We Were Warriors, Part III. Dir. Lane Nishikawa. Work in progress. 2001.

Studies of Lane Nishikawa

Breslauer, Jan. "Nephew of the Regiment." Rev. of *The Gate of Heaven. Los Angeles Times* 3 Mar. 1996: Calendar: 4.
Curcio, Chris. "*Gila River* Throws Open the Gates for Painful Look at Internment Camp." Rev. of *Gila River. Arizona Republic* 20 Feb. 1998: D11.
Drake, Sylvie. "Nishikawa on *A Mission From Buddha.*" Rev. of *I'm on a Mission From Buddha. Los Angeles Times* 14 Feb. 1991: F4.
Fox, Michael. "Pick Your War." Rev. of *The Gate of Heaven. American Theatre* Mar. 1994: 12.
Johnson, Wayne. "Nishikawa Presents a 'Hyphenated' View." Rev. of *Life in the Fast Lane. Seattle Times* 2 Mar. 1983: D8.
Leach, Anita Mabante. "WWII Japanese American Internment Retold in Play." *Arizona Republic* 28 Apr. 2000: 1. Rpt. as "Internment Tale Staged in *Gila River.*" *Arizona Republic* 3 May 2000: 3.
Lee, Joann Faung Jean. "Lane Nishikawa." *Asian American Actors: Oral Histories from Stage, Screen, and Television.* Jefferson, NC: McFarland, 2000. 188–94.
Nelson, Brian. "Introduction to *The Gate of Heaven.*" *Asian American Drama: 9 Plays from the Multiethnic Landscape.* Ed. Brian Nelson. New York: Applause, 1997. 158.
"Play Remembers 50th Anniversary of Dachau Liberation." *All Things Considered.* Transcript 1831–4. Prod. Robert Siegel. NPR. 28 Apr. 1995.
Rose, Lloyd. "Beyond the Barbed Wire." Rev. of *The Gate of Heaven. Washington Post* 25 Apr. 1995: D1+.
Shinomoto, Linda. "Turning Japanese." Rev. of *Life in the Fast Lane. Sampan* Feb. 1983: 27–28.
Smith, Mark Chalon. "*Mission* Accomplished? Not Yet, but Closer Theater." Rev. of *I'm on a Mission From Buddha. Los Angeles Times* 18 Apr. 1995, Orange County ed.: F2.
Viertel, Jack. "The High Price of Cultural Conglomeration." Rev. of *Life in the Fast Lane. Los Angeles Herald Examiner* 16 July 1982: D29.

Winer, Laurie. "A Common Ground in *Heaven*." Rev. of *The Gate of Heaven*. *Los Angeles Times* 9 Mar. 1996, Calendar: F1.

Winn, Steven. "The Many Faces of Asian Actor on a *Mission*." Rev. of *I'm on a Mission From Buddha*. *San Francisco Chronicle* 9 Mar. 1990: E10.

Dwight Okita
(1958–   )

John Jae-Nam Han

BIOGRAPHY

A sansei playwright, screenwriter, performance artist, and poet, Dwight Okita was born in Chicago, Illinois, on August 26, 1958. His father, Fred Yoshio Okita, and his mother, Patsy Takeyo Arase, originally came from Seattle and Fresno, California, respectively. After the Japanese bombing of Pearl Harbor, they were interned as enemy aliens, along with other Japanese Americans on the West Coast. After their release, they both moved with their families to Chicago, where they came to know each other, married, and settled in the city of Hyde Park. Fred Okita earned a bachelor's degree in anthropology at the University of Chicago, ultimately becoming a teacher. The playwright's mother worked as a bank accountant and later ran a variety of retail businesses.

Dwight Okita grew up in Hyde Park and later in Midlothian, attending public schools. He started writing short poems in the second grade; his first poem was about a penny-candy store. In high school, he developed a passion for reading, eventually earning the nickname "Words" due to his ability to use a very large vocabulary. Growing up, Okita also became acutely aware of his identity as an Asian American and a gay man. In 1966, when Richard Speck mass-murdered eight women, including three Filipino exchange nurses, just one block from Okita's residence on the Southeast Side of Chicago, he—a second grader—was terrified by the news. He was frequently subjected to racial slurs at school, where he was often mistaken for a foreigner. In his youth, he also discovered his homosexual orientation. At age sixteen, he informed his parents of the fact that he was gay; surprisingly, they were supportive of him (Chiu 108–11).

After graduating from high school in 1976, Okita attended the University of Illinois at Chicago, where he majored in theater. Intending to become a performance artist, he trained at various theaters in Chicago. At Steppenwolf Theater Company, Okita encountered John Malkovich and other talented actors. "I became so aware that there were really gifted actors for whom acting was effortless and that I should leave the acting to them," Okita recalls (qtd. in Chiu 112). Although he had already been admitted into an acting program at New York University, he decided to take writing as his profession. He earned a B.A. degree in creative writing at the University of Illinois at Chicago in 1983.

Okita has written several plays. *Dream/Fast* was produced as part of the Igloo Theater's New Works series in 1987. *Richard Speck*, a short play, was produced in 1991 as part of the American Blues Theater's "Monsters" show. *The Salad Bowl Dance* was commissioned and produced by the Chicago Historical Society in 1993. *The Rainy Season* was premiered in 1993 by the Zebra Crossing Theatre and North Avenue Productions. *The Spirit Guide*, Okita's brief monologue, was staged in 1994 as part of the HBO New Writers Project Festival at the Stella Adler Theatre in Los Angeles. *The Radiance of a Thousand Suns: The Hiroshima Project: A Drama with Music*, written in collaboration with three other playwrights, was produced in 1995 by Bailiwick Repertory to commemorate the fiftieth anniversary of the dropping of the atomic bomb. *Letters I Never Wrote* has yet to be produced, although it has had staged readings at Victory Gardens Theater and Chicago Dramatists.

Currently, Okita's focus is on writing nonfiction, memoirs in particular. *Serotonin City*, a book-length memoir of three years of mood swings, concerns the playwright's return to life after falling into the black hole of depression. Okita's current project is *A Life Must Have a Witness*, a memoir of roommates and soul mates. Both books are written in a humorous, mystical manner, but are not yet published.

Many writers and artists have influenced Okita's writing. They include singer Elton John, poet Philip Levine, and such playwrights as John Guare, Philip Kan Gotanda, and Tony Kushner. He also feels a strong bond with David Henry Hwang, the recipient of the 1988 Tony Award for best play for *M. Butterfly* (Chiu 113). Regarding literary influences on him, Okita writes for this sourcebook: "Simply put, I am more recently influenced by the magic realism of playwrights like Jose Rivera and Tony Kushner. . . . In the former work [*Richard Speck*], a woman is slashed by a knife, but birdseeds pour out instead of blood. She opens her mouth to scream and parakeets fly out, hummingbirds, toucans. In the latter work [*My Last Week on Earth*], a woman blows away on a busy street. A planetarium fills at night with people wearing masks. And a man finds his happiness just as he comes face to face with his death. Prose-wise, I am a fan of Chang-rae Lee's *Native Speaker*, and I think Amy Tan is amazing. Her wit, depth, and eccentricity [are] irresistible" (E-mail).

Literary and academic circles have recognized Okita's achievements. He won an Illinois Arts Council Fellowship for poetry in 1988 and was a panelist at the Asian American Renaissance Conference in 1992. The Association for Asian

American Studies also nominated *Crossing with the Light*, Okita's first book of poems, published in 1992, as the best Asian American literature book of 1993.

MAJOR WORKS AND THEMES

Okita has written eight plays that demonstrate his preoccupation with gay romance, the Asian (especially Japanese) American experience, death, and time. *Dream/Fast* (1987) is Okita's first produced play, in which he also performed. The work focuses on what two friends would do the night before a nuclear holocaust. *Letters I Never Wrote* (1991) and *The Spirit Guide* (1994) both focus on the lives of Asian Americans. The former work concerns a young Japanese American girl in the internment camps with the magical power to conjure letters to people. In the latter, an Asian American man goes on a cab ride with two people who just may be God and the devil, respectively.

Okita's play *Richard Speck*, published in 1991, consists of a short monologue by an Asian American woman who dreams that Richard Speck, the nurse killer, has come knocking on her door. The speaker of this darkly comic piece likes one Filipino nurse who, thanks to her instincts, escaped death. In her dream, however, the speaker is visited by Speck, who slashes at her with a pocketknife. After recounting the dream, she ponders how she cannot ignore the fact that three of the murdered nurses were Asian by race: "Those women he [Speck] killed, they weren't just nurses, you know—they were Asian Americans." She ends her speech with a mischievous remark: "I think when Speck comes back in his next life, he'll come back as something harmless. Something gentle. Maybe a parakeet. . . . I can hardly wait" (*Richard Speck*).

The Salad Bowl Dance (1993) concerns a Japanese American woman coming out of the internment camps and resettling in Chicago. The play was selected to be part of the HBO New Writers Workshop, with Tamlyn Tomita as the lead, in 1994. It was commissioned by the Chicago Historical Society and coproduced with Angel Island Theater in Chicago in 1993.

The Rainy Season (1993), included in *Asian American Drama: 9 Plays from the Multiethnic Landscape* (1997), deals with a gay Japanese American's four-week affair with a Brazilian man, Antonio. The protagonist, Harry, defines himself as "a romantic in an unromantic age [who has] a lousy taste in men" (261). Antonio tells him of the rainy season in his home country, when heavy rains rejuvenate the barren hearts. Their plan to visit Brazil for the summer is thwarted by Antonio's change of mind at the last minute. As Antonio visits him to say goodbye, Harry's dream of visiting the rainforests with his foreign lover is shattered.

The Radiance of a Thousand Suns (1998) looks at the birth of the nuclear age through the eyes of the scientists, the atomic-bomb survivors, and women of that era, as well as through an unusual episode of the 1950s television show *This Is Your Life*. In the show, eight actors perform a variety of characters, often switching race, gender, and political viewpoint from one scene to the next.

Finally, *My Last Week on Earth* (1998), the playwright's most recent script, concerns an unhappy man who visits a fortune-teller, who informs him that he has seven days to live. In his last week on earth, the man finds happiness. Okita wrote it as both a stage play and a screenplay and has had staged readings at Chicago Dramatists, where he is a resident playwright. *My Last Week on Earth* was a finalist in the Sundance Screenwriters Lab Competition in 1998.

Thematically, Okita's plays are both similar to and different from the writings by earlier Japanese American writers. In his preoccupation with the Japanese American experience, such as the internment during World War II and the atomic bombing, he is in line with older writers of Japanese ancestry. As a writer who was born in the United States in the late 1950s, however, he grapples with a younger generation's literary concerns such as gay romance and interracial dating. Stylistically, Okita's plays tend to be poetic. As he stated in his interview with Christina Chiu, "poetry infuses everything [he writes]" (qtd. in Chiu 113).

CRITICAL RECEPTION

Okita's plays have elicited mixed reviews from the critics. *Dream/Fast* received a favorable critical reaction from the *Windy City Times*, a Chicago newspaper for the gay and lesbian communities. The reviewer, Richard Warburton, commented that the play "fills its raw, small space at the Igloo Theater with wit, warmth and humanity. Even though we have been sitting in the dark with strangers, Okita's magic and universal emotions unite us all" (N. pag.).

Richard Speck earned terrific reviews. In the *Chicago Tribune*, Sid Smith observed, "Two of the best pieces come drenched in black. Lee Chen is exquisite in Dwight Okita's partly comic, partly scary reminiscence of growing up Asian American near where the Richard Speck murders took place" (26). Hedy Weiss, in the review article for the *Chicago Sun-Times*, wrote, "A young Asian American woman fantasizes in a magic realism style about the killer of Asian nurses" in Okita's play (" 'Monsters' " 23). In his article for the *Windy City Times*, Lawrence Bommer called the play "a burning portrait of a young Asian American woman . . . still haunted by the memory of growing up one block from where Richard Speck killed eight nurses" (*Richard* N. pag.).

Critical reactions to *The Rainy Season* were mixed. It received terrific reviews in the *Reader* and *Nightlines*. Justin Hayford, writing in the *Reader*, observed that the work "presents what few plays even approximate: an accurate, honest, compelling picture of life in our times. At the same time, Okita's poetic sensibility imbues this realistic drama with a nearly mystical quality" (32). In the review published in *Nightlines*, M.J. Hochberg called the work "a warm, funny and touching work filled with truisms that are as poignantly perceptive as they are commonly accepted" (23). In his editorial notes on the play, included in *Asian American Drama: 9 Plays from the Multiethnic Landscape*, Brian Nelson also praised the play's uniqueness as a work on gay issues. Okita is "strikingly free of bitterness and alienation"; Harry, an Asian American gay unlike stereotypical Asian characters, is not the exotic Other in the play (Nelson 211).

The Rainy Season, however, received lukewarm reviews from the *Chicago Tribune,* where Lawrence Bommer criticized it for its lack of action: "Chekhov wrote so strongly that his passive plots never dwindled into talk. [Okita] doesn't fare as well with *The Rainy Season,* a sweet-tempered, good-hearted play with little movement and a lot of undramatized longings" (" 'Rainy' " 13).

The Radiance of a Thousand Suns won a Joseph Jefferson Citation for Outstanding New Work in Chicago Theater. It received generally terrific reviews from many of the presses, including the *Chicago Sun-Times, New City,* and *Gay Chicago.* In the *Chicago Sun-Times,* for instance, Hedy Weiss called the work "a worthy, moving and intelligent meditation on all aspects of the event [the atomic bomb]" (" 'Hiroshima' " 28). Lucia Mauro wrote in *New City,* "Bailiwick's profoundly revelatory collective effect achieves what the canceled Smithsonian exhibit couldn't: it presents both sides of the atomic bombing of Hiroshima fifty years ago" (31).

Overall, Okita's plays have received favorable reviews for his realistic portrayal of modern life (especially as related to Asian Americans and gays) and for his profound wit and depth of feeling. Critics have also noted Okita's magical use of language, which recalls the writings of Gabriel García Marquez, a Latin American magic realist. On the other hand, however, Okita's theatrical works have occasionally been criticized for their lack of meaningful interactions among the characters. Indeed, his *Dream/Fast* and *The Rainy Season* occasionally rely on monotonous conversations.

BIBLIOGRAPHY

Works by Dwight Okita

Drama

The Rainy Season. Asian American Drama: 9 Plays from the Multiethnic Landscape. Ed. Brian Nelson. New York: Applause, 1997. 209–62.

The Radiance of a Thousand Suns: The Hiroshima Project: A Drama with Music. With Anne V. McGravie, Dwight Okita, Nicholas A. Patricca, and David Zak. Woodstock, IL: Dramatic Publishing Company, 1998.

Richard Speck. Riksha. Issue 2. 30 May 2000 <http://www.riksha.com/about.htm#currentissue>. Rpt. in *Yellow Light: The Flowering of Asian American Arts.* Ed. Amy Ling. Philadelphia: Temple UP, 1999. 256–57.

Asian Men on Asian Men: The Attraction. Monologue. *Yellow Light: The Flowering of Asian American Arts.* Ed. Amy Ling. Philadelphia: Temple UP, 1999. 258–59.

Unpublished Manuscripts

Dream/Fast. 1987.
Letters I Never Wrote. 1991.

The Salad Bowl Dance. 1993.
The Spirit Guide. 1994.
My Last Week on Earth. 1998.
Serotonin City. Memoir. 1999.
A Life Must Have a Witness. Memoir. 2000.

Selected Production History

Dream/Fast

Production. New Works series, Igloo Theater, Chicago, 1987.

Richard Speck

Production as part of the "Monsters" show. American Blues Theater, Chicago, 1991.

Letters I Never Wrote

Staged reading. Victory Gardens Theater, Chicago, 1993.
———. Chicago Dramatists, Chicago, 1993.

The Rainy Season

Production, dir. Marlene Zuccaro. Zebra Crossing Theatre and North Avenue, Chicago, 1993.

The Salad Bowl Dance

Production, Chicago Historical Society, Angel Island Theater, Chicago, 1993.
———, dir. Jenny Moy; perf. Tamlyn Tomita. HBO New Writers Workshop, Los Angeles, 1994.
———, dir. Chuck Smith. Columbia Theater, Columbia College, Chicago, 1995.

The Spirit Guide

Performance. HBO New Writers Project Festival, Stella Adler Theatre, Los Angeles, 1994.

The Radiance of a Thousand Suns

Production, dir. David Zak. Bailiwick Repertory Theater, Chicago, 1995.

My Last Week on Earth

Staged reading. Chicago Dramatists, Chicago, 1998.

Essay

"Response." *Yellow Light: The Flowering of Asian American Arts.* Ed. Amy Ling. Philadelphia: Temple UP, 1999. 250–55.

Letter

E-mail to the author. 29 May 2000.

Poetry

"The Art of holding On." *Breaking Silence: An Anthology of Contemporary Asian American Poets.* Ed. Joseph Bruchac. New York: Greenfield Review P, 1983. 209.
"Cross with the Light." *Breaking Silence: An Anthology of Contemporary Asian Amer-*

ican Poets. Ed. Joseph Bruchac. New York: Greenfield Review P, 1983. 210. Rpt. of *Crossing with the Light*. Chicago: Tia Chucha Press, 1992.

"In Response to Executive Order 9066: All Americans of Japanese Descent Must Report to Relocation Centers." *Breaking Silence: An Anthology of Contemporary Asian American Poets*. Ed. Joseph Bruchac. New York: Greenfield Review P, 1983. 211. Rpt. in *Yellow Light: The Flowering of Asian American Arts*. Ed. Amy Ling. Philadelphia: Temple UP, 1999. 259–60.

"Parachute." *Breaking Silence: An Anthology of Contemporary Asian American Poets*. Ed. Joseph Bruchac. New York: Greenfield Review P, 1983. 212.

"Poetry Video Comes of Age." *Letter eX* Oct. 1991. 19 May 2000 <http://community-2.webtv.net/LETTEREX/POETRYVIDEOCOMEOF/>.

"Notes for a Poem on Being Asian American." *Asian Pacific American Journal* 2.1 (1993): 45–46.

"Where the Boys Were." *Asian Pacific American Journal* 2.1 (1993): 47–49.

"Jellyfish." *Power Lines: A Decade of Poetry from Chicago's Guild Complex*. Ed. Julie Parson-Nesbitt, Luis J. Rodriguez, and Michael Warr. Chicago: Tia Chucha Press, 1999. 136.

Screenplay

My Last Week on Earth. Motion picture. Independent. 1998.

Studies of Dwight Okita

Applegate, Jane. "From Videos to Greeting Cards, Gay Clout Abounds." *Washington Post* 3 May 1993: F10.

Bommer, Lawrence. " 'Rainy Season' Dries Up after First Act." *Chicago Tribune* 25 Feb. 1993: 13.

———. Rev. of *Richard Speck*. *Windy City Times* 5 Dec. 1991. N. pag.

Chiu, Christina. "Dwight Okita." *Lives of Notable Asian Americans: Literature and Education*. New York: Chelsea House, 1996. 107–13.

Hayford, Justin. Rev. of *The Rainy Season*. *Reader* 26 Feb. 1993: 32.

Heintz, Kurt. "An Incomplete History of Slam: Slam Poetry in Print, on Disc, and in Video." 1999. 17 Mar. 2000 <http://www.e-poets.net/library/slam/publish.html>.

Hochberg, M.J. Rev. of *The Rainy Season*. *Nightlines* 10 Mar. 1993: 23.

Kondo, Dorinne. Introduction. *Asian American Drama: 9 Plays from the Multiethnic Landscape*. Ed. Brian Nelson. New York: Applause, 1997. ix–xiv.

Mauro, Lucia. Rev. of *The Radiance of a Thousand Suns: The Hiroshima Project: A Drama with Music*. *New City* 27 July 1995: 31.

Nelson, Brian. Editor's notes. *Asian American Drama: 9 Plays from the Multiethnic Landscape*. New York: Applause, 1997. 211–12.

Shirley, Don. "Monologues Highlight HBO New Writers Project Festival." *Los Angeles Times* 19 Oct. 1994: F-2.

Smith, Sid. " 'Monsters' Adds Up When Pieces Join Together." Rev. of *Richard Speck*. *Chicago Tribune* 20 Nov. 1991: 26.

Warburton, Richard. Rev. of *Dream/Fast*. *Windy City Times* 18 June 1987: N. pag.

Weiss, Hedy. " 'Monsters' Takes a Violent, Keen Look at Urban Creatures." *Chicago Sun-Times* 18 Nov. 1991: 23.

———. " 'Hiroshima Project' Hits Issues Head on." Rev. of *The Radiance of a Thousand Suns: The Hiroshima Project: A Drama with Music. Chicago Sun-Times* 28 July 1995: 28.

Han Ong
(1968–   )

John Jae-Nam Han

BIOGRAPHY

A playwright, performance artist, and novelist, Han Ong was born on February 5, 1968, to Chinese parents in Manila, the Philippines. He grew up and went to school there until 1984, when his family immigrated to the United States. He was sixteen at the time. The family settled in Koreatown in Los Angeles, California. His parents held jobs as blue-collar workers in Los Angeles while he went to Grant High School, a predominantly white school in the San Fernando Valley.

As a teenager, Ong experienced a tough time dealing with his puberty and a life on foreign soil. "Puberty plus a new country—both are tough enough on their own. The five of us children were very distinct individuals. It was pretty much each on his own," recalls Ong (qtd. in Chiu 59–60). He indulged in reading books, watching television, and watching music videos. But Ong developed an interest in theater while he was in high school, where he took a drama course. He wrote his first play at age seventeen. People began to notice his talent, which motivated him to write more plays. Eventually, Ong was admitted to a young playwrights' lab at the Los Angeles Theater Center. Because he did not feel that he was learning much from high school, he left it at eighteen without graduating. He earned a GED later. In order to support himself as a writer, he worked in a trophy-manufacturing factory and then at a Los Angeles theater as a clerk. He left his clerical jobs when he was awarded a commission from the Mark Taper Forum and a grant from the National Endowment for the Arts.

Ong's works were not fully recognized until he left Los Angeles for New York in 1994, where he won recognition from Robert Brustein, the artistic director of the American Repertory Theater (ART) and one of the most esteemed names of the American stage. In 1997, when Ong was twenty-nine, he was honored as one of twenty-three winners of the celebrated MacArthur Fellowships—the so-called genius awards—provided by the John D. and Catherine T. MacArthur Foundation of Chicago. The grant for Ong was $200,000. In an interview with Lonnae O'Neal Parker, Ong remarked, "I hope this MacArthur Fellowship demonstrates the importance of self-determination and the hunger for improvement for people of [my] generation. I didn't take being a [high-school] dropout as a measure of my intelligence or as a harbinger of my future" (qtd. in Parker E2).

Ong has written a substantial number of plays, almost all of which have yet to be published. In 1991, he wrote his first monologue, *Symposium in Manila*, which was presented at Highways in Santa Monica, California, and at the Joseph Papp Public Theater in New York. Ong's next piece, *Cornerstone Geography*, was performed at the Joseph Papp Public Theater in 1992 and at both the Portland Stage Company in Maine and then at Highways in 1993. In 1992, Ong had three productions in the San Francisco Bay Area running simultaneously: *Bachelor Rat; Reasons to Live. Reason to Live. Half. No Reason*; and *Symposium in Manila*. In 1993, the playwright collaborated with Jessica Hagedorn, another Filipino American writer, on a performance piece entitled *Airport Music* for the Los Angeles festival; in 1994, the two authors performed *Airport Music* again at the Public Theater and then at the Berkeley Repertory Theater. Meanwhile, Ong wrote two one-act plays, *In a Lonely Country* and *The Short List of Alternate Places*, collectively entitled *The L.A. Plays*. On April 8, 1993, *The L.A. Plays* was premiered at Boston's American Repertory Theater. Later that year, they were performed at the American Repertory Theater at Harvard University and then at the Almeida Theater in London. More recent plays by Ong include *The Chang Fragments* and *Swooney Planet*.

In addition to his plays, Ong has written two novels so far, *The Stranded in the World* and *Shank Rote*. They have yet to be published, although an excerpt from the former work is included in *Charlie Chan Is Dead: An Anthology of Contemporary Asian American Fiction* (1993), a much-praised collection edited by Jessica Hagedorn.

Many writers and artists have inspired Ong. Maria Irene Fornes, the Cuban-born American playwright, has had a particular influence on him. According to Ong, his own and Fornes's plays share a comparable "outsider observation of the way things are in this country" (qtd. in Kelly 30). In addition to Fornes, Flannery O'Connor, Georg Büchner, Wallace Shawn, Franz Xaver Koretz, Samuel Beckett, Harry Kondoleon, Rainer Werner Fassbinder, and Tennessee Williams all have had an impact on Ong's writing.

MAJOR WORKS AND THEMES

Set in an urban, multicultural environment, Ong's theatrical works can be generally divided into two groups: those exploring the issues related to immigration, such as the search for roots, clashes of culture, identity crisis, and the American dream, and those presenting the lives of nonstereotypical Asian American characters. Typical of the first group are *Symposium in Manila* (1991), *Airport Music* (1993), and *The Chang Fragments* (1996). In *Symposium in Manila*, for instance, a Filipino grandfather urges his grandson to return to his roots. *Airport Music* concerns both the immigrants' real arrival at the airport and their psychological arrival. *The Chang Fragments* deals with a Chinese immigrant family's gradual disintegration. Mr. Chang, who fiercely refuses to assimilate to American culture, leaves his family and hangs himself in a Los Angeles flophouse. Mrs. Chang, who constantly speaks surreal broken English, enrolls in a Boogaloo dance class "to [learn] how to forget" (Ong, *Mrs. Chang* 62). The couple's three children are problematic in their own ways: the oldest son, a workaholic, is stuck in a loveless marriage; the younger son, an ambitious artist, has dropped out of school and is emotionally unstable; and the rebellious daughter marries an older man who is a Japanese doctor.

The second group may include *Cornerstone Geography* (1992), *Bachelor Rat* (1992), *Reasons to Live* (1992), and *The L.A. Plays* (1993), all of which portray characters outside the stereotypes of Asian Americans. In the monologue *Cornerstone Geography*, a boy hooker works La Brea Boulevard in Los Angeles in defiance of an alcoholic, abusive father. *Bachelor Rat* concerns a young gay man, Dada, who has a series of sexual encounters in his squalid apartment with various people, including a married bisexual, a fussy older man, and a sensuous child. *Reasons to Live*, a tragic story written in free verse, is about an Asian male ex-convict who has no hope for the future. The protagonist, who has been doing time for ten years for killing his mother, is released from prison. His urge to murder, however, causes him to kill his girlfriend. *In a Lonely Country* and *A Short List of Alternate Places*, Ong's double bill, concerns the seedy life of a gay Asian American male prostitute. Ong's hero, nineteen-year-old Greg In, is an unhappy youth who suffers from horrifying dreams and attempts suicide. In writing this work, Ong was particularly interested in having an Asian character at the center of the play without creating an exclusively Asian play. Ong remarked in an interview, "Making him [Greg In] a male prostitute creates subtextual political messages: Giving sex back to Asian males and not making them be the good sons" (qtd. in Breslauer, "New" 5).

Overall, Ong's plays portray the dark, seamy side of Asian American life. The characters typically live in a depressing, sometimes-hopeless environment. They not only are alienated from society, but also suffer from a lack of mutual communication, respect, and warmth in their family lives. Ong is similar to Dwight Okita, a contemporary Japanese American playwright, in his theatrical use of gay characters. However, we do not find in Ong's plays the dreamy and romantic elements that permeate Okita's works.

CRITICAL RECEPTION

Once an obscure author/performer, Ong has secured an important place in Asian American theater. Various critics have recognized Ong's literary and artistic talent. In her 1997 introduction, Dorinne Kondo comments, "[With] post-1965 immigration, we are continuing to see the emergence of new playwrights from newer Asian Pacific communities, including the vibrant and exciting work of young playwrights and performance artists such as Rob Shin, Han Ong, Linda Faigao-Hall, Sung Rno and others" (x). David Henry Hwang similarly observes that Ong is one of the "younger, or 'Third Wave' Asian/Pacific playwrights" who, unlike their predecessors, refuse to focus mainly on racial issues in their works (viii). The Asian American Writers' Workshop calls Ong one of the "prestigious [Asian American] playwrights" along with David Henry Hwang and Philip Kan Gotanda in its online publications (screen 8). Finally, in her article on Los Angeles theater, Jan Breslauer calls Ong a "lyrical genius" ("They" 72).

Critics have also noted similarities between Ong and various writers. The American Repertory Theater's Robert Brustein describes Ong as "the most exciting new talent to evolve in years" without much formal education, "like Shakespeare" (qtd. in Koch 45). Steve Maler, a director in Harvard/ART's Institute for Advanced Theater Training, likens Ong to playwright Samuel Beckett: "Han writes with a Beckett-like economy and a poetic vision. That vision stays connected to people's lives, yet it's not a documentary. It's just shards of a life" (qtd. in Breslauer, "New" 5). In her comment on *Reasons to Live*, Breslauer also finds similarities between Ong and such well-known writers as Nathanael West and John Steppling: "Ong's characters are the disenfranchised. His universe is the low-rent world of back-door L.A., the same seedy byways and dingy apartments that have surfaced in works as various as Nathanael West's *Day of the Locust* and the plays of John Steppling" ("New" 5).

However, critical reactions to Ong's individual plays have been mixed. In her review of Ong's *Reasons to Live*, Judith Green writes that Ong is "an extraordinary playwright" and the work is "an unusual play" ("Hope" 3C). Green is equally impressed with *Bachelor Rat*, in which Ong "has a deft way with words: an ability to layer poetry on reality and an unusual appreciation of irony" ("Remembered" 7F). In his 1993 review of *The L.A. Plays*, however, Kevin Kelly is doubtful of Ong's genuineness as a dramatist. According to Kelly, Ong is "a quick-scene dramatist whose work is a dark blip from John Rechy's *City of Night* . . . and *The Sexual Outlaw*, both of which were graphic forerunners detailing the underground 'sexhunt' of homosexual life," and his best distinction is "brute observation, poetic sensibility, sharp characterization and cinematic skill" (30). As an actor, Kelly adds, Ong is "a fussy, low-level actor who uses too many gestures and too often settles for moony passivity" (30). In her comment on *Airport Music*, Judith Green is also critical of Ong: Although the piece is not completely without depth, it is "mostly about anger, which is a good servant but a bad master" ("*Airport Music*" 3C).

Still in his early thirties, Ong has secured a firm place as a representative Asian American playwright. Although he has often been criticized for lacking a clear-cut focus and for his angry tone, Ong still uses poetic language, irony, and dramatic skills in a brilliant way. The fact that he has acquired so much literary fame as a recent Asian immigrant is a telling testimony to his talent and potential.

BIBLIOGRAPHY

Works by Han Ong

Drama

Mrs. Chang. *Conjunctions* 25 (Spring 1995): 60–79.
Swoony Planet. *Tokens? The NYC Asian American Experience on Stage*. Ed. Alvin Eng.
    New York: Asian American Writers' Workshop, 1999. 41–144.

Unpublished Manuscripts

Symposium in Manila. 1991.
Bachelor Rat. 1992.
Cornerstone Geography. 1992.
Reasons to Live. Reason to Live. Half. No Reason. 1991.
The Stranded in the World. Novel. 1992.
Airport Music. With Jessica Tarahata Hagedorn. 1993.
The L.A. Plays: In a Lonely Country and *A Short List of Alternate Places*. 1993.
Shank Rote. Novel. 1995.
The Chang Fragments. 1996.

Selected Production History

Symposium in Manila

Production. Highways Performance Space, Santa Monica, CA, 1991.
———. Joseph Papp Public Theater, New York, 1991.
———. Marsh, San Francisco, 1992.

Bachelor Rat

Production, dir. Tony Kelly. Thick Description Theatre, San Francisco, 1992.

Cornerstone Geography

Production. Joseph Papp Public Theater, New York, 1992.
———. Portland Stage Company, Portland, ME, 1993.
———. Highways Performance Space, Santa Monica, CA, 1993.

Reasons to Live. Reason to Live. Half. No Reason

Production, dir. Brian Kulick. Magic Theater, San Francisco, 1992.

Airport Music

Production, perf. Jessica Tarahata Hagedorn and Han Ong. Los Angeles Festival, Los
    Angeles, 1993.
——, dir. Sharon Ott; perf. Jessica Tarahata Hagedorn and Han Ong. Joseph Papp
    Public Theater, New York City, 1994.
——, perf. Jessica Tarahata Hagedorn and Han Ong. Berkeley Repertory Theatre,
    Berkeley, CA, 1994.

The L.A. Plays: In a Lonely Country and *A Short List of Alternate*
Places

Production. American Repertory Theater, Boston, 1993.
——, dir. Steven Maler. American Repertory Theater, Harvard U, Cambridge, MA,
    1993.
——. Almeida Theatre, London, 1993.

The Chang Fragments

Production, dir. Marcus Stern. Joseph Papp Public Theater, New York City, 1996.

Novels

"Excerpts from *The Stranded in the World*, a Novel-in-Progress." *Charlie Chan Is Dead:*
    An Anthology of Contemporary Asian American Fiction. Ed. Jessica Hagedorn.
    New York: Penguin, 1993. 389–98.

Studies of Han Ong

Asian American Writers' Workshop. "Performance Series." *The Program Divisions*. New
    York: Asian American Writers' Workshop, 2000. 8 screens. 17 Nov. 2000. <http:
    //www.panix.com/~aaww/temp/programs.html>.
Breslauer, Jan. "The New (Real) L.A. Stories: Han Ong's Plays Aim beyond the We-
    Are-Downtrodden Agenda of Many Minority Artists to Chart the Complexities
    of Life in the City." *Los Angeles Times* 29 Nov. 1992, Calendar: 5.
——. "They Don't Get No Respect." *Los Angeles Times* 8 Nov. 1998, Calendar: 72.
Chiu, Christina. "Han Ung" [*sic*]. *Lives of Notable Asian Americans: Literature and*
    Education. New York: Chelsea House, 1996. 59–63.
Green, Judith. "*Airport Music* Never Really Arrives: View of Immigration Bogs Down
    in Griping." *San Jose Mercury News* 9 June 1994: 3C.
——. "Hope Crumbles for an Ex-Con in Poetic Drama." *San Jose Mercury News* 27
    Apr. 1992: 3C.
——. "Performer on the Edge." *San Jose Mercury News* 26 Apr. 1992: 3C.
——. "Remembered Places in a Young, Gay Life." *San Jose Mercury News* 15 Apr.
    1992: 7F.
Hwang, David Henry. "Foreword: The Myth of Immutable Cultural Identity." *Asian*
    American Drama: 9 Plays from the Multiethnic Landscape. Ed. Brian Nelson.
    New York: Applause, 1997. vii–viii.
Kelly, Kevin. "Ong's *L.A. Plays*: Snappy Scenes in Search of a Plot." *Boston Globe* 12
    Apr. 1993: 30.
Koch, John. "Grant Means Power, Plays for Art." *Boston Globe* 15 Jan. 1993: 45.

Kondo, Dorinne. Introduction. *Asian American Drama: 9 Plays from the Multiethnic Landscape*. Ed. Brian Nelson. New York: Applause, 1997. ix–xiv.

Parker, Lonnae O'Neal. "Out of the Blue Comes Green: 23 Artists, Authors, Academics, and Activists Are Surprised with MacArthur 'Genius' Grants." *Washington Post* 17 June 1997: E2.

Uma Parameswaran

(1941–)

Rashna B. Singh

BIOGRAPHY

Born in Madras (now called Chennai), Uma Parameswaran was raised in the central Indian city of Jabalpur, where her father was a professor of physics at Jabalpur University. It was at this university that Parameswaran matriculated. After receiving a B.A. degree, she went on to receive her M.A. and diploma in journalism from Nagpur University. In 1963, when she was awarded a Smith-Mundt Fulbright Fellowship, she proceeded to the United States, where she attended Indiana University, from which she received an M.A. with a concentration in creative writing in 1964, and Michigan State University, from which she received a Ph.D. in English in 1972. Prior to that, in 1966, Uma Parameswaran had taken up residence in Winnipeg, Canada, where she still lives. She has taught English at the University of Winnipeg since 1967, specializing in the literature of the Commonwealth and in creative writing. Parameswaran is the author of many critical studies as well as works of fiction, drama, and poetry. Her husband is a mathematician, and they have one daughter.

Parameswaran has been an active member of her community. Her causes and concerns reflect not only the preoccupations of her personal life, but also the main themes of her works. She has taken a leadership role in issues pertaining to women, especially immigrant women and women writers, and in the South Asian diaspora in Canada. She has served as chair, president, or board member of a number of committees, guilds, and associations. In addition, Parameswaran has been instrumental in bringing Indian cultural activities to Winnipeg and organized the first formal instruction in Indian classical dance for children.

MAJOR WORKS AND THEMES

Uma Parameswaran has explored a range of genres in her writing, experimenting with poetry, plays, and short fiction. She has published a volume of poems entitled *Trishanku*, a volume of plays entitled *Sons Must Die*, and a collection of short fiction, poetry, and drama called *The Door I Shut behind Me*, the title story of which won the 1967 Lady Eaton Award. Her most recent work is a collection of short stories entitled *What Was Always Hers*, which won the Canadian Authors' Association Jubilee Award for 2000. Parameswaran's plays explore multiple themes simultaneously as she takes up the conflict between countries, cultures, generations, and individual members of a family. What the author herself, in a statement that precedes her book of plays, *Sons Must Die*, refers to as her "dual cultural sensibility" is evident throughout her plays, both in theme and in structure (9). While plays such as *Meera* and *Sita's Promise*, both dance dramas, embody classical Hindu myths and legends, the influence of classical Greek drama and English narrative poetry is easily perceptible.

Sons Must Die (1985) is set against the backdrop of the disputed territory of Kashmir and the conflict of 1947–48, the first of many between India and Pakistan. It is a play about the "pity of war," the words of the poet Wilfred Owen that the author herself uses to describe the work. After gaining independence from British rule, the people of the subcontinent, who had lived in a fragile and frequently disrupted equilibrium, found themselves bitter enemies across a newly created border. Religion remained the great divide, and Parameswaran focuses on this by bringing together three women, two of whom are Hindu, but from different and disparate parts of India, and one of whom is Muslim. Motherhood becomes the only bond they share, and it is meant to transcend the communal, cultural, and political clashes that have culminated in this bloodshed.

While *Sons Must Die* vaguely recalls the narrative poetry of Matthew Arnold and Greek drama, it is written in somewhat stilted verse. There is a chorus consisting of old men, eight of them Muslim, two Hindu, and one Sikh, another obvious attempt to insist on communal harmony over communal dissent and destruction. A corpse who apparently comes alive and refuses to be dead is an interesting but risky device, for what is evidently intended as tragic veers dangerously toward the comic. The cadences of colloquial Indian English combine with those of classical verse to make this a somewhat strange yet ambitious work.

The two dance dramas that follow take up well-loved stories from Hindu legend. *Meera: A Dance Drama* (1972) tells the story of Meera, who went from Rajput queen to handmaiden of Lord Krishna, singing his praises in a most personal manner, an intimacy of worship that became the hallmark of the Bhakti movement. *Sita's Promise* (1981) is about the banishment into the forest for fourteen years of Rama, his wife, Sita, and his brother, Lakshmana. However, Parameswaran produces a Canadian twist to the old tale as she takes the trio to Canada in the tenth year of their exile, where Sita promises the Inuit children:

"I, through my people, shall surely come again and we shall build our temple and sing our songs with all the children of all the different lands who make this their home" (*Sita's Promise* 62). Both plays are rather clumsy contrivances to frame dance sequences, which seem artificially added on rather than integral to the action even though, in a staged presentation, they would probably overshadow it.

Dear Deedi, My Sister (1990) is a short play that takes up themes of dislocation and diversity. It is more a series of monologues than an actual drama. Each character delivers a monologue that then interlocks thematically with the next one. The result becomes a dialogue that is not sequential but spatially connected, an overlapping of commonalities based on the characters' experience of isolation and alienation in the cold country to which they have immigrated. The characters hail from India, Nicaragua, Kenya, the Philippines, Nigeria, Pakistan, and Sri Lanka, all "New Canadians / Come from faraway places" (*Dear Deedi* 72) only to find the faces of their young ones "Slapped by unthinking scorn, unfeeling barbs, / From closed fists and closed hearts" (73). The play ends on a note of hope and determination as the Indian woman resolves to build a temple at the confluence of two Canadian rivers that will be enriched and sanctified by the waters of the Ganges. The cultures of these new Canadians will thus be grafted rather than simply absorbed or annihilated.

The final play in the collection, *Rootless but Green Are the Boulevard Trees*, is probably Parameswaran's best known. It is also her most sustained and mature dramatic work and continues her preoccupation with aliens and alienation. The play takes place entirely within the home of an Indian immigrant family in Winnipeg, but the imaginary homeland of India becomes a simultaneous setting as the tensions between generations, cultures, value systems, and family members are played out. The boulevard trees, transplanted themselves, symbolize the struggle of the family and, by extension, of all immigrants to survive in spirit and to set down roots in an alien environment. Parameswaran's plays all have in common the idea of intersection, as the past and the present, old and new identities, contrasting cultures and clashing values all intersect to create a complex new sensibility.

CRITICAL RECEPTION

Critical reception of Parameswaran's work remains somewhat scant and sporadic, restricted to special issues of specialized journals such as *Canadian Theatre Review*, where her play *Rootless but Green* is explored in some depth in an article by Bina Mittal. A brief and not very positive review of the volume *Sons Must Die and Other Plays* by Susheela N. Rao is published in *World Literature Today*. An article entitled "Travelers between Cultures" by Roshni Rustomji appears in the *Toronto South Asian Review*. It explores Parameswaran's prose poems in the context of a dislocated consciousness and in conjunction with a contemporary expatriate writer, Meena Alexander. Diane

McGifford writes an entry on Uma Parameswaran that provides important biographical and thematic information in *Writers of the Indian Diaspora*, edited by Emmanuel Nelson. There have also been several papers presented on Parameswaran's works at Canadian studies conferences in India. In general, Parameswaran's works have received closer critical attention in India than they have in her adopted country of Canada, though her contribution to the range of contemporary Canadian literature is now being recognized to a greater degree.

BIBLIOGRAPHY

Works by Uma Parameswaran

Drama

Rootless but Green Are the Boulevard Trees. Toronto: Toronto South Asian Review Books, 1987. Rpt. in *Sons Must Die and Other Plays*. New Delhi: Prestige Books, 1998. 74–128.
Dear Deedi, My Sister. Sons Must Die and Other Plays. New Delhi: Prestige Books, 1998. 63–73
Meera: A Dance Drama. Sons Must Die and Other Plays. New Delhi: Prestige Books, 1998. 37–45.
Sita's Promise. Sons Must Die and Other Plays. New Delhi: Prestige Books, 1998. 46–62.
Sons Must Die. Sons Must Die and Other Plays. New Delhi: Prestige Books, 1998. 13–36.

Selected Production History

Meera: A Dance Drama

Production, dir. Kay Unruh; chor. Rubena Sinha. U of Manitoba Theatre, Winnipeg, 1972.

Sita's Promise

Production, dir. Uma Parameswaran; chor. Sarasi Raj. Winnipeg Art Gallery, Winnipeg, 1981.

Rootless but Green Are the Boulevard Trees

Workshop. Performing Arts and Literatures of India, U of Winnipeg, Winnipeg, 1984.

Sons Must Die

Staged reading. U of Winnipeg Creative Writing Forum, Winnipeg, 1985.

Dear Deedi, My Sister

Workshop. U of Winnipeg, Winnipeg, 1990.

Essay

"First Person Singular." Introduction. *Sons Must Die and Other Plays*. New Delhi: Prestige Books, 1998. 7–12.

Poetry

Cyclic Hope, Cyclic Pain. Calcutta: Writers Workshop, 1973.
Trishanku. Toronto: Toronto South Asian Review Books, 1988.
The Door I Shut behind Me: Selected Fiction, Poetry and Drama. New Delhi: Affiliated
    East-West P, 1990.

Short Stories

What Was Always Hers. Fredericton, NB: Broken Jaw P, 1999.

Studies of Uma Parameswaran

James, Jancy. "Remythologizing as Expatriate Vision and Art: An Intertextual Reading
    of Uma Parameswaran's *Sita's Promise* and *Meera*." *Writers of the Indian Di-
    aspora: Theory and Practice*. Ed. Jasbir Jain. Jaipur: Rawat, 1998. 199–208.
McGifford, Diane. "Uma Parameswaran." *Writers of the Indian Diaspora: A Bio-
    Bibliographical Critcal Sourcebook*. Ed. Emmanuel S. Nelson. Westport, CT:
    Greenwood P, 1993. 305–9.
Mittal, Bina. "Exploring the Immigrant Experience through Theatre: Uma Parames-
    waran's *Rootless but Green Are the Boulevard Trees*." *Canadian Theatre Review*
    94 (1998): 32–35.
Rao, Susheela N. Rev. of *Sons Must Die and Other Plays*. *World Literature Today* 73.2
    (1999): 344.
Rustomji, Roshni. "Travelers between Cultures." *Toronto South Asian Review* 7.2 (1989):
    86–92.

Ralph B. Peña

(1963–   )

Lucy Mae San Pablo Burns

BIOGRAPHY

Ralph Peña was born in 1963 and grew up in Manila, the Philippines. When he was ten years old, he and his siblings came to the United States to live with their father. He then went back to the Philippines to finish high school. In high school, he got involved with the Philippine Educational Theater Association (PETA). It was through PETA that Peña began to understand the dynamic and political potential of theater. PETA's main vision is to create a theater "truly expressive of the Filipino's national culture" (qtd. in Van Erven 33). Before the events that led to the 1982 People's Revolution, Peña was already finding in the barrios and on the streets the power of theater to inspire and to move people to action during a time of political unrest.

During the early 1980s, Peña began his training as a student actor at the University of the Philippines in Diliman but found himself, along with his fellow students, in the middle of the People's Revolution at Manila. They started asking themselves what they as theater artists might be able to contribute to the growing politicization of the people against the oppressive government. With the protest marches right on the streets of the university, Peña and his classmates could not justify getting back behind the safety of the theater's four walls. Thus Peña began creating and performing theater on the streets, in the rice fields, and during protests.

Peña and his colleagues were building a repertoire of street theater in Manila at the heart of the daily protests to oust the dictatorship of Ferdinand Marcos. They employed a variety of theater techniques such as the use of masks, mimes, and giant puppets. They traveled all over the Philippines and conducted theater workshops with farm workers, factory workers, parents, and children. These community-based theater workshops not only brought out the stories of the people and identified crises in a given community, but also served as calls to action.

In fear of his son's political involvement, Peña's father urged him to complete his studies in the United States. In 1984, Peña found himself in Orange County, California. The contrast between the tumultuous environment he had just departed and the sanitized Orange County left Peña unable to speak. Peña explained this aphasia as survival guilt during a recorded interview with the students in a drama class at the University of Massachusetts. He was "escaping to the bastion of Republicanism" while some of his friends were being imprisoned and others killed (Students' interview). As a theater artist, he did not quite know how he could work with productions such as *Fiddler on the Roof* (Students' interview). Therefore, he started a theater company focusing on the issues of the Philippines while he was still a student at the University of California at Los Angeles, but the effort was short-lived because he decided to pursue his theater training as a Birch Foundation scholar at the Circle in the Square Professional Actors' Conservatory in New York.

In 1991, Peña revisited the idea of a theater dedicated to the lives of Filipinos through the creation of the New York–based Ma-Yi Theatre Ensemble. Peña, along with his Filipino theater colleagues in the United States, established Ma-Yi for Filipino American theater artists and produced works that are complex and meaningful to the Filipino communities across the world. Peña still serves as Ma-Yi's artistic director. His association with other Asian American theater companies is most noted in his capacity of director and playwright.

MAJOR WORKS AND THEMES

As an artistic director, Peña has moved Ma-Yi Theater Ensemble into its ninth year of producing works by and about Filipino Americans. In its first few years, Peña and his fellow artists sought to re-create the theater they had in the early 1980s in the Philippines, focusing on the issues back in their homeland. But after examining what they had truly learned from their early works, they redirected the ensemble's focus to the experiences of Filipinos in the United States. Filipinos in the United States have their own issues and history that may be connected to the Philippines but certainly not in its margins or in its shadow. Under his directorship, plays like *Waiting for Lefty* by Clifford Odets, *Baby with Bathwater* by Christopher Durang, *Three Sisters* by Anton Chekhov, and *Almanac of a Revolution* by Nicholas Pichay as well as *Disyembre* and *Kuti-Kutitap* of his own have been either stage-read or produced. He is now involved in an initiative toward the development of Asian American directors.

Peña as a playwright engages his work with issues of displacement, exile, and alienation. In *Cinema Verite* (1991), Peña examines the dynamics of the Filipino gay community in the face of AIDS. The play is a solo piece with a gay porn actor who refuses to leave his world of pornography. Peña's human cartographies challenge the boundaries of race and sexuality as the play stages an immigrant narrative that is complexly queer. Peña's characters cannot be understood as traditionally "gay" but more as embattled protagonists. They struggle with balancing a language of desire with a language of belonging in a nation-space that both welcomes and minoritizes them as subjects.

However, *Flipzoids* (1996) is Peña's first play that truly broke ground across Asian American theaters in the United States and the Philippines. As the "ultimate identity piece," the play was his way to exorcise the turmoil of cultural schizophrenia from his perspective as an artist of color and as an immigrant (Burns 3). *Flipzoids* explores the subject of identity through three carefully constructed Filipino characters, all of whom are newly established archetypes in the literature of the Filipino diaspora. Aying is the unchanging elderly woman (the *lola* figure) who only knows the ways of the Philippines; Vangie, the middle-aged professional who insists on becoming "American" at the expense of the homeland; and Redford, the one-and-a-half-generation Filipino American who has heard of this not-so-distant country of the Philippines, but whose access has only been through other people's memories and stories. Peña says, "All three characters are refracted self-images" (*Flipzoids* 146). Struggling with their choice of living as part of the Filipino diaspora, they all search deep and wide for who they really are in a country that accepts them legally and rejects them culturally.

CRITICAL RECEPTION

Flipzoids has been received incredibly well in the United States and the Philippines. In the last three years, *Flipzoids* has been produced in San Diego Asian American Repertory Theatre, Kumu Kahua Theatre in Honolulu, and Northwest Asian American Theatre in Seattle, in addition to Ma-Yi's production in New York and its tour at the New WORLD Theater in Amherst, Massachusetts. In 1998, Ma-Yi brought this production to the Cultural Center of the Philippines. Doreen Fernandez, one of the foremost critics and scholars of Philippine theater, writes in a review, "Of all the explorations into the experience of Filipinos in America that I have witnessed—in stories, novels, poems, plays, lectures, analyses—I found this the most effective so far, luminous and eloquent, deeply moving" (7D). It was also named as one of the 1996 Best in Queer Theatre by Andrew Velez for the *Newspaper for Lesbian and Gay New York* (15). Ching Valdes was awarded a 1997 Obie Award, New York's most prestigious award for off- and off-off-Broadway theater productions, for her role of Aying in Ma-Yi's New York production.

Peña's works have been produced and commissioned by many, including the Rockefeller Foundation, South Coast Repertory, Joseph Papp Public Theatre, New York Ethical Society, the Henry Street Settlement, and Theatre for the New City. However, they have not yet received the kind of critical studies they deserve, partly because his works had not been available in print until 1999 when *Flipzoids* was first published, and partly because scholarship in Asian American theater remains a growing field.

BIBLIOGRAPHY

Works by Ralph B. Peña

Drama

Flipzoids. Tokens? The NYC Asian American Experience on Stage. Ed. Alvin Eng. New York: Asian American Writers' Workshop, 1999. 145–84.

Unpublished Manuscripts

Cinema Verite. 1991.
Kuti-Kutitap. Music. Lerrick Santos. 1993.
Disyembre. 1996.
Kape Barako. 1997.
December. 1998.
Full on Empty. 2000.
Loose Leaf Binding. 2000.
Sound of Falling Light. 2000.

Selected Production History

Cinema Verite

Production. Theatre for the New City, New York City, 1991.
———. Ma-Yi Theatre Ensemble, New York City, 1991.

Kuti-Kutitap

Production. Ma-Yi Theatre Ensemble, New York City, 1993.

Disyembre

Production. New York Ethical Society, New York City, 1996.

Flipzoids

Production, dir. Loy Arcenas. Ma-Yi Theatre Company, New York City, 1996.
———, dir. Ralph Peña. New WORLD Theater, U of Massachusetts, Amherst, MA, 1997.
———(tour), dir. Loy Arcenas. Cultural Center of the Philippines, Manila, 1998.
———, dir. Chil Kong. Northwest Asian American Theatre, Seattle, 1998.
———, dir. Naoko Maeshiba. Kumu Kahua Theatre, Honolulu, 1998.
———, dir. Randy Kaplan; perf. Michelle Hui, Jacalyn Lee, and Carl Marcelo. Robert Sinclair Theatre, State U of New York, Geneseo, 1999.
———, dir. George Ye. Asian American Repertory Theatre, San Diego, 2000.

Kape Barako

Production. Joseph Papp Public Theater, New York City, 1997.

Full on Empty

Production, South Coast Repertory, Costa Mesa, CA, 2000.

Interview

Interview by students in Roberta Uno and Harley Erdman's "Dramaturgy in Action." U
of Massachusetts at Amherst. Videocassette. 17 Oct. 1997.

Studies of Ralph B. Peña

Burns, Lucy Mae San Pablo. "Ralph B. Peña." Interview. *Notes for a New World: News-
letter of the New WORLD Theater* 20.3 (Fall 1997): 3.
Eng, Alvin, ed. *Tokens? The NYC Asian American Experience on Stage.* New York:
Asian American Writers' Workshop, 1999.
Fernandez, Doreen. Review of *Flipzoids. Philippine Inquirer* June 1998: 7D.
Manalansan, Martin F. "(Re)locating the Gay Filipino: Resistance, Postcolonialism, and
Identity." *Journal of Homosexuality* 26.2–3 (Aug.–Sept. 1993): 53–96.
Van Erven, Eugene. *The Playful Revolution: Theatre and Liberation in Asia.* Blooming-
ton: Indiana UP, 1992.
Velez, Andrew. "Arts for Lesbian and Gay New York: 1996's Best in Queer Theatre."
Newspaper for Lesbian and Gay New York 20 Jan. 1997: 15.

Santha Rama Rau
(1923–   )

Leela Kapai

BIOGRAPHY

Santha Rama Rau, the second daughter of Benegal and Dhanvanthi Rama Rau, was born on January 24, 1923, in Madras, India. She had a privileged upbringing by educated and enlightened parents; her father, educated at Cambridge, England, served in the highly selective Indian Civil Service during the British rule, and her mother was a college teacher of English literature before her marriage.

Santha Rama Rau matriculated from St. Paul's Girls' School, London, in 1939. Her vacation in South Africa, where her father was a diplomat, was interrupted when World War II broke out, and the Rau sisters could not obtain a return passage to England. Thus they spent the next two years with their mother in India. Staying with her orthodox Brahmin grandparents provided the anglicized Rau an opportunity to learn about her Indian heritage.

Because of the political unrest in India, Santha Rama Rau chose to go to the United States for further education in 1941. She majored in English literature and received a B.A. with honors from Wellesley College in 1944. The publication of her first book, *Home to India*, in 1945 started her on a writing career.

On her return to India in 1945, Rau worked as an editor for *Trend*, a magazine published in Bombay. After India gained independence in 1947, her father was appointed the first Indian ambassador to Japan. Santha Rama Rau accompanied him as his official hostess. Her stay in Japan and subsequent trips to China, Indochina, Siam, Indonesia, and later Russia provided the material for her other books.

Rau's success as a writer has earned her several honors. She was awarded honorary degrees by Bates College in 1961, by Roosevelt College (now a university) in 1962, by Brandeis University in 1963, and by Bard College in 1964.

MAJOR WORKS AND THEMES

Santha Rama Rau's claim to be a playwright rests solely on her acclaimed dramatization of E.M. Forster's novel *A Passage to India*. Rau recounts the genesis of her work in "Remembering E.M. Forster." In 1957, Cheryl Crawford of the Group Theatre in New York suggested that Rau dramatize *A Passage to India*. Though Rau had never written a play, she had always been interested in drama, so the thought intrigued her. The play that began as a mere literary exercise ended up earning Forster's unconditional approval. Forster signed an agreement for the Broadway production; however, the details did not work out, and the play remained shelved until 1959. Frank Hauser, the director of the Meadow Players, approached Rau about producing the play at the Oxford Playhouse. The play finally opened in Oxford on January 19, 1960, and was well reviewed by critics from London dailies and local magazines.

Turning a novel into a play understandably requires omissions and modifications, and Santha Rama Rau's dramatization of *A Passage to India* is no exception. It is remarkable how well she succeeds in preserving the spirit of the novel. Forster's novel has several themes: the relationship between the colonial masters and the native population, the effect of colonialism on the colonizers, the difficulty of understanding the complexity of India, and the almost impossible task of reconciling the East and the West. Forster also touches upon the theme of interpersonal relationships, not just between the British and the Indians, but among the ruling class as well. To maintain the unity of action, Rau chooses to focus on only one of these themes, the Aziz-Fielding friendship that epitomizes the relationship between the East and the West. She attempts to convey the rich texture of the novel by providing extensive stage directions.

The play is presented in three acts. Act 1, set in Fielding's residence, brings Aziz, Mrs. Moore, and Adela Quested together. Aziz is brought on the stage before the ladies arrive, thus allowing the audience to understand Aziz's enthusiasm, curiosity, and developing fondness for Fielding. By the end of the act, Aziz has set the stage for the ensuing tragedy by inviting everyone to a picnic at the Marabar Hills. Act 2 has two scenes: the first takes the audience to the caves, retaining the original details of Fielding's missing the train and arriving later. Rau takes the liberty of changing some details here. In the play, Adela Quested is rescued by Mrs. Callender, the civil surgeon's wife, rather than by Miss Derek, a secretary. The change allows a smooth transition to the next scene. The second scene takes place in the English Club, where the British reaction to this explosive episode is aired. Act 3 is set in the courthouse; Adela Quested, already doubting her memory of the incident, finally recants her allegation. The scene ends with the English ruling class deserting Adela Quested. The play comes full circle with the closing scene again between Fielding and Aziz. The use of the "punkah-wallah," the man who pulls the rope to move the fan, in the last scene is particularly effective, for it reinforces the image of unfathomable and unflappable India.

Though the play stays close to the original plot of *A Passage to India*, its limited scope diminishes the portrayal of Mrs. Moore and, to some extent, of Adela Quested. The omission of the last section of the novel—Fielding's marriage to Mrs. Moore's daughter and his later meeting with Aziz—certainly impoverishes the plot but does not affect the overall thematic emphasis.

Rau has also authored two novels, but she is primarily known for her travel writing. All of her works are variations on the theme of East-West encounter and are rooted in her experiences and travels. Santha Rama Rau's works are distinguished by her ability to capture the mood of the place she describes. Her sensitivity to people of all cultures is reflected in the sympathetic portrayals of people she met in all the countries during her travels. Her cosmopolitan background, in conjunction with a clear sense of her own heritage, gives a special edge to her writing.

CRITICAL RECEPTION

Widely acclaimed as a writer of travelogues, Santha Rama Rau has received very little critical attention as a dramatist. In the only book-length study of her works, S.K. Desai provides a critical summary of her works and devotes a short chapter to the dramatization of *A Passage to India*, comparing the novel and the play. Ragini Ramachandra notes very briefly Rau's success as a playwright in her article. Roshni Rustomji-Kerns focuses primarily on the travel books and fiction of Rau.

Most of the observations on Rau's playwriting skills come from the contemporary reviews of the play. The opening at the Oxford Playhouse in January 1960 drew very favorable reviews of her play. Walter Kerr for the London *Times* remarked, "Her rearrangement of his [Forster's] material is skillful, and the result is very far from being what is called, disparagingly, a novelist's play" (6). A.V. Coton paid tribute to Rau's "respect for the original and to her self discipline that she has not unduly rarefied, unbalanced or simplified this tragic-comic study of Anglo-Indian relations under the British Raj" (12). When the play moved to the Comedy Theatre in London, Kerr observed that the play "reflects clearly and excitingly remarkable sensitive and faithful rendering of the novel" (6). W.A. Darlington also spoke of "the miraculous ingenuity" with which "the adapter had kept within the author's reach" (14). Reviewing the Broadway presentation in 1962, Howard Taubman praised the "clever dramatization and its incandescent performance" (L23). Kerr commended Rau for accomplishing the most difficult thing, her rendering of the characters: "While talking a great deal about the mystery of India, she has almost surreptitiously dramatized the mystery of character" (6). These observations clearly confirm Rau's success in transforming *A Passage to India* into a play.

BIBLIOGRAPHY

Works by Santha Rama Rau

Drama

A Passage to India: A Play by Santha Rama Rau from the Novel by E.M. Forster. London: Edwin Arnold, 1960.

Selected Production History

A Passage to India

Production, dir. Frank Hauser. Oxford Playhouse, Oxford, UK, 1960.
————. Cambridge Arts Theatre, Cambridge, UK, 1960.
————, dir. Donald Albery. Comedy Theatre, London, 1960.
————, dir. Donald McWhinnie; prod. Lawrence Langner. Wilbur Theatre, Boston, 1962.
————; prod. Lawrence Langner. Ambassador Theatre, New York City, 1962.

Autobiography/Memoirs

Home to India. New York: Harper, 1945.
Gifts of Passage. New York: Harper, 1961.
"Remembering E.M. Forster." *Grand Street* 5.4 (Summer 1986): 99–119.

Novels

Remember the House. New York: Harper, 1956.
The Adventuress. New York: Harper, 1970.

Travel Books

East of Home. London: Gollancz, 1951.
This Is India. New York: Harper, 1954.
View to the Southeast. New York: Harper, 1957.
My Russian Journey. New York: Harper, 1959.

Studies of Santha Rama Rau

Coton, A.V. "A Passage to India." *Daily Telegraph* 20 Jan. 1960: 12.
Darlington, W.A. "A Passage to India." *Daily Telegraph* 21 Apr. 1960: 14.
Desai, S.K. *Santha Rama Rau.* New Delhi: Arnold-Heinemann, 1976.
Kerr, Walter. "A Passage to India." *Times* (London) 20 Jan. 1960: 6.
————. "A Passage to India." *Times* (London) 20 Apr. 1960: 16.
————. "A Passage to India." *New York Herald Tribune* 1 Feb. 1962: 10. Rpt. in *New York Theatre Critics Reviews* 23 (1962): 373.
Ramachandra, Ragini. "Santha Rama Rau: The Imagination of Fact." *Commonwealth Quarterly* 3.9 (1978): 204–23.
Rustomji-Kerns, Roshni. "Expatriates, Immigrants, and Literature: Three South Asian Women Writers." *Massachusetts Review* 29 (Winter 1988–89): 655–65.
Taubman, Howard. "A Passage to India." *New York Times* 1 Feb. 1962: L23.

Sung Jung Rno
(1967–   )

Daphne P. Lei

BIOGRAPHY

Sung Jung Rno (pronounced "no") was born in Minneapolis on July 29, 1967. His parents, both from Korea, came to the United States in the 1960s for graduate study. He grew up in Minneapolis and the suburbs of Washington, D.C., and spent his high-school years in Cincinnati. Rno credits his parents with introducing him to theater at an early age; he first saw *Waiting for Godot* when he was only five.

As a high-school student, Rno excelled both in science and in writing. He received his B.A. in 1988 in physics from Harvard University but went on to study poetry writing at Brown University. "I started out as an aspiring physicist who also wanted to write," but "gradually the writing desire became stronger" ("Interview One"). At a workshop with Paula Vogel at Brown in 1990, he wrote the first draft of *Cleveland Raining*. With Vogel's encouragement, Rno sent this play out and received immediate positive responses from the outside theater world. It received a staged reading at Pan Asian Repertory Theatre in 1990, won first prize at the Seattle Multicultural Playwrights' Festival in 1992, and premiered at the East West Players in 1995. Rno received his M.F.A. in poetry from Brown in 1991. Some of his poems have appeared in journals and anthologies.

The workshop at Brown proved to be a turning point in Rno's life. In the past decade, Rno has remained active in playwriting, but has also retained his interest in science. He received the Van Lier Playwriting Fellowship at New Dramatists (1993–1995) and at New York Theater Workshop (1995–1996) and was resident artist at Millay Colony for the Arts in 1994 and at Mabou Mines in 1999. He now lives in New York and is considering venturing into film and novel writing.

MAJOR WORKS AND THEMES

Rno's love of science and poetry is clearly reflected in his works. In his plays, he often interweaves dream and reality, absurdity and melancholy, science and poetry to create stylistically distinctive works, which Rno himself terms "metaphysical tragicomedies" ("Interview One"). His first play, *Cleveland Raining* (1990), remains his best-known play and his only published dramatic work. Set in a rural area south of Cleveland during an apocalyptic era, *Cleveland Raining* deals with a dysfunctional Korean American family. The Kims are "a family of leavers": "We leave Korea. Then we leave each other" (267). The immigrant parents have disappeared, leaving the second-generation children to deal with their abandonment, injury, pain, memories, and the mundaneness of daily life. The gloomy Mari, a failed pianist who also has given up her medical studies, is the family caretaker and is still searching for their missing father. Her brother Jimmy Rodin, a failed painter and fired stock boy (he sees a woman asking for bananas in the market as a kind of racial slur), is trying to be a prophet. He wants to build a Noah's Ark out of a Volkswagen because he believes that a deluge is going to bring the end of the world. The two siblings painfully cling to their broken home and to each other as two outsiders enter their lives. Storm, a leather-clad woman biker who denies her own Asian heritage, accidentally killed her own grandmother in a crash. Mick, the only non-Asian character, is the mechanic who is convinced by Jimmy to convert the Volkswagen into a boat. After numerous experiments, they discover that the only fuel to start this vessel is "emotional loss" (247). At the end, Jimmy reveals the note his father left for his children: "Remember to forget" (267). Rain begins to fall.

Although nature can be indifferent to humans, it is the various forms of human creation that are responsible for conflicts and sufferings in the modern world. Rno's plays of the early 1990s seem to share such a thematic focus. Adapted from short stories by the Korean writer Hwang Sun-won, the three plays collected in *Drizzle and Other Stories* (1992) deal with the origins of loss and pain. *In a Small Village, Drizzle,* and *Masks* depict nature and war as the sources of human suffering, both of them vast, alluring, and arbitrary. *Konishini, Mon Amour* (1993) focuses on the human creation of conflict in yet another form: representations and misrepresentations of Asians in the U.S. mass media. *New World* (1994) depicts various aspects of colonization and exploitation. But the disastrous nature of human demarcation is fully exposed on stage in Rno's next play, *Gravity Falls from Trees.*

Gravity Falls from Trees (1994), Rno's second most frequently produced play, deals again with the arbitrariness of human creation, namely, national boundaries. Eleven years after Korean Air Lines Flight 007 was shot down by the Soviets, the play is set in a hospital room, where Isabella, a Korean American woman, is seeking medical help for her mysterious "chills." Her body temperature reads symbolically 74.7 degrees Fahrenheit. Later the hospital room is transformed into a cloud and an apple is suspended in midair. Now Isabella's doctor Francis Park has become Captain Park, the pilot who was in charge of Flight 007, and his colleague Ike, the physicist Isaac Newton. They are trying to solve the mystery of Isabella's illness and the apple that defies gravity. Rno intriguingly links the idea of Cold War, human frigidity, the Flight 007 tragedy, and gravity. At the end of the play, Isabella finds the answer: "We have created a world where we can't just fly wherever we want to. We have to worry about boundaries. We have to worry about gravity." As the apple finally falls to the ground, Newton discovers his fourth law: "Gravity falls from trees."

Rno's more recent works tackle traditional themes with symbolism of a digital era. While *Principia* (1996) explores the law of the jungle in the world of scientific research, *wAve* (1999) is a futuristic version of Euripides' *Medea*. The Korean American woman M is betrayed by her husband Jason when he abandons their family computer business and falls in love with Marilyn II, an actress digitized and synthesized from Marilyn Monroe's DNA by media moguls. After destroying Marilyn II, M gets her revenge by herself becoming a movie star. *Yi Sang Counts to 13* (1999) goes one step further in Rno's experiment with the surrealist theater tradition in an Asian American context. In this play, Diet Coke, the symbol of modern Western capitalism and imperialism, is drunk in the style of the traditional Japanese tea ceremony.

CRITICAL RECEPTION

Since most of Rno's plays have only received workshops or staged readings, the critical response to his works consists of theater reviews, mostly of his two best-known plays, *Cleveland Raining* and *Gravity Falls from Trees*. In general, critics applaud Rno's witty and humorous dialogue and imaginative and original plots. His style of mixed fantasy and reality, absurdity and melancholy, reminds the audience of the works of Samuel Beckett, Jean-Paul Sartre, and Sam Shepard. His settings, whether a sky-blue Volkswagen in *Cleveland Raining* (the only real object against the fluid and ephemeral background) or an apple suspended above the hospital room/cloud in *Gravity Falls from Trees*, seem to be extremely effective. However, a number of reviews suggest that the structure of his plays is problematic and the endings are often unconvincing.

Writing about *Cleveland Raining*, Roberta Penn of the *Seattle Post-Intelligencer* sees Rno as "a sharp writer, weaving in humorous quips among the painful whiplashes of the characters' lives. But he doesn't know how to end the play" (C5). Penn believes that Rno has not supplied a real solution for the problems, and the unreal solution (the characters sail away in the Volkswagen-turned-boat) does not seem persuasive. Similarly, Misha Berson of the *Seattle Times* writes, "As trenchantly humorous as *Cleveland Raining* can be, it hangs in one key rather than modulating and developing its themes" (D24). However, critics generally like the intelligent dialogue and the ambiance Rno creates. Judith Green points out in her review in the *San Jose Mercury News*, "The charm of the play is in its flavor: dialogue that snaps and curls and tingles, like the kim chee [the spicy Korean version of sauerkraut] that Rodin eats for breakfast, lunch and dinner" (3D).

Gravity Falls from Trees also received mixed reviews. The play's grand questions—about the Cold War, gravity, dreams, and memory—are generally unanswerable. For some critics, the charm of the play lies in its elliptical approach; however, others believe that although various parts shine, they are pieced together rather mechanically and do not cohere well. The ending provides another problem. Steven Winn of the *San Francisco Chronicle* writes: "The resolution . . . is less than satisfying. . . . The apple finally falls, but without much dramatic effect" ("*Gravity*" D3). "The fourth law isn't well enough developed to sound like anything more than wishful thinking," according to Robert Hurwitt of the *San Francisco Examiner* ("Mystical" C1).

Rno's plays encompass a wide range of topics, styles, and scales, and it is not fair to evaluate his works as a whole by reading only the reviews of his two major plays. The critical reception of his two major works suggests that in general, audiences are enticed by the theatricality that Rno presents on stage: a world that is often both realistic and absurdly implausible and a mental state that exists between dream and scientific fantasies, presented in dialogue that is sharp, witty, and humorous. Although some critics are troubled by the way he structures his plays, Rno's problem is "on the side of creative excess," as Robert Hurwitt puts it ("Apocalyptic" C5). Although Rno has received mixed reviews of his works, he has clearly established his unique dramatic style, and with more plays produced, he is likely to enjoy greater successes in the very near future.

BIBLIOGRAPHY

Works by Sung Jung Rno

Drama

Cleveland Raining. But Still, Like Air, I'll Rise: New Asian American Plays. Ed. Velina Hasu Houston. Philadelphia: Temple UP, 1997. 227–270.

Unpublished Manuscripts

"This Light So Quiet." M.F.A. thesis. Brown U, 1991.
Drizzle and Other Stories. 1992.
Konishini, Mon Amour. 1993.
Gravity Falls from Trees. 1994.
New World. 1994.
Change. 1995.
Principia. 1996.

wAve. 1999.
Yi Sang Counts to 13. 1999.

Selected Production History

Cleveland Raining

Staged reading. Pan Asian Repertory Theatre, New York City, 1990.
Production, dir. Shishir Kurup; perf. Nelson Mashita, Peggy Ahn, Kei Rowan-Young, and Mark Bringelson. East West Players, Los Angeles, 1995.
————, dir. Octavio Solis; perf. Karen Lee, Michael Torres, Kelvin Han Yee, and Karen Amano. Asian American Theater Company and Thick Description, San Francisco, 1995.
————, dir. Manuel Cawaling; perf. Hans Altwies, Shirley Oliver, Kim Evey, and Jesse Wine. Northwest Asian American Theatre, Seattle, 1996.
————, dir. Andy Lowe; perf. Connie Kim, Robert Dahey, Norman Victor Mackinnon, and Kimberly Miller. San Diego Asian American Repertory Theatre, San Diego, 1999.

Drizzle and Other Stories

Staged reading, dir. Tzi Ma. East West Players, Los Angeles, 1994.

Gravity Falls from Trees

Production, dir. Lenora Champagne. Dance Theater Workshop, New York City, 1994.
————, dir. Karen Amano; perf. Steve Park, Rania Ho, and Michael Lopez. Asian American Theater Company, San Francisco, 1997.

New World

Staged reading. Public Theater New Work Now!, New York City, 1994.
Production, dir. Marcy Arlin. Immigrants' Theater Project, New York City, 1997.

Principia

Workshop, dir. Lenora Champagne. New York Theater Workshop, New York City, 1996.

wAve

Staged reading, dir. Jon Rivera. Mark Taper Forum, Los Angeles, 1999.
————, dir. Naoko Maeshiba. Arena Stage, Washington, DC, 2000.
————, dir. Chay Yew. Public Theater New Work Now!, New York City, 2000.
————, dir. Kelvin Han Yee. Asian American Theater Company, San Francisco, 2000.

Yi Sang Counts to 13

Staged reading, dir. Sung Rno. Mabou Mines, New York City, 1999.
Production, dir. Lee Breuer. Seoul Theater Festival 2000/Arts for Living, Seoul, Korea, 2000.
————, dir. Sung Jung Rno. Kraine Theater, New York City, 2001.

Essay

"The Fear of Being American." *Korean Journal* July 1994: 9.

Interviews

"Interview One." Personal interview. 22 Apr. 2000.
"Interview Two." Personal interview. 12 May 2000.

"Interview Three." Personal interview. 4 June 2000.
"Interview Four." Personal interview. 19 June 2000.

Poetry

"Another Place." *Dickinson Review* 24 (1990): 15.

"Window" and "Night." *Caliban* 11 (1992): 91–92.

"The Mounds." *Chaminade Literary Review* 6.1 (1992): 51–53. Rpt. in *Asian Pacific American Journal* 1.2 (1992): 48–49; *Premonitions: The Kaya Anthology of New Asian North American Poetry.* Ed. Walter Lew. New York: Kaya Productions, 1995. 514–16.

"Three Haiku" and "There was something in the air." *Asian Pacific American Journal* 1.2 (1992): 50–51.

"Spring" and "Not Weeds." *Asian Pacific American Journal* 2.2 (1993): 130–33.

"in the case of music gone wrong." *Asian Pacific American Journal* 2.2 (1993): 134. Rpt. in *The NuyorAsian Anthology: Asian American Writings about New York City.* Ed. Bino A. Realuyo and Rahna R. Rizzuto. New York: Asian American Writers' Workshop, 1999. 404.

"April." *Asian Pacific American Journal* 4.2 (1995): 79.

"But Perceived." *Asian Pacific American Journal* 5.1 (1996): 101–2.

"Country." *Premonitions: The Kaya Anthology of New Asian North American Poetry.* Ed. Walter Lew. New York: Kaya Productions, 1995. 517–18.

"Blue October," "Woolworth's," and "Icon," *The NuyorAsian Anthology: Asian American Writings about New York City.* Ed. Bino A. Realuyo and Rahna R. Rizzuto. New York: Asian American Writers' Workshop, 1999. 404–5.

Studies of Sung Jung Rno

Berson, Misha. "A Witty Get-It-off-Our-Chest Reverie, *Cleveland Raining* Searching for Story." *Seattle Times* 18 Jan. 1996: D24.

Green, Judith. "A Beetle's Big Part: Charming Little Play Needs No Plot to Fuel It." *San Jose Mercury News* 20 June 1995: 3D.

Hurwitt, Robert. "Apocalyptic Fun in the *Cleveland* Rain." *San Francisco Examiner* 14 June 1995: C5.

———. "Mystical Encounter with *Gravity*; Play's Layers Are Tough to Navigate." *San Francisco Examiner* 6 June 1997: C1.

Penn, Roberta. "*Cleveland Raining* Floats on Humor above the Murky Depth of Pain." *Seattle Post-Intelligencer* 11 Jan. 1996: C5.

Welsh, Anne Marie. "Uneven *Cleveland Raining* Still Manages to Intrigue Us." *San Diego Union-Tribune* 11 Jan. 1999: E4.

Winer, Laurie. "*Cleveland Raining* Driven by Memories at East West." *Los Angeles Times* 29 Mar. 1995: F2.

Winn, Steven. "*Cleveland Raining* Flooded with Talent." *San Francisco Chronicle* 16 June 1995: C10.

———. "*Gravity* Charming But Weightless; Sleek Production Never Builds Force." *San Francisco Chronicle* 12 June 1997: D3.

Dmae Roberts

(1957–   )

Gary Storhoff

BIOGRAPHY

Dmae Roberts is an Amerasian actor, producer, and playwright, born in Taiwan on November 29, 1957. The daughter of a Taiwanese woman and an Oklahoma GI, Roberts emigrated to America at the age of eight. She grew up in rural Junction City, Oregon, where, as the only multicultural family in town, they contended with "a ton of racism" (Telephone interview). After earning a journalism degree at the University of Oregon in 1984, she worked as a free-lance independent producer, moving to Portland in 1990. Her thirteen-part radio production *Legacies: Tales from America* was broadcast nationwide to more than one hundred stations on National Public Radio (NPR), for whom Roberts has written and produced more than three hundred radio productions.

In 1990, she received the prestigious George Foster Peabody Award for her autobiographical radio docuplay, *Mei Mei, a Daughter's Song*, which was also broadcast on NPR. Based on the docuplay, the Drammy-nominated *Mei Mei* was later produced onstage in Portland. In 1995, Roberts wrote and produced two plays, *Breaking Glass* and *Picasso in the Back Seat*. Considered for the Humana Festival of New Plays, *Breaking Glass* continues her interest in autobiographical drama, and Roberts explains that the play explores "the breaking points, the determinants that spark the individual will to survive" (E-mail). *Picasso* won the Portland Drama Critics Circle Award for Best Original Play and the Oregon Book Award for Best Play. The play dramatizes, Roberts notes, "the value of art in a society that doesn't seem to value the arts" (*Picasso* ii). In 1997, Roberts wrote and produced *Lady Buddha*, a multimedia theatrical work about Kuan Yin, the Asian goddess of compassion. *Tell Me, Janie Bigo* (1998) humorously combines the difficulties of young, single women with cultural issues confronting many Amerasians. Her most recent production, *Volcano Embrace* (1999), is a multimedia work that spans the ages.

Roberts's other awards include grants from the Corporation for Public Broadcasting and the National Endowment for the Arts, the Oregon Arts Commission Fellowship, the United Nations Silver Award, the Robert F. Kennedy Journalism Award, the Oregon Playwrights Award from the Oregon Institute of Literary Arts, the Casey Medal, and the New Langton Arts Fellowship. In 1990, she became the executive director and board chair of MediaRites, a nonprofit agency that promotes tolerance between diverse communities through artistic performance. In this capacity, she often works in schools, writing and performing drama with at-risk students. Roberts married Richard Jensen in 1998 and currently lives in Portland.

MAJOR WORKS AND THEMES

Dmae Roberts says that for her, "writing is a way to make sense of things that really don't make sense" (Telephone interview). Influenced by Maxine Hong Kingston, she feels that her work, along with Kingston's, expresses "a bicultural point of view that usually is not represented anywhere else" (Telephone interview). Like Kingston, Roberts integrates social commentary on biculturalism with fantasy, memory, dream, and wish. As a playwright, Roberts is creatively engaged with the stage's limitations and possibilities. Thus her plays are startlingly experimental as they transcend boundaries of culture, ethnicity, time, and space.

Mei Mei ("little sister") is an autobiographical exploration of a mother-daughter relationship. The play concerns a trip to Taiwan taken by the mother (Mei Jen) and her Taiwanese American daughter Cyndy, but as they visit Taiwan, the play reveals with flashbacks and "sideway turns in time" the young girl Mei Mei who would become Mei Jen. Mei Jen is a remarkable woman who overcame terrible ordeals: she was sold at the age of two, she survived starvation and World War II, and she made great sacrifices for her children. Dream sequences show both Lady Buddha and Ghostwoman keeping her from committing suicide, Mei Mei's perpetual wish. By splicing the adult character (Mei Jen) with her child-self (Mei Mei), Roberts imaginatively dramatizes the formative elements of the mother's character: her resourcefulness, initiative, and courage.

Perhaps because of Mei Jen's strength, she cannot empathize easily with Cyndy. Understandably, Mei Jen expects gratitude and devotion from Cyndy, but Cyndy has been assimilated and educated, and so—again understandably—Cyndy feels alienated from her mother. Cyndy's maturational task in the play is to overcome her emotional distance from her mother and to feel sincerely that they make a "good team." Their emotional union occurs only after Cyndy bravely admits that she uncritically absorbed American middle-class values that led her to look down on her mother. Acknowledging unattractive aspects of herself, Cyndy feels at one with her mother, symbolized by their shared laughter at the play's conclusion.

Mei Jen reappears in *Breaking Glass* (1995), another dramatic study of family dysfunctionality. This play complicates Roberts's domestic theme by introducing Mei Jen's husband, Buddy, a ne'er-do-well Caucasian salesman, and Mei Jen's son, Jimmy, an illiterate but endearing son. The daughter, Rickie, is forced to negotiate her multiple family loyalties while simultaneously creating her own identity; she is burdened by Mei Jen's constant demands, Buddy's pathetic neediness, and Jimmy's many vulnerabilities. The title implies that an individual's "break" from the family is essential for survival, and at the play's climax Mei Jen's ferocious ambition and suffocating love drive Rickie away.

The play's two most compelling characters are Buddy and Jimmy. Buddy is an "Oklahoma country boy" who brings his family to Junction City naïvely hoping to re-create his own idyllic childhood. But this is his tragic mistake: Buddy fails to understand the depth of racism in America, and he misunderstands his Amerasian children's pain. His death in the play is only partly attributable to his heavy smoking, for he cannot reconcile himself to his family's unhappiness. Like his father, Jimmy is likeable and generous. But like Laura Wingfield in Tennessee Williams's *Glass Menagerie*, Jimmy takes refuge from the world by playing with his stained-glass animals. As Rickie's foil, Jimmy fails to escape his home, and the play ends dramatically with his paralysis.

Picasso in the Back Seat (1995) marks an artistic departure for Roberts as she moves away from her autobiographical material to much more abstract themes. Based on a theft of a Picasso painting by two thieves who were caught with it in their car's back seat, the play interrogates art's transformative effect on people. The characters change when they appreciate Picasso's painting, entitled *Tete*. The two thieves, Stone and Finch, become more immediately human, as evidenced by Stone's suddenly acquired emotional capacity and Finch's reconciliation with his deserted wife and child. Moved by the painting, Streets, a homeless woman scarred from childhood, sees herself as spiritually beautiful. But perhaps the most important transformation occurs in Gillian, the museum curator who relentlessly searches for the stolen painting. She is afflicted with cancer, and her acceptance of *Tete*'s loss—and the painting's installation in an underground "museum" for street people—assuages her anguish over life's transitory nature. By understanding the centrality of art in a seemingly indifferent society, Gillian experiences her own spiritual and emotional renewal.

Picasso is also a transitional point in Roberts's career because of the play's radically innovative stagecraft. In a very original move, *Tete* the painting becomes a speaking character whose soothing effect on the characters encourages them to be their best selves. Roberts uses absurdist satire, lighting, dream sequences, illusory characters, and allusions to myth to elevate the play to an abstract level.

Lady Buddha (1997), *Tell Me, Janie Bigo* (1998), and *Volcano Embrace* (1999) continue Roberts's aesthetic experimentation. *Lady Buddha* and *Volcano*

Embrace are multimedia productions that employ dance, puppetry, music, photography, and drama. *Lady Buddha* is a meditation on the need for compassion in society. *Volcano Embrace*, telling the stories of victims of volcanoes since Mt. Vesuvius, makes a subtle connection between tectonic and social disruption. *Janie* is a generic experiment; ostensibly a mystery, it combines comedy, Broadway musicals, and romance with a commentary on the legacy of the Vietnam War. The plot concerns Janie, a Vietnamese American, and her search for her father who abandoned her in Vietnam at the war's end. Despite its comedic emphasis, the play challenges America's complacency about the orphaned children left behind in Vietnam.

In a very brief period of time, then, Roberts has evolved significantly as an artist. Moving from painfully autobiographical studies to impersonal studies of art, she continues to experiment with the possibilities of self-expression on the stage. She is currently writing her memoirs about her childhood and her mother.

CRITICAL RECEPTION

Roberts's work has been performed in Portland and Seattle, and a reading of *Breaking Glass* was presented in Los Angeles. Brief reviews of specific plays may be found in Portland's daily, the *Oregonian*. In general, the reviewers are enthusiastic about her acting, directing, and playwriting talents. The only play that received somewhat weak reviews was *Tell Me, Janie Bigo* for what the reviewer felt was a lack of dramatic cohesiveness (Kantor E4). In nontheatrical reviews, Laurie Winer complained that Roberts's *Breaking Glass* is marred by an overly simplistic analysis of character.

BIBLIOGRAPHY

Works by Dmae Roberts

Drama

Notes. *Picasso in the Back Seat*. Seattle: Rain City Projects, 1995. i–ii.
Picasso in the Back Seat. Seattle: Rain City Projects, 1995.
Breaking Glass. But Still, Like Air, I'll Rise: New Asian American Plays. Ed. Velina Hasu Houston. Philadelphia: Temple UP, 1997. 271–330.
Tell Me, Janie Bigo. With Brenna Sage. Portland: MediaRites, 1998.

Unpublished Manuscripts

Mei Mei, a Daughter's Song. 1990.
Lady Buddha. 1997.
Volcano Embrace. 1999.

Selected Production History

Mei Mei, a Daughter's Song

Production. Artists Repertory Theatre, Portland, 1990.

Picasso in the Back Seat

Production, dir. Staci L. Paley. Artists Repertory Theatre, Portland, 1995.

Tell Me, Janie Bigo

Production, dir. Carmela Lanza-Weil. Interstate Firehouse Cultural Center and Media-Rites, Portland, 1998.
Production. Northwest Asian American Theatre, Seattle, 1999.

Lady Buddha

Production. Interstate Firehouse Cultural Center and MediaRites, Portland, 1997.

Breaking Glass

Production. Artists Repertory Theatre, Portland, 1995.
Staged reading. East West Players, Los Angeles, 1996.

Interview

Telephone interview. 21 June 2000.

Letter

E-mail to the author. 26 June 2000.

Studies of Dmae Roberts

Fitzgibbon, Joe. "Dmae Roberts Seeks Peace and Justice through Drama." *Portland Oregonian* 1 Oct. 1998: 3.
Kantor, Jill. "Comedic *Janie Bigo* Can't Quite Hit Its Mark." *Portland Oregonian* 29 Sept. 1998: E4.
Watternberg, Richard. "Volcano Embrace Taps Tectonic Terrors." *Portland Oregonian* 12 Nov. 1999: E6.
Winer, Laurie. "A Collection with Much Missing." Rev. of *But Still, Like Air, I'll Rise: New Asian American Plays*, ed. Velina Hasu Houston. *Los Angeles Times* 31 Aug. 1997, Calendar: 42.

Edward Sakamoto

(1940–   )

Nikolas Huot

BIOGRAPHY

Born and raised in Hawaii, Edward Sakamoto grew up in the A'ala Park neighborhood in Honolulu, where his family owned a store. His interest in writing began in the ninth grade when he rewrote the end of Robert Louis Stevenson's *Treasure Island* for extra credit. Following enthusiastic reviews from his teacher, Sakamoto was "hooked for life" (Odo xx). At the University of Hawaii, Sakamoto briefly flirted with an acting career; however, the constant traveling and auditioning and, especially, the thought that Asian American actors were restricted to the same demeaning roles on the stage as in television and in the movies led him to abandon the stage. He later wrote to the *Los Angeles Times* about this typecasting in "Anna May Wong and the Dragon-Lady Syndrome." As a way of counteracting this absence of Asian Americans in substantial roles, Sakamoto decided to concentrate his energy on writing plays "where Asian Americans are the 'stars,' where the central characters were us and not them, and the stories revolved around us" (Odo xx).

His first play, *In the Alley*, was written while he was a junior at the University of Hawaii and was produced there after it received a campus prize. This was to be Sakamoto's last play written on Hawaiian soil. In 1966, four years after his graduation, Sakamoto moved to the mainland: "I had to. Hawaii seemed too small for a youthful dreamer. You have to go to the mainland to better yourself, to get opportunities unavailable here" ("Taste" B1). Sakamoto settled in Los Angeles, where he found work at the *Los Angeles Times*, and started to write again. His second play, *Yellow Is My Favorite Color*, was staged in 1972 by the East West Players and its artistic director, Mako. The relationship between Sakamoto and Mako's East West Players proved to be a lasting and valuable one, as the theater group has staged all but one of Sakamoto's fifteen plays at least once.

Even if his relocation to the mainland has been a right move for his career, Sakamoto's decision to leave Hawaii still haunts him: "If I stayed in Hawaii, I might have been happier. Or maybe I might have been frustrated. The point is I'll never know" (Oi). Wondering if he should have ever left and yearning to return home, Sakamoto has expressed more than once the "irreconcilable pain of displacement": "we don't belong on the mainland and we don't belong in Hawaii anymore" (Carroll, "Sakamoto" 6 and Gordon B6). Feeling "in limbo" as a Hawaii exile, Sakamoto admits that "every time someone calls him an 'ex-Hawaii' or 'former Hawaii' resident, a little piece of him dies" (Gordon B6). Yet Sakamoto wonders if exiles like him belong on the island and if they can ever find and reclaim the home they left behind. Although Sakamoto is determined to return to Hawaii, as he assured Franklin Odo in a personal interview, he still lives in the Los Angeles area and settles for writing about Hawaii and about the dilemmas and issues faced by expatriates like himself. Of the fifteen plays he has written, ten (*A'ala Park*, *Aloha Las Vegas*, *Dead of Night*, *In the Alley*, *Lava*, *The Life of the Land*, *Manoa Valley*, *Our Hearts Were Touched with Fire*, *Stew Rice*, and *The Taste of Kona Coffee*) are set in Hawaii.

MAJOR WORKS AND THEMES

As Dennis Carroll and other reviewers have noted, the process of at least one character exploring what "home" means is central to Sakamoto's plays set in Hawaii. In his ten Hawaiian plays, Sakamoto introduces a character who considers leaving Hawaii and settling down on the mainland. In this way, Sakamoto questions how far the concept of "home" is linked to a physical locale, whether one can carry "home" during one's relocation, how the vision of "home" changes while one is away, and, more importantly, whether one "can ever come 'home' again" (Carroll, "Sakamoto" 5). As Dennis Carroll writes in his introduction to *Aloha Las Vegas and Other Plays*, "the nature and extent of personal sociocultural transformation in a new home is one common denominator of all Sakamoto's Hawaii plays" (Carroll, "Sakamoto" 5). Specifically, this dilemma of home is presented in terms of the old against the new, Hawaii versus the mainland, and Japanese values versus American values.

If relocation to the mainland seems like a simple geographical move for certain individuals, for Sakamoto's characters it becomes an extremely difficult and crucial decision that will drastically change their lives and personalities. In his plays, Sakamoto underlines quite clearly the sacrifices that await the Japanese Americans who decide to move to the mainland. Indeed, the characters must not only leave behind their birthplaces, their families, and the support of their ethnic community, but must also abandon their unique culture to embark on a journey toward racism and acculturation. For Sakamoto's characters, "moving to the Mainland is as big a deal as it would be for an Italian or an Irishman to immigrate to the United States" (Drake 6). However, the European immigrants may not necessarily have to struggle with the questions like "whether to become 'haolefied' or assimilated into the 'white' culture, and to what extent" (Drake 6). Although most Hawaiians who relocate know of the cultural sacrifices involved in the move to the mainland (some actually look forward to them), none are fully prepared for what awaits them on the continent, nor are they prepared for their reception back in Hawaii.

Despite heartfelt attempts to fit in and embrace American values, Sakamoto's expatriates are always cast aside and looked down upon. As Russell in *Stew Rice* points out, "Sure, we try to fit in, we make believe like we're haoles, but the haoles will always look at us like we're foreigners, aliens with funny eyes and yellow skin living in their white society" (*Stew* 123). The expatriates are also received with the same kind of alienation and resentment on their return "home." On the island of Kona during a school break but anxiously waiting to return to the mainland to pursue his education, Jiro feels like he is "a stranger to [his] old friends and even [his] family": "When we were kids, [Tomiko] used to talk to me. But since I've been on the mainland, she treats me like an outcast. Other people do the same thing" (*Taste* 33–34). Spencer, in *The Life of the Land*, is also welcomed with resentment by his sister on his return: "You think you can come home and tell me wat I gotta do? Wat do you know about wat happened while you were having a good time on da mainland? Now I gotta listen to you, my wise little bruddah who went to da mainland?" (*Life* 129). Despite the alienation faced at home and the isolation and discrimination found on the continent, the mainland still appears the better place to live for individuals who are trying to define themselves in what they perceive as a culturally and geographically restrictive environment.

In his Hawaii plays, Sakamoto is also preoccupied with the cultural push and pull factors behind the relocations. The characters in these plays are either moving away from Hawaii because they want to "disconnect" from their Japanese heritage or are moving toward the mainland because they want to embrace the American culture. For many of Sakamoto's nisei and sansei, the way of the future lies not with traditional values in Hawaii, but toward progress and Americanization on the mainland. At the same time, however, the majority of expatriates are returning to Hawaii to get in touch with the culture and with parts of themselves they had forgotten or are moving away from the mainland because of discrimination and racism. Regardless of the reasons for relocating, on their return, the expatriates are always left wondering if they can ever reclaim Hawaii as their home.

CRITICAL RECEPTION

So far, only half of Sakamoto's plays have been published: *In the Alley* appeared in an anthology of plays produced by the Kumu Kahua Theatre (1983); *The Taste of Kona Coffee, Manoa Valley*, and *The Life of the Land* formed the

Kamiya family trilogy *Hawai'i No Ka Oi* (1995); and *A'ala Park, Aloha Las Vegas*, and *Stew Rice* were published in *Aloha Las Vegas and Other Plays* (2000). Upon *In the Alley*'s publication, Dennis Carroll, the director of the Kumu Kahua Theatre and editor of the play collection, commented that it was "possibly the best short play ever written in Hawaii on the dynamics of racial conflicts" (*Kumu Kahua Plays* 123). Besides praise, Sakamoto has received so far two Hollywood Dramalogue Critic's awards for outstanding achievement in writing for *Chikamatsu's Forest* and *Stew Rice*, the Po'okela Award for Excellence in Original Script for *Aloha Las Vegas*, and the Hawaii Award for Literature in 1997. He has also been the recipient of grants from the National Endowment for the Arts and the Rockefeller Foundation.

As would be expected from the acclaim Sakamoto has won, Sakamoto's plays have been well received by the public as well as by the majority of theater reviewers. The playwright's ability to write effective comedies where spectators "care about every [character] down to the last line" (Bruckner E5) and his great aptness at re-creating Hawaiian pidgin in the conversation-packed plays are among the most recurrent praises found in the critiques. Of course, not all comments are positive; some critics feel that the plays are lacking in their slow-pace actions, in the predictability of the scripts (Monji), and, according to mainland reviewers, in "Sakamoto lay[ing] on the local color a bit thick" (Foley, "*Aloha*" 7). However, even when these flaws are presented, the overall tone of the critiques is mostly positive.

Even if Sakamoto's plays "have been the backbone of the [Kumu Kahua Theatre]'s repertory since 1984" and have been regularly produced in Los Angeles, this Hawaiian playwright is for the most part still unrecognized on the mainland (Carroll, "Sakamoto" 1). Hopefully, the forthcoming publication of three more of his plays will change that circumstance. Until more of his plays appear in print, Edward Sakamoto is likely to remain the best unknown playwright of Hawaii.

BIBLIOGRAPHY

Works by Edward Sakamoto

Drama

In the Alley. Kumu Kahua Plays. Ed. Dennis Carroll. Honolulu: U of Hawai'i P, 1983. 123–42.

The Life of the Land. Hawai'i No Ka Oi: The Kamiya Family Trilogy. Honolulu: U of Hawai'i P, 1995. 91–138.

Manoa Valley. Hawai'i No Ka Oi: The Kamiya Family Trilogy. Honolulu: U of Hawai'i P, 1995. 49–90.

The Taste of Kona Coffee. Hawai'i No Ka Oi: The Kamiya Family Trilogy. Honolulu: U of Hawai'i P, 1995. 1–48.

A'ala Park. Aloha Las Vegas and Other Plays. Honolulu: U of Hawai'i P, 2000. 25–70.

Aloha Las Vegas. Aloha Las Vegas and Other Plays. Honolulu: U of Hawai'i P, 2000.
  131–90.
Stew Rice. Aloha Las Vegas and Other Plays. Honolulu: U of Hawai'i P, 2000. 71–
  130.

Unpublished Manuscripts

Yellow Is My Favorite Color. 1972.
That's the Way the Fortune Cookie Crumbles. 1976.
Voices in the Shadows. 1978.
Pilgramage. 1980.
Chikamatsu's Forest. 1986.
Our Hearts Were Touched with Fire. 1993.
Lava. 1997.
Dead of Night. 1999.

Selected Production History

In the Alley

Production, dir. Edward Langhans. U of Hawaii, Honolulu, 1961.

Yellow Is My Favorite Color

Production, dir. Mako. East West Players, Los Angeles, 1972.
————. Pan Asian Repertory Theatre, New York City, 1980–81.

That's the Way the Fortune Cookie Crumbles

Production, dir. Mako. East West Players, Los Angeles, 1976–77.

Voices in the Shadows

Production, dir. Mako. East West Players, Los Angeles, 1978–79.

Manoa Valley

Production, dir. Mako. East West Players, Los Angeles, 1979–80.
————. Pan Asian Repertory Theatre, New York City, 1984–85.

The Life of the Land

Production, dir. Mako. East West Players, Los Angeles, 1980–81.
————. Pan Asian Repertory Theatre, New York City, 1987.

Pilgramage

Production, dir. Mako. East West Players, Los Angeles, 1981.

Chikamatsu's Forest

Production, dir. Mako. East West Players, Los Angeles, 1986–87.

Stew Rice

Production, dir. Dana Lee. East West Players, Los Angeles, 1988.

Aloha Las Vegas

Production, dir. James A. Nakamoto. U of Hawaii, Honolulu, 1992.
————. Pan Asian Repertory Theatre, New York City, 1997–98.

Our Hearts Were Touched with Fire

Production. U of Hawaii, Honolulu, 1994.

The Taste of Kona Coffee

Production, dir. Mako. East West Players, Los Angeles, 1996–97.

A'ala Park

Production, dir. James A. Nakamoto. Kumu Kahua Theatre, Honolulu, 1997.

Lava

Production, dir. Shizuko Hoshi. East West Players, Los Angeles, 1998–99.

Dead of Night

Production, dir. James A. Nakamoto. Kumu Kahua Theatre, Honolulu, 2000.

Essays

"Anna May Wong and the Dragon-Lady Syndrome." *Los Angeles Times* 12 July 1987, Calendar: 40+.

Studies of Edward Sakamoto

Berger, John. *"Dead of Night* Powerful, Troubling Drama." *Honolulu Star-Bulletin On-line* 3 Nov. 2000. 17 Nov. 2000 <http://www.starbulletin.com/2000/11/03/features/story4.html>.

———. "Tribute to 100th, 442nd Is July 4 Fare with Impact." Rev. of *Our Hearts Were Touched with Fire*. *Honolulu Star-Bulletin Online* 3 July 1998. 17 Nov. 2000 <http://www.starbulletin.com/98/07/03/features/story2.html>.

Bowman, Pierre. "A Vivid Slice of Life from Hawaii of Old." Rev. of *A'ala Park*. *Honolulu Star-Bulletin* 21 Mar. 1984: B4.

Bruckner, D.J.R. "Where Hawai'ians Discover Paradise." Rev. of *Aloha Las Vegas*. *New York Times* 23 Apr. 1998: E5.

Burlingame, Burl. "A'ala Revisited." *Honolulu Star-Bulletin* 1 May 1997: B1.

———. "A Taste of Ed Sakamoto." *Honolulu Star-Bulletin* 15 Sep. 1993: B1+.

Carroll, Dennis, ed. *Kumu Kahua Plays*. Honolulu: U of Hawaii P, 1983.

———. "Sakamoto in the Theatre: Displaced Protagonists, Challenged Spectators." Introduction. *Aloha Las Vegas and Other Plays*. By Edward Sakamoto. Honolulu: U of Hawai'i P, 2000. 1–23.

Drake, Sylvie. *"Stew Rice*: Nostalgia and Reality." *Los Angeles Times* 11 Jan. 1988, Calendar: 6.

Foley, F. Kathleen. *"Aloha Las Vegas* Stays on Hawai'i Time." *Los Angeles Times* 20 June 1994, Calendar: 7.

———. *"Lava* Runs Deep in Comedy and Ecological Grievances." *Los Angeles Times* 18 Sep. 1998, Calendar: 27.

Gordon, Mike. "Haunted by Ghosts of His Past." *Honolulu Star-Bulletin* 5 May 1988: B1+.

Gussow, Mel. "Stage: Edward Sakamoto's *Manoa Valley.*" *New York Times* 23 Feb. 1985, sec. 1: 11.

Harada, Wayne. "Dark Tale of Unionization in Hawai'i Premieres Tonight." *Honolulu Advertiser* 7 Nov. 2000, Island Life: 18.

Loynd, Ray. "Sakamoto's *Forest* a Tapestry." Rev. of *Chikamatsu's Forest*. *Los Angeles Times* 18 Oct. 1986, Calendar: 9.

Miller, Daryl H. "*Fire* Tells of Japanese Americans' Heroism." Rev. of *Our Hearts Were Touched with Fire*. *Los Angeles Times* 21 Feb. 2000, Calendar: 13.

Monji, Jana J. "Embracing Hawai'i in *Manoa Valley*." *Los Angeles Times* 29 Sep. 1997, Calendar: 4.

Muromoto, Wayne. "Aloha, Ed Sakamoto." *Hawaii Herald* 2 Oct. 1992: A16.

Novick, Julius. "Paradise Island." Rev. of *The Life of the Land*. *Village Voice* 32.25 (1987): 98.

Odo, Franklin S. "Can You Go Home Again? Edward Sakamoto's Plays and Japanese Americans in Hawai'i." Foreword. *Hawai'i No Ka Oi: The Kamiya Family Trilogy*. By Edward Sakamoto. Honolulu: U of Hawai'i P, 1995. ix–xxv.

Oi, Cynthia. "Playwright Revisits Days of His Life." *Honolulu Star-Bulletin Online* 2 Nov. 2000. 17 Nov. 2000 <http://www.starbulletin.com/2000/11/02/features/story3.html>.

Preciado, Irma. "*Kona Coffee* in Hawaii Is Bitter-sweet." *Daily Sun Dial* 13 Feb. 1997, Entertainment: 5.

Romaine, Suzanne. "Hau fo rait pijin: Writing in Hawai'i Creole English." *English Today* 10.2 (Apr. 1994): 20–24.

Rozmiarek, Joseph T. "*A'ala Park* Is a Rich, Nostalgic Reflection on Life." *Honolulu Advertiser* 5 May 1997: C4.

———. "*Dead of Night* Is Dark, Turbulent—and Melodramatic." *Honolulu Advertiser* 7 Nov. 2000. 17 Nov. 2000 <http://www.honoluluadvertiser.com/2000/Nov/0711 7islandlife14.html>.

———. "The Local Appeal of Las Vegas." Rev. of *Aloha Las Vegas*. *Honolulu Advertiser* 22 Sept. 1992: B3.

———. "New *A'ala* Takes on Bitter Tone." *Honolulu Advertiser* 3 Nov. 1986: B3.

———. "Sakamoto's *A'ala Park*: A Gem." *Honolulu Advertiser* 21 Mar. 1984: C8.

———. "*Stew Rice* Goes Home Again—With Problems." *Honolulu Advertiser* 9 May 1987: D2+.

White, John W. "Revival of *A'ala Park* Funny but Too Focused." *Honolulu Star-Bulletin* 3 Nov. 1986: C3.

———. "*Stew Rice* Is a Tasty Recipe, but Needs a Little More Meat." *Honolulu Star-Bulletin* 8 May 1987: B2.

Winer, Laurie. "A Slow Cup of *Kona*." Rev. of *The Taste of Kona Coffee*. *Los Angeles Times* 6 Feb. 1997, Calendar: 26.

Bina Sharif

(1940–   )

Rashna B. Singh

BIOGRAPHY

Born in Lyallpur (now Faisalabad), Pakistan, in 1940, Bina Sharif has lived in America for the last twenty-six years. The middle of nine children, six girls and three boys, she was educated mostly in Pakistan, going on to receive her medical degree from the Fatima Jinnah Medical University in Lahore. By her own admission, she came to America to be an artist, but her father, a man of letters and a great source of strength and support in her life, feared that she would be unable to sustain herself in an artistic career. To allay those fears, she completed her education in America, taking a master's degree in public health from Johns Hopkins University, but then ended her medical career and turned to the intense pursuit of writing and theater. Sharif writes in part to emulate and honor one of her sisters who died at a very young age.

Like many immigrants, Sharif came to America in the pursuit of a dream and in the quest for freedom, equality, and justice, and, like many immigrants, she has felt disillusioned, for in America she has been categorized and confined by the very labels and groupings she sought to escape. "It amuses me sometimes that I had to leave my Muslim homeland and come to America to be labeled a Muslim woman playwright," she says in the artistic statement that precedes her play *My Ancestor's House* (Perkins and Uno 262–63). Confined by the petty limitations on women in her highly patriarchal homeland, Sharif crossed the ocean to separate herself from her society, but in doing so, found that she "would disintegrate in the deepest sphere of [her] psyche" (263). She felt as though she had lost the very nucleus of her existence and missed with a passion her loved ones: her parents, brothers, and sisters, as well as the sights and sounds of her childhood home.

Sharif now lives in New York City, where she not only writes but also acts, directs, and serves as cohost and theater critic on a show called *High Drama* that appears on Channel 57. She has had eight plays produced at Theatre for the New City in New York and four one-acts produced by Lower Levels of Society, also based in New York. She has had small parts in a few films, including *Side Streets*, directed by James Ivory, and *King of the Gypsies*, directed by William Friedkin, and a number of popular television shows, including *Law and Order, NYPD Blue, As the World Turns*, and *All My Children*. Sharif is the recipient of a wide spectrum of awards and grants for her work, including the Joseph Jefferson Award nomination from Chicago's Goodman Theatre, New York State Council on the Arts grants, Jerome Foundation grants, a Franklin Foundation Emerging Playwright grant, and the Pick of the Fringe Award of the Edinburgh Theater Festival.

MAJOR WORKS AND THEMES

What may be described as Sharif's most substantial and available work is the only one that has been published in full as part of a book. It is a two-act family drama called *My Ancestor's House*, which was published in *Contemporary Plays by Women of Color: An Anthology* (1996), edited by Kathy A. Perkins and Roberta Uno. The author describes it as a memory play where the actors are already in place when the audience walks in. There is a grave downstage, which, she specifies, must be of fresh real earth; a dimly lit apparition or dream figure that represents the dead sister, Deedi, hovers there. Another unconventional touch in the stage setting is the author's suggestion that the dying mother can also be downstage, lying on her deathbed while she watches the disintegration and metaphorical death of her family, which is unaware of her presence on stage.

Since this is July in Pakistan, all the characters are dressed in light subtle fabrics, while it is Deedi who wears the rich red and gold colors of a bride. The melancholy strains of the ghazal and the haunting call of the Muezzin, who calls the faithful to prayer, form the backdrop to the short first scene in which the family is gathered around Deedi's grave, and the only dialogue is the lamentation of one of the sisters who mourns that Deedi never hurt anyone but herself.

The play then proceeds back in time to a day earlier as an involved, intense family conflict plays out. At the center of the conflict is Bindia, one of the sisters, who has left her homeland for New York City and has come back because their mother is on her deathbed, as have two of her brothers who live in Denmark. Bindia admits to feelings of alienation and unhappiness in her life abroad, which prompts her older sister to ask why she lives there when she can live in her own country "as a perfectly decent human being" (268).

In an interesting reversal, Bindia describes America as a jungle, a "massive jungle of loneliness, of poverty, of disillusionment" (269). Guilt, shame, blame, and feelings of abandonment are among the emotions tossed around in a taut scene as the sisters gather around the breakfast table. Recrimination, remorse, rivalry, and resentment are added to the stew as a brother joins them in a later scene. The siblings argue about the care and attention (or lack of it) given to their mother by each of them, about their various spouses, and about life choices and decisions, while accusations are hurled and memories are retrieved. What emerges is a family that has turned on itself, that is without direction, moorings, or harmony as the matriarch lies dying. When the dreaded phone call finally comes, it is to convey the news of Deedi's death, not the mother's.

Deedi's despair and the family's disintegration become metaphors for the newly and artificially constructed country of Pakistan as it too struggles to establish an identity, find a purpose, and retain a sense of unity, only to find itself constantly torn apart by internal as much as external conflicts. Sahid, Bindia's brother, recognizes the enemy within when he says, "Yes, I know we never had any peace and warmth amongst us. We are empty souls, wandering around, trying to blame others for our vacuum. We somehow with all our education, creativity, and sensitivity have become emotionally crippled monsters incapable of having a healthy conversation without getting into a primal scream, which starts from nothing and turns into nothing!" (278). *My Ancestor's House* is a potent and powerful play that grapples with the tensions and turmoil of a family and, by extension, of the Indian subcontinent where they abide. It is, however, a play that depends greatly on the strength of the production for its impact on an audience. In the drama it wrests from familial friction and dysfunction, it is reminiscent of Tennessee Williams, a playwright Sharif much admires and has met.

All but one of Sharif's other plays have been published only in excerpts, mainly of monologues. The exception is *Love Is a Stranger in a Windowless Room*, a one-act play that was published in *Cinemastage: An International Magazine of the Arts*. It concerns the nature of relationships and the barriers that people erect between themselves. In an interesting and innovative departure, Sharif frames a dialogue and allows it to be spoken by three pairs of people: a straight couple, a lesbian couple, and a gay male couple. Even while the players change, the words remain the same.

Fire was conceived as a one-woman show, a series of autonomous monologues, one of which, "Bank Account," was published in *Movement Research Performance Journal* as well as in *Tribes: A Multicultural Literary Magazine of the Arts*. Another monologue from *Fire*, "Blow Job," was published in *Big Cigars*; "Blood Drop," another stand-alone monologue, was published in *Fruit*; and "My Chemical Mommy," an independent performance piece, was published in *Portable Lower East Side*. Excerpts from *Rats in the Tunnel* were published in *Optimism: A Poetry, Art, Prose Monthly*; excerpts from *Kill* were published in *Women and Performance: A Journal of Feminist Theory*. A common theme in all these plays and monologues is a sense of loss: the loss of a homeland, a family, an identity, a presence, and a sense of place. Alienation and the absence of acceptance in the New World accentuate that sense of loss because it becomes loss without the compensation of gain.

Sharif has also published two short stories: "The Black Fur Coat" in *Big Cigars* and "A Tremor in My Heart" in *Lower Levels of Society: A Literary Magazine*. In addition, she has conducted many theater and film interviews with established artists (including Emma Thompson and Bob Hoskins) and has published them in a variety of film, theater, literary, and arts magazines as well as in the *Times of Pakistan*.

CRITICAL RECEPTION

Bina Sharif's plays have been reviewed in a number of reputed journals in her profession, including the *Village Voice, Stages, Theater Week*, and *New York Casting*, as well as in newspapers such as *India Abroad, India West*, and the *New York Post*, which reviewed *One Thousand Hours of Love*. Sharif herself has been interviewed by the *Times of Pakistan* and *Little India*. The critical response to Sharif's plays has generally been enthusiastic. Critics have noted her creative approach to dramatic structure and setting, which stand in stark contrast to the classic themes projected by a play such as *My Ancestor's House*. Reviewers from the countries of the Indian subcontinent have commented on her courage in tackling themes and issues that are often taboo in her homeland.

BIBLIOGRAPHY

Works by Bina Sharif

Drama

Blow Job. 4 *Big Cigars: A Literary Magazine* (Winter 1989): 11–13.
"Bank Account Monologue" from the play *Fire*. *Tribes: A Multicultural Literary Magazine of the Arts* 2.1 (Apr. 1992): 38.
My Chemical Mommy. 9.1 *Portable Lower East Side* (Spring 1992): N. pag.
Blood Drop Monologue. *Fruit* (Summer 1995): 34–35.
Excerpts from *Kill*. *Women and Performance: A Journal of Feminist Theory* 7.2 & 8.1 (1995): 91–96.
My Ancestor's House. Contemporary Plays by Women of Color: An Anthology. Ed. Kathy A. Perkins and Roberta Uno. New York: Routledge, 1996. 264–79.
Love Is a Stranger in a Windowless Room: A One-Act Play. Cinemastage: An International Magazine of the Arts 1.1 (Jan. 1997): 12.
Excerpts from *Rats in the Tunnel*. 32 *Optimism: A Poetry, Art, Prose Monthly* (Prague) (1999): 4–6.

Unpublished Manuscripts

Watchman. 1989.
One Thousand Hours of Love. 1993.

Selected Production History

My Ancestor's House

Production, dir. Francisco G. Rivela; perf. Gleen Athaide, Rajshree Daryanani, Madhur
     Jaffrey, Sunita Mukhi, Karim Panjwani, and Sol Tamir. Theatre for the New City,
     New York City, 1992.

Love Is a Stranger in a Windowless Room

Production. Theatre for the New City, New York, 1994.

Interviews

"An Interview with Radical Playwright Bina Sharif." *Spectacle Arts and Entertainment
     Magazine* 30 Nov. 1989: N. pag.
Interview with Bina Sharif. 32 *Optimism: A Poetry, Art, Prose Monthly* (Prague) (1999):
     1–3.

Short Stories

"The Black Fur Coat." 5 *Big Cigars: A Literary Magazine* (Fall 1990): 21–22.
"An Tremor in My Heart." *Lower Levels of Society* 1.1 (Spring 1991): 9–12.

Studies of Bina Sharif

Dworkin, Norine. Rev. of *Fire. Village Voice* 36.5 (1991): 84.
Faber, Roderick M. Rev. of *Watchman. Village Voice* 34.43 (1989): 106.
Irani, Kaizad. Rev. of *One Thousand Hours of Love. India Abroad* 23.22 (1993): N. pag.
Khan, Seema. "Talk With Hesh Malkar and Bina Sharif." *Times of Pakistan* 28 Jan.
     1994: N. pag.
Melwani, Lavina. "Give My Regards to Broadway." *Little India* 5.1 (1995): 23.
Myers, Larry. "Immigrant Dreams Theme of New York Play." *India West* 1 Jan. 1993:
     41+.
———. Rev. of *One Thousand Hours of Love. New York Casting* 9 Mar. 1993: N. pag.
———. Rev. of *Watchman. Stages* (Dec. 1989): 47.
Steele, Tom. "Beyond Broadway." *Theater Week* 16 Mar. 1992: 33.
Tallmer, Jerry. "India under the Raj." Rev. of *One Thousand Hours of Love. New York
     Post* 22 Apr. 1993: 28.

R.A. Shiomi

(1947–   )

Josephine D. Lee

BIOGRAPHY

R.A. Shiomi was born in Toronto on May 25, 1947. In 1970, he received a B.A. from the University of Toronto, where he majored in history; in 1972, he earned a teaching certificate at Simon Fraser University in Vancouver. After traveling for two years in Europe and Asia (including one year teaching in Hong Kong), he returned to Vancouver and worked in the Asian Canadian community, including serving as coordinator for the Powell Street Festival and joining the Redress movement questioning the internment of Japanese Canadians during World War II. His first play was *Yellow Fever*, followed by *Rosie's Café, Play Ball*, and *Uncle Tadao*.

In 1992, Shiomi moved to Minneapolis and cofounded Theater Mu, an Asian American theater company. He is presently the artistic director and interim managing director of the company. His writing for Theater Mu has included *Mask Dance, River of Dreams, The Walleye Kid, The Raven in the Starfruit Tree, The Tale of the Dancing Crane*, and *The Song of the Pipa*. Shiomi directed *Mask Dance*, Theater Mu's first full-length production, as well as other works such as two segments of the *River of Dreams* trilogy at the McKnight Theater, *S.A.M. I Am* by the late Garrett Omata, *The Raven in the Starfruit Tree, The Walleye Kid*, and *The Tale of the Dancing Crane*. He has also directed at the Asian American Theater Company in San Francisco and at Interact Theater in Philadelphia. He has taught playwriting at the David Henry Hwang Writers' Institute in Los Angeles and in the Many Voices Program at the Playwrights' Center in Minnesota.

As a taiko performer, he began his career in the late 1970s with Katari Taiko in Vancouver, Canada. In the early 1980s, he studied and performed with the

San Francisco Taiko Dojo under Grandmaster Seiichi Tanaka. In the 1980s he also performed with Soh Daiko of New York and the San Jose Taiko Group and was a founding member of Wasabi Daiko of Toronto. He is now the founder and leader of Mu Daiko, a taiko group within Theater Mu. As an individual taiko performer, he played in the Ragamala Music and Dance Theater production of *The Return of the Rain Seed* by Veena Deo and Ranee Ramaswarny and was awarded a MSAB Cultural Collaborations grant to create a taiko and bharata-natyam performance with Ragamala Music and Dance Theater.

MAJOR WORKS AND THEMES

Shiomi's first play, *Yellow Fever* (1982), had successful runs at the Asian American Theater Company in San Francisco, the Pan Asian Repertory Theater in New York, and other theaters in the United States, Canada, and Japan. In this parody of the classic detective story, hard-boiled Japanese Canadian Sam Shi-kaze investigates the kidnapping of the Cherry Blossom Queen, only to uncover a more insidious strain of racism and police corruption. Sergeant Mackenzie and Superintendent Jameson are members of the white-supremacist group Sons of the Western Guard, whose rabid fear of "yellow fever" has led them to abduct the Queen in order to pin the blame on Chinese gangs. Shiomi's detective play provides history about Japanese Canadian internment during World War II, re-minds audiences about the persistence of racism even in a seemingly multicul-tural society, and teaches lessons about the importance of individual resistance and collective action. Set in Powell Street in Vancouver, *Yellow Fever* presents a Japanese Canadian community still coping with internment and relocation. While Sam remains wary of middle-class complacency and suspicious of au-thority, others such as Captain Kenji Kadota, Sam's ex-wife, and the Cherry Blossom Queen respond to racism by trying to assimilate. Even Sam, however, cannot work alone. Importantly, it is his connections within the Asian Canadian community and the help of lawyer Chuck Chan, local café owner Rosie, and reporter and love interest Nancy Wing that allow him to identify and subdue the perpetrators of the kidnapping.

Shiomi returns to *Yellow Fever*'s main characters and its Powell Street setting, not only in his 1984 sequel *Once Is Never Enough* (with Marc Hayashi and Lane Nishikawa) but also in *Rosie's Café* (1985). Set in the postinternment Japanese Canadian community, the play portrays Sam Shikaze and Kenji Kadota as younger police cadets who are drawn into investigating a mysterious series of robberies; the main suspect is the rebellious Michio, who is romantically involved with Rosie. Through its characterizations, the play contrasts instances of Japanese Canadian resistance with assimilation and complicity. Wartime anti-Japanese hysteria is also important to *Play Ball* (1989) and *Uncle Tadao* (1990). *Play Ball* depicts two white men who detain two young Japanese Canadians, Gordon and Kaz, under the wrongful charge of espionage; Kaz is ultimately murdered. Years later, Gordon returns to confront one of the men, now a prominent judge, with the crimes of his past. The family play *Uncle Tadao* also emphasizes how past injustices cannot be escaped. Despite his attempts to ignore his memories of internment and his brother Tadao's suicide, the middle-aged George is haunted by Tadao's ghost and his own repressed anger.

In 1993, Shiomi collaborated with Dong-il Lee and Joo Yeo No in order to write *Mask Dance*, which centers on the identity crisis of a young woman adopted from Korea by a Minnesota family. *Mask Dance* heralded some significant new developments in Shiomi's work: the use of interview and oral history, the adaptation of Asian folktales, and the incorporation of traditional Asian music and dance. Based on personal narratives from Korean adoptees, the play brings together elements of domestic realism, comic monologue, fairy tale, and traditional Korean dance. Shiomi has also crafted the life stories of recent Southeast Asian immigrants into the one-acts *Land of a Million Elephants* and *River of Life*, which were produced, along with Luu Pham's touching *Consecration*, as *River of Dreams* (1994). The first work, *Land of a Million Elephants*, is based on the life of Laotian dancer Pone Suryadhay (as the heroine Mali), who in the Ordway production performed several of the featured traditional dances. A narrator and other actors reenact her youth in Laos, her difficult marriage, and her eventual immigration to the United States. The final piece, *River of Life*, written in collaboration with Thonnara Hing, recounts the 1990 defection of Hing and his sister, both principal dancers in a Cambodian dance company; its dialogue is interspersed with dance sequences that present a history of Cambodia through a mixture of traditional and contemporary dance forms.

Shiomi again addresses the anxieties of interracial adoption in *The Walleye Kid* (1998), coauthored with Sundraya Kase. Humorous and touching, the play reworks the story of Momotaro, the Japanese peach-boy, into the tale of a Minnesota couple who discover a Korean baby inside an enormous walleye. When the child grows up and begins to cope with her cultural identity, the walleye transports her back to Korea to meet a shaman whose tales help her gain a new understanding of her own situation. Shiomi's fascination with Asian folktales is also evident in his 1999 plays, an adaptation of the Vietnamese tales *The Raven in the Starfruit Tree* and *The Tale of the Dancing Crane*. In the latter, Shiomi blends the Japanese story of a poor man, his selfish father, and his devoted and magical crane-wife with an autobiographical account of his early taiko training.

Shiomi's integration of multiple forms of action—personal stories, Asian folktales and literature, traditional Asian music and dance—is also evident in *The Song of the Pipa* (2000). Based on interviews with internationally renowned pipa player Gao Hong, the play presents the devastating effects of the Chinese Cultural Revolution on a young girl's family. Shiomi deftly weaves this account together with excerpts from the classical Tang Dynasty poem "The Song of the Pipa" and a story of its composition by exiled poet Bai Juyi. The recent Theater Mu production featured Hong's own brilliant musical performances, which took on even more emotional and historical significance within the context of Shiomi's play.

CRITICAL RECEPTION

In newspaper and journal reviews, *Yellow Fever*'s success has generally eclipsed that of Shiomi's other plays. For example, Edith Oliver says of *Rosie's Café* that the play, while "just as charming," is "not as sharp and sarcastic as *Yellow Fever*" despite the "stylish and clear" acting in the 1987 production at Playhouse 46 (130). Shiomi himself has been more concerned with public reception than with academic repute, commenting that "works for the stage aren't for the intellect" (Kaplan 100). Despite this, scholarly attention to Shiomi's work has recently begun to emerge. In their anthology *Playwrights of Color*, Meg Swanson and Robin Murray provide a useful introduction to *Yellow Fever* that includes background on the detective genre, San Francisco's Asian American Theater Company, and Shiomi's life. In *Performing Asian America: Race and Ethnicity on the Contemporary Stage* and the chapter " 'Speaking a Language That We Both Understand': Reconciling Feminism and Cultural Nationalism in Asian American Theater," Josephine Lee examines Shiomi's *Yellow Fever* in light of broader concerns about Asian American masculinity. Lee's article "Between Immigration and Hyphenation: The Problems of Theorizing Asian American Theater" uses *Land of a Million Elephants* and *River of Life* as part of its questioning of Asian American theater as "immigrant" theater.

BIBLIOGRAPHY

Works by R.A. Shiomi

Drama

Yellow Fever. Toronto: Playwrights Union of Canada, 1984. Also in *Playwrights of Color*. Ed. Meg Swanson and Robin Murray. Yarmouth, ME: Intercultural P, Inc., 1999. 657–686.

Unpublished Manuscripts

Once Is Never Enough. With Marc Hayashi and Lane Nishikawa. 1984.
Prime Time. 1984.
Rosie's Café. 1985.
Play Ball. 1989.
Uncle Tadao. 1990.
Mask Dance. With Dong-il Lee and Joo Yeo No. 1993.
Land of a Million Elephants. 1994.
River of Life. With Thonnara Hing. 1994.
The Walleye Kid. With Sundraya Kase. 1998.
The Raven in the Starfruit Tree. 1999.
The Tale of the Dancing Crane. 1999.
The Song of the Pipa. 2000.

Selected Production History

Yellow Fever

Production, dir. Lane Nishikawa. Asian American Theater Company, San Francisco,
    1982.
———. Pan Asian Repertory, New York City, 1982 and 1983.
———. Ryuzanjin Theater, Tokyo, 1994.

Once Is Never Enough

Production. Asian American Theater Company, San Francisco, 1984.

Prime Time

Production. Amass Music Theater, New York City, 1984.

Rosie's Café

Production. Pan Asian Repertory, New York City, 1985.
———, dir. Raul Aranas; perf. Carol A. Honda, Keenan Shimizu, Donald Li, Dalton
    Leong, Steve Park, John Quincy Lee, Mary Lee-Aranas, Ann M. Tsuji, and Mi-
    chael Arkin. Playhouse 46, New York City, 1987.
———, dir. Lane Nishikawa. Asian American Theater Company, San Francisco, 1989.
———. Firehall Theater, Vancouver, 1991.

Play Ball

Production. Pan Asian Repertory, New York City, 1989.

Uncle Tadao

Production. East West Players, Los Angeles, 1990.
———, dir. Lane Nishikawa; Asian American Theater Company, San Francisco, 1992.

Mask Dance

Production. Theater Mu and the Southern Theater, Southern Theater, Minneapolis,
    1993.
———. Theater Mu and the Southern Theater, Southern Theater, Minneapolis, 1995.

Land of a Million Elephants' and *River of Life* (with Thonnara
Hing)

Production as *River of Dreams*. Theater Mu and the Ordway, Ordway Center for the
    Performing Arts/McKnight Theater, St. Paul, 1994.

The Walleye Kid

Production. Theater Mu and Intermedia Arts, Intermedia Arts, Minneapolis, 1998.

The Raven in the Starfruit Tree

Production. Theater Mu and the Ordway, Landmark Center, St. Paul, 1999.

Tale of the Dancing Crane

Production. Theater Mu and Intermedia Arts, Intermedia Arts, Minneapolis, 1999.

The Song of the Pipa

Production. Theater Mu and the Southern Theater, Southern Theater, Minneapolis,
    2000.

Studies of R.A. Shiomi

Gussow, Mel. "Nisei Bogart." *New York Times* 2 Dec. 1982: C21.

Kaplan, Jon. "New York: Sam Shikaze, Private-Eye." Interview with R.A. Shiomi. *Canadian Theatre Review* 46 (Spring 1986): 98–100.

Lee, Josephine. "Between Immigration and Hyphenation: The Problems of Theorizing Asian American Theater." *Journal of Dramatic Theory and Criticism* 13.1 (1998): 45–69.

———. *Performing Asian America: Race and Ethnicity on the Contemporary Stage.* Philadelphia: Temple UP, 1997.

———. Rev. of Illusion Theater's *Undesirable Elements*, by Ping Chong, and Theater Mu's *River of Dreams*, by R.A. Shiomi, Luu Pham, and Thonnara Hing. *Theatre Journal* 47.3 (1995): 424–26.

———. " 'Speaking a Language That We Both Understand': Reconciling Feminism and Cultural Nationalism in Asian American Theater." *Performing America: Cultural Nationalism in American Theater.* Ed. Jeffrey D. Mason and J. Ellen Gainor. Ann Arbor: U of Michigan P, 1999. 139–59.

Oliver, Edith. Rev. of *Rosie's Café. New Yorker* 26 Oct. 1987: 130.

———. Rev. of *Yellow Fever. Contractor* 30 (1983): 86.

Swanson, Meg, and Robin Murray. "Introduction to *Yellow Fever.*" *Playwrights of Color.* Ed. Meg Swanson and Robin Murray. Yarmouth, ME: Intercultural P, 1999. 641–56.

Diana Son

(1965–)

Esther S. Kim

BIOGRAPHY

Diana Son was born in 1965 in Philadelphia and grew up in Dover, Delaware. Her mother was a nurse on exchange from Korea, and her father was a Korean foreign student at the Philadelphia College of Pharmacy. In Dover, Son lived in a racially mixed neighborhood where the numbers of blacks and whites were almost equal. To her and her friends, "race was not as important as whose basement had a ping pong table in it" (Jacobs 7). While she knew that she was different, she lived the typical suburban American life, which included shopping malls, K-Mart, and maypole dancing on May Day. Despite her occasional encounters with racism, she saw herself as an "insider" of the mainstream culture. From the fourth grade on, Son knew that she wanted to be a writer. Her teacher assigned the students a Thanksgiving essay that year, and Son wrote about her family and how grateful she was for her parents and older brother. Her essay was selected as the best in the class, and the teacher posted it for the entire class to read. For the first time, Son was recognized as being "something other than [her] older brother's little sister" (Janich 6Q). With this realization of self-identity, Son decided to become a writer.

Another crucial moment for the young writer came during her senior year of high school in Dover when she went on a field trip to New York City's Public Theater. She attended Joseph Papp's famous production of *Hamlet*, starring Diane Venora as the Danish prince. The experience was revelatory for Son. From 1983 to 1987, she attended New York University as a dramatic-literature major. During her first year at the university, she saw a production of Anne Bogart's *South Pacific* at the Experimental Theatre Wing at New York University. The production was set in a Vietnam veterans' hospital, and actors played patients with repetitive movements and speeches. Multiple actions took place on stage at once, and Son found the production confusing and enthralling. She wanted to understand it "emotionally, psychologically, historically, and theoretically" (Perkins and Uno 290). Other major influences on Son were Bertolt Brecht, Friedrich Düerrenmatt, and Harold Pinter.

In her last year in college, Son interned at La Mama Experimental Theatre Club, where she worked in the administrative office during the day and in the theater at night. After a season, La Mama mounted one of Son's plays, *Wrecked on Brecht*, in June 1987. Around the same time, Son graduated from NYU and began her career as a professional playwright. Supporting herself as a waitress and temp secretary, she continued to write plays and sought ways to stage them. In 1992, Son and her friends produced *Stealing Fire* at Soho Rep in New York City. From 1991 to 1992, Son studied directing composition with Anne Bogart at Playwrights Horizons Theatre School in New York City. In 1993, she attended the Iowa Playwrights Workshop at the University of Iowa but left without finishing her master's degree because she missed New York City. After returning from Iowa, she participated in the Asian American Playwrights Lab at the Public Theater. The workshop was organized by playwright and dramaturge Chiori Miyagawa, who invited Asian American playwrights to work on short pieces. At the workshop, Son developed *R.A.W. ('Cause I'm a Woman)*, her first work to address Asian American themes directly.

Artistic directors and literary managers around the country began to notice her work and encouraged her to write more plays. Michael Greif, the artistic director of La Jolla Playhouse in La Jolla, California, selected and directed *BOY*, Son's second full-length play, in 1996. For Son, it was "an amazing first professional experience," and she learned much from working with Greif (Ascheim N9). In 1997, Playwrights Horizons commissioned Son to write a new play. She wrote the first draft of *Stop Kiss* in six weeks and continued to revise it for the next ten months. In November 1998, the Joseph Papp Public Theater mounted the play, and the production became a surprising hit of the season and ran for nearly four months.

In 1999 and 2000, the play was produced by at least six companies, including Nora Theatre Company at Boston Playwrights' Theatre, Seattle Repertory Theatre, Oregon Shakespeare Festival, the Delaware Theatre Company, and Woolly Mammoth. Also, the play has been optioned for a film, and Son is writing the adaptation. Moreover, Son landed a job as a staff writer for NBC-TV's drama series *West Wing*. She moved to Los Angeles with her husband Michael Cosaboom in 1999, but in April 2000, she resigned from the television show and moved back to New York City. Son has received a National Endowment for the Arts/Theatre Communications Group grant to be playwright-in-residence at the Mark Taper Forum in Los Angeles, where she leads a writing workshop for caregivers. She is also working on two new plays, *Siberia* for the Public Theater and *Gold* for the Mark Taper Forum.

MAJOR WORKS AND THEMES

Consistent themes in Son's work include identity, transformation, and human connection. Son admits that she is "forced to think about identity because of her face" (Byrne, "Writer's" S09). "I am Korean and that's inescapable" (S09). For Son, identities are comprised not only of obviously visible characteristics such as ethnicity and gender, but also of complex, less obvious characteristics such as sexuality and humanity. Although her plays cannot be categorized singularly as "feminist," most of them address women's issues, including mother-daughter relationships, sisterhood, and gender discrimination. Her first full-length play, *Stealing Fire*, is a modern reworking of the Procne and Philomela myth, a story about two sisters. *2000 Miles*, a one-act play, tells the story of a young woman and her struggle with her past and her ill mother. In *R.A.W. ('Cause I'm a Woman)*, four Asian American women respond to the sexual stereotyping of them as geishas, exotic virgins, china dolls, and suicidal Miss Saigons. After reacting to these imposed stereotypes, the four women reveal their experiences as a preppie whose mother forbade her to eat kimchee, a woman who feels ugly because she does not look like the girl on the macadamia-nut bottle, a flirtatious lesbian who ends up dateless because no one suspects that she is queer, and a Korean American woman who does not understand it when her boyfriend tells her that he loves her in Korean. In the play, Asian women stereotypes are subverted by their real and diverse experiences.

Subversion of socially constructed identity is central to *BOY*, Son's second full-length play. *BOY* is about Mama and Papa Uber Alles, who desperately want a boy after having three daughters. When they realize that their fourth child is a girl, they immediately wrap her in a blue blanket, name her "Boy," and tell everyone that it is a boy. Boy grows up worshipped by her parents and envied by her sisters. Then, an unhappy family—an overly sexual mother and lonely daughter—moves in next door and forces the issue of Boy's sexuality. Boy falls in love with Charlotte—the daughter—and loses her, but only to find out that her feelings have stayed the same despite her efforts to be a woman. According to a critic, the play is a "subversive little dramatic cartoon," but also has an "ingratiating way of pulling you into its complex questions of gender construction and cultural identity, almost with a sense of fun" (Steele 5E).

Son has the ability to balance heavy-handed topical issues with a sense of humor and fun without losing sensitivity and sincerity. This balance is best demonstrated in *Stop Kiss*, a full-length play about gay bashing. Two heterosexual women—Callie, an insecure traffic reporter in New York City, and Sara, an idealistic schoolteacher from St. Louis—discover their attraction for each other. While they are walking in a West Village park late at night, Callie finally gets the courage to kiss Sara after many missed cues and opportunities, but a man witnesses the kiss and beats Sara. The carefully constructed play begins with the first meeting of Sara and Callie, and short scenes alternate between the past and present, leading to the title kiss at the climactic point. Son explains that gay bashing is only the context, not the focal point, of the play. For her, the play is a love story about two people who experience a "whole web of emotions that they're alternating giving into and fighting against" (Tanaka 27). The play also addresses Son's interest in the "conflict between how other people identify you and the more complex way you know yourself" (27).

Although the majority of Son's plays are not specifically about Asian American or Korean American experiences, she has been a strong advocate for diversity in casting. For *Stop Kiss*, she insisted that African American actor Kevin Carroll be cast as George and that the role of Sara be played by Sandra Oh, a Korean Canadian actor at the Public Theater. "What's crucially important to me is that actors of color get cast in this play, period" (Tanaka 27). By making the race of the characters in the play nonspecific, Son allows the play to be accessible to artists from different backgrounds. Also, Son sees no value in identifying the ethnicity of a writer. She questions the label "Asian American playwright" and finds it limiting. She is more interested in telling stories about people who come to New York City from small towns to "reinvent themselves as very different from the image that people had of them in their small towns" (Eng 418). Although her stories stem from her personal experience, her Korean American face is not a requirement in telling them.

CRITICAL RECEPTION

Since the early part of her career, New York City–based critics have called Son a "talented young playwright" and predicted her success. With *Stop Kiss*, Son received exceptionally warm responses from critics and audiences. The play was nominated for several awards, including the Outer Critics Circle Award for outstanding off-Broadway production and a Drama League Award for distinguished production of a play, and received the 1999 GLAAD (Gay and Lesbian Alliance against Defamation) Media Award for Outstanding New York Theatre Production on Broadway or Off-Broadway. She was also awarded the Berilla Kerr Award for Playwriting and was nominated for the John Gassner Playwriting Prize. In academia, most learned of her work after the publication of *R.A.W* (*'Cause I'm a Woman*). In Asian American studies, *R.A.W.* is described as a representative Asian American woman's play, while her other plays are often ignored. In mainstream theater scholarship, Son's plays are recognized for raising questions of identity and subverting social constructions of gender and sexuality, but, overall, there is little scholarship on Son and her plays.

BIBLIOGRAPHY

Works by Diana Son

Drama

R.A.W. ('Cause I'm a Woman). Contemporary Plays by Women of Color: An Anthology. Ed. Kathy A. Perkins and Roberta Uno. New York: Routledge, 1996. 290–96.

Rpt. in *Take Ten: New 10-Minutes Plays*. Ed. Eric Lane and Nina Shengold. New York: Vintage Books, 1997. 289–300.

BOY. Excerpts. *New Voices of the American Theater*. Ed. Stephen Vincent Brennan. New York: Henry Holt, 1997. 110–15.

Happy Birthday Jack. Humana Festival '99: The Complete Plays. Ed. Michael Bigelow Dixon and Amy Wegener. Lyme, NH: Smith and Kraus, 1999. 355–58.

Stop Kiss. Woodstock, NY: Overlook P, 1999.

Unpublished Manuscripts

Wrecked on Brecht. 1987.
Stealing Fire. 1992.
The Joyless Bad Luck Club. 1993.
2000 Miles. 1993.
Fishes. 1995.

Selected Production History

Wrecked on Brecht

Production. La Mama E.T.C., New York City, 1987.

Stealing Fire

Staged reading. Cornelia Street Café, New York City, 1990.
Production. Soho Rep, New York City, 1992.

The Joyless Bad Luck Club

Production. HOME for Contemporary Theatre at HERE, New York City, 1993.

R.A.W. ('Cause I'm a Woman)

Production. Joseph Papp Public Theater, New York City, 1993.
————. Columbia University, 1993.
————. dir. Lenora Champagne; perf. Kim Ima, Lisa Ann Li, Liana Pai, and Elaine Tse. Ohio Theatre, T.W.E.E.D. New Works Festival, New York City, 1993.
————. HOME for Contemporary Theatre at HERE, New York City, 1993.
————. T.W.E.E.D. Ten Year Reunion Festival, 1995.
————. Theater Mu, Minneapolis, 1995.
————. New WORLD Theater, U of Massachusetts, Amherst, 1996.
————. U of Chicago, 1996.
————. Smith College, Northampton, MA, 1996.
————. Asian American Theater Company, San Francisco, 1997.
————. Asian American Repertory Theatre, San Diego, 1997.

2000 Miles

Production. No Pants Theatre Company, New York City, 1993.
————. Under One Roof, New York City, 1993.
————. Ensemble Studio Theatre, New York City, 1993.

BOY

Staged reading. Dramatists, New York City, 1994.
————. New York Theatre Workshop, New York City, 1994.
Production, dir. Michael Greif; perf. Michi Barall, Cynthia Martells, Robert Dorfman, Alyssa Lupo, Amy Elizabeth McKenna, Melody Butiu, James Saba, Damen

Scranton, Mike Ryan, Kevin Berntson, Todd Cerveris, and Andrea Renee Portes. La Jolla Playhouse, La Jolla, CA, 1995.

Fishes

Workshop. Mark Taper Forum, Los Angeles, 1995.
Staged reading. Public Theater, New York City, 1995.
Production. New Georges, New York City, 1998.
————. People's Light and Theater Company, Philadelphia, 1998.

Stop Kiss

Staged reading. Playwrights Horizons, New York City, 1997.
————. Mark Taper Forum, Los Angeles, 1998.
————. Public Theater, New York City, 1998.
Workshop. Playwrights Center, Minneapolis, 1998.
Production, dir. Jo Bonney; perf. Jessica Hecht, Sandra Oh, Saul Stein, Saundra McClain, Kevin Carroll, and Rick Holmes. Public Theater, New York City, 1998.
Staged reading. Royal National Theatre, London, 1998.
Production, dir. Lee Mikeska Gardner; perf. Rhea Seehorn, Holly Twyford, Ian LeValley, Jeorge Watson, Doug Brown, and Desiree Marie. Woolly Mammoth Theatre, Washington, DC, 1999.
————, dir. Steven Dietz; perf. Amy Cronise, Jodi Somers, Mike Regan, Alban Dennis, Tamu Gray, and David Scully. Seattle Repertory Theatre, Seattle, 2000.
————, dir. Janet Morrison; perf. Nada Despotovich, Carolyn Roberts, Augustus Kelley, Barlow Adamson, and Monique Nicole McIntyre. Nora Theatre Company, Boston, 2000.
————. Delaware Theatre Company, Wilmington, DE, 2000.
————, dir. Abigail Morris; perf. Holly Aird, Georgia Mackenzie, Eric Loren, and Daniel Coonan. Soho Theatre Company, London, 2000.
————, dir. Loretta Greco; perf. Tyler Layton and Julie Oda. Oregon Shakespeare Festival, Ashland, OR, 2000.

Happy Birthday Jack

Production, perf. Jon Brent Curry and V. Craig Heidenreich. Actors Theatre of Louisville at the 23rd annual Humana Festival of New American Plays, Louisville, KY, 1999.

Essay

"Artistic Statement." *Contemporary Plays by Women of Color: An Anthology*. Ed. Kathy A. Perkins and Roberta Uno. New York: Routledge, 1996. 289–90.

Short Story

"Fireflies to Bittersweet." *Asian Pacific American Journal* 1.2 (1992): 9–14.

Studies of Diana Son

Ascheim, Skip. "Playwright Diana Son in Search of Identity." *Boston Globe* 5 Mar. 2000: N9.
Barnes, Clive. " 'Stop and Go See 'Kiss.' " *New York Post* 7 Dec. 1998: 42.

Berson, Misha. "The 'Kiss' of Success: Diana Son Embraces Her Good Fortune Writing for Stage and Television." *Seattle Times* 20 Jan. 2000: G26.

Brantley, Ben. "Comic in Spirit, Serious at Heart." *New York Times* 7 Dec. 1998, Arts Section 1: 6.

Byrne, Terry. "Crafty 'Kiss' Explores Light and Dark of Relationships." *Boston Herald* 16 Mar. 2000: O47.

———. "Writer's Success Sealed with 'Kiss.' " *Boston Herald* 10 Mar. 2000: S09.

Eng, Alvin, ed. *Tokens? The NYC Asian American Experience on Stage.* New York: Asian American Writers' Workshop, 1999.

Jackson, Erik. "Stop Kiss." *Time Out/New York* 168 (10–17 Dec. 1998): 147.

Jacobs, Tom. "Defying Assumptions." *Santa Barbara News Press* 19 Nov. 1999. 7–8.

Janich, Kathy. "A Conversation with *Stop Kiss* Playwright Diana Son." *Atlanta Journal and Constitution* 21 Apr. 2000: 6Q.

Kuchwara, Michael. "A Precise, Rewarding Comedy-Drama." *Buffalo News* 5 Jan. 1999: 6C.

Siegel, Ed. "Stage Review: Stop Kiss." *Boston Globe* 16 Mar. 2000: F2.

Steele, Mike. "*BOY* Explores Cultural Construction of Gender." *Star Tribune* (Minneapolis, MN) 30 Apr. 1999: 5E.

Tanaka, Jennifer. "Only Connect: An Interview with the Playwright." *American Theatre* 16.6 (July/Aug. 1999): 26–27.

Winer, Laurie. " 'BOY's' Search Leads Down a Funny but Rocky Path." *Los Angeles Times* 19 June 1996: F1.

Winer, Linda. "The Risk That Begins with a Kiss." *Newsday* 7 Dec. 1998: B9.

Alice Tuan
(1963–   )

Jie Tian

BIOGRAPHY

Alice Tuan was born in Seattle, Washington, on July 26, 1963. When she was five years old, her family relocated to San Fernando Valley, California. Her paternal grandparents moved from Taiwan to live with the family when she was seven. Tuan and her sister Susan grew up in a bicultural environment, with traditional Chinese culture at home and American culture outside home. "I feel a huge gap in my life," Tuan observed, "Chinese and American cultures are so opposite. American culture is aggressive and embraces instant satisfaction while Chinese culture reveres patience, suffering, and longevity" ("Beginnings" 1). Tuan first had the idea of becoming a writer during her high school years. She was inspired by existentialist philosophy and ideas of freedom, choice, and responsibility through the writings of Albert Camus, Jean-Paul Sartre, and Samuel Beckett.

Tuan majored in economics at the University of California at Los Angeles. After graduation with a B.A. in 1987, she went to teach English in Guangzhou, China, hoping to embrace socialism, ideas of community, and a nonmaterialistic culture. She returned to the United States a year later and studied teaching English as a second language (ESL) at California State University at Los Angeles. She earned an M.A. in ESL in 1991.

Tuan started playwriting in 1988 with a story about General Yeh Yeh. After submitting the play to the Mark Taper Forum, she was invited to be a member in the Mentor Playwright Program at Taper in 1991. Tuan wrote three plays at Taper: *Dim Sums, Kitpor*, and *Crown Goose*. In 1994, Paula Vogel invited Tuan to Brown University to be a fellow in its M.F.A. Playwriting Program. Tuan wrote five plays at Brown: *Ikebana, Some Asians, Iconana, mALL*, and *Coast-*

line, invented virtual hypertext theatre, and used her thesis play to experiment with computer simulation, creating a juxtaposition of the contrived with the human in a physical stage space.

After receiving an M.F.A. from Brown University in 1997, Tuan returned to Los Angeles. She is a vital part of the theater scenes in Los Angeles, New York, and Seattle. Tuan also teaches playwriting. She has participated in the Playwright-in-the-Schools Project of Audrey Skirbal Kenis Theater Projects (A.S.K.), a private theater service organization, and is currently the playwright-in-residence of the Los Angeles Theatre Center. She has taught at the David Henry Hwang Writers' Institute and is still a part of the Writers' Workshop at Taper. In June 2000, she became the latest recipient of the Robert E. Sherwood Award from the Mark Taper Forum.

MAJOR WORKS AND THEMES

Alice Tuan's plays are audacious and imaginative expressions and interpretations of history, contemporary American reality, and the immigrant experience. She employs in her plays rich collages and juxtapositions in bold, brisk, postmodern, and highly expressionistic style. Her characters are at the mercy of family, cultural, social, and political influences, sometimes dark and desperate, sometimes absurd and darkly humorous. The themes of her plays encompass both East and West, past and present, family saga and world history.

Tuan's plays are known for exploring the complex issues in immigration, cultural tradition, generational conflicts, and individual identity. *Last of the Suns* is centered in a Chinese American family in southern California's San Fernando Valley. China's political history coexists with contemporary American experience. Through the perils of the family, Tuan raises questions of the meaning of being an American, an Asian American, and an individual in an environment full of despair, isolation, and disconnectedness. The meaning of being Asian American is further confounded in *Ikebana*, in which Tuan utilizes the Japanese art of flower arrangement, ikebana, to tell the stories of a Chinese American family struggling with personal past and identity. Each of the fifteen scenes is named after a flower arrangement, and each is a play within a play. On a fundamental level, the play draws parallels between the experiences of immigrants and that of the cut flowers; both have been separated from their roots and placed in a new environment where they struggle to survive.

Beyond family and identity conflicts, Tuan's plays also cover broader issues quintessential to immigrant experience in America. In *New Culture for a New Century*, Tuan demonstrates a unique penchant for juxtaposition. The play layers the experience of different immigrant groups in one locale, the Lower East Side in New York. There an Asian immigrant girl to Chinatown pushes a dim sum cart at Wing Shoon Restaurant. That scene flashes back to earlier experiences of other immigrants: a "corn girl" pushing her wares on Hester Street, and then the revolutionary Leon Trotsky in the Garden Cafeteria in the same neighborhood. Tuan's textured scenes expound on the role of locale: the Lower East Side as a place that houses many different cultural experiences through time and history.

In *Some Asians*, Tuan's preoccupation with history and cultural interaction takes a humorous and sarcastic turn. Juxtaposing three disparate segments of history, the play uses historical incidents in an anecdotal and absurdist way: the reclaiming of Hong Kong by China after a ninety-nine-year lease, Marco Polo in China, and the fictional, opium-addicted Bong Dynasty. She illuminates the issues of exploitation, colonialism, and imperialism and suggests themes of cultural differences, misunderstandings, and intolerance in the exchange between East and West.

In summary, her plays project contradictory cultural identity, images, and experiences. Caricatures of culture and personality, fragments of history and facts, and juxtaposition of time and place mark an element of Tuan's originality. Defining her understanding of a new Asian American consciousness in her essay "The Crisis of Label," Tuan finds the economist Vilfredo Pareto's words most relevant: "Marx's words are like bats: one can see in them both birds and mice." Tuan urges people to move beyond the surface: "I wonder if it is possible to look deeper into Asian American works, for its sensibility rather than cultural ambassadorship . . . for its Paretoan 'batness' instead of either 'birdness' or mouseness." The same maxim would also help Tuan's readers and critics alike pin down the real meaning of Tuan's plays behind the seemingly absurd and melodramatic devices.

CRITICAL RECEPTION

Major critical response to Tuan's plays exists as theater reviews in various news sources. *Women Playwrights of Diversity: A Bio-bibliographical Sourcebook* by Jane T. Peterson and Suzanne Bennett is the first scholarly source to include an entry on Alice Tuan. This 1997 book is descriptive rather than analytical. In the professional theater circle, mentors and producers such as Oliver Mayer, Lisa Peterson, Paula Vogel, Aishah Rahman, and Chay Yew applaud Alice Tuan as a bold, brilliant, and passionate new playwright.

Theater reviews show mixed responses to Tuan's use of Asian imagery and folkloric figures. This technique strikes some as exotic and mysterious, while others see it as confusing and absurd. In the review of *Last of the Suns* for the *San Francisco Chronicle*, Octavio Roca is drawn to the mystical elements of the play and the employment of traditional Chinese folk imageries such as Eight Pig, the Monkey King, and a reincarnated Buddha (E1). In a similar way, reviewers are favorably impressed with Tuan's fifteen stylistic scenes in *Ikebana*, each named after a particular Japanese floral arrangement. In the *Los Angeles Times*, Laurie Winer remarks in her review of *Ikebana*'s production that Tuan succeeds in conveying the struggles and aspirations of an immigrant family (F1). However, some fail to see the connection between the titles of the scenes and the play's themes. "There is little this scheme adds by way of illumination," Charles Isherwood observes; "a tighter focus on the play's core concerns ... would enhance that play" (screens 2–3).

Tuan's experimental style breaks the boundaries of the traditional drama structure. As a result, it generates disputes among her critics and reviewers regarding the structure of her plays. Steven Winn of the *San Francisco Chronicle* comments on the "awkwardness" of the construction in *Last of the Suns* (D1). Reviewing the same play, Robert Hurwitt of the *San Francisco Examiner* finds it "hard to keep track of its central story" (C1). The three disparate history-based scenes in *Some Asians* also generate confusion for some. William K. Gale of the *Providence Journal-Bulletin* regards the play as obscure and "unknowable" and muses, "Maybe there's an East/West comment there?" (G1).

The most understanding analysis of Tuan's intent as a playwright comes from Aishah Rahman of the Perishable Theatre in Providence. Her introduction to *Some Asians* offers a lucid statement on the structure, subject, and innovativeness of the play. "Tuan unites both form and content into an organic ethnic interiority that looks into the face of the past, sifts through the illusions of our present and expresses ... the clash and merge of past and present, East and West. ... Tuan's layered and circuitous storytelling ... reveal[s] an innovative playwright's kaleidoscopic vision that insists on bursting through boundaries of theme, style, and language as well as those of structure" (*Some Asians* 20). Rahman's remark is equally apt for Tuan's work as a whole. While some reviewers might have missed the point of Tuan's experimental style, others like Rahman manage to see her work from an insider's perspective and contribute insightful observations to the meaningful discussion of Tuan's dramatic presentation.

BIBLIOGRAPHY

Works by Alice Tuan

Drama

Some Asians. Perishable Theatre's 5th Annual Women's Playwriting Festival. Seattle: Rain City Projects, 1997. 20–31.
"Organic Form." Excerpts from *Ikebana. Scenes for Women by Women.* Ed. Tori Haring-Smith. Portsmouth, NH: Heinemann, 1998. 158–62.

Unpublished Manuscripts

Dim Sums. Ms. 345. Roberta Uno Asian Women Playwrights Scripts Collection 1924–1992, Special Collections and Archives, W.E.B. Du Bois Library, U of Massachusetts, Amherst; also at the Joyce Ketay Agency, New York City, 1992.
Crown Goose. Ms. 345. Roberta Uno Asian Women Playwrights Scripts Collection 1924–1992, Special Collections and Archives, W.E.B. Du Bois Library, U of Massachusetts, Amherst; also at the Joyce Ketay Agency, New York City, 1994.

Kitpor. Ms. 345. Roberta Uno Asian Women Playwrights Scripts Collection 1924–1992, Special Collections and Archives, W.E.B. Du Bois Library, U of Massachusetts, Amherst; also at the Joyce Ketay Agency, New York City, 1994.

Last of the Suns. Ms. 345. Roberta Uno Asian Women Playwrights Scripts Collection 1924–1992, Special Collections and Archives, W.E.B. Du Bois Library, U of Massachusetts, Amherst; also at the Joyce Ketay Agency, New York City, 1995.

Iconana. Joyce Ketay Agency, New York City, 1996.

Ikebana. Joyce Ketay Agency, New York City, 1996.

"Towards Next Text: Three Plays: Some Asians, mALL, Coastline." M.F.A. thesis, Brown U, 1997.

Ajax. 1998.

New Culture for a New Century. Joyce Ketay Agency, New York City, 1998.

Cricket. Joyce Ketay Agency, New York City, 2000.

"The Crisis of Label." Essay. 2000.

That Race Place. Joyce Ketay Agency, New York City, 2000.

Selected Production History

Dim Sums

Staged reading, Mark Taper Forum, Los Angeles, 1992.
———. Cast Theatre, Los Angeles, 1993.

Last of the Suns

Staged reading. Mark Taper Forum, Los Angeles, 1993.
Production, prod. Sharon Ott. Berkeley Repertory Theatre, Berkeley, CA, Dec. 1994–Jan. 1995.
Staged reading. Public Theater, New York City, 1995.

Crown Goose

Staged reading. Cast Theatre, Los Angeles, 1994.

Ikebana

Staged reading. Public Theater, New York City, 1996.
Production, prod. Aishah Rahman. Brown U, Providence, RI, 1996.
———. East West Players, Los Angeles, 1996.

mALL

Production, prod. Paula Vogel. Trinity Repertory, Providence, RI, 1997.
———, prod. Mark Majarian. Cypress College, Cypress, CA, 2000.

Some Asians

Production, prod. Mark Lerman. Perishable Theatre, Providence, RI, 1997.
———, prod. Anne Hamburger. En Garde Arts, New York City, 1998.

Ajax

Staged Reading. Mark Taper Forum Writers' Workshop, Los Angeles, 1998.
———. Actors' Studio West, Los Angeles, 1998.
———. Public Theater, New York City, 1999.
———. Contemporary Theater, Seattle, 2000.

"Cricket" from The Square Project (Tuan, one of sixteen Asian American playwrights in a project of the Mark Taper Forum's Asian Theatre Workshop)

Production, prod. Chay Yew. Mark Taper Forum (Too at the Actors' Gang), Hollywood, 2000.

Interview

"Personal Beginnings." Telephone interview. 12 May 2000.

Studies of Alice Tuan

Gale, William K. "Women's Playwriting Showcases Acting Talent." *Providence Journal-Bulletin* 3 June 1997: G1.

Hayes, Steve. "Lisa Peterson: A Bird on a Wire." *American Theatre* 1 Apr. 1997: 28.

Hurwitt, Robert. "All in the Family." *San Francisco Examiner* 6 Jan. 1995: C1.

Isherwood, Charles. "Ikebana." *Daily Variety* 3 Dec. 1996. Dow Jones Interactive. 10 Jan. 2000 <http://nrstg1p.djnr.com/>.

Peterson, Jane T., and Susanne Bennett, eds. "Alice Tuan." *Women Playwrights of Diversity: A Bio-bibliographical Sourcebook.* Westport, CT: Greenwood P, 1997. 334–36.

Rahman, Aishah. Preface. *Some Asians. Perishable Theatre's 5th Annual Women's Playwriting Festival.* Seattle: Rain City Projects, 1997. 20–31.

Roca, Octavio. "A Young Playwright's Bright Horizon." *San Francisco Chronicle* 29 Dec. 1994: E1.

Uno, Roberta. Appendix. *Unbroken Thread: An Anthology of Plays by Asian American Women.* Amherst: U of Massachusetts P, 1993. 309–28.

Winer, Laurie. "Examining a Family's Roots." *Los Angeles Times* 26 Nov. 1996: F1.

W nn, Steven. "The Last of the Suns Is Hazy in Berkeley." *San Francisco Chronicle* 6 Jan. 1995: D1.

Denise Uyehara

(1966–   )

Yuko Kurahashi

BIOGRAPHY

Denise Uyehara was born in Tustin, California, in 1966 to Japanese American parents, Hajime and Joyce Uyehara. Her parents, who are both scientists, have an interest in the arts, history, and the sociopolitical condition. In 1976, the family moved to Westminster, California. In 1984, Uyehara attended the University of California at Irvine, where she started as a biology major, then changed to comparative literature. She studied fiction writing and playwriting, edited the Asian American newsmagazine and the university's literary journal, and actively participated in experimental theater performances and traditional storytelling. She obtained her B.A. in 1989. Shortly after, she moved to Los Angeles, where she worked as an arts administrator.

Uyehara continued to educate herself. She worked at the Asian American Theatre Projects headed by Dom Magwili. She studied playwriting more intensively as part of the Mark Taper Forum's Mentor Playwright Program and as a student at the David Henry Hwang Writers' Institute (East West Players). She wrote full-length plays such as *Hobbies, Hiro*, and *Jo & Millie Go to Church*. Her solo performances, which have been presented across the United States and internationally, include *Headless Turtleneck Relatives: The Tale of Family and a Grandmother's Suicide by Fire, Hello (Sex) Kitty: Mad Asian Bitch on Wheels*, and *Maps of City & Body*.

As she stretched intellectually, she also wrestled with her responsibility as an artist as it intertwined with her individual sexual and ethnic identity. Her efforts to work from specific stories about people, by their very nature, spoke to audiences of all kinds: queer, straight, women, men, of all racial backgrounds.

Uyehara genuinely believes in solidarity among artists and has proved her investment by consistently participating in collaborative projects. She is a founding member of the Sacred Naked Nature Girls, a culturally diverse experimental performance collective. The ensemble has explored the intersections of class, sexual orientation, and race (African American, Asian American, and European American). She also participated with other performance artists in *The Other Weapon*, an oral-history piece about the Black Panther party that was directed by performance artist Robbie McCauley and produced by the Arts Company. All along, Uyehara has continued to contribute to the Los Angeles community as an educator and artist. She has taught performance and writing to Asian Pacific Islanders, senior citizens, and various queer and women's communities. Her workshops include the Rad Asian Sisters Workshop, which was designed for Asian Pacific Islander women.

Uyehara has developed a series of unique projects that she refers to as "Public Art Investigations." There she collaborates with artists from various cultures and usually serves as artistic director. These investigations focus on bringing art into the public, instead of the public walking into a theater or gallery. For instance, in the first project, "Tell It Like It Is" (1994), Uyehara met with a group of seniors from Los Angeles Plaza and created a multimedia presentation of their own oral histories. In "Laundry/Cello/Rain" (1995)—a piece on which she collaborated with cellist Maria Elena Gaitan—Uyehara commemorated the bombing of Hiroshima through the act of "washing laundry on the rooftop and hanging it to dry over the audience in the gallery" (E-mail). "Kissing" (1996) is a series of interviews of those who witnessed the kissing of the couples whom Uyehara and her collaborator, Teri Osato, a visual artist, sent to various public places to "perform" kissing. "Lost & Found, Part I" (1997) took place at the Korean American Museum with John Song, Veronica Ko (artistic director), Jeff Matsuda, Lee B., and Uyehara. In "Lost & Found, Part II" (1998), Uyehara left objects all around the city of Helsinki, Finland, with messages on the objects. Citizens returned the objects to a central site, thus creating a "community of seekers and finders" (E-mail). Through these projects, Uyehara has explored people's verbal and behavioral responses to experimental work, which she believes is the core of our lives and arts.

MAJOR WORKS AND THEMES

Uyehara's first play, *Hobbies* (1989), deals with various obsessions of Asian characters. Beni, a Japanese American woman, wants to visit Italy. Her friends are a mixed-race Asian man who is an Asianophile and optimistic, a Chinese Japanese American man who picks up West African drumming in order to free his spirit, and the "Woman," a weathered, eccentric, homeless Asian who teaches Beni how to moon (E-mail). By fully employing absurd situations and characters, Uyehara questions the public's fear of ethnic fetish and its value judgment of it.

Her next full-length play, *Hiro* (1993), was originally developed at the East

West Players' David Henry Hwang Writers' Institute. Then Uyehara received the AT&T: On-Stage Production Award to produce the play at EWP. It portrays the bizarre family reunion of a young woman, Hiro, and her sister and mother. After a fifteen-year absence, Hiro visits her sister, Shell, and her mother, Queen T. Hiro has a supernatural power to fly and levitate, but mistakenly drops her father, who attempts to experiment the flight with her. Shell, an alcoholic, lives in an imaginary world where she can be a perfect southern belle. Queen T. also suffers from mental illness and denies the passing of the years and the death of her husband. Through absurd and eccentric dialogue, which takes place in the world of magic realism, Uyehara examines and criticizes many serious harms inflicted on Asian Americans who are culturally displaced and isolated. In this piece, her quest is to find her own identity, as well as freedom in the meta-physical realm—a task that is particularly demanding and reflective of most contemporary Asian American women's ambition to attain professional achieve-ment and emotional liberty.

In *Headless Turtleneck Relatives* (1993), Uyehara revives stories and her own memories of several generations of her family. She weaves a number of shock-ing, touching, and challenging images of Japanese Americans such as a portrayal of her grandmother who commits self-immolation in a car and a scientist father who belts out karaoke songs. Uyehara uses her astute sensitivity to revive the sense and emotion of her grandmother at the time of her death. The detailed description of the surroundings from her grandmother's viewpoint is followed by the graphic description of how she set herself on fire:

> The Sky is Blue
> And the dirt is brown
> And the windshield is clean
> And the canister is red
> Gasoline along the dash
> and it trickles down her forehead
> a pungent perfume
> that lifts her skin up
> it lifts her skin up
> and the sky is blue. (76)

Each vignette recalls the past, present, and future of the Japanese Americans who have been forced to be silent and to suppress their histories in order to survive.

Hello (Sex) Kitty: Mad Asian Bitch on Wheels (1994) deals with diverse issues in the Asian American community. Uyehara describes the piece as "more about all the things attached to sex—love, self-respect, honoring each other—than about sex itself. It's also about lust, respect, domestic violence, a woman's right to define her own image and access to her passions. It's about an Asian Amer-ican, a bisexual woman, and a human being" (*Hello (Sex) Kitty* 377). Through multiple characters whom she herself plays on stage such as "The Asian Chick,"

"DykeAsia," and "The Asian Guy," Uyehara probes issues of human sexuality, ethnic identity, gender relations, ethnic representations, and violence between women and men. Depicting heterosexual, bisexual, and homosexual relationships, she resists the norms of society that silence diverse voices and views of sexuality. "The Hello Kitty Girl," an Oriental Cherry Blossom archetype, recounts her first date with a white male who takes Polaroids of her while they reenact a tea ceremony. "The Asian Guy" talks about his "Joy Fucked Up Club" date from hell and criticizes the Hollywood films' negative depiction of Asian men and Asian women who date non-Asians (*Hello (Sex) Kitty* 392–93). Meanwhile, his date begins to talk back, creating a feisty dialogue between them. Through these characters, Uyehara attacks the dehumanization and desexualization that many Asian Americans have experienced and accepted silently. At the same time, she demonstrates the need for dialogue between men and women within a community of color.

In 1999, *Maps of City & Body*, which was commissioned by the Mark Taper Forum's Asian Theater Workshop, was produced at Highways Performance Space in Santa Monica, California, under the direction of Chay Yew. In that performance, Uyehara drew shimmering blue and green maps over her body and the back wall. The maps symbolized the collective experiences and memories of ethnically and racially diverse individuals and communities. Through the action of drawing colored lines on her body and the wall, Uyehara demonstrated the intersection of the memories and experiences of her family who lived through the internment camps and Jewish neighbors who survived the Holocaust. This piece once again affirms Uyehara's quest for more borderless identities for racially and sexually marginalized people such as Asian American, Jewish, and Chicana women.

CRITICAL RECEPTION

Uyehara speaks the speaking of the unspeakable and thus totally commits to examining honestly all types of taboos in American society. As she described in an interview with *Rafu Shimpo*, the core of her writing has always been the "Asian American experience," which she described as "what I am and the life that I've lived" (Yokota 2). Her works have been nationally and internationally performed.

Uyehara has received national recognition through various newspapers. Reviewing *Headless Turtleneck Relatives*, Jan Breslauer of the *Los Angeles Times* is impressed by her skillful writing, challenging performance, and "sharply realized point of view" (F4). "[H]er transitions are fluid and economical, the telling of her tales pointed and the performance itself pristine" (Breslauer F4). Connie Monaghan of *LA Weekly* remarks, "Uyehara's wonder as she explores the unknowable resonates beyond the theater's walls to the dark details that inhabit the corners of our lives" (106). Reviewing the production of *Hiro* in 1994, Laurie Winer of the *Los Angeles Times* praises "fleeting moments when one can envision a Uyehara character who one day might really fly" (F1). Praising Uyehara's attempt to break down imposed labels and boundaries, Jana J. Monji of the *Los Angeles Times* states, "Uyehara's concept of body memory and identity is intriguing in its refusal to clearly set up judgmental boundaries about sexuality and ethnicity" (F1).

BIBLIOGRAPHY

Works by Denise Uyehara

Drama

Headless Turtleneck Relatives. Excerpts. *Getting Your Solo Act Together.* Ed. Michael Kearns. Portsmouth, NH: Heinemann, 1997. 75–79.
Hiro. Asian American Drama: 9 Plays from the Multiethnic Landscape. Ed. Brian Nelson. New York: Applause, 1997. 385–421.
Hello (Sex) Kitty: Mad Asian Bitch on Wheels. O Solo Homo: The New Queer Performance. Ed. Holly Hughes and David Román. New York: Grove Press, 1998. 377–409.
Maps of City & Body and Other Tales. New York: Kaya Productions, 2001.

Unpublished Manuscripts

Hobbies. 1989.
Jo & Millie Go to Church. 1994.

Selected Production History

Hobbies

Staged reading. Senshin Buddhist Community Hall, Los Angeles, 1991.
———. Los Angeles Theater Center, Los Angeles, 1991.

Headless Turtleneck Relatives

Production. Institute for Contemporary Art, London, 1993.
———. Highways Performance Space, Santa Monica, CA, 1993.
———. Cleveland Performance Art Festival, Cleveland, 1994.
———. Walker Arts Center, Minneapolis, 1995.
———, dir. Valerie Curtis-Newton. Northwest Asian American Theatre, Seattle, 1995.

Hello (Sex) Kitty: Mad Asian Bitch on Wheels

Production. Institute for Contemporary Art, London, 1994.
———. Fourth World Conference on Women, Beijing, 1995.
———. Brown U, Providence, RI, 1995.
———. Asian American Theater Company, San Francisco, 1996.
———. Painted Bride, Philadelphia, 1996.

Hiro

Production, dir. Roxanne Rogers. East West Players, Los Angeles, 1994.
———. Northwest Asian American Theatre, Seattle, 1996.

Maps of City & Body

Production. Kiasma Museum of Contemporary Art, Helsinki, Finland, 1998.
———. Modern Language Association, San Francisco, 1998.
———. Los Angeles County Museum of Art, Los Angeles, 1999.
———, dir. Chay Yew. Highways Performance Space, Santa Monica, CA, 1999.

Letter

E-mail to the author. 5 June 2000.

Poetry

"Birdseed." *Asian Pacific American Journal* 3.1 (1994): 23–24.

Short Story

"Chasing Airplanes." *Asian Pacific American Journal* 5.2 (1996): 132–40.

Studies of Denise Uyehara

Breslauer, Jan. "Uyehara Paints an Arresting Dreamscape with 'Relatives.' " *Los Angeles Times* 11 Dec. 1993: F4.
Johnson, Glen. "Critical Performance." *Harvard Gay and Lesbian Review* 5.4 (1998): 60.
Monaghan, Connie. "Denise Uyehara." *LA Weekly* 10–15 Dec. 1993: 106.
Monji, Jana J. "*Maps of City & Body*: Memories and Identity." *Los Angeles Times* 12 Nov. 1999: F1.
Winer, Laurie. "*Hiro*: Reaching for Altitude." *Los Angeles Times* 9 July 1994: F1.
Yokota, Kaiann. "Speaking the Unspeakable." *Rafu Shimpo* 20 June 1994: 2.

Ermena Marlene Vinluan
(1949–   )

Theodore S. Gonzalves

BIOGRAPHY

Ermena Marlene Vinluan was born in Berkeley, California, and was raised in the nearby East Bay city of Alameda. She describes her father as a "first wave" Filipina/o immigrant, part of that early cohort of male laborers and students from the Philippines who came to the United States before World War II as subjects of the American empire and who worked in the agricultural and service trades (Chan 39–41). Vinluan's father worked as a farm worker, busboy, elevator man, and chauffeur until World War II broke out. After a brief stint in the U.S. Army, he worked as an air mechanic for the U.S. Navy for over thirty-five years. She describes her mother as a Filipino American "warbride" (Posadas 28) who hailed from Binmaley, Pangasinan, the same hometown as her husband.

In the early 1950s, Vinluan grew up in a mainly white, working-class community that was home to several families connected with the Alameda naval air station. Neighbors included recent immigrants from Portugal, Italy, and Byelorussia, but this did not stop some of the locals from disapproving of her family moving into the area. A group of homeowners actually passed a petition to demand that the outgoing owners of their new house not sell to a nonwhite family. There were few children of color in her elementary school. Nevertheless, she thrived, academically and socially. At the age of eight, she wrote, directed, and produced her first school play, regurgitating popular 1950s Disneyesque television fare. Later, in high school, she was drawn further to the arts: literature, creative writing, the glee club, the orchestra, and more theater.

Because the Filipina/o American community was small and geographically scattered, Vinluan claims that her "Filipino cultural identity and roots were sketchy" (Interview with Uno and Burns). There were communities that got together for birthdays, church meetings, and World War II veterans' group activities. "Unfortunately, these amounted to the traditional folk dancing programs, beauty queen contests, and dances to some excellent Filipino combos playing popular music from the 1930s and 40s" (Personal interview).

Vinluan enrolled at the University of California at Berkeley in the fall of 1967, initially declaring political science as her major to satisfy her parents' wishes that she study what they considered a "serious" field. She also remembers the ignorance of fellow students who spoke slowly to her, assuming that she spoke little English. "The very few people of color on campus were not American [citizens] but rich foreign students whose parents could afford to send them to school overseas and pay those exorbitant fees" (Interview with Uno and Burns).

The University of California at Berkeley was an alienating environment then for freshmen like Vinluan, but suddenly the campus community "exploded with radicalism—culturally and politically—as well as excessively with drugs and a new morality, the so-called 'free-love' of the flower power generation" (Personal interview). Amid the upheaval, Vinluan, who until then had been sheltered by strict immigrant parents, was obliged to leave for study in the Philippines for about a year and a half.

It was in the Philippines that she became familiar with her family's and the Philippines' long history from Spanish times to its neocolonial present. She also became involved in theater again, studying with Rolando Tinio at Ateneo University and with Father James Reuter at the College of the Holy Spirit in Manila, where she found the sisters in charge of the school trying to insulate their students from the growing nationalist movement. But the political activity was all over the city. Students were organized around several key issues: substantive land reform, the use of the Philippines as a staging ground for American violence in Southeast Asia, and the corruption of Philippine president Ferdinand Marcos. Being in the Philippines, Vinluan admitted, "dramatically helped fill out my roots" (Interview with Uno and Burns).

Vinluan also cites her exposure to the city of Olongapo as another lesson in her political education. Originally a fishing village, Olongapo was operated by the Spanish as a naval station. The Americans later developed the surrounding Subic Bay region into one of the largest American bases outside of the United States. In order to service the sexual appetite of its military personnel, "that fishing village had turned into the armpit of the Pacific. It was the playground of hundreds of thousands of GI's looking for entertainment or looking for temporary respite from a war that was becoming very unpopular" (Interview with Uno and Burns). For Vinluan, her witness to the events at Olongapo would confirm for her that a critique of the cultures of U.S. imperialism was necessary.

The United States, and especially the Berkeley campus, was a very different place when Vinluan returned. While all the major universities in the Philippines had become hotbeds of nationalist and radical protests against the Vietnam War, so too had the Berkeley campus turned fiercely against the war in Vietnam.

Along with the powerful anti-U.S.-imperialist movement, students working in racial and ethnic studies became politicized in the Asian American movement (Wei).

Vinluan's return to Berkeley marked her turn toward radical theater—the drama department was staging productions with antiwar and antiracist themes. She also was amazed to see that after the brief year and a half she had been away, there was now a visible presence of black, Latino, and Asian fellow baby boomers and a newly established ethnic studies program. She enrolled in the fledgling Philippine studies course, where her instructors, about her age, asked her to participate in the university's second annual Asian festival by coauthoring and directing a historical play. This was her first foray away from what she described as "Eurocentric" plays and toward her work in "ethnic theater." The piece—*Isuda Ti Imuna* (Those who were first)—was a sprawling, multimedia epic historical pageant. Filipino students from all the Bay Area colleges participated plus "several high schools and even 'manongs,' old-timers who used to play in the band at the community dances.....The performance, too, was a hit for the Asian students on campus, friends, family. But not a hit with the Theater Department" (Interview with Uno and Burns).

Vinluan's work in developing a radical voice in Filipina/o American theater drew further inspiration from several coordinates: her participation in the Chicano theater movement, especially El Teatro Campesino; the San Francisco Mime Troupe; and the cultural group of the National Committee for the Restoration of Civil Liberties in the Philippines. She was also motivated by stories she heard about a University of the Philippines–based agitprop group named Sining Bayan (Interview with Romero).

Such institutions and organizations laid the groundwork for an immigrant community's political education and served as indispensable venues for radicalizing the consciousness of the members of her cohort. The National Committee for the Restoration of Civil Liberties in the Philippines (NCRCLP), founded in the United States in 1971, used its Cultural Committee (1971–73) to perform critiques on the streets, at demonstrations, in programs, and at other public meetings (Personal interview). How these organizations functioned and what they accomplished for thousands of young folks in Vinluan's generation are part of the larger story of Filipina/o American history in the post–World War II period. Her artistic work is the result of mobilizing populations and communities that were deemed too difficult to organize—students, workers, immigrants, and racial minorities.

At the center of Ermena Vinluan's work was the formation of the Katipunan ng mga Demokratikong Pilipino (Union of Democratic Filipinos), or the KDP. Founded in 1973 in northern California's Bay Area, the KDP linked with other activists to develop the "cultural arm" of the Sining Bayan. The purposes of the group included educating its audiences and inspiring political mobilization through agitprop sensibilities. Sining Bayan's productions relied on many theatrical genres and always involved popular forms of music and dance. There were so few Asian professionals or students of the arts at that time that the troupe was comprised of amateurs for the most part. Between school, work, families, production meetings, and rehearsals, the KDP leadership of Sining Bayan organized music studies—from Woodie Guthrie to Jimmy Cliff—as well as outings to performances at the Ashland Shakespeare Festival. Sining Bayan not only emphasized the political conscientization of its audiences but also of its players. Vinluan and the other cultural activists regarded theater as a natural means of recruiting new activists or sympathizers for their cause (Personal interview).

MAJOR WORKS AND THEMES

The themes of Sining Bayan's work ran the gamut of Filipina/o American political history, its reckoning with what the group considered the important issues of the day, and the transnational political imagination of its artists. Although Sining Bayan's work was fostered in a collectivist setting, with several writers, directors, and other contributors often dropping in and out of the many projects, Vinluan is credited as lead writer and director for the group's work.

Isuda Ti Imuna (Those who were first, 1973) followed the stories of three brothers, loosely based on Filipina/o American Popular Front–era writer and activist Carlos Bulosan's text, *America Is in the Heart* (1946). The play combines several other narratives of the harsh experiences faced by Filipino laborers along the West Coast, such as underemployment, unfair labor practices, and racial scapegoating and violence directed against Filipinos. While *Isuda* was performed for aging agricultural workers in central California in the late 1970s, along with their families and the younger Chicano farm-working families, it spoke directly to the qualities that the younger generation ascribed to its Filipino "manongs" (elders, brothers)—cultural intransigence, tenacious organizing, and familial nostalgia. The play's material was developed out of the writers' oral history accounts, and the play featured several college and high-school students (Interview with Uno and Burns).

Sining Bayan's *Mindanao* (1974) was mounted for the University of California at Berkeley's third annual Asian festival. It was produced a year later for an eight-city tour in the United States and Canada. This play featured the interreligious and cultural conflict between Filipina/o Christians and Muslims. It drew attention to the latter as a beleaguered ethnic minority that would seek an alliance with their Christian counterparts to counter the land-grabbing schemes supported by the Marcos regime. According to Vinluan, "The production of *Mindanao* also made possible the first ever Kulintang music ensemble in the U.S. Young Fil-Am rock, jazz and salsa musicians had never heard, let alone set eyes on a set of kulintang gongs. The experience was a phenomenal cultural awakening to pre-Hispanic, native Filipino music and culture to not only these musicians but appreciative Filipinos and non-Filipinos in the audiences" (Interview with Uno and Burns).

Tagatupad (1976) was based on contemporary antieviction struggles of aging working-class Filipina/os living in the inner cities. The central characters, young Filipina/o Americans, helped to organize senior citizens in Seattle's International District around the preservation of low-income housing. *Visions of a Warbride* (1979) centered its narrative on a Pinay's politicization. The backdrop for the play included the lessons of the Philippine Huk resistance in World War II as well as the personalized politics played out in community civic organizations—attuned to and critical of its pettiness, colonial mentality, and divisiveness. Vinluan's text follows the main character through generations of political activity, entering the United States as a war bride but concluding as a mother, worker, and union organizer.

The Frame-up of Narciso and Perez (1979) was quickly written and staged in response to the uproar of real-life events in the Filipina/o American community. In 1979, two immigrant Filipina/o nurses were arrested and charged with the serial murders of their Ann Arbor, Michigan, patients at a Veterans Administration hospital. Through this piece, Sining Bayan boldly challenged the FBI's competence in the investigation of the murders. The play was part of a nationwide organizing campaign spearheaded by the KDP along with Filipina/o nurses groups who had already been organizing for labor immigrant rights. Within a few weeks of *The Frame-up*'s performances, the court released the two nurses and pronounced them innocent.

Ti Mangyuna (Those who led the way, 1981), Sining Bayan's last production, was a collaborative effort between the KDP and the International Longshoremen's and Warehousemen's Union's (ILWU) Local 142 of Hawaii. *Ti Mangyuna* retold the history of the emergence of the powerful labor-union drives in the 1930s. The play was a community event, a production that commemorated the seventy-fifth anniversary of Filipino immigration to Hawaii. The company played to more than 5,000 audiencegoers, touring high schools, community colleges, and hotel ballrooms on Oahu, the Big Island, Maui, Lanai, Molokai, and Kauai. Many in the audience saw their own stories retold onstage. Yet this proved to be tricky in its own right. The KDP's anti-Marcos politics challenged the rank and file of Hawaii's union membership, many of whom were Marcos supporters. To blunt that potential conflict, the KDP worked closely with the ILWU's leadership to highlight the heroic narratives of Filipina/o plantation labor while consciously avoiding what many activists saw as "counterprogramming" by Marcos supporters (Interview with Toribio). In line with Sining Bayan's theater's goals, this production aimed to galvanize an entire community, even with its diverse interests: "to start a network, to mine the community for people to become politicized and to become organized; to launch them into the movement at large" (Personal interview).

CRITICAL RECEPTION

A detailed survey of Filipina/o American theatrical work has not yet been written. Academic criticism of Vinluan's work is underdeveloped. However, during the staging of performances such as *Isuda Ti Imuna*, community activists and scholars criticized the historical accuracy of some of the play's details. For instance, community critics pointed out that the migration of laborers from the Visayan regions came before, not after, the rush of plantation-induced migration from the Ilocos region. Such criticism once again serves as a reminder that (1) artists do not always make the best historians; and (2) Vinluan's and Sining Bayan's work emerged during a time when art and culture making had specific burdens of representing the political aspirations of far-flung Filipina/o American communities in both the United States and the Philippines. Thus discussion of their work opens a larger field of investigation concerning the use of performing arts under the period of cultural nationalism.

Vinluan's radical voice in Filipina/o American theater also testifies to the fact that the historical legacy of American colonialism in the Philippines has been creatively generative. Artists like Vinluan address the historiographical gaps and distortions in the official record, dominant discourse, and popular culture. In doing so, they urge students of Asian American studies to insist on developing relevant criticism and historical accounts that foreground the cultures of U.S. imperialism.

BIBLIOGRAPHY

Works by Ermena Marlene Vinluan

Unpublished Manuscripts

Isuda Ti Imuna (Those Who Were First). 1973.
Maguindanao (also titled *Mindanao*). 1974.
Tagatupad. 1976.
The Frame-up of Narciso and Perez. 1979.
Visions of a Warbride. 1979.
Ti Mangyuna (Those Who Led the Way). 1981.

Selected Production History

Information unavailable.

Interviews

Interview with Roberta Uno and Lucy Mae San Pablo Burns. 1995.
Interview with Helen Toribio. 1998.
Personal interview. 1998.
Interview with Lesly Romero. Videocassette. Ms. 345. Roberta Uno Asian Women Playwrights Scripts Collection 1924–1992, Special Collections and Archives, W.E.B. Du Bois Library, U of Massachusetts, Amherst, n.d.

Studies of Ermena Marlene Vinluan

Bulosan, Carlos. *America Is in the Heart, a Personal History*. New York: Harcourt, Brace and Company, 1946.

Chan, Sucheng. *Asian Americans: An Interpretive History*. Boston: Twayne, 1989.

Fernandez, Doreen G. *Palabas: Essays on Philippine Theater History*. Manila: Ateneo de Manila UP, 1996.

Katipunan ng mga Demokratikong Pilipino (KDP). Event program. 1973.

Peñaranda, Oscar, Serafin Syquia, and Sam Tagatac. "An Introduction to Filipino-American Literature." *Aiiieeeee! An Anthology of Asian-American Writers*. Ed. Frank Chin, Jeffery Paul Chan, Lawson Fusao Inada, and Shawn Hsu Wong. Washington, DC: Howard UP, 1974. xlix–lxiii.

Posadas, Barbara M. *The Filipino Americans*. Westport, CT: Greenwood P, 1999.

Vallangca, Caridad Concepcion. *The Second Wave: Pinay and Pinoy, (1945–1960)*. Ed. Jody Bytheway Larson. San Francisco: Strawberry Hill P, 1987.

Van Erven, Eugene. *The Playful Revolution: Theatre and Liberation in Asia*. Bloomington: Indiana UP, 1992.

Wei, William. *The Asian American Movement*. Philadelphia: Temple UP, 1993.

Elizabeth Wong
(1958–   )

Randy Barbara Kaplan

BIOGRAPHY

Born in South Gate, California, to working-class Chinese immigrant parents, Elizabeth Wong learned early in life to internalize demeaning stereotypes of media-created Asians. As an adolescent growing up in Chinatown, she felt compelled to distance herself from the community in which she had come of age: "I didn't want to have anything to do with all these people who talked with accents, who didn't read the things that I read or see the movies that I saw. . . . I didn't have anything in common with these people. . . . I didn't feel I was like them, I didn't want to be associated with them, and I didn't know why" (qtd. in Uno, "Introduction" 262). Years later, in her essay "The Struggle to Be an All-American Girl," Wong remembered that "Nancy Drew, my favorite book heroine, never spoke Chinese. The language was a source of embarrassment . . . it was loud, it was unbeautiful. . . . not like the gentle refinement of the American South. Chinese sounded pedestrian" (B5).

After completing an undergraduate degree in journalism at the University of Southern California in 1980, Wong continued to struggle with issues of cultural self-denial. Feeling devalued rather than affirmed by her Chinese ancestry, she was unable to cherish it as an empowering means of bringing a unique perspective to her reporting. While she was working as field producer at KNXT-TV News in Los Angeles, where she remained for three years before accepting a reporting position first with the *San Diego Tribune* and subsequently the *Hartford Courant*, she acknowledged feeling resentful when she was assigned to cover "Asian stories." It was Asian American theater that taught Elizabeth Wong to embrace her ethnic heritage as a source of strength rather than an embarrassing flaw. In interviews with producer-director Roberta Uno ("Introduction"

262–63), Wong explained that seeing David Henry Hwang's *FOB* and Wakako Yamauchi's *And the Soul Shall Dance*, plays that treated Asian American themes with dignity, were instrumental in enabling her to legitimize her image of herself.

After eight years of news reporting, Wong found herself questioning the validity of the practice of journalism, which demanded that she confine herself to the objective reconstruction of facts without interpolating her subjective responses to them, especially those influenced by her personal cultural perspective. Her growing awareness of what she perceived to be the inherently restrictive nature of her line of work led her to a reassessment of her professional goals. Though she would eventually return to journalism for a brief time as an editorial columnist for the *Los Angeles Times* (1992–96), Wong discovered that her Asian American voice was an invaluable inspiration in the shaping rather than simply the reproduction of stories.

At the same time, Wong serendipitously came under the influence of several leading American theater artists and educators. Leaving the *Hartford Courant*, she moved to New Haven and devoted her time to sneaking a top notch education in playwriting at the Yale School of Drama, thanks to the generosity of Lloyd Richards, Leon Katz, and a number of its drama graduate students (Wong, "Artistic statement" 311). The experience emboldened her: with not a single theatrical credit to her name, she applied to New York University's graduate playwriting program, feeling somehow sure that theater was the artistic medium that could liberate her as a writer and that New York City was the place where this would happen. In order to be accepted into the program, however, she was required to submit an original script, something she had never before written. The result was *The Aftermath of a Chinese Banquet* (1988), which Wong describes as "my dysfunctional family drama." Wong's instincts served her well. She was accepted into NYU's Tisch School of the Arts, where she completed a master of fine arts in playwriting in 1991. It was there that she developed two of her most popular and oft-produced works, *Letters to a Student Revolutionary* (1989), about the Tiananmen Square massacre, and *Kimchee and Chitlins* (1990), about conflicts between Korean immigrants and African Americans in Brooklyn. Her playwriting career began to take off.

Several events returned Wong to her West Coast home in 1992, among them the death of her grandmother, with whom she had had an extremely loving and supportive relationship. Coincidentally, at the same time, the Asian Theatre Workshop at the Mark Taper Forum invited Wong to perform a reading of *Kimchee and Chitlins*. The reading, coming as it did mere weeks after race rioting in Los Angeles caused the destruction of over two thousand Korean-owned shops, in turn brought her to the attention of Disney Studios, which invited Wong to become one of three writing fellows for its Touchstone Television Division. Wong remained with Touchstone through 1995, becoming a staff writer for the short-lived *All-American Girl* (1994–95) starring Margaret

Cho, the first and only television situation comedy ever to revolve around an Asian American family.

Following the cancellation of *All-American Girl*, Wong added to her list of accomplishments the mentoring of younger playwrights. She had previously taught playwriting at East West Players' David Henry Hwang Institute (1993–94) in Los Angeles; now she joined the faculties of the University of California at Santa Barbara and her alma mater, the University of Southern California, as associate professor of playwriting.

Elizabeth Wong is the recipient of numerous honors and serves on the board of many theater organizations. A member of the Dramatists Guild, Writers Guild West, PEN West, the Circle Repertory Theatre Playwrights Project, and the Mark Taper Forum's Mentor Playwright Program, she has received fellowships from Yaddo, the Ucross Foundation, and Catawba College. She received the Playwright Forum Award from Theatre Works in Colorado Springs (1990) and a Margo Jones New Play Citation (1992) for *Letters to a Student Revolutionary* and the Association for Theatre in Higher Education's Jane Chambers Award for the abbreviated version of *China Doll* (1995). Wong serves on the advisory board of Theatre Emory in Atlanta along with distinguished playwrights Wole Soyinka, Wendy Wasserstein, and Alfred Uhry. In 1998, Wong's papers were established in the California Ethnic and Multicultural Archives at the University of California at Santa Barbara's Davidson Library.

MAJOR WORKS AND THEMES

Letters to a Student Revolutionary (1989), the first American play to dramatize events surrounding the Tiananmen Square massacre, is Wong's most popular produced work. The script was inspired by her real-life correspondence with a young Chinese woman beginning in 1984. After the massacre, Wong ceased to receive letters from her friend and never heard from her again. In Wong's theatrical rendition of the story, two women who have little more in common than their racial identity experience emotional and spiritual transformations through their decade-long exchange of letters. Bibi is the American-born mall junkie and news reporter who struggles with issues of identity and self-worth, as did Wong in her own earlier years. Bibi's Chinese counterpart is Karen, barely postadolescent and desirous of any and all things American, whom Bibi first meets in 1979 while accompanying her family on a trip to its ancestral home.

The women's lack of commonality as they engage in their correspondence is reflected in their consistent, oftentimes-humorous misreadings of each other, colored by Karen's earnestness contrasted with Bibi's cynicism. When Bibi, for example, suggests that Karen participate in an American national pastime as a way of chasing her blues away, Karen assumes that Bibi is referring to baseball; Bibi instead is actually referring to "retail therapy"—shopping (298). Their initial accidental meeting, ironically in Tiananmen Square, establishes Bibi's

American standard for "freedom" that places Karen, as a Chinese, squarely in the loser's position, even to the colors of her clothing. In post–Cultural Revolution China, where people are still suspicious of wearing anything but proper Maoist blues and grays, Karen sees Bibi, "in pink, lavender, indigo . . . a human rainbow" (270). Bibi is thus immediately established as the personification of individual empowerment by virtue of her "American" right to freedom, which turns out to be nothing more than instant sensual gratification—be it a Big Mac, a curly perm, or a well-built surfer in a wet suit. Karen is nevertheless mesmerized by Bibi, drawn to her as a moth to a flame. The danger of their contact, which exposes Karen to all the temptations of American "freedom," renders her potentially vulnerable to government reprisal.

At first, Karen misunderstands the significance of American liberties; she sees, for example, that Bibi can nonchalantly travel wherever her impulses take her, whereas her own movements are closely monitored and controlled by the Chinese Communist government. Bibi's sympathies for Karen are likewise misplaced; she perceives Karen's politically enforced lack of materialism as a denial of her fundamental human rights. To that end, Bibi tries to assuage Karen's deprivation by mailing American goodies: perfume, a tape player, fashion magazines.

As time progresses and Karen grows into young womanhood, however, her intellectual and spiritual positions begin to shift, almost imperceptibly at first, then with gathering momentum as they parallel the genesis and growth of China's student-driven democracy movement. Upon realizing that Bibi's right to flit from job to job and man to man is actually not freedom at all but rather a form of enslavement, Karen comes to understand that Bibi's is not a freedom to be emulated. Instead, she chooses to commit her energies to achieving true freedom for all Chinese citizens. When Karen urges Bibi to appreciate democracy for its enabling of the individual to count, Bibi responds, "That's funny. I never feel my vote counts for anything. It all happens without me" (298). Bibi, hoodwinked by the ersatz freedom of her credit-card culture, has judged her American right to vote and found it worthless compared with the liberty to spend, spend, and spend some more. Karen, reacting to Bibi's political emptiness, is unable to convince her friend that democracy and capitalism are not interchangeable. By the time a pregnant Karen takes her commitment to its logical and only possible end, she disappears in the mass of bodies and debris in Tiananmen Square. For Bibi, it will be too late to save Karen.

Letters introduces Wong's first use of a chorus as a character, a choice that provides significant aural texturing and vocal harmony to her play; she returns to this technique in several subsequent works. From time to time, each member of the four-person *Letters* Chorus portrays specific supporting roles. Chorus One, for example, also functions as both Bibi's boyfriend Charlie and Karen's fiancé Lu Yan; Chorus Two as Bibi's Father, Karen's Brother, and an I.N.S. Officer. While this approach certainly provides appealing challenges for Wong's

actors, it fulfills dramatic functions above and beyond showcasing acting prowess.

When the technique splits the Chorus into individual voices who are not
specific characters, such as Karen's Brother, but simply remain nameless Chorus
members who speak individually, it becomes a theatrical referent for Wong's
journalistic training. Most simply, the Chorus imparts information about dates
and timelines in the bare-bones style of a cub reporter. However, Wong develops
the Chorus's function in another, more complex way by using it as a means to
present simultaneous and multiple perspectives rather than limiting herself to
constructing a single linear narrative that proceeds from and is controlled by a
protagonist's sole point of view. The Chorus can therefore dramatize ambiguity,
inviting the audience to consider concurrent perspectives. When the Chorus describes the 1983 Chinese premiere of Arthur Miller's *Death of a Salesman*, three
speakers present three different Chinese responses to Miller's influential drama.
The first speaker echoes Biff's lines from Miller's Epilogue, "Willy Loman
didn't know who he was. He had all the wrong dreams." Subsequent speakers
follow:

Chorus Three: I have those same dreams.
Chorus Four: I don't know who I am. (292)

Bibi responds with "I don't know who I am," a motif that recurs in the two
women's letters four years later. Wong does not indicate through stage directions
Chorus One's identity or how he should read his line. Is he simply reiterating
Miller's famous lines for dramatic effect? Coming to an understanding of Willy
Loman that is in accordance with Miller's? Taking exception to Miller's lines?
Similarly, Chorus Three's line is open to interpretation: it may be that he shares
those dreams and is, like Happy in Miller's Epilogue, enthusiastic about pursuing them. Or he may be expressing defiance toward Biff. A third alternative
would be that he is realizing that having those same dreams aligns him with
Willy, a loser. Chorus Four is the only female chorus member; she may speak
for herself, for Karen, or for Bibi, who responds with her own "I don't know
who I am."

Alternatively, Wong uses the Chorus to create what she calls "a collective
consciousness, a barometer for ethical behavior for the other characters," much
in the tradition of classical Greek playwrights. In one of the opening scenes of
Letters, the Chorus becomes the manifestation of the faceless monolith that is
the Chinese Communist party, physically creating a human wall between Karen
and Bibi. One by one they decry the individuality manifested by Bibi's colorful
appearance and Karen's risky behavior in approaching her, describing both as
wild and unclean, not to be tolerated. Each Chorus member articulates different
party fears regarding Chinese contact with foreigners until their lines culminate
in a whispered refrain of "There is no you. There is no me. Only people. People

must prevail" (273). Late in the play, the Chorus transforms itself into the sea of dissidents who gave their lives at Tiananmen Square, shouting slogans made famous by that student movement.

Finally, by virtue of its journalistic "objectivity," the Chorus is enabled to stand outside the dramatic action and foreground the play's ironies as experienced by its main characters. The sad truth of *Letters* is driven home by the Chorus in the play's final moments: "And China has begun a policy of selective historical amnesia. And fast-food America has gone back to shopping" (308).

In her next play, *Kimchee and Chitlins* (1990), Wong examined the economic entanglements and cultural misunderstandings that provided the impetus for the 1990 boycott of Korean greengrocers by black communities in Brooklyn, New York. The play received its first reading at New York City's Primary Stages in June 1991 in the aftermath of the Brooklyn conflicts. However, *Kimchee and Chitlins* unexpectedly—and sadly—turned out to be a prophecy of the race riots in Los Angeles commemorated in the Korean community as *sa-i-gu* (literally, 2–9), which occurred barely ten months later on April 29, 1992.

With *Kimchee and Chitlins*, Wong made several innovative contributions to the field of Asian American dramaturgy. Asian American playwrights have never feared to address issues of interracial conflict, whether between Asian American characters and whites (R.A. Shiomi's *Uncle Tadao*, Philip Kan Gotanda's *Sisters Matsumoto*, and Genny Lim's *Paper Angels* are three examples that come to mind) or Asian American characters and non-Asian characters of color (Velina Hasu Houston's *Asa Ga Kimashita*, Gotanda's *Wash*). In *Kimchee and Chitlins*, however, Wong places overt antagonism between an Asian American population and a non-Caucasian community of color at the center of its dramatic action. Wong also broke theatrical ground with her depiction of an Asian American community that was of neither Chinese nor Japanese descent. Though protagonist Suzie Seeto is herself Chinese American, Wong's central positioning of Korean and Korean American characters predated the work of Korean American writers such as Harold Byun, Diana Son, Rob Shinn, and Sung Rno, playwrights who came to prominence during the mid- to late 1990s.

In *Kimchee and Chitlins*, Wong investigates a complex cluster of issues engendered by hatred rooted in cultural, ethnic, class, and sexual differences. A corollary to that theme is whether, given individual and collective perspectives that generate, justify, and maintain hatred, objective truth can exist and be defined. The play opens with a child's beginning: Suzie Seeto relates her eye-opening experience of her first encounter with an African American man, her first-ever awareness of racial difference. As she reports the incident, it was "no big deal" (5). However, the two Choruses, which remain onstage throughout the play to comment on its action, perceive the same incident quite differently. The Black Chorus agrees with Suzie, but the Korean Chorus, contradicting its Black counterpart, describes Suzie as frozen with fear at the sight of the African American "bogeyman" (6). From the very outset of the dramatic action, therefore, oppositional interpretations governed by individual and communal racial perspectives are established. These often-irreconcilable versions of truth drive the subsequent dramatic action toward its irreconcilable conclusion.

A Chinese American from Canton, Ohio, who prefers a burger to dim sum and a fork to chopsticks, Suzie Seeto is the polar opposite of her Caucasian boss Mark Thompson, a Buddhist Asiaphile who can order dinner in "perfect Thailandese" (67) and is "too Asian" (62) to suit Suzie's taste in men. As did Wong herself, Suzie struggles with self-definition when as an Asian American woman she is assigned "stories of color," stories she considers to be "soft news." She is thus less than thrilled at the prospect of covering the boycott of Key Chun Mak's grocery led by black activist Reverend Lonnie Carter. The assignment forces her to confront racism in her colleagues and her boss, in the black boycotters and the Koreans who defend their business, and, most importantly, in herself. She finally is brought face-to-face with her responsibility to the Asian American community upon witnessing four African American boys beating a Vietnamese youth they assume to be Korean with a baseball bat. As she records dispassionately the event for the nightly news, she realizes,

I was too busy, too preoccupied with disassociating myself from that squirming weak, yellow boy on the ground. Coolly, I hid behind my profession, thoroughly brainwashed by my complete-and-utter certainty that I could not and would not be hurt . . . because I was NOT like that kid. Those black boys with their baseball bat shattered my beautiful delusion once and forever. For if I wasn't yellow, then what color did I think I was? (82)

The Black and Korean Choruses chant in unison, whispering, "The bogeyman is here. Inside you. Inside me. . . . Make the bogeyman go away. Make the bogeyman go away" (83). That very "bogeyman," primogenitor of universal fear of the Other, has replicated himself in Suzie Seeto, so proud of her nonracist views, and, by extension, in all people. As he was present in the very first scene of the play in which Suzie the child saw her first black face, so he reappears at the play's conclusion, forcing her gaze upon the distasteful and inevitable truth, a truth from which she has long tried to hide.

Throughout *Kimchee and Chitlins*, Wong repeatedly demonstrates that the nightly news, a supposed repository of objective truth, is nothing more than a false construct. Through the juxtaposition of images, sound bites, and timely—or not so timely—questioning, the media empower themselves to create palatable "truths" that can be sold for profit. In a scene by turns cynical and hilarious, Korean grocer Key Chun Mak and African American barber James Brown fling accusations and insults at each other, but only for as long as they are guaranteed their fifteen minutes of fame: "We're taking a break. . . . When the red light goes on, we go on and when the red light goes off . . . forget it, Makie" (65).

Among Suzie's numerous conflicts with Mark Thompson is their disagreement over whether the media are entitled to sanitize news that is potentially inflammatory. If, as Thompson believes, the media are obligated to render information that could be construed as dangerous as palatable instead, it follows that the media are further empowered to manufacture a "truth" empowered to heal, as the conclusion of *Kimchee and Chitlins* seems to suggest. Wong, an expert at pulling the rug from beneath the audience's expectations, seems to suggest that neutralizing the bogeyman could be accomplished through the deliberate invention of a meaningful truth. To that end, the play is performed with two endings, one immediately following the other. In the first, "true-to-life" ending, grocer Mak, unable to withstand the financial blow caused by the boycott, prepares to sell his grocery, a business he has run for over ten years. Though barber Brown sympathizes, it is only moments before the two men resort to their old pattern of racially motivated recriminations, each accusing the other of having failed him. Suddenly, for the first and only time in the play, stage directions instruct the Black and Korean Choruses to stand intermingled onstage. In unison they announce that since reality is too depressing for popular consumption, a more uplifting outcome ought to be provided. The actors maneuver into position after the manner of images on a rewinding videotape to start the scene over. In the "instant replay," Mak's and Brown's dialogue changes completely: both men acknowledge that in order to make peace, they must break bread together. In this case, they agree to share a feast of the pungent kimchee and chitlins of the play's title that represent their cultures' shared qualities. Suzie sardonically remarks as the curtain falls, "Just goes to show, . . . the best stories are *invented*" (85), thereby reinforcing Wong's position that if truth can be artificially constructed for conflict's sake, there is no reason that it should not be possible or even advisable to manufacture it for healing's sake.

Wong's ability to render deeply serious material as wildly humorous without sacrificing the significance of its import is evident throughout the play. The story, which could easily disintegrate into pathos, is kept in check by what can only be described as Wong's wicked sense of humor, which short-circuits the audience's ability to wallow in that most undemanding and far too simplistic of emotional judgment calls, sentimentality. Suzie Seeto, ever confused as to which group she is ethically—and ethnically—obligated to represent more sympathetically on television, visits both sides of the black-Korean controversy. The Black Chorus acts out the Koreans' alleged attack on a Haitian immigrant that caused all the fuss; then the Korean Chorus takes its turn. Both versions of the incident, with the Black Chorus acting out its interpretation of "typical" Korean behaviors and attitudes and the Korean Chorus performing its own rendering of African American gangbangers and Haitian immigrants, evoke laughter, and although both reveal exaggerations and misunderstandings, both have some truth to them.

Indeed, at the conclusions of these choral scenes, just as Suzie is on the verge of uncovering the "truth," in typical television style, both scenes cut to a commercial. In the first, Mark and Suzie take turns relating ethnocultural myths. For Mark, the myth is the sexual availability of Asian women; for Suzie, it is the comic-book ethos of Superman, Lois Lane, and their journalistic adventures on the *Daily Planet*. Though neither myth has any realistic validity, both myths drive Mark's and Suzie's lives. In the second commercial, blonde, blue-eyed anchorwoman Tara Sullivan teaches the women of color in the play another enduring myth: no doubt about it, blondes do have more fun. But as for the truth, the real "truth," of what happened in Mak's store, that never comes to light—it simply is too clouded over with individual and collective perspective to be ascertainable.

The commercial breaks in the play give Wong an opportunity to confront the audience about its own "bogeymen," using humor to name aloud the secret prejudices many people harbor. In another commercial break, Tara Sullivan instructs the white folks in the audience on how to avoid feeling "queasy" around black people: "Just say, 'Hey, bro' whas' up' and give' em a high five. And all your fears will disappear . . . like magic" (41). No cow is too sacred to be the butt of Wong's jokes, even the most inflammatory of racial epithets. In the midst of slinging insults at each other, the Black Chorus, carried away by emotion and confusion, yells, "Black nigger!" at the Koreans, who, just as wound up, respond by shouting, "Yellow nigger!" Upon immediate reflection, the Black Chorus hurriedly corrects itself, "Well, you know what I mean," as the Koreans wonder aloud, "Did we say that right?" (59). Toward the end of act 2, after the opposing sides agree to talk about their differences, the potential for a storybook ending is undercut when the mediation session disintegrates into a wild free-for-all with both sides chucking every object in sight at each other and barely missing Suzie, who is attempting to cover the story and protect herself at the same time.

Wong's irreverent attitude to sacred cows surfaces throughout her plays and is especially evident in her later, short theater pieces. *Punk Girls: On Divine Omnipotence and the Longstanding Nature of Evil* (1997) is a philosophical debate about the existence of evil in the universe placed in the unlikely mouths of its purple and green spike-haired postadolescent protagonists. *Let the Big Dog Eat* (1998), which Wong wrote for Actors Theatre of Louisville's Humana Festival, effectively satirizes Ted Turner's billion-dollar contribution to the United Nations, placing him on a golf green with other money-making moguls who mightily resent him for making them look stingy.

Another significant work in progress is *China Doll*, Wong's homage to film star Anna May Wong, an Asian American pioneer in the entertainment industry whose courage and tenacity have long gone unrecognized. In its abbreviated version, the work was the recipient of the Association for Theatre in Higher Education's prestigious Jane Chambers Award (1995). The piece is a biographical dramatization and exposé of the racism and sexism that prohibited Wong from achieving her full creative potential, restricting her instead to playing "dragon ladies" and gangsters' molls.

Along with R.A. Shiomi and Cherylene Lee, Wong is one of the few Asian American playwrights to turn her attention to writing for young audiences, a field she never planned to enter but in which she has recently found both fulfillment and success. Her first effort, an adaptation of Oscar Wilde's short story

The Happy Prince (1998), was commissioned by the Kennedy Center for the Performing Arts. Its positive reception resulted in further commissions to produce works for young audiences, from the Denver Theatre Center for *Prometheus* (1999) and *Amazing Adventures of the Marvelous Monkey King* (2001); from Cincinnati's Playhouse in the Park for *Boyd and Oskar* (1999), a modern reworking of *The Happy Prince*; and again from the Kennedy Center for *The Happy Prince: The Opera!* (2002). Wong perceives the challenge of writing for this much-neglected audience as deriving from the need for playwrights to engage in a delicate balancing act of writing, creating work that is on the cutting edge but that does not sacrifice "subatomic energy," all the while influencing children to seek excellence and moral good within themselves.

CRITICAL RECEPTION

As with many other Asian American playwrights whose work came to prominence in the aftermath of David Henry Hwang's and Philip Kan Gotanda's commercial and artistic successes, critical consideration of Elizabeth Wong's works exists mainly in the form of newspaper reviews of her productions. An exception worth noting is Josephine Lee's "Asian American Doubles and the Soul under Capitalism" in her study *Performing Asian America* (1997). In her chapter, Lee considers the manner in which Asian American playwrights construct the technique of doubling, that is, positioning two Asian American characters as cultural opposites on a continuum of "Asianness" and the working out of the resultant conflict.

Lee begins with the concept of "doubling" defined by Sau-Ling Cynthia Wong in *Reading Asian American Literature* (109–12) as a metaphor for racial self-hatred in which one character, desiring to deny her ethnic identity, faces off with and rejects a second character who epitomizes that ethnic identity in some way—looks, dress, speech, values. However, Lee expands upon that concept of racial doubling by adding to the mix a consideration of economic pressures promoted by capitalist ideology. Thus Lee perceives the cultural schizophrenia of the Asian American character as "the result of . . . existence within a system that perpetuates self-individuation and consumerism as goals and encourages the replacement of other human bonds with purely economic relations" (168). In *Letters*, therefore, the American-born Bibi's initial condescension toward her root culture is indeed a metaphor for Asian American racial self-hatred. Bibi expresses revulsion toward Chinese food, Chinese music, and Chinese attitudes, comparing them to their American equivalents and finding them sadly lacking (much as Wong herself did in the essay "The Struggle to Be an All-American Girl"). Lee suggests that Bibi's cultural disgust repudiates "the threat of a shared Asianness" (169) that could topple the so-called normative American body politic with its collectivity of potential pan-Asian resistance to American options.

Bibi, a confirmed and joyful American consumer, undergoes her own process of enlightenment as she discovers that the more she shops, the less she is able to fill the hole that is at her spiritual core. For Karen, on the other hand, living under a totalitarian regime, consuming is neither an actual option nor a longed-for dream. Rather, Karen turns her sights toward self-realization in the communal struggle for liberty not grounded in freedom to spend. As Lee notes, the Chinese Communist government is a self-defined and out-in-the-open "machine of oppression," but American capitalism is perhaps a more insidious molder of character, seductively cloaking itself in a glittering come-on of materialism (185).

Lee perceives the outcome of *Letters* as suggesting an intraethnic unity that is unique and "potentially subversive," for it represents a new connection, an affirmation of commonality between a Chinese American woman and her Chinese double rather than a reinforcement of their disparities (188). Noting one of the final letters Bibi sends to Karen, in which Bibi tells her, "I am Chinese too and I feel a deep connection to you" (Wong, *Letters* 305), Lee sees the ties that bind Karen and Bibi as derived not from "family, nationalism or economic profit," but solely from a past and potentially a future grounded in honoring their shared and empowering identity as Chinese women (Lee 188).

BIBLIOGRAPHY

Works by Elizabeth Wong

Drama

Assume the Position. Script Magazine 1990: 42–84.

Letters to a Student Revolutionary. Unbroken Thread: An Anthology of Plays by Asian American Women. Ed. Roberta Uno. Amherst: U of Massachusetts P, 1993. 261–308. Rpt. in *Women on the Verge: 7 Avant-garde American Plays.* Ed. Rosette C. Lamont. New York: Applause, 1993. 277–334; Woodstock, IL: Dramatic Publishing Company, 1996; *Multicultural Theatre II: Contemporary Hispanic, Asian and African-American Plays.* Ed. Roger Ellis. Colorado Springs: Meriwether, 1998. 143–94; *Playwrights of Color.* Ed. Meg Swanson and Robin Murray. Yarmouth, ME: Intercultural P, 1999. 533–61.

Kimchee and Chitlins. Woodstock, IL: Dramatic Publishing Company, 1996. Rpt. *But Still, Like Air, I'll Rise: New Asian American Plays.* Ed. Velina Hasu Houston. Philadelphia: Temple UP, 1997. 395–450.

China Doll. Abridged version. *Contemporary Plays by Women of Color: An Anthology.* Ed. Kathy A. Perkins and Roberta Uno. New York: Routledge, 1996. 310–16.

Let the Big Dog Eat. Humana Festival '98: The Complete Plays. Ed. Michael Bigelow Dixon and Amy Wegener. Lyme, NH: Smith and Kraus, 1998. 357–67. Rpt. *Ten Minute Plays: Volume 5 from Actors Theatre of Louisville.* Ed. Michael Bigelow Dixon and Amy Wegener. New York: Samuel French, 2000. 141–49.

"Elizabeth Wong: *Inside a Red Envelope.*" *Playwriting Master Class: The Personality of Processes and the Art of Rewriting.* Ed. Michael Wright. Portsmouth, NH: Heinemann, 2000. 15–27.

Punk Girls: On Divine Omnipotence and the Longstanding Nature of Evil. Scenes and Monologues for Young Actors. Ed. Kent Brown. Woodstock, IL: Dramatic Publishing Company, 2000. 229–31.

Unpublished Manuscripts

The Aftermath of a Chinese Banquet. Ms. 345. Roberta Uno Asian Women Playwrights Scripts Collection 1924–1992, Special Collections and Archives, W.E.B. Du Bois Library, U of Massachusetts, Amherst, 1988.

Bu and Bun. 1991.

Reveries of an Amorous Woman. 1991.

The Concubine Spy. 1992.

"Young at Heart." *All-American Girl* (ABC television series). 1994.

"The Apartment." *All-American Girl* (ABC television series). 1995.

China Doll. Full-length version. 1995.

Alice Downsized. 1998.

The Happy Prince. Adaptation from Oscar Wilde's short story. 1998.

Boyd and Oskar: A Play Inspired by Oskar Wilde's The Happy Prince. 1999.

Prometheus. 1999.

Amazing Adventures of the Marvelous Monkey King. 2001.

Badass of the RIP Eternal. 2001.

The Happy Prince: The Opera! Work in progress. Commissioned by the Kennedy Center for the Performing Arts for 2002 production.

Selected Production History

Letters to a Student Revolutionary

Staged reading. Henry Street Settlement, New York City, 1989.

———. Pan Asian Repertory Theatre, New York City, 1989.

———. Theatre Works, Colorado Springs, 1989.

Production. Theatre Works, Colorado Springs, 1990.

Staged reading. Theatre in the Works, Amherst, MA, 1991.

Production. New WORLD Theatre, U of Massachusetts, Amherst, MA, 1991.

———, dir. Ernest Abuba; perf. Karen Tsen Lee and Mary Lum. Pan Asian Repertory Theatre, New York City, 1991.

———, prod. Pan Asian Repertory Theatre. Singapore Arts Festival, 1992.

———. Pan Asian Repertory Theatre National Tour, 1993–95.

———, dir. Szu Wang Wakeman; perf. Jennifer Fujii, Vicky Chow, Newton Kaneshiro, Art Desuyo, Rex Lee, and Janet J. Song. East West Players, Los Angeles, 1994.

———, dir. Manuel R. Cawaling; perf. Kathy Hsieh, Anthony Colinares, Dylan Okimoto, Lisa Nakamura, and Tiffany Saito. Northwest Asian American Theatre, Seattle, 1994.

———. Brecht Festival, Tokyo, Japan, 1997.

———, dir. Kathy Gibbs; perf. Jenny Selner, Karen Tran, Kurt Hirata, Cherry Rox Lorenzana, Arnold Marquez, and Phil Simon. San Diego Asian American Repertory Theatre, 1998.

———, dir. John Lim. Asian American Theatre Project, Stanford U, Stanford, CA, 1999.

———, dir. Due Quach; prod. Flora Kao and Carey Hsu; perf. June Mee Kim, Andy

Han, Maria Ho, Angela Hur, and Jared Green. Asian American Association Players, Harvard U, Cambridge, MA, 1999.

————, dir. Sonny Alforque; perf. Kyla Aquino, Bernadette Ang, Brian Doan, Israel Serrat, Eric Fong, and Katrina Ordonio. INTERact, Sacramento, CA, 2000.

Reveries of an Amorous Woman

Production. Bouwerie Lane Theatre, New York City, 1991.

Kimchee and Chitlins

Staged reading. Primary Stages, New York City, 1991–92.

————. Women's Project, New York City, 1992.

————. Actors Institute, New York City, 1992.

————. Mark Taper Forum, Los Angeles, 1992.

Production. Chameleon Productions, Chicago, 1992.

————. Victory Gardens Theatre, Chicago, 1993.

————, dir. Claudia Jaffee; perf. Julia Nickson, Nyra Crenshaw, Larry Gamell, Jr., Kevin E. Jones, Allison Sie, Benjamin Lum, and Eddie Mui. West Coast Ensemble, Los Angeles, 1994.

————. Theatre Emory, Atlanta, 1995.

Staged reading, dir. Randy Barbara Kaplan; perf. Sam Chan, Carl Marcelo, Hoang Trinh, Judy No, Sara Howard, Dan Saper, Ernest Wilson, Michelle Brummell, and Arthur Louissaint. GENseng, State U of New York, Geneseo, 2000.

"Young at Heart," episode of All-American Girl

Production, prod. Gary Jacobs; perf. Margaret Cho, B.D. Wong, Jodi Long, Amy Hill, and Clyde Kusatsu. ABC-TV, Los Angeles. 5 Oct. 1994.

"The Apartment," episode of All-American Girl

Production, prod. Gary Jacobs; perf. Margaret Cho, B.D. Wong, Jodi Long, Amy Hill, and Clyde Kusatsu. ABC-TV, Los Angeles. 11 Jan. 1995.

Let the Big Dog Eat

Production. New American Play Humana Festival, Actors Theatre of Louisville, KY, 1998.

China Doll (full-length version)

Staged reading, dir. Lee Ann Tzeng; prod. Flora Kao; perf. Jared Greene, Andy Han, Terry Chang, John Doan, Reihan Salam, Risha Lee, Alex Chen, and Alex Patterson. Asian American Association Players, Harvard U, Cambridge, MA, 1999.

————, dir. Tom Prewitt. Kennedy Center, Washington, DC, 2000.

Production, dir. Chay Yew. Northwest Asian American Theatre, Seattle, 2001.

Prometheus

Production, dir. Luanne Nunes. Denver Theatre Center, 1999.

Punk Girls: On Divine Omnipotence and the Longstanding Nature of Evil

Production. Jewish Women's Theatre Project, Los Angeles, 1999–2000.

————. Shalimar Theatre, New York City, 2001.

Amazing Adventures of the Marvelous Monkey King

Production. Denver Center Theatre Company, CO, 2001.

―――. Honolulu Theatre for Youth, HI, 2001.

Badass of the RIP Eternal

Production. Heaven/Hell Project, New American Play Humana Festival, Louisville, KY, 2001.

Essays

"The Struggle to Be an All-American Girl." *Los Angeles Times* 7 Sept. 1980: B5.

"The *Miss Saigon* Diaries." With Cecilia Pang. *American Theatre Magazine* Dec. 1990: 40–43.

"A Present for PoPo." *Los Angeles Times* 30 Dec. 1992: B7.

"A Real American Me at the Movies." *Los Angeles Times* 12 May 1993: B7.

"Double Decaf PC with a Twist." *Los Angeles Times* 16 June 1993: B7.

"But What about Michelle Kwan?" *Los Angeles Times* 18 Jan. 1994: B9.

"Artistic Statement and Production History." *Contemporary Plays by Women of Color: An Anthology.* Ed. Kathy A. Perkins and Roberta Uno. New York: Routledge, 1996. 310–11.

"Exercises." *Conducting a Life: Reflections on the Theatre of Maria Irene Fornes.* Ed. Maria M. Delgado and Caridad Svich. Lyme, NH: Smith and Kraus, 1999. 221–23.

Studies of Elizabeth Wong

Bommer, Lawrence. "Culture Clash." Rev. of *Kimchee and Chitlins. Chicago Tribune* 6 May 1993: 511C.

Collins, Scott. " 'Kimchee, Chitlins' Leaves a Mixed Taste." Rev. of *Kimchee and Chitlins. Los Angeles Times* 29 July 1994: F25.

Feingold, Michael. "Savage Tongues." Rev. of *Letters to a Student Revolutionary. Village Voice* 36.22 (1991): 99.

Foley, F. Kathleen. "Striking *Letters to a Student Revolutionary*." Rev. of *Letters to a Student Revolutionary. Los Angeles Times* 13 May 1994: F16.

Gussow, Mel. "Letters across a Cultural Divide." Rev. of *Letters to a Student Revolutionary. New York Times* 16 May 1991, current events ed.: C18.

Lee, Josephine. "Asian American Doubles and the Soul under Capitalism." *Performing Asian America: Race and Ethnicity on the Contemporary Stage.* By Josephine Lee. Philadelphia: Temple UP, 1997. 163–88.

Torres, Vicki. "Prophetic Drama Evokes Some Jitters." Rev. of *Kimchee and Chitlins. Los Angeles Times* 26 May 1992: B3.

Uno, Roberta. "Appendix: Plays by Asian American Women." *Unbroken Thread: An Anthology of Plays by Asian American Women.* Ed. Roberta Uno. Amherst: U of Massachusetts P, 1993. 309–28.

―――. "Introduction to *Letters to a Student Revolutionary*." *Unbroken Thread: An Anthology of Plays by Asian American Women.* Ed. Roberta Uno. Amherst: U of Massachusetts P, 1993. 261–63.

Wong, Saus-ling Cynthia. *Reading Asian American Literature: From Necessity to Extravagance.* Princeton, NJ: Princeton UP, 1993.

Merle Woo

(1941–   )

Janet Hyunju Clarke

BIOGRAPHY

Merle Woo is often described as a teacher and a writer; she is very much both. But her name is also associated with the term "fighter," for she has been a tireless combatant against racism, sexism, homophobia, and capitalism. Beginning in 1981, she successfully sued the University of California at Berkeley several times for discrimination in firing her. She is an active leader in the Freedom Socialist party and Radical Women. She is a breast-cancer survivor. She ran for governor of California in 1990 on the Peace and Freedom ticket. She believes in and participates in community activism. Woo is a vocal queer socialist feminist whose life experiences have borne out the courage of her convictions.

Woo was born in San Francisco, California, on October 24, 1941. Her father, Richard, an immigrant from southern China, was a ginseng salesman, Methodist minister, and store clerk. Though her Korean mother, Helene Chang, was born in Los Angeles, she lived in Shanghai until she was ten years old, when she was sent to an orphanage in the United States. She worked as a maid, waitress, salesclerk, office worker, and nurse's aide. Woo's parents were both detained at Angel Island when they entered the United States. One of Woo's early concerns was to give voice to her parents and their generation through her writings, as is evident in her essay "Letter to Ma" and the dramatic monologue *Home Movies*. She is the mother of two grown children, Emily and Paul.

Woo has taught ethnic and women's studies and creative writing at San Francisco State University and the University of California at Berkeley. She was a member of the Asian American Theater Company of San Francisco, where she performed in Amy Sanbo and Lonny Kaneko's *Lady Is Dying* in 1977, but her interest in writing plays was sparked by a new performance group of six Chinese American women called Unbound Feet. The group consisted of Nellie Wong, Kitty Tsui, Canyon Sam, Genny Lim, Nancy Ho, and later Merle Woo. She joined the group in 1980. There was a "desire to write and perform our own pieces," she emphasized during an interview, "to make them accessible to the community" (Telephone interview).

MAJOR WORKS AND THEMES

Woo is a prolific writer. Though she is known best for her essays and poetry, her dramatic work echoes the concerns she routinely addresses in her other writings, namely, the realities, struggles, and joys of life as a queer Asian American feminist, socialist, activist, mother, and daughter. She wrote a dramatic monologue, *Home Movies*, in 1979 and a two-act play, *Balancing*, in 1980. She sees her dramatic efforts in a larger framework of the general goals espoused by the now-defunct performance group, Unbound Feet, which were to produce pieces that expressed their own voices and concerns and to reach the community they belonged to.

In *Home Movies*, the speaker is an elderly woman with a "slightly Chinese accent" in a convalescent hospital. As she watches an old black-and-white film in which a white man is assaulting a young girl, she cannot help seeing a "family resemblance": she muses that the girl in the movie could be herself, or her daughter, or even her Ma-Ma. As the line between fiction and reality is blurred, the speaker not only identifies with the girl but also identifies the male character as her abusive employer, Mr. Kearney, from her own past. In the movie, the girl does what the man would not have expected of an Asian woman: she fights back. Indeed, he is not only surprised but dies a violent death at the girl's hands. As the speaker watches this movie, she herself goes through an emotional transformation: from apathy and lethargy to fear, then to anger and joy. When the man dies with "red foam streaming from the mouth," the speaker feels the "need to sing out! Now!" The monologue ends with the speaker singing in a "triumphant crescendo." The themes of this dramatic monologue resonate with a primary goal of Unbound Feet—that of fighting racism, sexism, and ignorance through self-affirmation and voice.

Moreover, the violence in this play suggests that this fight is a matter of life and death. In "Some Basic Ingredients for *Home Movies*," Woo writes that seeing her own "Auntie Lee-Ching" and other elderly women "silent and alone" in their "sterile, antiseptic rooms" at a convalescent home made her realize that many of their life stories would remain tragically untold. The act of writing and performing this dramatic monologue is, like her essay "Letter to Ma," which also addresses her parents' silenced generation, a tribute to the older generations and a small acknowledgment of their struggles in a hostile society.

Balancing can be seen in the framework of Unbound Feet's second goal—to make theater accessible to the people. This play presents a typical mother/

teenage-daughter struggle for love and acceptance, the child's assertion of independence, and the parent's inevitable sense of protectiveness and loss. But it also deals with a larger issue of community: that of the difficulties of coalition building among the diverse members of a community.

Balancing is a two-act play, of which scene 1 of act 1 is published. Though the cast indicates four characters, only two appear in this scene: Esther, a second-generation Chinese American who is a recovering alcoholic working as an alcohol-rehabilitation counselor, and Chris, her eighteen-year old daughter who is preparing to move out into her own apartment. Esther hides her sense of abandonment by lashing out at Chris's "new roommate," her Caucasian boyfriend Tony, whom Esther openly derides as a racist who has a "blank tape" for a head. Esther is a conflicted character. While she has a desire to do social good (as a rehab counselor and community activist), her previous experiences of being "messed over all [her] life by white bosses and [her] stupid white boyfriends" seem to preclude her from being able to trust Tony, "that white trash" (71–72).

Outspoken in her youthfulness, Chris exposes her mother's shortcomings: "You're always talkin' your talk about uniting oppressed people, but when it comes down to poor whites who've had it just as bad as the Third World people you treat, you wear blinders" (72). Yet by the end of the scene, Chris betrays her own intolerance by disparaging Esther and her lover, who are lesbians.

In her plays then, Woo worked against this kind of divisiveness, and in her essays today she writes about the power of coalitions. For example, Woo argues emphatically in "Forging the Future" that a multi-issue coalition among different areas of academic study is critical to the long-term survival of political enterprises such as multiculturalism and gay and lesbian studies.

CRITICAL RECEPTION

Since Woo's dramatic writings are not central to her life's work, it is perhaps more appropriate to consider them in the context of her works in general. Woo is widely recognized as a veteran activist and fearless fighter for social justice. Her writing is a testament to her tireless dedication to her revolutionary politics. While her essays and poetry continue to flourish and are regularly included in numerous anthologies, her most famous essay is "Letter to Ma," published in the groundbreaking anthology *This Bridge Called My Back: Writings by Radical Women of Color*. The simplicity, poignancy, urgency, and continued relevance of this epistolary essay, which discusses white feminist racism, Asian American male sexism, the need to write against the silencing of Asian American lives like her parents', and the need to build coalitions, make it a staple in college-course readers two decades later. True to her own ideals of multi-issue, coalition-building politics, her work has been used in women's and ethnic studies as well as Asian American studies, and even in critical race and legal studies. This is a testament to the wide-ranging relevance of her vision of revolutionary politics.

Woo's own courageous life has been an example of what she expounds in her writings.

BIBLIOGRAPHY

Works by Merle Woo

Drama

Home Movies: A Dramatic Monologue. 3 Asian American Writers Speak Out on Feminism. By Nellie Wong, Merle Woo, and Mitsuye Yamada. San Francisco: Radical Women Publications, 1979. N. pag.

Balancing. Act 1, scene 1. *Hanai: An Anthology of Asian American Writings.* Ed. Asian American Studies, U of California, Berkeley. Berkeley: Asian American Studies, Dept. of Ethnic Studies, U of California, 1980. 67–73.

Selected Production History

Information unavailable.

Anthology

3 Asian American Writers Speak Out on Feminism. With Nellie Wong and Mitsuye Yamada. San Francisco: Radical Women Publications, 1979.

Essays

"A Partial Bibliography of Asian American Women Writers." With Nellie Wong. *3 Asian American Writers Speak Out on Feminism.* By Nellie Wong, Merle Woo, and Mitsuye Yamada. San Francisco: Radical Women Publications, 1979. N. pag.

"Some Basic Ingredients for *Home Movies.*" *3 Asian American Writers Speak Out on Feminism.* By Nellie Wong, Merle Woo, and Mitsuye Yamada. San Francisco: Radical Women Publications, 1979. N. pag.

"Letter to Ma." *This Bridge Called My Back: Writings by Radical Women of Color.* Ed. Cherríe Moraga and Gloria Anzaldúa. New York: Kitchen Table/Women of Color P, 1983. 140–47.

"Lesbian and Gay Liberation: A Trotskyist Analysis." *Trotskyist and Revolutionary Socialist Conference, San Francisco, 30 November–1 December 1985.* Freedom Socialist Party. 14 July 2000 <http://www.socialism.com/library/perm1.html>.

"Our Common Enemy, Our Common Cause: Freedom Organizing in the Eighties." *Apartheid U.S.A.* By Audre Lorde. *Our Common Enemy, Our Common Cause: Freedom Organizing in the Eighties.* By Merle Woo. New York: Kitchen Table/ Women of Color Press, 1986. 12–23.

"Introduction." *Woman Sitting at the Machine, Thinking: Poems.* By Karen Brodine. Seattle: Red Letter P, 1990. xi–xiv.

"Is NOW the Right Group for Lesbians?" *Advocate* 17 Dec. 1991: 114.

"Forging the Future, Remembering Our Roots: Building Multicultural, Feminist Lesbian and Gay Studies." *Tilting the Tower: Lesbians, Teaching, Queer Subjects.* Ed. Linda Garber. New York: Routledge, 1994. 163–67.

"The Politics of Breast Cancer." *The Very Inside: An Anthology of Writing by Asian and*

Pacific Islander Lesbian and Bisexual Women. Ed. Sharon Lim-Hing. Toronto: Sister Vision, 1994. 416–25.

"Soul Food for Rabble-Rousers." Rev. of *Revolution, She Wrote.* By Clara Fraser. *Freedom Socialist* 19.1 (April–June 1998): 19 pars. 5 Apr. 2000 <http://www.socialism.com/fsarticles/Vol19no1/191_CF_book_review.html>.

"Three Decades of Class Struggle on Campus: A Personal History." *Legacy to Liberation: Politics and Culture of Revolutionary Asian Pacific America.* Ed. Fred Ho. San Francisco: AK Press, 2000. 159–73.

Interview

Telephone interview. 14 July 2000.

Poetry

"Poems for the Creative Writing Class, Spring 1982," "The Subversive," and "Yellow Woman Speaks." *Breaking Silence: An Anthology of Contemporary Asian American Poets.* Ed. Joseph Bruchac. New York: Greenfield Review P, 1983. 284–86.

Yellow Woman Speaks: Selected Poems. Seattle: Radical Women Publications, 1986.

Screenplays

American Chinatown. Narrator. Berkeley: U of California Extension Media Center, 1980.

Monterey's Boat People. Narrator. San Francisco: CrossCurrent Media, National Asian American Telecommunications Association, 1982.

Short Story

"Recovering." *Bridge: An Asian American Perspective* 6.4 (1978): 43–45.

Studies of Merle Woo

Averill, Linda. "Mumia Abu-Jamal: His Life Is in Our Hands." *Freedom Socialist* 20.2 (Jul.–Sept. 1999): 20 pars. 25 Apr. 2000 <http://www.socialism.com/fsarticles/vol20no2/hisLife.htm>.

———. "Three Decades of a Powerful Program and Decisive Achievements." *Freedom Socialist* 17.3 (Oct.–Dec. 1996): 29 pars. 25 Apr. 2000 <http://www.socialism.com/fsarticles/vol17no3/30yearEng.html>.

Chang, Robert S. "Toward an Asian American Legal Scholarship: Critical Race Theory, Post-structuralism, and Narrative Space." *California Law Review* 81 (1993): 1243–323.

Hayes, Loie B. "Merle Woo." *Gay and Lesbian Biography.* Ed. Michael J. Tyrkus. Detroit: St. James P, 1997. 464–65.

Matthaei, Julie, and Teresa Amott. "Race, Gender, Work: The History of Asian and Asian-American Women." *Race and Class* 31.3 (1990): 61–80.

"Merle Woo." *Almanac of Famous People.* Ed. Frank V. Castronova. 6th ed. Vol. 1. Detroit: Gale, 1998. 1808.

Nelson, Sandy. "Newsroom Heretic." *On the Issues: The Progressive Women's Quarterly. OTI Online* Fall 1996: 29 pars. 25 Apr. 2000 <http://mosaic.echonyc.com/~onissues/f96nelson.html>.

Ono, Kent A. "A Letter/Essay I've Been Longing to Write in My Personal/Academic Voice." *Western Journal of Communication* 61.1 (1997): 114–25.

Rogers, Ann, and Gil Veyna. "Unveiling Hidden Heroes: Four Women Who Have Shaken the System." *Freedom Socialist* 18.3 (1997): 18 pars. 25 Apr. 2000 <http://www.socialism.com/fsarticles/vol18no3/183VofCEnglishWeb.html>.

Wakako Yamauchi
(1924–   )

Douglas I. Sugano

BIOGRAPHY

Wakako Yamauchi was born to issei (first-generation) parents Yasaku Nakamura and Hamako Machida Nakamura on October 25, 1924. Yamauchi's parents were tenant farmers and later ran a hotel in Oceanside, California, for migrant Japanese farm workers. Raised in Westmoreland (near the California-Mexican border), an arid agricultural area in the Imperial Valley, Yamauchi grew to understand both geographical and racial isolation. Yamauchi's first language was Japanese, and she did not learn English until she attended school. She spent much of her childhood reading and making up her own stories, "white stories," she calls them. She adds that her childhood "heroes were white—Errol Flynn, Shirley Temple, all the matinee idols of her childhood. Shirley Temple embodied everything that was American to us. She was everything that we weren't—white, free, wealthy" (qtd. in Uno 53).

Yamauchi was seventeen when World War II began, and the internment experience was for her "a devastating lesson in the politics of economics and racism" ("Surviving" 30). Taken to Poston, Arizona, with many others, her family of six suffered from the incarceration within barbed-wire fences and guard towers, in facilities with poor sanitation and a humiliating lack of privacy. "We lost everything . . . but the two armloads we carried to camp. The evening we arrived, my father squatted on the dusty barracks for a long time, shoulders hunched, arms folded, his head deep in shadow" ("Surviving" 30). The internment had a lasting effect on Yamauchi's life. Her father died in Poston, and her mother still longed to return to an idyllic Japan. Toward the end of the war, in Chicago, Yamauchi packaged candy, attended art classes, and discovered the theater. All of these life experiences deepened Yamauchi's awareness of cultural differences in America.

In 1948, she married Chester Yamauchi, and they had a child, Joy, in 1955. During the 1950s, Yamauchi experimented with her writing, but did not pursue it seriously until the early 1970s. Yamauchi's lifelong friend, Hisaye Yamamoto, asked her to contribute a short story, "And the Soul Shall Dance," for the pioneering anthology *Aiiieeeee!*, which was published in 1974. That same year, Mako, the founding artistic director of the East West Players in Los Angeles, convinced Yamauchi to transform that short story into her first play. Her first three published plays—*And the Soul Shall Dance, The Music Lessons*, and *12-1-A*—are all autobiographical, the first one based upon her childhood experiences in the Imperial Valley and the latter two based on her life in Poston during the war. *And the Soul Shall Dance* was the second Asian American drama to be shown on national television on PBS in 1978. The best known of her plays, it has also been performed across the country, having premiered in Los Angeles and having been performed in Washington, D.C., New York, Hawaii, and Seattle. Her most recent published play is also a historical, but not autobiographical, piece, *The Chairman's Wife*, which premiered in 1990.

MAJOR WORKS AND THEMES

Yamauchi states that her early theatrical influences were varied works such as *Porgy and Bess, The Glass Menagerie*, and *Rebecca*. She reflects that in 1974, when she met with Mako, "I was sort of pushed into playwriting—blind and unaware" (Houston 36). Such statements suggest Yamauchi's modesty or Japanese *enryo*, an important concept for understanding her work. *Enryo* is a type of humility, a recognition of beings and forces greater than oneself. In short, her sense of *enryo* helps explain her perspective as a Japanese American writer: all of her characters are subject to relational and historical forces beyond their immediate control. Even if Yamauchi's self-deprecating statements about her influences and her introduction to playwriting are accurate, she is still speaking from a fairly typical nisei perspective that would appear to be, on the surface, passive and accepting. Accused by younger Japanese American critics of being silent on the internment experience, Yamauchi argues that the nisei were "overwhelmed by a current of events we could neither understand nor stem" and that "deep inside something tells us we could have been braver, or stronger . . . and what good does it do to bring back those events that might prove that we could have, should have, behaved more courageously?" (Kim 137). Throughout her career as a playwright, Yamauchi has striven to understand these larger historical forces such as racism, the internment experience, and radical social change through characters who faced each challenge with a particular kind of courage.

Yamauchi's best-known work, *And the Soul Shall Dance* (1974), was first produced at Los Angeles's East West Players in 1977. The play concerns the Muratas and the Okas, two Depression-era farming families in California's arid

Imperial Valley. The first scene opens as the Muratas and Mr. Oka discuss the fire that destroyed the Muratas' bathhouse. Through the expository conversation, Oka reveals that he was forced to marry his deceased wife's younger sister (Emiko) and has a daughter from a previous marriage. In subsequent scenes, it becomes apparent that Oka is also hiding Emiko's desperate unhappiness in America, their problems with alcohol, their poverty, their respective lost loves, Oka's physical abuse of Emiko, and Emiko's fragile emotional state. Emiko later reveals to Masako (the Muratas' teenaged daughter) her desire to return to Japan, back to her long-lost love. "I must keep the dream alive," Emiko wistfully states. "The dream is all I have" (*Songs* 180). The play exposes tension not only between the issei (first-generation Japanese immigrants) and nisei (second-generation Japanese Americans), but between a nostalgic view of Japan and a bleak present and future for Japanese Americans as a whole. In a major confrontation from the second act, Oka, who is aware of Emiko's homesickness, tells Emiko, "I don't care what you do. Walk. Use your feet. Swim to Japan. I don't care" (202). In the haunting last scene, Masako witnesses Emiko in her formal kimono, carrying a sage branch, singing the title song and dancing into the desert, presumably dancing her way back to her past, back to a Japan and a love that no longer exist.

Yamauchi's second play, *The Music Lessons* (1977), premiered at the New York Public Theater in 1980. Set about the same time and place as *And the Soul Shall Dance*, this play is, again, about the survival of body and soul. The theme of budding sexuality, seen latently through Masako and Kiyoko in the previous play, is brought to the fore in *The Music Lessons* through Aki, the teenaged daughter of the issei widow Chizuko Sakata. With her two teenaged sons, Chizuko is struggling to make ends meet in a backbreaking agricultural setting. Kawaguchi, a migrant worker, appears on the scene to work in exchange for room and board. What begins as an innocent set of misunderstandings in the first act—Kawaguchi's small gifts such as a book of poetry for Aki and small acts such as giving her violin lessons—eventually accrues romantic significance for Aki and leads to Chizuko's jealousy. In the last two scenes, during a music lesson, Aki and a slightly drunk Kawaguchi discuss love and eventually kiss, only to be seen by Chizuko. During a heated argument with them, Chizuko reveals her own weariness of her life in America and her loveless marriage and then commands Kawaguchi to leave the premises. Despite Aki's protestations and promises to follow him, Kawaguchi departs alone. The play ends tensely, suddenly, and with uncertainty for the Sakatas and for Kawaguchi, symbolic of the societal and psychological limbo for two generations of Japanese Americans.

Yamauchi's next drama, *12-1-A* (1981), is set only seven years later, in May 1942 in the Poston, Arizona, internment camp. The play's time encompasses slightly longer than a year, from the internees' arrival into camp to the later recruitment of nisei males into the U.S. Army. More of an ensemble piece than the previous two plays, this one revolves around the lives of the Tanakas, the Yoshidas, and the Ichiokas, who live in barrack 12-1-A. Understandably, the play problematizes notions of citizenship and nationalism (which are also mentioned in the other plays). All of the families struggle with the poor housing and sanitation, lack of furnishings, deplorable food, and psychological depression. Toward the end of act 1, Koko Tanaka, the teenaged daughter of an issei widow, wonders as if speaking for two generations: "Maybe it's the weather. . . . Maybe it's this place. Maybe it's the world. . . . You're shut out from the outside and inside everyone pretends like nothing's wrong" (64–65).

While act 1 presents a relatively placid facade, act 2 reveals the worst facets of the internment experience. Mrs. Ichioka, the issei mother of Ken, maintains her confidence in Japan's eventual victory; the administration has jailed men who have beaten up informants; dissidents are sent to Tule Lake; and army registration has begun. This last issue brings all of the internees' feelings to the surface because the recruits, in order to enlist in the armed forces, need to disavow all loyalty to Japan and pledge their undivided devotion to America. All families, not just the recruits, are torn by these loyalty oaths. At the end of the play, Ken Ichioka decides to enlist, and the play closes sardonically with his departure while the audience hears the retarded Harry Yamane sing, "Yes sir, that's my baby." After Ken departs on the recruits' bus, the last lonely scene is dominated by the sight of the guard tower and the sound of the desert wind.

The Chairman's Wife (1988), which premiered at East West Players in 1990, focuses upon Chiang Ching, Mao Tse-tung's widow. Rather than an autobiographical memory piece, this play, set during the Tiananmen Square demonstrations, inhabits the stage of Chiang Ching's tortured mind. Ching, imprisoned for her "crimes against the people," revisits significant events in her life, prompted by the guards' poignant intrusive queries. She recounts her childhood memories of preindustrial China (1919), her career as an actress, her touring for the party in the 1930s, her imprisonment, her romantic affairs, and her eventual marriage to Mao. For most of the play, the guards are largely unaware of her internal monologues and take her ruminations as mad chattering.

In her exchanges with the guards, she reveals her twenty-eight-year struggle in the Revolution, recalling Mao's various weaknesses and excesses. In the middle of act 2, the two young guards discuss Ching's insomnia and her constant reminiscing, especially her inciting the Red Guard to action. After the guards hear (from others) of the current Tiananmen Square massacre, Ching taunts them, "One day I'll be out and you'll put up a statue of me . . . in Tiananmen Square. . . . Politics is like fashion. Styles change. Yesterday I was in fashion. Today you. Tomorrow me, again" (149). As in her other plays, Yamauchi again composes a memory piece that depicts characters at the mercy of sweeping historical forces.

CRITICAL RECEPTION

As Velina Hasu Houston points out in her anthology *The Politics of Life*, Momoko Iko and Yamauchi represent the first wave of Asian American playwrights (23). These pioneers, along with Frank Chin, have had to fight to win acceptance with an American audience. Before her first work was produced, Yamauchi was told that she likely would not succeed because her plays did not have a "drawing card"—a white actor or star (Uno 57), and no one "cares about a bath house burning down, referring to the events in *And the Soul Shall Dance*" (Uno 58). Fortunately, Yamauchi's work has been produced to appreciative American audiences, but there has been little written about Yamauchi and the other pioneers of Asian American theater. In essence, there appear to be two critical responses to her dramatic work, all of which have more to do with the critics than with the works themselves. For those theater and literary critics who are still discovering the Japanese American internment, Yamauchi's work appears as naturalistic, historical slices of life that seek to inform the audience of a tragedy in American history. For those already aware of the internment experience, it is the larger historical forces such as racism, war, and radical social change that take the center stage in her works.

It was not until the 1980s when critics noted different forms of identity issues in Yamauchi's plays. The most obvious are the discussions about racism in *The Music Lessons* (act 1, scene 3, in the pool hall). The second form of identity that Yamauchi discusses is intergenerational tensions between the immigrant issei and the native-born nisei. Many nisei writings about internment are attempts "to create a past that was governed by Issei elders, the standard-bearers of Japanese American cultural integrity," Elaine Kim observes. "Wakako Yamauchi and Hisaye Yamamoto reveal the Issei world through the eyes of young nisei narrators and observers" (261).

A third type of identity is found in the tension between Yamauchi's nisei (teenaged) characters and their parents such as Koko Tanaka in *12-1-A*, Aki Sakata in *The Music Lessons*, and Masako Murata in *And the Soul Shall Dance*. Hongo notes this tension as the nisei characters strive for a new, more fulfilling identity than their parents have: "[*The Music Lessons*] depicts the Issei generation dedicated to material survival—the men functioning as beasts of burden and the women as . . . a kind of servant and manager at the same time" (12). Hongo develops this line of reasoning further in his analysis of *And the Soul Shall Dance*. The play "elevates Emiko . . . into a spellbinding martyr for art, culture, and independence of mind. . . . For the young Masako, madwoman Emiko functions as a troubled model of imaginative freedom in a time and culture in which the roles of women are highly bound by their circumstances, race, and gender status" (15). But, in addition to the identity issues, Yamauchi's works really attempt to reflect "that delicate balance between the sustaining of dream and coping with reality that allows human beings to survive" through all of her characters, as Velina H. Houston has noted (41).

BIBLIOGRAPHY

Works by Wakako Yamauchi

Drama

And the Soul Shall Dance. Excerpts. *The Best Plays of 1976–77.* Ed. Otis Guernsey, Jr.
New York: Dodd, Mead & Co., 1978. 36–49. Rpt. in *The Big Aiiieeeee! An
Anthology of Chinese American and Japanese American Literature.* Ed. Jeffery
Paul Chan, Frank Chin, Lawson Fusao Inada, and Shawn Hsu Wong. New York:
Meridian, 1991. 193–215.

And the Soul Shall Dance. Full length. *West Coast Plays 11–12.* Ed. Rick Foster. Berke-
ley: California Theatre Council, 1982. 117–64. Rpt. in *New Worlds of Literature.*
Ed. Jerome Beatty and J. Paul Hunter. New York: Norton, 1989. 64–107; *Staging
Diversity: Plays and Practice in American Theater.* Ed. John R. Wolcott and
Michael L. Quinn. Dubuque, IA: Kendall/Hunt, 1992. 339–66; *Literature: A Con-
temporary Introduction.* Ed. James Hurt. New York: Macmillan, 1994. 1223–62;
Songs My Mother Taught Me: Stories, Plays, and Memoir. Ed. Garrett Hongo.
New York: Feminist P, 1994. 153–208; *Imagining Worlds.* Ed. Marjorie Ford and
Jon Ford. New York: McGraw-Hill, 1994. 540–79; *The Creative Spirit: An In-
troduction to Theatre.* Ed. Stephanie Arnold. Mountain View, CA: Mayfield,
1998. 126–51.

The Chairman's Wife. The Politics of Life: Four Plays by Asian American Women. Ed.
Velina Hasu Houston. Philadelphia: Temple UP, 1993. 101–49.

*The Music Lessons. Unbroken Thread: An Anthology of Plays by Asian American
Women.* Ed. Roberta Uno. Amherst: U of Massachusetts P, 1993. 53–104. Rpt.
in *Songs My Mother Taught Me: Stories, Plays, and Memoir.* Ed. Garrett Hongo.
New York: Feminist P, 1994. 51–97.

12-1-A. Politics of Life: Four Plays by Asian American Women. Ed. Velina Hasu Houston. Philadephia: Temple UP, 1993. 45–100. Excerpts. *Great Scenes from Minority Playwrights.* Ed. Marsh Cassady. Colorado Springs: Meriwether, 1997.
245–96. Rpt. in *Playwrights of Color.* By Meg Swanson and Robin Murray.
Yarmouth, ME: Intercultural P, 1999. 213–60.

Unpublished Manuscripts

Shirley Temple Hotcha-Cha. Ms. 345. Roberta Uno Asian Women Playwrights Scripts
Collection 1924–1992, Special Collections and Archives, W.E.B. Du Bois Library, U of Massachusetts, Amherst, 1977.

Not a Through Street. Ms. 345. Roberta Uno Asian Women Playwrights Scripts Collection 1924–1992, Special Collections and Archives, W.E.B. Du Bois Library, U
of Massachusetts, Amherst, 1981.

The Trip. Ms. 345. Roberta Uno Asian Women Playwrights Scripts Collection 1924–
1992, Special Collections and Archives, W.E.B. Du Bois Library, U of Massachusetts, Amherst, 1982.

A Good Time. Ms. 345. Roberta Uno Asian Women Playwrights Scripts Collection 1924–
1992, Special Collections and Archives, W.E.B. Du Bois Library, U of Massachusetts, Amherst, 1983.

The Memento. Ms. 345. Roberta Uno Asian Women Playwrights Scripts Collection 1924–1992, Special Collections and Archives, W.E.B. Du Bois Library, U of Massachusetts, Amherst, 1983.

Songs That Made the Hit Parade. Ms. 345. Roberta Uno Asian Women Playwrights Scripts Collection 1924–1992, Special Collections and Archives, W.E.B. Du Bois Library, U of Massachusetts, Amherst, 1988.

Stereoscope I: Taj Mahal. Ms. 345. Roberta Uno Asian Women Playwrights Scripts Collection 1924–1992, Special Collections and Archives, W.E.B. Du Bois Library, U of Massachusetts, Amherst, 1988.

Selected Production History

And the Soul Shall Dance

Production. Northwest Asian American Theatre, Seattle, 1974 and 1993.
———. East West Players, Los Angeles, 1977, 1978, and 1996.
———. U of Hawai'i at Manoa, Honolulu, 1978 and 1981.
———. Kauai Community Theatre, Kauai, HI, 1979 and 1980.
———. Pan-Asian Repertory Theatre, New York City, 1979 and 1990.
———. Asian American Theater Company, San Francisco, 1980.
———. California State U Asian American Theatre, Los Angeles, 1985.
———. Asian Theatre Productions, Hilo, HI, 1994.
———. Asian American Repertory Theatre, Stockton, CA, 1995.
———. Morgan-Wixon Theatre, Santa Monica, CA, 1998.
———. Tsunami Theatre, Washington, DC, 1999.
———. Interactive Asian Contemporary Theatre, Sacramento, CA, 2000.

The Music Lessons

Production. New York Public Theater, New York City, 1980.
———. Asian American Theater Company, San Francisco, 1982.
———. California State U Asian American Theatre, Los Angeles, 1982.
———. East West Players, Los Angeles, 1983.
———. Asian Theatre Productions, Hilo, HI, 1995.

12-1-A

Production. East West Players, Los Angeles, 1982.
———. Asian American Theater Company, San Francisco, 1982.
———. Kumu Kahua Theatre, Honolulu, 1990.
———. UCLA Freud Theatre, Los Angeles, 1992.
———. USC Theatre, Los Angeles, 1993.
———. Teoriza Company, Tokyo, 1995.
———. Northwest Asian American Theatre, Seattle, 1995.

The Memento

Production. Pan Asian Repertory Theatre, New York City, 1984.
———. East West Players, Los Angeles, 1986.
———. Yale Repertory Theatre, Winterfest, New Haven, CT, 1987.

The Chairman's Wife

Staged reading. East West Players, Los Angeles, 1989.
Production. East West Players, Los Angeles, 1990.

————. Kumu Kahua Theatre, Honolulu, 1990.
————. East West Players, Los Angeles, 1991.

Anthology

Songs My Mother Taught Me: Stories, Plays, and Memoir. Ed. and Intro. Garrett Hongo; Afterword by Valerie Miner. New York: Feminist P, 1994.

Autobiography

"Makapuu Bay." *Songs My Mother Taught Me: Stories, Plays, and Memoir.* Ed. Garrett Hongo. New York: Feminist P, 1994. 211–18.
"Old Times, Old Stories." *Songs My Mother Taught Me: Stories, Plays, and Memoir.* Ed. Garrett Hongo. New York: Feminist P, 1994. 224–30.
"Otoko." *Southwest Review* 77.2–3 (1992): 338–48. Rpt. in *Songs My Mother Taught Me: Stories, Plays, and Memoir.* Ed. Garrett Hongo. New York: Feminist P, 1994. 237–44; *Into the Fire: Asian American Prose.* Ed. Sylvia Watanabe and Carol Bruchac. Greenfield Center, NY: Greenfield Review P, 1996. 149–60.
"Surviving the Wasteland Years." *Christian Science Monitor* 8 Nov. 1988: 30. Rpt. in *Home Forum Reader: A Timeless Collection of Essays and Poems from the Home Forum Page of the Christian Science Monitor.* Ed. Frederic Hunter. Boston: Christian Science Monitor, 1989. 87–90.
"That Was All." *Charlie Chan Is Dead.* Ed. Jessica Hagedorn. New York: Penguin, 1993. 551–56. Rpt. in *Songs My Mother Taught Me: Stories, Plays, and Memoir.* Ed. Garrett Hongo. New York: Feminist P, 1994. 46–50.

Interview

"A Conversation with Wakako Yamauchi." Interview with William P. Osborn and Silvia Watanabe. *Into the Fire: Asian American Prose.* Ed. Sylvia Watanabe and Carol Bruchac. Greenfield Center, NY: Greenfield Review P, 1996. 163–73.

Short Stories

"And the Soul Shall Dance." *Rafu Shimpo Holiday Supplement.* (Los Angeles) 19 Dec. 1966, sec. 2: 9+. Rpt. in *Aiiieeeee! An Anthology of Asian-American Writers.* Ed. Frank Chin, Jeffrey Paul Chan, Lawson Fusao Inada, and Shawn Hsu Wong. Washington, DC: Howard UP, 1974. 191–200; *Solo: Women on Woman Alone.* Ed. Linda Hamalian and Leo Hamalian. New York: Dell, 1977. 232–39; *Six Short Stories by Japanese American Writers.* Ed. Iwao Yamamoto, Mie Hihara, and Shigeru Kobayashi. Tokyo: Tsurami Shoten, 1991. 11–23; *Women of the Century: Thirty Modern Short Stories.* Ed. Regina Barreca. New York: St. Martin's, 1993. 178–85; *American Dragons.* Ed. Laurence Yep. New York: Anchor, 1993. 144–54; *Growing Up Asian American.* Ed. Maria Hong. New York: William Morrow, 1993. 65–73; *Songs My Mother Taught Me: Stories, Plays, and Memoir.* Ed. Garrett Hongo. New York: Feminist P, 1994. 19–24.
"Otoko." *Into the Fire: Asian American Prose.* Ed. Sylvia Watanabe and Carol Bruchac. Greenfield Center, NY: Greenfield Review P, 1996. 149–60.
"Rosebud." *Southwest Review* 81.1 (1996): 28–43.
"The Sensei." *Yardbird Reader* 3 (1974): 245–55.

Songs My Mother Taught Me: Stories, Plays, and Memoir. Collection of 14 short stories by Wakako Yamauchi. Ed. Garrett Hongo. New York: Feminist P, 1994.

Television

And the Soul Shall Dance. Dir. Paul Stanley. Prod. KCET. Hollywood Television Theatre. Perf. Sab Shimono, Pat Li, Denise Kumagai, Yuki Shimoda, Diane Takai, and Hunani Min. Los Angeles. 7 Feb. 1978, 15 July 1978, and 11 Nov. 1979.

Studies of Wakako Yamauchi

Adcock, Joseph. "Season Openers Touch on Nostalgia, Tragedy." *Seattle Post-Intelligencer* 8 Oct. 1993, final ed.: 7.

———. "Small Personal Dramas Take on Large Import in *12-1-A.*" *Seattle Post-Intelligencer* 18 Oct. 1995: C9.

———. "*Soul Shall Dance* Moves Deeply; Immigrant Tale Is a Touching One." Rev. of *And the Soul Shall Dance. Seattle Post-Intelligencer* 16 Oct. 1993, final ed.: C3.

Arnold, Stephanie. "Dissolving the Half Shadows: Japanese-American Women Playwrights." *Making a Spectacle: Feminist Essays on Contemporary Women's Theatre.* Ed. Lynda Hart. Ann Arbor: U of Michigan P, 1989. 181–94.

———. "Producing *And the Soul Shall Dance.*" *The Creative Spirit.* Ed. Stephanie Arnold. Mountain View, CA: Mayfield, 1998. 151–64.

Berg, Christine G. "Voices from the Gaps: Wakako Yamauchi." U of Minnesota, Minneapolis. 19 May 2000 <http://voices.cla.umn.edu/authors/wakakoyamauchi.html>.

Berson, Misha, ed. "Wakako Yamauchi." *Between Worlds: Contemporary Asian-American Plays.* New York: Theatre Communications Group, 1990. 128–31.

Bledsoe, Sheri. "Artist Directory Series." 15 Dec. 1999. Arizona State U, Tucson. 19 May 2000 <http://www.public.asu.edu/~dejesus/210entries/yamauchi.htm>.

Cassady, Marsh, ed. *Great Scenes from Minority Playwrights: Seventy-four Scenes of Cultural Diversity.* Colorado Springs, CO: Meriwether, 1997.

Holden, Stephen. "Trying to Adapt to Inhospitable Terrain." Rev. of *And the Soul Shall Dance. New York Times* 25 Mar. 1990, late ed.: 63.

Hongo, Garrett, ed. Introduction. *Songs My Mother Taught Me: Stories, Plays, and Memoir.* New York: Feminist P, 1994. 1–16.

Houston, Velina Hasu, ed. "Wakako Yamauchi." *The Politics of Life: Four Plays by Asian American Women.* Philadelphia: Temple UP, 1993. 33–43.

Kim, Elaine H. *Asian American Literature, an Introduction to the Writings and Their Social Context.* Philadelphia: Temple UP, 1982.

McDonald, Dorothy Ritsuko, and Katharine Newman. "Relocation and Dislocation: The Writings of Hisaye Yamamoto and Wakako Yamauchi." *MELUS* 7.3 (1980): 21–38.

Osborn, William P., and Sylvia Watanabe. "A *MELUS* Interview: Wakako Yamauchi." *MELUS* 23.2 (1998): 101–10.

Partnow, Elaine T., and Lesley Anne Hyatt. "Wakako Yamauchi." *The Female Dramatist: Profiles of Women Playwrights from the Middle Ages to Contemporary Times.* By Elaine T. Partnow and Lesley Anne Hyatt. New York: Facts on File, 1998. 223–24.

Pollard, Lauren Ray. "*12-1-A*: Revisiting the Internment Tragedy." *Seattle Times* 17 Oct. 1995, final ed.: F4.

Uno, Roberta, ed. "Wakako Yamauchi." *Unbroken Thread: An Anthology of Plays by Asian American Women.* Amherst: U of Massachusetts P, 1993. 53–58.

Watanabe, Sylvia. "Japanese to American: An Unsentimental Look." Rev. of *Songs My Mother Taught Me. Boston Globe* 11 Sept. 1994, sec. A: 21.

Wood, Joe. "Cameos: *And the Soul Shall Dance.*" *Village Voice* 35.14 (1990): 110.

Yogi, Stan. "Rebels and Heroines: Subversive Narratives in the Stories of Wakako Yamauchi and Hisaye Yamamoto." *Reading the Literatures of Asian America.* Ed. Shirley Geok-lin Lim and Amy Ling. Philadelphia: Temple UP, 1992. 131–50.

Laurence Michael Yep

(1948–   )

Uppinder Mehan

BIOGRAPHY

Laurence Michael Yep was born on June 14, 1948, in San Francisco, where he "was raised in a black ghetto but commuted to a grammar school in Chinatown" and "did not really meet white culture until [he] went to high school" (Commire 206). As a third-generation Chinese in America, Yep grew up speaking little Chinese and largely ignorant of Chinese myths and legends. High school came in the form of a Jesuit school, from which he went to Marquette University in 1966 in order to study journalism. In 1969, his first science-fiction story, "The Selchey Kids," was included in *World's Best Science Fiction of 1969*. He received his B.A. from the University of California at Santa Cruz in 1970 and started working on his Ph.D. at the State University of New York at Buffalo. Over the next few years, he published a number of science-fiction short stories. His first children's book, *Sweetwater*, was published in 1973. In 1975, Yep not only received his Ph.D. from SUNY Buffalo, but also published his most acclaimed children's book, *Dragonwings*. Since then Yep has written at least thirty works of fiction for both children and adults (many of which have won prestigious prizes), and, most important, for this volume, he has written three plays: *Pay the Chinaman* (1987), *Fairy Bones* (1987), and an adaptation of *Dragonwings* (1992). Yep is currently writer-in-residence at the University of California at Santa Barbara.

MAJOR WORKS AND THEMES

Although Yep is a prolific fiction writer, he has written only three plays, one of which, *Fairy Bones*, has not been published. In response to an actor's question during a rehearsal of *Dragonwings* about the propriety of a Chinese father publicly displaying affection to his son, Yep wrote, "Windrider must perform the same juggling act in his family life as he does in his identity and interests. . . . Definition and re-definition [of his identity] take place continually. What is important is to maintain some connection to the past to provide not only continuity but vitality as well" (Yep, *CMLEA* 9). The necessity of maintaining some connection to the past while adapting to the present is the major theme of all of Yep's writing, whether the form it takes is science fiction, fantasy, conventional bildungsroman, or dramatic dialogue, as is the case with his first play.

At the explicit level, *Pay the Chinaman* (1987) is a story of two Chinese con men, each trying to cheat the other out of his money. The play is set in the period of the last two decades of the nineteenth century when smaller Chinatowns all over the American West were erased through massacre and forced exile. The two attempt to cheat each other at various games of chance against a backdrop of the increasing violence against the Chinese in the United States, the tensions between Chinese of different generations, and the gap between the expectations and the reality awaiting the Chinese in the United States. The characters' lack of names (one is called "Con Man" and the other "Young Man") signals that the play is less concerned with individual psychology and more with the community.

In an introduction to the play, Yep tells that the phrase "pay the chinaman" comes from West Coast lumber camps, where it means to settle accounts. In Yep's play, the phrase comes to be "symbolic of Chinese immigrants who managed to manipulate the American environment and come out ahead" (Berson 178). But that manipulation and the continual distrust it requires of the motives of others exact a price. The character Young Man, as Yep puts it, "denies the past, and any sense of having roots" (Berson 178). While it certainly is the case in the majority of Yep's work that those who deny their heritage are just as lost as those who seek to reconstruct entire their Chinese homes in America, Young Man is only too aware of the project he has undertaken of crafting a new identity for himself out of his past and his present. In a play where the audience is never certain when the characters are speaking the truth of their experiences of survival in a strange land and when they are manipulating the telling in order to cheat each other, it becomes impossible to differentiate between a denial of the past and a strategic rethinking of it.

At one point, Con Man and Young Man seem to play their respective generational roles, with the older one warning the younger one not to be fooled by the present:

CON MAN: This place is one big gamble. White demons all around us.

YOUNG MAN: Americans.

CON MAN: Always been white demons.

YOUNG MAN: Names are power. Call them demons and they are demons.

CON MAN: This is the third Chinatown. First one used to be over there in the demon town. But a mob of demons burnt it down. So the Chinese built a new one on this side of the river. And the mob torched that one down. So the Chinese put up a third. Stubborn. (Berson 188)

The implication in this scene is that Young Man risks his death by forgetting the past behavior of the Americans, but, as we discover later, Young Man is only too aware of the danger. In fact, he is pretending to be naïve in order to fool Con Man into mistaking him for a newcomer to the area.

It could be argued that Con Man wants to make money in order to send it back home and therefore is cheating Chinese in the western Chinatowns for the sake of his family, but Young Man wants to make money for himself, and that therein lies the difference. Ultimately, both characters have the same motive, survival, but differ in their generational understanding of the roles of fathers and sons. Despite Con Man's unorthodox manner of making a living, he still expects fathers to sacrifice their own needs for those of their sons and for the sons, in turn, to obey them unquestioningly, whereas Young Man sees that traditional familial structure as the barrier that keeps the generations from fully understanding and working with each other.

Dragonwings (1992) starts with the adult Moon Shadow in 1928 introducing the audience to himself as a young boy in 1905 with his mother in China. We quickly learn that his father Windrider is in the United States, the land of the Golden Mountain, and that he will return when he has made enough money. We find that Windrider is working in his Uncle Bright Star's laundry in San Francisco and has just sent for Moon Shadow to join him. As father and son reacquaint themselves with each other, Windrider reveals his dream to someday build and fly an aeroplane. After an earthquake forces everyone to start all over, Windrider and Moon Shadow leave the familiarity of Chinatown and the laundry in pursuit of this seemingly quixotic venture. They spend the next three years in Oakland living in a barn and working odd jobs so they can devote their energies to constructing the plane. Uncle Bright Star and Miss Whitlaw, an elderly white woman who had befriended them earlier, come to help launch the plane from a hilltop. Windrider accomplishes his dream of flying as the plane soars into the sky. The flight is cut short by a structural defect, and the plane crashes, with Windrider suffering a few broken bones. As he heals, he tells Moon Shadow of his plan to join Uncle Bright Star as a partner in the laundry, whereby he will be able to bring his wife to the United States, and they can then be a family together.

The greatest obstacle to the father and son's attempt to realize the dream of flying is not the white Americans who more or less confine all Chinese to Chinatown or who seize their land after the earthquake, but the disaffected son of Uncle Bright Star, Black Dog, who sees nothing but discrimination and toil in San Francisco. He chafes at his father's boundary of Chinatown but is chased by mobs when he goes to white San Francisco. He develops an addiction to opium and robs Windrider and Moon Shadow of their rent money, leaving them nearly destitute. Black Dog is disowned by his father and is never heard of again. The shadow of Black Dog is a reminder that the multiculturalism that asks of the minority culture that it accept the conditions of the majority culture and work diligently and without complaint exacts a price.

It is abundantly clear in *Dragonwings* that success in America means moving outside the bounds of Chinatown and interacting with the larger community. Moon Shadow and Uncle Bright Star discover a friend in Miss Whitlaw; Mr. Alger makes it possible for Windrider to make a living as a handyman; and the family will make its home in the United States rather than Windrider and Moon Shadow ultimately returning to China.

CRITICAL RECEPTION

Laurence Yep has garnered numerous prizes and lavish praise for his fiction. His plays, however, have gone largely unnoticed. The few reviewers who have written on his theatrical works comment on different aspects of his plays.

In his review of *Dragonwings* in the October 20, 1992, issue of the *Washington Times*, Hap Erstein calls it a story of "the cultural chasm between China and the United States, underlining the ethnic prejudices against the Asians" (4). He finds that the staging has "beautiful Asian theatre touches" (whatever those are) and that the choreography is "splendid" (4).

In reviewing *Pay the Chinaman*, Linda Sarver sees the play as an "acerbic and frequently comic" reminder that not much has changed for recent Asian immigrant arrivals to the United States, where survival is still paramount (147). Mel Gussow points out more insightfully that Con Man and Young Man "have learned to conceal their true feelings, which is in itself a form of lying," for survival (11). The most substantial review of the play comes from Una Chaudhuri, who finds that it underscores the multicultural "paradox of simultaneous sameness and difference" through its doubling of characters, action, and setting (232). The play refuses to substitute an ethnic group identity for an American individualist identity, just as it refuses an easy identification between any home and certainty (Chaudhuri 238). Although Yep's theatrical works have not generated the kind of critical response his fiction has, the few reviews clearly reveal the impact his plays can make on the audience beyond the Asian American community as they keep on the stage the cultural paradox of assimilation and individualism in America.

BIBLIOGRAPHY

Works by Laurence Michael Yep

Drama

Pay the Chinaman. Between Worlds: Contemporary Asian-American Plays. Ed. Misha Berson. New York: Theatre Communications Group, 1990. 180–96.

Dragonwings. American Theatre 9.5 (1992): 1–13. New York: Dramatists Play Service, 1993.

Unpublished Manuscript

Fairy Bones. 1987.

Selected Production History

Fairy Bones

Production, dir. Andrea Gordon. Asian American Theater Company, Zephyr Theater, San Francisco, 1987.
———, dir. Tina Chen. Pan Asian Repertory Theatre, Playhouse 46, New York City, 1992.

Pay the Chinaman

Production, dir. Lane Nishikawa. Asian American Theater Company, San Francisco, 1987.
———. Zephyr Theater, San Francisco, 1987.
———, dir. Tina Chen. Pan Asian Repertory Theatre, Playhouse 46, New York City, 1992.
———. Lab Theatre, Salt Lake City, 1994.

The Age of Wonders (an integration of *Pay the Chinaman* and *Fairy Bones*)

Production, dir. Cynthia Wallis. New WORLD Theater, U of Massachusetts, Amherst, 1989.

Dragonwings

Production, dir. Phyllis S. K. Look. Berkeley Repertory Theatre, Berkeley, CA, 1991.
———. Honolulu Theatre for Youth, Honolulu, 1994–95.

Anthologies

The Rainbow People. New York: Harper, 1989.
Tongues of Jade. New York: HarperCollins, 1991.
Tree of Dreams: Ten Tales from the Garden of Night. Mahwah, NJ: BridgeWater Books, 1995.

Children's Books

Sweetwater. New York: Harper, 1973.
Dragonwings. New York: Harper, 1975.
Child of the Owl. New York: Harper, 1977.
Sea Glass. New York: Harper, 1979.
Dragon of the Lost Sea. New York: Harper, 1982.
Kind Hearts and Gentle Monsters. New York: Harper, 1982.
The Mark Twain Murders. New York: Four Winds Press, 1982.
Liar, Liar. New York: Morrow, 1983.
The Serpent's Children. New York: Harper, 1984.
The Tom Sawyer Fires. New York: Morrow, 1984.
Dragon Steel. New York: Harper, 1985.
Mountain Light. New York: Harper, 1985.

The Curse of the Squirrel. New York: Random House, 1987.
Dragon Cauldron. New York: HarperCollins, 1991.
The Lost Garden. Englewood Cliffs, NJ: Messner, 1991.
The Star Fisher. New York: Morrow, 1991.
Dragon War. New York: HarperCollins, 1992.
Butterfly Boy. New York: Farrar Straus Giroux, 1993.
Dragon's Gate. New York: HarperCollins, 1993.
The Man Who Tricked a Ghost. Mahwah, NJ: Troll, 1993.
The Shell Woman and the King. New York: Dial Books, 1993.
The Boy Who Swallowed Snakes. New York: Scholastic, 1994.
The Ghost Fox. New York: Scholastic, 1994.
The Junior Thunder Lord. Mahwah, NJ: BridgeWater Books, 1994.
Tiger Woman. Mahwah, NJ: BridgeWater Books, 1994.
The City of Dragons. New York: Scholastic, 1995.
Hiroshima: A Novella. New York: Scholastic, 1995.
Later, Gator. New York: Hyperion Books for Children, 1995.
Thief of Hearts. New York: HarperCollins, 1995.
Ribbons. New York: G.P. Putnam's Sons, 1996.
The Case of the Goblin Pearls. New York: HarperCollins, 1997.
The Dragon Prince. New York: HarperCollins, 1997.
The Khan's Daughter. New York: Scholastic, 1997.

Novels

Seademons. New York: Harper, 1977.
Shadow Lord. New York: Pocket Books, 1985.
Monster Makers, Inc. New York: Arbor House, 1986.

Short Stories

"The Selchey Kids." *World's Best Science Fiction of 1969.* Ed. Donald A. Wollheim
    and Terry Carr. New York: An Ace Book, 1969. 216–40.
"In a Sky of Daemons." *Protostars.* Ed. David Gerrold. New York: Ballantine, 1971.
    29–69.
"Looking-Glass Sea." *Strange Bedfellows: Sex and Science Fiction.* Ed. Thomas N. Scor-
    tia. New York: Random House, 1972. 165–77.

Studies of Laurence Yep

Berson, Misha, ed. *Between Worlds: Contemporary Asian-American Plays.* New York:
    Theatre Communications Group, 1990.
Chaudhuri, Una. *Staging Place: The Geography of Modern Drama.* Ann Arbor: U of
    Michigan P, 1995.
Commire, Anne, ed. *Something about the Author.* Vol. 7. Detroit: Gale, 1975. 206–207.
Erstein, Hap. "*Dragonwings* Lift Youngsters to Joys of Books." *Washington Times* 20
    Oct. 1992, final ed.: E4.
Gussow, Mel. "Outwitting a Variety of Demons." *New York Times* 11 May 1992, late
    ed.: C11.
Johnson-Feelings, Dianne. *Presenting Laurence Yep.* New York: Twayne, 1995.

Khorana, Meena. "The Ethnic Family and Identity Formation in Adolescents." *The Child and the Family: Selected Papers from the 1988 International Conference of the Children's Literature Association, College of Charleston, Charleston, South Carolina, May 19–22, 1988*. Ed. Susan R. Gannon and Ruth Anne Thompson. New York: Pace U, 1989. 52–58.

"Laurence (Michael) Yep." *Contemporary Literary Criticism*. Vol. 35. Ed. Daniel G. Marowski. (1985): 468–74.

Liu, Fiona Feng-Hsin. "Images of Chinese-Americans and Images of Child-Readers in Three of Laurence Yep's Fictions." Diss. Pennsylvania State U, 1998. *DAI* 59 (1998): 06A.

Sarver, Linda. "Between Worlds: *The Sound of a Voice* and *Pay the Chinaman*." *Theatre Journal* 47.1 (1995): 145–48.

Yep, Laurence. *CMLEA Journal: Official Journal of the California Media and Library Educators Association* 15.1 (Fall 1991): 8–10.

Chay Yew

(1966–   )

Josephine D. Lee

BIOGRAPHY

Chay Yew was born in Singapore. At the age of sixteen, he came to the United States to attend Pepperdine University, where he studied theater. After two years, he returned to Singapore and wrote his first play, *As If He Hears* (1989), for Theater Works in Singapore. This play was later banned by government censors for its sympathetic portrayal of gay characters. He moved back to the United States in 1988. Subsequent plays such as *Porcelain, A Language of Their Own, Wonderland* (originally titled *Half Lives*), and *Red* have been produced at numerous theaters in the United States, Canada, the United Kingdom, and Singapore, including the Royal Court Theatre, the East West Players, the La Jolla Playhouse, the Intiman Theatre, the Public Theater, the Long Wharf Theatre, and the Manhattan Theatre Club. He has won a number of awards, including the 1993 London Fringe Award for Best Play for *Porcelain* and the George and Elisabeth Marton Playwriting Award and the Gay and Lesbian Alliance Against Defamation (GLAAD) Media Award for Best Play for *A Language of Their Own*. Yew directed a production of Prince Gomolvilas's *Big Hunk o' Burnin' Love* for East West Players in 1998. Recently, he has written work for the Seattle Playwrights Alliance New Waves Radio Series—a live broadcast of short works by contemporary dramatists—adapted and directed Federico García Lorca's *House of Bernarda Alba* for the National Asian American Theater Company, and cocreated *The Square* with Lisa Peterson. He is a resident artist and director of the Asian Theatre Workshop at the Mark Taper Forum and the artistic director of the Northwest Asian American Theatre.

MAJOR WORKS AND THEMES

Yew first conceived of the idea for *Porcelain* in a screenplay written for his master's degree at Boston University. He later wrote *Porcelain* (1992) for the Mu-Lan Theatre Company in London, where he was a resident playwright. Mu-Lan's production played to sold-out audiences at London's Etcetera Theatre and the Royal Court, and the play was awarded the 1993 London Fringe Award for Best Play. *Porcelain* concerns the shooting of a white man, William Hope, in the stall of a public bathroom. As the play begins, tabloid newspapers market their sensationalized version of the story, while journalists, hungry for details for their television documentary, interview Dr. Worthing, the criminal psychologist working on the case. His interviews with the suspect, John Lee, and a series of flashbacks reveal a complex set of circumstances. John, a young student, is estranged from his Chinese family because of his homosexuality; he also has trouble forming more stable relationships because of racism within the gay community. When he meets William in a casual sexual encounter at a public lavatory, he is surprised when William invites him out for a drink. They begin an ongoing affair. Despite William's abusive behavior, John falls in love with him and becomes distraught when William breaks off their affair. John follows William back to the scene of their initial encounter and shoots him. Yew's nonrealistic staging, music, and poetic language heighten the intensity of John's tragedy. The play emphasizes his centrality by using a chorus of white male characters to play the various roles of Dr. Worthing, William Hope, and other characters. Throughout the play, John folds red origami paper cranes, symbols of passion and blood, hope and freedom, until the stage is littered with them.

Yew has noted the difference between his writing and Asian American plays of the past: "No more, thank God, Japanese internment camp dramas, intergeneration family melodrama or Chinese railroad stories. Been there, done that. Instead of letting our history and mythology determine the nature of our plays, we're digging up our own issues and problems. Being Asian then ceases to become a central issue; instead, it's the tone, part of the landscape" (Drukman 59). But this does not mean that racial and ethnic identities are only incidental to his plays. *Porcelain* concerns itself with the complexity of love not only as it is mixed with anger, possessiveness, and insecurity, but also as it is complicated by the awareness of racial difference. John fears that he can only be seen as an Oriental fetish, that his Chinese body will never be truly accepted by the other men he desires; similarly, his homosexual body is rejected by his Chinese father.

Yew's *A Language of Their Own* (1994) also emphasizes the interconnections between racial identity, emotional needs, and sexual desires. The play depicts the relationship between Oscar and Ming, two Chinese American men whose long-term relationship becomes strained when Oscar learns that he has AIDS. After Oscar ends the relationship, the two eventually pair up with other lovers,

Ming with Robert, a white headwaiter, and Oscar with Daniel, a young Filipino student. However, their attraction to one another does not end, as evidenced by their intense encounter at a party where they revisit their old bonds. Ming and Robert move to Venice, California, where Ming's discontent with Robert grows deeper; they begin seeing other men. Oscar and Daniel's relationship remains more stable, although Daniel becomes weary of Oscar's growing neediness. Oscar, health failing, intentionally overdoses on sleeping pills. In his final moments, he fantasizes about his past relationship with Ming. Robert breaks up with Ming in order to live with Pran, a Vietnamese man with whom he has begun another relationship; however, the ending of the play suggests a possible reconciliation between Robert and Ming. Yew's couples lay out the parameters of their relationships in extraordinarily original and nuanced conversations, both shared and private. The lyrical dialogue of A Language of Their Own examines intimacy, passion, mourning, and loss in ways that move beyond simple categorizations of race and sexuality. At the same time, the play also carefully dissects some of the racial dynamics of gay relationships, skewering stereotypes and questioning the nature of desire and commitment.

The politics of racial identity as played out in the most private dimensions of life is a common concern of all three plays of the Whitelands trilogy, which includes Porcelain, A Language of Their Own, and Half Lives (1996, later rewritten as Wonderland). Wonderland looks more closely at how racial politics in the United States is linked with global capitalism, labor, and immigration. Each of the members of the family is caught by his or her own misguided faith in the American dream: the father (Man) is trapped by his professional aspirations and corporate dreams, the mother (Woman) by her empty life of domesticity and consumerism, and the son (Son, Young Man) by the absurd contradictions between his parents' disappointed hopes and his own reality. The play moves through the story of the Asian American father's trip to Singapore, where he launches his career as an architect and meets his future wife, a Singapore Chinese. Once in the United States, the woman projects her fantasies of American life onto her son, while the father becomes increasingly absorbed in his vision of corporate success and distanced from his family. The son grows up and becomes a frustrated actor whose homosexuality alienates him even further from his parents; he eventually loses himself in drugs and hustling. At the center of the play is the Whitelands Mall, a project that embodies the empty hopes of each family member; by the end of the play, the mall itself literally crumbles, signaling the final deterioration of the family. Yew's staging moves between memory play, movie fantasy, and flashback, illustrating the many sides of both the family history and the dreams and myths that bring that story into being.

Wonderland picks up a number of the themes of Yew's earlier plays: the connections between racial and sexual identity, the estrangement between parents and children, and the movement of contemporary Asian American lives. In A Beautiful Country (1998) and The Square (2000), Yew also revisits some of these concerns, this time presenting a broader perspective on Asian American history and experience. *A Beautiful Country* combines satire, tragedy, music, and dance and video, written scenes, and monologues that survey nineteenth- and twentieth-century Asian American histories; disparate pieces such as a staging of Henry Grimm's exclusion-era play *The Chinese Must Go*, a dramatization of the 1941 *Time* magazine story "How to Tell Your Friends from the Japs," a poetic depiction of Filipino migrant workers, and a set of contemporary first-person testimonials are held together by the perspective of Miss Visa Denied, an immigrant drag queen. *The Square*, cocreated with director Lisa Peterson, is a collaboration that includes short works by sixteen contemporary playwrights, all set in Manhattan's Chinatown; Yew's contribution, *Scissors* (2000), set in the 1920s, tells the story of a white man and his Chinese barber.

A more explicit political commentary is also revealed in Yew's *Red* (1998), which tells the story of a legendary Peking opera singer, Hua Wai Mun, who is murdered for his allegedly counterrevolutionary art during Mao's Cultural Revolution. The story is told from the contemporary perspective of Chinese American Sonja Wong Pickford, a best-selling romance author (à la Barbara Cartland) who is working on a biography of the performer. Pickford has traveled to Shanghai to complete her research; she discovers Hua Wai Mun's ghost haunting the abandoned theater where he was killed. Hua Wai Mun was betrayed at the hands of his daughter, who joins the Red Guard; ultimately the audience learns that Sonja and the daughter are the same, and that Sonja's current commercialism is a response to her personal involvement in the tragedies of the Cultural Revolution. Yew has told reporters from the *New York Times* and the *Straits Times* (Singapore) that he wrote *Red* out of a sense of protest against Republicans in Congress who have sought to regulate artists by reducing support for the National Endowment for the Arts. His character Hua Wai Mun muses, "I am always amazed at how a simple photograph or a play can threaten people, topple governments, religions, moralists"; in such moments, *Red* draws out thought-provoking connections between the past horrors of the Cultural Revolution in China and the more recent acts of political censorship in the United States.

CRITICAL RECEPTION

Reviews of Yew's work and interviews with Yew have appeared in numerous newspapers, journals, and other periodicals, including the *London Guardian*, the *London Independent*, the *London Times*, the *New York Times*, the *Los Angeles Times*, the *Seattle Times*, the *Village Voice*, the *Straits Times* (Singapore), the *North American Review, American Theatre*, and the *Lambda Book Report*. Critics have hailed *Porcelain* and *A Language of Their Own* for their complex treatment of gay Asian male characters and for their nuanced uses of poetic language and dramatic metaphor. Malcolm Rutherford, writing for the *Financial Times* (London), finds the "harrowing" subject matter of *Porcelain* to be "immaculately handled" (11); Pamela Sommers, of the *Washington Post*, calls *A Language of Their Own* an "unusual and affecting chamber piece" that uses language "as weapon, caress, palliative, barrier" (BIO). Stagings of *Wonderland* again prompt praise for Yew's lyrical uses of language and staging; this and later works such as *A Beautiful Country* have also inspired more pointed reflection on Asian American history, immigration and migration, and racial politics. David Román's scholarly analysis of *A Beautiful Country* examines the play's numerous scenes and its central figure, Miss Visa Denied, through a broader theoretical lens. Reviewers of *Red* have sought to tease out the historical and autobiographical sources for the play's political conflicts, as well as understand its fusing of Chinese and Chinese American concerns.

BIBLIOGRAPHY

Works by Chay Yew

Drama

A Language of Their Own. But Still, Like Air, I'll Rise: New Asian American Plays. Ed. Velina Hasu Houston. Philadelphia: Temple UP, 1997. 451–513.
Porcelain and A Language of Their Own: Two Plays. New York: Grove P, 1997.

Unpublished Manuscripts

As If He Hears. 1989.
Wonderland. Originally *Half Lives.* 1996.
A Beautiful Country. 1998.
Red. 1998.
The House of Bernarda Alba. Adaptation of the play by Federico García Lorca. 2000.
Scissors. As part of *The Square*, with Lisa Peterson. 2000.

Selected Production History

Porcelain

Production, dir. Glen Goei and Stephen Knight. Mu-Lan Theatre Company, London, 1992.
———, dir. Adele Prandini. Theater Rhinoceros, San Francisco, 1993.
———, dir. Van Riley. Woolly Mammoth, Washington, DC, 1993.
———, dir. Ivan Spiegel. Burbage Theater, Los Angeles, 1993.
———, dir. Robert Joseph. Diversionary Playhouse, San Diego, 1994.
———, dir. Tim Dang. East West Players, Los Angeles, 1996.
———, dir. Steven Maler. SpeakEasy Stage Company, Boston, 1998.
———, dir. John Mandes. Theatre on Broadway, Denver, 1998.
———, dir. Joyce Casey. Dobama Theatre, Cleveland Heights, 1999.

A Language of Their Own

Production, dir. Tim Dang. Celebration Theatre, West Hollywood, 1994.
———, dir. Ong Keng Sen. New York Shakespeare Festival, New York City, 1995.

————, dir. Jose Carrasquillo. Studio Theatre's Secondstage, Washington, DC, 1995.
————, dir. Tim Dang. East West Players, Los Angeles, 1996.
————, dir. Tim Dang. Asian American Theater Company, San Francisco, 1996.
————, dir. Jose Carrasquillo. Group Theatre, Seattle, 1997.
————, dir. Janet Lo. Tarragon Theatre Extra Space, Toronto, 1997.

Whitelands Trilogy (*Porcelain, A Language of Their Own*, and *Wonderland*)

Production, dir. Tim Dang. East West Players, Los Angeles, 1996.

Wonderland

Production, dir. Tim Dang. East West Players, Los Angeles, 1996.
————, dir. Lim Kay Siu. Theatre Works, Singapore, 1997.
————, dir. Lisa Peterson. La Jolla Playhouse, San Diego, 1999.

A Beautiful Country

Production, dir. Chay Yew. Cornerstone Theatre, Los Angeles, 1998.

Red

Production, dir. Lisa Peterson. Intiman Theatre, Seattle, 1998.
————, dir. David Petrarca. Long Wharf Theater, New Haven, 1999.
————, dir. David Petrarca. Manhattan Theater Club, New York City, 1999.

The House of Bernarda Alba

Production, dir. Chay Yew. National Asian American Theatre Company, New York City, 2000.

Scissors (as part of *The Square*)

Production, dir. Lisa Peterson. Actors' Gang, Los Angeles, 2000.

Studies of Chay Yew

Drakes, David. "Fusion: David Drakes Interviews Playwright Chay Yew." *Lambda Book Report: A Review of Contemporary Gay and Lesbian Literature* 7.4 (Nov. 1998): 6–8.
Drukman, Steven. "Chay Yew: The Importance of Being Verbal." *American Theatre* Nov. 1995: 58–60.
Kaiden, Elizabeth A. "It's like a Meihua Blossom." *Straits Times* (Singapore) 2 Mar. 1999, life sec.: 4.
Marks, Peter. "Parable Set in a Reign of Terror." *New York Times* 25 Mar. 1999: E5.
Reynolds, Michael. "Review, 1996 East West Players Production of Yew's *Whitelands* Trilogy." *Theatre Journal* Mar. 1997: 75–79.
Román, David. "Visa Denied." *Queer Frontiers: Millennial Geographies, Genders, and Generations*. Ed. Joseph Allen Boone, Martin Dupuis, Martin Meeker, and Karin Quimby. Madison: U of Wisconsin P, 2000. 350–64.
Rutherford, Malcolm. "Excellence on the Small Stage—Theatre." *Financial Times* (London) 10 Aug. 1992, arts sec.: 11.
Sommers, Pamela. "Tangled 'Language' of Love." *Washington Post* 11 Oct. 1995: B10.
Swarns, Rachel L. "An Outsider Determined Not to Be Someone He's Not." *New York Times* 21 Mar. 1999, sec. 2: 8–9.

Selected Bibliography

ANTHOLOGIES

Berson, Misha, ed. *Between Worlds: Contemporary Asian-American Plays*. New York: Theatre Communications Group, 1990.

Cassady, Marsh, ed. *Great Scenes from Minority Playwrights: Seventy-four Scenes of Cultural Diversity*. Colorado Springs: Meriwether, 1997.

Champagne, Lenora, ed. *Out from Under: Texts by Women Performance Artists*. New York: Theatre Communications Group, 1990.

Chan, Jeffery Paul, Frank Chin, Lawson Fusao Inada, and Shawn Wong, eds. *The Big Aiieeeee! An Anthology of Chinese American and Japanese American Literature*. New York: Meridian, 1991.

Chin, Frank, Jeffery Paul Chan, Lawson Fusao Inada, and Shawn Hsu Wong, eds. *Aiiieeeee!: An Anthology of Asian-American Writers*. Washington, DC: Howard UP, 1974.

Dixon, Michael Bigelow, and Amy Wegener, eds. *Humana Festival '99: The Complete Plays*. Lyme, NH: Smith and Kraus, 1999.

Ellis, Roger, ed. *Multicultural Theatre II: Contemporary Hispanic, Asian, and African-American Plays*. Colorado Springs: Meriwether, 1998.

Eng, Alvin, ed. *Tokens? The NYC Asian American Experience on Stage*. New York: Asian American Writers' Workshop, 1999.

Gotanda, Philip Kan. *Fish Head Soup and Other Plays*. Introduction. Michael Omi. Seattle: U of Washington P, 1991.

Houston, Velina Hasu, ed. *But Still, Like Air, I'll Rise: New Asian American Plays*. Philadelphia: Temple UP, 1997.

——, ed. *The Politics of Life: Four Plays by Asian American Women*. Philadelphia: Temple UP, 1993.

Hwang, David Henry. *Trying to Find Chinatown: The Selected Plays*. New York: Theatre Communications Group, 2000.

Lane, Eric, and Nina Shengold, eds. *Take Ten: New 10-Minutes Plays*. New York: Vintage Books, 1997.

Nelson, Brian. *Asian American Drama: 9 Plays from the Multiethnic Landscape*. New York: Applause, 1997.

Perkins, Kathy A., and Roberta Uno, eds. *Contemporary Plays by Women of Color: An Anthology*. New York: Routledge, 1996.

Swanson, Meg, and Robin Murray. *Playwrights of Color*. Yarmouth, ME: Intercultural P, 1999.

Uno, Roberta. ed. *Unbroken Thread: An Anthology of Plays by Asian American Women*. Amherst: U of Massachusetts P, 1993.

SECONDARY SOURCES

Bryer, Jackson R., ed. *The Playwright's Art: Conversations with Contemporary American Dramatists*. New Brunswick, NJ: Rutgers UP, 1995.

Chan, Mimi, and Roy Harris, eds. *Asian Voices in English*. Hong Kong: Hong Kong UP, 1991.

Cheung, King-Kok, ed. *Words Matter: Conversations with Asian American Writers*. Honolulu: U of Hawai'i P, 2000.

DiGaetani, John L. *A Search for a Postmodern Theater: Interviews with Contemporary Playwrights*. Westport, CT: Greenwood P, 1991.

Hart, Lynda, ed. *Making a Spectacle: Feminist Essays on Contemporary Women's Theatre*. Ann Arbor: U of Michigan P, 1989.

Hong, Maria, ed. *Growing up Asian American: An Anthology*. New York: W. Morrow, 1993.

Kamp, Jim, ed. *Reference Guide to American Literature*. 3rd ed. Detroit: St. James P, 1994.

Kolin, Philip C., and Colby H. Kullman, eds. *Speaking on Stage: Interviews with Contemporary American Playwrights*. Tuscaloosa: U of Alabama P, 1996.

Kondo, Dorinne. *About Face: Performing Race in Fashion and Theater*. New York: Routledge, 1997.

Kurahashi, Yuko. *Asian American Culture on Stage: The History of the East West Players*. New York: Garland, 1999.

Lee, Joanne Faung Jean. *Asian American Actors: Oral Histories from Stage, Screen, and Television*. Jefferson, NC: McFarland, 2000.

Lee, Josephine. *Performing Asian America: Race and Ethnicity on the Contemporary Stage*. Philadelphia: Temple UP, 1997.

Lim, Shirley Geok-lin, and Amy Ling, eds. *Reading the Literatures of Asian America*. Philadelphia: Temple UP, 1992.

Ling, Amy, ed. *Yellow Light: The Flowering of Asian American Arts*. Philadelphia: Temple UP, 1999.

Maufort, Marc, ed. *Staging Difference: Cultural Pluralism in American Theatre and Drama*. New York: Peter Lang, 1995.

Moy, James S. *Marginal Sights: Staging the Chinese in America*. Iowa City: U of Iowa, 1993.

Palumbo-Liu, David, ed. *The Ethnic Canon: Histories, Institutions, and Interventions*. Minneapolis: U of Minneapolis P, 1995.

Partnow, Elaine T., and Lesley Anne Hyatt. *The Female Dramatist: Profiles of Women Playwrights from the Middle Ages to Contemporary Times.* New York: Facts on File, 1998.

Peterson, Jane T. and Suzanne Bennett, eds. *Women Playwrights of Diversity.* Westport, CT: Greenwood P, 1997.

Revilla, Linda A. Gail M. Nomura, Shawn Wong, and Shirley Hune, eds. *Bearing Dreams, Shaping Visions: Asian Pacific American Perspectives.* Pullman: Washington State UP, 1993.

Said, Edward W. *Orientalism.* New York: Vintage Books, 1979.

Savran, David. *In Their Own Words: Contemporary American Playwrights.* New York City: Theatre Communications Group, 1988.

Trudeau, Lawrence J., ed. *Asian American Literature: Reviews and Criticism of Works by American Writers of Asian Descent.* Detroit: Gale Research, 1999.

Uno, Roberta, ed. *The Color of Theatre: A Critical Source Book in Race and Performance.* London: Athlone, forthcoming.

Uno, Roberta, and Lucy Mae San Pablo Burns, eds. *The Color of Theater: Race, Ethnicity and Contemporary Performance.* London: Continuum, forthcoming.

Williams, Dave. *Misreading the Chinese Character: Images of the Chinese in Euroamerican Drama to 1925.* New York: Peter Lang, 2000.

Wolcott, John R., and Michael L. Quinn. *Staging Diversity: Plays and Practice in American Theatre.* Dubuque, IA: Kendall/Hunt, 1992.

Wong, Sau-ling Cynthia. *Reading Asian American Literature: From Necessity to Extravagance.* Princeton, NJ: Princeton UP, 1993.

PERIODICALS

Amerasia Journal (semiannual).

American Theatre (monthly).

Asian Pacific American Journal (quarterly).

Bamboo Ridge: Hawaii Writers Quarterly (semiannual).

Canadian Theatre Review (quarterly).

Critical Arts: A Journal for Cultural Studies (semiannual).

The Drama Review: TDR (quarterly).

Hitting Critical Mass: A Journal of Asian American Cultural Criticism (semiannual).

Journal of Asian American Studies (three issues annually).

Journal of Dramatic Theory and Criticism (semiannual).

Journal of Ethnic Studies (quarterly).

MELUS: Journal of the Society for the Study of the Multi-Ethnic Literature of the United States (quarterly).

Modern Drama (quarterly).

Mosaic: A Journal for the Interdisciplinary Study of Literature (quarterly).

Race, Gender and Class: An Interdisciplinary Journal (quarterly).

Theater (New Haven) (three issues annually).

Index

Page numbers for main entries appear in **boldface** type.

About the Editor and Contributors

VICTOR BASCARA is Assistant Professor in the English Department at the University of Georgia, where he teaches courses in Asian American literature and culture. He received his Ph.D. from Columbia University and has published in *Amerasia, Critical Mass, Q&A: Queer in Asian America*, and *Jouvert*.

LUCY MAE SAN PABLO BURNS is pursuing her doctoral degree at the University of Massachusetts at Amherst. She is currently working on a dissertation focusing on Filipino American theater. Her works have been published in the *Journal of Asian American Studies, Asian Pacific American Journal, BTNetwork (Black Theater Network)*, and the *North American Review*. She coedited the collection *The Color of Theater: Race, Ethnicity, and Contemporary Performance* (forthcoming) with Roberta Uno. She was the former literary manager at the New WORLD Theater.

JANET HYUNJU CLARKE is a librarian at State University of New York at Stony Brook, New York.

MARTHA J. CUTTER is Associate Professor of English at Kent State University. Her book *Unruly Tongue: Identity and Voice in American Women's Writing, 1850–1930* was published in 1999. Her articles have appeared in *American Literature, MELUS, Women's Studies, African American Review, Criticism*, and numerous other journals.

ELIZABETH BYRNE FITZPATRICK is a reference librarian at the University of Massachusetts at Amherst. She received her master's degree in comparative literature there in 2000, specializing in Indonesian literature.

THEODORE S. GONZALVES is a doctoral candidate in the Program in Comparative Culture at the University of California at Irvine. He has taught courses in literature, history, and Asian American and ethnic studies at several colleges and universities in California. Gonzalves is also a composer and producer.

JOHN JAE-NAM HAN earned his M.A. and Ph.D. from Kansas State University and the University of Nebraska at Lincoln, respectively. He is currently Assistant Professor of English at Missouri Baptist College, where he teaches modernist literature, minority literature, world literary types, creative writing, and history of the English language.

GUIYOU HUANG is Associate Professor of English and teaches American and ethnic American literatures at Kutztown University of Pennsylvania and Asian American studies at Lehigh University. He is the author of *Whitmanism, Imagism, and Modernism in China and America* (1997) and *Asian, Asian American, American: Texts in Between* (forthcoming) and editor of *Asian American Autobiographers* (2001) and *Asian American Poets* (forthcoming); he is also the author of many articles on Walt Whitman, Ezra Pound, Maxine Hong Kingston, and Frank Chin in English, as well as essays, reviews, and translations in Chinese.

SHUCHEN S. HUANG was born in Taipei and earned a B.A. from National Chengchi University, Taiwan. From 1991 to 1994, she studied at Universität Freiburg, Germany. Currently a Ph.D. candidate in the Comparative Literature Department at the University of Massachusetts at Amherst, she is writing her dissertation on Asian diasporan experiences.

NIKOLAS HUOT is a doctoral candidate in English at the University of Massachusetts at Amherst.

LYNN M. ITAGAKI is currently pursuing her doctorate in English at UCLA and received her M.A. from the UCLA Asian American Studies Program. Her current projects examine the developing political ideology of multiculturalism and the rise of the Asian American "neoconservatives" in recent Asian American fiction and nonfiction.

MELINDA L. de JESÚS is Assistant Professor of Asian Pacific American studies at Arizona State University. She teaches and writes about Asian Pacific American literature and culture, U.S. third-world feminist theory and literature, and new media pedagogy. Her work has appeared in *Works and Days, Delinquents and Debutantes, Sisters Uprising*, and *Women Artists of Color: A Biocritical Sourcebook to 20th Century Artists in the Americas*. She is currently editing a volume of oral histories of Filipino Americans.

LEELA KAPAI holds a Ph.D. in English literature from Howard University. She is Professor of English at Prince George's Community College in Largo, Maryland. She has published several articles on multicultural literature.

RANDY BARBARA KAPLAN is Assistant Professor of Theatre at the State University of New York at Geneseo, where she teaches Asian American theater and directs GENseng, Geneseo's Asian American Play Reading Series. In addition to publishing on Asian American theater, she has curated "Casting Discrimination against Asian and Asian American Actors: A Time Honored Tradition on the New York Stage," a photographic exhibit that is now archived at Ohio State University's Theatre Research Institute.

ESTHER S. KIM is Assistant Professor of Theater at the University of Illinois at Urbana-Champaign. She teaches theater history, literature, and criticism. Her specialization areas include Asian American theater, American theater, and dramatic theory. She is the author of the forthcoming book *Finding a Voice: Asian American Theatre History from 1965 to 1999.*

YUKO KURAHASHI was born and raised in Tokyo, Japan. She holds a Ph.D. in theater from Indiana University and is Visiting Assistant Professor at Miami University, Oxford, Ohio. Her interests are in dramaturgy, Asian American theater, and Latino American theater. Her book *Asian American Culture on Stage: The History of the East West Players* was published in 1999.

SANSAN KWAN is a doctoral candidate in performance studies at New York University. She danced with Maura Nguyen Donohue from 1995 to 2000. Her dissertation is entitled "Choreographing Chineseness: Space, Commodity, and Performance in the Production of Ethnicity."

JOSEPHINE D. LEE is Associate Professor of English at the University of Minnesota. Her book *Performing Asian America: Race and Ethnicity on the Contemporary Stage* was published in 1997. She is coeditor of *Re/collecting Early Asian America: Readings in Culture History*, a forthcoming interdisciplinary collection of essays. She has written numerous essays on modern and contemporary American and British theater and is currently completing a book on racial politics and contemporary American theater.

DAPHNE P. LEI holds a Ph.D. in drama from Tufts University. Currently she is teaching in the Drama Department at Stanford University on a Mellon Postdoctoral Fellowship in Humanities. She is a scholar in Asian, Asian American, Chinese, and intercultural theater.

MILES XIAN LIU is Assistant Professor in the English Department at Holyoke Community College, Massachusetts. He is a Faulkner scholar. His specialties include Asian American and twentieth-century American literature and cross-cultural theories. His publications appear in the *Faulkner Journal, Asian American Novelists* (2000), *Jordan Creek Anthology*, and the *International Students' Guide to the U.S.A.* (1996–97).

UPPINDER MEHAN is Assistant Professor in the Department of Writing, Literature, and Publishing at Emerson College, Boston. He is a specialist in postcolonial, particularly South Asian, literatures.

SEAN METZGER is a doctoral candidate in the department of theater at the University of California at Davis. He has published essays and reviews in the

Journal of Homosexuality and *Theatre Journal*. His dissertation is entitled "In the Realm of the Rice Queen: Fetishism, Diaspora, and 'Chineseness.' "

LOUIS J. PARASCANDOLA is Associate Professor of English at Long Island University's Brooklyn Campus. He holds a Ph.D. from the City University of New York Graduate School. His publications include an edition of the writings of Harlem Renaissance author Eric Walrond and a monograph on Victorian novelist Captain Marryat as well as three editions of Marryat's novels.

RASHNA B. SINGH was born and raised in India, where she obtained her B.A. (honors) degree in English from the University of Calcutta. She came to the United States for graduate study, earning her M.A. in English from Mount Holyoke College and a Ph.D. from the University of Massachusetts at Amherst. She is the author of one of the first studies of British fiction on India, entitled *The Imperishable Empire*, and is Professor of English at Holyoke Community College, where she has taught for ten years.

ANDREW L. SMITH teaches creative writing at Holyoke Community College in Massachusetts. His research interests range from hypertextuality to Spanish poetry to Asian American theater. He writes poetry and creative nonfiction, which have appeared in numerous literary journals. He is currently completing a collection of memoirs titled *The Children of Sinking Creek*.

GARY STORHOFF is Associate Professor of English at the University of Connecticut, Stamford Campus. He teaches American literature and has published on a variety of American writers, including William Faulkner, Toni Morrison, Richard Wright, and Louise Erdrich.

DOUGLAS I. SUGANO is Professor of English and teaches early British, multicultural American, and Asian American literatures at Whitworth College. He has published a book and several articles on medieval English drama and several articles on Asian American literature.

JIE TIAN is a reference librarian at California State University, Fullerton. She holds a B.A. and M.A. in English, an M.A. in American studies, and an M.L.S. in library and information science. Her research interests are user studies, electronic resources, and cultural studies. She also writes essays, short stories, and poems.

ROBERTA UNO is the artistic director of the New WORLD Theater and Professor of Theater at the University of Massachusetts at Amherst. She is the editor of *Unbroken Thread: An Anthology of Plays by Asian American Women* (1993), coeditor of *Contemporary Plays by Women of Color* (1996), and editor of the forthcoming *The Color of Theater: Race, Ethnicity, and Contemporary Performance*.

MASAMI USUI, born and raised in Kobe, Japan, holds a Ph.D. in English from Michigan State University. She has published articles on Virginia Woolf and

Japanese American writers in Japan, the United States, and England. She is Associate Professor of English at Doshisha University, Japan, but taught at Hiroshima University from 1990 to 1999.

YUPEI ZHOU has an M.A. from the University of Akron. She is now a teaching fellow and a doctoral candidate in the Department of English at Kent State University.